MR. LEAR

ALSO BY JENNY UGLOW

George Eliot

Elizabeth Gaskell: A Habit of Stories

Henry Fielding

Hogarth: A Life and a World

Cultural Babbage: Time, Technology and Invention
(with Francis Spufford)

Dr Johnson, His Club and Other Friends

The Lunar Men: Five Friends Whose Curiosity Changed the World

A Little History of British Gardening

Nature's Engraver: A Life of Thomas Bewick

Words & Pictures: Writers, Artists and a Peculiarly British Tradition

A Gambling Man: Charles II's Restoration Game

The Pinecone: The Story of Sarah Losh,
Forgotten Romantic Heroine—Antiquarian, Architect, and Visionary

In These Times: Living in Britain
Through Napoleon's Wars, 1793–1815

MR. LEAR

A LIFE OF ART AND NONSENSE

JENNY UGLOW

FARRAR, STRAUS AND GIROUX
NEW YORK

Farrar, Straus and Giroux
175 Varick Street, New York 10014

Printed in the United States of America
Originally published in 2017 by Faber and Faber Limited, Great Britain
Published in the United States by Farrar, Straus and Giroux
First American edition, 2018

Library of Congress Cataloging-in-Publication Data
Names: Uglow, Jennifer S., author.
Title: Mr. Lear : a life of art and nonsense / Jenny Uglow.
Description: First American edition. | New York : Farrar, Straus and Giroux, 2018. |
"Originally published in 2017 by Faber and Faber Limited, Great Britain"—ECIP
galley. | Includes bibliographical references and index.
Identifiers: LCCN 2017058631 | ISBN 9780374113339 (hardcover)
Subjects: LCSH: Lear, Edward, 1812–1888. | Poets, English—19th century—Biography. |
Artists—Great Britain—Biography.
Classification: LCC PR4879.L2 Z94 2018 | DDC 700.92 [B] —dc23
LC record available at https://lccn.loc.gov/2017058631

Our books may be purchased in bulk for promotional, educational, or business use.
Please contact your local bookseller or the Macmillan Corporate and Premium
Sales Department at 1-800-221-7945, extension 5442, or by
e-mail at MacmillanSpecialMarkets@macmillan.com.

www.fsgbooks.com
www.twitter.com/fsgbooks • www.facebook.com/fsgbooks

1   3   5   7   9   10   8   6   4   2

For Steve

The Scroobious Pip from the top of a tree
Saw the distant Jellybolēe, –
And all the birds in the world came there,
Flying in crowds all through the air.
The Vulture and Eagle – the Cock and the Hen,
The Ostrich, the Turkey, the Snipe and the Wren,
The Parrot chattered, the Blackbird sung,
And the Owl looked wise but held his tongue,
And when the Peacock began to scream,
The hullabaloo was quite extreme.
And every bird he fluttered the tip
Of his wing as he stared at the Scroobious Pip.

At last they said to the Owl, – 'By far
You're wisest Bird – you know you are!
Fly close to the Scroobious Pip and say,
"Explain all about yourself we pray! –
For as yet we have neither seen nor heard
If you're Fish or Insect, Beast or Bird!"'

The Scroobious Pip looked gaily round
And sang these words with a chirpy sound –
    'Flippetty chip – Chippetty flip –
    My only name is the Scroobious Pip.'

EDWARD LEAR

CONTENTS

Prologue: 'It's Absurd . . .'   1

I FLEDGING

  1 One Foot Off the Ground   9
  2 With the Girls   21
  3 'O Sussex!'   35

II PERCHING

  4 To the Zoo   45
  5 Knowsley   66
  6 Tribes and Species   74
  7 Make 'Em Laugh   84
  8 Mountains   98

III FLYING

  9 'Rome Is Rome'   109
 10 Happy as a Hedgehog   120
 11 Third Person   131
 12 Excursions   139
 13 Derry down Derry: *Nonsense*, 1846   150
 14 'Something Is About to Happen'   161
 15 'Calmly, into the Dice-box'   175
 16 'All that Amber'   189

IV TUMBLING

 17 The Brotherhood   201
 18 Meeting the Poet   213
 19 An Owl in the Desert   224
 20 Half a Life: Corfu and Athos   234
 21 Bible Lands   251

CONTENTS

22 A Was an Ass   262
23 Home Again, Rome Again   270
24 No More   283

V CIRCLING

25 'Overconstrained to Folly': *Nonsense*, 1861   297
26 'Mr Lear the Artist'   311
27 'From Island unto Island'   320
28 'What a Charming Life an Artist's Is!'   333
29 'The "Marriage" Phantasy'   341
30 'Gradually Extinguified'   352

VI CALLING

31 Sail Away: Cannes, 1868–1869   375
32 'Three Groans for Corsica!'   388
33 *Degli Inglesi*   395
34 *Nonsense Songs* and *More Nonsense*   407
35 Restless in San Remo   424
36 India   435
37 Families   446
38 *Laughable Lyrics*   456

VII SWOOPING

39 Shocks   469
40 The Villa Tennyson   480
41 'As Great a Fool as Ever I Was'   494
42 *Pax Vobiscum*   513

Acknowledgements   523
List of Illustrations   525
Abbreviations   529
Select Bibliography   530
Notes   534
Index   583

PROLOGUE: 'IT'S ABSURD...'

There was an Old Man of Spithead,
Who opened the window, and said, –
'Fil-jomble, fil-jumble, fil-rumble-come-tumble!'
That doubtful Old Man of Spithead.

Every time I look at Edward Lear's nonsenses, as he called his limericks and songs, I am amazed afresh. They make me laugh with surprise. They are full of joys, shocks, rule-breaking freedoms and assaults. They open a window onto another world. Lear's poems exist both within and outside the rules. They follow the logic of syntax, the linking of rhyme and off-rhyme, the strict dance of rhythm, but are peopled by oddities whose actions are bizarre, upsetting their neighbours. Where do they come from, the stubborn eccentrics, the animal- and bird-like humans? Later, Lear's creatures took on another life in his beautiful and melancholy songs – the Dong with the Luminous Nose searching by lake and shore, the Owl and the Pussy-cat under the stars, the sweet, long lines lapping like waves on their pea-green boat. His people exist nowhere else in literature. Some are gentle, some are violent, some are musical, some are wild. They slide between sky, earth and sea. Even when they are peaceful, like the fishing daughters of Marseilles, they are exceedingly strange.

There was an Old Man of Marseilles,
Whose daughters wore bottle-green veils;
They caught several fish, which they put in a dish,
And sent to their Pa' at Marseilles.

Lear wrote nonsense alphabets, botany and cookery, and marvel-filled travel journals. He was a great letter writer, sprinkling the pages with sketches or fat self-portraits of the bespectacled artist followed by Foss, his cat with the cut-off tail. A letter could itself be a drawing. Lear could fly, as he does, rotundly, in a note to his friend, the 'beneficial & brick-like Baring', or his letter could crawl – snail-mail.

Lear's youthful drawings of animals and birds are almost hyper-real, as if he wanted to free the creatures from the page. Chronically short-sighted, in the landscapes that he painted he looked always into the distance, to towering mountains or far horizons. He was roused to rage by religious intolerance yet yearned for an afterlife: one thing he always believed in was forgiveness. All his life he depended on patrons and moved in establishment circles yet never truly belonged among them. He loved men yet dreamed of marriage, and remained, it seems, wrapped in himself, alone yet surrounded by friends.

There was an Old Man of Whitehaven,
Who danced a quadrille with a raven;
But they said – 'It's absurd, to encourage this bird!'
So they smashed that Old Man of Whitehaven.

That last line has a real thump of surprise, of violence delivered with gusto. Such a satisfying verb, 'smashed', a word for six-year-olds to shout as they bash the hedges with a stick. But why Whitehaven? Perhaps the bird came first – few places rhyme with raven. When Lear sketched in the Lake District as a young man, Whitehaven lay on the coast in the corner of his map, yet his rhyme gives the stress to White-*haven*, a safe harbour – one that proves not so safe after all. Lear knew his birds, and as he walked the fells he watched ravens soaring above the crags in aerial acrobatics, rising, falling, swooping, turning, tumbling. He could hear their hoarse 'caw caw'. In this nonsense dance – a couple in a quadrille designed for four – he shows the raven's excited cawing, the man with coat-tails like wings and nose in line with the bird's open beak. The raven takes off, and the man, too, is almost – almost – in the air. Below them comes the rhyme. Eyes and mind jump between image and word, challenging each other: the delight of the image, the shock of the verse.

3

When Lear was nearly fifty he added this rhyme to his *Book of Nonsense*. It is one of many unlikely pairings: man and bird, owl and cat, daddy long-legs and fly, duck and kangaroo. And it is one of many appearances of the disapproving 'they', who turn up again and again in his nonsense. 'They' don't, we notice, damn the dancing itself but say 'It's absurd to encourage this bird', to make it at odds with its place in nature. Yet absurdity is the essence. Many writers quote this particular limerick (a later term, first recorded in 1898, but one we can use) to illustrate Lear's attack on the invisible, pettifogging crowd, 'The legions of cruel inquisitive They', as W. H. Auden called them, or in George Orwell's words, 'the realists, the practical men, the sober citizens in bowler hats who are always anxious to stop you doing anything worth doing'. But are we too part of the common-sensible 'they', who so often turn against the odd and the outsider? And sometimes, when the limericks confront Lear's own fears – loud noises, scary dogs, fierce women – are 'they' the author himself?

In this case 'they' miss the point, as they often do. The wonder is not that a raven should dance but that a man can join it: a Lear-like longing. As a child I was fascinated by Lear's limericks and songs, and sometimes scared. I loved the unexpected rhymes, the exotic and ordinary places and the strange words: intrinsic, scroobious, dyspeptic, abruptious. They meant nothing to me but were fat and full and good on the tongue. In the late songs, I heard Lear's music, the jerky sharpness of Mr and Mrs Discobbolos, the yearning of the Dong with the Luminous Nose. I pored over the pictures while my grandmother read and I still wonder if sometimes the image came first, a doodle in a margin, a crafty portrait, a feature or expression, then a rhyme to go with it.

Lear's scratchy figures play a harp with the chin, nurse fishes in the sea, wear a wreath 'Of lobsters and spice, pickled onions and mice'. Even an aunt can reach excess.

There was a Young Girl of Majorca
Whose aunt was a very fast walker;
She walked seventy miles, and leaped fifteen stiles,
Which astonished that Girl of Majorca.

Astonished I was. But children, used to fairy tales and nursery rhymes, rarely question stories. The impossible becomes possible, as it was for the Jumblies: 'They sailed away in a sieve, they did, they sailed away in a sieve'. They did. Every time one returns to the limericks one can find something new: the gap between the characters, never quite touching, the action suspended in time; the darkness and anger. A whole world is here: nonsense beings come from Hull and Harrow, Parma and Paris, Cairo and Crete, while the late songs inhabit a geography of their own, the land where the Bong Tree grows, the hills of the Chankly Bore and the great Gromboolian plain.

There are other Lears. One is the young painter of birds and beasts: toucans with huge beaks, like his own big nose, flaming red parrots, the horned owl with ruffs round his eyes, the wildcat with its soft fur. Another is the landscape artist, painting ruins in Rome, rivers in Albania, boats like moths on the Nile. Lear saw himself as a Romantic wanderer and wrote dramatic, self-mocking, quirkily evocative travel journals, letting us feel rain and heat, and evoking the structure and life of a land. Beyond these, his passion for Tennyson's poetry prompted him to explore the kinship of the arts, and in illustrating lines from Tennyson he created a unique visual autobiography. How do these worlds fit together?

Because memories were important to Lear, I want to follow his life straightforwardly, to see how the layers are laid down, how they overlap and twist like strata. He was always involved with the lives of his friends and also always slightly apart. One of his fantasies was of living on top of a tree, like a bird in a nest, looking down at the ground, but he enjoyed small, daily things: food and drink, sunshine, odd comic happenings, curious words, turning them over like stones. He is like the sandpiper on the edge of the sea in the poem by Elizabeth Bishop, one of Lear's great admirers:

> On his left, a sheet
> of interrupting water comes and goes
> and glazes over his dark and brittle feet.
> He runs, he runs straight through it, watching his toes.

Lear ran. Back and forth over the silent-roaring ocean. He travelled to Italy, Greece and Albania, to the Levant and Egypt and India. For most of his life, he was a self-appointed exile, spending the winters abroad and returning like a reluctant swallow in the summers. But what was he flying to? Or what was he fleeing *from*? If we follow him across land and sea, to the borderlands of self, can we see where the art and nonsense are born? This is what, in my sieve of words, I am setting sail to find out.

I. FLEDGING

1: ONE FOOT OFF THE GROUND

O Brother Chicken! Sister Chick!
O gracious me! O my!
This broken Eggshell was my home!
I see it with my eye!
However did I get inside? Or how did I get out?
And must my life be evermore, an atmosphere of doubt?

Lear was intrigued by beginnings: the growth and structure of plants, the inherited make-up and habits of birds, animals and humans, the child's acquisition of language. He was moved by the way civilisations rose and faded, and by the progress of life itself, evolving from primitive forms, crawling from the sea. He wrote his lighthearted verse of the chicken and the egg in his late sixties. Accepting mystery, fluidity, doubt, he came to the conclusion 'that we are *not wholly* responsible for our lives *i.e.*, – our acts, *in so far as* congenital circumstances, physical or psychical over which we have no absolute control, prevent our being so.' We have partial control, but it is too hard, too late, as adults, 'to change the lines we have early begun to trace and follow'. He was formed, he felt, by a mix of nature and nurture, setting him always at variance with 'they'.

The first 'they' were his family. He was small and they were many, talking, bossing, teasing, ignoring. He was a part, yet set apart. His mother,

Ann, had been pregnant almost constantly after she married his father, Jeremiah, in 1788. The babies came year after year, and names were used and reused until one survived, a litany of hope. Thus: Ann, Sarah, Sarah, Sarah, Mary, Henry, Henry, Eleanor, Jane, Harriett, Cordelia, Frederick, Florence, Charles, Catherine, Edward, Catherine. Different lists are confused as to whether there were seventeen, nineteen or twenty-one babies (as Lear often claimed). The first Catherine, born about 1811, must have died just before or while Ann was pregnant with Edward: death and birth, burial and cradles, so close together, a conjunction that perhaps spurred rejection.

The Lear family were nonconformists (Lear often jumped angrily to defend dissenters against complacent Anglicans, 'bigots and fools'), and most of the children were baptised by Joseph Brooksbank, the pastor of the Independent church that met in Haberdasher's Hall in Staining Lane, off Wood Street in Cheapside. In this respect they were city babies, christened in the street where Wordsworth's 'Poor Susan' heard the song of the thrush and thought of her mountain home. Edward, the thirteenth baby to live past infancy, was born late at night on 12 May 1812 – four months after Dickens, a few days after Browning. Until his middle age, he kept his birthday on the 13th, but then started to celebrate it on the 12th. Was he ducking an unlucky day? He was born, he told a friend, at half past eleven at night, so late that it seemed to the busy household like the next day. He looked up through a ladder of brothers and sisters, the nearest to him being Charles, aged three when Lear was born, Florence, six and Fred, who was seven. Within months his mother was pregnant again – her last child, a second Catherine, arrived the following November.

In late middle age Lear began to look back on his life, he said, as 'a series of pictures seen through "Memory's Arch"'. Often, when his mind went back to these days, he was feeling sad, or ill, and muddled the dates. And he made things up for fun, like the family descent from a Dane called Lör, who had allegedly changed his name, in graphic Lear style, by removing a horizontal line and sliding Lör to Lear. 'As for memory,' Lear quipped when he was seventy, 'I remember lots of things before I was born, & quite distinctly remember being born at Highgate 12 May 1812.' Nonsense, of course, but what he did remember were the stories told by his eldest sister, Ann, who grew up in his father's golden days.

Jeremiah Lear's great-grandfather was a Dorset butcher's son who came to London in the late seventeenth century and set up first, the story goes, as a gingerbread baker in Soho. To succeed in this mercantile city it was useful to belong to a livery company, and in the 1720s the baker's son, George, joined the Fruiterers' Company, one of the oldest guilds, becoming a Freeman and eventually Master. From this point on, making a lucrative move into sugar refining, the family ran a firm on the London wharfs, importing raw sugar from Jamaica and re-exporting to Hamburg. Strict dissenters, they built links with the Hamburg Lutheran Church in Trinity Lane – something that Lear, who had a rooted, if mysterious, dislike of Germans, chose to blot out, as he did any mention of money based on slavery. George's grandson, Jeremiah, joined the family sugar-boiling business run by his widowed mother in Thames Street. At thirty-one, he married the nineteen-year-old Ann Clark Skerrett from Whitechapel, but Ann felt herself above the London trades, mourning a lost inheritance from forebears on her mother's side, the Brignalls of Sunniside, south-west of Gateshead in the Durham coalfields.

The couple were always said to have eloped, and the truth, if less dramatic, still suggested parental disapproval: a quiet wedding in Wanstead, away from their home parish, with only the clerk and a passer-by for witness. Jeremiah brought his bride sugar, if not honey, and plenty of money. In 1799, when his oldest daughter Ann was eight, and Sarah and Mary were four and three, he became a Freeman of the City and Master of the Fruiterers. For the girls there were glimpses of City pomp, of their father setting off in his livery with the Master's badge, an oval of Adam and Eve with the apple. Every November the Fruiterers marched to present the Lord Mayor with twelve bushels of apples, packed into white baskets from Faringdon market, and then to a banquet in the columned Egyptian Hall of the Mansion House, with servants scurrying beneath the swinging chandeliers.

Although Jeremiah went on attending at the Fruiterers', he left sugar refining to become a broker in the City: the family home was in Pentonville, on the northern outskirts, while the business address was now 'Pinner's Court, Broad Street and Stock Exchange'. In the long years of the French wars, from 1793 to 1815, the City grew in strength, with issues of bonds and raising of loans, but business was risky. Men could make a fortune but they could easily go bankrupt, as Jeremiah's young nephew Henry Chesmer did after speculating in Spanish wool, becoming embroiled in a court case that would go on for years. Jeremiah was lucky, at least to begin with. He took a share when the stock exchange became a formal subscription body in 1801, to raise money to build a new Exchange in Capel Court, and in 1806 he moved his family west to Bowman's Lodge, a villa in Holloway. On today's map it would be at the Nag's Head crossroads, where the Seven Sisters Road joins the Holloway Road. But then the Seven Sisters Road did not exist: beyond the side garden there was only a narrow alley, cutting through to the old Heames Lane. It felt like the country.

This was where Lear was born. In 1863, when he was fifty, after his sister Ann died, he went back to look at their old house, finding that roads now covered the garden and paddocks, and men were demolishing the house for building materials. He had been to look at 'old Bowman's Lodge, & its Limes' five years before when he happened to be nearby, but this time a woman showed him round. It was like a parody of the broken eggshell from which he emerged. Some of the steps were gone and so were small rooms like the study and conservatory, the 'greenhouse room'. New buildings were all around. But the parlour, he said, 'at once annihilated 50 years': the room was empty, but there were the two bookcases, '& the old "Secretary" my father used to write at – I saw every possible evening for years. Would I could see the pictures as they were!!' An inventory made in 1845, when the house was sold to become a girls' school, describes the fittings: 'Two mahogany

Bowman's Lodge

doors, Recess Bookcases with glazed doors, secretaire drawers, paneled doors under, & shelves'. It was a fine place for the master of the house, the collector of pictures. Lear went upstairs, past the drawing room, and found:

My room – ehi! ehi! – Henry's – Mary's – Mother's, and the spare room. Down stairs again – the nursery, a large low room – just as it was – only with no view. Dear Ann's – & the painting room – the happiest of all my life perhaps – the 'dark room' and the 'play ground' . . . Gave the woman 2 shillings – a cheap & wonderful lesson.

'No view'. In his childhood there had been views in every direction: west across flat fields to the slopes of Camden, north to Highgate, east to the market gardens, and south to the spires and smoke of the City. From the windows he could see lights glimmering in the dusk, lighting the roads to the river and the docks, filled with ships sailing to unknown lands.

When these smart Regency villas were built, Holloway was still a village on the Great North Road. One stagecoach a day went into town from the Plough Inn. Shepherds herded flocks down the street, and the remains of the old moated manor house could still be seen. A scattering of houses lined the road and the Lear children could walk up Highgate Hill or across into Hornsey Wood, where families came on trips to Eel-Pie House, with its pleasure grounds along the New River. Up the hill, Highgate had a new theatre, a library and smart monthly assemblies, and this was where the Lears felt they belonged – Lear always said he came from Highgate, rather than Holloway. By contrast Holloway was almost industrial. Near the end of Heames Lane Elizabeth Duke ran a manufactory 'wherein clothes and other articles were rendered water-proof', making cloaks and greatcoats for Wellington's army in the Peninsula.

Lear was born in the year of Wellington's victory at Salamanca and Napoleon's retreat from Moscow, when the fortunes of war seemed to turn. His first real memory, so he said, was of the end of the war. Writing to a friend in 1884, four years before he died, he said:

I think a great deal in these later days of all my life, *every particle* of which from the time I was 4 years old, I, strange to say, can perfectly remember. (Even earlier for I well remember being wrapped in a blanket & taken out of bed to see the illuminations in the house at Highgate, on the Battle of Waterloo occasion – and I was then, 1815, just 3 years and odd weeks.)

The Waterloo fireworks were a signal of joy. But within months the slump came. No troops needed waterproofs now, and trade collapsed at the Heames Lane manufactory. In 1816, the year without a summer, when the skies were black after the eruption of Mount Tambora in the East Indies, the streets were full of demobilised soldiers and sailors hunting for work. With a huge national debt to be paid, taxes rose, loans were called in, and investors stayed away. In the City great firms like Barings and men like Nathan Rothschild could make fortunes, but smaller brokers suffered. Jeremiah Lear was a defaulter, owing £2150 11s. 1d., his name called out loud to blows of a hammer on the wainscoting of the Exchange, and written on the blackboard for all to see. This was a ceremony 'so very awful' for the defaulter 'that he always takes care to be at a reasonable distance from the house on the occasion . . . and dare not show his face in the house until he gets his affairs managed'. In this case, a friend settled the debt, with the creditors accepting 2s. 6d. in the pound. Jeremiah could show his face again.

For a time the Lears had to let their house. It seems that they packed their bags and trundled off to the family's old properties in the City, where the sugar houses smoked in the narrow streets by the quays. Their exile was not long: back they moved to leafy Holloway. Yet by 1820 the Lears were in trouble again. Lear once wrote bitterly of a local woman who might remember that his father was imprisoned 'for fraud and debt'. Exaggerated family stories talked of Jeremiah as a debtor in the King's Bench prison, of his wife carrying him six-course dinners in gaol, of the older girls becoming governesses and dying in distress. None of this was true. They kept afloat: Mrs Lear had some money, Frederick went to work as a Stock Exchange clerk and Henry briefly joined the army.

An image recurs in Lear's limericks of men feeding queues of hungry offspring: this is what Jeremiah managed to do, although the upheaval was too much for his wife, who clung to the mirage of a different life, the one they could have, should have, led.

There was an Old Man of Apulia,
Whose conduct was very peculiar;
He fed twenty sons, upon nothing but buns,
That whimsical Man of Apulia.

During the turmoil of moving out and moving back four-year-old Edward was handed over to his eldest sister Ann, who was twenty-five in 1816. She may, indeed, have been responsible for him since he was born and she became, he always felt, his true mother. Ann and his other elder sisters played with him, read to him, and he learnt his letters with them, peering myopically at the alphabet books with their squares of letters illustrated by crude animals and birds – A is for Ass, C for Crow, Z for Zebra.

Ann was fun and liked to laugh, and, despite the family piety, for Lear as for all well-off children there were games and jokes, nursery rhymes to sing and books to read, like *The Butterfly's Ball and the Grasshopper's Feast*, written by the MP William Roscoe for his ten children, with every small page showing insects, animals and birds thronging to the feast. A host of small pleasures: birthday dinners of bacon and beans, and his sister Sarah teaching him to draw in the small parlour downstairs. But a year or so after their return, when Edward was five or six, it became clear that something was wrong. He had bronchitis and asthma, frightening for children who find themselves gasping, feeling that a monster is sitting on their chest. Worse still was the onset of some kind of fits – he remembered these clearly from the age of around five, but sometimes thought that they may have occurred earlier, even at one. These would last all his life, and he marked their onset and severity with 'X' in his diary. In his early fifties, mid-August 1866, after a bibulous dinner, Lear jotted down a grim 'XX 5', with a note, 'very unwell all night'. He rose late:

more or less stupefied all day. But, before I rose – reflected on days long gone – when I was but 8 – if so many years old. And this demon oppressed me then, I not knowing; its worry & misery. Every morning in the little study when learning my lessons – all day long: & always in the evening & at night. Nor could I have been more than 6 I think – for I remember whole years before I went to school – at 11.

The attacks were a form of epilepsy. Lear did not usually experience grand mal seizures, where the electric discharge affects the deep structure of the brain, bringing full-scale convulsions without warning. More often he had what are now called 'complex partial seizures', focal epilepsy affecting the temporal lobe, involved in processing memory, smell, taste, music and language. Sufferers experience a powerful 'aura', a wave of overwhelming dread, or a surging thrill of ecstatic joy, or a tremor of physical excitement. As this spreads, it can bring a rush of strange sensations, hallucinations of smell or taste, distortions of memory such as *déjà vu* or *jamais vu*, a sense of shrinking and expanding like Alice (Lewis Carroll was also a sufferer), of spinning through space, watching the self from above or dissolving in a storm of images. This state can be linked, too, to violent emotions, and – as for Lear – it can bring confusion, twitching and strange, jerky movements. Lear almost always felt the fits coming and could hide himself away. His bad times tended to come when he was tired or resting: the seizures lessened in adolescence then returned when he was about twenty and increased in force in later life, often arriving suddenly, marked by a swimming head and a feeling of nausea, '– & frightful dyspepsia – no relief till sudden X6. Then as usual deep sleep for ¾ hr. more epileptic then and later.' He was quick to spot signs in others. Visiting one family he noted, 'breakfast & after that, came George W. the second son – they told me he had "fallen on the stove – or grate" – & his face was dreadful to see. I have an impression he may have had epileptic fits . . . There is great sadness in this house, evidently.'

For a small boy it was terrifying, more so as he had seen his sister Jane, who was about seventeen when he had his first fits, suffer severely. Thinking about her years later, after a short midday fit, he wrote, 'How I remember my sister Jane's epileptic attacks, now! Child as I was then, & quite unable to understand them. The wonder with such attacks with me is the way wh. I have nearly always been able to be aware of the time they come to prevent publicity accordingly.' Jane was not looked after by her mother but by kindly 'Aunt Knight', a fixture in the family. Although epilepsy no longer carried the stigma of demonic possession, fits were still a cause of shame, linked to lack of will power, thought to be caused by masturbation, private pleasure, jerking off in secret. For a while Edward's sister Harriett shared his room, bossing him out of his 'impurity'. 'The strong will of sister Harriett put a short pause to the misery – but very short,' he wrote. With extraordinary strength he kept the seizures hidden. 'It is wonderful', he wrote in old age, 'that these fits have never been discovered – except that partly apprehending them beforehand, I go to my room.' He had been told, he said, of a doctor who was periodically mad, '& always knows beforehand when he will become so'. Lear's epilepsy, and the secrecy with which he guarded it, set him apart: it was the root of the profound loneliness he felt all his life.

Even as a small boy he was on guard, fearful of his own body. He lived with apprehension, hoping he would grow out of the fits, or could reduce them by walking, exercise, diet. He was vulnerable too because he was so shortsighted – much of his childhood was, literally, a blur. In his late thirties, when he reminded Ann jokingly of their trips to Margate together (fresh sea air and sea bathing was thought good for lung ailments like bronchitis), he tossed out a scatter of images: Mr Cox's hawk, colliers unloading coal at the pier, windmills, and a chimney sweep that Ann teasingly made Edward walk round 'to be sure he was not smoking – shocking. My imperfect sight in those days – antespectacled – formed everything into a horror.'

When the Lears returned to Bowman's Lodge after a few months away, with no spare cash for carriages and grooms, or tutors or governesses, life was simpler. Ann looked after Edward. She taught him about plants, insects and birds, and she and Sarah drew with him in the painting room across the hall from the nursery. She read him Greek myths, stories and poetry – the eighteenth-century favourites, Gray, Collins, Thomson's *Seasons*, and the new poets, especially Byron. She gave him her own love of the exotic: when he saw the statues of Abu Simbel in Egypt, a sight that took his breath away, he wrote of it as 'a place earliest known to me from the tales of my dear sister Ann – 48 years ago'. He thrilled to Thomas Stodhard's illustrations to *Robinson Crusoe*, which made him long to see 'similar realities'. Ann understood this. She painted a portrait of him when he was nine, in a dark-blue velvet coat, Sunday best, with a ruff like a miniature clergyman, his brown hair swept forward in a fashionable Napoleonic style, his long nose and gentle mouth already recognisable features. The setting was not Holloway fields but a land-scape with jewel-like flowers and a gushing waterfall, with a glimpse through the trees of pink sunset, smooth seas and spouting whales. Behind the boy, hidden by tree trunks and vines, is a rough structure, like Crusoe's hut. He is holding his flute, to charm the beasts.

The duo of Edward and Ann formed a family within a family. In the background moved his shadowy mother, who had no time for him, and his father, who was rarely there. Lear never forgot or forgave, or really understood, his mother's rejection. In all his work, although birds and animals snuggle up together, Lear never drew parents and children embracing. When he noted her birthday in his diary, as he did for all his family, he put 'mother', in eloquent quotation marks. His father too was distant. Looking at a miniature of him, Lear thought it was not as 'agreeable in the face' as he really was. 'Agreeable' is a remote term. It suggests a man he never really knew, who was either in the City, or in his study, or in his fabled workshop or laboratory in the attic.

Lear remembered odd scenes with Jeremiah, like driving through Holborn one day, 'remembering my father & a gig – a gray mare, Peggy – driving me by Theobald's Road, & shuddering about a murder close by . . .' One memory, often quoted, was of Jeremiah taking him to see some travelling showmen in a field near Highgate. Such shows had tumblers and acrobats, barkers shouting out the acts, music and gravity-defying feats on the slack rope and tight rope. 'Equilibristes' stood on their heads on the wire, or balanced in a tottering pyramid, the women were tinselled and daring. In the dusk they looked entrancing. When he thought of this in March 1877, Lear was going through a bad phase: on the top of the diary page he scrawled 'XX 3', and 'The Demon chain though loosened for 16 days'. He was feeling great swoops of mood and that evening he added, 'One had hoped to have got into smoother waters at 65; but not so.' Next day he went to a sociable dinner and played the piano: he put on a good front, he knew, 'but the heartache of many phases of life breaks one to pieces'. Then he went on:

The earliest of all the morbidnesses I can recollect must have been somewhere about 1819 –when my father took me to a field near Highgate, where was a rural performance of gymnastic clowns &c. – & a band. The music was good, – at least it attracted me: – the sunset & twilight I remember as if yesterday. And I can recollect crying half the night after all the small gaiety broke up – & also suffering for days at the memory of the past scene.

The yearning for vanished happiness swamped his delight in the music and the spinning acrobats. But the perilous, ecstatic balance would return in his nonsense, where people could still leap and cavort with one foot – two feet – off the ground.

2: WITH THE GIRLS

Lear's favourite early books were myths and poems, stories of travel and distant adventures. He idolised Byron for his bravura defiance of 'they', for his struggle for Greek independence, and for his poetry. He loved the music, wit and wide horizons of *Childe Harold's Pilgrimage*, *The Giaour*, *The Bride of Abydos* and *The Corsair*, which, as Francis Jeffrey wrote in the *Edinburgh Review*, 'spread around us the blue waters and dazzling skies – the ruined temples and dusky olives – the desolated cities, and turbaned population, of modern Attica'.

It was not surprising that Edward dreamed of distant lands. Something strange happened in Bowman's Lodge just before his tenth birthday, surfacing in his diary decades later when he heard of the death of a cousin, Frederick Harding. 'It is just fifty years since he did me the greatest evil done to me in life', he wrote '– excepting that done by C: – which must last now to the end – spite of all reason and effort.' Fifty years back was Easter Monday 1822, when Frederick was staying with the Lears. Lear never clarified this, or identified 'C' – perhaps his brother Charles. But the event was clearly momentous, inviting speculation that this must have been abuse of some kind, which he related to his own difficulties with relationships and sex – Lear rarely writes of touch, or physical desire. Once the memory surfaced he returned to it constantly, marking the date in his diary each year.

He went away to school, briefly, when he was eleven and twelve, and hated it, leaving no account except of hearing of Byron's death, 'in a crowd of horrid boys at the dreadful school of ——'. For many nights, he remembered, he did not sleep, and could not talk without crying. Elsewhere he wrote of his memory of a pale, cold moon and the yard and passages where he sat looking at the stars, 'when I heard that Ld Byron was dead, stupefied & crying'. Lear does not say he was bullied, but a weeping, poetry-loving eleven-year-old is an easy target, and his experience at school, like the incident with Harding, left deep scars. Indeed the scar tissue was building: the fits, the financial crash, his mother's rejection, the Harding incident and now the school. In later life, when he scratched these memories, he bled.

It was a relief to come home, away from the schoolboy 'they', and he had good local friends, the artistic Robert Leake Gale and William Nevill, with whom he stayed close all his life. Like many boys unhappy at school Lear built an inner life and learned that one way to be accepted was to make people laugh, to become an amiable buffoon. While he fretted about being 'half-educated' he was glad, he said later, to have escaped the straitjacket of conventional teaching, as so many of those who had been laboriously and expensively educated lost their learning, '& remain like Swift's Stullbruggs – cut & dried for life, making no use of their earlier-gained treasures: – whereas I seem to be on the threshold of knowledge'.

Lear's life was shaped less by school and childhood friends than by his sisters. If his Byron-worship spelled adventure, sex and glamour, his Holloway world was that of modest, accomplished girls. His elder sisters, Ann, Sarah, Mary and Eleanor, were Regency girls, born before Victorian proprieties took hold, high-spirited and zestful despite their evangelical faith. In teaching Edward they passed on their own education, on the lines that Miss Bingley in *Pride and Prejudice* lays down to merit the adjective 'accomplished', to wit 'a thorough knowledge of music, singing, drawing, dancing, and the modern languages'. They appeared at dinner in white dresses with blue sashes. They played the piano and shared the current taste for Thomas Moore's *Irish Melodies* like 'The Minstrel Boy' and 'Oft in the Stilly Night'. Lear had a natural ear and could play the small guitar, flute and accordion and pick up any tune on the piano. This gift would serve him all his life as a social, convivial skill, being a good man to have around, but music was also a private solace and pleasure: he composed his own settings, and his love of playing and singing flows through his poetry. The songs of Moore, Byron's friend and first biographer, remained an echo in his head and while he copied the popular parodies, the romantic melancholy of Moore's songs, like 'The Boat' of 1807, settled even deeper in his mind.

> I saw from the beach, when the morning was shining,
> A bark o'er the waters move gloriously on;
> I came when the sun o'er that beach was declining,
> The bark was still there, but the waters were gone.
>
> And such is the fate of our life's early promise,
> So passing the spring-tide of joy we have known;
> Each wave that we danced on at morning ebbs from us,
> And leaves us, at eve, on the bleak shore alone.

Lear often saw himself on this bleak shore.

His fear of being cast out was also heightened by his family's evangelical religion: the dread of losing heaven's 'golden shore', promised by the hymns. For his sisters, Sunday services, daily prayers and Bible reading were backed by a strong ethic of charity, hard work and self-improvement, and although Lear came to reject their fervent piety, he kept some of the habits ingrained in childhood: the self-examination of the diary, the dedication to work, the importance of 'improvement'. 'I lead as quiet a life as I can,' he once wrote, during some rare weeks of calm, 'being strongly convinced that a regular application to some kind of self-improvement by way of work is more necessary to ensure comfort than any variety of social fuss.'

He was happy with his sisters, taught by the older ones and tolerated by the younger. But gradually the family changed. In 1821, when Edward was nine, Ann was thirty, Sarah twenty-six, Mary twenty-five and Eleanor twenty-two. Then all in a rush, three of them found husbands. That same year Mary married Richard Shuter Boswell, who worked in the Bank of England; a year later, in 1822, Sarah married Charles Street, a Sussex banker's clerk, and a year after that Eleanor married William Newsom, the son of old sugar-house friends, who also worked for the Bank of England.

The house was emptying of the young women who petted and played with Edward. Mary and Eleanor's marriages strengthened the family's evangelical strain: the kindly William Newsom was a staunch Calvinist and Richard Boswell would become accountant and assistant secretary of 'The Language Institution, in Aid of the Propagation of Christianity' (whose vice presidents included William Wilberforce and Stamford Raffles), founded in 1826. By contrast, Sarah's marriage was less solemn, and it came with a good story. Walking through the City her father had seen a name-plate for 'Jeremiah Lear' and on impulse he introduced himself to his namesake. The two families were unrelated but came to know each other well and the wealthier Jeremiah welcomed the Holloway Lears at his country house, Batsworth Park, near Arundel in Sussex. Here Sarah met Charles Street, the fifth son of a Surrey squire, and a clerk in the bank in town.

From now on Edward often took the coach down to stay with Sarah and Charles in Arundel. But his London life was still shaped by Ann. Together they pored over his father's collection of pictures and prints, like the ambitious Boydell Shakespeare with its engravings of works by contemporary artists, including Fuseli, Romney, Benjamin West, Angelica Kauffman and Thomas Stothard. Other prints looked back to great artists of the past and Lear grew up with a love of superb, meticulous drawing. Many years later, between trains in Vienna, he spent a day in Duke Charles's gallery, and wrote to Ann:

I had folio after folio of Albert Durer's drawing all to my blessed self. I never looked at anything else, but passed the whole morning on the old Nuremberger's works, getting a good lesson as to what perseverance & delicate attention to drawing may do. You would have liked to see some of the wonderfully beautiful sketches of weeds – flowers, & birds, which were there – much reminding me of certain hedgehogs, shells, flies, & pole cats etc. etc. – of other days.

With Ann, too, Lear read classics, travel books and the poetry of Byron, Keats and Shelley, giving him a yearning for liberty and a sense of glory past, as well as of the fleeting nature of happiness. (He was thrilled, years later, to meet Shelley's son Percy and play him his setting of 'O world! O life! O time!'.) He and Ann also enjoyed the spoofs of Byron's orientalism, Wordsworth's ballads and Tom Moore's songs in *The London Magazine*, whose authors included De Quincey, Hazlitt, Lamb, and Thomas Hood, especially the parody and puns of Hood's light verse, like the lament of Mary's ghost, her corpse seized by the body-snatchers:

> The arm that used to take your arm
> Is took to Dr Vyse;
> And both my legs are gone to walk
> The hospital at Guy's . . .
>
> Don't go to weep upon my grave,
> And think that there I be;
> They haven't left an atom there,
> Of my anatomie.

'An atom . . . anatomie' is exactly the kind of punning word division Lear made his own. Lear admired Hood all his life, and Hood's sense of language as alive and fluid, his grotesquery, his sense of fragmentation and blurring of boundaries between animal and human, as well as his edgy violence, seeped into Lear's writing from the start.

Even as a boy, encouraged by Ann, he wrote parodies. When he was thirteen, he turned the disaster of his father's defaulting and the flight from their home into a comic saga in imitation of 'Hassan: or, the

Camel Driver' from William Collins's *Persian Eclogues* of 1742. He copied the length, eighty-two lines, and echoed Collins's dynamic rhyming
couplets, undercutting the high-flying original with prosaic details and
bathetic rhymes. In place of Hassan trekking across the scorching sands
with his camels,

> In dreary silence down the bustling road
> The Lears – with all their goods and chattels rode;
> Ten carts of moveables went on before,
> And in the rear came half-a-dozen more.

Just as Hassan strikes his breast in a mournful refrain: 'Sad was the
hour, and luckless was the day/When first from Schiraz' walls I bent
my way,' so the Lears, doomed to stay in 'thrice odious New Street',
tortured by fears of radical mobs, burglars and house fires, wail: 'Sad
was the hour – and luckless was the day/When first from Bowman's
Lodge we bent our way.'

He teased his mother's delusions of lost grandeur too, in 'The Sunny
Side of Durham', and became adept at bravura word games, odd diction
and bad rhymes. In 1826, when he was fourteen, he gave Ann a poem
for her thirty-fifth birthday:

> Dear, and very dear relation,
> Time, who flies without cessation, –
> Who ne'er allows procrastination, –
> Who never yields to recubation,
> Nor ever stops for respiration,
> Has brought again in round rotation
> The once a yearly celebration
> Of the day of thy creation . . .

His own 'dire depauperation', with no money to buy her a present,
pushed him back on his own resources, wrenching his imagination to
ensure that in all the poem's 110 breathless lines, 'every termination/
To every line should end in -ation'. Beginnings and ends come together

as the teenager collects existing words and tumbles into coinages and inventions. He imagines her life fading: may Ann be loved with veneration, 'towards the life's advesperation', but also ponders her nearer future: 'If as report gives intimation/You are about to change your station', he wishes her bliss in 'matrimonial elevation'. That 'report' came to nothing. Although Ann did love one man, a Major Wilby, and turned down a proposal from another, she never married. Her life was bound up with her brother.

Apart from odd hints, Lear stayed quiet about the darker sides of childhood. In 1868, enjoying the beauty of a spring day in Cannes, he wrote, 'Considering all I remember to have passed through from 6 years old to 15 – is it not wonderful I am alive? – far more to be able to feel & write.' The significant age, '15', saw the end of the Holloway years. In 1827, when Jeremiah Lear reached seventy and his wife was entering her sixties, they left London and retired to Gravesend. Florence and Catherine went with them and the rest of the family scattered. Ann took lodgings for herself and Edward on the top floor of 38 Upper North Place, off Gray's Inn Road, using a small annuity of £300 a year from a trust set up by her maternal great-grandmother. Four years later Lear complained bitterly of being someone who, 'at the age of 14 & a half, was turned out into the world, *literally without a farthing* – & with nought to look to for a living but his own exertions'. Elsewhere the farthing became a halfpenny, or a penny.

Central London was dark with smog from coal fires, its streets crowded, its slums riddled with disease. The city's population had soared to two million, and in the long depression thousands of Londoners were driven to emigrate, joining the rural poor and the paupers from the industrial towns. By those standards Ann and Edward were comfortably off, although the gulf between their family and the Sussex Lears of Batsworth Park became even more obvious. This year, 1827, George Lear from Arundel started work with the lawyers Ellis and Blackmore in Gray's Inn: in May, the fifteen-year-old Dickens, Lear's contemporary, joined the firm as a clerk. Dickens put George into the *Pickwick Papers* as the 'Articled Clerk' who has paid a premium, runs a tailor's bill, receives invitations to parties, 'and who is, in short, the very aristocrat of clerks'. For his part, George thought he knew London, 'but after a little talk with Dickens I found I knew nothing . . . he knew it all from Bow to Brentford', and could imitate every kind of street-seller in town. Edward Lear's London was nearer to that of Dickens than that of George – he too was a boy scurrying to make a living. Later letters to Ann hum with London memories; Bologna is 'as full of beggars as Russell Square used to be'; the stern palaces of Florence look like Newgate; the streets of Tivoli, however beautiful its gardens, are as narrow and filthy as the dog-leg alleys behind Gray's Inn Road. His nonsense language often has the Cockney twang and glottal stops of Dickens's madder characters, splitting and combining words: 'a nother taito', a 'chikki-boan', and dropping or adding 'h's. In his fifties, he came out with a bravura diary entry about a Mrs Deaking:

Mrs D. has haspirated her haitches more amazingly than ever: she said 'the Hice-hickels ung hin hevery hexposed helevation, & on hall hobjects'. Really I never did hear such pronunciation, & hit hoppresses me.

Wherever he travelled, Lear stayed a Londoner.

Ann faced noisy inner London head on, if modestly. 'How you used to swear: such oaths!!! – don't you recollect? – "by the soldiers!"' Lear teased her. Since money was short, he turned to the one thing he was good at: in about 1827 he began to draw, he said, 'for bread and cheese . . . but only did uncommon queer shop-sketches – selling them for prices varying from ninepence to four shillings: colouring prints, screens, fans: awhile making morbid disease drawings, for hospitals and certain doctors of physic'. At times he sold his drawings to passengers in the inn-yards waiting to change coaches.

The medical drawings, perhaps studies of different conditions as a guide to diagnosis, perhaps drawings to teach students, or advertisements for medicines (like the 'Propter's Nicodemus Pills' he mentions in his poem 'Uncle Arly'), were a training in precise observation and anatomy, useful to Lear in natural history painting. But with the coloured prints and painted screens and fans he was still with the girls. He had learned from the drawing manuals published for women like his sisters, with etchings to copy after old masters, and from the lessons in drawing and watercolours in magazines like *Ackermann's Repository of Arts* and the *Ladies' Monthly Museum*, squeezed between fashion plates, new songs and household hints. Now he began teaching well-off girls hardly younger than himself, sometimes on their own, sometimes in groups of six or eight. He remembered one group in St James's, presided over by the daunting Madame Zielske in her turban; his sister Cordelia gave him instructions on how he should behave when he went into the drawing room. He enjoyed teaching, although his friend Daniel Fowler found it agony: 'Every teacher will have a parcel of young girls on his hands, who have not the remotest idea what art means,' Fowler groaned.

They do not, and never will, begin at the beginning. They must do something that looks pretty; some copy that they have made, with about as much comprehension of it as a parrot has of the speech it learns. This is the case with ninety-nine out of a hundred young ladies who take it up as an accomplishment, so called, I suppose, because nothing is accomplished.

Several of Lear's pupils lived in smart London streets and squares but one, Miss Fraser, came from the old Highgate milieu. He gave her an album as a 'First Drawing Prize', a gift that fitted a current craze. A poem on the first page of one album belonging to Robert Southey's daughter Edith summed up the form:

> What is an album? Tis a thing
> Made up of odds and ends,
> A Drawing here and there, and Rhymes
> By dear poetic Friends.

> Wit thinly scatter'd up and down,
> And lines of every measure,
> A Tree, a Butterfly, a Flowr
> Compose the motley treasure . . .

In 1827 Charles Lamb fled Islington, he said, to escape 'Albumean persecution'. Sighing that albums would pursue him to the uttermost parts of the earth, he published *Album Verses* in 1830. Ten years later, in 'A Shabby Genteel Story', Thackeray's Miss Caroline 'had in her possession, like almost every young lady in England, a little square book called an album, containing prints from annuals, hideous designs of flowers, old pictures of faded fashions, cut out and pasted into the leaves; and small scraps of verses selected from Byron, Landon or Mrs Hemans'.

On Miss Fraser's opening page Lear drew a vignette of a lyre, an open book with a sketch of hummingbirds, and a palette surrounded by a colourful swag of flowers, with a rhyme:

> My album's open, come and see: –
> What, won't you waste a thought on me:
> Write but a word, a word or two,
> And make me love to think on you.

Inside, he gummed in paintings of birds against palm-studded scenery, joined by his own sketches of a beady-eyed tiger, a peasant woman, rococo flowers, and the 'Temple of Jupiter, Aegina', copied from a print, with mournful, but heartfelt, sub-Byronic verse:

> But Greece has fallen, like thee, –
> Desolate – wildly lone; –
> Her sons – the brave and free,
> Forgotten and unknown . . .

Lear knew how to charm. And the flowers he drew showed genuine skill. Sometimes they resembled embroidery designs – curling convolvulus, sprays of apple blossom – but several detailed studies suggest he was copying the classic *Bowles's Drawing Book for Ladies; or Complete Florist*, which gave precise rules for drawing flowers, with plates of examples.

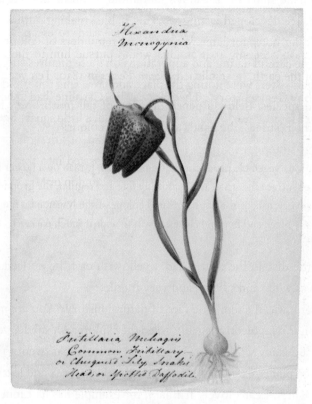

Hexandria Monogynia, 'The Common Fritillary'

Sarah was the most knowledgeable botanist among the Lear sisters, and the finest painter. In her late fifties, writing to her brother Fred about his daughter, she exclaimed:

gladly would I supply little Rosita with a Book of drawings, if you were more accessible, for it is such a delightful, as well as inexpensive amusement. I hope, if spared she will make progress in it, and copy Flowers, Houses, Trees, etc. from Nature for if she inherits the taste for it some of our family possess, it may in some future day be very useful.

Ann too was skilled at drawing plants, in elegant, formal compositions, noting that one flower was picked in a garden at Hackney, and
signing another 'Drawn from Nature, Holloway A.L.' Edward painted
an exquisite study of 'Eleanor's Geranium' from nature when he was
sixteen. He developed lasting working habits, making outline sketches
and adding notes for later watercolours, reminders of colour and texture. The careful dating and annotations on these pictures suggests that
he and his sisters were noting the place and flowering time, and the gen-
era and species. Below a pencil drawing of tall mushrooms he wrote
about their 'striae', the bands and stripes of colour:

This curious vegetable production I found, May 1st, 1828 on a flower bed – On
the upper surface the striae are beautifully fine and regular, the ground being of
a pale, silvery, ash, as is also the ground colour of the lower side, but the striae
being very black and fine and close cause it to appear much darker.

The little disc in the centre had a yellowish cast, he noticed, and the
stem was white and silvery, and very fragile.

Botany was the feminine face of natural history: 'You are interested
in botany?' Napoleon allegedly asked the explorer Alexander von Hum-
boldt. 'So is my wife.' Women read and wrote books, went to lectures,
collected plants, examined them through microscopes and learned their
Latin names. Lear's lovely fritillary, for example has its Linnean label,
'*Hexandria Monogynia*', with common names beneath: 'Fritillaria Mili-
agris. Common Fritillary or Chequered Lily, Snakes Head, or Spotted
Daffodil'. This was the taxonomic pigeonholing that he would mock
affectionately in his nonsense botany, in the surreal *Piggiwiggia Pyramidalis*, and *Phattfacia Stupenda*, and *Manypeeplia Upsidownia*, like
Solomon's seal with tiny suspended people. These were his own inven-
tions, but they reflected reports of travellers and plant hunters, of plants
full of mimicry and odd relations with the animal and insect worlds.
Amid all this, why should there not be a Bong Tree, or a fly-guzzling
Bluebottlia Buzztilentia?

He ridiculed the exaggerated passion for flowers in an early nonsense rhyme, where the flower-lover's waistcoat matches the lily's marks, rousing the bees:

There was an old person so silly,
He poked his head into a lily;
But six bees who lived there, filled him full of despair,
For they stung that old person so silly.

Yet athough he laughed Lear rejoiced in flowers and trees all his life: wild flowers like a Turkish carpet, cypresses against blue sky, palms on the Nile.

After they moved to Gray's Inn Road, Ann and Edward shared large, leather-bound scrapbooks, sticking in some of Sarah's paintings as well as their own. There were drawings and paintings of shells and exotic birds: a pair of Indian bee-eaters on a branch, doves on a nest, a golden pheasant (signed 'A. Lear') before a landscape that looks like the South Downs with palms. A smaller notebook, with different coloured pages, contains the usual amateurish sketches and pasted-in butterflies with tissue-paper wings: then suddenly, there is a dynamic watercolour of a duck in flight.

The duck, and other elegant, delicately careful bird paintings from the late 1820s, were very different in style from the stylised humming-birds. They showed how far he had moved on. Yet models for these too could be found in the sisters' magazines, which had embraced natural history eagerly for a generation, printing articles that were unafraid to give technical details. Birds figured large when Ann was a girl, in Ann Murry's serial 'The Moral Zoologist' in *The Lady's Magazine*, which laid out clearly the current debates about classification, drawing on a mass of ornithological experts: Edwards and Latham, Buffon, Albin, Brisson and Sloane. One set of Murry's articles was on parrots: lorys, macaws, and red-headed and blue-headed parakeets, with details of plumage, size, colour, habits and habitat, accompanied by large, clear engravings. These were the kinds of pictures that Edward copied. This was the kind of artist he was going to be. His education with the girls was far from frivolous: by his late teens he had an eye for detail that would make him one of the finest natural history painters of his day.

3: 'O SUSSEX!'

In contrast to Gray's Inn Road, Sussex was light and air and views and space, broad fields of corn, grassy slopes, clumps of trees, with farms nestling beneath. Edward spent many holidays with Sarah and her husband Charles Street in Arundel, in their tall red-brick house on the quay, at the foot of the High Street that climbed from the river to the walls of the castle grounds. In summer he walked through lanes like green tunnels, emerging high on the downs to see the Arun snaking across the plain to the sea. In winter he strode along the muddy river bank, where frost silvered the reeds and teazles and the castle shimmered across the water meadows like a mirage.

Sussex meant family and friends, free of constraints. To call on the wealthy Lears at Batsworth Park, a mile or so east of Arundel, he crossed the fast-flowing river, where flocks of seagulls flew up with the tide, walked along the flood-plain and then took a steep lane into the woods. If he followed the curving loop of the Arun before he reached the Batsworth lane he could visit new friends, the Drewitts, who lived at Peppering House just beyond the small village of Burpham. All these families were involved in the town's finances, Charles Street as a clerk, Jeremiah Lear as a trustee of the Savings Bank and John Drewitt in the bank formed with his brother-in-law in 1827: Hopkins, Drewitt and Wyatt.

Edward met the Drewitts when he was eleven, the time of his unhappy stay at school: of their three children, Fanny, who took him under her wing, was then nineteen, Robert was fourteen and Eliza twelve. Their father, John, was a naturalist, an expert on birds, insects and plants, interested in geology and fossils. Six years before he had inherited a collection of eight hundred species of butterflies and moths, in their cabinet of forty-four drawers, from his cousin William Jones, a pioneering entomologist and one of the first members of the Linnean Society. To Edward the house was full of treasures, alight with happiness and new discoveries. Later, in a moment of nostalgia, he wrote to Fanny, 'How clearly just at the moment is before me the first morning I was ever there – when I had so much delight in looking over the Cabinet – & when I fancied one would always live in the sunshine one felt then!' A drawing of Peppering House, with its plain Georgian front shaded by trees, is his first surviving landscape. It was, and still is, a beautiful, open place, on a spur of the hill above the river with views on three sides, north up the valley to the downs, west across the river to the wooded slopes, and south towards the sea with the castle silhouetted against the light.

Peppering opened his eyes to the natural world. He walked and looked, high up into the great trees, and for the first time, he remembered, he heard the voice of the rooks. But it was also a place of stories, like that of the Knucker, a dragon who crept from a bottomless pool to slaughter livestock and people. Legend and reality seemed to touch, too, in the discovery of bones nearby: the Lewes doctor Gideon Mantell, who uncovered giant lizards and iguanodon in central Sussex, noted that 'the bones, and several grinders of elephants, have been found in a bed of gravel, on the estate of John Drewett, Esq., of Peppering'. Lear could also feel more recent history: in 1826 a rare coin turned up in a field on the Drewitts' farm, bearing the head of Edward I, as Duke of Aquitaine. With its busy farm and evocative past, Peppering was a rich second home throughout Lear's adolescence, where he could be as moody and wild and odd as he pleased. He grew fast, with long thin legs and flailing arms. The tolerant Drewitts knew about the family troubles, and about his illness – a few years later he sent an unembarrassed message to Eliza, apologising for not seeing her off in the coach, explaining, 'I was taken ill – with my old complaint in the head – so much as to be unable to walk home.'

Arundel widened his horizons. He was throwing off his family's chapel-going zeal, and as a fan of Byron and Shelley, he was scathing about political corruption and attempts to 'christianize the nation'. At fourteen, he wrote an accomplished parody, part radical drinking song, part spoof evangelical hymn: 'Ye who have hearts – aloud rejoice,/For Oligarchy trembles'. In that summer's election the Tories under Lord Liverpool had trounced the Whigs and Lear's song echoed the appeal of radical candidates like Henry 'Orator' Hunt and William Cobbett 'to strike always at the head of that insolent and rapacious oligarchy who make us burn with shame and indignation at the disgrace and bankruptcy and misery' they have heaped on the nation. But while Lear mocked this rhetoric, he was parodying the language of Methodist or Universalist/Unitarian hymns – 'Rejoice aloud! Rejoice aloud!' – and of charismatic preachers like Edward Irving, who was drawing huge crowds to his Caledonian chapel in London. Lear often heard Irving preach, remembering him walking round the square, 'reading a Bible over the head of his baby'. An odd prophetic note sounds here too: one election song of this year had the tune 'Derry Down', close to the mummer's name 'Derry down Derry' that Lear later chose for his nonsense, and its refrain was loud in defiance of the powerful 'they' who stifled the people: 'Derry down, down, oppression lie down'.

As a teenager in Sussex, however, Lear was drawn into conservative rather than radical circles, and was more concerned with his future as an artist than with religion or politics. The Drewitts and the Batsworth Lears were important local families, welcomed at assemblies at the castle (Robert Drewitt would later lead the young Queen Victoria up the narrow winding stairs of the keep). Through them a web of connections spread outwards. Lear made a lasting friend in George Cartwright, son of the vicar of Lyminster. They went sketching together, and through the Cartwrights he met the young Robert Curzon, who would one day become Baron Zouche and inherit nearby Parham, a golden stone Elizabethan house dreaming in its deer park. Lear came to understand the use of such a chain of connections, and as he walked the countryside, in love with the great trees and downland views, he began to think, idly, of drawing landscapes.

He was already considering an artist's life and was on his best behaviour at Batsworth Park on a bitter Sunday morning in November 1829, where he told Ann in a long verse letter:

> Called at Lyminster – John at home
> Looked at the plates of Rogers' Italy –
> Talked of reform and Chancellor Brougham –
> Back to Arundel made a run, –
> And finished a lunch at half past one.

Reform was the topic of the day: a month before, an article in the *Westminster Review* had attacked the proposals for law reform put forward by Jeremy Bentham and Henry Brougham (soon to be Lord Chancellor). But 'Rogers' Italy' intrigued Lear more. Samuel Rogers had visited Italy after the Napoleonic wars, celebrating it in a long poem weaving his own ecstatic response with stories from history. Its reception was flat, and to gain more attention a disappointed Rogers commissioned vignettes for a luxury edition. Early copies appeared in late 1829, and the publishers also produced separate portfolios of the plates. These included twenty-five engravings of watercolours by Turner, whom Lear came to admire more than any living artist, from Lake Como and the Roman Campagna to the Temples of Paestum under lightning-rent skies – all places that Lear would later see and sketch.

As it happened, when Lear looked at Rogers's *Italy*, Turner was not far away. George Wyndham, third Earl of Egremont, who owned the great house at Petworth in West Sussex, had first commissioned him to paint landscapes twenty years earlier, but it was not until 1829 that Turner became almost part of the household, using the library as his studio, painting the lake, grounds and distant views. Petworth was packed with glorious paintings, including Van Dycks and Claudes, and the genial, lackadaisical earl opened his house to friends, artists and musicians, as well as his own entangled family, too diverse to count. (A few years before, Lord Blessington had written: 'Nothing will persuade me that Lord Egremont has not forty three children . . . when quarrels arise, which few days pass without, each mother takes part with her progeny, bursts into the drawing room, fights with each other, with Lord E., his children, and I believe the Company, and makes scenes worthy of Billingsgate or a Madhouse.')

Egremont was a model of the eccentric aristocratic patron, and Lear also came into the orbits of two more Turner patrons. One was John Leicester, Lord de Tabley, co-founder in 1805 of the 'British Institution for Promoting the Fine Arts in the United Kingdom' – or 'The Pall Mall Gallery', as it was known – where shows of living British artists alternated with old masters. Leicester also opened his own house in Berkeley Square to the public, but such a passion was expensive – when he died in 1827, a year after the fourteen-year-old Lear met him, his finances were in tatters and his executors immediately sold his great collection.

The other Turner connection was with the family of Walter Ramsden Fawkes, Turner's friend and patron for sixteen years. By the mid-1820s Fawkes, like Leicester, was almost broke: when his daughter Anne married her cousin Godfrey Wentworth in 1822 he had to borrow £8000 from a neighbour for her dowry. 'Anne and Godfrey married,' wrote his wife Maria. 'A very long day. Had a large party to dinner. All tipsey.' Turner was one of the guests. Mrs Wentworth was a friendly, open woman, interested in art and in natural history – her husband's relation Lord Fitzwilliam had a famous menagerie at Wentworth Woodhouse in Yorkshire. She admired the young Lear's drawings and used her London connections to get him introductions. He always believed that she had started him on his way, and in April 1830 he gave her an album with seventeen paintings of birds against pencilled landscapes with a grateful inscription.

This was almost the last period when artists could hope to make a living through painting for patrons, and Lear, a young amateur still in his teens, would of course try to find financial backing. He already had a facility for fitting into any group, any situation. By 1829, when he was seventeen, Sarah and Charles Street had two children, Charles Henry, now five, and Fred, who was two. That winter he sent Ann a verse diary from Arundel, beginning with the freezing coach journey from London. Cleverly, he mimicked Moore's comic 'intercepted letters' from an Irish family in 'The Fudge Family in Paris', a satire of the tourists rushing to France after the Napoleonic wars. Other writers transported the Fudges to Edinburgh, Dublin and Washington, but Lear felt Arundel would do just as well. He wrote of walks beneath leafless trees, boys skating, tea and backgammon, party games with neighbours, children and a new baby:

> Saw the baby – that unique child
> Who squeaked – and stared – and sniffed – and smiled.

With the Streets and their friends Lear was the high-spirited uncle, who jokes and plays and throws shrieking children in the air. At Batsworth Park, by contrast, he was the polite young visitor, interested in politics, engravings and art. At Peppering he was like a beloved cousin, flirting with Fanny and Eliza, running races with Robert, charming the older generation with his interest in the farm, the village and their natural history pursuits. He amused the family with poems like 'Peppering Roads', a sharp picture of his struggle to see them on a winter holiday, his coach jolting on the steep rutted roads:

> The coachman who opened the door
> Found us tangled so very topturvy –
> We rolled out in a bundle, – all four.
> And then we were so whisped together,

> Legs – dresses – caps – arms – blacks and whites
> That some minutes elapsed before ever
> They put us completely to rights! –

Nonsense is almost here. He wrote too, of slithering in the melting ice and claggy chalk of the lane:

> Oh the Peppering roads! Sure 'tis fit there
> Should be some requital at last
> So the inmates you find, when you get there
> Amply pay you for all you have passed.

They did repay him. The Drewitts' concerns became his; he composed a sad poem when their King Charles spaniel Ruby was shot by accident, with a little watercolour that they kept carefully among their letters. He wrote about the turkeys attacking gulls in the garden – to the tune, he said, of the song 'Shades of Evening' – catching the household chaos:

> Down rushed Fanny and Eliza; –
> Screams and squawks and yowlings shrill, –
> Gulls and turkeys with their cries a-
> round them echoed oer the hill: –

At Peppering Lear was allowed to play the fool, '3 parts crazy – & wholly affectionate'. At seventeen he was a bundle of mobility, physically and mentally restless. But sometimes when he was leaving Sussex he stopped and looked back. In a verse letter to Eliza, sending some magazines from London, he described watching her set off home from the ridge of Bury Hill. He missed the Drewitts when he was away, especially Fanny. In another poem he wrote of the view from the same ridge at sunset 'on a calm summer's eve'. In times of grief, he wondered,

> Will not memory turn to some thrice hallowed spot,
> That shines out like a star among years that are past?
> Some dream that will wake in a desolate heart,

Every chord into music that long has been hushed.
Mournful echo! – soon still – for it tolls with a smart,
That the joys which first woke it, are long ago crushed.

He was borrowing phrases from 'Troubadour' by Laetitia Landon, the massively popular 'L.E.L.', who described the singer's burial in 'a thrice hallowed spot', but the sentiment that he often mocked is serious here.

The following September he wrote to Fanny begging for a letter – he had heard nothing from the Drewitts for two months – putting her silence down to the work of 'that wretched little fat Person, who has lately made so much confusion in Sussex', adding a drawing of a plump Cupid with bow and arrow and an ironic PS: 'Of course you have heard of my marriage.' That year Fanny married George Coombe, a local landowner. (For her wedding Lear wrote a comic poem about the cracked church bell.) She moved from Peppering to another romantic house, Calceto, in the marshy valley of the Arun, where Queen Adelisa had established a priory on the causeway seven hundred years ago. A chapter was over, but the friendship was not lost. Lear remained close to Fanny and to her husband George, a keen bird-watcher and fossil collector. He was godfather to their son Percy, an adopted uncle to their daughter Laura, and he kept in touch with Fanny all her life.

In his poem, as he looked down from Bury Hill over the plain to the sea, an enduring emotional geography, a map of longing, began to take shape. Returning here in 1862, when he was fifty, climbing to the top of the downs, Lear wrote in his diary, 'O Sussex! – & *what* a sunset!! . . . – Ai! – E! come passano, i dì felici!" said I – remembering years – nearly 40 – ago!!' How they pass, the happy days.

II. PERCHING

4: TO THE ZOO

There was a Young Lady whose bonnet,
Came untied when the birds sate upon it;
But she said, 'I don't care! all the birds in the air
Are welcome to sit on my bonnet!'

Surely this is the most joyful of all Lear's limericks. Like the young lady, he was always happy with birds. In the middle of one of his early sketchbooks, solid on the page, sits a pair of green parrots, bold and companionable, looking slightly bored. Further on there is a watercolour of a blue macaw, and two carefully painted feathers. A pencil sketch shows another parrot perching on a branch against flowing, willow-like foliage; other drawings, more careful still, are of a greater bird of paradise and a citrus-crested cockatoo from Indonesia.

In the summer of 1830, parrots were Lear's companions. In the hazy mornings, in his narrow trousers and frock coat, he dashed across town from Gray's Inn Road, past Coram Fields and north through Bloomsbury to the ivory Nash terraces by Regent's Park. He was heading for the zoo, and the parrot house, where, that June, the London Zoological Society had given him permission to sketch. If botany was for women, ornithology was for men: birds opened the way for Lear to join them. Soon after he and Ann moved to Gray's Inn Road, he presented himself as an artist that naturalists could turn to, making a fine *trompe l'œil* painting of his card, with a tiny black feather from a Siberian ruby-throat and a large jay's feather, miraculously real.

If he wasn't at the zoo he was at the society's museum at Lord Berkeley's town house, 33 Bruton Street, where some birds were kept until new aviaries were built, and where the skins and specimens were stored – by 1828 these had reached an astonishing six hundred mammals, four thousand birds, one thousand reptiles and fish, and thirty thousand insects. At the end of 1830, writing a quick verse to a friend, Harry Hinde, accepting an invitation to tea, Lear broke off to 'go to my dinner':

> For all day I've been a-
> way at the West End,

Painting the best end
Of some vast Parrots
As red as new carrots, –
(They are at the museum, –
When you come you shall see 'em, –)
I do the head and neck first; –
And ever since breakfast
I've had one bun merely!
So – yours quite sincerely
E.L.

The appetite for books on birds and animals had grown since the voyages of Captain Cook in the 1760s and 70s, as more and more expeditions brought back unfamiliar plants and specimens of animals, birds, reptiles and fish. Passionate devotees worked to keep pace, diligently labelling species, trying to tie down the profusion, grotesqueries and marvels of the natural world. System was all; from Linnaean categories of flora and fauna to Lavoisier's ordering of elements and gases, from the mapping of land to new standards of measurement and weight. The world expanded before the eyes of Western savants and they wanted not only to order and name new species but to see them, and even to possess them. The public had always been thrilled by wild animals, as ferocious as possible: they could see these at the Royal Menagerie in the Tower of London, and at 'Exeter Change' in the Strand, now run by Edward Cross. In Lear's early teens this was famous for its great elephant, Chunee, who turned violent in 1826 and was executed by firing squad – a great London drama. Two years later all the beasts were paraded down the Strand to the King's Mews, when the old Exchange was demolished. At around the same time, the Surrey Zoo opened next to Vauxhall pleasure gardens, with lions, tigers, kangaroos, and a giant tortoise giving rides to children, as well as a lake and a model of Vesuvius: a site of spectacle and entertainment, of balloon ascents, concerts, fireworks and panoramas.

With a very different approach, in April 1828 the Zoological Society of London opened its zoo as a serious centre for research. The society was founded in 1826 by Sir Stamford Raffles, former governor of British territories in South East Asia, and Humphry Davy, successor to Joseph Banks as president of the Royal Society – empire and science hand in hand. The Crown Estates allotted a triangular plot in Regent's Park (the same area covered by the zoo today), and in 1829, when the Crown granted a Royal Charter and transferred the Royal Menagerie from the Tower, Regent's Park stood out as the pre-eminent British zoo. Members of the society, their families and friends and holders of special tickets, could wander along gravelled paths between low-built animal houses and aviaries, past ponds filled with wildfowl. There were kangaroos and llamas, monkeys and bears and even a hippopotamus, not seen in Europe since the Romans. But if the zoo showed off the beautiful, sensuous emblems of empire and exploration, it also stressed Britain's civilising mission: the most ferocious animals, even lions and wolves, the society claimed, were milder when bred in captivity. A guide for children proclaimed that the zoo's animals were 'not only beautiful but happy . . . gentle, tender, compassionate, sympathising and benevolent, or at least innocent, like the best, and like the fairest, among ourselves'.

Mrs Wentworth managed to get Lear an introduction as soon as the zoo opened – a rare privilege, as other artists were denied entry – and at once he began to draw. A lemur and his favourite blue-and-yellow macaws were both used for wood engravings in *The Gardens and Menagerie of the Zoological Society Delineated*, a small two-volume work for the general public, edited by the society's secretary, Edward Bennett. This was another chance to learn, as the leading London illustrator William Harvey – a former apprentice to the great wood engraver Thomas Bewick and a kindly, hard-working man, always generous to young artists – was in charge of the illustrations. Whenever he could Harvey drew from living creatures rather than stuffed specimens, and dropped the conventional side view of birds and animals, making them lively as well as lifelike. In both approaches Lear would follow him. Perhaps persuaded by the publisher Rudolph Ackermann, he even considered publishing lithographs of his own sketches of the animals, like those used in Bennet's book, and on a proof title page he included the study of the lion, camel, tiger and other creatures that he had pasted into one of his notebooks, the 'peaceable kingdom'. But he then set this aside, and decided to create a more ravishing work and publish it himself. The subject, he decided, would be parrots.

It was a move of astounding ambition. First, he had to find subscribers to fund such an expensive work. He approached friends, who in turn roped in others: the list began with Mrs Wentworth, followed by her daughter and sisters; then came the Zoological Society's key figures, including Nicholas Vigors and Lord Stanley, President of the Linnean Society and soon of the Zoological Society, and leading naturalists such as Sir William Jardine and the Northumberland squire Prideaux John Selby. Selby's fellow grandees from the north-east were there, including the Duke and Duchess of Northumberland, and the Sussex connection was strong too, from the Earl of Egremont and the Duke of Norfolk to the Wardropers and Mrs Hopkins, the Streets' Arundel neighbours. Old friends from Holloway signed up, and parents and teachers of his pupils, like Madame Zielske of Tavistock Square. But the seriousness of the enterprise showed in the subscriptions from societies: the Linnean, the Society of Arts and the Zoological Society itself.

To satisfy them Lear had to produce something special. His plan was that *Illustrations of the Family of Psittacidae, or Parrots* would appear in fourteen numbers between 1830 and 1832, with subscribers paying ten shillings for each of the promised parts: all of this showed a surprisingly entrepreneurial, practical-minded side to his nature. Even bolder, he chose a large folio size, a format no one had used before: *Parrots* was a turning point in ornithological illustration. The only man to go further was Audubon, with his huge 'elephant folio' plates for *Birds of America*, which had just begun publication in 1827. When Lear got to work, Audubon, now in his fifties, was lecturing in Britain and Europe, hunting for good printers and drumming up his own subscribers, including many of those named in Lear's list. He met Lear at the zoo, and his example may well have inspired the idea of *Parrots*: they became friends and Lear was especially close to Audubon's sons, Victor, three years his senior, and John, exactly his age. When *Parrots* was published as a book in 1832, Audubon bought a copy, admiring Lear's art in comparison to the new flood of popular bird books, 'cheap as dirt and more dirty than dirt'.

As well as using a novel format, Lear was a pioneer in concentrating on a single species. The choice of parrots was inspired: decorative and entertaining, brilliantly coloured, admired for their mimicry, they were fashionable pets, seen in many contemporary portraits, and their shimmering feathers nodded from the headdresses of fashionable women. The Parrot House was one of the biggest draws at the zoo and if Lear could not find a species there or in Bruton Street, he begged entry to private collections, especially those of Lord Stanley, the dealer Benjamin Leadbetter and the naturalist Vigors. As a last resort, he turned to the stuffed birds of the taxidermist John Gould, the zoo's first 'Curator and Preserver'. The final touch of novelty was Lear's insistence, following Harvey, in drawing from live birds wherever possible. At the zoo, he measured wingspan, length and legs while the young keeper Goss held the birds still. He chose their most striking, defining pose (and in his paintings they do seem to pose), then he sketched them – perched on branches, preening, nodding and blinking at the artist before them – in countless rough drawings, surrounded by jotted notes. He caught the arc of movement and the tilt of heads and drew their graduated feathers and soft down with painstaking accuracy, noting the smallest gradations of colour and texture. He made test sheets of colour, dabbing the tints around the sketches as a guide. But he also gave the birds character: the green and red Kuhl's parakeets seem to talk to each other; the salmon-crested cockatoo appears blushingly vain; the great red and yellow macaw turns its head with a wary, arrogant glance and the blue and yellow macaw leans forward, its feathers ruffled and high. It is hard to tell who is the observer, artist or bird. 'A huge Maccaw is now looking me in the face as much as to say – "finish me",' he groaned in one letter, looking at the uncompleted work filling his room.

MACROCERCUS ARACANGA.

Red and Yellow Macaw.

J.G. Natl. Sci.

To save money Lear decided to produce his own lithographic plates, another brave move. Lithography, invented in the mid-1790s by the German Alois Senefelder, was hardly used in Britain until 1819 when Rudolph Ackermann published Senefelder's *A Complete Course of Lithography*, and the landscape painter and printer Charles Hullmandel set up a studio. Hullmandel's *The Art of Drawing on Stone* of 1824 became 'the Bible for budding lithographic artists'. Artists liked the technique, based on the simple fact that oil and water repel each other, because they could make the plates themselves, without employing an engraver. Using a greasy wax crayon or chalk they could draw or trace directly onto the smoothly ground piece of limestone. The stone was 'cooled' with a mix of nitric acid and gum arabic, so that the parts not covered by the greasy drawing were etched away, then moistened so that when an oil-based ink was applied the water repelled it and the ink stuck only to the crayoned lines. Hullmandel kept the blocks at his studio at Great Marlborough Street, off Regent Street, hiring them out at rates from 4d. to 18d. per month, according to size. The studio became another place that Lear dashed to: drawing, supervising proofs, getting specialist letterers to add the titles. Here too he was a trendsetter: so far, lithography had been used for landscapes and portraits but only in a handful of natural history books.

Lear had to learn many things: how to use the different grades of crayon, making sure they did not break; how to avoid smears; how to put a bridge – a piece of wood – across the stone to prevent smudging; how to mix crayon and ink for dark areas or lines; how to create highlights by scraping with a sharp tool. He shrugged his first failures off and carried on. He liked the freedom; he liked the 'sculptural' feel, using the grain and grit of the stone; he liked drawing directly so that his plates kept their liveliness. Once the prints were made – mirror images of the drawings – Hullmandel's assistants applied watercolours to match Lear's original, ending with a whisk of egg white to give sheen to the plumage and glint to the eye.

On 1 November 1830 Lear published Parts I and II. The next day three distinguished zoologists, Nicholas Vigors, Thomas Bell and Edward Bennett, put his name forward as an Associate of the Linnean Society: he was still only eighteen. As the following parts came out his subscribers were thrilled. William Swainson, once a pupil of Audubon, asked for duplicates of two plates, which 'will then be framed, as fit companions in my drawing room to hang by the side of a pair by my friend Audubon'. Prideaux John Selby went further, finding Lear's plates 'beautifully coloured & I think infinitely superior to Audubon's in softness and the drawing as good'.

Lear had designed wrappers to send out the separate parts, changing these when he obtained permission to dedicate the book to Queen Adelaide, wife of William IV. He sent some parts out himself and distributed others through Ackermann or local booksellers, but the cost was horrendous and since he couldn't afford to hire the stones for long, he erased the drawings as soon as he had made the 175 prints he needed. 'I have pretty great difficulty in paying my monthly charges,' he told the Newcastle bookseller Charles Empson in October 1831, 'for to pay colourer & printer monthly I am obstinately prepossessed – since I had rather be at the bottom of the River Thames – than be one week in debt.' Many subscribers paid late, and though Lear exaggerated for comedy's sake, his panic conveyed the state of his life. 'Should you come to town,' he told Empson, '– I am sorry that I cannot offer you a home pro tempore':

– pro trumpery indeed it would be, if I did make any such offer – for unless you occupied the grate as a seat – I see no probability of your finding any rest consonant with the safety of my Parrots – seeing that of the six chairs I possess – 5 are at present occupied with lithographic prints: – the whole of my exalted & delightful upper tenement in fact overflows with them, and for the last 12 months I have so moved – looked at, – & existed among Parrots – that should any transmigration take place at my decease I am sure my soul would be very uncomfortable in anything but one of the Psittacidae.

By this time he was exhausted. That autumn, to make it easier to run back and forth to the zoo, he moved to 61 Albany Street, tucked behind the smart terraces on the east of the park. But early the next year the money finally ran out and his *Parrots* ground to a halt. He had promised to bring out fourteen numbers, but had to stop at twelve, having published forty-two plates, without any accompanying text. As he later told Sir William Jardine, 'Their publication was a speculation which – so far as it made me known & procured me employment in Zoological drawing – answered my expectations – but in matters of money occasioned me considerable loss.'

For two years Lear had been preoccupied with parrots. He turned his back on the political storms preceding the Great Reform Act of June 1832; he ignored the debates about the Poor Law; he shrugged off the fear of a cholera epidemic sweeping down from the industrial cities of the north. At London Zoo, safe from mobs and disease, he found a home and a bevy of patrons.

His work was part of the drive to describe, present and label the natural world. Watching eager label readers on a visit to the zoo in 1836, the journalist Leigh Hunt described one typical species spotter dashing from beast to bird, 'and giving little self-complacent stops at each':

'Hah!' he seemed to be saying to himself, 'this is the panther is it? *Hm* – Panther. What says the label here? "Hyaena Capensis." *Hm* – Hyaena – ah! A thing untameable. "Grisly Bear." Hah! – grisly – *hm*. Very like. Boa, "Tiger Boa" – ah! – Boa in a box – *Hm* – Sleeping, I suppose. Very different from seeing him squeeze somebody. *Hm*. Well! I think it will rain. Terrible thing *that* – spoil my hat.'

The parakeets and macaws, Hunt thought, seemed the happiest birds there, flaunting and chattering: 'Does their talk mean to say anything of this?' he asked. 'Is it divided between an admiration of one another, and their dinner? For assuredly, talk they do, of something or other, from morning to night, like a room-full of French milliners.' Lear too felt the birds talked to him, and that in some sense he belonged with them, an exhibit himself. Visitors gawped at the gangly young man with his large spectacles and furrowed brow. '*Hm* – an artist – hm.' Often, as he made his preliminary drawings, he included their curious, peering faces. They were outside the cage: Lear was inside, with the birds.

Birds gave Lear joy all his life, not in cages but in the freedom of the skies, lakes and rivers, forests and gardens. Every journey he made was crowned with birds. In Albania, twenty years later, he dashed down to look at some white stones by a lake:

when – lo! on my near approach, one and all put forth legs, long necks, and great wings, and 'stood confessed' so many great pelicans, which, with croakings expressive of great disgust at all such ill-timed interruptions, rose up into the air in a body of five or six hundred, and soared slowly away to the cliffs to the north of the gulf.

Again and again, birds left him speechless. He counted them and gave them characters wherever he found them, in Greece, in Italy, in Egypt: '4 black storks – one legged: apart – 8 pelicans – careless foolish. 17 small ducks, cohesive. 23 herons – watchful variously posed: & 2 or 3 flocks of lovely ivory ibis.' And he used his compulsive counting in his nonsense.

There was an Old Man with a beard,
Who said, 'It is just as I feared! –
Two Owls and a Hen, four Larks and a Wren,
Have all built their nests in my beard!'

There the birds are. (In 1860 Lear asked Holman Hunt, 'How, my dear Daddy, is your paternal beard? Do the little birds nest in it yet? & if so, is their innocement & periseminating twitter pleasant to your benevolent heart?') They nest and fly and swim through Lear's rhymes and alphabets, stories and songs. And just as he renders the birds human, so people begin to look like birds: the long-legged Old Man of Dunblane, 'Who greatly resembled a Crane'; the Old Man of El Hums, who ate nothing but crumbs, 'Which he picked off the ground,/With the other birds round'; the depressing Old Man of Crowle, who lived in a nest with an owl; the long-necked Old Person of Nice:

There was an old Person of Nice,
Whose associates were usually Geese;
They walked out together, in all sorts of weather,
That affable Person of Nice!

Wherever they appear, the birds' sidelong glances make them look considerably wiser than the men. And just as Lear perched in the aviary so in his drawings he took on avian shape. In doodles in his letters he leans forward with his frock coat flung out like a tail and his long nose a beak; he hovers in the air, a rotund bird with feathery wings and tiny legs; he swims solemnly on with the geese from Corfu; he nests in a tree, or struts and bends his head as if to peck.

When he finished *Parrots*, the young Lear, with his domed head and his spectacles perched on his large nose, was feeling hard pressed, hopeless in matters of money. Others, like the ambitious John Gould, were far shrewder. Gould had started a taxidermy business in Windsor in 1824, beginning work for the Zoological Society three years later, and publishing *A Century of Birds from the Himalaya Mountains*, based on a hundred skins of Indian birds that he had been sent, in 1830–1. Noting the success of *Parrots*, Gould planned a series of works on Lear's model, using Hullmandel as his printer – he eventually produced forty volumes over twenty years. He was not an artist or a naturalist but he was determined and enthusiastic and had a good business head. He was, Lear told George Coombe in 1833, 'a man who without any prospects or education, has by dint of a singularly active mind, good talents, & uncontrollable perseverance (not to say impudence backed by no little good luck) – risen in the world beyond belief for the last ten years'. Eager for work, Lear helped Gould with illustrations for the five-part *Birds of Europe*, from 1832 to 1837. He also taught lithography to Gould's wife, Elizabeth, who drew the smaller birds while Lear took on the larger, more striking ones and did all the backgrounds and touchings up. He was fond of Elizabeth, 'an exceedingly pleasant & amiable woman', and drew a little study of her own pet vole, inscribed 'Portrait of Mrs Gould's Pet'. (When she died in 1841, Lear was genuinely saddened, asking for a sketch of her, as a person he 'esteemed & respected so greatly'.)

In March 1833, when Lear was desperate to get rid of unsold copies of *Parrots*, as he still owed money for their printing and 'they were always before me like a great nimbus or nightmare or anything else very disagreeable & unavoidable', Gould bought the stock and all rights in the plates for £50, on condition that Lear went to the Continent with him, to draw in the zoos of Rotterdam, Berne, Berlin, Frankfurt and Amsterdam. Then came delays – Elizabeth went into premature labour, the whole Gould family had flu, and the trip was put off. Suddenly, Lear collapsed. He went down to Arundel, where Sarah stuffed him 'with puddings – chops – cutlets – and pies', as he told Ann:

> Exceedingly careful were they of my health,
> And I scarcely left home at all, saving by stealth;
> – They never allowed me to walk by the river
> For said they – 'Lest the fogs disagree with your liver!' –

When he wrote this he was at Peppering with the Drewitts, drawing 'a very magnificent pigeon'. He came back fatter and better, ready to work again. Finally, in July, off he went with Gould to all those places, the first time he had been abroad. In Amsterdam he made a more binding agreement to complete a specific number of drawings, which he later regretted. In all he contributed sixty-eight plates to *Birds of Europe*, for which Gould acknowledged his help, and at least ten more for Gould's book on toucans, 1833–5, including some of his liveliest, most mischievous birds: but although he signed several plates in the first edition, in the second edition of 1854 his signature was silently erased.

EAGLE OWL.
Bubo maximus (Sibbald)

While Lear felt disgruntled he also felt obliged to Gould, who employed him and paid him well. And although he was often hasty and careless, Gould was in the centre of this world – he was the one who identified Darwin's bird specimens from the Galapagos not as a mixed lot but as thirteen distinct kinds of finch, setting Darwin on his long musings about their adaptive evolution. In later life Lear was less impressed, and less grateful. Gould was 'always a hog', he decided, and it was a wonder 'as to how *such* a man could portray humming birds or anything refined'. When Gould died in 1881 Lear dismissed him as 'one I never liked really, for in spite of a certain jollity & Bonhomie he was a harsh & violent man . . . ever the same, persevering, hard working toiler in his own (ornithological) line, – but ever as unfeeling for those about him'. Yet the birds he drew for Gould are wonders: fat pigeons and fierce marsh harriers, long-legged storks, great pelicans with huge beaks and the majestic eagle owl, with its ear-like tufts of feathers and soft ruffs around piercing golden eyes.

Gould was not his sole employer. Soon he was much in demand. The members of the Zoological Society who saw his drawings and admired his *Parrots* turned to him for help with their current work, and soon he was drawing reptiles and animals as well as birds. He contributed, for example, to the illustrations for accounts of great expeditions such as Captain Beechey's three-year voyage across the Pacific to the Bering Straits and Alaska.

Lear already had connections in this world, particularly with the gentleman naturalist and collector Prideaux John Selby, a friend of Mrs Wentworth's brother Walter Ramsden Fawkes. Since Lear was sixteen, he had been sending Selby watercolour sketches for his *British Ornithology*, which was published in nineteen parts, mostly plates, between 1821 and 1834. In the past generation Thomas Bewick's exquisite *History of British Birds* had introduced native species to a wide general public, but rich families with large libraries wanted more lavish volumes, leather-bound and finely printed, with hand-coloured plates on thick paper. Selby worked on this grander scale, and his *British Orni-thology* was an airy and elegant production with characterful, life-size illustrations. After he began work at the zoo his reputation spread. Nicholas Vigors introduced him to Selby's collaborator, Sir William Jardine, and Lear painted delicate watercolours for their *Illustrations of Ornithology*, which appeared from 1825 to 1843, and for Jardine's work on the duck tribe. He also made drawings for the wood engravings in Jardine's popular *Naturalist's Library*, especially of pigeons and parrots: 'Parrots are my favourites,' he told Jardine, '& I can do them with greater facility than any other class of animals.' His continuing fondness and familiarity show in his work, like this conversation between two macaws, painted in May 1836.

Selby and Jardine were both enchanted with his work, and took his scientific expertise seriously, as well as his art: he always remembered their kindness. And while he worked at the zoo other experts sought him out. In July 1832 he wrote comically to the Coombes' baby daughter, begging her to ask for a letter in return ('If you cannot yet speak your ideas – my love – you can squeak them you know') and appealing for specimens from Fanny Coombe's brother Robert Drewitt:

only because I feel more pleasure in drawing from those given me by my intimate friends – than I could do from those otherwise come by – not from my being unable to get at specimens. – Having rather a Zoological connexion – & being about to Publish British Quadrupeds – I have now living – 2 Hedgehogs, all the sorts of mice – weasels – Bats &c – & every beast requisite except a Pine Marten, – all of which, my dear child, – I should be glad to present you with – did I suppose you could make the slightest use of them whatever.

Tortoises were also on his mind: Eliza Drewitt's tortoise had just died and he was making lithographs from James Sowerby's sketches of tortoises and terrapins, with their wonderfully patterned shells and beady eyes, for Thomas Bell's great study *A Monograph of the Testudinata*. He also worked on Bell's 1837 *History of Quadrupeds*, writing across several plates in his own copy, 'drawn from nature also on wood by me'. Bell was one of the trio who had put his name forward to the Linnean Society and Lear felt a true affection for him, often visiting him in later years, especially after Bell moved into Gilbert White's old house in Selborne.

This was a good, sociable time. Lear had work, and a growing reputation. 'I am up to my neck in hurry', he told George Coombe in April 1833, '– & work from 5AM – till 7 P.M without cessation: – my lute & my flute are locked up.' He saw his old friends, as well as his new ones from the zoo and the artists' studios. One Sussex friend, Bernard Senior (who later took the name of Husey Hunt, for inheritance reasons), a year older than Lear, was now at the law firm of Ellis and Blackmore's in Gray's Inn, where George Lear worked. Lear often went on the town with him and Henry Greening, a young lawyer from Lincoln's Inn. Almost fifty years later, when he saw a notice of Greening's death in *The Times*, he wrote, '*What* days, (& *what* nights) we used to share so long ago as 1830 or even earlier. Harry Greening was in those times the life of all our parties, albeit through him partly I got into bad ways.' There are other hints that around this time Lear's life became tangled. When he set off with Gould to the Continent he mentioned 'some circumstances which had just occurred' that made him glad to leave England. In a late diary, when he found his servant Giorgio's son crying from shame because he thought he had syphilis (it turned out to be a plain abscess), he commented, 'Considering that I myself in 1833 had every sort of syphilitic disease, who am I to blame others, who have had less education & more temptation.' Lear was consistently evasive about his sex life, even in his diary: this is one of the rare occasions that he even mentions having one. He doesn't say if he went to brothels, or picked up rent boys – or both. He doesn't specify the nature of his 'disease' and it is likely to have been bacterial gonorrhoea, treatable with arsenic and mercury, rather than the more deadly syphilis (at the time the two were thought to be connected, with syphilis a later stage), but this would still be enough to cause years of problems and to make him anxious in the future, especially about marriage.

In 1833 his father, Jeremiah, died of a heart attack, aged seventy-six, but Lear's relationship with his mother remained cool. He was dutiful, went down to Gravesend to see her and later sent money when he could, but there was no warmth between them. In his view, he and his sister Ann were still on their own. In the New Year of 1834 Lear moved to rooms at 28 Southampton Row which soon became as crammed with books, prints, plates and drawings as his old lodgings: 'It must be a very thin man to live in these rooms as there are only a few weasel like corners not filled up,' he told Fanny Coombe later. One escape was Hullmandel's labyrinthine studio. Acutely intelligent and a fine linguist, Hullmandel liked to encourage young artists, though he was 'decidedly caustic', Dan Fowler thought: 'If you made a blot in his presence, he was sure to find it; withal, as it was his business to be, an excellent judge of art.' This summer, feeling he needed proper formal training, Lear also enrolled in Sass's School of Art in Charlotte Street, Bloomsbury.

Started by Henry Sass, a friend of Turner and Landseer, the school prepared students for entrance to the Royal Academy Schools, copying old masters, studying perspective and drawing from antique sculptures. Pupils included William Powell Frith, Augustus Egg and John Everett Millais, and like Hullmandel's studio, Sass's was a social hub. Frith, who was there that summer, remembered 'A series of *conversazioni*, at which great artists and other distinguished men were present . . . Etty, Martin (certainly one of the most beautiful human beings I ever beheld), and Constable were frequent visitors. We had dinners and dances, too. Who that had once seen Wilkie dance a quadrille could ever forget the solemnity of the performance.' The lithographer George Barnard also noted these conversations, 'and the society of most of the Royal Academicians, such as Stanfield, Turner, Westall, Landseer &c'. Lear heard Turner singing at one party, belting out 'And the world goes round a-bound, a-bound'.

But Lear did not stay long at Sass's; he was older than most of the pupils and had no cash or time for a long, expensive course. He had proved himself at London Zoo, with his work for the naturalists, and with his own amazing plates of the parrots – and now he had new commitments, to his most important patron so far, Edward Smith Stanley. Lord Stanley had chaired the meeting of the Zoological Society that granted Lear permission to draw the parrots in the zoo, and had become president of the Society in 1831, a post he held until his death. Lear had included two of his birds in the *Parrots*, an iridescent green and pink Stanley parakeet and a red-capped parakeet, and had also made several drawings for him at Knowsley, the Stanley family's Lancashire estate just north of Liverpool. And now, after Stanley inherited his father's title in 1834, becoming the thirteenth Earl of Derby, they would work even more closely together.

5: KNOWSLEY

At Knowsley everything was on a grand scale. When Lear went up for an extended stay in the summer of 1835, he looked out from his window over fields and copses, across the plain to Liverpool and far beyond to the west, to the marshes and dunes where the Mersey met the cold Irish Sea. He painted this view, his first known landscape in watercolour, a pattern of brown and gold cornfields and clumps of dark trees under a huge, billowing sky. It was not picturesque: 'The rain is coming down in torrents,' he wrote to George Coombe, 'and the vast pancake of land-scape from here to Liverpool is all in a beastly grey mist.'

All that flat pancake belonged to the Stanleys. They were stagger-ingly rich – by far the richest family in the north-west – with money pouring in from coal mines and from property in the growing industrial towns of Preston and Bury, and on the Liverpool quays. The house was a vast pile, a jumble of styles from Tudor times on, its Georgian front and portico mixing with new neo-Gothic additions. The twelfth earl was a rip-roaring liberal Whig, a close ally of Charles James Fox and a great gambler and man of the turf, founding the Oaks (named after his Epsom estate), the Derby, and the Grand National at nearby Aintree. By contrast, the new Lord Derby was quiet, even shy, finding animals and birds easier to deal with than people. He had been an MP for over thirty years, from the age of twenty-one, but his reputation and his spirits were badly bruised by his support of his local yeomanry at the inquiry after the massacre of Peterloo in 1819, and as soon as he entered the House of Lords in 1834 he stood back from politics. He hated London and avoided the season. His son Edward made up for this: 'a lively rattling sportsman', according to the gossipy Charles Greville, 'apparently devoted to racing and rabbit shooting', he entertained the Fancy, the sporting aristocracy, for the Liverpool races and would become prime minister three times in the 1850s and 60s.

Derby's passion for natural history baffled his rackety father: he rarely went racing and instead, said Greville, 'spent a million on kangaroos'. Knowsley's 170 acres were a vast private zoo, for which Stanley sent collectors across the globe, to South Africa and India, South America and Australia; at Knowsley at dawn the screeches and hootings of the birds almost drowned the bellowing of the wild Brahmin cattle. The collecting was not without mishap: one hungry ship's crew devoured the precious birds; a vicuña tried to eat paint; efforts to send kiwi birds from New Zealand 'by shipping them with a supply of worms mixed with chicken entrails' failed entirely. The animals that did arrive needed a large staff to undertake odd tasks: the blacksmith pared the zebra's hooves; a local surgeon operated on an antelope's cataracts; gangs of men clipped reluctant alpacas; garden boys tended reptiles and tropical fish in warm tanks in the plant houses. Derby also employed taxidermists, including Gould, and his museum on the first floor of the house was full of stuffed birds and animals, cabinets of skins, trays of insects and plant specimens. He became an expert in identifying species and amassed an extraordinary collection of rare books, botanical and zoological paintings and engravings, hiring artists to paint his living specimens.

When Lear was asked to contribute to this great visual filing system, he began, not surprisingly, with a bird: a tiny chestnut-belted gnateater from the Amazon, sketched in 1830. Many ravishing watercolours in the great folios of his work at Knowsley are dated 1831, among them Stanley's golden parakeet and a pretty blue and green bird from eastern China, soon named 'Lord Derby's parakeet', *Paleornis Derbianus*: when

Lear painted this from a skin at the Knowsley museum it was the only example of the species in Britain. Derby paid him well, far better than Gould had, beginning at £3 for each painting, and Lear was touched by his open acknowledgement, as he told Fanny Coombe, 'such as at the Gardens & Zoological Meetings – shaking hands with me before all the great bodies – & in calling & sitting for a long half hour at 28 Southampton Row'. He was wryly grateful for such attentions 'from people of rank – to us small fry of artists'. The gulf was bridged by Derby's humanity. Lear told Fanny of 'an opportune misunderstanding when Lord D called – through his dreadful deafness: "My Lord" – said I – "I hope your head is better" – for he had had a bad headache the day before. "Oh" – replied he – "I have found a remedy for that. I have taken out all the little birds & put in one Cockatoo & three large Red Macaws."' The absurdity, and Derby's vulnerability and generosity, won Lear's devotion.

Offering to send William Jardine some pictures of Lord Derby's 'novelties', Lear added, 'He will have great pleasure in your having them, I am sure – indeed, a more liberal and amiable collector (you know we naturalists have a selfish reputation), does not exist.' During his stays at Knowsley he worked for Derby with immense patience, drawing from life if he could, making many pencil studies, with notes on colour and on texture, silky or rough. He turned a turtle upside down, painting its soft belly and wriggling legs. He learned about anatomy, feeding habits, mating rituals, and his humour showed through as he caught the shrewd gaze of the spectacled owl, and the angular pride of the great crowned crane. His watercolours were far more than an accurate depiction of plumage, markings and anatomy. They displayed a tenderness, an intimate perception, a feeling for the fast beat of a heart, the wetness of a twitching nose, the stress of animals far from their familiar habitat.

As the birds and animals died, their cabinet skins piled up in Derby's museum: they are now in the Liverpool Museum, which he endowed in his will. Many skins are those of individuals that Lear knew personally, from the stately, embarrassed-looking crowned crane to the Orinoco

Spectacled Owl, Wattle-crowned Crane and *Quebec Marmot or Weenusk*
(*Arctomys Empetra*), watercolours made at Knowsley

goose. This goose was one of Lear's favourites. He loved to see the courtship display: the male and female standing tall with wings widespread, flinging their heads back and puffing their chests in and out, whistling and chuff-chuffing. Derby noted that Lear 'was much amused by its manner of swelling out the breast like a Pouter Pigeon, which he represented'. The skins of the mammals he painted are in this museum too: a fat little woodchuck from Alaska with its quivering nose; a perky 'tree rat' from Central America, with its tail curled round a branch (later named as 'Lord Derby's Woolly Opossum'); a black giant squirrel from the high canopies of Asian forests. Painting these birds and animals, Lear touched distant lands and different ways of inhabiting the living world, and he knew that however meticulous his drawings, his flying, jumping, leaping subjects would always remain mysterious.

Malayan Giant Squirrel (1846)

He looked carefully, paying close attention to details like the way an animal's hair fell over its toes or the creases on a paw. When he sent sketches from London of the *Trionyx*, the soft-shelled turtle from the Nile, and the beautiful little South American wildcat *Leopardus yagoua-roundi*, he wrote:

I took the sketches very carefully from the living animals, but owing to their not being in a good light, I have had very great trouble in getting the drawings to look satisfactory: even now, only the under side of the Trionyx is what I really like. The cat was very difficult to represent, & the Trionyx, although James Hunte held it for me for two whole mornings – not much less so.

Similarly, when he tackled the Eastern quoll from Australia – his 'Manges Opossum' – with its delicately spotted pelt, he explained that he had taken great pains, and trusted that Derby would think he had tried 'to imitate the fur more nearly'.

These Australian species enthralled him: a little later he drew a page of 'Portraites of the inditchenous beestes of New Ollond' including kangaroos 'in their proper propperportions', a platypus and porcupine, a bandicoot and a grinning 'common or Natur Catte'. When the Goulds set off to work there, he sounded rather envious.

All the species – familiar and unfamiliar – had to be fitted into the Linnaean taxonomy that Derby and his colleagues favoured, according to strict rules. Species were arranged in orders – for instance the largest order of birds was the *Passeriformes*, the songbirds – then families, and then by genus and species. To establish a 'type', or type series, specimens that would form the standard for a new species or variant, the describer had to produce a detailed document, which must be published to be valid. In the description, the scientific name, such as *Passer domesticus* (house sparrow), could be derived from any language or from the name of a person but it had to be Latinised and followed by the date of publication (so we have '*Passer domesticus*, Linnaeus, 1758'), and then it had to be checked against other closely related species, to note any difference or variation.

Lear had no background in this work and sometimes grew impatient with the disputes over naming, but he did try to identify the birds he painted, and as some of them were new to science, he was 'the first describer'. Three birds were named after him: the blue Brazilian parrot, 'Lear's macaw', *Anodorhynchus leari*, 'Lear's cockatoo', *Lapochroa leari*, and *Platycercus leari*, a red and green Tabuan parakeet from Fiji. He also named some birds himself, from specimens that he recognised as

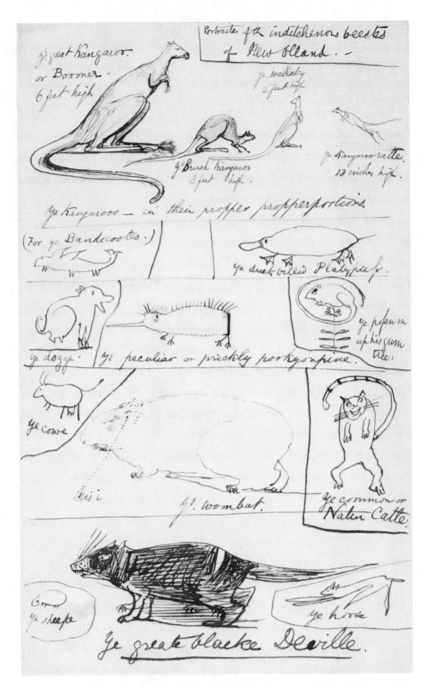

'Portraites of the inditchenous beestes of New Ollond'

belonging to undescribed species, like the long-billed black cockatoo, *Calyptorhynchus baudinii*, which he named after Nicolas Baudin, the leader of a French scientific expedition to Australia in 1800. But many birds and animals also arrived with names from their country of origin, or given by settlers and hunters. These rolled off the tongue, different and alien: the whiskered yarke and the eye-browed rollulus, the pur- plish guan and the aequitoon, the ging-e-jonga and jungli-bukra. The music of strange names, never forgotten, echoes in Lear's late songs, granted to the Fimble Fowl with a corkscrew leg and the others who flock to the Quangle Wangle Quee:

> And the Golden Grouse came there,
> And the Pobble who has no toes, –
> And the small Olympian bear, –
> And the Dong with a luminous nose.
> And the Blue Baboon, who played the Flute, –
> And the Orient Calf from the Land of Tute, –
> And the Attery Squash, and the Bisky Bat, –
> All came and built on the lovely Hat
> Of the Quangle Wangle Quee.

In his poems, Lear had his own menagerie where all the creatures were free.

6: TRIBES AND SPECIES

The Kicking Kangaroo
Who wore a pale Pink Muslin Dress
With Blue spots

Lear drew this kangaroo for two children, Daisy and Arthur Terry, at a hotel in Italy in August 1870. In his illustrated alphabet the Kicking Kangaroo was joined by the Jubilant Jay, who did up her hair with 'a Wreath of Roses, Feathers and a good Pin', the Melodious Meritorious Mouse, who played a merry minuet on the piano, and many others, all mimicking accomplishments and fashions that also – as with the Jay's feather headdress – showed how the smart set exploited them.

In the mid-1830s, as Lear watched the kangaroos lolloping around the grassy fields at Knowsley, he also watched the human menagerie of the great country house with their dress suits and muslin gowns, music and picnics and play. When he had first come to Knowsley in the time of the old twelfth earl, he had soon learned the complicated family history. Despite wedding celebrations so glittering that they became a legend, the twelfth earl's first wife ran off with the Duke of Dorset, with whom she had a daughter, and was banished: twenty years later, within three weeks of his wife's death in 1797, the earl married his great love, the Irish comic actress Elizabeth Farren (many caricatures by Gillray show the short, stubby, 'baby-faced' earl dwarfed by the tall, willowy actress). Derby and his sister Charlotte, then in their twenties, lived on with the children of the new marriage in their father's boisterous household. Kind, crude in the old Regency style, prone to teasing young women about their looks and lovers, and incurably hospitable, the earl added a vast panelled dining room in the Gothic style, hung with portraits of ancestors, its high curved ceiling disappearing into a mist above the chandeliers: his dinners often seated between forty and a hundred. In this tribe, the Stanleys were frequently outnumbered by their cousins the Hornbys, linked through marriages of two generations. Friends, cousins, children, nephews and nieces, grandchildren and great-grandchildren filled the house. It was for those children that Lear wrote the first of his nonsense rhymes.

Knowsley Hall from the west (1835)

In June 1835, when Lear set off for his long summer stay at Knowsley, he squeezed into the last cheap seat on the coach, behind the box, singing to the mildly drunk coachman and reaching Birmingham, 'perfectly frozen, to make a beastly breakfast of far gone eggs'. Near Knowsley he left his bags to be collected and walked through the park, later telling George Coombe loyally that the trees were mere gooseberry bushes compared to those of Sussex. He was conscious of his odd status, neither servant nor guest, and went round to the back door to meet the housekeeper, who showed him 'my *rooms*'. These were gratifyingly lavish, in the great front of the house looking west into the sunset: 'Grand piano book case – sofa – fire &c – with lots of Orthodox furniture'. At dinner in the housekeeper's room, he reported:

all things were going on swimmingly – when lo! A messenger from Lord D. begged me to come immediately to him. To my surprise his Lordship was in the Passage, where he gave me a regular *shake* of the hand, & apologised for my having been put where I was. 'I intended of course,' quoth he – 'that you should have been *one of us* – & not dine with the servants.'

So after the meal he left the servants' quarters, 'to the eminent opening of eyes of the good people assembled', and was shown to the drawing room, full of assorted Stanleys and Hornbys, 'a legion to themselves'. He clearly enjoyed this story and told it again to Dan Fowler, who remembered it with amusement, but added shrewdly, 'His career was founded on patronage, and under that he was content to enter upon it. It was, too, more or less patronage all his days, but he proved himself worthy of it, if any man ever did.'

Lear was not really '*one of us*'. His letters from Lancashire were forerunners of later reports from foreign countries on their people, customs and tribes. On his first day in 1835 he reported the routine. At ten, a bell summoned the household to prayers, the guests in the library, the servants in the hall; then came breakfast in 'the enormous dining room – a good one you may guess'. At noon, keen to see the changes since his last visit, Lear toured the aviaries, finding them 'incredibly altered and improved'; after lunch he talked for two hours to Derby's nephew Robert Hornby – later a good friend and patron – and sketched until five. At half past six a bell rang for dressing and at seven the company processed into the dining room: dinner, coffee, tea, then Derby played patience with the ladies. Then bed. It looked as though he was in for a quiet time and as it was too wet to work in the aviaries he planned to ask Derby if he could sketch a bird or two indoors, 'as I want to do 4 every week for him'.

He was young, middle-class, nervous in his new clothes, working hard to fit in. At dinner with the housekeeper, 'as I saw how matters were going to be – I took all the pains in the world to make myself pleasant'; at dinner with the earl, 'I behaved myself however – very decently during dinner, & devoured some of the good things with great complacency.' There were some horrors, like putting up with guests who were only civil, he felt, because the Stanleys and Hornbys liked him. There were moments, too, of pure bafflement, as when the visiting Earl of Wilton, clad like a Van Dyck painting in crimson and a black velvet waistcoat, insisted he drink champagne with him. 'Why?' Lear asked another guest, 'and she began to laugh, and said, because he knows you are a clever artist and sees you always look at him and admire him: and he is a very vain man and this pleases him, and so he asks you to take wine as a reward.' While he was watching them, they were watching him. Like the animals in the zoo, the artist was a different species, a curiosity, caressed by some and ignored by others. At times, he wrote, 'the uniform apathetic tone assumed by lofty society irks me *dreadfully* – nothing I long for half so much as to giggle heartily and to hop on one leg down the great gallery – but I dare not.'

The quiet vanished in late July when the crowd came up for the races:

Another! – Another!! – & Another!!! – the rattling & bustle is very superlative: – at the moment I am writing no less than 3 carriages & 4 – four carriages & 2 – 2 Phaetons with white ponies – 1 Gig – & 3 Grooms with single horses are congregated before the awful door: surely out of all the contents there must be something good at the dinner party – I am sick of splendour – vomiting with excess of pomp – longing for a little porter out of a pewter pot – & some bread and cheese eaten with my fingers . . . as soon as one gets to like one Sett of people – away they go – & a perpetual change keeps one in a froze. – Would I live so! – St Peter! –

Yet despite his sardonic 'very superlative', Lear was impressed, and his protests gave way to a torrent of name dropping. He listed visits to old Cheshire houses like Tabley Hall, where he gorged on raspberries, joined outings, and shared a gipsy picnic in the ruins of Beeston Castle. The high-born women were like exotic specimens, described in general terms rather than in detail: 'Everybody ought to see Lady de Tabley before they die – she is a most glorious creature: – & not less delightful than beautiful,' or Sir Philip Egerton's wife, 'who is *preterpluperfection*, (she used to be called the "pride of Cheshire")'.

At Knowsley more visitors arrived, in bursts of sound: 'the noise of children, the hurrying of valets – the bustling of ladies' maids – the orderings of housekeepers – the stumping & squawking of Sir J. Shelley – the giggling of Miss – & the volubilities of My Lady – the barking of six dogs'. Then came shooting parties, ironic in a park devoted to preservation. 'Rabbit slaughter began two days ago. 138 were demolished in one evening. "Great Fun", as Lady Shelley says.' Next there was a new craze: cricket. In the mornings children and women joined in, and 'after luncheon – the males rush out again, & then there is a match general – grooms – riders – footmen & aristocrats all in a bundle'. The mix of gentlemen and players was not wholly equal. Every time Lear looked out of the window one of the gents was at the wicket.

As he described this in his letters, life at Knowsley was moving towards caricature, even fantasy. He knew that Fanny Coombe loved a good comic disaster, and when a fire broke out as he was writing to her, he seized the moment: 'Featherbeds are rolling down the stairs – curtains – clothes – books – furniture are being tossed from windows – the heat is dreadful – the women are losing their presence of mind.' The blaze was small, so Lear could turn it into farce, with the housekeeper deluging him with water, featherbeds felling a cook, the fat butler rolling over four bricklayers and two grooms, and soot-covered gentry passing buckets from the ponds: 'Lady Ellinor & 20 Gardeners command a regiment of watering pots.' He enjoyed seeing this well-ordered milieu thrown into chaos. But in a house run like clockwork, butlers and footmen were soon carrying their trays, backs straight, noses in the air, eyes raised above a floor carpeted with beds and books, as if nothing had happened at all.

Next Lear was swept into an excursion by steamer to Puffin Island off Anglesey with Lord D. and several Hornbys who planned to shoot the puffins that bred there in their millions. They were too late in the season: the puffins had vanished and the rain poured down. But for Lear, the scenery made up for all. Escaping a dinner party, he walked to the Menai bridge, gazing at the mountains in the distance: 'beyond all glorious. Eat hearty supper after 10 miles walk & then sang with accordion & flute till 2 in the morning on the beach.'

Lear's status as a hired artist was offset by his reputation as a naturalist. After the Anglesey trip he went to Dublin with four members of a different branch of the family, the Stanleys of Alderley. The leading spirit was the Reverend Edward Stanley, author of *A Familiar History of Birds* and soon to be president of the Linnean Society; with him came his sons Charles Edward and Arthur Penrhyn Stanley. Three years younger than Lear, Arthur became a close friend, although sadly their letters are lost: at the time of this trip he was a student at Balliol, and later he became a noted liberal theologian and Dean of Westminster. The final member of the Irish party was Edward Leycester Penrhyn, Revd Stanley's brother-in-law, and husband of Derby's daughter Charlotte – a double connection. They were heading for the annual meeting of the British Association for the Advancement of Science, founded four years earlier as a counter to the conservative Royal Society, 'to give a stronger impulse and a more systematic direction to scientific enquiry'. (In 1837 Dickens lampooned the BAAS as 'the Mudfog Association for the Advancement of Everything', giving it five sections including two Lear-sounding disciplines, 'Umbugology' and 'Ditchwateristics'.)

When Lear was in Dublin the Association was made up of four sections: Physics, Chemistry, Geology and Natural History. Stars among the founders were the polymath William Whewell – who coined the word 'scientist' – William Buckland, who had worked on the great dino-saur fossils, and was now putting forward his theory of the 'catastrophic' creation of the earth, and Charles Babbage, inventor of the Difference Engine and the Analytical Engine. The hottest subject was geology, and the most debated work was Charles Lyell's *Principles of Geology* (1830–3), which argued for the gradual and continuing formation of the earth over millennia, perhaps as long as 300 million years. Alarmed at such thinking, for the past few years authors of the eight ecclesiastically sanc-tioned *Bridgewater Treatises*, including Buckland, had presented Nature as the creation of a God who intervened constantly in its workings. In 1837, Babbage would attack this in his pertly named *Ninth Bridgewater Treatise*. There was no need, he said, for divine miracles to create new species or adaptations. Instead, his 'Creator' was a kind of divine legis-lator, or clockmaker, who designed successive species to appear at set times, and let them progress and change without intervention.

The delegates heard learned arguments, toured the zoo and feasted in marquees in the Botanical Gardens. Alexis de Tocqueville, the first volume of whose *Democracy in America*, published in 1835, was making waves, reported to his mother, 'We found there at least five hundred people; a great deal of noise and little work, as it happens generally in assemblies so numerous.' Lear enjoyed the noise and talk, and was enrolled as a member of the BAAS. But a kind of unease affected him. Current arguments about design, creation and the long history of the earth still placed mankind at the top of a pyramid, with all other crea-tures below. As he drew and painted the animals and birds and reptiles, Lear was not so sure about man's assumed dominion. The oppression of captivity was less obvious at Knowsley than at London Zoo – Derby valued the animals' need for space and had no big cats pacing behind bars, no polar bears stuffed into cages – but still the zebras and antelopes in the park could not race in great herds across the plains. And the more Lear looked at the smart society set on the one hand, and the animals on the other, the more he seems to have asked, 'What does it mean to be human?'

One touching watercolour from 1835 showed a chimpanzee in a dress, holding a hoop, with gnarled, curved toes peeping under the dimity hem. Lear was clearly fascinated, and another sketch shows the chimp's pensive head bending heavily over the childish collar. Beneath the dress the chimp has its own, individual consciousness. And surely, without much effort, you could reverse this and see the humans as the animals they were beneath their clothes, their wrinkles and spotted skin hidden by their dresses and suits, their passions and anxieties tucked beneath accepted social manners?

Lear's dizzying sense of the overlap between animal and human looked back in part to Thomas Hood, who often drew this resemblance – a tall visitor to the zoo exchanging stares with a giraffe, a fat man with outspread coat-tails like a bird – and to George Cruikshank, who showed members of the Zoological Society as hippos, monkeys, lions and cranes. In Hood's 'Pythagorean Fancies' the narrator prefers the idea of 'inhabiting the body of a bird' (like Lear), but notes how many people seem 'semibrutal . . . What apes, foxes, pigs, curs and cats, walk our metropolis.' Conversely many of Lear's watercolours of birds and animals look curiously human, like the little Scops-eared owl, then called 'Ephialtes', who looks anxiously upwards like a man whose toupée is about to slide off.

Comic as such paintings are, Lear was scrupulously accurate, and he knew the rules of scientific writing as well as drawing – using it in topsy-turvy form in his nonsense. In standard natural history texts the format was a picture followed by a physical description and account of the habitat and habits, including odd traits and actions. Like an echo of this, Lear's limericks list different species, Old Persons and Young, identified by place and behaviour. The human world, Lear implied, was quite as bizarre and protean as the animal. As humans and animals face each other, their likeness is clear. The beasts do sometimes get their own back.

There was an Old Man of the Cape,
Who possessed a large Barbary Ape;
Till the Ape one dark night, set the house on a light,
Which burned that Old Man of the Cape.

But sometimes, too, with the help of music, real, if noisy, happiness can be achieved.

There was an Old Person of Bray,
Who sang through the whole of the day
To his ducks and his pigs, whom he fed upon figs,
That valuable Person of Bray.

Perhaps fearing the effect of the figs, or exhausted by the songs, the neatly lined-up pigs and ducks are unimpressed. It is easy to see which is the odder species. 'Goodbye, love to all,' Lear ended one gossipy letter. 'Must go & draw a Kangaroo.'

7: MAKE 'EM LAUGH

At Knowsley, Lear told George Coombe in June 1835, the place and the gossip were the bright side; 'the darks I don't bother you with'. 'I think my stay here will make me burst to have some fun,' he sighed. 'I long to have a good laugh.' The darks were his feelings of panic, of always having to be on good behaviour, of an inner loneliness, but his beguiling, fun-loving side was hard to keep down. From boyhood he had found that making people laugh won him acceptance, like his talent with music (and the two often went together). The first comic pieces he wrote and drew were parodies and illustrated songs for his family and friends. Then, at Knowsley in the 1830s, he found a new form: his nonsense rhyme, or limerick. And these, to begin with at least, were for the children.

From the age of thirteen, when he wrote the parodic account of the exodus from Bowman's Lodge, Lear found that effervescent word-play and humour, pushed to absurdity but controlled by form, could deflect despair, loneliness, rejected affection. Sometimes a bizarre simile was both funny and an accurate description of feeling: 'I must leave off, I feel like 5 nutmeg-graters full of baked eggshells – so dry & cold & miserable.' He used nonsense to avoid sounding too serious, or too emotional, or too self-important, and in the process he often revealed the fears or emotions he wanted to hide. He also had fun. In his letters, for example, his exaggerated stories gave him control over a world in which he was marginal: his account of the fire at Knowsley was like a comic strip, scene after scene – it begged to be turned into drawings.

He was already turning stories and songs into drawings, especially songs. Lear was always ready to sing, to sit down at the piano, to bring out his flute, guitar or accordion. At Tabley Hall in 1835, he wrote, 'Lady de T. & I duet wonderfully – & I only marvel at my not being hired as nurse to the baby – who was always quieted by my playing the Accordion.' Like laughter, singing crossed barriers of class, race and culture. Travelling in the Abruzzi in the 1840s, staying with an oddly mixed group of people, Lear explained:

The only way to be comfortable was to adapt oneself to circumstances, so I did as everybody did after supper – namely, sang songs and played on the guitar perpetually, and was constantly pestered for 'un'aria Inglese' every five minutes. Two widows from Aquila were incessant in their requests for 'Ye banks and braes' but 'Alice Gray' had the greatest number of votes. Thus the evening went by merrily enough . . .'

Throughout life he would adapt himself to circumstances. 'Alice Gray' was a romantic ballad ('But her heart it is another's/She never can be mine') that cried out to be made fun of. Lear could recognise excess sentiment perfectly, as in 'The Bride's Farewell', a favourite of the singer John Barnett:

> Farewell Mother! Tears are streaming
> Down thy pallid tender cheek,
> I, in gems and roses gleaming,
> One eternal sunshine dreaming,
> Scarce this sad farewell may speak.

As the lachrymose verse rolls on, it's clear that the bride is far from sad at leaving her sobbing family for a life of jewels and comfort. Sung for the Drewitt girls, this mock ballad demands a turn at the piano with screwed-up face and sobs. Fanny Drewitt, in particular, appreciated Lear's dark visual/musical burlesque: if she had written these poems herself, we would read them as fiery feminist outbursts against convention, family and stifling moral codes.

Instead of providing new words for well-known songs, a popular musical game, often Lear simply illustrated them, with pictures disquietingly out of key with the lyrics. For Fanny, Lear wrote and drew 'Miss Maniac', in a little notebook, with a plate signed to 'Miss Drewitt, with his respects' and a slightly sinister self-portrait. In the late eighteenth century, before the Romantic co-option of madness to the visionary bard, writers had poured out verses and stories demanding sympathy for animals, children, the weak and the mad. There were many 'maniac poems', telling of insanity brought on by hard luck, poverty or lost love, and evoking volcanic eruptions of feeling:

> Shall I tell what fetters bound me;
> Fetters forged by sorrow's hand?
> Shall I say how mercy found me,
> Friendless on the naked strand . . .
>
> Belching torrents meet the sky,
> Rocks the heavenly ramparts dare;
> Then her mad convulsions die,
> Wasted in the yielding air . . .

A maniac story even appeared in *The Lady's Magazine* (oddly, right next to Ann Murry's article on parrots), where the heroine, Selina, is abandoned by her sweet-tongued suitor for a richer bride: 'Fair maniac! May the God of mercy soon release thy fetter'd brain, restore thy wandering sense, and lull thy pure, untainted soul to happiness and peace!' Lear's parodic version went further, embracing a tougher melodrama of seduction and parental rejection, using the stock tropes of a moral tale; the stern father banishes his pregnant daughter, who has been seduced and deserted by a stereotypical bounder (Lear shows him with eye-glass, curly beard and eerily fixed smile). Cast out, she wanders restlessly until a final descent into madness. From her madhouse cell she tells her story in couplets, their scansion perhaps echoing Hood's mock-dramatic 'The Demon Ship'. ('What darksome caverns yawn'd before! What Jagged steeps behind!') But Lear's drawings, with something of the scratchy young George Cruikshank and something of Hood's punning sketches in *Whims and Oddities*, transmuted her harrowing tale into black comedy.

'O – thou who falsely lured my frail fond heart astray/
Then left me like a broken flower, alone to waste away'

The counterpoint of picture and verse echoed the doubleness of Miss Maniac's own thoughts. It was funny, but only just. There was real sadness here; real fear; real hatred of the scoffing crowd.

'Still – still I feel the scoffs of those who, with a cruel scorn,/
Made doubly sad the memory of hours for ever gone, –'

There is tenderness, too, for the baby sleeping in its mother's arms, then cast aside on the ground: a kind of fellow-feeling.

'I longed for morn yet feared it, and I wandered on and wept/
Till, worn with sorrow and fatigue, – careless I sat me down . . .'

Above all Lear showed the terror of madness and the disappearance of self:

> Around my brain there is a chain, and o'er my fevered soul
> A darkness like that solemn gloom which once through Egypt stole;
> Sometimes I feel, but know not why, a fire within me burn,
> And visions fierce and terrible, pursue where'er I turn;
> Then I forget that earth is earth, and that myself am life,
> And nature seems to die away in darkness, hell and strife.
> But when my phrenzied fit is o'er, a dreary hour comes on, –
> A consciousness of unknown things, – of reason overthrown.
> Cold runs my blood from vein to vein – all vacant is mine eye,
> And in my ears a sound of death, and dread eternity!

Beneath his parodic wit the anxiety showed through. Here too he was one with the girls, no longer painting flowers, but writing of banishment, madness and loss.

A darkness underpinned these early picture-songs. Among the

scariest images were his surreal illustrations to Lady Anne Lindsay's 'Auld Robin Grey'. In this popular dialect ballad the heroine's lover drowns when his ship goes down, but although she cries 'my heart was in the sea', her poverty-stricken parents persuade her to marry a well-off neighbour, Robin Grey. Lear shows us her underwater love, as her tears flow down, with her feet below the tide-line and the fish swimming below, while her mother looms over above her. 'My mother did not speak', runs the line, '*But* she looked in my face, till my heart was like to break.'

A more terrifying image of parental pressure is hard to imagine. The monster parents win: a bearded Robin Grey pours booze down the father's throat and spoons soup into the mother: 'he fed them both', runs the song. But where have they come from, in Lear's imagination, these nightmare figures devouring their daughter's life?

Scoffing at intense emotion and clichéd tales, Lear explored the threats of family demands, romance and sex, entrapment and rejection. In 1835, after the Dublin conference, he went walking in the Wicklow mountains with Revd Stanley and Arthur. It was an opportunity for landscape drawing, his new interest, but a chance for comedy too. The Stanleys had estates in Ireland and Lear had become intrigued by Irish traditions, legends and songs: one of the poems he illustrated, his pictures fiercely undermining nostalgia for childhood, began:

I slept – and back to my early days
Did wandering fancy roam
When my hopes were light and my fancy bright
And my own a happy home.

This seems to have been a parody of a poem in the *Dublin Magazine* of 1833 by George Fenton, whom Lear would know later as the chaplain in San Remo. And at Knowsley he drew quick, crude illustrations for two stories, 'The Adventures of Daniel O'Rourke' and 'The Adventures of Mick,' based on published folk tales.

He was well primed for Irish fantasy on this trip. At the romantic valley of Glendalough their guide, shouting 'at the top of his voice' according to Arthur Stanley, recited Tom Moore's poem of St Kevin (or Kiven), who flees to his cave and rocky bed above the lake, to avoid the 'unholy blue' eyes of the beautiful Kathleen. The guide persuaded them to twine their legs round a stone cross, a sure way to win a fortune and a beautiful wife, he said. Lear won neither, but he did draw a version of Moore's poem:

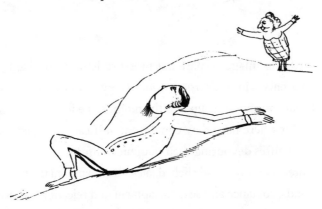

Here at least, he calmly said
Woman ne'er shall find my bed
Ah! the good saint little knew,
What that wily sex can do. –

Hunted down, Kevin takes drastic action.

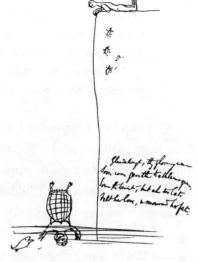

Ah! yes saints have cruel hearts –
Sternly from his bed he darts
& with rude repulsive shock
Hurls her down the beetling rock.

Glendalough, thy gloomy wave
Soon was gentle Kathleen's grave,
Soon the Saint, but ah too late
Felt her love, & mournd her fate.

Kathleen's beaming ghost glides round the lake: there is no escape after all.

The nursery and schoolroom at Knowsley were full of children bursting from the effort of being polite in grown-up company. Lear did not seek children out, as Lewis Carroll did small girls, and he was far from sentimental about childhood. He felt for their untamed innocence and lamented its loss as they grew up, but he never believed in pure, untarnished souls 'trailing clouds of glory'. He would never write, like Wordsworth, 'Heaven lies about us in our infancy', or like Carroll, 'Their innocent unconsciousness is very beautiful and gives one a feeling of reverence, as at the presence of something sacred.' If anything, it was the animal side of children he liked, not the 'sacred'. He watched them, enjoyed the chaos they caused and could see that they were sometimes pests. At nineteen, writing to Ann about their sister Sarah's boys, he summed them up in rhyme:

Little Charles – I must say, seems improved on the whole
But at books he's extremely dull – poor little soul!
But the other child – Freddie – is noon night and morn
The most horrid young monkey that ever was born –
Such violent passions and tears in an ocean,
He kept the whole house in a constant commotion.

With children Lear did not have to put on airs. He could be one with them, without effort: 'Never was there a man who could so live into the feelings of a child,' remembered Mary Crawford, who knew him when she was a girl. Children loved to watch him draw, and he made them feel he was specially theirs: 'He grew to be so much our own,' Mary wrote. Robert Francillon (the nephew of Lear's old friend Robert Leake Gale) never forgot Lear's first visit, when he drew an Eastern landscape for him, with camels and palms: 'I treasured it as long as the wear and tear of nurseries and schoolrooms allowed.' Robert and his sisters watched Lear doing drawings for his limericks, standing by his knee, and when the collection was published, they felt oddly bereft because now it 'was no longer our very own, that we had watched flow for *us* from the pen'. Because Lear felt easy with children, they responded in kind. They felt safe and were always drawn to him: 'And children swarmed to him like settlers,' as Auden put it. 'He became a land.'

If Lear was a land, at this point he was a country of misrule, nonsense, larking about, and only later a landscape of loneliness, courage and endurance. One visitor attributed Lear's invitation to the family dinner table not to a nervous, kindly gesture of Lord Derby, but to his grandsons' insistence on speeding away from the dining room because it was 'so much more amusing downstairs'. Why? 'Oh, because that young fellow in the steward's room who is drawing the birds for you is such good company and we like to go and hear him talk.' So Lear, allegedly, was summoned upstairs, to make the adults laugh too.

Being 'much more amusing' made him good company. The 1830s were years of games after supper, of silliness and risqué inventiveness, of blowing feathers round the room, men kneeling on all fours carrying women on their backs, word games like 'The Three Kingdoms' – animal, vegetable, mineral. There was even one called 'Nonsense', with '*cross questions* and *crooked answers*', where players gave their neighbour an answer word, secretly, and the conductor put questions:

PETER: Mr Charles, what do you think matrimony is like?
CHARLES: A mouse-trap.
PETER: You were at the last Lord Mayor's ball, Miss Martha: what sort of stuff was Lady Nudeley's petticoat made of?
MARTHA: A fig-leaf.
PETER: So, Master Simon, you went to the dentist this morning, what did he order you to pick your teeth with?
SIMON: A soup-ladle.

The Young Person at table, who picked at his teeth with a ladle, sounds like a Lear character. Another popular game, Aldiborontiphoskyphorniostikos, involved shouting out the names of invented characters faster and faster. The players then told the stories of these crazy characters at speed, with actions. From this, Lear made up his own, long nonsense name, varied over the years – 'Mr Abebika, Kratoponoko, Prizzikalo, Kattefello, Ablegorabalus . . . Otherwise – Edward Lear'.

Storytelling, madness and speed came easily to him. And in his own – though unreliable – memory he found the perfect form at Knowsley almost by chance. 'Long years ago,' he wrote in 1872,

in days when much of my time was passed in a Country House, where children and mirth abounded, the lines beginning 'There was an old man of' were suggested to me by a valued friend, as a form of verse lending itself to limitless variety for Rhymes and Pictures; and thenceforth,the greater part of the original drawings and verses for the first 'Book of Nonsense' were struck off with a pen, no assistance ever having been given me in any way but that of uproarious delight and welcome at the appearance of every new absurdity.

Lear's model 'There was an Old Man of Tobago' came from Richard Scrafton Sharpe's *Anecdotes and Adventures of Fifteen Gentlemen*, published by John Marshall in 1822 with illustrations by Robert Cruikshank. The book parodied *The Adventures of Fifteen Young Ladies* and *A History of Sixteen Wonderful Old Women*, from Marshall's competitor John Harris, who had taken over the firm of Newberry, publisher of nursery rhymes, stories and alphabets. Similar forms can be traced back in time, for example to medieval French nonsense poems, but these were more like the bouncing nursery songs, tied to a place, that summon a character and tell a story with no explanation:

> Doctor Foster went to Gloucester
> In a shower of rain.
> He fell in a puddle right up to his middle
> And never went there again.

Lear's verses shared other elements with the old lore of children: word-play, jingles, strange pairings and impossibilities. 'Hey diddle diddle, the Cat and the Fiddle, the Cow jumped over the Moon' was one of several rhymes he illustrated later for children. His nonsense had the arbitrary numbers, sudden surprises, disasters and attacks of those rhymes: Four-and-twenty Blackbirds bursting out of a pie and pecking off a nose: Three Blind Mice and the farmer's wife, who cut off their tails with a carving knife; Humpty Dumpty, cracked for ever after his fall.

To begin with Lear treated 'There was an Old Man of Tobago' as he did the parlour ballads, illustrating it with three numbered scenes (later pasted into an album made from a pattern-book for swatches of material from a Manchester firm not far from Knowsley). Sharpe's rhyme satirised fashionable non-meat diets, but it also touched on one of Lear's pet subjects, the greed of the glutton. In his pictures a man with a hamster-like face and an old-fashioned bob-wig sits forlornly before bowls of sago and rice; in walk the physicians in boots and spurs, and as soon as they give him the go-ahead he attacks the huge leg of lamb, teeth first, waving knife and fork like weapons.

> There was an Old Man of Tobago
> Who lived on rice, gruel and sago
> Till one day to his bliss
> The Physicians said this
> To a roast leg of mutton you *may go*.

Lear had a go at another of the *Fifteen Gentlemen*'s rhymes, 'The old soldier of Bicester', this time drawing only two scenes. Then came the moment when he realised that one picture alone would do. The verse form he chose did not follow the pattern of the Old Man of Tobago, but that used in *Wonderful Old Women*. In this, the character was introduced by a place, followed by a distinguishing action (often employing the terrible rhymes Lear enjoyed), and concluding with a statement of its effect – 'which sadly annoy'd', 'which rejoiced' – or a summarising final adjective – 'worrying', 'whimsical', 'provident', as in this rhyme from the original book:

> There was an Old Woman of Norwich
> Who lived upon nothing but porridge.
> Parading the town,
> She turned cloak into gown
> That thrifty Old Woman of Norwich.

The short verse concertinaed a narrative: person, place and event, followed by consequence or judgement: no motive, no past, no future. The rhyme worked like a jack-in-the-box, springing a character into

95

life, then snapping the box shut as it returned to the place of the opening line. Children would laugh, adults could make up their own meaning. And some of Lear's rhymes were gleefully awful: 'There was an Old Man of Kamschatka,/Who possessed a remarkably fat cur'; 'There was an Old Man of Columbia,/Who was thirsty, and called out for some beer'. This playful rhyming often seemed to look back to Byron, his childhood idol, who compared the softness of Italian to 'our harsh Northern whistling, grunting guttural/Which we're obliged to hiss, and spit, and sputter all'.

The nonsenses were always a performance. Holman Hunt talked of how Lear 'beat out' his rhymes, reciting them with a thumping rhythm on their walks. The rhyming words were the kind that children loved to invent, and the weird happenings were very different to their usual fare of moral tales and the enjoyable yet didactic stories of Maria Edgeworth and others. Like Catherine Sinclair's exuberantly original novel *Holiday House* with its noisy, mischievous, anarchic children, published at the end of this decade, Lear's limericks challenged the teaching designed, as Sinclair said, 'to stuff the memory, like a cricket ball, with well known facts and ready-made opinions'. Nonsense persons disdained facts. They were eccentric, mindless, violent, vague, sometimes peaceable, often cross. They had false teeth and gammy legs. They ate muffins and crumpets, fish and beans, tea and toast. They longed to escape but often failed: they set off, gave up and came back. They said what they thought and were rude. Their demands were infantile, their ambitions wild. There was ghoulish stuff here too, another childish taste of which adults disapproved: blood, amputation, screaming, dismemberment, 'accidental' baking in a cake.

In a nursery, designed to mould infants into rational shape, nonsense was a dance of unreason, showing strait-laced grown-ups dancing jigs, sleeping on tables, falling down volcanoes, climbing up trees. But they were not always happy.

There was an Old Lady whose folly,
Induced her to sit in a holly;
Whereon by a thorn, her dress being torn,
She quickly became melancholy.

This could work well to console a small girl for spoilt dresses and hurt feelings, but it could equally well be a dig at a disapproving aunt, who pursed her lips as though she had thorns up her dress. Yet there is sympathy and affection here too: in Lear, folly and melancholy often go together. What was the Old Lady's 'folly'? What form does her 'melancholy' take? Will she ever get down from this tree?

8: MOUNTAINS

Lear's enthusiasm, his love of the ridiculous and his sense of wonder won him many friends. But he also liked being on the move. Doctors had decreed that exercise reduced the risk of epileptic seizures, and in his twenties he longed to get away from aviaries and studios and drawing rooms, to walk the country and sketch.

One way to combine freedom with an artist's career was to take up landscape painting. This would also release him from exploitation by Gould, who was becoming increasingly demanding and impatient, and from the strain of such detailed, close work: 'My eyes are so sadly worse', he told Gould in the autumn of 1836, 'that no bird under an Ostrich shall I soon be able to do.' With this in mind, Lear became more and more interested in topographical art, accurate delineations of place inflected by atmosphere. This would suit him. As well as working to commission artists could sell watercolours and oils at London exhibitions and publish books of their sketches, as Samuel Prout did in the mid-1820s and early 1830s with the *Landscape Annuals* and *Facsimiles of Sketches Made in Flanders and Germany*.

Lear particularly admired James Duffield Harding, who took over from Prout as chief illustrator for the *Landscape Annuals*, and drew the landscapes for Hullmandel's books: in 1830, he published his own Italian sketches on tinted paper, the start of a new vogue. Lear followed

Harding's style, particularly in his drawings of trees, balancing accurate depiction of form and bark against airy, impressionistic foliage. He used Harding's recommended materials, graphite with highlights of white chalk on grey-tinted paper, and on a summer visit to Arundel in 1834, the year that Harding published his book *Elementary Art: or, the Use of the Lead Pencil Advocated and Explained*, he launched into landscapes: hedges in a country lane, the church at Peppering and the yard with its turkeys, the huge trees in the park at Parham. (Lear was always moved, and soothed, by trees, making them the focus of many works, and painting and drawing them separately all his life.)

Friends encouraged Lear's interest, like Robert Leake Gale and his engaging future brother-in-law Daniel Fowler; both had been Harding's pupils before going on a sketching tour of Holland, the Rhine, Switzerland and Italy. Lear saw them both at Hullmandel's. Fowler came from a well-off family who lived at Downe in Kent, Darwin's later home. (His widowed mother had paid £300 for three years in Harding's studio, the kind of training Lear could never afford.) The Gales became another family, as the Drewitts had been in Sussex: Robert's nephew, the writer Robert Francillon, noted that 'an almost brotherly and sisterly relation grew up between him and the group of bright young girls who then filled with life the house in Queen Square'. In old age Lear remembered sitting in Queen's Square with Gale's sisters, Lucy and Elizabeth (who married Dan Fowler in August 1835), reading Dan's letters from Italy under a mulberry tree. When Fowler came back to London, with a face pitted by smallpox and an armful of sketches, an excited Lear thought his drawings 'without *exception the finest sketches* I ever saw from any artist's portfolio'.

In the week of Dan's return Lear was planning a party. He had asked seven friends, including Robert Gale, thinking eight was the most he could squeeze into Southampton Row. Then in rushed Fowler, 'red hot from Rome. – of course if he could be split into 10 – he must all come.' Next Hullmandel asked to bring a foreign visitor;

then Bernard Senior said his 'only Brother in England' was coming for the night – could he bring him too?

I own my blood curdled at this last volunteer . . . Conceive – for they can't be described – the momentous cogitations with my landlady which ensued – the cleanings – the hurryings – the widening of table & multiplication of dishes, – & above all – add the misery of an Irish servant who almost always misunderstands whatever you say.

The Gales sent arack for punch and lent him a punch bowl, but then he found at the last minute that all his landlady's ladles had been 'smished'. In a panic Lear sent round 'the following pathetic stanzas':

> My dear Mrs Gale – from my leaving the cradle
> Till now I have never such agony known
> What use is a Punch bowl without any ladle, –
> Be it Ivory – Silver – Wood – China – or Bone? –
> My landlady rushes & foams in a flurry
> Her ladles for Punch & her Ladles for Soup
> Besides all her Ladles for Butter & Curry
> Are all, she vows – 'smished' in one family Group.
>
> Then dear Mrs Gale – have a little Compassion
> – If it's only a Ladle full – Send me in one! –
> And I'll ever proclaim you in my estimation –
> The most '*Ladle-like*' personage under the sun!

Fowler always remembered these early days, the start of a lifetime friendship. Lear 'must have then been about twenty', he thought. 'Tall, not handsome, and rather ungainly in figure, he was very agreeable and genial in manner. There indeed was partly the secret of his great success in life; he was all things to all people.' He greatly admired Lear's parrots, 'drawn with great precision, truth and accuracy', and loved his nonsense too, full of covert humour: 'The astonishing vigour and drollery of the intentional bad drawing are quite past description.'

Later that summer, Lear was in Dublin, being 'all things' at once:

naturalist, humorist, walker, and now landscape artist. In his brief tour with Revd Stanley and Arthur he drew the towers of Clondalkin and the valley of Glendalough, the cliff-top banqueting house of Bellevue and the crowded streets of Bray. It gave him a taste of something different, and he could not wait to set out with his sketchbook to draw mountains and mist again.

That summer a plan had been mooted that he might go on a painting trip with Audubon in the States. Audubon was kind, but tactfully pointed out to Lord Derby that the strain on Lear's health would be simply too much. The idea was shelved. He was not done with painting animals. In early June 1836 he sent Derby an excited account of London Zoo's first giraffes, the sensation of the year, whose arrival drew a crowd of nearly four thousand. 'I never imagined any thing living of such extreme elegance,' wrote Lear.

By the end of that month he was in Lancashire again for another long stay: 'I never remember passing so happy a consecutive 6 weeks as I did this year at Knowsley.' In early August, with Derby's blessing and pockets stuffed with invitations to Stanley and Hornby connections in Westmorland and Cumberland, he set off on his own on a tour of the Lakes. At twenty-four, he could become a landscape artist.

A trip to the Lakes was a must for any aspiring artist, treading in the steps of Gainsborough, Constable and Turner. Lear knew what was expected, making several sketches from exactly the same position as the prints in contemporary guidebooks. But he was also agog for new impressions and keen to stray off prescribed routes. On his way he stayed with Derby's nephew Edmund Hornby, who was Constable of Lancaster Castle and also had a home on Windermere. He summed up his visit in self-mocking raptures: 'Mrs Hornby – the mountains of Westmoreland – the Castle – & the Lunatic Asylum – are all balanced in my mind – you might see them all at once – & each was perfection in its way.'

The perfection was marred by the fact that everywhere he went, it rained. On Saturday 20 August, he made a little drawing, wryly entitled

Umbrellifera, a record of Kendal on market day, a huddle of women under umbrellas. 'Nature's slopbasin', Lear called the town, 'where it always rains', where babies were born with fins. The clouds followed him to the southern flanks of the Lake District, where he sketched the abbeys of Cartmel and Furness in a deluge. He was still looking forward to the high mountains. 'I have now been a month in the Lake Country', he lamented in early September, '– & have seen nothing of a Lake at all! . . . almost all this time I have only made studies of rain.' There were, however, some magical compensations, especially the Elizabethan Levens Hall, the home of Fulke and Mary Greville Howard, for whom Lear had been doing lithographs in London. He had met Mary Howard when he was eighteen, and thought her 'one of the finest specimens of the Grand English lady of olden time'; she was fond of him in return, a friendship that would last until her death in 1874.

At Levens it still rained but he loved everything about the place, from the gardens to the dancing in the hall, 'where ghosts are as common as mice, – & you sit among armour & starched ruffs till you find even your own limbs growing stiff & mouldy'. He enjoyed the absurd, like the great yew trees, '30 or 40 feet high – cut into cows – bottles – hats – & every possible shape – unaltered by an inch since 1680!! Imagine turf between walls of high beech trees – all magically shorn quite even – & looking like fable & nonsense!!' There were more jollities – the daughters of Colonel Thomas Bradyll at Conishead Priory near Ulverston were '20 degrees beyond perfection – & what with all sorts of singing & music with them, their father, & brother, & Admiral Sotheran – a band of 2 accordions, flute, harp, guitar & piano – we minded not the rain a tittle'. At Alexander Nowell's Underley Hall near Kirkby Lonsdale, luxury replaced music. Nowell, he explained, 'is a rich possessor of East Ind. Property, and the valuable splendour beats credibility! – & such living! Curries! Pilaus! champagnes! – Dear Me!'

At last, after that first rainy month, he reached the fells that were his real goal. On 9 September, he was at Storrs Hall on Windermere and from then on he refused further invitations. 'This sort of life is all very fine,' he decided, tongue in cheek, 'but very improper.' Instead he packed his bag, put on his boots, and set out.

He took with him a portfolio with blue-grey paper, a supply of pencils and stump, wad for shading and white chalk for heightening. His sketches, dated and numbered in pen and brown ink, showed a landscape at once familiar and strange. They began with a standard tourist view from Lowood on the eastern shore of Windermere, looking across the lake and up the valley beyond to the Langdale Pikes, their peaks emerging from drifting clouds. Then Lear went north, past Wordsworth's home at Rydal Mount, through Grasmere and over Dunmail Raise, the old county border between Westmorland and Cumberland. Sometimes he hired a horse or took the coach but usually he walked. In mid-September he was high among the crags. 'I know every corner of Westmoreland,' he wrote later. 'Scawfell Pikes is my cousin, and Skiddaw is my mother-in-law.'

Scafell Pike from Styhead Pass, 19 September 1836

From Wasdale he marched over the old packhorse route of Styhead Pass to Borrowdale, sketching the view back towards Scafell Pike.

This was not a guide-book standard but an out-of-the-way view, and Lear conjured the great fells and the cloudy skies with simple, broken pencil lines and shading. The looseness and freedom of his drawing was itself a holiday, after years of detailed, intricate natural history work. Stopping in lonely uplands to sketch marshes and tarns, waterfalls in spate and the jagged crags silhouetted against the sky, he zig-zagged across the mountains. In his final few days he strode over to Ullswater before circling back over the Kirkstone Pass to Windermere. Now his great tour was over. By 30 October he was back at Knowsley.

He had managed at least six sketches a day, and had learned how to convey hazy distances, wind and storm, clouded heights and shimmering lakes. 'Really it is impossible to tell you', he wrote to John Gould, '*how, & how enormously* I have enjoyed the whole Autumn':

The counties of Cumberland & Wstmd are superb indeed, & tho' the weather has been miserable, yet I have contrived to walk pretty well over the whole ground, & to sketch a good deal beside. I hope too, I have improved somewhat – (hard if I haven't after slaving as I have done) but you will judge when I get back.

He had improved. The sketches showed a young artist finding his way, deft, accurate and atmospheric – he found he could get a sense of the misty air and gradations of tone by rubbing the graphite with a finger or leather pad. Some views were delicate, others were bold, impressionistic notations of striking forms.

In theory the trip put money in his purse. Lake District prints were popular and lithographs would be a useful money-spinner. But although he made notes on colour and texture and planned to work them up over the winter, only one print survives, *Wastwater & the Screes, from Wastdale*, and only one finished watercolour, *Wastwater*, a variant of the same scene, a hazy view in brown and gold, textured with scratching and gum arabic, which he gave to the Hornbys of Windermere. He abandoned the idea of prints, and over the years he gave his drawings on their blue-grey paper to his old Holloway friend Bill Nevill and his sons Allan and Ralph. Within months, Lear had set the Lake District aside: he had other plans.

Winter set in early at Knowsley. On 31 October, when he told Gould about his trip, he painted two watercolours of the flat Lancashire view, with streaks of red in the sky and clouds piling in from the west. He headed his letter to Gould 'hail-snow-frost- &desolation', and ended it with a PS, 'This place is colder than Kamschatka!' He had a cold that made him feel half blind, as well as a cough and sore throat. He remained at Knowsley to finish some work for Derby, and was touched to be invited to stay on after Christmas and 'to come when I please without being asked'. But he had work to do in London. He took the coach south through the New Year blizzards, 'miles of a sort of lane between snow walls 10 or 12 feet high'; the coach overturned twice and he arrived in Southampton Row without his luggage, which was 'still frozen up in a filthy Leicestershire canal'.

He saw no chance of getting down to Sussex. There was so much to do: a trip to Paris with Gould as well as orders for lithographs and watercolours. He was working by candlelight every evening, turning down invitations, and 'leeching & sitting up with my old friend Hullmandel who is very ill'. Illness was all around: his sister Kate, the youngest of the Lear siblings, was suffering from consumption. She died by the end of the month. 'I do not know when I have been so unhinged & miserable,' Lear wrote. And he feared there would be another death too. 'Before long I fear, for my sister Florence is but a shadow.'

By now he had moved again, to 36 Great Marlborough Street, just down from Hullmandel's studio at no. 49. (Charles Darwin, back from his voyage, had rooms here at the same time: did they pass on the stairs?) But although the lodgings were comfortable, he was not well and the doctors advised him to go south, away from the chill east winds. The chance came within a month. Led by Derby and Robert Hornby, a group of thirty subscribers – or so his benefactors told him – combined to commission drawings 'to be executed in Rome'. This hugely generous gesture was a measure of the Knowsley group's fondness, showing how much they valued him as a person, as well as an artist. For Lear a long-nursed dream, of studying for two years in Italy, was on the verge of becoming a reality.

He paid farewell visits and travelled up to Knowsley 'in a chariot drawn by four horses, accompanied by 2 postillions & 2 domestics, – & containing Lord Derby – myself – 6 cloaks – one jerboa – 3 pigeons – 20 or 30 books – some bread & biscuits, – a roast fowl & a bottle of wine'. As he looked around at the old red drawing room, the red-and-white-striped chairs, the bookcases and window seats with their fat cushions, the lawn sloping down until it was lost in the meadows, he suddenly felt sad. He would always look back on this as the best home he had ever met with, he told Fanny: 'I don't half like going out of England, now it comes to the point.'

He planned to travel with Daniel Fowler, and by midsummer their passage was booked. After stopping for two days with Ann, who was in Bath, he went down to Bovisand on Plymouth Sound to stay with Captain Phipps Hornby and his large family. They walked and swam, sailed up the Tamar and paddled in the sea, the women with their skirts gathered up around their knees. In the evenings they took their guitars down to the rocks: '& there we sate singing to the sea & the moon till late'. Back in London, where the city was agog at the death of William IV and the accession of his eighteen-year-old niece Victoria, Lear packed his bags. And then, he told Fanny on 7 July, 'I sail next Sunday on the Antwerp packet.'

III. FLYING

9: 'ROME IS ROME'

What did it mean to be a landscape artist? Who would he meet, and how would he live? When Lear sailed for Antwerp on 16 July 1837, the day after the funeral of William IV, it felt like the start of a new era for him, as well as for the country. With Dan Fowler and Robert Gale he set off to sketch first in Brussels and Luxembourg, but there Fowler became ill and from Coblenz he headed home. Gale left too, and from mid-August Lear drifted through Germany alone. He was happy being on his own, as he had been in the Lakes. He sketched the market squares of Coblenz and Trier, the timbered buildings of towns on the Mosel, the fairytale turrets of Eltz and the canopied shop-fronts of Frankfurt. Despite his yearning for training, his drawings were detailed and exquisite, full of atmosphere, as if they had simply sprung out of him, the product of a natural talent. In early September he reached Geneva. At last, white-capped mountains appeared in his sketches. Aged twenty-five, Lear crossed the Alps.

Ann was also now on the Continent: often in these years, through contacts in the local churches, she stayed in France or Belgium where life was cheaper. Now she was in Brussels, where, Lear joked, 'by your praises of the Beer there, I fear you have taken to drinking'. His long letters were alive with new scenes. He reached Milan, and then, taking only his knapsack and sketchbook, he set off for Como, where he met a fellow pupil of his own age from Sass's, Sir William Knighton (the son of George IV's private secretary, who had been burdened with trying to control the king's debts). Kind though the Knighton family were, Lear longed to be on his own again. He dashed off to Domaso at the head of the lake, where the scenery *was quite beyond anything I had seen*; the dark blue lake reflects the white houses of Domaso – and over them enormous Alps, Jiggy-Jaggy – shut out the Italians from Switzerland'. He walked high into the mountains and back along the lake, watching peasants bring in the grape harvest, seeing his first olive trees and struggling to describe them: 'I think they are very beautiful – more like a huge lavender bush – or a fine gray willow than anything else, and all over little shiny green olives.' Then, after a trip to Lugano, he picked up his gear in Milan and drove slowly south along the poplar-lined roads across the Lombardy plains. From Bologna he joined a crowd of British tourists struggling over the snowy Apennines: their string of eight coaches were hauled up by oxen, '– and all the passengers walking. So much for the loneliness of mountain passes! – at the place we lunched – 32 people – all English, sat down together.'

All these English travellers were heading for Florence, where Lear found 'cards and notes left as if one were in Sherrard Street still . . . The whole place is like an English watering place.' (Ten years later, Anna Jameson warned the Brownings – in vain – against settling there as it was 'British to the teeth and bursting at the seams with balls and hoopla'.) Lear found rooms and pupils and began to settle down. But November brought icy winds and despite the cheap roasted chestnuts – 'I eat them perpetual' – Florence, he felt, was no place for the winter. Defying rumours of cholera in the cities and robbers on the roads, he would go on, as an artist should, to Rome.

He left Florence with regret, looking back at the magnificent bridges and tall medieval buildings, but remembering the cold above all:

the clear lilac mountains all round it – the exquisite walks on every side to hills covered with villages, convents and cypresses, where you have the whole city beneath you – the bustle of the Grand Duke's court and the fine shops – the endless churches – the Zebra Cathedral of black and white marble – the crowds of towers and steeples – all these make Florence a little Paradise in its way – if it were but hotter. – Oh! How I used to go shivering about!

By mid-December Lear was in Rome. The sculptor William Theed, who travelled with him from Florence and had lived in Rome for ten years, helped him hunt for lodgings, and he found a study and bedroom, with a small balcony, at no. 39 Via del Babuino – 'Baboon Street', he told Ann happily. It was close by the Piazza di Spagna, the favourite area of the English and the artists, and he found friends there already, including the Knighton family. Soon his days fell into a pattern:

At 8 I go to the Café, where all the artists breakfast, and have 2 cups of coffee and 2 toasted rolls – for 6½ d. and then – I either see sights – make calls – draw out of doors – or, if wet – have models indoors till 4. Then most of the artists walk on the Pincian Mount (a beautiful garden overlooking all Rome, and from which such sunsets are seen!) – and at 5 we dine very capitally at a Trattoria or eating house, immediately after which Sir W. Knighton and I walk to the Academy – whence after 2 hours we return home.

Joseph Severn – Keats's friend, who had been at his deathbed next to the Spanish Steps in 1821 – had started 'the Academy' with the support of the Royal Academy, anxious to rival the French in Rome after the Napoleonic wars. Artists collected tickets before they left England, but, as Lear and Knighton discovered, the Academy was small, an evening school offering only a life class, a few models and casts and skeletons: the real meeting places were informal, in trattorias and studios, galleries and parks. In Rome, instead of attaching himself to a particular family or clan, as he had in Sussex and Lancashire, Lear found the closeness he needed in the international community of artists.

British artists had come to Rome for many years, to learn from the great paintings and sculpture that filled the churches and palaces and to fulfil commissions for collectors and aristocrats on their Grand Tour,

recording scenery and antiquities and making copies of Italian old masters. From the mid-eighteenth century, the British public, whose vision
of Italy had been previously governed by the idealised scenes of Claude
Lorrain, Salvator Rosa and Nicolas Poussin, began to see it afresh in
the topographical paintings of Richard Wilson and William Pars and
the evocative views of John Robert Cozens – 'all poetry', as Constable
called Cozens's work. In Lear's youth John 'Warwick' Smith, Samuel
Prout and others had exhibited their Italian watercolours in London,
while engravings of scenes by Turner and many others appeared in
works like Rogers's *Italy*, which Lear had pored over in Arundel.

The sculptors, in particular, came and stayed for years, inspired by
Canova and the Danish sculptor Bertel Thorwaldsen, who lived near
the Spanish Steps until his return to Denmark in 1838. Lear's new friend
William Theed had trained under Thorwaldsen and his marble statues
and busts were soon bought with enthusiasm by the British royal family. Through Theed, Lear met Richard James Wyatt and John Gibson
– 'Gibby' as Turner affectionately called him. Now in their forties, admired for their elegant neo-classical statues – Venus, Aurora, Pandora –
and for their modern portraits, with clear profiles and flowing drapery,
Wyatt and Gibson had studios opposite each other in the Via della Fon-
tanella Barberini: 'I thank God', wrote Gibson, 'for every morning that
opens my eyes in Rome.' A model for other artists, their life was simple:
rising early, breakfasting in the Caffe Greco, reading the newspapers
and walking in the Pincian gardens before a long day in the studio. And
although they were shrewd businessmen they set a casual style. Meeting Gibson in Naples, William Dean Howells described him as 'dressed
with extraordinary slovenliness and indifference to clothes, had no collar, I think, and evidently did not know that he had none'.

Painters and sculptors from Britain, France, Germany and Scandi-
navia clustered around the Piazza di Spagna: in 1834 it was reckoned
there were over five hundred foreign artists, musicians and writers in
Rome. The French, notorious for dallying in taverns and downing
the sparkling white *orvieto*, had their academy in the Villa Medici: the

Norwegians, Swedes and Danes had their own book clubs and reading rooms; the Germans and Scandinavians formed the 'Ponte Molle' society, laying on parties on the river banks near the bridge and running the Cervarofeste, a boozy annual fancy-dress procession to the Cervaro caves. Hans Christian Andersen, remembering his arrival in 1833, described Italy as 'the country of my longing, and of my poetical happiness . . . a new world of art'. The Caffe Greco, a fug of tobacco smoke with separate rooms for Germans, French and the English, rang with arguments over art and politics. This was an easy-going world, tolerant of affairs with both sexes and marked by intense friendships. It was coloured, too, by a tendency – which Lear shared at first – to romanticise the Italian peasantry, embodied by the local women paid to pose in their studios, 'an unfortunate class of females who make a trade of *attitudinizing* to artists'.

This was a speciality of the Welsh painter Penry Williams, ten years Lear's senior, who set up his studio in the late 1820s, attracting British visitors with his views of Italy and scenes of Roman life. Lear came to know him well, 'always the same even & quiet man', and praised him as the most conscientious painter of the Italian peasantry, whose colour 'was always truthful & lovely, & his delineation of scenery on the Roman Campagna & in the neighbouring mountains absolutely perfect'. With his guidance, Lear began to work in oil, and although he came to feel that Williams's appreciation of other artists was too narrow and regretted blindly following his lead, in these golden years his teaching was an inspiration.

Established stars like Wyatt, Gibson and Williams drew younger artists into their orbit, like the landscape painter Charles Coleman, the sculptor Frederick Thrupp and his friend James Uwins, the quiet, good-tempered nephew of the watercolourist Thomas Uwins who had lived here in the previous decade. 'The artists especially are a delightful set,' Lear told Ann, 'Gibson, Wyatt and Theed, Williams, Coleman and Uwins particularly.' As an artist, Lear was small fry, with his Harding-esque sketches, but he was keen to learn. His health was better, he told

Derby, and 'For improvement – I say little as yet: I try hard enough & if improvement in art *must necessarily* follow, I shall be sure to have it, – but I think sometimes, one bird drawing was worth 2 landscapes – I go on hoping nevertheless.' The Derby connection served him well and he went to assemblies and balls in rambling old palaces with wealthy British families wintering in Italy. He made firm friends, like the kindly Lady Susannah ('Susan') Percy, niece of the Duke of Northumberland who had subscribed to his *Parrots*, who had lived in Rome for forty years, and Charles Knight and his sisters: Isabella, an invalid who languished stylishly on her couch until a fine old age, and Margaret, who married the Duke of Sermoneta, from the great Caetani family.

As in Florence, the British community was insular. They read the London papers – admittedly rather late – in the reading rooms in the Piazza di Spagna, held their own parties and ran their own excursions. Gentlemen went to the English Club, whose membership excluded professionals such as doctors and artists. They also had an English chapel near the Via Condotti, where Lear went on Sundays: most remained firmly Protestant, although they did accept tickets from the Vatican for special services (a few years later English ladies gained a reputation for whispering and eating biscuits, and the Vatican sent round a notice asking for decorum in Holy Week). They left their money in English banks, and shopped at the English shoemakers, bakers, tailors and saddle-makers who clustered in the nearby streets. In the coming years Murray's *Handbook to Italy* noted: 'we would advise our countrymen to employ English tradespeople when possible; they are more to be relied upon for punctuality, good attitudes and honesty, than the native shopkeepers.' Arthur Clough, who came to Rome a few years later, at the age of nineteen, caught the mood exactly in the breathless letters of Georgina Trevellyn in his *Amours de Voyage* – very much Lear's tone when he describes the arrival of exuberant English visitors:

> At last, dearest Louisa, I take up my pen to address you.
> Here we are, you see, with the seven-and-seventy boxes,

Courier, Papa and Mamma, the children, and Mary and Susan:
Here we all are at Rome, and delighted of course with St Peter's,
And very pleasantly lodged in the famous Piazza di Spagna.
Rome is a wonderful place, but Mary shall tell you about it;
Not very gay, however; the English are mostly at Naples;
There are the A.'s, we hear, and most of the W. party.
George, however, is come; did I tell you about his mustachios?

Dividing his time between the artists and the British residents and visitors, the people Lear did not get to know were the Romans themselves – he didn't even know his landlady's name; 'very likely she has none at all,' he joked. Ten or twelve families shared the tall house he lodged in, with its seven floors, but they rarely spoke: 'All strangers they call only "Forestieri" – unless they have lived many years in Rome, and then they say "Signor Riccardo Scultore" – "Sign. Giovanni Pittore" – or "Sign. Giorgio Inglesi," but they never take the trouble to learn surnames.'

Many Inglesi arrived for 'the Season', from January until April, enjoying the masked parades, balls and fireworks of Carnival and the dramatic Easter processions. Lear flung himself into the Carnival uproar with the Knightons, bombarding passers-by with *confetti*, filled with flour:

having disguised ourselves as women of Albano (fancy me with a red bodice, and green skirt – with a white scioccatura which is the name of the beautiful headdress the women wear . . . besides a black mask!!), we hired a coach and pelted away famously. But on the last evening is the best fun of all. Directly after the horse race, dusk begins and by degrees every door and window all down the long and narrow Corso becomes illuminated with candles called 'mocoli'. The houses being of such vast height – the effect is wonderfully beautiful.

The streets were full of people carrying candles. The game, he explained, was to keep your own candle alight while extinguishing others with great cries and shouts: 'It is as like magic as anything you can fancy.'

'One may be very gay if one pleases,' he admitted, downplaying his excitement. 'At Torlone's, the rich bankers, the other night nearly all

Rome was present: cardinals – priests – Russians – English – French & Germans – all the world in fact. But I am pretty well sick of these things. When I come home at night with my key I often think of Gray's Inn Road & Albany St!' But he was fascinated by the people and their costumes, and by the flocks of priests of different orders, 'white – black – piebald – scarlet – cinnamon – purple: round hats – shovel hats – cocked hats – hoods and caps', cardinals and friars, bishops and monks, all in their own colours. He told Ann of the sleek grey cattle pulling carts, decorated with bells and ribbons, and of the Neapolitan pipers with peacock feathers in their caps who came to play for the Virgin at Christmas. And beyond the crowds, he was amazed at the way old ruins were mixed up with modern buildings, and stunned by the grandeur of the Coliseum and the Forum: 'judge how bewildered one's noddle becomes! – for my part, I am taking things very quietly – and like better to poke about over and over again in the Forum, than to hurry with the stream of sight-seers all day long.' Soon Lear would paint the Forum with the Temple of Venus, in the golden evening light.

Temple of Venus and Rome (1840)

There were grim sides to city life, especially the ravages of the recent cholera epidemic, but Lear was in love with it all. The January weather was mild as May, and he dreamt of bringing Ann out to join him '– so – if I were you, I would get up my Italian . . . Other folks have sisters and wives and mothers here, so I don't see why I should not too.' Ann did think about coming, amusing him with her poor Italian geography when she suggested she might travel via Naples. But although he sent her details of ships and prices, in a way he was happier that she was at a distance. Money was short and by the following March he admitted that 'coming here, at present, is I think out of the question'. Still his family and friends were always in his mind. His letters to Ann were filled with references to their sisters Ellen and Sarah, Florence and Harriett, and to old London friends like the kindly Nevills. He kept in touch too with the Sussex Coombes and with George Cartwright and his wife Henri-etta, who visited him in Rome, 'two of the best and nicest people I have known', he told Fanny Coombe. He enjoyed gossiping to Fanny, telling her things that would make her gasp:

Last Friday a Roman Lady of 50 – in love with a soldier, threw herself out of a window in the next street – & on Monday a younger damsel from the same cause (Roman also) did just the same a few doors off, her lover taking poison just after; they talk of English suicides but all I can say is that these make up the 7th that have occurred in a space not larger than that from you to the Norfolk Arms, dur-ing the 2 years I have been here!! – Yesterday a poor English woman suffering from tic doloreux – Mrs Dunbar, next door but one to me – also killed herself in a paroxysm of insanity. There! I think I have given you sufficient horrors.

In a different vein, he tried to keep up with natural history interests as a way of expressing his gratitude to Lord Derby, to whom he also sent many drawings and watercolours. He had promised to look for specimens and to tell Derby about the collection of the naturalist Joseph Lucien Bonaparte, Napoleon's nephew, now Prince of Musignano. In time he came to know the Bonaparte family well, staying with them at their villa in the country, but for the moment the prince was in France and Lear had nothing to report: little birds were scarce, he explained, as thousands were shot for daily food and there were no new canaries or parrots in the bird markets. He was reduced to telling Derby of Italian practices like the skinning of frogs in Milan – he watched them capering about as if nothing had happened – and the clipping of cats' tails (a fate that later befell his own cat, Foss), so that 'they will never forsake the house in which they have lost that useful member'. In Rome, he confessed, 'my zoological notes are at a most deplorably low ebb'. When he wrote this on a cold February day, his spirits were also low: 'It is all very beautiful and wonderful here, – but – it is not England, & I am stupid enough to get into very homesick fits sometimes.'

Apart from occasional homesickness, Lear was happy. He drank in the beauty and history of the city, the blue blaze of the sky, the water splashing in mossy fountains, the long shadows of columns in the gold light of sunset. He illustrated his letters with sketches, of Holy Week fireworks at the Castel St Angelo, of Maecenas's villa, of the avenues and fountains of Tivoli. Lear loved Tivoli, as all the artists did, painting identical views of the great cypress avenues and fountains of the Villa d'Este: 'I used to stay there constantly,' he told a friend, '& one year for 8 months as it is cool in the summertime.' The place that moved him most, however, was the Campagna, the great plain between the city and the encircling hills. In ancient times this had been a fruitful area, rippling with corn, but the Goths had smashed the Roman aqueducts that brought water from the mountains and over the centuries the flooded fields had declined into wastes and malarial marshes. The bare Campagna was a glory of wild flowers in spring, but arid under summer sun and menacing and gloomy when dusk fell. There were few houses or huts, Lear noted, only herds of buffaloes and great flocks of sheep 'guarded by horribly fierce dogs – which it is not safe to go near'. He thrilled to the scattered ruins and arches and fallen aqueducts:

The ancient tombs & old Roman roads are just as they were, in some places. You don't meet peasants as you seem to think, for it is loneliness itself; foxes &

hawks – tortoises & porcupines, are the only inmates . . . The mighty aqueducts, the umbrella pines, the blue mountains beyond, the colours shining in the clear atmosphere . . . It is impossible to give any good idea of the amazing wildness and beauty of these plains.

Campagna of Rome from Villa Mattei, from *Views in Rome and its Environs* (1841)

In the mid-seventeenth century Claude Lorrain had painted the Campagna and had included these scenes in his *Liber Veritatis*, the 'Book of Truth' of almost two hundred drawings. Engraved and published in three volumes between 1778 and 1819, Claude's drawings inspired Turner to create his own series of prints, his *Liber Studiorum*, from 1806 to 1824. For Lear, Claude and Turner were inspiring models. 'You have little notion how completely an artist's paradise is Rome', he told Ann vehemently, '– and how destitute all other places would be of capacities to study and prosper. Rome is Rome – do not think about the future; let us be thankful that so far all is and has been so much better than we could ever have expected.'

10: HAPPY AS A HEDGEHOG

There was an Old Man of Vesuvius,
Who studied the works of Vitruvius;
When the flames burnt his book, to drinking he took,
That morbid Old Man of Vesuvius.

In early May 1838 Lear left his paintings with William Theed and headed for Naples with James Uwins. They took the inland route, walking through the mountains and staying in country inns where they shared a single echoing room with family, servants, animals and fleas. Writing on his birthday, 13 May ('26 today'), he told Ann:

In England you would be shocked to catch 5 in a morning – here 100, are nearer the mark. The only way to get rid of them is this, which I adopt very frequently: strip entirely, & then shake out your clothes well & then walk up & down the room barefooted – presently the creatures settle on your feet like mites on a cheese, & you may kill them by dozens.

Setting off at dawn they watched people come down from the hills to work, men carrying tools, women balancing cradles on their heads, knitting or spinning as they went. Day after day they walked on, over rocky passes where eagles soared, through oak forests, across torrents and past castles and villages, eventually climbing up to the convent on the precipice of Monte Cassino, ravaged by the French but with its famous library intact. In this rough country they found no real hardship, only pigs and spinning wheels and fat children: 'rollypoly babies abound'. '*And universally*', Lear wrote, 'the people are as kind, obliging, & respectful as it is possible to wish. So much for the "dangers and difficulties of walking among Italian mountains"!! What stuff! Clapham Common is at least doubly awful.'

By contrast Naples was a nightmare. Its surroundings were paradise, 'but the town itself is all noise, horror – dirt, heat – & abomination – & I hate it.' Writing to Ann, he evoked the cacophony of the main street, the Toledo:

They yell & shout – nobody in Naples speaks – in a manner quite superhuman. They allow themselves no repose. If you empty all the streets of the capitals of Europe into one – then turn in some thousand oxen, sheep, goats, monks – priests – processions – cars – mules – naked children & bare legged mariners – you may form some idea of the Toledo . . . yet at 8 o'clock people lounge & eat ices at every door although the noise is like all the thunder in the world.

The chaos was made worse by the royal family charging up and down in carriages, escorted by soldiers and kettledrums. At the market, too, Lear was deafened:

As you pass, every woman screams out – 'will you sit?' 'will you drink?' 'will you give me something?' 'anything?' 'a grana?' Signor, Signor, Signor, Water, Water, Fish – Meat – muscles – oysters – baskets – eggs – roses – apples – cherries? – while every man steps before you overwhelming you with the most tremendous shouts of 'Come along Sir – come; a boat! a boat! – instantly – now – this minute – this minute! To Capri – to Vesuvius – to Sorrento – to wherever you please – a boat, boat boat boat!!!'

By chance, Lear and Uwins were in the same hotel as the artist Samuel Palmer and his wife Hannah ('Anny'), in the middle of their two-year Italian honeymoon. Palmer was thirty-two and Anny nineteen and they had arrived in Rome the previous winter, finding their feet at the same time as Lear. 'Italy – especially Rome, is quite a new world,' Palmer thought. In the brilliant sunlight he produced vibrantly colourful paintings, a complete change from his earlier work. 'Much as I love England, I think every landscape painter should see Italy,' he wrote. 'It enlarges his IDEA of creation and he sees at least the sun and air fresh as from the head of their maker.'

The windows of the Hotel de la Ville de Rome looked across the bay, and the sea at night, said Anny, lay 'like a sheet of glittering silver with the beautiful full moon'. Lear too thought the bay was fine and Vesuvius was beautiful, green at the foot and lilac on the heights. But although he saw a fine eruption, an unforgettable midnight display, he ended by calling the volcano a 'filthy old mountain', cursing its grumblings and complaining that its bad air nearly killed him. The sulphur springs of Pozzuoli also made Lear ill and breathless, and he was glad to escape. For clear, cool air, he and Uwins headed to the walled town of Corpo di Cava, at the head of a high wooded valley looking down to the Bay of Salerno. It was a place 'always held in high admiration by the admirers of picturesque scenery', as Richard Colt Hoare had put it in 1819: 'To these sequestered scenes both Gaspar Poussin and Salvator Rosa directed their attention; and the modern landscape painter, who is anxious for improvement, cannot employ his time better than following in their footsteps.' Lear was certainly anxious for improvement, and – perhaps influenced by James Uwins, whose uncle Thomas Uwins had painted here a decade before – on this trip he switched from soft chalks to harder, crisper pencil, giving bolder outlines and sharper detail. He penned in his sketches in the evening in sepia ink, keeping his scribbled notes on colour, tone, shadow and detail.

Lear's ambition was changing subtly: he was now increasingly keen to use his sketches as the basis for oils, and for larger, more finished watercolours that he could paint when he was back in his studio. At Corpo di Cava, he worked on his first oil paintings: fluent studies of rocks and trees, a still life and a glimpse of a girl in a lane. The village seemed to encourage experiment: the Palmers also came up here and

Amalfi, July 1838

Samuel painted the 'Titian-like' mountains in the crimson glow of sunset.

In the mountains Lear heard birdsong rather than street cries and feasted on macaroni soup, strawberries, cherries and wine. His botanist self revelled in the aloes in bloom, the figs and oranges, pomegranates full of scarlet blossoms, wild red lilies, larkspur, roses and myrtle, and the chestnut woods echoing with cuckoos and nightingales. After they left he and Uwins went on, restored, to Salerno, Eboli and Paestum with its 'monstrous yet exquisitely beautiful temples' on the plain by the sea. Then, after another cool week in the mountains, they explored Sorrento and Amalfi, where Lear sketched the houses clinging to the rocky cliffs.

At Amalfi they lodged for three weeks in the Albergo Cappucini, writing their names in the guest book as '*Pittori Inglesi. Contentissime*'. Their stay overlapped with that of two Italian painters, Achille Vianelli and Ercole Gigante (also '*sempre contentissimi*'). Both were members of the School of Posillipo, based on the Neapolitan waterfront, and the accurate outlines, hazy reflections and golden light of their water-colours were interestingly similar to Lear's style.

He was overwhelmed by impressions, particularly when they visited Pompeii, feeling that everything he had read fell short of the reality: Pompeii alone was worth a journey from England. It was quite different, he insisted, to see the details of life stopped in a moment – marks where the wineglasses had been set down, still wet, the bones of men in the stocks, the names of shopkeepers written on the walls 'just as you see them now, all over Italy'.

Rumours reached England that Lear was seriously ill in Amalfi, with signs of consumption, even spitting blood, but he soldiered on, and never reported this to Ann. The two friends returned slowly to Rome, travelling by the easier coastal route, resting like snails in the sweltering middle of the day. 'What do you think of my new address?' Lear asked Ann in September. On his return, finding that his landlady had doubled her prices, he had moved to rooms over a cafe in the Via Felice, near the Pincian gardens, where his fellow lodgers included the topographical artist Thomas Hartley Cromek, his wife Anastasia and his mother, a quiet, thrifty, household who became his good friends.

'Rome continues to fill', he wrote that autumn, 'though there is no more room. It was never so full before.' Half the English peerage seemed to arrive daily and his diary was packed with dinners and evening parties. If the previous winter had been costly, now he had some money in his purse, from lessons and commissions for studio drawings, done in soft pencil on half-tone paper, with white highlights. These drawings sold so well that to his delight he could put £100 aside to pay for travel in the summer. He also sent money home to his sisters and, despite their estrangement, to his mother. Some friends had left, including William Knighton, who gave up ideas of becoming an artist and became engaged to 'a fooly Scotchwoman': she never took to Lear, nor he to her. James Uwins too, went back to England and at first Lear missed him badly, but he went out to the country with Penry Williams and the sculptors Wyatt and Thrupp: 'I am never very much alone,' he crowed.

Lear was indebted to Williams, above all, for introducing him to Civitella and Olevano, hilltop towns high in the Sabine hills fifty miles east of Rome. On his way south to Naples, Lear had admired Civitella perched above its rock staircase, with ancient stone walls all around 'like Stonehenge . . . older by many hundreds of years than the Romans', and had stopped in Olevano, crowned by its castle, where noisy children mobbed the artists as they sketched. These towns, gazing across the Serpentara forest to the mountains, topped with snow from October to May and hazy blue in midsummer, had long been a favourite retreat from the city heat: Coleridge had come here with his sculptor friend Washington Allston, writing in his notebooks of the dramatic views, forests and ravines. Lear joined the artists in the 'grandeur and mountain solitude' of late spring and early summer and at the vintage in September, 'surrounded by chestnuts and olives and looking over boundless views – most of them exactly like pictures of Claude, who studied hereabouts'.

Among the crowd there in June 1839 were the Palmers and their friend Albin Martin. 'We are every day in a large party of artists of different nations,' Anny Palmer wrote home. 'The scenery here is very very beautiful,' the air fresh and delicious;

we are perched on a mountain and look down into a most lovely fertile valley bounded on one side by a wooded mountain and on the other by rich little hills on whose tops and sides stand other little wild villages and over them you can see the campagna of Rome bounded by more distant mountains and then stretching far away the glittering Mediterranean.

The artists copied the locals, rising at dawn and taking long siestas, and it was easy to lose track of time. One day Anny was up at four, ready to sketch, thinking it was a Saturday, until 'Mr Lear, an artist here who keeps a journal', told her it was Sunday. But it made little difference:

The sentiment here of a quiet Sunday is not to be found – there were 12 or 14 artists and one lady here last Sunday and at night I was asked at dinner to join in a Ball which I declined – but Mr M. looked on and said it was capital fun and well done. Mr Lear plays very well on the flute so altogether they got up a row.

Penry Williams, *Civitella Gazette*, 1 July 1839. 'View of the Serpentara'. Samuel Palmer is on the rock at the left, with Anny in her bonnet. Lear, with his long legs and large nose, is at the foot of the rock in centre right.

Lear's life developed a pattern: winters in Rome, spring and autumn in the mountains and summer spent travelling. But he still struggled with his landscapes and regretted his lack of training, unable to see exactly how good his work already was. 'I hope ultimately to paint something or other,' he told Gould. 'It takes a long while to make a painter – even with a good artist's education – but without one – it tires the patience of Job: – it is a great thing if one does not go backward. – Meanwhile I am extremely happy – as the hedgehog said when he rolled himself through a thistlebush . . .'

The winter and early spring of 1839–40 passed with feasts and carnivals, rainstorms and pale sun, and strange days, like one in March that brought a sudden blizzard, turning the whole land white and forcing Lear and a friend to trek back from the Campagna through blinding snow. By now, to justify his Italian stay to his patrons, he had decided to put together a book: a tangible thing, a testament to what Italy had done for him. With his book in mind, Lear made more trips, painting Roman remains, castles on rocks, lakes in the old volcanic craters. His sketches piled up, annotated with jottings. On a drawing of Roccagorga in the Sabine hills he dashed down 'snow', 'thick wood', 'brown earth', 'road', 'foot path', 'dark', 'red', 'weeds grass', 'all mist', 'trees', 'shrubs', 'red earth bank', 'stream', 'stones'. Increasingly, he used his own phonetic shorthand: 'rox' for rocks, 'flox' for sheep. And for Lear words and pictures were never quite separate. His notes seemed part of the drawing: 'Olive' waving like branches, 'O! path!' leading along a track, 'River' written flat so that the word forms, in itself, a ripple of water.

He kept putting off his return to England. In the summer he was at Civitella again. He did not want to leave Italy, and he did not want to leave his friends: 'I know all the English artists – who are universally kind to me – as well as everybody else,' he wrote.

'Everybody else' included the Danish painter Wilhelm Marstrand, who came to embody this time in Lear's memory. Small and blond and witty, 'Willi' Marstrand, later a leader of Denmark's 'Golden Age' painters, had arrived in Rome in 1836 and was now painting exuberant scenes of festivals and peasant life. Twenty years hence, revisiting Lake Nemi, where a great hoopoe suddenly flew up before him, Lear was touched to see the landscape unchanged, 'all as when *W. Marstrand* & I used to be always together!! – It seems indeed but a week ago – yet it was in 1839!! & 1840!!' Later, on a fine sunny day, he thought again of '*Those Civitella days of old*. When one sate from noon to 3 listening to songs coming up from the great silent depths below the rock!' As Marstrand knew no English they spoke Italian, the language 'soft as kisses', as Byron called it, that 'sounds as if it should be writ on satin/With syllables which breathe of the sweet South'. Lear felt that he was cutting quite a dashing figure. 'Do you know I wear very considerable moustaches now?' he asked. 'But I cut them off in the winter.' His floppy moustache is there in Marstrand's pencil portrait, his thick hair pushed back, his gaze pensive behind his oval spectacles.

In 1840, when Marstrand left to study in Munich before returning to Denmark, Lear burnt his diary, giving no reason. Marstrand does not figure in his letters to Ann or to Fanny Coombe: Lear did not spill all the details of his Roman life. And although his escape to Italy felt like a flight from the restrictions of English society, any serious sexual encounters went unrecorded. Lear was good company, with an infectious capacity for fun, and on the whole, it seems that however intense his attachments were most of his friendships remained just that, alliances of pure enjoyment, with physical desire suppressed. He hardly mentions the handsome Swiss guards or the young boys lolling by the Tiber who thrilled other artists and writers. 'All kinds of young men,' wrote John Addington Symonds, 'peasants on the Riviera, Corsican drivers, Florentine lads upon Lungarno in the evenings, *facchini* at Venice, and especially a handsome Bernese guide who attended to the strong black horse I rode – used to pluck at the sleeve of my heart.'

Lear never writes in this way: his fantasies are hidden, even from his diary. His sexuality was fluid, uncertain. His homosexual longings are clear but he was also drawn to elegant, intelligent women, and there are hints of casual sex with women. His letters emphasise the grace of the peasant girls, their dress and hair, their walk and stature. In the same vein, always partly in jest, he presented himself as a man in need of a wife: 'Though I be not yet arrived at that keystone of hope – matrimony, I anticipate firmly the chance of a Mrs Lear in 40 years hence at least.' Writing to Fanny – apologising for his scrawl, but his eyes were sore, his ink mouldy, his pen like a pin – he exclaimed at the many marriages among their friends. 'St Peter help me! – how the world does go on! Is Robert likely to marry? I wish he would: I am sure I shall, one of these days.' Rome was lovely, he added, even in winter 'when all the city is golden and lilac – beautiful Rome!'

– There is only one thing wanting – my old complaynt – a wife. I have said to everybody that in 5 years I will be married – to my landlady even be she who she may – item very horrid, You may expect to hear of me rashly rushing into matrimony – some penniless governess – or ladies maid. I really think I shall marry some such person, because the refined peoples of rank & the rich lower ones are equally inaccessible & so I won't wait, & I will have a mendicant wife – & in about 5 years time you will be all sitting at dinner at Peppering when a long beggar with a ragged woman all over small children will interrupt you – & that you'll see will be me.

He took refuge in nonsense, often a cover for anxiety. But even in jokes his fantasy wife resembled sisterly figures like Ann and Fanny – kindly and caring, hardly an object of desire. 'I wish to goodness I could get a wife!' he lamented to Gould in 1841. 'You have no idea how sick I am of living alone! – Please make a memorandum of any Lady under 28 who has a little money – can live in Rome – & knows how to cut pencils & make puddings.'

11: THIRD PERSON

By early 1841 Lear was ready to return, although 'What I shall do in England I have no idea,' he wrote, except 'run about on railroads – & eat beef-steaks'. He was in London by early summer, collecting stones for lithographs from Hullmandel. And he did run about on railroads: he was a man in a hurry, in tune with the spirit of Turner's *Rain, Steam and Speed* of 1844. In years to come he hurtled around Britain and took long journeys across the Continent and later across India. Train travel annoyed him with delays and minor crashes, lost tickets and luggage, but it gave him freedom and often amused him: his letters and diaries were full of chance encounters and odd details, like the tins of hot water in French railway carriages in winter, a good idea, 'but you are apt to sprain your feet if you don't take care – for they are often round and rolly-polly'.

The Grand Junction Railway from Euston to Warrington, with a link to Liverpool Lime Street, had opened in 1837 and Bradshaw's first *General Railway and Steam Navigation Guide*, with timetables and maps, appeared two years later. Lear quickly became adept at timetables, and in August he puffed north from Euston towards Knowsley. He was keen to see Derby, who had suffered a stroke and was confined to a wheel-chair, but was happy surrounded by his children and grandchildren and his animals and birds. In his old haunts, preparing his lithographs, Lear turned his Italian sketches into fine reversed drawings on the stone.

In the autumn Hullmandel printed the plates, and in December *Views in Rome and Its Environs, Drawn from Nature and on Stone* was published in a luxurious folio edition by Thomas McLean, in the Haymarket, its title page bearing the artist's name: 'Edward Lear'.

The twenty-five prints contained views that tourists would know well, with ripples of distant views. After scenes of Rome from the outskirts the journey stretched further out to the Campagna, Tivoli, Lake Nemi, and Civitella and Olevano. By now he had mastered a variety of effects in his lithographs, using tint stones – painted all over in cream or buff except for white areas where the colour of the paper showed through – giving a pale grey or warm, yellowish background, with subtle shading and highlights. As with the *Parrots*, the book was funded by subscriptions – 209 sets were printed – and Lear paid the costs.

He wooed subscribers with a four-page prospectus, with short accounts of each view, and his efforts worked: the subscription list, headed by the queen and Prince Albert, was stuffed with earls and dukes. And unlike the *Parrots*, his *Views in Rome and Its Environs* made a profit. 'My "publishing transaction" is all "signed and sealed",' he wrote in relief to Fanny Coombe as he headed back to Rome, '– & what is more I have £300 of the money – £200 of which I leave behind as clear profit – & £100 goes in bill paying and the journey.' The book gave him confidence that he could pay his way in Rome. 'I feel I ought to go, & I must go,' he wrote; 'staying among friends alone – however delightful – is quite against an Artist's steady progress in his Art.' He had a sudden attack of nerves on leaving, 'as if I was about to be executed' – but he set off, with Frederick Thrupp, at the start of December.

Lear's return to Rome in late 1841 was a deliberate decision to make a life abroad, a voluntary exile. The reasons were not solely artistic: he wanted to escape the pressure of family and social life in England, to escape the shackles of convention, to find himself abroad. He used the word 'exile' in a long letter to Lord Derby the following June, a month after his thirtieth birthday. Derby was a patron but also a father figure, and in his letters to him Lear tended to emphasise his love of England and Knowsley. This time, he wrote, 'I have not become so foreignized as before – that is – I hope I am always *an Englishman*.' His great pleasure, he said, was news from Hornby friends, and he looked nostalgically at old Knowsley sketches of 'the puffin geese –the darling old Spectacle owl – or the Stanley cranes'. 'I sometimes please myself with thinking that I shall not be able to bear exile more than another year – & so that I shall perforce set off for the North – next – or the summer after – but this I know is wrong, & I ought to remain more settled for a longer time to come.' Like the birds, Lear would never remain settled. He was always eager to fly further.

He was also breaking old links, and his 'exile' had something of the cavalier brio of Byron in *Beppo*, the ironic rejection of corrupt politics, high taxes and prices, beef-steak and beer and rain:

> I like the weather – when it is not rainy,
> That is, I like two months of every year.

But Lear was also genuine in his sense of loss. His deepest regret on leaving England, he told Fanny Coombe, was not having seen Peppering. But the idyllic Sussex of his youth had vanished. John Drewitt was ill and the family bank was in trouble: John would die bankrupt in 1842, leaving his son Robert to take over the farm. George Coombe was also ill – Lear recommended Buxton or Torquay – and the family were leaving Calceto. In the summer of 1841 Fanny was on her own in Arundel, with the four younger children, including Lear's godson Percy. Looking back he was full of emotion, remembering the morning he met the family, reminding Fanny how he was amazed by the curiosities in the cabinet (which was included in the Coombes' possessions put up for auction the following year).

Most probably I owe a great deal to you – to all of you – for had I not then known you – my school companions would have led me into a different way of life. At thirty I see this clearer than in earlier days. I shall – if it pleases God to give me health – most probably be a successful landscape painter & have a number of friends given to but few in the world: – on the other hand, I am but too certain of living alone throughout life – a fate for which my sensitive mind ill enough prepares me –

The vision of a life alone, which he had not formulated so clearly before, was a central, crucial confession. But again, when matters got personal, he tumbled into nonsense. He wrote this rigmarole, he said, because Fanny had known him so long, '& should have written more if 2 abominable housemaids had not entered the room & are poking & scratching & slapping the furniture about in a manner not to be believed'.

From now on his letters were full of concern for Fanny's health and the children, and he saw her almost every time he came back. But he no longer fitted into the old life. The same went for his own family. He loved Ann, and part of him genuinely wanted her to come to Rome, and when their mother died in 1844, at the age of eighty, his first instinct was to tell her to come out at once. But his eagerness was clouded: how would she fit in? Although they would be in mourning, he wrote rather brutally, 'I hope you will dress very nicely.' She should buy new boots and shoes in Paris, 'and good *warm clothing*, and if you want any handsome, plain shawl or dress in Paris (not odd-looking, my dear old sister!) buy it, and keep it as a present from me. You know that I am very much known here, and live in the "highest respectability" – and so you must not be too dowdy.' Ann did not come.

Easing himself out of old bonds to family, to Sussex and to Knowsley, Lear began to draw a line around his own image, like a cut-out figure, a semi-cartoon. There were versions for different audiences. The public Mr Lear was a young artist, determined to learn more, taking on pupils and displaying his work to potential patrons and buyers. In 1839 Gladstone dropped by his studio, jotting in his diary that Lear 'draws beautifully', and four years later Murray's *Handbook* for 1843, extolling the charm of visiting artists' studios in Rome, mentioned him as 'an artist of great promise'. The private Lear of his letters was a man lucky in his friends, happy in his travels but dreaming of domestic bliss – or at least of puddings and sharp pencils. Beneath this ran the admission that he was in essence a man who would live his life alone, and, perhaps, lonely.

There was, however, a third Mr Lear, displayed to a wider circle to amuse and entertain: the outsider, the peripatetic artist, the court jester. Staying with Edward Penrhyn and his young family at East Sheen in October, he produced two comic Roman histories. Four surviving drawings of Romulus and Remus show the beaming babies floating on the Tiber, meeting a jovial-looking wolf in boots and spurs, and growing up to be remarkably unprepossessing shepherds.

The other story was *The Tragical Life and Death of Caius Marius Esqre late her Majesty's Consul-general in the Roman states: illustrated from authentic sauces*. In one scene in this nonsense history in twenty-three sketches, cooked up from dubious 'sauces', a lugubrious Marius, 'not feeling himself comfortable, places himself in the marshes of Minturnum, all among the bullfrogs' – with bull-headed frogs leaping around his half-doused head.

These 1841 children's stories were absurd and sweet, lacking the anger of many of the limericks. He sent similar letters to his kindly Rome patron, Lady Susan Percy, a talented artist herself. One was 'Mr Lear recovers his hat'. In a flowing sequence of drawings the bespectacled author loses his hat in a gale, turns his umbrella upside down like a kite to fly after it and, as in Lear's happiest dreams, flies with the birds, 'joined in the chase of his lively hat by some familiar & affectionate jackdaws'. (Lady Susan, like Lear, loved birds, dying in a limerick-like way in 1847 while 'feeding her canary birds' before breakfast.) Finally two fat, eager 'ingenious infants' hand his lost headgear back, with a large hole turning it into a high collar, which ends up jammed round his knees.

This was a dreamlike concoction, a forerunner of today's children's books. Lear would fly with the birds in other picture stories. But it was also a self-presentation: the most comical character was 'Mr Lear' himself. This persona turned into pictures the bungling, anxious figure of the letters – the boy in the topsy-turvy coach to Sussex, the nervous young man at Knowsley staring in horror at the fowls he was supposed to carve: '2 live tigers would have been a farce to it – I could eat nothing – drink nothing – do nothing but perspire with horror at those 2 boiled fowls!' During his recent visit to Knowsley he had gone walking in Scotland with Phipps Hornby, recording their adventures in thirty drawings, like a cartoon strip: 'P & L being hurried insert the remains of their lunch in their boots'; 'L – on ascending the cabin stairs – nearly loses his eye by the abrupt and injudicious promission of a new broom in the hands of a misguided infant'; 'L's portmanteau rushes wildly about the deck'; 'L endeavours to eat a piece of oatcake'. Lear as fool also appeared in a picture-apology for missing an appointment with Captain Phipps Hornby at Woolwich Dockyard. The drawings showed his thin, long-legged self being dragged off by a sentry and learning from harassed clerks that Captain Hornby was in the 'basin' – the slang term for the dockyard, an unmissable visual joke.

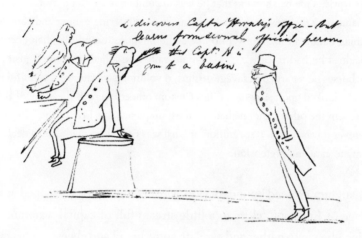

Over the next few years Lear drew more cartoon misadventures. In Italy in July 1842, planning a trip with his friend Charles Knight to the hills of the Abruzzi, he realised he must learn to ride. In over thirty scratchy drawings, he recorded his trials when Knight gave him riding lessons, from 'L contemplates a ferocious horse with feelings of distrust', through gallops and falls, immersion in quagmires and encounters with bushes, until he reaches an unsteady, but manageable pace. Lear was clumsy, prone to falling – off horses, down stairs, over branches: long ago he had described himself as having crooked knees, a long neck, 'a most elephantine nose, and a disposition to tumble here and there owing to being half blind'. This clumsiness, like his nose, became a comic feature.

From time to time, he drew more of these happy travel sketches. In 1847, touring Sicily with John Proby, he drew them fleeing beggars, dodging mosquitoes and, stepping into fantasy, nursing a troglodyte infant and peering at a 'hen trinacria' (the three-legged symbol of Sicily) sitting on her eggs. The cartoon journeys were presents for friends. In these drawings, so different from the formal lithographs, Lear created the hapless wanderer who would appear in poems, letters and journals. Holman Hunt described Lear staying in Sussex in 1852, where he told stories of his travels, Hunt said,

and surprised me by showing that he was uncombative as a tender girl, while at the same time the most indomitable being in encountering danger and hardship. Nothing daunted him, and yet no one could be more fearful than he of certain difficulties he had to face . . . He would rather be killed than fire a pistol or gun; horses he regarded as savage griffins; revolutionists, who were plentiful just then, he looked upon as demons, and Custom officers were of the army of Beelzebub. On the other hand, he had the most unquenchable love of the humorous wherever it was found. Recognition of what was ridiculous made him a declared enemy to cant and pretension.

Laughter crossed boundaries. In Albania in 1848 Lear stopped at the village of Episkopí, 'close to a little stream full of capital watercresses which I began to gather and eat with some bread and cheese'. This provoked the bystanders 'to extatic laughter and curiosity':

Every portion I put into my mouth, delighted them as a most charming exhibition of foreign whim; and the more juvenile spectators instantly commenced bringing me all sorts of funny objects, with an earnest request that the Frank would amuse them by feeding thereupon forthwith. One brought a thistle, a second a collection of sticks and wood, a third some grass; a fourth presented me with a fat grasshopper – the whole scene was acted amid shouts of laughter, in which I joined as loudly as any. We parted amazingly good friends, and the wits of Episkopí will long remember the Frank who fed on weeds out of the water.

If Lear was an artist of promise, a talented, published lithographer, he was also, in the third person, already the 'Mr Lear' that children, friends and strangers would love: comical, accident-prone, and nonsensically pleasant to know.

L. declares that he considers his horse far from tame.

12: EXCURSIONS

Lear saw how Ann and his friends enjoyed his accounts of Italy. (In one early letter he included a sketch of Ann devouring his letters, munching the pages.) This gave him a new ambition: Lear as travel writer, parallel to Lear as landscape artist. His time in Italy was for learning, and making money from paintings and lithographs, but he also liked travel for its own sake – it gave him freedom, excitement, variety, and a way of assuaging loneliness. He wrote later to his friend Chichester Fortescue: 'if you are absolutely alone in the world, & likely to be so, then move about continually & never stand still. I therefore think I shall be compulsed & more especially by things on the horizon.'

Compulsed, he went to Sicily in the spring after his return to Italy – the trip was supposed to last only a month, but 'delays & ill fortunes' stretched it to ten weeks. He went with Peter Leopold Acland – the son of a Devon MP – who had stayed in Tivoli with him and Uwins in 1838. The Moorish tone of Sicilian life fascinated Lear and so did the waves of invasion and layers of history, from legendary Cyclops and cave-dwellers to Greeks and Romans, Normans, Spanish and French. He loved the wild beauty of the northern coast and the temples of Selinunte and Agrigento in the south, and was astonished by the ravines on the slopes of Etna, a volcano that smoked and growled but was quiet compared to Vesuvius. And he found the absurd here too:

Just above Taormina on a perpendicular rock of vast height is a town called Molia – where we had heard that all the babies were tethered to door posts by strings round their waists – for fear of falling down the precipice: – so we made an excursion there, to seek for all or any such babies – but – after diligent search – none were to be found: only – just as we were giving up the scrutiny – Lo! – one solitary piggywiggy – tied by its body – & fallen just 3 feet over the end of the rock – being the full length of its cord!

A tethered pig apart, he found little in the zoological way, he told Derby, but was thrilled by 'that brilliant bird the Roller – which flew like glittering jewels in the morning sun – round & round the old temples: – I suppose they build there.' There were eagles in lonely places too, and herons, and birds he could not identify.

Back in Rome, as he listened to the owls hooting, and watched the bats flitting round the houses in the evening, he thought of eagles soaring in the Apennines and of flights of birds crossing the Campagna to their winter feeding grounds on the vast Lake Fucino. He did not need to fly far to find a wilder Italy. In July 1843, after his riding lessons, Charles Knight lent him his Arab horse, Gridiron, and they set off together to explore the three provinces of the Abruzzi, south-east of Rome. This was then part of Neapolitan territory, reaching from the Apennines to the Adriatic coast, and much planning was required, as they needed permission from the Neapolitan minister in Rome to take their horses across the border from the Papal States. Nationalist feeling was rising and with it came fear of spies. At one point the police detained them for two nights before they could travel on, and later Lear could only obtain his pass to move from one province to another by facing an entire room of townsfolk:

These people cannot imagine one's motives for travelling to be simply the love of seeing new places, &c; and the more one strives to convince them that it is so, the more certain are they that one has other designs. 'Where are you going!' they scream out, if one goes but a foot's length out of the highway to seek a point for drawing.

But difficult borders were part of the attraction – this was a relatively unknown territory to British visitors and thus a good subject for Lear. This time, he thought, he would revise his journals as a travel book with his lithographs and call it *Illustrated Excursions in Italy*.

Travel books were popular in Britain and if Lear could not offer adventures with tigers, or voyages through deserts and jungles, he could at least reveal an Italy that lay off the beaten track and people to whom 'an Englishman' was a strange being. He knew that his readers would expect descriptions of landscape and local life, mingled with history. This he could easily give them, describing the mountain passes, the great valley with its wine and corn, olives and melons, and the streets of Sulmona, birthplace of Ovid. He did his research carefully, acknowledging Sir Richard Colt Hoare and Richard Keppel Craven who had written on the Abruzzi before him, and including extracts from authorities and footnotes acknowledging a wide range of sources, many in Italian. But if he was not the first to describe the region, he was a pioneer as an artist: his illustrations, he could claim, 'are, I believe, the first hitherto given of a part of central Italy as romantic as it is unfrequented'.

Lear's response to the region was unusually personal and lively. At Lake Fucino the recorder of history gave way to the naturalist, the artist and the dreamer. As he sat in the sunshine gazing on the still water and the peaks beyond, 'brilliant with the splendour of an Italian morning', he brooded on the contrast between the lake's glory as the site of Roman holidays and festivals and its air of solitude today. He felt a spell of enchantment, heightened by the presence of the animals and birds:

A herd of white goats blinking and sneezing lazily in the morning sun: their goatherd piping on a little reed; two or three large falcons soaring above the Lake; the watchful cormorant sitting motionless on its shining surface; and a host of merry flies sporting in the fragrant air, – these were the only signs of life in the very spot where the thrones of Claudius and his Empress were placed on the crowd-blackened hill: a few distant fishing boats dotted the Lake where, eighteen centuries ago the cries of combat rent the air, and the glitter of contending galleys delighted the Roman multitude.

This lake, illustrated in his book, has since vanished. In Roman times Claudius had tried to control its constant flooding by digging a tunnel, and almost two millennia later, a quarter of a century after Lear's visit, the whole lake was drained to create a fertile plain.

Lago di Fucino, from *Illustrated Excursions in Italy* (1846)

As they travelled on, Lear described the rugged landscape like a lyrical geologist, but also like a painter, noting detailed foregrounds giving way to the interest of the middle plane and then to distant horizons. Among the bare, rugged peaks surrounding the mountain of the Gran Sasso, 'the monarch of the Abruzzi', they looked out, he wrote, over 'a wild chaos of mountain tops, ridge above ridge, peak above peak . . . a dark purple world, still and solemn, outlined with the utmost delicacy against the clear sky, where the daylight yet lingered along an horizon of golden red'.

Travel books needed the drama of obstacles and Lear provided these: rocky passes and dense woods, fierce storms and summer heat. But readers also wanted to see the life of the people, so he wrote of the peasants in their colourful dress and painted brilliant word-pictures of feasts and processions, like his memory of the first time he saw the annual feast at La Mentorella, near Subiaco, when men and women chanting

litanies and prayers carried huge stones from the summit to a pile below the town. The chapel on its rock, backed by the sombre mountains,
'was crowded with peasants, kneeling or sleeping under its dark arches;
forming altogether so wild a scene that, unable to tear myself away, I remained wandering from fire to fire, among the groups of people, nearly
the whole night through.'

He wrote too of eccentric aristocratic hosts, echoing inns and heavy
meals. He was delighted when the constant macaroni and 'Pomi'd'oro'
was unexpectedly replaced by 'a positive plain English-looking roast
leg of mutton' with boiled potatoes, served by Prince Giardinelli,
whose cook, like the prince himself, had been in England. He was delighted too by odd culinary suggestions. In the shady valley of Antro-
doco, 'I was sauntering by the brawling river, when a little boy passed
me carrying a dead fox. "It is delightful food (*cibo esquisito*)", said he,
"either boiled or roast". Said I, "I wish you joy".' He took joy, too, in
the animals, like the torrent of black pigs rushing into Avezzano to be
fed: 'How we did laugh, to the diversion of half the rabble of the town,
who had come to gaze on us, as the immense current of grunters burst
from the long street into the market-place, with a wonderful hubbub,
and ran shrieking through all the lanes of the place.'

As they crossed the borders, Knight became ill and returned to Rome,
taking Gridiron with him. Riding a solid grey mare, Lear wandered on
through the mountains, enduring earthquakes and answering everlasting questions about Brunel's Thames tunnel, which had just opened in
1843. He was touched by the hospitality of the people, although some
hosts were disconcerting, like Don Constantino in the hill village of Aba-
dessa, where the looks of the inhabitants, Lear thought, betrayed its past
as a Greek colony. The stay was a catalogue of oddities: first, Don Constantino hit his five beautiful daughters if they spoke Albanese rather
than Italian; next a young blind man came in 'to see the Englishman'
and sang twenty interminable verses of a Greek song about the battle of
Navarino; and finally, when the family went to bed, 'Don Constantino
and a very old hideous female domestic followed me into my chamber,

the latter of whom proffered her services to "undress me", which offer I respectfully declined, though she again entered to tuck all the sheets round the bed, an operation I could not prevent as the doors of all the rooms were open . . .' Often, as here, picturesque artist, hapless traveller and nonsense writer came together. Could it really be that on one night cats ran in and out perpetually and the doves called without cease: 'two turtles remained stationary on the top of the bed, moaning dismally'?

The following year Lear was 'over head and ears in painting', affectionately treated by the established Rome artists – Richard James Wyatt gave him a four-volume set of the *Arabian Nights* in 1843, which he kept all his life. He travelled down to sketch again on the Amalfi coast and came back to stay with the artists in the mountains:

out before sunrise, watching the sun catch peak by peak . . . the little village of Civitella di Licenza, perched on its peaked hill, which rises out of a long line of folds so blue. Olive gardens still sleeping in shade . . . paths, with crisp brown & green fern, hanging over the gardens below from the mossy old bits of stone. Not a sound, but the cry of the Jay, of the woodpecker, & the gay yellow oriole.

But then in September, news came of his mother's death – for which he showed no grief, apart from wearing a mourning suit – and once he had got over the flurry of Ann's potential visit, he wanted to travel again. 'Now you are not coming,' he wrote to her, with scarcely hidden relief, 'I think I shall run into the Abruzzi to see some places I did not go to last year.'

Almost as soon as he wrote he was off. From this second trip, he included the story of his border crossing at Civita Ducale, when he was stopped by a *carabiniere* convinced that he was Palmerston, whose name, as Foreign Secretary, was written on Lear's passport in large letters, and who was known to support the insurrectionary movement. Lear argued and cajoled to no avail. 'You great fool! I thought: but I made two bows, and said placidly, "take me to to the Sott' Intendente, my dear sir, as he knows me very well".' Triumphantly, the *carabiniere* paraded him through the town, Lear feeling a great fool himself: 'Some have greatness thrust upon them. In spite of all expostulations Viscount Palmerston it was settled I should be.' Soon, however, all was sorted: 'So I reached Rieti by dark, instead of going to prison.'

San Vittorino (2 May 1845). Notes: 'very bright', 'bright far', 'blue!!!!!' . . . 'field', 'olive wood deep shadow', 'red rox', 'olives', 'light trees', 'roofs yellow red – houses gray & ochre', 'O! path!' . . .

That winter Lear thought briefly that he might illustrate the seventh book of Virgil's *Aeneid*, where the landing of the Trojans gives rise to vivid descriptions of central Italy. In the spring, thinking of this, he toured the Volscian mountains but then he went back to the Abruzzi, collecting still more hidden places, like the hamlet of San Vittorino, on the site of the ancient Roman city of Amiternum. Only a few of these, however, would find a place in his *Illustrated Excursions*, the project uppermost in his mind.

In England, in the summer of 1845, he went to work on his drawings at Knowsley. He had hoped for quiet, but Knowsley, like the rest of the country, was abuzz with politics. Lord Derby's son Edward, Lord Stanley, had been Colonial Secretary in Peel's government but had resigned after arguments over Ireland and the Corn Laws: soon he would lead the Protectionist party, which included the young Disraeli. Not far away the Lancashire mill towns were afire. Three years before, when the Chartist petition was rejected, soldiers had opened fire on a crowd in Preston and now poor harvests sparked more agitation. Knowsley rang with arguments and in the autumn Lear came down to London to find quiet, staying at Robert Hornby's house, 27 Duke Street in St James's.

He still had work to do on the text and plates, and on the vignettes that would appear as wood engravings. Side by side with these, as a relaxation, Lear gathered together the nonsense rhymes that he had written from time to time since his first experiments at Knowsley, ten years before: urged by friends, he had decided to publish them, just for fun. But the serious work was always the *Excursions*, and when he came to publish this he added an unusual addition, an Appendix of music (he thanked unidentified 'Ladies' for writing out the arrangements). He was a pioneer, as the collecting of folk music was only just getting underway in Britain, and the tunes he published were a tribute to his memories of evenings of song in the Abruzzi: a song to a swallow, the '*bella Rondinella*'; a dance tune; a chanting song of women carrying cloth to a shrine. His first setting was one of the tunes played by the *pifferari*, the pipers Lear had heard in Rome who came down from the mountains during Advent to play *novenas* in pairs, one playing a wooden flute or *piffero*, a kind of oboe, the other bagpipes made of goatskin. The bagpipe drone had often been associated with the pastoral; Handel had used the 'pifa' to introduce the shepherds in the *Messiah*, and the tunes of the *pifferi* also inspired Berlioz and Mendelssohn. Lear liked their primitive, rural, ancient tone: in his own nonsense there is often something Orphic about music, as if it could soothe the animal in all of us, scaring away the serpents of lust and fear.

Since Lear was planning a luxurious production for *Illustrated Excursions in Italy*, costing four guineas, he wrote to his long list of connections, asking for subscriptions. When their numbers were known, Hullmandel printed the plates and Bentley the text and finally, in April 1846, Thomas McLean published his book. Lear dedicated it 'most respectfully and gratefully' to Lord Derby, his patron and friend. The text was full of unusual, entertaining detail, and the thirty plates conjured up views of high mountain ranges, villages clinging to the hillsides, lonely churches and narrow passes between great rocks, as well as groups of peasants, men tending goats and women in elaborate headdresses carrying loads on their heads. He felt he was among a new generation of artist-writers.

The same month saw the publication of the second volume of John Ruskin's *Modern Painters*, in which Ruskin made a distinction between the old masters, like Claude and Poussin, and the new, like Turner, who had a different understanding of 'truth to nature', not as a following of convention but as profoundly imaginative, displaying a moral as well as material truth. This idea caught Lear's heart. In 1880, after he went to see the Turners that Ruskin had donated to the Taylorian in Oxford, he wrote to tell him that this was 'a treat for which I may also take this opportunity of thanking you, as I often do mentally for having by your books caused me to use my own eyes in looking at Landscape, from a period dating many years back'.

Among the admirers of Lear's *Views* and *Excursions* was the young Queen Victoria and in July 1846 she asked Lear to give her drawing lessons. Since her marriage to Albert in 1840, Victoria had had five children in rapid succession – the oldest, Vicky, was now six, and the latest, Helena, was born in late May. This summer she was at Osborne House in the Isle of Wight, to recuperate and get back her boundless energy and also to escape, at least briefly, from the keen eye of the public and the tussles of politics. On 25 June, Peel's government had collapsed after a vote on Ireland, and much to the queen's dismay a new Whig government came in, under Lord John Russell.

At Osborne, by contrast, all was peace, except for the noise of builders, and she confided in her uncle, Prince Leopold, how 'snug and nice' she found it 'to have a place of *one's own*, quiet and retired'. Victoria and Albert had bought the house the previous year, and Albert had immediately drawn up designs for rebuilding it in an Italianate style, with a tower looking over the gardens to the sea – he said the view of the Solent reminded him of the Bay of Naples. Sixteen years later, after Albert's death in December 1861, Lear remembered how he had showed him a model of the new house '& particularly a Terrace, saying – "This is what I like to think of – because when we are old, we shall hope to walk up & down this Terrace with our children grown up into men & women."'

Victoria liked to breakfast on the terrace and spend the morning painting. Encouraged by Albert, who was a talented amateur artist, she was keen to learn. She had been taught as a child by Richard Westall, and in the early 1840s both she and Albert practised etching with George Hayter and Edwin Landseer (who found her 'all whim and fancy', while she found him annoyingly unreliable). Lear turned up at the back door of Osborne in mid-July, six weeks after Helena was born, to begin his lessons. Lear's nerves disappeared, perhaps remembering his years of teaching well-bred young women in St James's, and the lessons were a success. Their sessions were squeezed between government business, drives in the country and visits to the children in the nursery, and Victoria noted that Mr Lear 'teaches remarkably well, in landscape painting in watercolours'. A diligent pupil, she copied Lear's drawing and he, hardly surprisingly, was pleased and encouraging. 'Gave Vicky her religious lesson, as most days,' she wrote on 17 July. 'Had another lesson with Mr Lear, who much praised my 2nd copy. – Later in the afternoon I went out and saw a beautiful sketch he had done of the new house.' Next day, 'had another drawing lesson, and am, I hope, improving'. When she returned to London, Lear gave her more lessons at Buckingham Palace: she even fitted one in on the morning of Helena's christening, a grand occasion, with the little girls in satin dresses, Bertie in a white merino blouse and 'little Alfie' looking lovely 'in a white frock trimmed with silver . . . The Baby 1st cried & then (shocking to relate) proceeded to suck her thumb, but looked very dear.' Amid this mix of domesticity and state affairs, Lear taught Victoria how to select her composition without cramming everything in and introduced her to ink and wash. Although she went on to study for many years with the Scottish painter William Leighton Leitch, her watercolour style stayed faithful to Lear's: trees in the foreground, flat horizontal planes, and hills in the distance.

Lear was touched when Victoria sent an engraving of one of his drawings of Osborne to him in Rome, but he was determined not to boast about this, or about all the commissions he had, warning Ann against mentioning it lest his success brought 'complaints from those who are more skilful & yet have little to do'. But he did dine out on stories of being shooed sideways when he stood with his back to the fire – not the place to stand in front of royalty – and of his famous gaffe when the queen proudly showed off her display cases. 'Oh! how *did* you get all these beautiful things?' he asked, to which she replied mildly, 'I inherited them, Mr Lear.'

In his preface to the *Excursions* in April, Lear had hinted that if the book should 'meet with approbation' a second volume might follow. And it did, a few days after his last lesson with Victoria on 6 August, this time dedicated to Derby's son, Lord Stanley, with a text giving short descriptions of the scenes. And if the books were a success so were the travels themselves, in a more personal sense. Lear valued his tours of the Abruzzi, he said, less for the landscape, which was often too barren to provide 'picturesque' subjects, than for its novelty and for the warmth of the people. Over the next couple of years he sent drawings of their towns or churches to the families he had stayed with, 'and every day there come such nice letters from those good people who are quite delighted with these trifling presents'. He knew that he would never forget the time he had spent with them, 'and should I never revisit this part of Italy, I shall not cease to cherish the memories of my stay in the three provinces of Abruzzo'.

13: DERRY DOWN DERRY: *NONSENSE*, 1846

There was an Old Man of the West,
Who never could get any rest;
So they set him to spin, on his nose and his chin,
Which cured that Old Man of the West.

Chichester Fortescue, who met Lear in mid-April 1845 before his return to England, caught his amiable, music-loving, companionable spirit straight away. 'I like what I have seen of him very much,' he wrote soon after they met, 'he is a good, clever, agreeable man – very friendly and *getonable* with.' Fortescue was twenty-two, a brilliant student with a First in Classics from Oxford, shy, with an occasional stutter but easy-going among his friends: he would soon plunge happily into an affair with Polly Fleming, the star equestrienne of Astley's circus. As the son of an Irish MP he was destined to enter politics himself and was touring with his friend Cornwall Simeon while waiting for the next election, due in 1847. Lear took the two young men sketching, explored Tivoli and the Campagna, rode out to villages and dined with gaggles of their friends. Lear was, Fortescue thought, 'full of *nonsense*, puns, riddles, everything in the shape of fun, and *brimming* with intense appreciation of nature as well as history. I don't know when I have met any one to whom I took so great a liking.' When Lear left for England, Fortescue was full of laments: 'I have enjoyed his society immensely and am very sorry he is gone. We seemed to suit each other capitally. Among other qualifications, he is one of those men of real feeling it is so delightful to meet in this cold-hearted world. Simeon and myself both miss him very much.'

The *Views* and *Excursions* showed Lear's appreciation of nature and of history, and his humour and capacity for feeling. And the second volume of the *Excursions* also carried an advertisement for a completely different kind of book without naming the author: *A Book of Nonsense*. This had appeared in February, with Lear paying the costs, published by Thomas McLean in two volumes, each carrying thirty-six rhymes, priced at three shillings and sixpence (a marked contrast to the four guineas for *Excursions*).

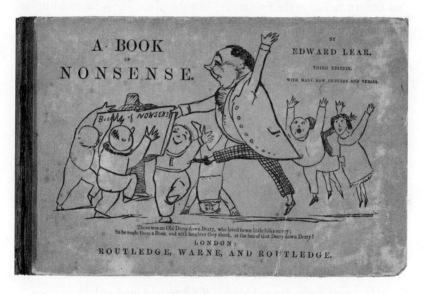

'There was an Old Derry down Derry,/ Who loved to see little folks merry;
So he made them a Book, / And with laughter they shook,
At the fun of that Derry down Derry!'

Lear's name did not appear on the cover until this third, expanded edition of 1861. But on all the editions, the author, toes pointed, feet off the ground and arm raised, bounds into a group of eager children, so excited that one boy stands on his head and the others rush forward shrieking with pleasure. Their delight was understandable: the books were quite unlike the standard fare, positively naughty. They looked different for a start, like rectangular sketchbooks, with drawings that raced right across each page, open and unframed. Each right-hand page carried a separate image, so that when you turned the page a surprise leapt out at you. The pictures caught the eye first: below them the verses, printed in sloping capitals, ran in three lines, not the four of later versions used here. The whole effect was freewheeling, anarchic, full of fun.

Nonsense never seemed to cause Lear trouble or headaches. In his drawings he ushered forth old men and young women, pigs and ducks, rabbits and bees, in untidily effortless lines. He wrote and drew them fast. His preliminary drawings have a marvellous free-hand vivacity that cannot fail to make one smile, like the plain, large-busted Euphemia (not living up to her name 'of good report'), who runs off, clearly pleased, with her long-haired crook clutching the family silver:

There was an Old Man of Bohemia,
Whose daughter was christened Euphemia;
Till one day, to his grief, she married a thief,
Which grieved that Old Man of Bohemia.

Lear took up his nonsense when tired, or bored, or when it was too dark to paint, images and words swimming up from a realm below reason. Sometimes a name, a place passed or mentioned, prompted a rhyme, which might grow into a verse or be casually abandoned. Answering an invitation from a friend, he once wrote:

I shall come up from Barnes and hope to be with you at 6 –
> There was an old person of Barnes
> Whose stockings were covered with darns: –
A new idea & good for my new publication . . .

Since he composed his first 'Old Persons' at Knowsley a decade before, Lear had occasionally put together a book for friends, giving one manuscript to the Phipps Hornby family and another to Lady Duncan in Rome. He played with the detail of illustrations and tinkered with his verses: in Lady Duncan's draft, for instance, the Old Lady of Prague, whose language was horribly vague (suggesting an interesting contemporary pronunciation of 'Prague', which Lear rhymes elsewhere with 'plague'), appeared as an 'ambiguous old creature', not as 'an oracular Lady' as in the published book:

> There was an Old Lady of Prague,
> Whose language was horribly vague;
> When they said, 'Are these caps?' she answered, 'Perhaps!'
> That oracular Lady of Prague.

But with publication the text was relatively fixed, and the nonsense was open to a wider audience. What would they make of it? With 'Derry down Derry', an old ballad refrain, Lear placed himself in a line of performers descending from the mummers' plays at medieval Christmas feasts and the later versions that toured England and Ireland in the eighteenth and nineteenth centuries. These were popular, democratic entertainments, like the acrobats' show that Lear saw as a child on Highgate Hill: class and snobbery, his mummer's name implied, will be banished. The players – like Lear at this point – were anonymous and masked, and their songs were a call to fun:

> With hey dum dum, with hey dum dum,
> With hey dum dum dee derry,
> For we be come this Christmas time
> A purpose to be merry.

In a deep way, hard to articulate, Lear's nonsense is comprehensible as both the foolery of childhood and the foolery of carnival, turning the world upside down. Adult readers in a serious mood can trace a tradition of nonsense from the Greeks, finding it in ancient riddles, in Renaissance poems, in the word-play of Elizabethan verse, in the fools of Shakespeare's plays. But Lear, though he sometimes refers to Shakespeare's fools, never talked of past tradition in relation to his work. He had learnt from the parodies, comic poems and drawings of Hood and others that were popular in his youth, and had loved word-play and absurdity since his early teens. The discovery of *Anecdotes and Adventures of Fifteen Gentlemen* at Knowsley gave him a form, but his invention was his own.

The key quality of the nonsense rhymes is surprise: this is what makes us laugh. They ask us to believe in peculiar people, to accept strange happenings, to inhabit a world where butter is used to cure plague, a hatchet to scratch a flea.

In his landscapes Lear's people are small and rather formal, partly because he found it hard to draw them properly, but also to show how often they were dwarfed by the grandeur of their surroundings. But in his nonsense drawings, caricatured though they are, his strange people become touchingly real, alarming, intriguing. They step forward without awkwardness. Place names bestride the world; all borders can be easily crossed, including those between humans and animals. Lear's drawings are full of movement, bursting across the white space, free of perspective, while the verse with its bounding rhythm is mobile and unconfined.

The verses worked quite simply, at least on the surface. The bald, storytelling openings like 'There was a Young Lady of Russia', with their implied 'Once upon a time', seem to promise a connection between person and place. Yet the link is purely arbitrary. Of all literary forms, nonsense demands the strongest suspension of disbelief; but while we read, we do 'believe', entering a land where anything can happen. Lear's wonderland, however, is always tied to the real, like a kite whirling on a string, held down by those precisely named places. In this first book a cluster of Scottish and Italian names were playful mementoes of recent tours: Gretna, Bute and Dundee; Leghorn and Vesuvius, Ischia, Apulia and Parma. And while children enjoy the odd names without question, adults (and critics) can read them for local and historical references or for the sexual innuendo of large noses and pointing limbs. Lear must have searched hard for a rhyme for Abruzzi, before landing on something so daftly and deftly suggestive:

There was an Old Man of th' Abruzzi,
So blind that he couldn't his foot see;
When they said, 'That's your toe,' he replied, 'Is it so?'
That doubtful Old Man of th' Abruzzi.

We wouldn't read it as suggestive, however, if it weren't for the picture. Constantly, in these rhymes, the interpretation ripples like this, between image and text.

In the limericks there is no logic of cause and effect, merely a story to follow, contained in a rolling circle where the last line returns to the first.

But something has always happened in between, so that we read the final line differently to the first. In terms of action, the limericks teach us to live with the unlikely. Things happen fast in these short poems and consequence is briskly suggested by a final verb: 'which cured', 'which grieved', 'which displeased', 'which saved', 'which drowned', 'which astonished'.

And what of the odd people? How responsible are they for their fate? The nonsense people rage against conformity. But although there are many confrontations, the scornful or oppressive 'they' are as much puzzled and frightened as they are shocked and disapproving. True, they can be violent, but sometimes they run away, and sometimes they behave rather kindly, in a baffled way. They feed cake to the Old Person of Rheims, who is troubled by terrible dreams; they cure the Old Man of the West. They ask curious, concerned questions: 'Does it fit?' they ask the man in the plum-coloured vest; 'Is it hot?' they ask the Old Person of Gretna who tumbles down Etna. The replies they get are often angry, or mendacious, or both. The dangers, the verses suggest, come as much from the nonsense persons themselves as from the chorus of 'they'.

Sometimes the characters simply embody their situation. They may just be unfortunate, like the tiny Old Man of Leghorn ('quickly snapped up he, was once by a puppy'). But while some nonsense persons are victims of accident or chance, others are given a dominant trait, obscurely responsible for their actions and dilemmas. They may be small and thin or stout and 'globular', possess a huge mouth or waving arms or spindly legs – but more often they are identified by feelings or behaviour. Some sit on chairs or columns and stay there (they like to be up high), but many, like the Old Man of Coblenz, striding with his long legs from Turkey to France, are diagrams of movement. They point at each other with arms, feet, legs or paws or look out into space, off the blank page, like the Old Man of the Hague, riding in his balloon, gazing through his telescope at the moon.

The nonsense people's gestures imply things we cannot see, and their expressions can suggest a story or mood subtly at odds with the words. But several of them shrug off their fate, like the heavy drinker of Hurst – 'When they said, "You'll grow fatter," he replied, "Does it matter?"' – or this blithe Scandinavian heroine:

There was a Young Lady of Norway,
Who casually sat in a doorway;
When the door squeezed her flat, she exclaimed, 'What of that?'
This courageous Young Lady of Norway.

Lear often grants courage to women, like the cheery Young Lady of Hull who cries out 'Who's afraid?' waving her spade at the bull, or the laudable cook who springs to the rescue.

There was an Old Man of the North,
Who fell into a basin of broth;
But a laudable cook, fished him out with a hook,
Which saved that Old Man of the North.

Other women are alarming, frivolous or boring – they bake men in ovens, wear oversized bonnets and weep at the weather. But several, often rather mermaid-like in their appearance, are artistic or musical, sweeping a lyre with a broom, playing the harp with their chin. The feminine Lear, nurturing and murdering, is alive in variety and oddness.

Sometimes Lear leaves us with no judgement or consequence at all, simply an exclamation that is hard to decipher:

There was an Old Person of Tartary,
Who divided his jugular artery;
But he screeched to his wife, and she said, 'Oh, my life!
Your death will be felt by all Tartary!'

What does she mean? He husband may screech, but he looks calm – and he still has his pince-nez on. And will all Tartary be sad, shocked, or pleased – as she appears to be? In Lear's violent verses, horror is often offset by the smiles, the satisfaction, on the faces of those involved. Here we are left puzzled. Metaphors and morals are absent. Whatever Lear's struggles with faith there is no God here, no *deus ex machina*, no abstract justice. Yet many of the verses are metaphors in themselves, images of fleeting states of mind: anger, curiosity, ingenuity, foolishness and pride. Where there is a 'judgement' – and this is often elusive – it resides with the telling adjectives. These can be positive – amusing, courageous, ingenious – but just as often devastatingly negative: capricious, surprising, deluded, horrid, wayward, distressing, doubtful, bewildered, angry, mendacious, whimsical, vague. All our weaknesses are here.

Within the nonsense world, of course, we shouldn't take those judgements too seriously.

There was an Old Person of Rhodes,
Who strongly objected to toads;
He paid several cousins, to catch them by dozens,
That futile Old Person of Rhodes.

Is he futile simply because there will always be *more* toads? Or, as the picture suggests, because the marching female cousins with their froggy burdens fill him with even more fear?

The mood of Lear's final lines is always unpredictable:

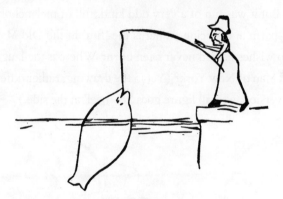

There was a Young Lady of Wales,
Who caught a large fish without scales;
When she lifted her hook, she exclaimed, 'Only look!'
That extatic young lady of Wales.

She could have been horrified – but Lear lets her rejoice. Far from an unthinking, easy return to a first line, his endings cleverly cast a mood back on the whole.

The flat tone makes the implausible sound 'sensible', and this fracture of reason makes the world dangerous, unsettling, even frightening.

There was an Old Man of Nepaul,
From his horse had a terrible fall;
But, though quite split in two, by some very strong glue,
They mended that Man of Nepaul.

The glue of the rhyme sticks the pieces together – but in the drawing the man's two halves are still wide apart. As Derry down Derry, Lear promised 'fun'. But it was fun of a very odd kind, full of melancholy, murder, panic, self-harm and suicide. What is the 'fun' in the Old Man of Cape Horn, who wishes he had never been born? Where is the laughter in the lonely Old Man of New York? (Yet in the drawing, rather different to the published version, a small figure goes 'tee-hee!' at the side.)

There was an old man of New York,
Who murdered himself with a fork;
But nobody cried – tho' he very soon died, –
That unlucky old man of New York.

14: 'SOMETHING IS ABOUT TO HAPPEN'

> There was an Old Person of Gretna,
> Who rushed down the crater of Etna;
> When they said, 'Is it hot?' he replied, 'No, it's not!'
> That mendacious Old Person of Gretna.

For Lear 1846 had been a year of work and publication. And before he left in December yet another book appeared, the lavish two-volume *Gleanings from the Menagerie and Aviary at Knowsley Hall*. The first volume contained lithographs of Lear's paintings of birds and small mammals, the second of ungulates, hoofed mammals, by Benjamin Waterhouse Hawkins. Lord Derby had wanted a permanent record, and John Edward Gray of the British Museum, who wrote the text, was so impressed by the liveliness, grace and accuracy of Lear's work that he had argued for separate volumes, lest Lear's illustrations make Hawkins's look weak. So in this single year Lear appeared in print in all his dimensions: naturalist, lithographer, landscape artist, travel writer and creator of nonsense.

He was particularly pleased by the acclaim for *Illustrated Excursions in Italy* in the *Quarterly Review* the following year, where the anonymous critic (actually Richard Ford) reviewed it alongside Fanny Kemble's account of her Italian travels. Ford had, he said, begun by looking at the engravings expecting 'the annual experience of the stereotyped stuff'.

Then a sentence or two caught his eye, and 'We found ourselves tempted on – and so on, until we read the entire letter-press – to be well repaid by much new observation, nice marking of manners, genuine relish for nature and quiet dramatic humour.' Lear was welcomed as a writer at last, and as an artist who 'has enrolled his name high in art – in that city where art is most appreciated'. 'The review seems written by someone of great kindness and cleverness,' he told Ann, 'but who is not quite *right* about me – as you will acknowledge when I tell you he talks about my "*unruffled temper*"!!!!!!!!!! – I hope we shall not happen to travel together if I am to keep his good opinion; I fear he would alter his decree.'

At the end of 1846 Lear travelled back to Rome the modern way, by train and steamboat, only to be held up by engine trouble and gales – 'I am crawling on like an old snail,' he moaned from Florence on Christmas Day. But at 5 a.m. on 29 December he was safe in the Via Felice. His friends cheered his return and he grew fat on the parties, but he already planned to get away, hoping to travel in May. He worried about how much work he could fit in before then, about the strain on his eyesight, and most of all about money. He might make £120 this year, he reckoned, to add to the £100 from his books, and could not save much.

In the long dark winter and early spring, when the rain poured, the snow came and the streets were a river of ice and mud, he wrote to Ann, sounding slightly homesick, asking for news of family and friends and fretting about her health – she had trouble with the nerves of her face and problems with her eyesight. He pressed her to get her portrait painted, teased her about thinking there were wolves in the Apennines, followed her charitable work with the blind and with coal and blankets for the poor, and told her of the Rome collection for the Irish famine. In March he wrote whimsically, that 'please God', five or six years ahead, he might live comfortably in London: 'when I trust you will live with me. We shall be very cosy & antique. I shall be 40 – or 41 – you – 60 or 61. We must have an old cat, & some china: – & so we shall go on smoothly. My dear Ann, this is all nonsense – but you must see I'm half asleep – so there's my apology.' They would never live together again. Ann drifted from place to place, blown here and there 'like thistledown', she said, often staying with friends, but nothing stopped her writing to her dear Edward.

Lear was gentle about Ann's faith, describing his own church-going and warding off her religious tracts. He could do without Griffith's *Spiritual Life*, he wrote; 'To tell you the truth, as I know you would wish me to do, I find the prayer book with all the lessons my most useful companion, & next to that, Abercromby's Essays.' And he warned her, lightly, against too many Mrs Jellyby-like ventures. Distressed cottagers were fine, but 'With regard to the Madagascar peoples, I am afraid I do not take much interest in them; you know they are quite black & I do not think they are quite respectable enough to be distressed about':

Seriously, there are so many poor & forlorn, & unenlightened, close beneath our eyes, that it seems to me one is looking through a telescope & yet blindfolding ones eyes to all round us, when one takes so long sight. This however, does not ever apply to you who always find someone to be of use to where ever you are. Tell me what cottages you find to visit, for, to one's shame, one requires, or thinks one requires, to feel an interest however little, in people before one gives them anything.

He was always curious about individuals, the way they worked, treated their families, talked, dressed, ate and played. In his travel journals, as in his limericks, he homed in on detail, like the Reggio official 'who had perched himself at the top of a totally dark and crooked staircase, the ascent of which was disputed step by step by an animated poodle', or the old French gentleman whom he found 'playing at whist, double dummy'.

Delight in the particular and avoidance of the general was one reason that Lear, warm-hearted as he was, turned his back on politics. He also hated confrontation and wanted anxiously to be accepted by all, whatever their stance or creed. His dissenting background placed him in a line that had always been outside the establishment, barred from political office and from taking degrees at Oxford and Cambridge. But

Lear liked moderation: at the end of his life he declared himself 'an out-sider and by nature and habit a Liberal', who felt that both 'gross and violent Radicals' and 'virulent Tories' should be kept from governing. Yet if he had managed to sweep aside rows over Ireland and Corn Law campaigns when he was in England, it was impossible to ignore the tension in Italy in 1847. He was glad that Ann had not come, he said, not only because of the cold: 'Many other causes, more serious, but of which I do not choose to write, confirm me in this view of things.' Much of the country was ablaze with nationalism, and the last two years had seen several failed uprisings. In July 1844, when Lear was heading back to the Abruzzi, two young Venetians, the Bandiera brothers, had led a doomed raid to free political prisoners in the Kingdom of the Two Sicilies. A month after their death by firing squad he wrote to Ann that 'although no war will probably break out *as yet* – two or more years will possibly upset everything'.

In 1847 matters were indeed upset. 'Italy' was a patchwork of sep-arate regional states and small kingdoms, and the drive for unification had been gathering force since the end of the Napoleonic wars, given new force by the European revolutions of 1830. A first aim was to expel the Austrians in the north and the Bourbon rulers in Naples and Sicily, but the ultimate goal was to create a complete nation. Radical leaders like Mazzini and Garibaldi dreamed of a single federal republic; others envisaged a conferacy of separate states, led by Piedmont. Under pres-sure, in Rome, the new Pope, Pius IX, elected in July 1846, gave an am-nesty to political prisoners, introduced more liberal press laws and set up a power-sharing Council of State. Leading exiles were full of hope: from London Mazzini supported the reforms and Garibaldi wrote from South America offering to provide the Pope with his legion to fight for unification. British interest was intense. Many Catholics, including John Henry Newman (who came out to Rome that year to be ordained as a Catholic priest), were anxious to restore the old Roman Catholic hier-archy in England, while the British government hoped the Pope might use his influence to calm discontent in Ireland. There were rumours of establishing new diplomatic relations – from Pisa, Robert Browning offered to be secretary of the new embassy and once settled in Florence the Brownings flung themselves into the cause of Italian liberty. All this Lear ignored. Instead he sent Ann engravings of the Pope to show her friends, writing only of his popularity, piety and person, 'large and portly (at least he looks so in his white and scarlet robe, as one meets him walking), and of the most cheerful and benevolent countenance possible. He very frequently walks about the roads just outside the Gates with his attendants and carriages – no guards.'

In the troubled city, Lear's spirits rose when spring came, turning the Campagna purple and gold: 'Thus – climate & beauty of atmosphere regain their hold on the mind – pen – & pencil.' He was ready to be off. 'I shall write before I go to Calabria, if I do go there at all.' But before Calabria, which he hoped to explore with Chichester Fortescue, he planned to revisit Sicily, travelling with the twenty-four-year-old John Proby. Proby (heir to the Earl of Carysfoot, as Lear later discovered) was another young Irishman who had aimed to become an MP, like Fortescue: when he failed to win a seat in 1846 he came to Rome to study painting and after spending the winter ill with 'Roman fever', a vicious strain of malaria affecting Rome and the Campagna, he rashly thought a trip would do him good. Lear met Proby in Palermo in late April, supplied with letters 'to half the grandees & merchants & bankers of Sicily & Naples & what not'. Over the next few weeks they walked and rode from dawn to dusk, seeing cornfields inland and temples on the coast.

Lear was horrified by Sicilian poverty but entranced by the ruins and the flora: the enormous prickly pears, the wildflowers carpeting the ground at the temple of Segesta, the oleanders and myrtles, figs and acanthus making 'such hedgerows as cannot be looked at without wonder'. Even the ancient quarries of Syracuse, where the Athenian prisoners had suffered, were now gardens. In the late 1850s, working with Holman Hunt, he would base one of his finest oil paintings on his sketches and watercolour studies of these quarries.

Syracuse quarries, 12 June 1847

The climax of the trip was their climbing of Etna. Starting at midnight they reached the snow-line at dawn, where Lear found it hard to keep his footing on the frozen snow. 'Sometimes I rolled back as far as 20 minutes had taken me up,' he wrote. As they struggled higher, now plunging up to their knees in ash, the thin air stopped his breath, but the view was worth it – from the summit Sicily lay below them like a pink map surrounded by blue sea and purple mountain shadows. Although the heat was intense and the sulphur burned their clothes,

Yet one was too glad to bury one's hands in it – one's body & head being wrapped up in cloaks & plaids through all which one shivered in the icy wind which blew like knives from the North (Etna you know, is nearly as high as Mt Blanc). We came down ridiculously fast: you stick your heels in the ashy cone, & slide down almost without stopping to the bottom, – & with a spiked stick you shoot down the icy hill we had taken so long to surmount – in 10 minutes.

His exaggerated account of the descent was like the slipping, sliding, tumbling of his nonsense figures. The exhilaration mixed with fear at the heat and cold, the heights and depths, the gasping and falling, suggests his own fluctuating moods – as well as the turbulence of Italy erupting into violence around him, and the flames, house fires, burning ovens of his limericks.

The travelling was hard, the food atrocious, the fleas and mosquitoes intolerable, and Proby fell ill. In their final week in Palermo, where the city was 'crammed full, full, full' due to the presence of the king and queen and the French fleet, their tempers frayed. But by the end they were friends again, and when they reached Naples and Lear realised that Chichester Fortescue could not come to Calabria, as he would have to stay in Britain for the coming election, he and Proby set off together, to the toe of Italy. Among the orange groves of Reggio, they collected more introductions and hired a guide, Ciccio – short for Francesco – who replied to all their plans with a single short sentence:

ending with – 'Dogo; dighi, doghi, daghi, da' – a collection of sounds of fre-quent recurrence in Calabrese lingo, and the only definite portion of that speech we could ever perfectly master. What the 'Dogo' was we never knew, though it was an object of our keenest search throughout the tour to ascertain if it were animal, mineral, or vegetable.

With his nonsense-speak, Ciccio was a success. He chivvied them on, found the best routes, solved problems, grimaced at things he disliked and was quick to laugh. When they parted at the end of the trip, he wept.

This region, even more than the Abruzzi, was largely unknown to British travellers and readers, but Lear did not publish his journal im-mediately. Instead he waited until 1852, when the political storms were past. He called it *Journals of a Landscape Painter in Southern Calabria and the Kingdom of Naples*, and in his Preface he wrote, 'Wishing to confine these journals strictly to the consideration of landscape, I have said as little as possible of events which occurred in 1848, and their sequel.' He wanted readers to travel with him not as a political commentator but as a painter, following his hunt for a good view, his dashes to sketch before sunset, his penning-out of drawings at night. His judgements were painterly, often referring back to his favourite artists, Claude

Lorrain, Salvator Rosa and Poussin. He expresses his frustration at lack of a 'Claudian foreground', his delight at Bruzzano, 'placed as if arranged by G. Poussin for a picture, on the edge of a great rock arising out of the plain', his joy at the woods in the morning light:

None of your dense carpet-forests – your monotonies of verdure, but made up of separate combinations of pictorial effect, such as one can hardly fancy – Claude and Salvator Rosa at every step. All the morning we drew in this beautiful place, and little enough could our utmost efforts make of what would occupy a regiment of landscape painters for years, if every one of them had as many arms and hands as Vishnoo.

The journal was alight with colour, flashes of blossom against dark rocks, women in deep blue dresses with orange and pink borders. All the senses were here: the feel of cactus prickles and burning heat; the perfume of amaryllis, the earthy scent of animals, the poisonous stench of soaking hemp; the taste of macaroni, figs and ricotta; the sound of waterfalls, crying children, squeaking pigs, barking dogs, and cicadas, 'who buzzed and fizzed, and shivered and shuddered, and ground knives

Palizzi, from *Journals of a Landscape Painter in Calabria*

on every branch above and around'. Lear's metaphors made grandeur intimate: a village 'crushed and squeezed into a nest of crags'; the great rock of Palizzi 'like a king of nine-pins, set edgeways against the sky'.

The sensuous, hurrying text reflected their journey. Lear and Proby were always on the move. They never knew what the day would bring or where they would stay – a palazzo on a precipice, a barn or a taverna outhouse, 'loaded with rolls of linen, guns, gourds, pears, hats, glasses, tumblers, puppies, jugs, sieves &c.' They speculated with amusement on the next set of hosts and whether they could stay awake long enough to be civil. Some stops were an ordeal, like 'Silkworm Hall', where every room was festooned and the stink of caterpillars was overwhelming: 'Supper and silkworms once again; screaming children and howling dogs; the fat lady shouted and scolded, and anathematised the daddy-long-legs who flew into the candles.' But they made many friends and met characters who remained in Lear's mind, like the garrulous baron who 'bustled about like an armadillo in a cage'. And Lear made careful studies of the people he met, drawing aprons and caps and children shyly proud of their best dress.

Lear knew that his readers would have preconceptions: 'Calabria! – No sooner is the word uttered than a new world arises before the mind's eye, – torrents, fastnesses, all the prodigality of mountain scenery, – caves, brigands, and pointed hats, – Mrs Radcliffe and Salvator Rosa – costumes and character, – horrors and magnificence without end.' He was not, however, setting out to find this southern Gothic. When he finally came across some 'real, positive, pointed hats', they did not belong to Calabrians at all, but to goatherds from Catanzaro, while a mysterious midnight noise, like an echo of Mrs Radcliffe's horrors, turned out to be a tame sheep huffing and sobbing under the bed.

As a sop to Gothic tastes, Lear includes a couple of tales of mad aristocrats, murdered lovers and crumbling castles – and he did visit the castle of Malfi, home of Webster's doomed duchess, soon to be utterly swept away in the terrible earthquake of 1851, just before Lear published his book. But his real interest was in the mundane life of the region. And he soon came to realise that it was he and Proby who were the oddities; to the local people, England, not Calabria, was an exotic place, a land of mystery. Did they have no rocks in England, that they must come here to draw them? How could there be a country that did not grow rice, or make wine? At the mountain convent of Polsi the Father Superior explained to his monks that England was very small, about a third the size of Rome, and the people were a sort of Christians 'though not exactly so', as their priests married – a ridiculous and shocking practice. And here too, as in the Abruzzi, tales circulated of Brunel's great achievement: 'The whole place is divided into two equal parts by an arm of the sea, under which there is a great tunnel,' the priest explained. At Rocella, fruit growers informed them that England had no fruit, only potatoes, and laughed off Lear's accounts of gooseberries and greengages: 'So we ate our supper in quiet, convinced almost that we had been telling lies; that gooseberries were unreal and fictitious; greengages a dream.'

Some enquiries were more disquieting. From the start, mystified by the idea of an artistic tour, people fired questions at them: 'What are you doing? Where are you going?' as if the only reason they had come was to spy. As they turned back towards the western coast, the unease grew. A spherical baron at first refused to welcome them and pursued them with a breathless interrogation: '*Perche?*' 'Why, what for?' Their passports were examined, their steps were followed, they were badgered about news from Reggio. By now even Lear, firm 'in the habit of studiously remaining as far as I could in ignorance of all political acts or expressions', felt increasingly that 'something is about to happen'. After a trip across the straits to Messina, where Proby stayed behind, Lear returned to the mainland to find his host and family agitated. Guns were heard, a messenger arrived: '*E gia principiata la revoluzione!*' – the revolution has already begun. In the published journal, moving to the present tense, Lear evoked the drama and his predicament: 'As for me, revolution or no revolution, here I am in the toe of Italy all alone, and I must find my way out of it as best I may.'

In Reggio armed men roamed the streets with banners declaring '*Viva Pio IX*' or '*Viva la Costituzione*'. The concierge at the hotel where Lear had left his luggage refused to give him his key: '*Non ci sono più chiavi,*' screamed the excited *cameriere*; '*non ci sono più passaporti, non ci sono più Ré – piu legge – più giudici – più niente – non x'è altro che l'amore, la libertà – l'amicizia e la costituzione – eccovi le chiavi – ai! o-o-o-o-o-orra birra bà!!*' – no more keys, passports, kings, laws, judges . . . nothing but love, liberty, friendship and the constitution. The Bourbon government was suspended and the friends and officials who had given Lear and Proby introductions were perplexed and distressed. Hearing that Messina, too, was in revolt, with considerable courage Lear persuaded a boatman to row him across to find Proby, and they eventually boarded a steamer to Naples, leaving sad scenes behind: 'Gloom, gloom, overshadows the memory of a tour so agreeably begun . . . The bright morning route of the traveller overcast with cloud and storm before mid-day.'

The tour was not altogether finished. Proby had another month to pass before heading north, so from Naples they decided to tour Basilicata for three weeks. But the scenery was not so grand, the clouds came down, and despite lovely mountain towns and kindly hosts their mood was shaken. They returned to Rome in mid-October.

Lear reassured Ann that he would leave if trouble threatened: 'Most people who intended to winter here have turned back; there is I believe no real alarm, but families do not like to take risks. Rely upon it, whenever it is necessary, I shall move in time.' In November he packed a huge box of books to send home, cheered by the arrival of Ann's miniature: 'it is exactly like looking at you through a diminishing glass.'

Ann Lear, by Mrs Arundale (1847)

Proudly keeping his long Calabrian moustaches, on Wednesdays he opened his studio to visitors, making enough to send small sums back to his sisters for Christmas. Although many people had left, he was still out to supper four or five times a week and his letters were sprinkled with names. Younger visitors in particular sought him out, men in their twenties, who looked up to him, as Proby had done, for his art, his ease, his knowledge of the language and his energetic travelling. Some would remain friends for life, like Lord Eastnor, later Lord Somers, and Fortescue's Oxford crony, the fair-haired, handsome Thomas Baring, 'an extremely luminous & amiable brick', Lear decided, '& I like him very much'.

Although he was busy, he felt increasingly unsettled, unsure what to do or where to go. The previous autumn George Bowen, President of the Ionian Academy, the University of Corfu, whom he had met in Rome, had invited him to stay on the island. The idea was tempting, as he wanted to see Greece, but he was also fascinated by the idea of Egypt, and by Syria and Asia Minor: 'You see therefore in how noxious a state of knownothingatallaboutwhatoneisgoingtodo-ness I am in!' When Lear wrote this in February 1848, one of his new friends, twenty-five-year-old Charles Church, was leaving Rome for Athens. Charles's uncle was the extraordinary Sir Richard Church, a Quaker who had defied his family to fight in the Napoleonic wars and had organised the Suliot defence of the Ionian islands in 1809. Later the Greeks asked him back to lead them against the Turks. Charles Church encouraged Lear to go to Greece. 'I am very sorry to leave Rome and many friends there, especially Edward Lear,' he wrote:

I spent my last evening in his studio, Lear diligently penning out his sketches, full of quaint and ludicrous stories of people who came to his studio; I and another man looking through portfolios, had coffee, smoked and chatted, Lear telling, among other things, about Ruskin and Tennyson, quoting piece after piece of Tennyson's early poems, and finally taking down his guitar, he sang off half of 'Locksley Hall', with voice pathetic and plaintive but not melodious. He is doubtful about coming to Greece, but has not given it up.

While Lear mulled over his next move, Italy became still more unsettled. The riots that he and Proby had seen in Reggio and Messina had been suppressed by the military but they were a harbinger of things to come: an uprising in Palermo in early January 1848 spread fast over Sicily, prompting riots on the mainland. King Ferdinand granted a new constitution in the Kingdom of Naples and the English rushed north to Rome. 'What do you think of the Sicilians?' Lear asked Fortescue. 'Brave fellows are they not?' Trouble was not confined to Italy. On 22 February, Parisian crowds poured onto the streets. Barricades were erected and soldiers fired on the crowd, then the troops mutinied and

Prime Minister Guizot resigned. Next day Louis Philippe abdicated and fled to England and the monarchy was replaced by the Second Republic. In London that week Marx and Engels published the Communist Manifesto, commissioned by 'The League of the Just'. London was full of rumours of approaching Chartist mobs and the army was on the alert. In fact the Chartist demonstration on 10 April was peaceful and the British panic faded, but in this 'Year of the People' insurrections flared across Europe – in Austria, Germany, Denmark, Hungary, Poland, Belgium. In Italy revolts in the north led to months of fighting against the Austrians. To begin with Pius IX supported the nationalist struggle, but in May he withdrew his troops, nervous of losing the war. His support in Rome collapsed after this apparent betrayal and in November he was forced to leave: the following February Mazzini and Garibaldi would set up the short-lived Roman Republic.

By the time of the Pope's flight, Lear was long gone. Finally, he decided to accept Bowen's invitation to Corfu. In late March 1848 he sold his furniture and sent his books and drawings and paintings home, apart from a couple of canvases that he thought he might return to Rome to finish. Since the steamers from Trieste had been stopped by the Austrian war, he set off for Naples to sail from there via Malta. 'It would be quite impossible', he told Ann after taking the boat south,

to make you understand how a few short months have changed all persons & things in Italy for indeed I hardly believe what passes before my own eyes. Restraint & espionage have given universal place to open speaking & triumphant liberal opinion. One of my fellow passengers was a Neapolitan noble, exiled for 17 years – when he saw Vesuvius first, he sobbed so that I thought he would break his heart.

Lear's sympathies were with the reformers, but when he sailed for Malta, on 7 April 1848, he was glad to leave the land he had come to love. This was not from fear of danger, he said, but because 'the whole tone of the place is worry, worry, worry – & I am sick of it, having lived in it so long in quieter times'.

15: 'CALMLY, INTO THE DICE-BOX'

'Daybreak and wailing; wailing at night, wailing at morn. Shrieks and Khimara will ever be united in my memory.' The lament for the dead, taken up by wives, daughters, sisters and the women around, echoed for days in the Albanian mountains. Lear felt it in his bones, yet the more he was surrounded by danger and death, the more alive he felt.

Leaving Italy, caught in the undertow of the great wave of revolutions, Lear found himself travelling through lands of earlier struggles and battles for independence. After a brief stay in Malta – too white, too bright, too treeless to attract him – he crossed the Ionian Sea in a storm, before sailing through the islands in a moonlit calm. He passed Missolonghi, where Byron died, and sailed on to Ithaca, 'Ulysses island, – & later to Leucadia whence Sappho leaped into the sea'. Early on the morning of 19 April 1848 his boat anchored in the beautiful bay of Corfu. But within days he was off again, sailing south to find his host George Bowen, who was visiting other islands, and then wandering on through Cephalonia and Ithaca.

Britain had gained six Ionian islands in 1810 during the Napoleonic wars, adding Corfu on Napoleon's defeat in 1815, and although they were technically independent, not colonies but British protectorates with their own senate and constitution, real power lay with the British High Commissioner. Lear found that while Corfu buzzed with a large expatriate community, this was only the latest layer in the island's culture. The architecture of the port, with its citadel, colonnaded streets, markets and squares, bore witness to the centuries of Venetian control up to 1797; many of the island's aristocrats, intellectuals and poets still spoke and wrote in Italian. A third of the population was Greek and another third Jewish, living in an area like the Venetian Ghetto, called the Hebraica. The rest were a galaxy of Mediterranean peoples from Albania, Malta, Dalmatia and Italy. The British were a mere crust floating on top of this rich mix, insular and snobbish, keeping to themselves, like the community Lear had known so well in Rome.

It was high spring, and Lear basked in the sun, the wild flowers and white villages. Gazing at the mountains across the straits, he saw the country that Byron had hymned in Canto II of *Childe Harold*, published in 1812, when Lear was born:

> Land of Albania! let me bend mine eyes
> On thee, thou rugged nurse of savage men!
> The cross descends, thy minarets arise,
> And the pale crescent sparkles in the glen,
> Through many a cypress grove within each city's ken.

'If I go to Albania I shall send you a daily journal,' he promised Ann. But then he accepted an invitation from the ambassador to Turkey, Sir Stratford Canning and his wife, old friends from Rome, now staying in Corfu, to go with them to Constantinople, spending a week in Athens on the way. And off he went again.

The Acropolis left Lear astounded: 'Poor old Rome sinks into nothing by the side of such beautiful magnificence.' In the sunset many owls, the bird of Minerva, came and sat near him as he drew.

With his usual precipitous enthusiasm Lear was now in love with Greece. Determined to explore at least some of it before he went to Turkey, he decided after all that he would travel with Charles Church, who could speak modern Greek and was full of the classical education Lear had never had. The trip began inauspiciously, with Lear crashing

from his horse and spraining his shoulder, then being bitten by a centipede so that his leg swelled up. But with a guide, who found horses,
cooked meals and arranged lodgings in village houses, they carried
on. They passed Marathon, where the Greeks defeated the Persians.
They rode past towns destroyed after the modern fight against the
Turks. But Lear was happy, careering through 'fields of pink hollyhocks, yellow and lilac thistles, clover and convolvulus, and rejoicing
in the storks of Lamia, that nested on every house and minaret, clattering with their beaks so that it seemed the whole town was playing
backgammon'.

Athens, 23 July 1848

At Thermopylae, Church read his pocket Herodotus while Lear
sketched. In the burning midsummer Lear was busy, Church remembered, 'from 3 in the morning, only resting during the midheat – among
the crowds in the market-place, among the soldiers – only intent upon
his work, with infinite patience and unflagging good humour and patience'. This took its toll. Another insect bite brought fever, probably
malaria. By early July Lear was delirious and had to be carried back to
Athens, 'brought here', he told Fortescue cheerfully later, 'by 4 horses on
an Indiarubber bed'. There he recovered slowly under the care of Lady
Canning, supported by 'books, jelly, porter & visits continual' from
English residents. By mid-July he felt better, so hungry, he said, that he
could eat an ox.

Soon he was strong enough to sail to Constantinople, but at the embassy at Therapia on the Bosphorus he collapsed again. It was not until

late August that he explored the city and could watch the sultan's procession to Santa Sophia, a display of power with horses caparisoned in velvet and gold, and pashas and officials in diamond-studded turbans. At the climax, there was a long, silent pause, and then 'surrounded by scarlet & gold dressed guards, with halberts or pikes, carrying most wondrous crescent-like plumes of green & white feathers', in rode the Grand Seigneur, 'as if he were in a grove of beautiful birds'. Seeing the ranks hurl themselves on the ground before the young sultan, Lear told Ann, 'gave one a wonderful idea of the Barbaric despot sort of thing one has read of as a child'.

Excited, he spent a week sketching and buying presents for his sisters: printed muslin with gold and blue flowers, silks for a dress, scented pastilles and bracelets, and a little Persian writing box, 'good for knitting needles'. By the time he described these on 9 September, Lear had already left. Well-off friends had sent money for him to travel, and he was on the Austrian steamer *Ferdinando* on his way to Salonica. The steerage was crammed with Turks, Jews, Greeks and Bulgarians, like herrings in a barrel, but Lear shared the first-class deck with the Austrian consul's family and a Turkish harem, 'who entirely cover the floor with a diversity of robes, pink, blue, chocolate and amber, pea, sea, olive, bottle, pale and dark green'. When the women rose, they moved like a bed of tulips in a breeze. He watched the towers of Constantinople fade into the distance: 'first pale and distinct in the light of the rising moon, and then glittering and lessening on the calm horizon, till they, and the memory that I have been among them for seven weeks, seem alike part of the world of dreams'.

When he came to write up his travels, Lear felt experienced enough to hand out advice. Travellers in this region should abandon firearms and gifts to the natives (including portraits of the queen). They should hire a good dragoman and take 'cooking utensils, tin plates, knives and forks' as well as a light mattress, sheets and blankets, capotes and plaids, 'two or three books; some rice, curry powder and cayenne; 'a world of drawing materials – if you be a hard sketcher'. Take as few clothes as possible, he added, but put something in for meeting beys and dig-nitaries. Most vital was 'some quinine made into pills (rather leave all behind than this)'. Cramming all this into heavy leather bags, Lear planned to meet Church in Salonica, to visit Mount Athos with him and then travel round Greece, continuing the explorations of the spring. He had been reading the many volumes of Colonel William Leake's travels in northern Greece and the Morea, published in the 1830s, and though he admired these books, he felt the lack of pictures. Greece, he thought had been only 'imperfectly illustrated . . . The vast yet beau-tifully simple sweeping lines of the hills have hardly been represented I fancy', he mused to Fortescue, 'nor the primitive dry foregrounds of Elgin marble peasants &c. What do you think of a huge work (if I can *do* all Greece)?' He clung to this idea for some years, sending sketches to Byron's publisher John Murray, who was depressingly cool, feeling Greece had been well covered already.

On this trip, he particularly wanted to go to the monasteries of Mount Athos. Then, to his dismay, he found that cholera had broken out in Sa-lonica: the monks had barred the peninsula and Church was trapped in the south beyond a *cordon sanitaire* of closed villages. In the city Lear met ominous silence, sultry, oppressive heat, and biers passing with corpses in the street. He longed to leave, and as his only way out was to the north-west he thought he might travel across country to Yannina (Ioannina), where he could meet Church. Or – and it was a formidable 'or' – should he travel on, to Elbasan and the wilds of Albania? 'Make, I thought to myself no definite arrangement beyond that of escape from Salonica; put yourself, as a predestinarian might say, calmly into the dice-box of small events, and be shaken out whenever circumstances may ordain: only go, and as soon as you can.' He made a rough plan. After Elbasan he would head north to Tirana and Skodra (modern Shkoder, or Scutari, the border-town in the Albanian Alps). Then he would trek south, before heading east across Greece, back to Mount Olympus.

It was Lear's first solo journey outside Italy, and he faced a landscape more hostile than any he had known. Autumn was coming, with rain and cold. He did not know the language, and was unfamiliar with the customs – he found it agony to sit cross-legged like a Turk to eat, and ended lying sideways on the ground. (Although the Turks were so polite, he thought, that they would show no amazement even if you took your tea suspended from the ceiling.) For a man recovering from fever this was a foolhardy choice. But Lear rested if he felt symptoms returning, and he had good support in his servant, a man from Smyrna who spoke ten languages and was his 'dragoman, cook, valet, interpreter and guide'.

The post-boy, the *soorudji*, in his jacket with blue embroideries, led the baggage horse heading their small procession. The omens were good, for Lear rode into a world of birds: 'Countless kestrels hovering in the air or rocking on tall thistles: hoopoes, rollers, myriads of jackdaws, great broad-winged falcons soaring above, and beautiful grey-headed ones sitting composedly close to the roadside as we passed.' There were vultures, too, and 'now and then a graceful milk-white egret, slowly stalking in searchful meditation'. The flight of birds was an avian commentary on human struggles below: coots circling and diving at a falcon, desperate to drive off the predator; eagles soaring above an abyss, then suddenly swooping to snatch a screaming chicken from the market place.

In the bazaars of Monastir, a barrack town on the border with Montenegro, Lear found 'an endless kaleidoscope of pictures', but a taste of difficulties ahead came with the crowds who mobbed him as he drew: one man wrenched his book away, saying, '*Yok, Yok!*' – No, no! Would this grow worse as he rode further into Albania? It was a Muslim country, and the Prophet had decreed that those who made images of living creatures – people, animals or birds – would be punished for imitating the creation of Allah. He soon forgot his fears, or set them aside. Reaching the fortress of Akhridha (modern Ohrid), its lake shimmering under stormy skies, he was astonished and delighted, he said, at every step: at the beech trees clothing the heights, at Lake Peupli clouded with flocks of birds; at the men in their fur-trimmed overcoats, purple, crimson or scarlet. But his own dress did not suit. His white hat offended the orthodox and bystanders pelted him with stones and lumps of mud.

And, said his guide, 'unless you take to a fez, Vossignoria will have no peace and probably lose an eye in a day or two.' Lear bought a fez, unhappy that it did not shade his eyes or protect him from the rain like his old wide-awake hat.

Monastir, 17–18 September 1848

They travelled on, across precipices and chasms into the country of the Gheghes people. 'At length, thought I, these are fairly the wilds of Albania.' But to the inhabitants, it was Lear who seemed dangerous. At Elbasan a shepherd, seeing the sketch of the castle, shrieked, '*Shaitan!*' and fled 'as from a profane magician', and when people saw Lear coming they rushed screaming into their houses, 'drawing bolts and banging doors with the most emphatic resolve'. As he drew, boys whistled through their fingers like 'the butcher-boys in England'. The vision of himself sketching while a great crowd whistled at him with all their might struck him so forcibly, he wrote,

that, come what might of it, I could not resist going off into convulsions of laughter, an impulse the Gheghes seemed to sympathise with, as one and all shrieked with delight, and the ramparts resounded with hilarious merriment. Alas! This was of no long duration, for one of those tiresome Dervishes – in whom, with their green turbans, Elbasan is rich – soon came up, and yelled

'*Shaitan scroo! – Shaitan!*' in my ears with all his force; seizing my book also, with an awful frown, and pointing to the sky, as intimating that heaven would not allow such impiety.

A shower of stones drove Lear to a quieter spot. But still he drew.

Although this was a nuisance, verging on frightening, Lear was intrigued: the stone-throwing mob were like the 'they' of his limericks, the god-fearing majority offended by the deviant, whom they genuinely want to smash. It was odd to be in this position. But he was also moved by the idea that an artist was not 'drawing' in an innocuous Western sense, but writing – '*scroo*' – recording a place, a way of life, and in so doing he had an almost magical power. The hostility was not only religious. 'We will not be written down,' people insisted – perhaps Lear was a Russian spy, sent to take notes so that the sultan could sell them to the Russian Emperor? The Gheghes were suffering in the aftermath of a rebellion against Turkish rule in north-western Albania that had been ferociously suppressed. Many of the beys, their local leaders, had been exiled and their men killed, or condemned to the galleys or drafted into the sultan's armies. Those who survived were taxed beyond endurance and forbidden to carry arms. Under the straw matting roofs of Elbasan's dark bazaars, Lear noticed especially the lanes of the tanners and butchers, 'dogs, blood, and carcasses filling up the whole street and sickening one's very heart'.

He was conscious of danger, of blood, yet he preferred to travel rough. He had a letter from the sultan and could have stayed with local beys, but their ceremonious meals and endless pipe-smoking left him no time to sketch. For a landscape painter, he concluded, travel in Albania offered 'luxury and inconvenience on the one hand, liberty, hard-living, and filth on the other; and of the two I chose the latter, as the most professionally useful, though not the most agreeable'. One exception moved him, the eighteen-year-old Bey of Kroia in his galleried palace under the crags, who made Lear describe steamships and trains, and imitate their noises, over and over again, '"Tik-tok, tik-tok, ly, tokka, tokka, tokka, tokka, tokka – tok (crescendo)", and "Squish-squash, squish-squash, squish-squash, thump-bump" for the land and sea engines respectively.'

He preferred to stay in the khans, roadside inns where horses were stabled and travellers slept in a gallery above. These were often ramshackle and filthy, but he described even the worst with a relish that reached its height in a long passage with the refrain 'O khan of Tyrana', where his long, despairing sentences moved towards music.

O khan of Tyrana! Rats, mice, cockroaches and all lesser vermin were there. Huge flimsy cobwebs, hanging in festoons above my head; big frizzly moths, bustling into my eyes and face, for the holes representing windows I could close but imperfectly with sacks and baggage: yet here I prepared to sleep, thankful that a clean mat was a partial preventive to some of this list of woes, and finding some consolation in the low crooning singing of the Gheghes above me, who, with that capacity for melody which those Northern Albanians seem to possess so essentially, were murmuring their wild airs in choral harmony.

As in a scene from a dark *Arabian Nights*, he watched through a chink in the wall as an elderly dervish hummed and whirred and whirled and danced alone.

Everywhere, Lear was surrounded by noise, the clucking of hens, the snorting of pigs, the barking of dogs. Even the music seemed strange and dissonant. One night, trying to sleep, he was kept awake by Albanians in the room next door: 'Four begin to form a sort of chorus; one makes a deep drone or bass; two more lead the air; and the remainder indulge in strange squeaking falsettos, like the whinings of uneasy sucking pigs.' At dawn, the muezzin often woke him, 'the wildest of singular melodies'. But other sounds roused him too, like the rain drumming on the roof: 'It is half past four A.M. and torrents of rain are falling.'

At Skodra, the northernmost point of his tour, the skies darkened, the thunder roared and the river swelled beneath the bridge, whose painted arches reminded Lear of a Gothic cathedral. He found friends here, including a grumbling Capuchin friar whom he knew from Rome, and the British vice consul, the Corfu-born Signor Bonatti, whose wife and ten children moaned of their exile among the mountains. Poor Signora Bonatti and her daughters, Lear thought – isolated as Greeks and as Christians and unable to show their faces (in some places both Christian and Muslim women were veiled). Staying with the Bonattis Lear painted a Gheghe chief in traditional finery and one of the daughters modelled a local wedding dress for him. He was fascinated by the glamour that the local women hid beneath their veils, 'a magnificence of costume almost beyond belief'.

Much lay beneath the surfaces. The mood of Skodra was black, he was told – '*vendette, nasconderie, sospetti, incendie*' – intrigue, suspicions, incendiaries. It held 'the extremes of revolutionary and despotic, Turk against Christian, Latin opposed to Greek – no place seems more fully fraught with the evils of life'. But was this so very different from 'civilised' states? When Lear finally got some German newspapers on the coast in Avlona, he devoured news 'of the most extraordinary events occurring throughout all Europe'. Returning three weeks later he found his German hosts full of Emperor Ferdinand's flight from Vienna (in December he would abdicate in favour of his son Franz). As they thumped the table, 'predicting with sinister glee all sorts of bloodshed and downfall of tyrants' and launching into tirades against England, Lear abandoned his role of passive listener and demanded 'that we might henceforth talk about pelicans, or red mullet, or whatever they pleased, so that we eschewed politics'. (The shy pelicans feeding on the salt-marsh pools near the sea were his special joy: he had thought them white stones when he first saw them, and then, like a magical metamorphosis, he later told Lord Derby, 'I rode up to them, when lo! They were all pelicans! & away they flew . . . I never was more amused in my life than at seeing so many thousand Pelicans all together.')

Between his two stays in Avlona, Lear left his guide behind and hired an elderly local man, Anastasio – who turned out to be related to almost everyone they met – to steer him over the crags of Acroceraunia, opposite Corfu. Beyond these moutains, in Khimara, lay the most unexplored and romantic place of his wanderings, the hidden gulf of Dukhades: 'Shut out as it stood by iron walls of mountain, surrounded by sternest features of savage scenery, rock and chasm, precipice and torrent, a more fearful prospect and more chilling to the blood I never beheld – gloomy and severe – so unredeemed by any beauty and cheerfulness.'

Khimara, 25 October 1848

That night, in the khan, Anastasio arranged for gipsies to play and sing. In the flickering light of wood torches, people crowded in, and the music rose to a climax, a *capo d'opera*,

till at the conclusion of the last verse, when the unearthly idol-gipsy snatched off and waved his cap in the air – his shining head was closely shaved, except one glossy raven tress at least three feet in length – the very rafters rang again to the frantic harmony: Bo, bo-bo –bo, bo-bo-bo, bobobo, BO! – the last 'Bo' uttered like a pistol-shot and followed by a unanimous yell.

Next morning Lear woke before daylight to a piercing scream, 'repeated with a force and sharpness not to be recalled without pain', the wild wail for the dead, echoing from the rocks around.

In this obscure region Lear was jolted by domestic as well as political oppression. He watched women carrying heavy burdens up the mountains, while their men walked: '"Heavens" said I, surprised out of my wonted philosophy of travel, which ought not to exclaim at anything. "How can you make your women such slaves?"' The explanation was simple: there were no mules in Khimara and 'though far inferior to mules, women were really far better than asses or horses'. Even Anastasio, whom he liked greatly, treated women like this. Lear was also dismayed at the arranged marriages that condemned a girl to live with an old man she hated, and at the punishment for infidelity: death for the woman, but not for her lover.

Everywhere, Lear found degrees of slavery, scales of violence. The Khimariots and the Suliots, whose region Lear visited next, had never recovered from the ravages of Ali Pasha, the 'Lion of Yannina'. In the 1780s, the sultan had made the brigand Ali a local governor, a pasha, in order to enlist him in the fight against the Austrians, but then Ali rampaged through southern and western Albania, carving out his own coastal kingdom. Stories of Ali's atrocities multiplied until finally the Ottomans attacked and in 1822 they sent his head to the sultan on a silver platter. Visiting his rock fortress of Tepelene, Lear found a 'a dreary, blank scene of desolation, where once, and so recently, was all the pomp of Oriental despotism'. The twenty-four-year-old Byron had met Ali Pasha here in 1809, admiring his splendour while knowing him to be barbarous and cruel:

> In marble-paved pavilion, where a spring
> Of living water from the centre rose,
> Whose bubbling did a genial freshness fling,
> And soft voluptuous couches breathed repose,
> ALI reclined, a man of war and woes:
> Yet in his lineaments ye cannot trace,
> While Gentleness her milder radiance throws
> Along that aged venerable face,
>   The deeds that lurk beneath, and stain him with disgrace.

Byron's visit was the stuff of myth: one of the few portraits that he allowed to be engraved was of himself in Albanian or Suliot dress, haughty in his loose turban and robes of red and gold. But the teasing flirtation between Byron and the powerful pasha was all in the past: 'The poet is no more; the host is beheaded, and his family nearly extinct; the palace is burned to the ground.' The abandoned palace was the most telling place, he said, of anywhere he had been.

Through the cold November rain Lear trekked back to Yannina, and then quickly down to the coast to take a boat to Malta – his post had brought yet another invitation, to visit Cairo, Mount Sinai and Palestine.

Suli, 5–6 May 1849

The following spring he returned, crossing the Pindus mountains in torrential rain to see the rocks of Meteora, with their crumbling monasteries perched on top like storks' nests, and to journey through the Vale of Tempe to Mount Olympus. On this second trip too, he followed a trail of blood. Ali Pasha had defeated the Orthodox Christians of Suli in 1803, and Lear passed the rock where desperate Suliot women had flung their children to the crags below, then joined hands and sang as they danced to the edge of the cliff, throwing themselves one by one to their deaths. But still, as he travelled, music followed him and the birds and animals woke him. One night, he listened to the 'wild octave singing of the Albanians below, till the arrival of midnight, silence and sleep', but the room was so dark that it was 'only by the sudden and simultaneous clattering of storks, twittering of swallows, bleating of goats, and jingling of mules' bells, that a man is advised of the coming day'.

Such details of life and landscape and history were thrilling to readers. Lear's *Journal of a Landscape Painter in Greece & Albania* was written with a new, passionate confidence. Lear had learnt how to mould his experiences into a narrative full of suspense, presenting himself both as artist and as 'innocent' recorder of people, places and culture. The innocence was artful. He knew now how to prune the detail that crammed his long letters to Ann. He made his journey immediate and vivid, beginning and ending each day in the present tense, so the reader would wake and sleep with him. He could command different registers, comic, reflective, moving or 'sublime', and enliven his vocabulary with Muslim and Albanian terms. He described Albania's soaring ranges, crashing waters and busy towns, its people, costumes and song, but he wrote also of its sufferings and defiance of tyranny. In this year of revolutions Lear showed how the violence of despots – the cruel Ali Pasha, the repressive Sublime Porte – could damage the spirit of a people. At the Suliots' final mountain stronghold, he wrote, 'I gazed on the strange, noiseless figures about me, bright in the moonlight, which tipped with silver the solemn lofty mountains around. For years those hills had rarely ceased to echo the cries of animosity, despair and agony; now all is silent as the actors in that dreadful drama.'

16: 'ALL THAT AMBER'

John Cross, a friend from Knowsley days, a fervent Christian who wanted to explore the lands of the Bible, had invited Lear to meet him in Malta and travel over the winter of 1848 from Cairo through the Holy Land to Syria and the Lebanon. Lear, the experienced traveller, seemed the ideal companion, and Cross was happy to pay his expenses, although 'The matter is a *secret*', Lear told Ann, '& I am supposed to be spending from my own purse.' He dashed away from Albania in November, only to be held back by nine days of quarantine on the island of Santa Maura (ancient Leucadia, now Lefkas) and then by 'high winds and hurricanes'.

When he arrived in Malta the Jerusalem party had already left. He stayed a week, meeting friends from Rome and dithering about whether to go back to Corfu or even to England. The island was full of talk about the upheavals in Europe and changes in Malta itself, with promise of constitutional reform. The chief secretary to the government was Henry Lushington, appointed in 1847 – Lear had met some of the family that May among the English visitors in Naples. Full of interest in the French Republic, the Italian Risorgimento and Hungarian nationalism (and alarm at the number of exiles arriving in Malta), Lushington was proposing a new code of laws, arguing for religious equality and educational reforms. He was helped in the Villa Giuseppe, among the pines on the cliffs outside Valletta, by his sisters Emily and Maria, and then, when Maria went home ill, by Louisa. His younger brother Franklin spent long holidays there, sailing and enjoying the heat.

Malta was a stopping point for Mediterranean journeys and when Lear decided to sail on to Egypt he left his books and clothes in Valletta to pick up on his return. After landing in Alexandria he joined a crowded steamer to Cairo. Egypt was one of the places Lear had dreamed of before he left Italy: 'I am quite crazy about Memphis & On & Isis & crocodiles & opthalmia & Nubians, – & simooms & sorcerers, & sphingidae', he wrote flippantly to Fortescue, and now Cairo amazed him. 'I shall never be surprised at anything after the streets of Cairo':

If you think one picture of a costume curious – what must the scene be which is composed of thousands of thousands of the most magnificent & strange varieties? The Arabs, blacks, Copts, Greeks & Dervishes etc etc!!!! – the astonishingly narrow streets full of galleries & beautiful stone work – the mosques, the shops – in a word every possible hue & form of novelty.

He loved the Sphinx and the pyramids, but was wary of the snarling camels. Riding a camel, he told Ann, was like riding a rocking chair. Perched up high on a kind of table 'made up of pillows, & coats, & carpets & saddlebags: – we sit crosslegged – or opposite each other, or we turn round – just as we please, & we lunch or read as quietly as if we were in a room. Nothing can be more charming.'

Cross had organised things well. When they set off across the desert they slept in tents, cared for by Arab guides and servants. These included Ibrahim the dragoman, an eclectic cook who conjured up Irish stews, pancakes and macaroni amid the sands, and a baggage train that carried food, beds, carpets and other luxuries, 'so I fear there will be no romance of hardships in the desert'. Lear felt that he cut rather a dashing figure, with a hat lined with green, and a green gauze veil and a cloak. The aim was to follow the path of the Israelites fleeing Egypt: 'You must begin at the 14th Chapter of Exodus to know our route.' They rode across gravelly plains to green oases, through brilliant sun and sudden rain, between bare, shimmering blue mountains.

Outside the Walls of Suez, 8:30 a.m., 17 January 1849

The climax was Sinai itself, a place of 'excessive & wonderful grandeur'. In his watercolour sketches, Lear caught the atmosphere while never sacrificing accuracy. He never took any credit for this particular achievement, thought Franklin Lushington, looking back. Lear called

Near Wadi el-Sheikh, 8 a.m., 30 January 1849. Notes: 'dark brown',
'sky pale blue', 'brown', 'rox', 'sand pale shining, mountains dark purple'.

himself a topographical artist, 'and the phrase was neither an affectation
of false modesty nor in any sense untrue':

Nothing could have induced him to give to his landscapes any effect of form,
colour, light, shade, or other detail which did not actually belong to the scenery
of the particular region. The lines of hill and mountain, the depths of valley,
the breadth of plain, the character of foreground, were reproduced with stern
exactness in his vigorous and delicate drawing.

Lushington noted that the geologist Sir Roderick Murchison used to say
that Lear's sketches always accurately revealed a region's geology: 'Yet
his sketches were not mere photographs. They were full of the intui-
tively true imagination of an artist who had studied the features of the
land till he knew them by heart.'

Lear immersed himself in the lines, textures, shadows and light. But
although the plan was to cross to Gaza, travel to Jerusalem and then
work slowly north through Palestine to Beirut, in early February Lear
suddenly cut his trip short. His excuse was a severe cold. He wrote air-
ily about abandoning Cross, 'I decided it would be more kind to leave

him than to accompany him.' This did not altogether ring true. Before
he had even reached Egypt Lear thought that he might skip Mount
Sinai, try to see Mount Athos in the spring, and 'wind up all my Thessaly, Albanian and Greek tour before I come home in the summer'. By
early March he was writing from Patras, 'Here I am you see in Greece
again.'

Greece was where he wanted to be, and this time his fellow traveller
was 'Mr F. Lushington – the government secretary's brother at Malta –
a very amiable and talented man – to travel with whom is a great advantage to me, as well as pleasure'.

The pleasure was obvious; this was the kind of young man he took to
his heart. Lear was now thirty-six and Frank Lushington was twenty-
six, good-looking in a similar way to Fortescue, tall and dark-haired.
Although he lacked Fortescue's Irish warmth, in Greece he was on
holiday, light of heart and full of fervour for the classical world. Lear
was always concerned about his lack of education, and prepared for
his trips meticulously. Before visiting any country, Lushington wrote
later,

he studied every book he could lay hands on that would give him the best in-
formation as to its physical characteristics and its history; and he appreciated
instinctively the truth and accuracy of travellers' descriptions. His habit of ac-
cumulating a store of knowledge before setting out made him a valuable and
delightful fellow-traveller to those whose tastes and objects were to any degree
in unison with his own. He knew what he wanted, and followed it up with energetic determination.

The short reading list that Lear sent Ann in January this year, so
that she had some idea of what he was up to, revealed the work he
put in: 'Doctor Holland's narrative of a Tour in Albania – Urquhart's
Spirit of the East – Walsh's residence in Constantinople (excellent) –
also his journey thence. Lanes's Customs & Manners of the Modern
Egyptians, Lord Lyndsay's Holy Land – Robertson's Palestine is the

best of all, but is voluminous.' But this reading was no substitute for the deep knowledge of the classical Greek world that Charles Church and the Lushington brothers had imbibed since childhood: 'One of the most delightful recollections of one particular holiday of my very young days', Frank Lushington remembered, was 'hearing Edmund and Harry translate the *Odyssey* for the benefit of Maria and Emily and us little ones'. Travelling with Frank, Lear could breathe in a bit of this knowledge like the sunlit air itself.

Frank Lushington, *c.*1840

The two eldest Lushington brothers, Edmund, now Professor of Greek at Glasgow, and Henry ('Harry' or 'Hal'), Lear's exact contemporary, were brilliant classical scholars. The much younger Frank had followed in their footsteps at Trinity College, Cambridge, coming first in the Classical tripos, winning the Chancellor's Medal and quickly being elected a Fellow. At Cambridge all three brothers were members of the Apostles as their father had been. Membership of this exclusive club of twelve was a stamp of brilliance: in 1851, when the critic William Bodham Donne had to speak at the annual dinner, he confessed, 'I had rather address a Norwich mob than the "Apostles", not that I mean to compare them, but they are so formidable.' The Lushingtons were doubly appealing to Lear, as Edmund and Harry were extremely close to their fellow Apostles Arthur Hallam and Alfred Tennyson, Lear's favourite poet. Their home, Park House near Maidstone, was a stone's throw from Boxley Hall where the Tennyson family lived after they left Lincolnshire, and in 1842, Edmund had married Tennyson's younger sister, Cecilia, a wedding celebrated at the end of *In Memoriam*, the sequence born of Hallam's early death.

> O true and tried, so well and long,
> Demand not thou a marriage lay;
> In that it is thy marriage day
> Is music more than any song.

When Frank reviewed *In Memoriam* in *Tait's Magazine* in 1850, he called it 'one of the most touching and exquisite monuments ever raised to a departed friend'. His own beloved friend was Hallam's younger brother Henry. Friendship (as well as high-minded duty) was central to the Apostles: they discussed the form it had taken in the past and its meaning today and saw nothing as more important. This was something that Lear could understand.

Frank was running to keep up with his brothers' standards: his father had died when he was fourteen, his mother four years later, and Edmund had been the head of the family ever since. But on holiday Frank shrugged off the sober ethos of the Lushingtons. The weather was glorious, and since he wanted to sketch as much as Lear, there was no awkwardness. Lear drew swiftly and confidently, noting the place, date and often the time of day, numbering his drawings, then penning in outlines and applying colour washes. 'I do not know when I have enjoyed myself so much,' Lear wrote; 'we only complain that the days are too short.' After landing at Patras and visiting the convent of Megaspelion, 'a wondrous place containing 200 or 300 monks – in a large cave', they headed south into the Morea, the heart of the Peloponnese, the ancient Arcady, home of Pan. 'The beauty of this part of Greece can hardly be imagined, as all the exquisite plains of the coast are seen through the magnificent forests of ilex and oak,' Lear wrote. 'At Bassae on the 18th – we went to the temple of Apollo – perhaps the finest Greek ruin after the Parthenon. I never saw such a beautiful landscape.' Their dragoman, though elderly, fat and unsteady, knew every winding path. From Bassae, where a sudden snowstorm stopped Lear sketching, he guided them to Sparta and the plains of Argos, 'where you know Agamemnon & all those people lived', Lear reminded Ann casually.

If Albania was a country of birds, Greece was a land of flowers. After a rare day of rain 'The ground has been literally covered with flowers; I wish you could see them; – sometimes it is quite pink with Hepaticas – scarlet & blue, – Anemones – Yellow Euphorbias – Cistus – & several hundred kinds of flowers.' The whole earth was like a garden, or a rich Turkish carpet: 'As for Lushington & I, equally fond of flowers, we gather them all day like children, & when we have stuck our hats & coats & horses all over with them – it is time to throw them away, & get a new set.' And nonsense rode with them too. 'I remember one night in Greece', Lushington wrote many years later,

when, after scrambling for fifteen hours on horseback over the roughest mountain paths, we had dismounted and were waiting in black darkness for our guide to find among a few huts a tolerably weather-tight shelter for us to sleep in, Lear, who was thoroughly tired, sat down upon what he supposed to be a bank; but an instant grunt and heave convinced him of error as a dark bovine quadruped suddenly rose up under him and tilted him into the mud. As Lear regained his feet he cheerily burst into song:

> There was an old man who said, 'Now
> I'll sit down on the horns of that cow!'

Frank could not remember if this was published, but the moment lay behind a verse in Lear's next nonsense book:

There was an Old Man who said, 'How, –
Shall I flee from this horrible Cow?
I will sit on this stile, and continue to smile,
Which may soften the heart of that Cow.'

Circling back, flowers in their hats, they saw the ruins of Mycenae and crossed the Gulf of Corinth to Athens. Then they headed west to Thebes and Mount Parnassus, the home of the Muses, sacred to Dionysus, where Apollo gave Orpheus his golden lyre, and on to Delphi, the seat of the oracle. At the end of April Lushington left for Malta from Patras, and next day Lear took the steamer north.

The tour in Greece was a rare time of true happiness: 'I really never remember having had so delightful a trip.' Nothing had happened, yet everything had happened. Lear had fallen in love with this younger man, and it would shape his life. The Delphic oracle uttered no warning of what lay ahead.

Lear now went back to finish his journey through Albania. In the journal of this second tour a new name crept in, condensed to initials: 'F.L., my Greek companion, is obliged to return to Malta, so I set out alone.' Lear wrote of the circling dance of peasant women that they had seen near Parnassus, and described a dangerous pass where the baggage horse stumbled and all the plates and dishes 'which F.L. had bequeathed to me at Patras' tumbled into the abyss. The trip had a melancholy air from the beginning. 'Late at night', he wrote in his journal for 6 May,

I strolled on to the bright sands, and enjoyed the strange scene: air seems peopled with fireflies, earth with frogs, which roar and croak from the wide Acherusian marsh; low-walled huts cluster around; Albanians are stretched on mats along the shore; huge watchdogs lie in a circle round the village; the calm sea ripples, and the faint outline of the hills of desolate Suli is traced against the clear and spangled sky.

When he crossed northern Greece to Mount Olympus, the gods were hidden in cloud. He could make only one sketch of 'dark Olympus' before a thunderstorm and a deluge drove him in. He wrote of the rain and the woes of Thessaly, and the loneliness he felt brought the familiar fear of happiness found and lost. It had been a year of friends, he noted:

Any one – it is certain – more quiet and good and full of all sorts of intelligences and knowledges than Lushington a man could not travel with. Charles M. Church, John E. Cross and F. Lushington are the companions within 12 months such as few could fall in with. How this fly got into all that amber, I can't understand.

It was time to go home. Lear collected his belongings in Malta and took back to England his Albanian studies of minarets and markets, his sketches in browns and greys, misty and mysterious, of mountains, rivers and towns. From Egypt he took his drawings of sulky camels and his glowing watercolours. He packed his views of the Acropolis and the heat-shimmering Greek plains. From these he would paint beautifully finished studio watercolours. But would this vision, too, pass away? It would be difficult, he thought, to recall the clarity of the Greek landscape and to transfer it to paper or canvas. 'What scenery is this Greece!' he sighed. 'Shall I remember these lovelinesses, these pure grey-blue seas, these clear skies, cut chiselled hills, and bright white sails, and glittering costumes, and deep shadows, when I am far away from them?' Could he keep these safe from the lapse of time, preserved in the amber of his art?

IV. TUMBLING

17: THE BROTHERHOOD

Lear arrived in England in the late spring of 1849 determined to make plans for his future career. He needed to work up his watercolours, revise his journals and make lithographs for his planned books on southern Italy and Albania, but what he wanted most was to gain some training and to become a respected, exhibited artist. The previous summer, lying ill in Athens, he had written:

What to do, my Dear Fortescue, when I return to England!!?? ?–¿!! (expressive of indelible doubt, wonder, & ignorance.) London must be the place, & then comes the choice of two lines; society, & half days work, pretty pictures, petit-maître praise boundless, frequented studio &c. &c, wound up with vexation of spirit as age comes on that talents have been thrown away: – or *hard study* beginning at the root of the matter, the human figure, which to master alone would enable me to carry out the views & feelings of landscape I know to exist within me. Alas! If real art is a *student*, I know no more than a child, an infant, a foetus.

He had no real home here. He was not the only one of the Lears to flee England: all his three brothers were now abroad. The eldest, Henry, had sailed to the West Indies in the early 1830s, and lived for ten years in Cuba before moving to New York with his wife Jemima and children. They were now in Brooklyn. Ten years hence Henry and his eldest son were described as painters, while the second son was a lithographer and the third a brass finisher: later Henry became a distinguished map- and globe-maker. Fred, who had been an exuberant elder brother when Lear was small, was also in America, engaged in ventures as a mining engineer, most of them disastrous, and now living near St Louis with his wife Rosa and their children, and Rosa's sister Fanny. Charles, the closest in age to Lear, went as a medical missionary to Sierra Leone. (According to family stories, he was sent home with malaria, but as the captain would not take him without a nurse, the local girl who had looked after him, Adjouah, came forward. Charles immediately married her for 'propriety' and brought her to his sister Ellen, who sent her to school: Adjouah then became a missionary herself.)

Lear was rarely in touch with his brothers. As for his sisters, he was devoted to Ann, but could not live with her, and he never thought of staying with the pious Ellen and Mary. When Ellen and her husband William Newsom searched for a house, 'There was an objection of some sort to all they saw; if the situation suited, there was no Chapel in the place: if there was a Chapel, there was no Garden, or the situation would not suit.' Eventually they settled on Leatherhead. ('What a funny dear old couple of larky birds are those two!' Lear wrote fondly.) Mary and Richard Boswell were in Margate and Harriett in Lanarkshire. Sarah, always the jolliest sister, was living near Ellen now that Charles Street had retired from the Arundel bank. A proud grandmother, Sarah kept up her music and drawing and loved her cottage with its apples and plums. 'Gardening', she told Fred, asking him to shake a few American seeds into his next letter, 'is my never failing pleasure.'

Sarah also passed on news of Lear's travels: 'He has arrived last from a visit to Egypt – Cairo – Mount Sinai – the Wilderness – Constantinople – and the Grecian Isles – and now intends to settle in England. The day before yesterday he surprised the Newsoms with an early visit, to breakfast, having walked over from Ashtead, where he was staying at the seat of Lady Howard.' A rapid visit was clearly enough. The family would scatter further when Sarah emigrated to the South Island of New Zealand with her son Charles and his wife Sophie, leaving her ill husband behind. Lear was fascinated by her farm near Otago and for once he sounded envious. 'The more I read travels, the more I want to move,' he told Chichester Fortescue. 'Such heaps of N. Zealand as I have read of late! I know every corner of the place.' He read too about Borneo, Australia and Tasmania. Three years later when Lord and Lady Somers were planning to go to India and asked Lear to come too, he thought seriously about it: 'I might see Sarah perhaps,' he mused to Ann, 'for from India to New Holland is now only a run. But there is time enough to think of this.' Some years later Ellen and William Newsom and Mary and her husband would follow Sarah to New Zealand, but the Newsoms stayed only briefly, returning with relief to civilised Leatherhead.

Lear was always attentive, sending money to Mary, helping Sarah settle her affairs, asking about Ellen, worrying that Harriett looked ill. But his world was now with his patrons – like Lady Howard – and with the artists. At the start of 1849 he was in debt, worrying about his future, but in June his immediate problems were solved. Over the past few years, encouraged by Ann, he had become a diligent correspondent of Mrs Courtney Warner, an elderly family friend. When she died that year she left him £500. Most of her fortune of nearly £50,000, said Sarah, went to '30 poor widows of the City of Bath – so that each is to have £40 per annum for life', a bequest that made Lear joke that he had thought of marrying one of the 'viddies' himself, until, he said, he realised she would then no longer be a widow.

The bequest let him pursue an old dream, to enrol in the Royal Academy Schools. It was hardly sensible, given that he was thirty-seven and the RA course lasted ten years, with students only moving to the 'Preliminary School of Painting' after three years of copying from the antique and studying anatomy, but this was what his heart was set on. As he had to submit drawings for selection in January, he signed on again at Sass's school in Bloomsbury, and before the term began he visited friends, old and new, 'in a constant state of happiness'. Old friends included Lord Derby and Robert Hornby: 'Immense fun we have had, one has done little but laugh, eat, drink and sleep.' New acquaintances included the Lushingtons at Park House: far less fun. Edmund, the Glasgow professor, spent half the year here with the children and Cecilia (a true Tennyson, hypochondriac and melancholy), and his sisters Ellen, Emily and Cissy. The household was inward-looking, high-thinking and earnest. The Lushingtons had a habit, as Emily Tennyson said, of treating all outsiders as 'mere mortals' and the Frank whom Lear saw here was ominously different from the high-spirited traveller in Greece.

After these visits, Lear settled into rooms at 17 Stratford Place, off Oxford Street, just opposite Bond Street, decorating them with stuffed birds, sent by Lord Derby, which he displayed in glass cases. He went to Sass's and in January 1851 he told Fortescue with delight that the Royal Academy had accepted him: 'I tried with 51 – little boys – & 19 of us were admitted. And now I go with a large book and a piece of chalk to school every day like a good little boy.' In this letter he sent his drawing of infants buzzing like flies round his easel. He was a probationer until April, when his drawings were examined, but although he was then approved for the full training, he did not stay much longer: he needed to make money. Yet a few years later, drawing two Arabs for a sketch, he thought that his 'slavy labours at anatomy in 1849–50' had been worth it, 'for small progress as I made – I can make something like figures now – & never could before'.

In the cold early months of 1851 London life was wretched, but in April the publication of *Journals of a Landscape Painter in Greece and Albania* brought '*heaps & loads* of compliments & congratulations', and good reviews in the *Athenaeum* and *Tait's Magazine*. London was *en fête* for the opening of the Great Exhibition in Joseph Paxton's amazing glass and iron palace in Hyde Park: the great machines and manufactures in its shining nave proclaiming the triumph of British industry and trade. People poured in, from the wealthy and the famous to cheap day-trippers on special trains. Ann and Sarah went soon after it opened, staying from ten in the morning to seven at night when 'The Queen and family were there, and 50,000 persons, but no crowding!'

Lear, however, was more concerned with his painting than with the Exhibition's excitements, working on a large oil of the road to the Acropolis at dawn and putting in more figures to please Lord Derby. (To his great distress, Derby died in June the following year, just after Lear had finished the painting and was on his way to Knowsley to present it.) As the summer passed he escaped the heat and stench of London, but only for a wet stay in Devon. Determined to paint despite the rain, he found unexpected light relief in the tipsy church clerk reading the psalms, telling Fortescue: 'He said last Sunday, "As white as an old salmon", instead of white as snow in Salmon), "A lion to my mother's children" (for alien) & "they are not guinea pigs", instead of guiltless!' He enjoyed the nonsense innocently invented by a real, instead of a clever, fool. He had fun with the local accent too, and sent a transcript in the same letter:

Enter Mary
  'Mary, has the boy come back from the Post with the letters yet?'
  'Noa zur, hiss be drewndid!'
  'He's what Mary?'
  'Hiss be drewndid zur in the pewerfil rain.'
  'Well it certainly does rain Mary but I hope he ain't drowned, for all that.'
Exit Mary
  Re-enter Mary.
  Here be tew litters zur: – the boy is all queet drewndid zur as ever you see!'

But at heart, after a joyless week in Cornwall with Frank Lushington, and a return to Devon (it was still raining), Lear felt low. The post cheered him and Fortescue was kind about his painting. 'I hope to go on', Lear responded, 'but only by the same road, i.e., *constant study* and perseverance.' He needed a new direction.

In the coming year he found it. Instead of copying the antique in dusty classrooms he found a teacher who took him into the open air, rain or not: William Holman Hunt. When Lear was making plans to enrol at the Royal Academy Schools in the summer of 1849, John Everett Millais's *Isabella* and Hunt's *Rienzi* were on show at the Academy, and Dante Gabriel Rossetti's *Girlhood of the Virgin Mary* was included in a Free Exhibition in Hyde Park. All these paintings were a novel mix of symbolism and detailed realism and all were signed with the cryptic initials 'PRB', the mark of a revolutionary movement, the Pre-Raphaelite Brotherhood.

Millais, Hunt and Rossetti, who had formed the group the previous autumn, were startlingly young: Millais nineteen, Hunt twenty-one and Rossetti twenty. All had been students at the RA Schools. Millais had been enrolled at eleven, the youngest pupil ever; Hunt was accepted on his third attempt in 1844 after enduring a four-year stint in a City office to please his father; Rossetti had studied there from 1845 to 1848. It was Rossetti's idea to form a secret brotherhood, modelled on the German Nazarene painters. Soon their numbers grew to seven, and in the spring of 1850 they published a magazine, *The Germ: Thoughts towards Nature in Poetry, Literature and Art*. Rejecting the idealising tenets of Reynolds and the Royal Academy, they were responding to Ruskin's call in the first volume of *Modern Painters* – a book that Lear had admired since its publication in 1843 – urging young artists to 'Go to Nature in all singleness of heart, and walk with her laboriously and trustingly, having no other thoughts but how best to penetrate her meaning, and remember her instruction; rejecting nothing, selecting nothing, and scorning nothing, believing all things to be right and good, and rejoicing always in the truth.'

The stated aims of the PRB were to express genuine ideas, to study nature, 'to sympathise with what is direct and serious and heartfelt in previous art, to the exclusion of what is conventional and self-parodying and learned by rote', and – simply – to produce good painting and sculpture. They would paint outdoors and use new pigments to create brilliant, glowing effects, and their concern for the 'pure' art of the distant past would be combined with modern subjects and a fervent scrutiny of nature – the curl of a leaf, the sheen of a pebble, the oily roughness of a sheep's wool. To begin with, the critics were merely

curious, but after the Academy show in the summer of 1850, the outbursts began. The centre of the storm was Millais's *Christ in the House
of His Parents*, denounced by Dickens in *Household Words* as both ugly
and blasphemous: Christ was a hideous, blubbering boy and 'Such men
as the carpenters might be undressed in any hospital where dirty drunk-
ards, in a high state of varicose veins, are received.' When the attacks
continued, Ruskin, in two letters to *The Times*, leapt to the new painters' defence, and became a friend.

Lear's oil of *Claude Lorrain's House on the Tiber* was on show in that
controversial Summer Exhibition of 1850. His style, with its debt to
Penry Williams and earlier landscapists, was very different, but he was
fascinated by the PRB. Holman Hunt recalled how his pupil Robert
Braithwaite Martineau took him to Stratford Place to see Lear's drawings, 'which were in outline, with little to indicate light or shade':

Lear overflowed with geniality, and, at the same time, betrayed anxiety as we
turned over the drawings, avowing that he had not the ability to carry out the
subjects in oil: in some parts of them he had written in phonetic spelling the
character of the points which the outlines would not explain – 'Rox', 'Korn',
'Ski', indulging his love of these vagaries.

As he was leaving Lear asked Hunt's advice: could he make good pictures from these sketches? '"For when I set myself to try", he added, "I
often break down in despair."' Candidly, Hunt replied that he would
not dream of painting from such skeleton outlines in a studio: Lear must
work outside. But there was no need to go back to Sicily. Looking at the
sketch of *Syracuse quarries* he suggested that Lear could perfectly well
find the rocks and skies he needed in England, and on impulse he invited
him down to Fairlight in Sussex, where he was planning to work on the
painting that became *Strayed Sheep: Our English Coasts, 1852*.

Lear found them lodgings at Clive Vale Farm near Fairlight, then
startled Hunt by writing nervously that to avoid friction perhaps they
should have separate rooms and meet only at meals. This may have been
alarm at needing somewhere to escape to if he felt a fit coming on, but it

was also typical of his mixture of gregariousness and private wariness. Hunt wrote later that when he and Rossetti's brother William Michael arrived, 'It was curious to see the unexpected guardedness of Lear's reception of us, but he gradually thawed, and by the end of dinner he was laughing and telling good stories . . . The proposed separate apartments soon became a joke.' For the first ten days Lear watched Hunt paint, then began to try himself, making notes on Hunt's approach, system and pigments and use of colour in *Ye Booke of Hunte* (now lost). In the early mornings he wrote letters, sometimes thirty before breakfast, said Hunt – probably quick notes to potential subscribers to his Calabria journal. Then they spent the day sketching. In the evenings Lear penned out his drawings, and 'In the intervals of working, with a good deal of joking he exercised me in Italian and beat out new Nonsense Rhymes which afterwards found a place in his well known volumes.' Thackeray and John Leach visited, William Rossetti helped Lear correct the proofs of *Journals of a Landscape Painter in Calabria* and Millais joined them for a while, prompting Lear's bad pun about bringing in a 'Millaisneum' of art, and his query about Millais, 'Is he disposed to lord it over others?' Well, thought Hunt, there were some men who were all good nature but still had a knack of getting others to carry their parcels. 'Oh but I won't carry his,' said Lear. 'Yes you will,' replied Hunt. The next day, inevitably, Millais cajoled Lear into carrying the cuttlefish shells that littered the beach: '"He doesn't carry his own cuttlefish", passed into a proverb amongst us.'

Many of the Brotherhood and their circle became Lear's friends, including William Rossetti, Thomas Woolner, Ford Madox Brown, Thomas Seddon, Robert Martineau and Augustus Egg. Lear admired Hunt's dogged sticking to principles, his precision, his brilliant colour, his scrupulous studies of stone, plants and water, his skill in capturing the pearly sheen of the sea beyond the russet downs. Hunt was keen on traditional pigments, Naples yellow, Chinese vermilion, Venetian red, Cologne earth and the beautiful, expensive ultramarine blue, but to gain intensity he would mix in some of the new chemical colours like the artificial cobalt blue and emerald green. Lear took note, and in exchange introduced Hunt to music and literature, as well as teaching him Italian. By the end of their three months together, Hunt found him 'beyond doubt the most considerately kind, and good natured man alive'. They discussed travelling to Egypt, Palestine and Syria together and their friendship would endure for over thirty years. Although Lear was forty, fifteen years older, they had much in common: both largely self-taught, they understood what it was to long for proper training, to feel isolated, to suffer depression. In January 1853 Hunt wrote Lear a letter that sounds like a brief for a limerick with its misunderstood artist, a whirling acrobat, taunted by 'they': 'I have for the last three weeks been like one of those street tumblers who spinning a wheel of sharp knives, are unable to look to the right or to the left, for fear of dangerous tools coming down upon their bare heads.' With this he drew a baffled head, dodging knives marked 'patrons', 'models', 'critics' and 'Ruskin's charity'.

The painting Lear was now determined to work on was that of his Syracuse quarries. When the ceiling of his London lodgings collapsed in January, he went back to Hastings, 'where at least there are fresh air, and muffins'. A month later he moved into new lodgings at 65 Oxford Street, near Hyde Park, paying for the move from the sale of his *Mount Parnassus* to Sir Richard Bethell, the Solicitor General. There he worked in his new Hunt-influenced style on oils of Reggio, Venosa and Thermopylae, and developed his Syracuse scene on a five-foot canvas: *The City of Syracuse from the Ancient Quarries where the Athenians Were Imprisoned BC 413*. He carried the PRB use of foreground detail and brilliant colour into all his large-scale paintings of the time, and every now and then in later life he returned to these tones: in 1871, he was working, 'off & on – at Corfu Citadel, Ventimiglia, Lerici, Megaspelion, Palermo – blue, pink & yellow – a la Holman Hunt'.

In December 1852, sending Hunt his *Nonsense*, Lear wrote, 'I really cannot help again expressing my thanks to you for the progress I have made this autumn . . . if the Thermopylae turns out right I am a P.R.B. forever – Indeed, in no case, shall I ever return to the old style.' When

The Mountains of Thermopylae was exhibited at the British Institution the following February he told William Rossetti that any praise of its colours was owing to Hunt, 'Not but that I dare say 99 out of a hundred will blame & not praise the colour – how green! How Blue! How queer!' But he made the point that these mountains were hard to draw: he had studied them carefully and understood the Mediterranean atmosphere after living there for thirteen years.

The Mountains of Thermopylae, 1852

Though *Thermopylae* was a success he still wanted Hunt's help with *Syracuse*. How should the shadows of the ravens fall? How to vary the too-similar colour of the shadows of the rocks?

Altogether I foresee the possibility of this picture being a failure & remaining unfinished, unless you can help me out of this mess. – It has been so completely impossible even to see nature lately – much more to paint from it, that the poor beast of a painting has not had fair play. This however by no means weakens my faith in the proper way of painting – had I really been able to follow it out.

Although he felt it was still not completely finished, he submitted it for selection in April 1853 and it was hung in the RA Summer Exhibition, receiving the Art Union Prize. When it sold for £250 to Henry Lygon, heir to the Earl of Beauchamp, his delight made Lear want to hop on one leg all the way to Hastings.

This success seemed to vindicate his new loyalties. But he found the PRB's *plein air* approach maddeningly difficult: to exhibit seriously he had to work on a large scale and found himself lugging huge canvases out of doors in all sorts of weather. That summer, working on another painting of Windsor for Edward Stanley, now the new Lord Derby (he became prime minister in June, with Disraeli at his side), Lear lamented that the beastly blue-black skies made it 'utterly impossible to do this view on a strictly P.R.B. principle, – for supposing a tree is black one minute – the next it's yellow, & the 3rd green: so that were I to finish any one part the whole 8 feet would be all spots – a sort of Leopard landscape.' As for the sheep in the foreground, the first lot were wild and would not be caught, and although his Hastings friend Frederick North bought some Southdown sheep specially, these too would not do. They kept changing, what with shearing and lambs insisting on growing – in the end he decided to put them all in the distance. (To Hunt, he declared that instead of sheep, 'I shall put in a drove of Apes from the Zoological Society.')

While Lear groaned about the 'infinite obstacles' he enjoyed feeling part of the group, joining his new allies in attacking the great and good of the Academy. He was scathing, for instance, about the 1854 Academy exhibition: Maclise 'wants nature and variety'; Landseer had 'a canvas full of slosh'; Sir Charles Eastlake, soon the first Director of the National Gallery, showed 'a "Giorgione & water" female head, – more like a piece of boiled veal than a woman'. Yet although he applauded his Pre-Raphaelite approach, Lear did not always agree with Hunt's practice. In 1853, for example, he worried that Hunt's *The Awakening Conscience* – where the 'fallen woman' leaps up from her lover's knee, stricken by remorse after singing Moore's 'Oft in the Stilly Night' – did not have a sufficiently 'high' theme. Hunt responded calmly. He saw the painting as a pendant to his *The Light of the World*, in which Christ knocks at the long-unopened door of the conscience: that was a spiritual scene and this would transfer it to the material world. It was, he said, prompted by a verse in Proverbs, '"As he that taketh away a garment in cold weather, so is he that sings songs to a heavy heart" . . . my desire was to show how the still small voice speaks to a human soul in the turmoil of life.' This was in Hunt's mind when he painted Lear's setting of Tennyson's 'Tears, idle tears', flung on the carpet.

Three years later, when Ann went to see Hunt's *The Scapegoat* at the Academy, Lear agreed with her 'in not liking the subject'. But, he wrote loyally, it was a wonderful picture and 'Where the skill & genius which Hunt possesses is so immeasurably in advance of that of the mass of painters, we must take what we can get.' Lear would always be wary of Hunt's biblical subjects, but he continued to think himself Hunt's junior as a painter. In this respect, as he told Fortescue, he was a child. From an early stage he began to address Hunt as 'dear Daddy', and Millais and Woolner as his 'Uncles'. As a painter in oils, Lear was transformed by his time with Hunt. In the end he found the Pre-Raphaelite palette too bright and the technique too arduous and fussy, yet under this influence his painting became more powerful, less conventional, utterly his own.

18: MEETING THE POET

'Illyrian woodlands, echoing falls . . .' In Sussex in the autumn of 1852 Lear was painting a fig tree in the overgrown garden of the Hastings MP Frederick North, lodging in the gardener's cottage. The fig was perfect for the Syracuse canvas, but as he also wanted a group of ravens he wired a stuffed bird on the apple tree opposite his window – hardly strict painting from nature. While there he met North's two daughters: Marianne, later famous for her paintings of flora, from California and Brazil to the East Indies and New Zealand, and Catherine, who would become a friend of Lear's later years. Marianne remembered how he would drift into their sitting-room at dusk:

and sit down to the piano and sing Tennyson's songs for hours, composing as he went on, and picking out the accompaniments by ear, putting the greatest expression and passion into the most sentimental words. He often set me laughing; then he would say I was not worthy of them, and would continue the intense pathos of expression and gravity of face, while he substituted Hey Diddle Diddle, the Cat and the Fiddle, or some other nonsensical words to the same air.

Lear had admired Tennyson's poetry since he read the two-volume *Poems* of 1843. One volume contained unpublished works from the past decade such as 'Ulysses', 'Locksley Hall' and 'Break, break, break', and the second held a selection from Tennyson's earlier collections of 1830 and 1833, including 'The Lady of Shalott', 'Mariana', 'The Palace of Art' and 'The Lotos Eaters'. Tennyson returned constantly to his earlier work, and all these poems had been heavily revised for the new edition: 'You will see and groan!' Browning wrote to a friend. 'The alterations are insane. *Whatever* is touched is spoiled.' But to Lear they were all wonderful. Seduced by the glorious excess, the echoing assonance and swooping cadences, he fell under the spell of Tennyson's melodic gift. He saw the sonorous phrases as summoning up the mood of scenes, like the gleaming river of 'The Lotos Eaters', 'rolling a slumbrous sheet of foam below'. The sounds did the work, almost regardless of meaning. Tennyson himself implied this when he remembered the lines he composed as a boy of eight, that he thought 'grander than Campbell, or Byron, or Scott. I rolled it out, it was this "With slaughterous sons of thunder rolled the flood" . . . great nonsense of course, but I thought it fine.'

Charles Church had remembered Lear setting half of the lengthy 'Locksley Hall' to music, an intriguing choice, especially on a guitar. (Lear was fond of 'spreading chords' on the piano, so he may have done the same with the guitar, more reciting than singing.) Though widely popular, the poem was controversial, with its bitter narrator, unhinged by loss and sexual jealousy, railing about fleeing to India where he was born.

> Or to burst all links of habit – there to wander far away,
> On from island unto island through the gateways of the day.
>
> Larger constellations burning, mellow moons and happy skies,
> Breadths of tropic shade and palms in cluster, knots of Paradise . . .
>
> There the passions cramp'd no longer shall have scope and breathing space;
> I will take some savage woman, she shall rear my dusky race.

Tennyson showed a man full of self-loathing, his imperialist tirade coming from the brink of madness. Yet Lear understood the drive to self-exile and the rejection of Victorian England and the mechanical 'march of mind' of steamship and railway. He was sensitive to Tennyson's

swerving attitude to progress, at once welcomed for the general good yet
regretted for the loss of the old. He felt, too, the underlying melancholy
and the curious stasis, the waiting and the lingering, the way that heroic
narrators like Ulysses might remain on the shore as if paralysed.

Tennyson's childhood outstripped Lear's for misery – his father was
a violent alcoholic and his family was haunted by feuds and madness –
but both men were nostalgic for a childhood that they had never really
had. 'Tears, idle tears' touched Lear's sense of happiness snatched away
but alive in memory – the acrobats of childhood, the days at Peppering,
the summers at Civitella:

> Tears, idle tears, I know not what they mean,
> Tears, from the depth of some divine despair
> Rise in the heart, and gather to the eyes,
> In looking on the happy Autumn-fields,
> And thinking of the days that are no more.

Although Lear hugely enjoyed life, and vividly described this enjoyment, he really did believe, as he once told Emily Tennyson, 'that I
enjoy hardly any one thing on earth while it is present: – always looking
back, or frettingly peering into the dim beyond'. This would always be
a feature of his emotional life: in 1881 he wrote to Chichester Fortescue,
'I am always fancying, and fancying in vain, that something different to
the life of the moment would be more endurable.'

For Tennyson 1850 was a miraculous year. In May he published *In Memoriam*, seventeen years in the writing; in June he finally married Emily
Sellwood, whom he had loved for almost as long; in November he succeeded Wordsworth as Poet Laureate.

Lear knew that the Lushingtons had played a crucial role in these
triumphs. Over the years, Edmund, Tennyson's fellow Apostle, had
read the poems prompted by the death of Arthur Hallam that would
become *In Memoriam*: Tennyson celebrated their friendship, 'the imperfect gift' of a grieving man, and Edmund's marriage to Cecilia gave

the poem its closing note of hope. The family, so fond of serious discussion, had also influenced *The Princess* in 1847. In the same year, Edmund and Cecilia brought Tennyson and Emily briefly together at Park House, the start of their rapprochement seven years after their early engagement had ended.

Lear met the Tennysons in the stormy late summer of 1850, when he and Frank Lushington called in on them at Tent Lodge, on the Marshalls' estate at Coniston in the Lake District. Lear was shy and eager, knowing that Tennyson, 'fiery Son of Gloom', as Thomas Carlyle called him, could be unpredictable: charismatic and affable or sardonic and critical. He looked alarming too, a towering figure, dishevelled and unkempt. While Lear and Tennyson got on amicably, they never really understood each other. By contrast, Emily was easy to like. Carlyle reported to his wife Jane that marriage had made Tennyson far more cheerful and 'Mrs T also pleased me: a freckly, *round*-faced woman, rather tallish and without shape, a slight lisp too.' There was something '*kleinstadtisch*' – provincial – and unpromising about her at first, he thought, 'but she lights up bright glittering blue eyes when you speak, has wit, has sense'.

In the early spring of 1851, Emily had a still-born son and to help her recover the Tennysons went to northern Italy (avoiding Rome because of unrest and Venice because of fever), and stayed with the Lushingtons at Park House on their return while they looked for a house. Knowing of their Italian trip – though 'it seems rather late in the day to beg you & Tennyson to accept a small "wedding present"' – in December Lear sent Emily his *Illustrated Excursions in Italy*, and told her that long ago he had meant to do some landscapes to illustrate Tennyson's poems. He had set this aside – 'A thousand things have stepped in between me & my wishes,' he wrote – but 'There have been but few weeks or days within the last 8 years, that I have not been more or less in the habit of remembering or reading Tennyson's poetry, & the amount of pleasure derived by me from them has been quite beyond reckoning.' He hoped to call on them in Twickenham, but in the cold and fogs of a London winter he had resorted to 'a kind of hybernating tortoise-ship'.

Emily immediately asked him to stay for the weekend, 'and we will try to get Frank Lushington to come too that you may have the more agreeable recollections of Twickenham and be tempted to come again and again'. She soon became a confidante. That winter, working alone in Sussex, he confessed all his self-doubts to her: 'It is a sad evil with me that I think I can do so much more than I ever can do: & that I have so little faith in my power of improvement. Whether I shall ever see my-self in a fair groove of improvement is very doubtful now.' ('Groove' is such a Tennysonian word.)

Emily, then, was a woman he could talk to, but he also hoped that she might act as a bridge between him and Tennyson. Even on his first reading of the *Poems*, he explained later, 'I thought that if I tried to illus-trate portions of the Tennyson Poetry by combining Poetical treatment with Topographical accuracy, I might eventually produce an original & beautiful work.' That idea drew on a popular format of the 1830s, often involving several illustrators, such as Rogers's *Italy*, Charles Tilt's *Land-scape Illustrations* of Scott's Waverley novels, and William and Edward Finden's *Landscape and Portrait Illustrations of the Life and Works of By-ron.* (This included several subjects by Turner, who went on to illustrate the many volumes of Scott's *Poetical Works* and *Prose Works*.) But by the time he met Tennyson, Lear's project had evolved into a different form.

In the autumn of 1852, when he was staying with Holman Hunt – also an avid Tennyson fan – he outlined his idea to Emily. He had arranged many subjects for illustration, he said, and recently he had:

extracted & placed in a sort of order all the lines which convey to me in the most decided manner his genius for the perception of the beautiful in Landscape, & I have divided them into 'suggestive' and 'Positive': & altogether there are 124 subjects in the 2 volumes. (I have not included the Princess or In Memoriam). By 'suggestive' I mean such lines as
  'vast images in glittering dawn' —
  'Hateful is the dark blue sky —
  &c&c&c – which are adaptable to any country or a wide scope of scenery.
  By 'positive' – such as —

— 'The lonely *moated grange* —
— 'They cut away my tallest *pines* —
— 'A huge *crag platform* . . .
'The balmy moon of blessed *Israel* —
&c &c – which indicate perforce certain limits of landscape.

He was more qualified than most to illustrate these, he thought, as he already had many sketches from nature, from many countries.

Lear's odd idea of taking single lines and painting landscapes that matched them was curiously in tune with the way Tennyson himself thought. Later in life, Tennyson told his son Hallam that in a kind of re-verse process, he had once jotted down responses to landscape as inspi-ration for poems. Passages were not suggested to him by Wordsworth or Shelley or another poet, he insisted:

There was a period in my life when, as an artist, Turner for instance, takes rough sketches of landskip, etc., in order to work them into some great picture, so I was in the habit of chronicling, in four or five words or more, whatever might strike me as picturesque in Nature. I never put these down, and many and many a line has gone away on the north wind, but some remain: e.g.
A full sea glazed with muffled moonlight.
Suggestion.
The sea one night at Torquay . . . The sky was covered with thin vapour,
and the moon behind it.
A great black cloud
Drags inward from the deep.
Suggestion.
A coming storm seen from the top of Snowdon.

By contrast, Lear looked at his own sketches for scenes that 'sug-gested' the lines to him as a reader. Offering to send Emily a list, he said that he had begun three or four subjects and hoped for Tenny-son's permission to continue. She responded at once, and kindly. A week later, Lear invited them down to spend Sunday at Clive Vale, telling Tennyson that there was a cliff 'on purpose to smoke on – &

nobody near'. That November, when they took a house not far away at Seaford, escaping London once Tennyson finished his 'Ode on the Death of the Duke of Wellington', his first work as Poet Laureate, Lear dashed over to see them. He had missed Hallam's christening in October, and now brought what Emily called a 'Roman Catholic doll' for him, that 'A. said perverted our Hallam from the pure protestant worship of morning light on the bedpost.' Lear was in a happy mood, illustrated by one of his flying drawings: 'I shall come all crookedwise a wandering about the hills . . . How windy it will be on those downs.'

Their first meetings were warm but they hardly felt momentous. At one point in the rush of laying out his grand scheme, Lear drew breath: 'But of that there is time enough to think.' Time there was – this would be a lifetime's work. Other illustrators, including Lear's Pre-Raphaelite friends, focused on Tennyson's characters: in 1850 Hunt drew the Lady of Shalott caught in her web, recoiling from the curse, her story told in roundels encircling the broken mirror. A few years later, in 1857, the Brotherhood drew many illustrations for the woodcuts in Edward Moxon's illustrated edition, and Hunt contributed six, with a new Lady of Shalott laden with Christian and magical symbolism. (Tennyson was baffled: 'I must now ask you', he pressed Hunt, 'why did you make the Lady of Shalott, in the illustration, with her hair wildly tossed about as if by a tornado?' and 'Why did you make the web wind round and round her like the threads of a cocoon?')

Lear's interest was not in character but in Tennyson's mood pictures in sound. He chose lines with echoing vowels, evoking sea and shore, mountain and cliff, dusk and twilight: 'A cedar spread his dark green layers of shade', 'A light upon the shining sea', 'Rosy blossom in hot ravine', 'of shadowy granite in a gleaming pass'. In particular, over time, he illustrated a lyrical poem addressed to himself – 'To E.L. on His Travels in Greece', which Tennyson wrote after reading his *Journal of a Landscape Painter in Greece and Albania*, in 1852.

Illyrian woodlands, echoing falls
Of water, sheets of summer glass,
The long divine Peneian pass,
The vast Akrokeraunian walls,

Tomohrit, Athos, all things fair,
With such a pencil, such a pen,
You shadow forth to distant men,
I read and felt that I was there:

This is almost self-mockingly 'Tennysonian' but it is also a nod to Lear's own love of onomatopoeic diction, like the craggy, rocky 'Akrokeraunian' range hiding the gulf of Dukhades.

With the pivotal line, 'I read and felt that I was there', Tennyson moved from writer to reader, from record to feeling. His reading of Lear was partial and personal, as his title suggested with its casual relocation of Albanian places to 'Greece', and the inclusion of Athos, which, of course, Lear had not reached. Tracking Lear, Tennyson stepped towards his own 'classic ground', a sensuous, unspecific pastoral:

And trust me while I turn'd the page,
And track'd you still on classic ground,
I grew in gladness till I found
My spirits in the golden age.

For me the torrent ever pour'd
And glisten'd – here and there alone
The broad-limb'd gods at random thrown
By fountain urns; – and Naiads oar'd

A glimmering shoulder under gloom
Of cavern pillars; on the swell
The silver lily heaved and fell;
And many a slope was rich in bloom

From him that on the mountain lea
By dancing rivulets fed his flocks,
To him who sat upon the rocks,
And fluted to the morning sea.

The land is both timeless and full of motion – torrents pouring, Naiads
rowing, lilies heaving, streams dancing – and at the end, perhaps, we
meet Lear again, the man who played his flute or guitar by the sea and
marked the 'rox' so carefully in his sketches.

The exchange turned each man's gaze back on himself, but though
flattered, Tennyson was always a little remote from Lear's passionate
project. Lear 'has painted one very fine picture "Morn broaden'd on
the borders of the dark", from a landscape near Rome,' he told Emily
in 1864, apparently forgetting he had seen a version almost ten years
before. The line, from 'A Dream of Fair Women', Lear said, seemed to
describe exactly 'what I had so often watched in other days, that Darkness, edged with broadening light, which I had seen through so many
summer and autumn months during years of Italian wanderings, and
most of all from the neighbourhood of Civitella'. This became one of
the key drawings of his Tennyson series.

Over the coming year, as he struggled with Pre-Raphaelite dictates about painting outdoors, and with his own longing to recreate the closeness to Frank Lushington that had made him so happy in Greece four years before, he began to long to leave rainy, stressful England. He started to look for escapes. In October 1853, he told Hunt that Charles Church had asked him to go up the Blue Nile – but he was also dreaming of Athens, Spain or Malta.

As he wrote, the country was heading towards war. Russian determination to break the Ottoman Empire had become ever clearer, and Turkish ships in the Black Sea were now under attack. The British government, worried about the threat to trade routes through the Mediterranean, had already sent a fleet to the Dardanelles. Lear joked about fighting the Russians – or going to Australia – when he told Emily that he longed to earn a living that would let him get away:

But stay here I *won't*, to be demoralised by years of mud & fog & gnats and rheumatism & small beer & stupid boors and coalfires and choleramorbusses and income taxes and Calvinists and steel forks and midnight atmospheres all the year round – I have had enough of it, & forthwith I am growing moustaches in sign of going elsewhere.

It would be a wrench to leave, he admitted to Hunt, but 'nevertheless I have not shaved my upper lip for a fortnight'. (He grew moustaches and a beard on his travels, but always shaved them off when he got back.)

At the end of October his lungs and throat were worse and he insisted to Emily that he was off at once, 'to see "the Palms and Temples of the South"'. The allusion was to Tennyson's 'You ask me, why'. England was a land of progress, the poem insisted, of 'sober-suited freedom', of liberty of speech, of empire building,

> Yet waft me from the harbour-mouth,
> Wild wind! I seek a warmer sky,
> And I will see before I die
> The palms and temples of the South.

Lear took the train to Southampton, to sail to Alexandria. Before he left he worked on his settings of four Tennyson songs. 'I have left a set of songs with Frank Lushington, for your acceptance,' he told Emily. He had been working on these all summer. They were to be published as a volume, 'inscribed to Mrs Alfred Tennyson', but also sold separately as sheet music for two shillings each. When he sent them to the printers he begged for 'Tears, idle tears' to be done first.

19: AN OWL IN THE DESERT

There was an Old Person of Philae,
Whose conduct was scroobious and wily;
He rushed up a Palm, when the weather was calm,
And observed all the ruins of Philae.

The next two years were ones of travel and work, and, in Lear's emotional life, of a deepening closeness to Chichester Fortescue and Emily Tennyson, as well as a frustration that he could not regain his intimacy with Frank. Travel came first, escape from the cold. In January 1854 Lear was sketching in the sun on the small island of Philae on the the Nile, with 'enough to occupy an artist for months'. His party left their boats and took everything they needed to sleep and cook, sweeping out rooms in the great temple. English visitors arrived all the time, he told Ann:

so we have dinner parties, & music every evening nearly. As for me I have been at work every day throughout the whole daylight hours, & so charming is the place & the climate that I shall be very sorry to leave it. It is impossible to describe the place to you, any further than by saying it is more like a real *fairy island* than anything else I can compare it to. It is very small, & was formerly all covered with temples, of which the ruins of 5 or 6 now only remain.

As he wrote he was sitting on the terrace of the Temple of Isis, watching the Nile flow round the rocky islets, with the desert and the hills of Aswan beyond: 'at morning & evening the scene is lovely beyond imagination'. On the oil painting of Philae that he made on his return, he wrote his Tennyson line: 'Philae – "I will see before I die/ The Palms & Temples of the South"'. He gave up trying to paint in oils as the colours dried too fast in the heat, the tubes stuck and the sand got into them. Watercolours were difficult too but he made many drawings, happy to return to his old ways. He was entranced by the colours, particularly the lingering light after the sun set, leaving the sky 'all in broad stripes of lilac, green, rose, & amber'.

His journey out had been surprisingly smooth, indeed 'perfectly wonderful'. A Hornby nephew and niece and Chichester Fortescue's nephew were on board, 'so we make up a very pleasant party of our own'. The Biscay storms held off, the meals were good and there was 'a piano and all sorts of games'. As he walked on deck his anxieties fell away. In Cairo, he met up with the painter Thomas Seddon and over Christmas they waited for Hunt to join them. In the meantime Lear painted, tried to learn Arabic, and met the mysterious Sir Richard Burton, who had left his job with the East India Company to go on the Hajj to Mecca, disguised as a pilgrim. Seddon sketched him, and Lear painted two watercolour sketches of him in Arab dress, vividly sombre.

Impatient at Hunt's delay while he finished *The Light of the World*, Lear joined a flotilla of English tourists sailing up the Nile to Aswan. 'Don't laugh!' he told Ann, but they would start '4 boats together, & 3 more go before, & 5 or 6 follow after!!' Heading slowly up the great wide river they slept in villages under a brilliant moon and woke to drink fresh buffalo milk for breakfast. Lear wore a flat leghorn hat covered with white calico for the shade: seeing him, a small boy said '"oh thou! Who wearest a turban resembling a dinner table" – so I am called "the father of the dinner tables" ever since!' He walked on the banks through green corn and broad-bean fields in bloom, but the most beautiful feature, he thought, was 'the number of boats, which look like giant moths'. Around and above him were birds, milk-white

herons, pelicans and cranes, eagles and hawks: 'Turtle doves, King-
fishers & Hoopoes are like flies in number, & Pigeons in vast flights of
hundreds. But today I heard a universal quacking, & looking up, saw
one of those astonishing flights of geese so remarkable here. *All the sky
was covered with a web.*'

On their way back they stopped at Luxor, the ancient Thebes, and
at the ruins of Karnak, 'a great forest of columns grown out of the
ground'. In Cairo Lear overlapped with Hunt, who was finally on his
way to Palestine. Lear dithered, but decided not to go with him: instead
he would go home.

Lear was back in London in late April 1854, fitter and fatter, with a
huge bushy beard and a portfolio stuffed with sketches. But he was still
restless and impatient, and by midsummer he was abroad again, walking in the Bernese Alps with Bernard Husey Hunt ('Bern', formerly
Bernard Senior), trekking up to the Reichenbach Falls that Turner had
painted, and past the Rhône glacier, 'like a ladies "goffrée" frill or
ruffle – all of ice – 20 miles long!' After Bern went home, Lear walked
on alone to Interlaken, always hoping that Frank would come and join
him, an idea mooted before he left. Earlier they had planned to go to the
Pyrenees together, but instead Frank and his sister Ellen had gone to
Malta to bring back their ill sister Louisa: she died in Frank's arms in
Avignon on their way home, and now he was plunged in grief.

With his nonsense rhymes Lear often drew a figure in a tree, on a
wall, up a ladder – somewhere up high, looking down, surveying the
scene in calm weather. But in his Philae limerick his 'scroobious and
wily' old man looks apprehensive: when you are high up, you can fall.
In the autumn after Lear returned from the Alps England seemed a land
of fogs and icy winds and sadness. Emily invited him affectionately to
come for Christmas but as the cold set in and his asthma grew worse,
he holed himself up until spring came. Over time, he saw that his depressions were often linked to winter darkness: 'I have been wondering
if on the whole,' he wrote a few years later, 'the being influenced to

an extreme by everything in natural or physical life, *i.e.* atmosphere, light, shadow, and all the variety of day and night, – is a blessing or the contrary – and the end of my speculation has been that "things must be as they may", and the best is to make the best of what happens.'

It was hard to make the best of things, and lack of sun was not the only cause of gloom. The whole country was preoccupied by the conflict with Russia. In the spring French and British troops had been sent to Gallipoli to counter the threat to the Balkans and the Danube, while a naval force confronted the Russian navy in the Baltic. Many debated the wisdom of this involvement, and Lear found it hard to discuss. He could not share the wholehearted enthusiasm for war expressed by Frank and Henry Lushington. When the first troops went out, Frank wrote two patriotic poems, one on the Baltic fleet and the other on 'The Muster of the Guards', coloured, perhaps, by a sedentary lawyer's envy for a life of action:

> Cheer boys, cheer! Till you crack a thousand throats,
> The cannons are God's preachers, when the time is ripe for War.

There was little movement over the summer but in September British troops landed in the Crimea, aiming to take the vital port of Sebastopol. Great battles followed: Alma in September; Balaclava in October; Inkerman in November. In response, the brothers wrote more poems, Henry on Inkerman and Frank on Alma, with bloodthirsty gusto:

> Charge! Up to the belching muzzles – charge! Drive the bayonet home:
> Oh God, do we live or die? What's Death, what Life, in the cry
> As we reel to the gory summit, all fire with the murderous climb.

Tennyson's 'Charge of the Light Brigade', on the remaining battle, Balaclava, was published in *The Examiner* in December. When the War Office circulated copies to the troops it became widely known as 'Someone had blundered'.

This was the first time that war correspondents in the field sent news humming across telegraph wires to London and the accounts of the battles and the year-long siege of Sebastopol shocked the public. As people learned of the freezing cold, the casualties, and the dysentery, malaria and cholera that left over fourteen thousand British troops in the camp hospitals, feelings ran high against the war. But Henry and Frank still argued loudly for British aggression. The Preface to their poems, collected as *Two Battle Pieces*, was a bold rallying cry: 'We are united as a people: that is, we are at war, and we all wish to win. Traitors in England there are none, except *Indifference*.' This was no time for agonised reflection: 'For a moment, dearly as we love him, let Hamlet stand aside . . . we want Fortinbras just now.'

Turning his back on war and politics, over the winter of 1854–5 Lear stayed in his studio, painting watercolours and warming himself with memories of the Nile and the sun. Many people had commissioned paintings based on his sketches, including Harriet, Lady Ashburton, who wanted an oil of Philae: Lear painted *The Approach to Philae* for her, the landscape of a dream, its temples moored like a great boat among the rocks.

Philae (1863)

But although he worked hard and visitors called constantly, he felt marooned and lonely, and when he went out he was on edge. Once,

after Fortescue invited him to a dinner with Lady Waldegrave, he realised that he might have offended her by refusing to sing when asked.
Mortified, he pleaded that he was ill from the bitter east winds, '& so
completely uncertain whether I had any voice or not, that I thought it
better not to sing, than to go to the piano & be obliged to quit it. I felt
like a cow who has swallowed a glass bottle – or a boiled weasel – &
should probably have made a noise like a dyspeptic mouse in a fit.'

The whimsy was telling: when he was low Lear always felt closer
to the animals than to the smart people around him. It was hardly surprising that he quailed at being driven to the piano as his hostess, the
blonde, flamboyant Frances, Lady Waldegrave, was the daughter of
the famous tenor John Braham, and her brother Charles was an opera
singer. In her early thirties Frances was already on her third husband.
Her first, John Waldegrave, illegitimate son of the sixth Earl Waldegrave, had died in 1839 within a year of their marriage, and then she
swiftly married his half-brother George, the seventh earl. He too died,
in 1846 from cirrhosis of the liver, leaving her all the family estates, including Horace Walpole's Strawberry Hill. The next year, she married
the widower George Harcourt MP, thirty-six years her senior, son of
a former Archbishop of York and a sober contrast to the wild Walde-
graves. At Nuneham in Oxfordshire and at Strawberry Hill, which
she restored in great style, she became a dazzling hostess, and made
their London house in Carlton Gardens a leading salon for the Liberal
leaders. Fortescue had fallen in love with her in 1850 when he saw her
bowling down Piccadilly in her carriage with her back to the wind.
(Trollope allegedly used her as the model for Madame Max Goesler
in his Palliser novels, and Fortescue for Phineas Finn.) Ever since, he
had followed her with devotion, included in all her parties but kept at
arm's length. Lear was a sympathetic confidant to his apparently hopeless passion, suggesting a remedy that he had tried for himself – work.
'By the bye', Fortescue wrote, 'I admire the excellence of your advice
to me touching occupation. I am putting it in practice and so fighting
against indescribable feelings which sometimes assault me.'

Lear was rather pleased that Fortescue whisked him into the Walde-grave world, so much brighter and livelier than that of the Lushingtons. In the Park House atmosphere Frank seemed withdrawn and lacking direction. He was now thirty-three and in the spring of 1855, encour-aged by Lear, who sought Fortescue's influence as an MP, he applied for the post of judge to the Supreme Court of Justice in the Ionian islands, based in Corfu. Yet when the post was offered he hesitated, until it seemed it might go to someone else, when he finally accepted. He sailed in May, and Lear joined the goodbye parties to see him off from Dover. In the weeks after Frank sailed, Lear tried to shore up his place as a family friend by looking after Cecilia and Edmund's ailing son Eddy, giving Cecilia an album of drawings, making a nonsense alphabet for their daughter Zilly's tenth birthday. In London, he met up with the Lushingtons and Tennysons among the groups going to see the Crystal Palace on its new site on Sydenham Hill. And at Frank's suggestion he invited Edmund, Tennyson and friends to come and see his Nile draw-ings. 'I of course would be happy to make friends with the Nile,' replied Tennyson, fitting this in with a trip to the dentist and then realising next day that he had promised to see Carlyle: 'Don't bore yourself to give a dinner. I love you all, as well undined.'

Lear was trying to be sociable and cheery, as all his friends expected him to be. In June Wilkie Collins gave a party for Millais, who was off to Scotland to marry Effie Ruskin, and Lear went along. But he was a lot older than this starry, laddish gang of young artists and writers, and confessed in a letter to Tennyson that he felt out of it, on the fringes, 'woundily like a spectator . . . very little an actor. David's particular Pelican in the Wilderness was a fool to what I have been all my days, whether in a crowd or not.' The reference, which he used more than once, was to the most desolate of psalms:

Hear my prayer, O Lord, and let my cry come unto thee.

Hide not thy face from me in the day when I am in trouble; incline thine ear unto me: in the day when I call answer me speedily.

For my days are consumed like smoke, and my bones are burned as an
  hearth.
My heart is smitten, and withered like grass; so that I forget to eat my bread.
By reason of the voice of my groaning my bones cleave to my skin.
I am like a pelican of the wilderness: I am like an owl of the desert.
I watch, and am as a sparrow alone upon the house top.

In the same letter, he wondered if there was a farmhouse or an inn
near the Tennysons ('a Pharmouse or a Nin' – his nonsense a sign of
nerves) where he could stay and paint. The Tennysons' summer was
fraught, troubled by attacks on the newly published *Maud*, but Lear
did visit them briefly at Farringford, the cliff-top house that they were
renting at Freshwater in the Isle of Wight, which they bought the following year.

Then came a blow. In July the Lushington family heard that Henry
had fallen ill in Malta. He was trying to make his way home but when
his close friend George Stovin Venables met him in Arles, he found him
weak and gaunt, and by the time he reached Paris he was clearly dying.
While Edmund and his sister Emily rushed over to Paris, Lear hurried
down and joined the family in their summer home at Eastbourne. It
was awkward, and he felt hurt and rebuffed, as if his presence was a
nuisance. He asked Emily Tennyson miserably if he should go or stay.
He was right to stay, she insisted: 'As Frank's friend you could not, I
am sure, be in any place where you would so much wish to be.' It was
true that he was useful: 'Mr Lear is very good and kind to us all,' Cecilia
told Edmund. Frank himself hurried back from Corfu, but Henry died
in Paris on 11 August, the day before he arrived. When the brothers
brought the body home the atmosphere was increasingly dark and Lear
worried that he should leave. Once again Emily Tennyson cheered him:
'Frank will make it all easy for you and you will find you are a comfort
and blessing,' she wrote, the day after Henry's funeral: 'You must be
good and not morbid and be with him as much as you can. I feel one, or
at least I myself, often errs grievously through what in worldly parlance

one calls shyness, what in higher and sterner language is want of faith in God and Man.' She was sure the Lushingtons were 'at heart grateful and sympathising, though the gift of utterance is except upon rare occasions denied them'.

Frozen by the silence, Lear dashed up to see Fortescue, who was staying at one of Lady Waldegrave's mansions, Dudbrook Hall in Essex. Lear was in low spirits, Fortescue noted, and revealed 'more of himself, his secret feelings, than he has ever done, showed me a good deal of his great and self-tormenting sensitiveness'.

Trying to salve Frank's deep distress, and to cheer Lear up, Emily invited them both to Farringford, warning Lear briskly that he had hard work ahead. 'Not only are you to be sofa to my shyness and Frank's silence, but you are to be yourself wellest and freshest and happiest.' They put the visit off until mid-October, and by then both men had relaxed. It was a happy time: Frank walked the grounds with Tennyson and his neighbour Sir John Simeon, and Emily arranged a dinner, only to be overwhelmed that she had overlooked Simeon's Roman Catholicism and forgotten 'Friday and fish'. Luckily, 'Mr Lear's singing made us forget this, whatever else it brought to mind. He sang for two or three hours.' (What did she mean by 'whatever else it brought to mind'?) Many listeners admired Lear's settings of Tennyson – including Tennyson himself, who said they were the only arrangements he liked – but some of the more musical ones winced. Millais thought he hummed rather than sang, and Charlotte Schreiber dismissed the songs briskly: 'They are mostly pretty things but he has no voice, and, on the whole, it is rather painful to listen to him.' But on this visit, Lear's music made one guest, Miss Cotton, the daughter of a local landowner, so transported that she spent a sleepless night. Reporting Lear's success as 'a hero of romance', Emily was, perhaps, trying to make a match. Frank, amused, encouraged the idea, but Lear shrugged it hastily off, slipping into an image that implied, almost openly, that his appearance might deceive: 'Alack! For Miss Cotton! And all admirers. But we all know about the beautiful glass jar which was only a white one after all, only there was blue water inside it.'

They left early in a morning mist, with Tennyson and Emily watching their boat through their telescope. A week later Emily wrote to Lear, 'I am afraid you are in some mischief as we do not hear from you, gnawing your own heart or doing some other cannibal thing of the kind.' It was true, he agreed, he had been 'jarry & out of tune'. Yet, he reassured her, he remembered every detail of their visit: the mushrooms at breakfast; the boy dashing in; 'You, Alfred & Frank begin to talk like Gods together careless of mankind.'

I even complain sometimes that such rare flashes of light as such visits are to me, make the path darker after they are over: – a bright blue & green landscape with purple hills, & winding rivers, & unexplored forests, and airy downs, & trees & birds, & all sorts of calm repose – exchanged for a dull dark plain, horizonless, pathless, & covered with clouds above, while beneath are brambles & weariness.

The pathless plain was a rural version of Tennyson's image of loss: 'On the bald street breaks the blank day'. As consolation for the lost mirage, Lear spun a brief fantasy about the future, imagining the Tennysons settling near Park House, and himself in his old age, going 'cripply cripply' across the hills to see their grandchildren and Frank's grandchildren '& so slide pleasantly out of life'.

After Henry's death, a major question was whether Frank should return to Corfu. Lear thought he should go, before he was warped by life at Park House, but his sisters wanted him to stay. After terrible tension, Frank decided to go. For a time it seemed that his sister Ellen could go out to look after him, but rumours of cholera scotched this. Instead Lear would travel with him: the prospect was exactly what he dreamed of – sunshine, Greece, and Frank. Before they left he read a last letter from Emily: 'You are not alone, Mr Lear,' she wrote, 'you cannot be while you can be so much to those so very dear to you, to those to whom so few are anything but the mere outside world. But one would be all and in that one cannot be, here is the loneliness . . . God bless you, dear Mr Lear,' she ended, 'and prosper you in your labour of love.'

20: HALF A LIFE: CORFU AND ATHOS

On 21 November 1855 Lear sailed from Dover with Frank Lushington, carrying in his pocket a conker that little Hallam Tennyson had given him. After a long train journey they reached Prague in blinding snow, before circling round to Vienna and south to Trieste. 'Was there ever such luck as mine in sailing!' wrote Lear, as they steamed down the Adriatic. 'The sea was perfectly smooth, so that one ate & drank, & read & wrote & slept just as if in a house.' But Corfu, which he had looked forward to so eagerly, was full of troops on their way to the Crimea, and George Bowen, now chief secretary to the government of the Ionian islands, only had room to put up Lushington. On their first night Lear struggled to find a bed. Then it was tricky to rent good rooms. Officers and their families had taken houses, prices had risen and those remaining were 'some too high up – some too low down – some with wrong lights – some too dear'. When Lear finally found rooms overlooking the harbour, the rain fell, lightning flashed and winds blew.

Beneath the surface Corfu was tense. The war was on everyone's mind. The islanders supported the Russians, their fellow Christians, and were horrified by British support of their old enemies the Muslim Turks. The British stuck closely together, ignoring the islanders. At the palace the ease and friendliness Lear remembered from 1848 had given way to 'great etiquette and gaiety', and he missed the bustle of London, the twice-daily post, the newspapers, the casual calling in and flow of invitations. With Frank caught up in official business – 'Poor boy, such loads of work' – he was so lonely that he begged Ann to write once a week, even a single line.

It seems that Lear had hoped that in Corfu he and Frank would become closer, perhaps becoming a couple, at least reaching the 'philosophical' love of the Apostles' circle, the love of Tennyson for Arthur Hallam, of George Stovin Venables for Henry Lushington, of Frank himself for Henry Hallam – whose friendship, he wrote, had been 'a necessity of existence'. But to Frank Lear was a different kind of friend, an older, kindly, amusing mentor. Frank's reserve also held him back: he could never match Lear's craving for affection, his desire to be needed. He was moody, insecure, over-serious. 'I suppose there is such an immense "fonds" of discontent at the bottom of my character', he confided to Emily Tennyson, 'that no possible combination of present and future will satisfy me.' No diaries for these years or letters between them have been found, and many papers were destroyed. Only Lear's account survives.

When Lear saw that the intimacy he longed for was impossible, his spirit crumbled. He paced his rooms weeping, lay and stared at the ceiling, unable to paint, and brooded on going home or back to Rome. He would always look back on this winter as the darkest time of his life. Slowly, he pulled himself back by focusing on his art and on Corfu itself: 'I certainly should like to do one or 2 large paintings of Corfu – for no place in all the world is so lovely, I think.' He looked across to the mountains of Albania, covered in snow, '& though there were still storms about, every part of this beautiful island was like purple & blue & gold & crimson velvet as the sun went down'. Walking up to the village of Ascension (Análipsis), he decided that this was the best view of the town and the bay, and made sketches that would be the basis of many paintings over the years.

On the steep hill to Ascension, Lear rediscovered his love of oddity and detail:

On the way up, I saw 2 gentlemen digging in a bank, & found they were looking for the Trap spiders so common here; these make a long nest, & shut it with a door, out of which they bound, upon flies & beetles, – but if you try to open it they stick their claws into little holes & prevent you. I shall try to get one, to send poor little Eddie Lushington.

Corfu from Ascension (1862)

Slowly his bounce came back. He got to know his landlord, Demetrius Kourkoumeli, and his family, especially his tall, dark-eyed daughter Effrosini, 'Foffy', a good friend for many years. He painted, braced himself to make calls, congratulated Bowen on his engagement to Contessa Diamantina di Roma, daughter of the Senate president. At the weekly palace receptions people asked him to dinner and parties and he grew to like the army officers and the civil officials, particularly the Chief Justice, Sir James Reid, and his wife: 'They are very nice, plain, kind people and asked me to come often.' Best of all, he saw more of Frank: they took long walks, dined together and went to the opera, and Lear sympathised with his anxieties. The weather cheered up and he drew outside in the sun among trees full of tiny green frogs which filled the air with duck-like quacking. On a cloudless Christmas Day Frank gave him a gold watch with a silver chain, valuable in itself but more so to Lear, because it had been Frank's own, and the watch chain had belonged to Harry: it seemed that he was, after all, being drawn into the family.

When the New Year came anemones and violets began to appear. Lear watched the boats bringing cattle, horses, pigs and sheep from Albania, tipped into the sea to swim ashore: 'Just now', he wrote at the end of January 1856, 'all the harbour is full of black pigs – swimming away like a shoal of porpoises!' He began to sell small views and these, plus his larger pictures of Philae and Parnassus, more than paid his rent. He felt more hopeful about his art, and when he was offered the post of director at a School of Art in the university, with a house and a salary of £100 a year, he turned it down, feeling sure that his 'progress as a painter would be wholly knocked up'. (A pity, as the Ionian Academy was a colourful place, established by the Philhellene Frederick North, Earl of Guilford, a convert to the Greek Orthodox Church: the poet Andreas Kalvo taught there and its pupils 'bound their hair like Hermes' and wore tunics and cloaks, and knee-high, red-leather buskins.)

Lear was fascinated again by the local people, the women in their colourful costumes, the bearded, black-robed priests and the kilted Albanian shepherds. His sketches showed that he could, when he wanted, draw people extremely well. With the sunshine the anxious letters to Ann dropped back to every two weeks, and then three. 'All the Court (as I call it) came to my rooms in a body on Thursday,' he reported. Lady Young, wife of the High Commissioner, was particularly keen: her husband Sir John told Fortescue that they found Lear 'a great addition to our society, and we all like him very much – especially Lady Young, who has taken to sketching with great ardour'. A couple of months later the big room at the palace was 'all over Lear', since she not only hung her own purchases but borrowed other people's to copy. But there were drawbacks :

the Court has taken a whim of coming to see me sketch, which disturbs and annoys me. That is to say Lady Young & her suite – galloping furiously on 12 or 16 horses, come rushing through my quiet olive groves, & quite destroy the repose of the landscape. However they are soon off again for Her Ladyship (our gracious sovereign) seldom remains long in one place.

Ann was not to report this in case it circled back: 'this is *such* a place for gossip!' 'We Corfiotes', he wrote once, 'seize a bit of local news with great avidity, & I think of ruminating cattle when I find the same atom of speculation coming up over & over again 10 times a day.'

Lear quite liked being a big fish in this small pond. In April Frank told Emily,

Lear having for the first month he was here asserted that he hated music more than any thing in the world, has now become the most admired musician in Corfu – a very much more natural position for him to occupy than that of a music-hater. He has done a good deal for the spreading of Alfred's reputation in these benighted shores.

By this point, when the countryside was a mass of wild flowers, he seemed thoroughly settled: 'all the fields have ceased to be green & are sheets of pink & lilac & yellow & blue. I never beheld anything so amazing.' He even went sailing – a proof of devotion from a man who hated boats – in *Midge*, Henry's old yacht that Frank had brought over from Malta. *Midge* was supposed to be comfortable, but Lear could not sleep for the 'screwy & squashy & fidgety noises'; he disliked the wind, and the dead calm even more: 'roll, roll, pitch, pitch, creaking, flapping and bumping till I could have thrown myself overboard'. When they landed in his favourite bay of Palaiokastritsa with its little monastery high on the cliff above, he uncurled gratefully after a week of knocking his head in a cramped cabin.

More enjoyably, they walked in the hills, exploring distant parts of the island. By now they had actually talked about sharing a house, and the difficulties that prevented it. And although Lear agreed it would not be wise to live together, as they were both nervous and fidgety and emotions could run high, they often behaved like a couple – without the sex – constantly bickering and making up. On dull days Lear wrote letters and read all the books at hand, old and new: the novels of Trollope and Bulwer Lytton, the poetry of Matthew Arnold and Clough and, of course, Tennyson. Frank, determined to educate him more seriously, said, 'I have set Lear upon Carlyle's *Past and Present*, as the easiest dose I could give him – and on his expression of a wish for more gave him the *Sartor Resartus* to try but I am afraid that has rather choked him off, to use the vulgar phrase.'

Lear studied Greek, took new rooms and hired a servant. 'Yorhi', soon 'Giorgio', Kokali had been born in Corfu after his Suliot family fled there during the civil war, and spoke Albanian, Greek and some Italian. He would work for Lear for the rest of his life.

In early summer Lear left for the hills to paint, following his old Civitella regime: rising early to sketch, reading, writing letters and practising his Greek, sleeping in the heat of the day, then sketching again until sunset, supper and bed. After a few weeks he moved on, to other remote hamlets, and finally back to Ascension. At the village fete he watched the women dancing in slow circles, in gorgeously coloured dresses, loaded with gold necklaces and heavy rings. It was a magical time: 'Last night the mountains at sunset were of the purest vermilion rose I ever saw! – & all the sea like glass or oil, was amber colour, reflecting the sky.'

Old friends appeared, including Charles Church, and, to his amazement, James Uwins, sporting a great grey beard: 'It seems but the other day – though really 19 years ago exactly that I walked from Rome to Naples with him.' But Lear also made new friends, like the Cortazzis, who lived in town in Condi Terrace but had a summer villa in Ascension. John Cortazzi was the British consul in Corfu: his wife Marianne was a Hornby and his sister had also married into the Hornby family, so for Lear the connections were close. He often called in to see them, 'though I am beginning to call the house "Castle Dangerous"', he said, 'because of the 2 young ladies, – & of the difficulty of getting away when one has gone there. If I were not such an ancient owl, I believe I should fall victim to the eldest, – but I am resolved to run if I find myself growing silly.' The younger sister, Madeleine, was prettier, but the older, Helena, intrigued Lear more, though she was 'not thought half as much of as that large Miss A.Z. who can only talk English and dance polkas'. Helena translated Tennyson into Italian, set his poems to music and knew every word of *In Memoriam*, or so Lear told Emily, who was, of course, delighted. He told Holman Hunt too about the girls:

so full of poetry & good taste, & grace & all the nettings whereby men are netted – I begin to think I must either run for it or rush into extremes – & as neither they nor I have money, am I not a fool for thinking about it? Yet sometimes at 43 I cannot help believing that life as half life will get too wearisome to bear ere long. The elder is my alarm – but the younger is prettier – o papa! What a blasted old ass your son is.

Lear chewed over this dilemma, mulling over the declaration in *The Princess*,

> Either sex alone
> Is half itself, and in true marriage lies
> Nor equal, nor unequal . . .

Helena was twenty years his junior and the idea of union, of Tennyson's perfect 'two-celled animal', was hard to envisage. His interest was genuine but the impulse to run was stronger. He had once told Fortescue in a sour mood that if married he would paint less well 'and the thought of annual infants would drive me wild. If I attain to 65, and have an "establismt" with lots of spoons &c to offer – I *may* chain myself: – but surely not before.' And, seriously, he asked, when he looked around at the married couples they knew, 'do I see a majority of happy pairs? No, I don't.' Yet he did not brush off Helena's spell straight away. Two years later, after Mrs Cortazzi's death, the family went to Odessa, but when they returned to England Lear tried to track them down in Manchester and Brighton: 'A world of thought about H.C.' he wrote.

Lear encountered another disturbing half-life in late summer. Frank was planning to cross to Albania and Lear decided to go with him and then to travel on to Yannina and, if possible, 'the long desired Mount Athos', the Holy Mountain. This mountainous, densely wooded peninsula on the northern Greek coast had been a monastic enclave since the eighth century, blessed, according to legend, when the Virgin Mary and St John the Evangelist were blown off course on a voyage to Cyprus. It was the Virgin's sacred garden, and no other female, human or animal, was allowed to enter there.

To make his way across country, Lear obtained papers from the British consuls who had been sent to Albanian towns during the Crimean war in an effort to keep the country neutral. Then he and Giorgio set off. They began by staying with Jaffier Pasha in Philates (modern Filiates, opposite Corfu). In his old Turkish courtyard house, its high walls black with jackdaws and towers white with storks, Lear fell down a flight of stone stairs and sprained his back, but he knew, he said, that the best thing was to go on – and so they did, crossing the mainland to Katerina on the Aegean coast, where they lingered hungrily waiting for a boat to Salonica. From there he could write letters to worried friends. He had been away for a month, Frank reported to Emily:

verifying Alfred's's poem about his travels – i.e. at last visiting Mount Athos. I heard from him a few days ago from Salonica – I was very glad to hear from him as he was not at all in condition for hard travelling when he started through a very rough & not always safe country . . . he began unluckily with a fall and after a fortnight still had to be lifted on & off his horse for fear of re-straining the muscles.

Still, Frank admitted fondly, 'He is one of the people pre-eminently gifted with a genius for travelling – and Athos is what he has always wanted to see.'

After a fifty-mile walk, Lear could at last glimpse Mount Athos, 'a high peak on a bluer sea – seen above the most wondrous forest of beech I ever beheld'. The Holy Synod that controlled the peninsula made them welcome, but the constant prayer and chanting and the 'atmosphere of falsehood and ignorance' irritated Lear beyond bounds. He became 'positive that living alone – banishing all women whom God has made to be our equals & companions', utterly reversed God's will. Then Giorgio fell dangerously ill with fever, and Lear succumbed too, but in the end they managed to visit all the western monasteries. These were 'wondrous' and the scenery was stupendous, he wrote, but he would not go again to the Holy Mountain 'for any money, so gloomy, so shockingly unnatural, so lonely, so lying, so unatonably odious seems to me all the atmosphere of such monkery'. A Turk with six wives or a Jew working to feed his family would be more pleasing to God 'than these muttering, miserable, mutton-hating, man-avoiding, misogynic, morose, & merriment-marring, monotoning, many-mule-making, mocking, mournful, minced fish & marmalade masticating Monx. Poor old pigs! Yet one or two were kind enough in their way – dirty as they were: but it is not them, it is their system I rail at.'

His nonsense speech was uncomfortably, excessively intense in its alliterative insults. Did Lear recognise something of himself in the monks, something that he would rather not see? A few months later he joked that Fortescue should get Parliament to send out all the distressed needlewomen in Britain. They must be landed at once, '4000 at least', and make a rush for the nearest monastery.

Lear came back from Mount Athos with fifty images of this hidden world: later he would paint several watercolours and at least ten oils of the Athos peninsula. This was the strangest, most unsettling of his trips. Images of death and staggering beauty jostled in his mind.

I never saw any more striking scenes than those forest screens & terrible crags, all lonely lonely lonely: paths thro' them leading to hermitages where these dead men abide, – or to the immense monasteries where many hundred of these living corpses chant prayers nightly & daily: the blue sea dash dash against the hard iron rocks below – & the oak fringed or chesnut covered height above, with always the great peak of Athos towering over all things, & beyond all the island edged horizon of wide ocean.

He was horrified to think how 'many many thousand monks live on through a long long life of mere formal blank. God's world maimed &

The Monastery of Zografu, Athos

turned upside down'. 'Blank' was one of Lear's darkest negatives, used when he was at his lowest. In this sacred mountain, a place where he had looked for spiritual qualities, he had found only horror. Would his own life be a 'mere formal blank', a hermit's dead existence? His counter to 'blank' was not 'happy' or 'full' but 'wondrous', a vision of beauty beyond sense – and he found that in Athos too.

Writing to Emily during the long quarantine off Corfu, imposed due to new fears of cholera, he told her about his frustration with Frank, who would always assume he knew all the family news – like the illness of Eddy, who would die that October – yet neglected to tell him what was going on. There were rows:

The impetuosity of my nature cannot however always be controlled & we have had one or two sad antagonisms – tho we are perhaps better friends afterwards: but our natures are so different, & he is so changed since I first knew him, while I have remained so absurdly the same – (I mean, he has become 70 – & I have stuck at 20 or any boy-age all through my life –) that I feel convinced we are best when not with each other.

Yet even as he wrote, a letter arrived from 'Franky' full of the news that Lear thought he was holding back. Then Frank himself sailed over, bringing books, wine, meat and fruit. 'I am a beast and ought to be squashed,' Lear wrote remorsefully.

When an earthquake shook his rooms he jumped at the chance of moving to the smart Condi Terrace on the ramparts, next door to Frank and near to the Cortazzis. He had a huge airy room with a lovely north-eastern light to paint by. He liked all his neighbours. The flat up-stairs was taken by Major John Shakespear, who had fought at Alma, Inkerman and Balaclava, and had now been posted to the Corfu garri-son, and his wife Louisa, whom Lear thought one of the nicest women there, if not the nicest. He spent Christmas Day with the Cortazzis and Shakespears and the latter's new baby Ida, for whom he asked Ann to send a coral rattle with silver bells and a handle: 'Major Shakespear has been so good natured in helping me with my easel, that I want to make them some return, & as their little girl is my "Alarum" in the morning, I fixed on this little present-trifle.'

Franklin Lushington   Edward Lear   Revd Sydney Clark   Major Shakespear
Sir James Reid Mrs Shakespear Jemmy Mary and Helen Reid Lady Reid

In a brief spell of calm in early January 1857 Lear crossed to Albania with Frank: it rained but on the whole, Lear thought, 'this queer Albanian trip did me a deal of good'. At least it was a change: in Corfu he was bored of palace gaiety, 'dancing & rushing about pauselessly & continually. I suspect Lady Young would not be happy in heaven if she did not get up an immense ball & land & water picnics, among the angels.' In mid-April he went again to Albania, sailing with Frank in *Midge* and sketching with James 'Jemmy' Edwards, godson of an old Knowsley friend.

But Lear still felt unsatisfied, woeful about Frank. He told Fortescue that he would come home for the summer to make lithographs of his Corfu and Athos sketches, and to see his sisters, as Ellen too was now going to New Zealand. The chief reason, however, was his own half-life: 'Why are you coming say you – ? – Because I can't stay here any longer – without seeing friends & having some communion of heart & spirit – with one who should have been this to me – I have none. And I can't bear it.' This, perhaps, was his most self-revealing moment.

Frank was going home for the summer break, and they left together on 19 May 1857, steaming through calm seas to Trieste, which seemed huge, busy and modern after 'poor, mean, dirty, uncomfortable, quoggly, boggly, old Corfu'. Then they went to Venice, which, to everyone's surprise, including his own, Lear disliked – no trees, no green, no colourful costumes. From there, Lear took the train back to England, bringing with him a large bag of presents and, in a red Albanian box, a small Corfu tortoise.

By 1857 he had decided that he would come back to England every summer, to make sure he was included in the exhibitions in Manchester and Liverpool and London and to show his sketches and paintings. This would, he hoped, make enough in sales and commissions to fund life abroad in the winter, avoiding 'the whitening of the ground & blackening of the sky: – the starving & deaths of birds; – the columns of deaths in the Newspapers: the railway & skating accidents "through the seasonable weather"'.

Although he always made room to go away and paint in peace, he spent most of his English summers scurrying between visits. He ricocheted round the country, north, east, west and south: he was always on trains, with the wrong ticket and smuts in his eyes, jolting his back when his train shunted backwards into a goods train. These journeys and visits allowed him to see friends and patrons across the country. When he was away he assiduously stayed in touch, noting letters received and sent. In Corfu he watched the Trieste steamer coming in with a leap of excitement, wondering if it brought post, and in quarantine in October 1856, he wrote to everyone he could think of. 'Why has Fanny Coombe not written to me?' he asked, and was relieved when a long letter came full of news. Apart from a couple of people, he told Ann, 'I have now letters, from all my old friends I think, I do not know what I should do without letters.' But letters were nothing in comparison to staying with them, talking to them, singing and showing them his pictures. He made his living through this wide net of friendship, and the circles grew.

He made sure to see the grand folk, although 'Very possibly', he confided to Fortescue, 'the small dinners of highly intelligent or scientific middle class friends are about the really best society going, though you might not think so, as Diamonds & Marchionesses hardly ever enter into these more vulgar Kingdoms of Heaven, nor are Duchesses or Princes frequent.' He was happy in London when the Season was over, feeling that 'of all things to be remarked, this is a fact: – the middle classes – professional & otherwise, are by far the best fun for pleasure & knowledge as to converse. The big folk are in most cases a norful bore.' But the 'big folk' bought his pictures – and Lear did enjoy his weekends in beautiful country houses. He liked sinking into the leather chairs in well-stocked libraries, he appreciated the smooth routines, the quiet hours when everyone retreated to their rooms and the maids plumped up the cushions in the drawing room, and was amused by the chatter and the music in the evenings. Most of all, his spirit expanded as he walked through the great parklands with their spreading lawns, a landscape he evoked in a painting of Nuneham for Lady Waldegrave, with sheep in early morning light, a scatter of birds over billowing trees, and the flow of the clouds above.

Nuneham (1860)

Many of his purchasers were diplomats or MPs, or sat in the House of Lords – all his Baring friends eventually became lords, as did Henry Bruce from south Wales, and Fortescue himself. The fourteenth Earl Derby had been in and out as prime minister, leading a minority government with Disraeli as his right-hand man: in 1855 he had declined to take office again, and when the elderly Palmerston took over, Fortescue became Under-Secretary of State for the Colonies. But the whirligig went on. Derby and Disraeli were back in 1858 – and Palmerston was back the year after that.

Lear's visits of 1857, however, were dominated not by domestic politics but by events in India. From May onwards, when sepoys in the East India Company army mutinied, *The Times* and other papers demonised the mutineers and published graphic accounts of massacres. Many of Lear's friends had relatives caught up in the Indian Mutiny. Fortescue's nephew John Hamilton was an engineer in Benares; Lady Reid's stepson Captain James Dalzell would be killed at Lucknow. The Lushington family had long connections in India and Ceylon (now Sri Lanka), and Frank's brother Tom worked in the colonial service. Home on leave after seven years, with his wife and five children, Tom was recalled in a hurry in December.

Lear felt guilty at enjoying life while others suffered. But enjoy himself he did, and for once, he had the promise of money. The MP T. William Evans bought his hastily finished *Corfu from the Village of Ascension, Evening* for five hundred guineas, a coup Lear trumpeted to Ann in capital letters, ending, 'HURRAH!' He set aside plans for his Athos lithographs and journal in a rush of visits. He spent three weeks in Ireland with Fortescue at Ardee, enjoying the wit of Fortescue's elderly aunt, Mrs Ruxton. 'He talked a good deal about F.L.', noted Fortescue, 'with whom he has had a misunderstanding from the entire diversity of their characters.' One afternoon, they had their portraits done by a travelling Glasgow photographer: 'Aunt much amused,' wrote Fortescue. (A few years later, when Lear had another portrait done, Frank said it looked like 'a mixture of Socrates, Sir John Falstaff & Sancho Panza'.)

Lear and Fortescue at Ardee, September 1857

From Ireland Lear crossed to Liverpool, stopped at Knowsley and saw his *Quarries of Syracuse* in the crowd-pulling Manchester Art Treasures exhibition, organised by Thomas Fairbairn, another good friend and purchaser. He went to south Wales to see Henry Bruce, later Lord Aberdare, and to Somerset to stay with Charles Church, now a canon of Wells Cathedral. He sank back and relaxed with his oldest friends, like William Nevill, now a widower: Lear took his godson Allan out and gave him the tiny Corfu tortoise. Another haven was Bern Husey Hunt's home near Lewes, where he walked on the downs, ate good dinners and read by the fire. 'The H's are always the same,' he wrote contentedly. But late summer brought sadness too: George Coombe died, after years of illness, and Lear called on Fanny, now living in the grand but still unfinished Trafalgar Square, while the next month saw the death of Robert Hornby, who had helped send him to Rome twenty years ago.

1857 was the year of Moxon's illustrated edition of Tennyson, and in November Lear dined at the Tennysons' with Woolner, Dante Gabriel Rossetti and Hunt. 'All pleased with Mr Lear's singing,' noted Emily. 'A. reads "Morte d'Arthur" & "Break, Break, Break" after he has sent me to bed.' That was one of Lear's last London outings. By now, as well as settling into this pattern of winters abroad, he had become an experienced traveller, keen on modern comforts. On his way across Europe he sent Ann an account of continental trains. He was in Vienna, having changed at Frankfurt before another '16 hours rattle':

These railway matters are so different to ours! A half hour before starting time everybody meets in a large room – each class separately; this room is full of couches – tables – chairs – & mirrors – & is like a drawingroom, & everybody sits or walks about with their bags & cloaks etc allowed in the train. Then a bell rings – ¼ hour before the time – & the doors are opened which lead on to the platform, when everybody rushes to the carriages & gets settled as best he or she may. Very few travel first class & in this instance I had a whole carriage to myself – so spread out my rugs & cloaks (did I not tell you that W. Nevill kindly gave me such a magnificent soft wool railway rug! Immensely large – black outside, & with a beautiful leopard woven inside –) & got my bag of books, & so became quite comfortable. I read away at the life of Charlotte Bronte – a most interesting biography – & I was so pleased with it . . .

He was back on Corfu at the end of November, finding that nothing had changed: 'The ludicrous sentiment of standstill & stagnation was truly wonderful.' Even when he tried to read he hopped from book to book: 'Some Greek of St John – some of Robinson's *Palestine*, some *Jane Eyre*, – some Burton's *Mecca*, – some *Friends in Council*, some Shakespeare, some *Vingt ans après*, – some Leake's *Topography* – some Rabelais – some Tennyson – some Gardner Wilkinson, – some Grote, some Ruskin – & all in half an hour.' To begin with he found the slow pace of life frustrating but he worked on his pictures and joined friends at dinners, lamenting that he talked, ate, drank and smoked too much. Yet as he settled back into the Corfu rhythm, he rather enjoyed the gossipy palace dinners. The island was like a jotting in the margins of empire and he liked to hear the stories of the eagle-sharp Lord Canning, his host in Constantinople a decade ago, and of Lady Headfort, widow of William Hay Macnaghten who had been assassinated during the Afghan War of 1842. Lady McN., as Lear called her, was always smothered in jewels, allegedly smuggled out in the retreat.

The only disappointment was that Frank became increasingly taciturn, ground down by petty island politics and pushed around by the domineering Bowen ('a man of rhinoceros-like insensibility'). It was Frank's thirty-fifth birthday on 4 January 1858, a cold day, threatening snow. 'Somehow I did nothing this day,' Lear noted. 'Wrote Greek: fidgetted for letters – had bookshelves put up: – prepared to paint. At 2½ Lushington called – but anything sadder or more unsatisfactory than his visit could not be.' Although they went walking together, these days, Lear wrote bitterly, 'it is a weary silent work, & now that he has got a dog, one cannot help feeling how far more agreeable it is to him to walk with that domestic object, to whom he has not the bore of being obliged to speak'. He winced at Frank's 'millennial, corpse-like stiltiness'. He knew that the only remedy was to move away, to move on.

21: BIBLE LANDS

Lear had wanted to go to Palestine for years, talking it over with Holman Hunt, who drew a fine portrait of him this year. He asked Hunt if he could provide any introductions in Jerusalem: 'Tell them you introduce a most irregular & uncomfortable fool – partly swell – partly painter, who will never do any good – to himself or anybody else: & advise them parenthetically to stop his unpleasant rumblings by instantly emptying a large bucket of water on his noddle.'

Lear's frivolousness and restlessness irked Frank, who planned his days in a straight line, without deviation. He realised that Lear's huge picture of Corfu from Ascension would lie unfinished if the Jerusalem trip came off, 'but I suppose that to make artists work straight on end at one thing like ordinary people till they have finished is a work beyond the reach of art'.

In the winter of 1857–8 Lear read as much as he could about Jerusalem and the Holy Land, from the fourth-century text of the 'Pilgrim of Bordeaux' and the medieval extravaganzas of John Mandeville to recent books like William Lynch's account of Jordan and the Dead Sea, the travels of the American clergyman Edward Robinson, and Félicien de Saulcy's tour to the 'Bible Lands'. He thought it could be a profitable venture, as the work of David Roberts in this region in the 1840s had proved immensely popular, particularly his dramatic prints of Petra.

At dinner at the palace he eyed Lady Hertford's 'turquoises & emeralds & bangles & spangles & chains', fantasising about turning them into cash for his trip.

By the end of February 1858 he had worked out his route, reassuring Ann that he was taking an enormous box of medicines. Reports of attacks on travellers in Palestine warned him that the trip might be dangerous, so he made his will, with Lushington and Husey Hunt as executors. Frank also insisted that he learn to shoot. 'O! here is a bit of queerness in my life. Brought up by women – & badly besides – & ill always, I never had any chance of manly improvement & exercise, etc – and never touched firearms in all my days.' Now he was packing a five-barrelled revolver. He set off alone. The omens were not good: 'Weather frightful, pouring rain & wind . . . O wind! Wind! Wind!' On the evening of Sunday 13 March he walked down through the quiet Jewish quarter to meet his servant Giorgio and his brother Spiro: 'Row over to harbour, & alongside steamer, to Bombay. Nearly fell into the water, & so did Spiro – I not seeing the steps . . . So begins my Syrian tour.'

A bundle of motives lay behind his trip: an escape from Corfu and getting away from Frank, a new set of subjects and most of all the longing to see new places – perhaps write another journal. But what did it mean to him to be in the 'Holy Land'? What did he believe? He had rejected his evangelical childhood, although his elder sisters were still devout chapel-goers. 'I hope you have the pleasure of hearing some good Ministers,' Ellen wrote to Fred's family in America. 'It must be a comfort to you if you have public worship regularly – but if outward means fail, I trust you may enjoy that inward peace, a deep sense of the love of God, that cannot be destroyed by the changes & trials of this present life.' Lear never wrote like this. After going to church with the Nevills at Stoke Newington he exploded about the complacent congregation of 'monstrous old men & gorgon-like elderly women', the endless hymns and the long sermon on the Athanasian Creed, damning non-believers. He railed against narrow-minded sectarian disputes, obsession with rituals, and smug protestations of 'love thy neighbour' that smacked of the hypocrisy of the 'Anglo-Saxon' (a frequent term of abuse).

A couple of years from now he would stop going to church in England altogether. Staying with Bernard Husey Hunt in Sussex, he wrote, 'Sleep and deadly Anglo-Sunday God hating idolatrous puritan Pharisee silence and sermonreading. At 6 dinner, & better fun. But I weary of English Sundays & must break off from lying conventionally.' He did, however, go to Anglican services while abroad. In 1861 he had dinner with the Revd Woodward, the chaplain in Rome:

After dinner a most sad dispute occurred: a real annoyance. Nor can I well remember what was its first origin except that Presbyterians & Dissenters coming to church was spoken of, & I vindicated their doing so on the grounds of there being but one Church in Rome. – All 4 flew at me & pointed out the Prussian, & the American services – I said, if you think it is inconvenient for dissenters to go to our church, it would be better that it were generally known that you disliked their coming. 'What do you mean by it being better that it were generally known –' said Mrs. W. – angrily? – 'In order that they might be more consistent, said I. Mrs. W. said then things about Quakers & Presbyterians – 'they may be called Xtians' – &c. &c. of so shocking a nature that I was really perfectly disgusted & distressed. The poor fool evidently supposes no one but 'Anglicans' can be saved – & W. said – 'the Q. of E. has no more right to go to a Scotch kirk than to a mosque.' 'Church? said Mrs. W. – it is not a church at all – it is a kirk.' – I scarcely spoke again all the evening, – tho' a Mr & Mrs Meynall came: – & I believe I shall never go to see them again – since the company of bigots & fools is not good for anyone who can avoid it.

Lear turned his back on intolerant bigots, just as he had shuddered at the misogynistic monks on Athos. He was, however, interested in spiritual matters. He had a sense of a transcendent being, or at least of a power suffused in the universe; he accepted Christ as a teacher, and he clung to the hope of an afterlife. But he had no time for doctrines of original sin, judgement and hell. He cringed at the Athanasian Creed, which decreed that the conditions of being 'saved' were belief in the

Trinity, the incarnation of Christ and the Second Coming, when 'All men will rise again with their bodies; And shall give account for their own works. And they that have done good shall go into life everlasting; and they that have done evil, into everlasting fire.' To Lear this showed that priests were guilty of blasphemy and lying, 'or they would not say that the Almighty damns the greater part of his creatures'. He joined many in his generation who rigorously questioned the 'truth' of the Bible. The Mosaic account of the Creation and the Deluge had long been overturned by geology and the fossil trail, and in biblical studies, certainties were shaken by works like David Friedrich Strauss's three-volume *Life of Jesus* of the mid-1830s, which applied historical method to the Gospels and set aside the supernatural elements as mythology, and Ludwig Feuerbach's *The Essence of Christianity*, published in 1841, which stressed love and sympathy rather than vengeful justice. (Both were translated by Lear's contemporary, Mary Anne Evans, later George Eliot, in 1846 and 1854.)

Years later, Lear reminded his sister Eleanor that Ann used to say to him, 'A man's life proves his religion.' Lear disagreed. 'I think this is a mistake. There may be excellent moral conduct, without any heartfelt spiritual knowledge of the Truth.' His historicist, humanist approach led to differences with the profoundly religious Holman Hunt, who believed in sacrifice and redemption, miracles and grace. Lear agreed with Hunt on many points, he said, but he needed 'to express my own preference for such subjects in the life of Christ as are universal & of daily interest & other than those more occult & dogma-breeding points which do not suit all minds':

Nor do I for one cling to the miraculous & supernatural, thinking that I observe from all history the torrents of blood & the cries of torture which have arisen from *disputable* 'idols' of belief. Christ pardoning the woman taken in adultery, Christ blessing the children & hundreds of ministries of exquisite goodness & wisdom appear to me as being incapable of failing in attracting *all* suffrage. *Nobody* doubts mercy, or affection, being good, but the world will never – as it has never agreed – agree on much that has been written on abstruser subjects, such subjects being (*selon moi*) of far less importance than the facts & rules Christ lived to order & exemplify.

He did not, then, set off for the Bible lands as a spiritual pilgrim, but he had been learning Greek assiduously and the fact that he could now read both the Old and New Testament in Greek spurred his desire to see the places mentioned in the Bible, and the sites in Josephus' *History of the Jews* (a staple on Victorian bookshelves). He did this in the same spirit in which he tracked the places mentioned in Greek myths, or in the *Odyssey*, or in Byron's poems. And by the time he left, his Greek studies had taken him in a new direction. He was reading Plato's arguments for the afterlife of the soul, reading his *Phaedo* all through the night and marvelling at the death of Socrates. 'How is it', he asked Fortescue, 'that the thoughts of this wonderful man are kept darkly away from the youths of the age? (except they go to the universities, & then only as matters of language or scarcely more) because Socrates was a "Pagan"?'

When Lear landed at Alexandria and discovered that the boat for Jaffa would not arrive for a week, he went to Cairo. On the slow train journey he burst with enthusiasm, vivid with joy in the birds and animals:

Renewal of Egyptian impressions, the immense green plains! The birds – Zikzacs & white egrets, hawks, herded crows, gulls, plovers, ducks! – Camels, in those long streams – asses, sheep in black masses, – spotted goats – horses, oxen, – buffali – : those endlessly varied costumes & figures! – the mud villages – pigeon houses, palm trees, Forts & Sycamores, & canals – dogs – &c., &c – the great moving panorama, delighted me. I am thankful today, just as in 1848.

After a week of tourism and sketching he boarded the little steamer, packed not only with 'English & Americans – Prussians & Austrians etc – but actually 20 different languages all going to Easter in the Holy City'. Luckily the sea was calm and after the scramble in the port at Jaffa, his party rode out onto the great coastal plains, an unbroken sea of bright green corn. Heading for Jerusalem, they climbed the stony hills on their mules and on the afternoon of the second day, 27 March 1858, Lear wrote, 'I saw all the places I at once recognised as portions of the scene I so long have desired to paint, – & when we were opposite the west side of the city – I at once found it far more beautiful than I had expected.'

It was Palm Sunday and when Lear went to the English church for once he was intrigued by the sermon, 'of a kind I had not looked for – & one which gave me great pleasure'. The text, from Luke's Gospel, was Christ's answer to Martha's complaints: 'Martha, Martha, thou art careful and troubled about many things. But one thing is needful: and Mary hath chosen that good part, which shall not be taken away from her.' This was a text that was often preached on, Lear knew, 'But I do not remember to have heard it treated before, as teaching that "the one thing" should be looked on as real practical life-religion; & that the spiritual mind may be cumbered by what it thinks spiritual "many things" to wit, party religion – forms – theologies – & all the Pharisaecalities Christ so pointedly condemned.'

Lear's 'life-religion' was practical in this sense, a matter of ethics and loving-kindness. But it was also full of poetry. Keen to see places he had heard of since childhood, he went twice to the Mount of Olives to find the spot where Christ must have been when he saw the city on coming from Bethany. To his friend Thomas Seddon, such a view was a religious experience; 'One cannot help feeling that one is treading upon holy ground; and it is impossible to tread the same soil which Our Lord trod . . . and follow the very road that he went from Gethsemane to the cross, without seriously feeling that it is a solemn reality, and no dream.' To Lear, who so often turned back from sacred sites – from Jerusalem, Mount Athos, Mount Olympus – the views were endowed with a different kind of sublimity, that of nature itself. At the top of the Mount, turning round, he exclaimed: '– lo! The Dead Sea! – clear pale milky far blue, with farther off all rosy mountains – fretted & carved in lovely shadow forms – their long long simple line melting into air towards the desert'. The next day, after dining with his new English acquaintances, he wrote: 'Afterwards – as I came up the stairs, how glorious was the full moon of blessed Israel – & how beautiful the dim pale film of Moab! – the round domes of the city & a thousand other glorious quietudes recalling older days.'

To escape the Easter crowds he hired a local dragoman, Abdel, and set off for Bethlehem and Hebron. Here Abdel made an arrangement with the Sheikh of the Jehaleen – who had been the guide to Edward Robinson in 1838 and to de Saulcy – to take Lear to the ancient Nabatean capital of Petra, then on to the Dead Sea and Masada: he would need an escort of fifteen men, the sheikh announced, for a cost of £30, to include the camels. It was expensive and Lear was not sure he trusted him but he accepted and after a night broken by the cries of jackals his small procession rode out into the hills of Moab, 'pure and beautiful in colour and simple in form'. Their six camels were impressive, if not biblical. His own was handsome and young; Giorgio's looked shaved, and 'a great white Hubblebubble' carried difficult goods, but refused the hens that gave Lear eggs for breakfast, 'as an uncamellike & undignified burden. Altogether the din of snarling, growling, screaming, and guggling was considerable.'

On they went, over carpets of hepatica and pale asphodel and out into an open plain where a thousand camels grazed. At night they camped in hollows in the sandy hills: 'The fires are lit, dinner & pipes discussed, firearms discharged to warn possible robbers. Starlight; and the vast desert silence.' The silence was broken only by the whirring of grasshoppers among the shrubs, reminding Lear of summer nights in Calabria. Riding up the rocky limestone tracks of the Edom mountains, watching his camels creeping like flies through the narrow defiles below, Lear was astonished by the colours, the forms, the views:

But what a scene of stoniness & craggyness, – points & chasms, – black grimness, exquisite colours, & strange, wild forms! What strata of giant boulders and rock-forms below! What tawny vastness of lion-coated ridges above! all lit up with the golden light of the afternoon sun, – a splendour of wonder, – a bewildering, dream-like, unfinished world, – bare, terrible, stupendous, strange, & beautiful!

During five days' hard travel, made worse by worry about water, feuds among the Arabs and rushes for guns when strangers were seen, he often wondered if the journey was worth the expense. These doubts vanished as they wound through the narrow entry of the Siq and saw before them the rose-coloured facades of Petra.

As he looked at the rainbow-hued cliffs and the dark mouths of the rock-hewn tombs, Lear sensed a terrible loneliness in these scenes of vanished glory with their scattered pillars and capitals and ruined temples. He had found a new world, he wrote in his journal, yet one that he could never fully convey: 'Who could reproduce the dead silence & strange feeling of solitude . . . What art could give the star-bright flitting of the wild dove & the rock-partridge through the oleander gloom, or the sound of the clear river rushing among the ruins of the fallen city.'

He sketched in the valley, full of flowering shrubs, and then higher up by an ancient temple, until the sun went down and the great eastern cliff became a wall of fiery-red stone. The purple shadows lengthened and the cliffs grew darker and darker, 'silent & ghostly-terrible'. As Lear kept on drawing in the creeping dusk Abdel pointed up to a rock terrace, and he saw ten black figures squatting in a line above their tents: '"Who are they Abdel, & what do they want?" said I. "He is of the Arab, & is asking for the money."' Local Bedouin were demanding a tax for crossing their land. Lear had already paid the Sheikh of Haweitat but these men were from different hill-villages and wanted a separate payment: if Lear did not pay they would be back with fifty men. He refused, saying the sheikh must divide the money with them. Then he went to bed. At midnight the fifty men appeared with loud shouts, settling round the fires to wait until morning. More and more men drifted in, cheerfully asking for sugar, coffee, bread, and at four in the morning Lear packed his saddle-bags. Then twenty retainers of the Sheikh of Haweitat arrived and briefly it seemed all would be solved. Leaving Giorgio to watch the tent, Lear went off to draw, fearing that it might be his last chance, climbing the cliffs to the highest temple, the monument of the Deir.

The theatre, Petra, 14 April 1858

On his return he found the camp flooded with two hundred violently quarrelling men, the sheikh in the middle, riding a white horse and dressed in scarlet robes. Quickly, he ordered the tents to be struck, then went off to sketch again, scrambling up to the top of the theatre: at the 'Kasne' – the so-called treasury, or Khazneh – he wrote his name on the wall so that if the worst happened it would be clear that he had got this far. When Giorgio and Abdel came to rescue him with the camels, men rushed past them, pushing Lear and pulling at his clothes: yet still he could see the absurd: 'One struck me in the face with one of my own hens, adding insult to injury.' Even the intense rage on the faces of his attackers would have been a study for a painter 'had the circumstances permitted'. As the arguments raged he was hustled and dragged and grabbed until men, 'holding my arms and unbuttoning all my clothing, extracted in a twinkling everything from all my many pockets, from dollars and penknives to handkerchiefs and hard-boiled eggs, excepting only my pistols and watch'. Finally the sheikh said he could help no more: Lear must pay their assailants twenty dollars. He paid, and the Bedouin wheeled and left. Within a quarter of an hour his party was on the move, pursued from time to time by more men demanding money. He paid them all.

Lear wrote about this with warmth and wit, but he was shaken and short of funds and set off quickly back to Jerusalem. He stopped on the way to sketch at Masada, the last stronghold of the Jews in AD 72–3, who chose mass suicide rather than surrender in their struggle against Rome. He would develop one Masada sketch into a fiery scene for Lady Waldegrave, who had commissioned two paintings from this trip.

Masada (1858)

Lady Waldegrave's second request was for a painting of Jerusalem, and Lear was soon back there, stopping briefly by the Dead Sea – the taste of the waters, he told Ann, 'you may imitate if you like by putting a little bark mustard, & cayenne, with Epsom salts'. Lear could explore Jerusalem properly now that the Easter crowds had left. He found it beautiful, but recoiled from the squalor and despaired at the squabbling of the Christian churches – Roman Catholic, Russian Orthodox and Protestant. Even more absurd was the mission to convert the Jews: with their rich heritage, why should they take up with 'a religion professing to be one of love & yet bringing forth bitter hatred & persecution'? Yet he found every corner of Jerusalem moving, 'forcing you to think on a vastly dim receding past – or a time of Roman War & splendour – (for Aelia Capitolium was a fine city –) or a smash of Moslem & Crusader years – & the long long dull winter of deep decay through centuries of misrule'.

From here he planned a northern trip. He got as far as Jericho, but after an encounter with yet another group of Arabs demanding money, he turned back again without seeing the Sea of Galilee and Nazareth. Instead, he took a steamer up the coast from Jaffa to the Lebanon. On 13 May, his forty-sixth birthday, he was in Beirut, wandering past dusty lemon groves and mulberry gardens. From the heights in the evenings, 'the Lebanon is white & pink & receded – & you see all the multitude of wrinkles & villages in the nearer hills – All the foreground is gray & cadmium, & dark Cologne earth.' At every stage, Lear thought as a painter, his 'Cologne' being a rich deep brown, and in the Lebanon he found a supreme subject, fusing natural grandeur with Biblical echoes: the great cedars. He sketched these among bare, snow-topped peaks, forming an amphitheatre above the dark grove, silent except for the birdsong, and his drawings would form the basis for his most ambitious painting. But the move from torrid cities to icy crags, so cold that he could not hold his pencil, made him ill. He travelled on to the temples of Baalbec (too florid, he thought, and not a patch on Egyptian temples), and by the time he reached Damascus, where it was too hot even to draw outside, he was exhausted. Beautiful though the city was with its gardens and glittering river, it was time to leave.

22: A WAS AN ASS

A was an Ass,
Who fed upon grass
And sometimes on Hay
Which caused him to bray.
A!
What a good Ass

In June 1858, with Palestine and the Lebanon behind him, Lear sailed back across the eastern Mediterranean, through the Cyclades and round to Corfu. Within hours of landing he was dining with Sir James Reid as if he had never been away. Island politics were now so bad that Frank Lushington had resigned: in August they would travel home. As the heat rose, Lear packed, made his last calls and sold his piano.

Many Corfu friends bought his pictures of Italy and Greece, Athos and Egypt, but some families also had more informal offerings, his alphabets. He had drawn these little gifts for several years, a habit of friendship. In 1846, the year of the first *Book of Nonsense*, he sent one to a friend, Sam Sandbach: 'My dear Sam,' he wrote, 'I send this alphabetic nonsense for the future amusement of your little boy,' telling him that the loose pages should last a long time, if pasted on linen. He made others for the de Tabley children – the house where ten years earlier he had quieted the baby by playing his accordion – for the children at Tatton

Hall and for the Tennyson boys, three-year-old Hallam and the baby, Lionel. At Christmas 1855, Tennyson tried sticking the pages onto linen himself: 'The pasting and the ironing have been by no means so successful as they ought to have been,' confessed Emily, 'but then I hope you will consider the remarkable fact of the Poet Laureate being seen ironing by nearly the whole household as something of a consolation.'

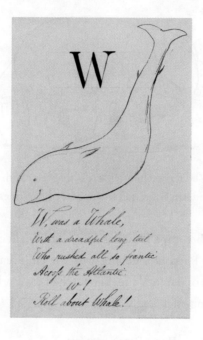

In his letters from Corfu he made these sound a chore: 'Now I finish 3 Alphabets for children – and so get pretty wearied by the end of the week.' But his invention and his pleasure were plain to see. The possibilities were endless: 'B' could be bee, bird, bat, butterfly, broom, book; S could be snail, spider, shoe, swallow, sugar-tongs, slipper, spoon, soup, screw; 'U' could be ukase, uppercoat, urn. Only one letter was constant – X was always for Xerxes, Lear's favourite villain. As in his limericks, the last line often circled back to its subject, now given an imaginative identity. The pages were packed with miniature stories of insects, fans and hats, ice creams and puddings, full of wonder at nature, bafflement at fashions and delight in bad rhymes, like the U for urn, 'with hot water in it/ To bubble and burn/ And make tea in a minute', or the W for whale, who 'rushed all so frantic/ Across the Atlantic'.

Some later alphabets were more fantastical, with illogical, logical-sounding juxtapositions, and gleeful alliterative word-making: 'The Dolomphious' Duck', the frisky, finny 'Fizzgiggious Fish' and 'The Enthusiastic Elephant',

Who ferried himself across the water with the Kitchen Poker and a New pair of Ear-rings.

Another alphabet, for a father and his children, became a set of very simple stories of Papa, a touching way for children to laugh at and share the oddities of parental life: his starched cravat, his bottle of beer, his hat and walking stick and watch:

H was Papa's new Hat,
He wore it on his head;
Outside it was completely black,
But inside it was red.

The alphabets were perfect to read aloud. By attaching the letter to an animal, or a cake, a doll, or a kite, Lear could tumble out rhymes for small children to join in.

The rhymes, 'Hairy! Beary! Taky Cary!' or 'mousey, bousey, sousey', were the kind of nonsense words that parents speak to babies, often the first words they hear, and all the more alluring – and important – for that reason.

But adults could play with alphabets too. In one letter, asking a friend to see his drawings of Corsica, Lear ebulliently proclaimed their delights by running down the alphabet, sloping across the page, sometimes using the sound, sometimes the letter's name, from 'A – mazing' and 'B – wildering' to 'Y – ld, & savage' and 'Z – edekiah perplexing'.

Quick and funny, the alphabets let us hear how Lear spoke. They show, too, how clever he was at introducing the building blocks of writing, hinting at how the names of consonants differ from their sound, or how vowels can be flat or round, short or long – as in his Ass, who eats grass, or hay. He enjoyed the way that splitting words made easy riddles and puns. Inviting a friend round, he wrote, 'Are you a tome or R U knot? – come & have dinner.' And he particularly liked question riddles:

> What would Neptune say if they deprived him of the sea?
> 'I haven't a n/otion!'

> What letter confounds Comets and Cookery?
> *G* – for it turns *A*stronomy into *G*astronomy.

Letters have a life of their own, they can jump and change the sense, or speak in different tones. In Lear's poem 'Mr and Mrs Discobbolos', he could make the final letters of the alphabet into a fluttery sigh, a gasp of amazement, or a muttered curse:

> Mr and Mrs Discobbolos
>> Lived on the top of the wall,
>> For twenty years, a month and a day,
>> Till their hair had grown all pearly gray,
>> And their teeth began to fall.
> They never were ill, or at all dejected, –
> By all admired, and by some respected,
>> Till Mrs Discobbolos said,
>> 'Oh! W! X! Y! Z!
> It has just come into my head,
> We have no more room at all –
>> Darling Mr Discobbolos.

Lear also liked to play with the function of letters in building words, and with the rules of grammar in making 'sense'. Even as a boy he grasped that if the common rules of word-making are followed – like adding 'ly' for an adverb – then a word will be accepted even if it's nonsense, as in his packing 'furibondiously'. Similarly, if a sentence sticks to accepted syntax, it will 'sound' like sense, whatever words are used, as in: 'It's as bright and cold & icicular as possible, and elicits the ordibble murmurs of the cantankerous Corcyreans.'

He could break the rules successfully because he knew them so well. His language is alive, protean, ever evolving. Words mutate and evolve, finding new endings and appendages, like new limbs. He delighted in children's mishearings and battles with speech and spelling, so similar to his own nonsense slippages. 'I went up a mounting & made a sketch.' His coinages work not only because he used conventional word formation but also because his phonetic spelling and forms, which looked so odd, genuinely evoked the sound, as in 'ordibble' for audible, 'Orgst' for 'August', or 'So I came moam & rote this'.

Nonsense forms could embody situations in sound. They became a kind of Joycean, or Gerard Manley Hopkins-esque, shorthand in Lear's letters and diary: 'a horridodious earthquake', 'dimmy-scirocco early', 'the wind shaken shutters bebother', 'the soft hushy ripple'. He found he could use this style in many ways to give a feeling of texture and atmosphere: struggling round Lago di Paola in the Pontine marshes near Rome, he described it as surrounded by 'immense lots of tangle jungle bungle greedy reedy grogorious stuff . . . very wild and uncomfortably tangly'. In 1861, when he was writing to Emily Tennyson, suddenly 'horrible borrible squashfibulus migoposhquilous sounds were heard', he wrote, 'ever increasing, like 5000 whales in hysterics': 'The – huming screams & shouts. – Then stamping: – roaring: – rushing: – bouncing: – Booming: by-go-bustling: – O – the great cistern, along of the sudden thaw – had bust all the pipes – which spouted forth, arm-broad torrents of water like fire from cannons.' The labials and sibilants were themselves an aural waterfall. And nonsense forms could evoke the visual as well as the aural, as in his disarmingly vivid description of the view from Fortescue's house at Ardee where he watched 'the perspective struggling milkly enthusiastic calves afar off'.

The playful mix of images and sounds that make Lear's alphabets so alive leaps to an extravagant length in one joyfully hectic picture-poem, 'Ribands and pigs', in which unrelated words and pictures bang against each other, setting the unnamed hero spinning like a top.

> Ribands & pigs,
> Helmets & Figs
> Set him a jigging & see how he jigs.

The combinations seem random – 'Trumpets & Guns, beetles & buns' – but the clashing nouns create a chain, like free association: 'knives' rhymes with 'hives', 'hives' lead to bees, to 'set him a stinging and see how he stings', and so on. As the paired nouns are matched by paired verbs, stinging moves to weeping, weeping to staring, hopping to sailing, screaming to howling:

Lobsters & owls,
Scissors & fowls,
Set him a howling & hark how he howls! –

The whole performance is driven by the energy and motive power of simple nouns: puddings, beams, cobwebs, creams; pancakes, fins, roses, pins; bonnets, legs, steamboats, eggs. And the drawings have their own oddity: all the creatures and objects appear in pairs as in a dance. The effect is dizzying, as if the world is in perpetual motion. The poem rolls on like the ball on this slope, beautifully balanced above the thistles and moles, crumpets and soles (or Souls?) below:

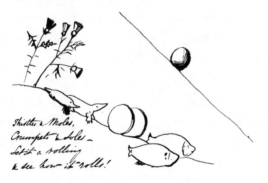

Thistles & Moles
Crumpets & Soles –
Set it a rolling & see how it rolls!

The drawings of the thistles and moles seem to have escaped from an alphabet to claim a life of their own. Such drawings could indeed make an alphabet: ant, bear, cat, dog. Small children could 'read' them, just as they could read Lear's drawings for nursery rhymes – 'Humpty Dumpty', 'Sing a Song of Sixpence', 'Hey Diddle Diddle' – so that once they knew the songs they could follow the sequence. Drawings could act as words: in Albania, when Lear drew, the dervish had cried out, '*Scroo! Scroo!*': you are writing us down.

On the simplest level, pictograms could be a parlour game. Late in life, Lear wrote a pictogram letter to Hallam and Lionel Tennyson, drawing his address in Duchess Street, Portland Place with a fat duchess and a bottle of port, and using a lion's curling tail for 'dear Lionel'. Lear's own signature was also a picture of a sort, in the monogram that he began using in the late 1850s. 'That's my new assygram,' he wrote as he signed a letter to Chichester Fortescue. Joining initials in a pattern, the monogram was an ancient device, used on Greek and Roman coins, royal seals, by artists like Dürer and Rembrandt, and now, in Victoria's age of affluence, on the silver plate of the rich as well as in the cryptic initials of the PRB, the looped Hs of Holman Hunt, the crown-like M of Millais. In Lear's monogram he caught the E in a curving L, like an open bubble blown into the air, as if 'Edward' was almost swallowed by 'Lear'.

A letter could be a person. Tennyson became a tall A with a hat; Fortescue a curl of Ps and Fs. When he drew the seating plans at dinner-tables, he did not put 'me', but his balloon-like EL. At huge parties at Strawberry Hill, his monogram looked like a snail sheltering in a shell; at cheery meals with Millais and Thackeray it expanded a bit; with friends like Emily and Lionel Tennyson, or Frank, it opened happily, like a boat on the sea, and occasionally, if he dined alone, he seemed to carry the whole table on his head. As in his alphabets, his initials usher in a trail of rhymes – an eerie, queery, sometimes weary, sometimes cheery Edward Lear.

Single letters could speak. Lear's alphabets, which he wrote to entertain, were also serious – letters were tools to open a door for children into the land of language, rhyme, story and feeling; the world of imagination.

23: HOME AGAIN, ROME AGAIN

There was an Old Man with a nose,
Who said, 'If you choose to suppose
That my nose is too long, you are certainly wrong!'
That remarkable Man with a nose.

At the end of the 1850s Lear was circling between Britain and the Continent, pushed around by European politics and swept by his own restless need. Returning to London in August 1858 he leapt like a diver into his British social life. On his first day he dashed to leave cards, rushed to Camden Town in search of Holman Hunt, jumped on an omnibus to see the Tennysons at the Great Northern Hotel, got money from his banker, marched to the framers, Foord and Dickinson off Wardour Street, who had taken over from McLean as his picture dealers, and bought brushes and colours from Winsor & Newton. On the same breathless day, he saw Fanny Coombe and his old Rome friend John Proby, now sick and skeletal. (When Proby died on 19 November, one of his sisters blamed their Sicilian trip for ruining his health, but another, Isabella, sent details of John's death, 'because I know you loved him'. And it was true, Lear wrote, 'I did love him very much.')

Wherever he went, the welcome was warm: at Wansfell, at Knowsley, in Liverpool and Manchester and Sussex. Everywhere, he found music, good talk, 'much fun and laughter'. Yet for some reason he felt weary – it must be the climate, he thought. In truth, a depression was building. At Portman Square in September he hired a piano and settled down to his commissions, including the paintings of Jerusalem and Masada for 'good, kind, wonderful' Lady Waldegrave. He showed his work in his studio and was often asked to bring his box of drawings on visits and to dinner parties, a tiresome business but he was pleased that his Palestine pictures were admired. 'They are the most beautiful things he has ever done,' Thomas Woolner told Emily Tennyson; 'if you have not seen them I hope you will, for they would give much delight and interest you extremely, not only for the mystery and history attached to the places themselves but also for the excessive fineness, tenderness and beauty of the art displayed in them.'

He had requests for many watercolours and was now painting large Palestine oils, asking advice from Holman Hunt, his admiration undiminished: 'He is *the* painter these days.' He left his large canvases in Hunt's studio at Tor Villa in Kensington and worked on them there almost every day, while other artists swept in and out: Ford Madox Brown, William Rossetti, Woolner, Egg and Martineau. When he stayed with Hunt he was, he said, 'happier than in most places', yet he knew Hunt would prove impossible to live with. Hunt's obsessive side came out in long talks late into the night about his woes over Annie Miller. He had found Annie, with her heavy-lidded eyes and tumbling hair, when she was a barmaid in Chelsea in 1850, making her his model for *The Awakening Conscience* and the Moxon *Lady of Shalott*. He firmly believed that he was 'rescuing her' by arranging her education and paying her bills and had expected her to stay faithful when he went to the Middle East; instead she whirled around with the painter George Boyce and with both Rossetti brothers – she was Dante Gabriel's model for several pictures including *Helen of Troy* – and she was also involved with Lord Ranelagh. On Hunt's return there were storms. In 1859 he would break off the relationship and, some years later, when he fell in love with Fanny Waugh, he scraped Annie's face off *The Awakening Conscience* and replaced it with Fanny's.

'Much conversation with H.H. on certain subjects – greatly disturbing to myself – thereof I say little to him,' Lear scribbled in his diary.

Hunt's attitude to Annie bothered him, as well as his views on religion. Lear was half-heartedly still thinking of Helena Cortazzi, but really he was trying hard to put his own obsession behind him – nearly ten years of brooding about Frank Lushington. They did not see each other often, but wrote constantly. One letter forwarded from Beirut showed that Frank had tried to tell Lear all his reasons for leaving Corfu, with 'many true & kind words. Poor dear F.: I wish his life were brighter: yet it is good: – & what more should we desire?' That year the Lushingtons suffered yet another blow: Tom died of fever on his way back to India and was buried in Ceylon. In June Frank hurried anxiously to meet his widow and five children off the boat.

To Lear's dismay Frank moved into chambers in the Temple with Henry's friend George Stovin Venables, who had always resented Lear's closeness to the family. Lear slept badly and had horrible epileptic nights. He began to hate his appearance: worried that his hair was thinning, he kept his moustaches and grew a bushy beard; he put on weight and became ever more conscious of his owl-like glasses and his large nose. By early October he was feeling very odd: 'unhinged – unhooked, unhappy – un-everything'. He thought he looked hideous and no one could love him. At a dinner with Fortescue, although the evening was easy and enjoyable, inside he felt 'more and more isolated'. A few days later he opened his eyes on a bright, fine day:

Wake, to impatience blindness & misery. Incapable of deciding whether life can be cured or cursed – I totter giddily, refusing to take any road, yet agonized by staying irresolute. To go to Brighton? To see H.C. – To take a place at the I. of Wight – & dismiss Giorgio? – To start at once for Rome with unfinished work? – To go to Madeira? – To try to complete the 5 paintings here? To be involved in new debt? To attempt the Palestine small drawings? — I cannot fix any point – but meanwhile groan.

At the end of November finally he fixed on Rome.

There were bright spots in this gloom. Lear had been fascinated by the Irish-English speech he heard when staying with Fortescue at Ardee, and amused too, by his friend being the Member of Parliament for Louth. When he was wheezing in a London winter, about to set off for Italy and hoping they might meet before he left, he pulled the Irish echoes and his own idiosyncratic language together in a ballad (or a pastiche of Isaac Watts) with clarity and smoothness.

> O! Mimber for the County Louth
>   Residing at Ardee!
> Whom I before I wander South,
>   Partik'lar wish to see; —
>
> I send you this – that you may know
>   I've left the Sussex shore,
> And coming here two days ago
>   Do cough for evermore.
>
> Or gasping hard for breath do sit
>   Upon a brutal chair,
> For to lie down in Asthma fit
>   Is what I cannot bear.
>
> Or sometimes sneeze: and always blow
>   My well-developed nose,
> And altogether never know
>   No comfort nor repose . . .
>
> But if you are not coming now
>   Just write a line to say so –
> And I shall still consider how
>   Ajoskyboskybayso.
>
> No more my pen: no more my ink
>   No more my rhyme is clear,
> So I shall leave off here I think. —
>   Yours ever,
>   Edward Lear

In the last week of November he set off to wander south. Borrowing £50 from Bernard Husey Hunt, he went to Margate to see Ann and then crossed the Channel with Samuel Clowes, an old Knowsley friend with whom he had once planned to go to Palestine. After a day of Paris tourism they took the night train to the Midi, a journey of impatience and amusement:

A very ugly woman, & a roaring baby & nurse, & a militaire our companions. At first, along of the child's screams, we anticipated a night of terror, but the enfant did us great good, as after frightening all people away – was itself silent: so we slept. – After midnight 2 people rushingly invaded us – one, a lady – drew a crinoline all 'athwart' the carriage, – but finding it intractable, left us.

2 Americans were our next lot, the baby waking up at intervals & conducting herself with great propriety.

After sailing from Hyères they finally reached Rome in a mighty thunderstorm, and Lear collapsed at his hotel with a large glass of brandy. Next morning he opened his shutters to find he was right opposite Penry Williams's studio, as if stepping back in time. Williams was delighted to see him, and all his old friends, like the sculptor John Gibson, James Uwins and the Knight family, were equally affectionate: '& it does seem most wondrous to me that all are so to me!'

Rome had been peaceful since French troops reinstated Pius IX in the summer of 1849 and the English had returned in droves. At first, in the bright sunshine and surrounded by friends, Lear felt huge joy and resurrection of spirits, as he put it. But after the high came the low. His days were ragged, with epileptic turns coming suddenly at night and in the afternoons. Clowes fell off his horse, broke his collar-bone and retired to bed, and letters from Ann and Fortescue made Lear cry like a child. 'A deep black bitter melancholy destroys me,' he wrote in his diary. Stoically he took a three-year lease on a suite in a large palazzo on the Via Condotti off the Spanish Steps. On Christmas Eve Giorgio, who had been summoned from Corfu, suddenly turned up at his door: 'Indeed, indeed, this is a great blessing.'

With Giorgio there, Lear cheered up. He always enjoyed furnishing his rooms, as if he were going to stay for years, not flit in and out. In Corfu he had bought rugs and put up prints, and now, while Giorgio sewed dish-cloths in the kitchen, he summoned workmen to hang grey cotton over the ghastly wallpaper in the drawing room, which became his studio. He had a dining room-cum-library, a small room where he could display his pictures, a kitchen and a room for Giorgio. In a great bustle the rooms were carpeted, the blinds put up, and they rushed out and bought coffee pots and plates: to begin with they lived in a very 'hoky poky' style, with Giorgio bringing in salt on a piece of paper and saying, 'We are in the desert Sir.' But a companionable routine resumed: at seven ('dreadful late hour') Giorgio opened the shutters and shouted at Lear in Greek to get up, 'So I do; & when I am up, I find the study fire quite lit, & I write or shuffle about there, or polyponder till 8.30.' Then came breakfast, the answering of notes and invitations, and work until noon. Each Wednesday and Saturday at noon, the door-bell rang:

From 20 to 30 people rush up the stairs. Giorgio lets them into my show-room, where a fire is lit, & there are chairs set before my folio stand, & he comes & says with a grave grin 'the Arabs are come'. (One day there were '4 male & 6 female Arabs' and another time 'one old Arab on 4 legs' – an old man on crutches.)

Lear saw new people too, and finally met Browning, who came to see his pictures in late January 1859. For the last few years the Brownings had spent the winters in Rome to escape the chill winds of Florence, although Elizabeth Barrett Browning often wearied of the sociable city: 'a great roaring watering place . . . Cheltenham or Baden Baden – How the Caesars can sleep through it is hard to fancy. But I can't work through it.' Lear also met the Brownings' American friend, the sculptor William Wetmore Story, who had finished his famous marble statue of Cleopatra the previous year and lived with his family in the Palazzo Barberini. This brought introductions, in Story's words, to 'the harem (scarem) I call it – and the emancipated females who dwell there in heavenly unity', including the actress Charlotte Cushman and her current lover, the sculptor Harriet 'Hatty' Hosmer. (Lear was astounded when the Prince of Wales commissioned one of her giant sculptures: '& one from Hosmer!!!!!!!!!!!') He hugely enjoyed Cushman's dinners, and revelled in her company and her singing: 'The Cushman sings savage ballads in a hoarse, manny voice', wrote Story, 'and requests people recitatively to forget her not. I'm sure I shall not.'

These Americans had lived in Rome on and off since the start of the decade (this is the world of Hawthorne's *Marble Fawn*, and Henry James's *Roderick Hudson*), but they still saw Italy as a place of romance and glorious light, of rambles over the Campagna with thunderstorms looming, of trips to Frascati and the Alban hills. When Elizabeth Gaskell stayed with the Storys, escaping the fuss over her *Life of Charlotte Brontë*, she was ecstatic. 'Oh I so long for Italy and Albano that it makes me ill,' she wrote on her return. 'I think Rome grows almost more vivid as the time recedes.' She remembered her time there with 'an ache of yearning'. Lear knew that ache of yearning. Sometimes as he walked the streets he was suffused with memories, full of the longing Henry James would attribute to 'the lover of Italy, the survivor of changes, extinctions, young intensities, the spirit haunted by the sweeter, softer, easier, idler Rome, of greater and stranger differences'.

On crisp January days Lear rode into the Campagna, the light shining on silver snow, and walked on the Pincian hill, empty of tourists and bitterly cold. In contrast to the weather, having lugged his canvases up the stairs, he was painting the sunlight in Palermo and the baking heat of the Dead Sea, Masada and Jerusalem. He kept up his twice-weekly viewings, showing his Palestine drawings and talking for an hour or so, after which, he said, everyone shook his hand and went away. In fact his pictures sold well, supporting him through the winter. His visitors included lords and ladies, Russian princesses and eventually the seventeen-year-old Prince of Wales, whose visit to Rome thrilled the British community: a prepossessing youth, Lear thought, '& very much like his mother, God help her'. Having said he didn't care 'a millionth of a button' whether the prince came or not, Lear was clearly pleased when he turned up in late March after an enquiry from his tutor, Colonel Bruce. Giorgio, dressed in his best, opened the door and Lear met him on the landing: 'I shewed him the Greek pictures, & all the Palestine also – & the whole of the sketches, & when I said, "please tell me to stop, Sir, if you are tired by so many" – he said – "O DEAR, NO!" in the naturallest way.'

If British royalty was entertaining, the government's policies with regard to Italy were disturbing. Piedmontese troops had supported the allies in the Crimean war and ever since, Victor Emanuel, the king of Piedmont-Sardinia, and his prime minister, the Count of Cavour, had argued for British support for unification. This winter Cavour turned instead to France, signing a secret treaty with Louis Napoleon to drive the Austrians from Venetia and Lombardy. 'To tell truth, we *are* getting a bit fidgetty from day to day,' Lear admitted. 'If war really breaks out, there will be no living here, and I can't see any chance of its not breaking out.' In April 1859, border skirmishes deliberately provoked an Austrian ultimatum and a declaration of war. In May the French crossed the border. 'All public news are most disastrous,' Lear wrote in his diary, '– The Emperor landing at Genoa – "hostilities" commenced, – part of the army marching to Ancona.' Garibaldi was back too, siding with Cavour and leading his three thousand volunteers, the *Cacciatori di Alpi*, against the Austrians in the Alps.

Angry supporters of the Risorgimento believed clearly that the British, deaf to their appeals, were siding with the Austrians. The English fled Rome. Civita Vecchia was packed with people fighting to get on the boats and although he despised the panic, Lear saw that there was no point staying with no one left to buy his pictures. Giorgio took up the carpets and Lear started packing. He had three full 'lots' to take home, stuffing in clothes and socks between painting materials:

LOT 1. 4 cases of drawings – (one contains 5 book folios & 2 flannel waistcoats.)
LOT 2. 1. case – 2 pictures, framed & glazed.
4. Folios

4 Arab dresses. 1 cloak. 2 pr. trousers. 2 waistcoats.

Carton of Corfu – in 3 pieces. 3 rolls of Gk. paper.

Petra, & 16 small books

LOT 3. 1 large wood case – (6 canvasses.)

2. case – 6 small canvasses – 3 books. 3 Rulers

    5 book folios. 3 Nos. of Roberts.

    6 pairs of drawers. 3 paper cutters.

3. case 3 folios – 2 prs of drawers.

    8 prs socks – 1. sketching stool.

4. case – 2 pictures

5. Knapsack, couches, 2 diaries (1855–1858) &c. &c.

6. Boxes of paintbrushes.

7. a cloak

8. a capote.

On 15 May he was on the steamer north, and Giorgio was on his way to Corfu, waving his hat from the boat.

Lear left many things undone. In London this summer he wrote up the journals of Athos, and of Palestine and Lebanon – neither would ever be published. 'At present I am doing little, but dimly walking on along the dusky twilight lanes of incomprehensible life,' he wrote mock-humorously to Fortescue. 'I wish you were married. I wish I were an egg and was going to be hatched.'

He stayed with friends, including the Tennysons, and looked for rooms in London, declining Fortescue's offer of a loan, 'for my whole life from 14 years has been independentissimo'. In July he went to St Leonards in Sussex, where he could breathe, feel calmer and work peacefully. When tired he read Sophocles or composed songs, and in the evenings he would potter to the post 'or puddle along the shingly beach' in the dusk. That shingly beach would return in Mr Yonghy-Bonghy-Bò's lament:

> I am tired of living singly, –
> On this coast so wild and shingly, –

In July, with both sides in the Italian conflict weakened after the bloody battle of Solferino (the Swiss tourist Henry Dunant's experiences there led to the founding of the Red Cross), the French and Austrians signed the Peace of Villafranca, leaving Cavour enraged. Furious at British indifference, Elizabeth Barrett Browning cried against this 'peace':

> There *is* no peace, and shall be none.
> Our very dead would cry 'Absurd!'
> And clamour that they died in vain,
> And whine to come back to the sun.

In a proclamation, Tuscany refused to countenance Austrian rule. When he heard of this Lear fretted, 'Tuscany is at present a beautiful, but lonely beacon of hope – alas! Who knows if fated to burn or die out?'

Although the tension remained, by the end of the year Lear felt that Rome was peaceful enough for him to return, away from the cold. London was encased in ice: on 18 December he walked across Hyde Park to the Serpentine, where thousands were skating. In the snowy days before Christmas he crossed the Channel. On board the ferry he met Thackeray, who gave him an early copy of the first issue of *The Cornhill Magazine*, which he was editing, to take to his friend Story. (Five years before, Thackeray had supported the Storys when their son died, and had composed 'The Rose and the Ring' to entertain their ill daughter Edith.) The train to Marseilles was followed by a stormy voyage, rocking every atom of Lear's body:

Bowels, stomach, toes, mind, liver, – all mixed together, it does not seem to me that actual death can be more horrible! – All became dark & terrific alas! – as I counted those dreadful moments hour after hour till the light went out. – The shrieks & hysterics & vomitings all round were most fearful, as the wind increased & the sea was fearful.

But then the wind ceased and he went on deck: '– & then came the golden sunset, calm, & with one long purple, orange lighted cloud above,

& many a golden flecked streak at the water edge – the sun going down one full orb of sublimity – : above the delicate new moon, & one star'.

In Rome he left romantic sublimity behind. French troops filled the streets and there were fewer English residents to buy his work. Looking at the Roman nobles and middle classes stuck in 'stagnation of pride & ignorance & superstition', Lear despaired: 'I believe, if God Almighty were to come down Himself, they wouldn't have a single benefit from him if He were not a "Roman".' 'I deeply hate this place,' he wrote in February. He was already thinking of taking Giorgio to England for the summer. Once there, he would paint a large Cedars of Lebanon for the Manchester exhibition, and perhaps a Baalbek for Liverpool – then off to Palestine.

Then came an unexpected shock. 'Have I ever lied to you in the four years I have been with you?' Giorgio asked one evening, before announcing that he had been married for nine years, and had three children, a boy of eight and two girls of six and three (later two more sons were born). All this was news to Lear. Yet once the astonishment passed, he was glad, he realised, that Giorgio had a family, and as he was clearly homesick Lear decided to send him to Corfu soon. His ideas grew more drastic: he would let Giorgio go altogether and head far away – to India, or America, or Australia. Better never to have been born, he wrote in his diary, quoting Sophocles in Greek: but the next best, if he was to be alone, was to be alone. Then in March, a letter came from Giorgio's brother Spiro – Giorgio's daughter, six-year-old Elisabetta, was dead. Lear had to break the news and when he saw his intense grief, 'actual as a wall or a house', he took him away to the Alban hills to distract him, feeling more and more concerned at the sacrifices Giorgio had made to be with him.

Lear often dined alone, cooked for by Giorgio, but sometimes he had meals sent up from Spillmans, the restaurant below, or ate at his favourite cafe, Falcone's. It rained constantly and he had colds and asthma, but he still saw his friends, visiting Isabella Knight, housebound by illness, and trying to help the landscape painter Charles Coleman, who was seriously ill. More happily, he saw a great deal of the older artists, especially Penry Williams, and the American set (although he ducked out of meeting Harriet Beecher Stowe). At a small dinner at Charlotte Cushman's, the other guests were her new partner the sculptor Emma Stebbins, the diplomat Odo Russell, 'so kindly without shame, & clear without sharpness', the archaeologist Sir Charles Newton — who had just excavated the mausoleum at Halicarnassus and was briefly consul in Rome, before becoming Keeper of the Antiquities at the British Museum — and Robert Browning. Browning was 'all fun':

foaming with spirit; — his anecdote of Carlyle — (wh. he hesitated ere giving,) — how he & C. went to Boulogne, C. for the first time abroad: — when, on see- ing the first Crucifix — C. calmly & feelingly said — — — — 'Ah! poor fellow! — I thought we had done with him!' Great mirth & roaring. Dinner especially good — oysters & peaches from America. Champagne & all things very excellent, but all in perfect taste. Miss C. with her plain broad kindly heartedness & good strong common sense, cultivated & refined taste, is assuredly a very No 1 woman.

Altogether 'the evening was splendidophoropherostiphongious'. He was less thrilled by his visit to Elizabeth Barrett Browning, who had collapsed after the Treaty of Villafranca in July, and was still frail, surrounded by admirers and hangers-on. 'What good does one get of anyone's society', he asked Emily Tennyson, 'when it is merely like a beautiful small rose tree planted in the midst of 43 sunflowers, 182 mar- igolds, 96 dahlias and 756 china-asters?'

Although supportive, Lear was sometimes unnerved by the rising nationalist fervour. On Garibaldi's birthday on 19 March crowds took to the streets, fighting with the police. Afterwards Lear told Giorgio that when he went out he should take a basket to put his head in, in case it was cut off: 'On which he said, "No sir, I take soup tureen — hold him better."' Soon the papers were censored and no news came through. Lear began to pack again. Troops were everywhere, including a thousand Irish who came on a mission to help the Papal States. On

11 May 1860 Garibaldi landed in Sicily with his 'Thousand Men' and took Palermo. A week later Lear and Giorgio sailed up the coast to Livorno and spent a few days exploring the Carrara mountains and the Gulf of Spezia, stopping at Lerici to pay tribute to Shelley and Byron. Before he left for England, Lear saw Giorgio onto the boat for Corfu. He watched him through his telescope until he disappeared from view, standing at the bowsprit, 'calmly enough & perobbably smoking'.

24: NO MORE

There was an Old Man of Lodore,
Who heard the loud waterfall roar;
But in going to look, he fell into a brook,
And he never was heard of no more.

Part of the reason that Lear enjoyed exploring the Bay of Spezia with Giorgio was that everything was new, not burdened with memories. In his middle forties he was suffering more and more from a feeling of transience, mourning a lost past.

Even his friendship with the Tennysons seemed to be slipping into this misty realm. He stayed with them at Farringford in Freshwater in the summer of 1859, a glorious June week. He read 'Guinevere', which he thought the loveliest of the new poems in the first tranche of the *Idylls of the King*, and walked on the downs with Tennyson: 'who read out the Lady of Astolât, – another version of Lady of Shalott: – most wonderfully beautiful & affecting – so that I cried like beans. The gulls on the cliff laughed.' He loved the boys, and Emily noted that as he left, Lionel, now aged five, 'looking out of the window says "How I like him" & one echoes the words in one's heart.' But Lear found it hard to get on with the poet, and thought Emily seemed pale and tired, underrated by Alfred: 'I should think computing moderately, that 15 angels, several hundreds of ordinary women, many philosophers, a heap of truly wise and kind mothers, 3 or 4 minor prophets, and a lot of doctors and school-mistresses might all be boiled down, and yet their combined essence fall short of what Emily Tennyson really is.'

Oscar Gustave Rejlander, *The Tennysons at Farringford* (*c*.1862)

That spring, with the organist Edward Francis Rimbault helping him with the arrangements, Lear published five more Tennyson songs. When the Tennysons received them – on a day when Charles Dodgson was visiting them – they both agreed that 'The time draws near' and 'Come not when I am dead', were 'the best & wonderfully beautiful'. The following year his settings from *Idylls of the King* appeared, including Elaine's heartsick song for Lancelot:

> Sweet is true love though given in vain, in vain;
> And sweet is death who puts an end to pain:
> I know not which is sweeter, no, not I.

In June 1860 Lear went to Farringford again. But this time Frank Lushington was coming too, a troubling reminder of having loved in vain. From the moment that he boarded the train at Waterloo with Frank and 'a party of Prinseps', coming down to see Julia Margaret Cameron, he felt overwhelmed. Julia and Sara, the latter married to Henry Thoby Prinsep, an East India Company director and Persian expert, were two of the seven famous Pattle sisters, born in Calcutta to an Anglo-Indian merchant and his aristocratic French wife. Sara Princep ran her own literary salon at Little Holland House, where the artist G. F. Watts, whom they had taken in when he was ill, stayed for many years. Among the other sisters were Virginia, Lady Somers, whom Thackeray thought too beautiful even to imagine falling in love with, and whose husband was one of Lear's patrons; Maria, grandmother of Virginia Woolf and Vanessa Bell; and Sophia, 'the improper Monte Carlo Great Aunt'. (Virginia Woolf imagined them all wafting by, 'robed in splendid Venetian draperies . . . talking with foreign emphatic gestures'.)

The tempestuously generous Julia – who had not yet been given the camera that would make her famous – had been very taken by the Isle of Wight when she visited the Tennysons and promptly bought a house nearby as a retreat for herself, her husband and their six children, naming it Dimbola Lodge after her husband's tea plantation in Ceylon. For Lear, it was a daunting gathering. Mrs Cameron, 'rushing al solito', met them at the harbour and whisked him off in a fly to Farringford. With Alfred and Emily, Frank and the boys, the evening would have been a happy one, he thought, 'only at 10, Mrs. C. & her train came & odious incense palaver & fuss succeeded to quiet home moments'.

Lear and Frank walked on the downs again with Tennyson, but this time they heard no booming poetry. Tennyson, instantly recognisable in his flowing cloak and broad-brimmed hat, was weary of admirers rushing up to him on walks or craning over his garden fence. Today he was at his 'most disagreeably querulous & irritating', and as soon as he saw people coming he wanted to go home. 'But F.L. would not go back, & led zigzag-wise towards the sea – A.T. snubby & cross always.

After a time he would not go on – but led us back by muddy paths (over our shoes,) a short-cut home – hardly, even at last, avoiding his horror, – the villagers coming from church.' Next day Tennyson and Frank walked alone, and later Lear sang to much applause at Mrs Cameron's. Soon after they returned, Emily noted:

I hear a trampling on the drive when I am resting before dinner and think it is Americans coming as seven did the other day to ask for admittance but find it is Mrs Cameron's Grand Piano which she has most kindly sent for Mr Lear. It is pleasant to see the surprise of each one coming in & seeing it. The Camerons in the evening. Mr Lear sings a long time.

Everyone complained that the Tennysons' own piano was out of tune, and a couple of years later Lear suggested they should buy Mrs Cameron's grand to replace their 'ancient & polykettlejarring instrument'. But although his singing went well, after the awkward walk on the downs he had already decided that this was probably his last visit. In his diary he wrote, 'We come no more to the golden shore, where we danced in days of old.'

Lear's sketch of Farringford, 1864

A few months later, Lear met Tennyson in London in one of his more affable moods, and was relieved that he had not been swallowed up in

'Pattledom'. Though now wary of the man, he still admired the poetry and kept to his plan for the illustrations. But once, when he wrote out his quotes he made a telling slip: instead of the lines from 'Ulysses',

> But all experience is an arch wherethro'
> Gleams that untravelled world whose margin fades
> For ever and forever as I move . . .

Lear wrote, 'But all remembrance is an arch wherethro''. The misquotation could have been his own motto. Sympathising with Fortescue's feeling of being in a vacuum, he had said that he too felt this intensely:

there is nothing of which I have so distinct a recollection as the fearful gnawing sensation which chills & destroys one, on leaving scenes & persons, for which & whom there are no substitutes till their memory is a bit worn down. I say, there is nothing I so distinctly remember, because these feelings are with me already taking the form of past matters, never again to recur, like cutting one's teeth, measles &c.

The childhood images of teeth and measles gave him away. His memory was constantly jolted, as if tripping over a branch in a path, by a place, news of a death, a change in the weather. When he met people or arrived somewhere, he would count the years since a first meeting or visit – twenty, thirty, now even forty. Life seemed fleeting, ungraspable. He recognised Sir James Reid's feeling after leaving his post as Chief Justice of Corfu 'that his twenty-one years seemed already like a dream'. But if the past was a dream, 'Where then are the realities? & why seek for any?'

Writing his diaries late at night Lear included backward looks like a haunting refrain:

7 June. Samuel Clowes comes round: & as it hardly rained, we walked to the Z. Gardens. The Balœniceps was the most curious brute there. – The few – 4 I think – older keepers, sadly strangely recall those early days of Z. drawing: – so narrow does the ruin of life gradually seem to become.

22 June 1860. [Visiting Frank Lushington's new lodging in the Temple] His rooms, – wh. I had never been in – strangely recalled past years: – the same objects & similarly placed.

2 July. [Reading the paper] I saw in the paper — died – ... Somerville, formerly Inspector of Hospitals, & later, chief Physician at Chelsea Hospital, at Florence, in his 93rd year. Whereon the Garden at the Nemi, & the walk at Genzano rise to sight.

14 November. [Painting an oil of Philates, on the coast opposite Corfu] – & how completely the carrying out the sketch brings the life of those days of August 1856 back again – strangely dreamy! – when lame & ill, I lay on the rugs over the door of Jaffier Pashas palace, & watched the Albanian Evening life.

Lear validated his sadness by clothing it in Romantic diction, as if he was mourning the beauty and innocence of the universe itself. It was like Tennyson's repeated 'no more'. And even the person remembering was the same but not the same.

He saw, too, that throwing off this sadness would mean losing the intensities of feeling that made him what he was. His dark moments were also part of him. He looked back at moments of apprehension from childhood on. Ten years hence, after walking though the pinewoods near Cannes, he would write: 'it is not easy to say why that scene of pines & far hills is so lovely now . . .'

What a mingling of sadness & admiration of landscape botheringly will persist in existing! All the unsought morbid feelings – (certainly unsought – for I knew not what even the meaning of morbid was in those days,) of past years crop up at once – such as the Hornsey fields & Highgate archway, & the sad large Thorn tree at Holloway about 1819 or 1820 . . . the Mill at Arundel, or Peppering in 1824 & 5 – the heights above Plymouth in 1836–7 – the Godesberg – 1837 – Civitella 1839 & Nemi – all were with me at once. How far is it right or wise to get rid of or crush the morbids altogether? – I can't tell. Yet I have tried & do try to do so – tho' I crush a good deal else with them – because I have a feeling that to encourage 'morbids' is wrong.

Lear had had enough of grinding away at his easel. In early July he sent Fortescue another verse letter, a parody of Arthur Clough's mock-Byronic verse novel in letters, *Amours de Voyage*, with its failures and misunderstanding and pungent picture of Rome. Pinching Clough's conversational tone and long hexameter, he wrote with deliberate bathos not of lost grandeur but of a borrowed handkerchief, of brushing his beard, breakfasting and reaching the station, ruefully thinking of Tennyson's pension of £200 a year and going back to the rant of 'Locksley Hall':

> Bother all painting! I wish I'd 200 per annum!
> – Wouldn't I sell all my colours and brushes and damnable messes!
> Over the world I would rove, North South East and *West* I would –
> Marrying a black girl at last, and slowly preparing to walk into Paradise!

He signed off, 'Yours with a lot of affection – the globular foolish Topographer.' He was worrying about the future: money, loneliness, travel, his career as an artist. He had a long list of commissions for watercolours and oils: three Bassaes, two Campagnas, one each of Civitella, Interlaken, Zagori, Philae, Bethlehem, Beirut and Damascus, and many more. He had done rather well in the big exhibitions, and this year his large oil of Bassae was bought for the Fitzwilliam Museum in Cambridge by a subscription raised among his patrons.

Now he wanted to aim higher, to do a truly grand painting. At the time he was concerned about the civil war in the Lebanon, following the suppression of Maronite Christian rebels. Early July saw massacres in Damascus, and after reading about these in *The Times*, then waking from an afternoon sleep, Lear wrote, 'Worked suddenly at a sketch for the cedars of Lebanon.' Behind his tranquil scene of trees in high mountains lay rivers of blood.

Lear read Colonel Charles Churchill's account of his ten years in the Lebanon: 'I am wretched about all those places,' he sighed. Now he set about hunting for good cedars to paint on all his visits to friends.

The Temple of Apollo at Bassae (c.1854–5)

There were beautiful trees at Weybridge in Surrey, and Lear stayed nearby at Ockham Park with Frank's elderly relation Dr Stephen Lushington, 'a wonderfully fine cheerful good learned fine old man'. This was a very different household to Park House: Stephen Lushington, now in his late seventies, had been a passionate anti-slavery advocate and a lawyer, then judge in the ecclesiastical court – he had acted for Lady Byron in her separation from Byron, and had been counsel to Queen Caroline in her dispute with George IV. His twin sons, Vernon and Godfrey, were both fervent advocates of positivism (Vernon was also close to the Pre-Raphaelites: he introduced Rossetti to Edward Burne-Jones, and his daughters knew Holman Hunt as 'Uncle Hunt'). Lear enjoyed being with this lively family, especially as they walked across to Painshill where they found 'Great & fine Cedars', coming back 'with much fun – pun – laughter & talk of all kinds'.

Eventually Lear found his trees in the grounds of the Oatlands Park Hotel near Weybridge. Oatlands was originally a royal palace built by Henry VIII, and Charles I, it was said, had planted the cedars in 1640. His room was light and airy, and he was woken by the songs of birds, which he fed from his window. He felt so well that one day, he said, 'I was seized with incapacity to work, – & foolishness of high spirits. – So off I walked – all along to Hersham, & to Esher – (how beautiful is the home on a hill with hanging woods close to the village!)' Occasionally he went up to London or friends came down to see him, but most of the time he worked on the *Cedars* and *Masada*. Both were huge: the canvas for *Cedars* was nine feet long and that for *Masada* was seven.

He was at Oatlands in the bitter January of 1861, when the snow fell and the Thames froze. He met working men in tears, begging on the road, and walked with them to Chertsey to buy loaves of bread for their families, returning to feel guiltily lucky in his warm room. Then came a thaw, the sudden bursting of the cistern and the deluge of the 'arm-broad torrents of water'. His own room was unscathed but the sawing and knocking of repair work drove him back to town. In February his huge *Masada* was exhibited at the British Institution, and a review in *The Times* called it the most noticeable painting there, 'for truth and conscientious work'. Other reviews were not so kind, but Lear was pleased. Determined to get up to date with London life he marched off to the Royal Society to sit, at first patiently, to hear the 'diabolical Professor Tindall rave on gases, figures & the deuce knows what. At the end of an hour I felt I was growing actually mad, – & flew the brutal torture. Meanwhile, I had seen AT come in & sit afar far off! –' Next day he met Tennyson at dinner. As a change from the Oatlands quiet he enjoyed the smart London dinners, meeting Gladstone and other luminaries.

Things were going well. The MP Sir Francis Goldsmid, the first Jew to be called to the English bar, bought his painting of *Civitella* for 150 guineas, and people came in droves to his studio at Stratford Place. He sold two paintings straight away: 'so I shall pay all my debts,' he told Emily Tennyson, and 'if there is any overplus, buy a pleasing tabby cat, or a guitar, or some currant jelly: – but I don't think there will be anything over.'

A nagging worry remained: Ann's health. She was seventy in January and her eyes and the nerves in her face had been bad for some time: '– poor dear – her face is very sad: – & so is her loneliness at the dark end of life,' Lear had written in 1858; 'I soon made her laugh by talking of her not studying the Bible properly – yet it seems to me more sad this year than in any yet.' Their sister Harriett died in Scotland in July 1859, and Ellen's husband William Newsom in December. Lear had liked William, and sent constant messages via Ann: 'My kind love to Ellen, & tell her to look sharp after you, for you are always full of mischief.' One consolation was that Sarah planned to come back from New Zealand to send her granddaughter Emily to school, and to try to persuade her husband Charles to go back out with her. 'She will bounce into your quiet room one day,' he promised Ann, 'clad in a New Zealand flax garment & otherwise wholly amazing!' So she did, and Lear often found her in the house that Ann shared with two old friends in Stonefield Street, Islington.

Whenever Lear was in London he took the bus to see her, or she came to his studio and chatted while he worked. One snowy day in mid-December 1860 she walked all the way, not trusting carriages on the slippery roads, and told him curious stories of life in Pentonville in 1800, before the family moved to Bowman's Lodge – one basis for his claim that he knew everything that had happened before he was born. A few weeks later, on 1 February 1861, they spent another evening with Sarah:

Ann – dear Ann so old! —
& Sarah – quieter.
This evening was passed really pleasantly. The talk of N. Zealand – & my nephew &c. &c. &c. all very straight & true & right.

He was still lured by the thought of the South Pacific. At Oatlands he read the new edition of Herman Melville's *Typee: A Peep at Polynesian Life*, where savages are noble and Europeans are not. But Ann's increasing weakness cancelled all thought of travel.

In early March a painful swelling appeared on the back of Ann's neck and she began vomiting. Within a week Lear was consulting the doctor daily. She was always pleased to see him: 'what a blessing you are here! – not among the Arabs! . . . bless you my dear Edward! What a comfort you have been to [me] all your life!' On 8 March he took her flowers: 'her pain is dreadful. But she never swerves in the least iota from cheerfulness, affection – patience . . . O! O! O! O! O! O!' Two days later she was still full of concern for them, sending Ellen to bed, asking the nurse if she had had supper, and 'Edward my precious – take care you do not hurt your head against the bed iron.'

Next day, 11 March, she slid into a coma. Lear went home, came back, walked the night streets, went up to the Nevills in Highbury, came back again. Unable to face seeing her die he paced the pavement outside. At noon he saw the blinds pulled across the windows. Ann died in her sleep, without pain.

In his letters and diary Lear painted her end as a classic Victorian deathbed scene, selfless and sustained by faith. She had talked of dying, he said, 'as a change to bring about such great delight' that she had to check herself from thinking about it: 'She has always been indeed as near Heaven as it was possible to be.' Sorting her possessions he found that she had kept his drawings since the age of five, and all his letters and the presents he had bought in Rome, in Sicilian markets, in the souks of Constantinople and Cairo. A week after her death, he told Fortescue: 'I am all at sea & do not know my way an hour ahead. I shall be so terribly alone. Wandering about a little may do me some good perhaps.' Emily invited him down, but he found the house full, with Tennyson's brother Horatio and his family, and left upset. He drifted between friends – to Bath, Torquay, Cheltenham. Perhaps after all, he wrote, 'the less one stays in places one likes the better – & so one escapes some pain. Therefore wander.'

He did wander, always looking back. At Woolwich in mid-May, he remembered the Hornbys' son, Phipps, killed in Montreal in 1848. 'There, on as bright a day as in years gone, I crossed the Artillery ground. There Phipps was alive, Lina & Susan & all: & dear Lady Hornby. All things seemed gay & bustling as then: yet how much of the "then" exists no longer – in myself as elsewhere?' At the end of the month, when Holman Hunt was going to Denmark, Lear gave him a letter of introduction to his beloved friend from the early days in Italy, Wilhelm Marstrand, asking him to write some day: '*Mandate mi un lettera un giorno.*' Adding a cartoon of his overweight self, he ended, '*Vostro affezionato sempre, Oduardo Lear*'.

Lady Waldegrave helped him in his distress by sending him to Florence to paint two views. He drew cypresses between showers of rain, and managed to get into the Villa San Firenze at San Miniato, looking down across the city, 'the *real* view of Turner. It is very glorious & I shall set to work at it thoroughly.' Still, grief pursued him and being unable to write his long letters to Ann made the time feel strange and blank. In Florence his heart bled for Browning, distraught at Elizabeth's death. Then Sarah wrote, telling him that their sister Mary had died on her way home from New Zealand and been buried at sea: 'The dead weary thinking of Ann, & now of Mary every now & then seems to exhaust all nature within me.' That summer, he would hear that his brother Henry's four boys were fighting for the North in the American Civil War, while Fred's son had joined the Confederate army. 'I suppose all my 5 nephews were in the last battle, a curious state of unpleasant domestic romance.' In a June dusk full of fireflies, he scribbled lines from Shelley's 1821 'Lament': 'Out of the day & night, / A joy hath taken flight!'

He missed Ann badly, and his memories of her were always fond. Four years later, on her birthday, 17 January, he wrote in his diary, 'Ever all she was to me was good, & what I should have been unless she had been my mother I dare not think. She would have been 74 today.'

V. CIRCLING

25: 'OVERCONSTRAINED TO FOLLY':
NONSENSE, 1861

There was an Old Man of the Isles
Whose face was pervaded with smiles;
He sung high dum diddle, and played on the fiddle,
That amiable Man of the Isles.

Lear liked children, their spontaneous affection, their cheerful lust for violence, their acceptance of the odd. He avoided the Victorian double-think that saw children as both innocents to be cherished and savages to be tamed: he just saw them as individuals and tried to enter their world. He was entertained by their curiosity, their language-struggles and non sequiturs. They made him laugh.

Now that Ann's death threw him back to his own childhood, he noticed children more than ever, but he was thin-skinned from exhaustion and shock and sometimes family life was too much. In Cheltenham Lucy Francillon's boys were delighted with his nonsenses, and Lucy herself, whom he had known as Lucy Gale in his early days in London, was 'always so quiet and sensible that her company *exactly* suits me now'. In the same town, though, staying with the Reids, he wrote:

Jemmy – (who is supposed to be unwell,) screaming in the next room – Helen practising below – (scales,) & Mary on the other side.
One day of this house is enough – basta I live thro' it! – Breakfast at 8 – but hurried – & piggish: it is wonderful to me how people can live so, taking

no care of the very days of boyhood & girlhood that make all their future life good or evil.

Afterwards he saw that it was his own ragged state that made this unendurable. By contrast, visiting George Clive and his wife at Perrystone near Ross on Wye, he found their small daughter Kathleen charmingly odd. In the evening, 'Little Kathleen came & amused us all. She sang "I am a Nemesis & a Fury rolled into one" – with a queer spirit enough to kill a man outright: – I thought I should never have been able to stop laughing.' The liking was mutual. Kathleen promised, he said, that 'she will go to Timbuctoo with me in 20 years, "if she is not ill"'. A few weeks later, on a train at the end of May he noticed that the juddering made two children, in the care of their nurse: 'not frightened, but half ill. So I took the boy – 4 years old, on my knee, & the girl in my arms, & told them my long name & all kinds of nonsense – till they forgot the shaking bother . . . I *never* saw 2 sweeter & more intelligent children than those 2: & I *longed* to keep them both.' Entertaining them he turned easily into the clown, the singer of songs, the maker of nonsense. Later in the year, calling in at some friends, and finding 'no one in but the baby', he asked, 'I wonder why I love children so?'

Gradually, as he came to terms with Ann's death, Lear's sense of being alive came back. On 1 September, at St Leonards, he wrote:

Assuredly one of the purestly loveliest days it is possible to see on earth. From sunrise all day & evening & night hardly a breath of air, & the sky pure blue – a few bright clouds at sunset: the sea a perfect mirror, – hardly rippled, & almost noiseless. – Rose at 7 – after a sleepless night. No letters. Placed outlines of Mt. Athos, Schloss Elz, & Matterhorn on canvass, & then wrote – absurdly & continually all day long – till 6. Posted 24 letters. During the day, the bathers, walkers, churchgoers, sprawlers on the sand, sitters on the shingles, loiterers on the benches, – were all happy to see.

At this point he was working on the proofs of a new *Book of Nonsense*. Despite his offhand attitude to his nonsense, he was proud of it, and took great care with the limericks and his later songs. Ten years hence he would admit that 'bosh requires a good deal of care, for it is a sine qua non in writing for children to keep what they have to read perfectly clear & bright, & incapable of any meaning but one of sheer nonsense'. But he was aware that the book was not only for children. A week after he smiled at the sprawlers on the sand, he went to stay in Kent with the Goldsmids, who had become good friends. He was smitten by Sir Francis's sister Julia, a clever woman of thirty-eight, in the Helena Cortazzi mode: 'Such a distracting Miss G. with such a face, like Mary Queen of Cotts!' After dinner he showed his nonsense drawings: '– gt. Laughter –. Sang a good deal: & Lady G played. Altogether happier than for many a day.'

Nonsense and the Goldsmids gave him heart. Instead of making his own lithographs he took his 1846 book to the Dalziel brothers, engravers who worked with the Pre-Raphaelite artists as well as for *Punch* and the *Illustrated London News* (and, in a few years' time, for the Alice books), explaining that he wanted to produce a new, cheaper edition. They found him 'a landscape painter of great distinction, a naturalist, a man of high culture, and a most kind and courteous gentleman', and agreed to cut the blocks, print and produce the book, and offered to buy his rights for £100. Lear declined, but asked if they could find a publisher. He had persuaded McLean to give up his rights in return for a promised book on Corfu, and had already approached Smith & Elder, who said no. The Dalziels now approached Routledge, Warne & Routledge, who would not publish, but agreed to sell a thousand copies on commission at three shillings and sixpence, a shilling higher than Lear suggested ('A wary Scotsman is Routledge').

Lear copied all his drawings afresh, so that the skilled wood engravers could get to work – sometimes shadowy pencilled lines showed second thoughts, later erased. There were small disputes with the Dalziels about the cutting and printing – he was very particular about the detail – but on the whole he was extremely pleased. On 16 December he wrote in amazement, 'Book of Nonsense is published & 500 sold already.'

There was a young Lady of Lucca, whose lovers completely forsook her. She ran up a tree, and said, "Fiddle-de-dee"! — Which embarassed the people of Lucca.

For the new book Lear dropped three limericks – including the Old Man of New York, who murdered himself with a fork – and added forty-two. Some seemed to show himself over the years as he grew his beard, put on weight and became more obsessed with his nose – a lasting invitation to phallic readings. His restless travels were there in the Old Man on a Hill, who seldom if ever stood still and the man fleeing the cow recalling his sitting on one by mistake in Greece with Frank. He was there, too, in the 'scroobious', wily palm-climber of Philae and in the struggling scholar of Greek:

There was an Old Person of Cromer,
Who stood on one leg to read Homer;
When he found he grew stiff, he jumped over the cliff,
Which concluded that Person of Cromer.

'Concluded' is nice. But is he dead, or skipping on the sand beneath, having finished reading and hopped down?

In the rhymes that Lear added to his book people balance, swing, teeter on their toes, or fall. The drawings show even more unnatural poses than the first book, people with their legs in the air, upside down, stretching, pointing, swinging on a bell-rope. They are like actors performing before a critical 'they', and yet they also reflect back, in exaggerated form, the 'normal' oddities Lear saw around him. He was very aware of dress and found that looking hard at fashions made them powerfully strange. Writing to Fortescue about a photograph of Lady Waldegrave, he noted that 'the large dresses of the day never look well photographed, for in themselves they are so monstrous that only the movement of a live woman can make them approximate to a figure at all ... the portrait of a sitting lady in a crinoline always looks as if she were a dwarf walking'. Later he was amused by the new fashion for dresses narrowing at the ankle, so that now women could 'postulate theirselves upside down with impunity, and no fear of petticoatical derangement'.

There was an Old Man of Melrose,
Who walked on the tips of his toes;
But they said, 'It ain't pleasant, to see you at present,
You stupid Old Man of Melrose.'

'They' are more confrontational, more violent in 1861 than in the earlier limericks. They smash the man from Whitehaven with his raven, and the old man with the gong ('But they called out, "O law! You're a horrid old Bore!'"). He seems not to mind, being ecstatically involved in his playing, and nor does the Old Man of Melrose, dancing on despite the abuse. But although many characters are defiant, like the girl with the birds on her bonnet, shouting back, 'I don't care' – many do care. There are dark encounters: the man who shuts his wife in a box; the women who swap barbarities:

There was a Young Person of Smyrna,
Whose Grandmother threatened to burn her;
But she seized on the Cat, and said, 'Granny, burn that!
You incongruous Old Woman of Smyrna!'

That last adjective makes one pause. 'Incongruous' is hardly apt for a woman who wants to burn her granddaughter: yet it means exactly that, not fitting, out of place.

The drawings, feeding off slips of sound, like visual puns, are as slippery as the words. Looking at the Old Person of Ewell, we can see that 'mice' won't make his soup 'nice', but does the word on the bowl read 'Gruel', or 'cruel'?

There was an Old Person of Ewell,
Who chiefly subsisted on gruel;
But to make it more nice, he inserted some mice,
Which refreshed that Old Person of Ewell.

Some limericks and drawings flirt openly with uncertainty, like the man in a boat, a rhyme that critics often return to with furrowed brow.

There was an Old Man in a boat,
Who said, 'I'm afloat! I'm afloat!'
When they said, 'No! you ain't!' he was ready to faint,
That unhappy Old Man in a boat.

Is he ready to faint from despair or relief? Is he 'unhappy' in general, or just in this dilemma? His boat seems both on the water and the land. Perhaps 'they' are teasing, and he is floating after all? And why does he look as though he has just fallen into the boat? Why are they leaping with their feet in the air? Boundaries between land, water, air disappear. Lear leaves us afloat on riddles, while the mechanics of the poem, the accelerating rhythm and slow return, work to prevent a capsize.

In early March 1861 Lear told Emily Tennyson how he waited for people to come and see his pictures but sometimes no one came for three hours or more: 'so then I partly sleep, & partly draw pages of a new Nonsense book. If I sleep, I wake savagely at some newcomer's entrance, & they go away abashed. If I write nonsense I am pervaded with smiles, & please the visitors.' Like the amiable Old Man of the Isles, playing his fiddle, 'pervaded with smiles', Lear was a skilled performer. But a licensed fool tells truth: his nonsense is serious. Some years on, raging at a doctrinaire sermon, he exploded, 'Perhaps it is better that I should altogether stay away, since one day, if I am so overconstrained to folly, I may get up and snort & dance & fling my hat at the abomination of sermon preaching where sermons are simply rot.' His nonsense verse was an anti-sermon, the explosive expression of an outsider who had to smile and sing for lords and ladies, bishops and bankers. Fortescue once ticked him off for being easily bored by people, and in London in 1862 after a dull posh lunch, he admitted, 'I am come to a point of life when the restraint of aristocratic society is a fearful bore, & one not at all wants entertaining.' In Corfu he scrawled on the corner of a letter to Emily, 'I have decided to go to the Palace in dirty boots: to eat my fish with my fingers: & to spit in the tumbler: – on wh. I shall never be asked again.' Nonsense let him snort and fling his hat, make faces in church, fulfil his old urge to jig down the stately corridors of Knowsley. It defied gravity, in all senses, even if it risked a fall.

There was an Old Man at a casement,
Who held up his hands in amazement;
When they said, 'Sir, you'll fall!' he replied, 'Not at all!'
That incipient Old Man at a casement.

The *Book of Nonsense* sold fast and its readers now spread far beyond Lear's circle of friends. His purchasers were still a well-heeled bunch: three shillings and sixpence was a lot to pay for a children's book. But why did this semi-private pleasure become such a public hit? Perhaps

George Routledge, that canny Scotsman, was just a better publisher than McLean, more adept at marketing. But perhaps, too, the time was ready for nonsense: Lear, the man of feeling, and then in 1865 Lewis Carroll, the man of mind. Lear read *Alice in Wonderland* without comment. He did not have Carroll's logical genius, but both writers created an escape into time-free imaginary worlds. Both were shrewd about contemporary modes, conventions and beliefs, sharing a parodic brilliance, an eye for the absurd and an inspired verbal liberty, rousing simultaneous surprise and recognition. Looking back on Lear's 1861 book, the writer of a long *Spectator* article noted in 1870 that he had 'seen an eminent statesman, great in finance, unequalled on the Bank Act, laugh over it the whole of a summer morning (when out of office)'. More seriously, he worked out that although Lear's rhymes and pictures 'defied sense – which is just what nonsense ought to do . . . the defiance was in itself at once acknowledgment and rebellion. What we want from Nonsense is exactly this – a gay rebellion against sense. But there is no relief to the mind unless there be enough sense in the nonsense to make the nonsense visible.' All nonsense, the review concluded, 'should be audacious and capricious defiance of sense, but never go far enough from sense to lose the feeling of delightful freedom which is implied in the rebellion'.

Lear's limericks, which he had been writing now for twenty-five years, both recognised and defied social rules. This was a concern that fitted these uneasy decades. Notions of British superiority and empire had been shaken by the Crimea and the Indian Mutiny, and the queen herself would soon be sunk in mourning after Albert's death in December 1861. Fantasy and irreverent nonsense were a relief, a way of reading a world out of joint. Charles Kingsley turned to an underwater world in 1863 for his fable of reform and his moral 'Do as you would be done by'. (Lear read Kingsley's Christian Socialist essays and *The Water-Babies*, and wrote to express his appreciation for all his works 'perhaps above all – "Water Babies", which I firmly believe to be all true'.)

Lear was not alone in worrying that the rules 'they' imposed to maintain order could throttle individuals, or in his concern with society's failure to absorb the 'different', the foreign, the odd and disruptive. In *On Liberty*, in 1859, John Stuart Mill despaired at the way people always looked first to see what others were doing, instead of thinking like individuals. 'Even in what people do for pleasure, conformity is the first thing thought of; they like in crowds; they exercise choice only among things commonly done; peculiarity of taste, eccentricity of conduct, are shunned equally with crimes.' Mill linked this to the Puritan heritage, where the one great offence was 'Self Will', and all human good was comprised in 'Obedience'. Such narrow conformity led, he was sure, to a withering and starving of human capacity.

In art and literature, this generation, poised between the defiance of the Romantics and the counter-cultures of the *fin de siècle*, had little time for oddity. The past decade had seen outbursts against the Pre-Raphaelites in 1850, and against Tennyson's *Maud* in 1855, when one critic exploded, 'If an author pipe of adultery, fornication, murder and suicide, set him down as practiser of those crimes.' How dare the Poet Laureate offer such a picture of decline into madness and self-loathing?

> Till a morbid hate and horror have grown
> Of a world in which I have hardly mixt,
> And a morbid eating lichen fixt
> On a heart half-turned to stone.

Maud was a disturbing picture of the fragmentation of self, full of social as well as personal anger against the rottenness of politics, the poisonous gases of the mines, the adulteration of bread for the poor so that 'the spirit of murder works in the very means of life'. Yet just as upsetting to many readers, the cure that Tennyson offered was to plunge his tortured individual back into the mass, marching off to the Crimean war. Lear never offered such a parable of reintegration: his inventive, free-spirited outsiders, facing hostility and loneliness, remain outside.

Arguments about the individual and the species also coloured the debates about evolution that Lear had followed over the last thirty years. Fifteen years before, in April 1845, Lear and his friends were caught up in the excitement following Robert Chambers's *Vestiges of the Natural History of Creation*, which posited the development of the whole natural world from earlier forms, from stars and planets to plants, fish, animals and humans. In the same year, the revised edition of Darwin's researches on the *Beagle*, especially on the Galapagos finches, a single species 'modified for different ends', had given glimmerings of a theory of natural selection. Lear's limericks had always been taxonomic, a gallery of odd types, and his people were curiously fluid, morphing into animals and birds, with elongated limbs, arms turning into wings, noses into beaks. His nonsense people, ill-fitting folk pushed out by the herd, also evoked the ruthless process that made Tennyson long to believe 'that nothing walks with aimless feet,/ That not one life shall be destroy'd,/ Or cast as rubbish to the void'.

> Are God and Nature then at strife,
> That Nature lends such evil dreams?
> So careful of the type she seems,
> So careless of the single life.

On 22 November 1859 Darwin's *On the Origin of Species by Means of Natural Selection* sold out overnight. For Darwin's supporters, the words 'natural behaviour' no longer had a fixed meaning, defined by a Creator. The book created rifts between those who accepted the complex, stumbling 'progress' of nature, with its leaps and dead ends, and those who clung to the belief that the world was ordained by God, in general and in detail. In June 1860 at the British Association of Science meeting, a ferocious argument took place between Darwin stalwarts, led by T. H. Huxley, and the believers in divine design, headed by Bishop Samuel Wilberforce ('Soapy Sam'): the 'Darwinists' triumphed but the row was far from over.

In the 1860s, however, church circles were riven by different schisms, with the Anglican establishment gathering their skirts against critics. The Darwin furore was almost pushed aside by the row the following year over the mildly titled *Essays and Reviews*, whose authors, dubbed by opponents 'The Seven against Christ' (six were clergyman and one a lawyer and Egyptologist), spoke out roundly against belief in miracles and for a critical reading of the Bible. Benjamin Jowett, Master of Balliol, argued that the scriptures should be read as a book like any other, taking account of context and the author's intention. The *Essays* went through ten editions in two years, selling in equal numbers to the *Origin of Species*, and provoking equally furious attacks: a letter to *The Times* signed by the Archbishop of Canterbury and twenty-five bishops threatened to pursue the authors through the ecclesiastical courts. The paper war raged for five years in around four hundred books and pamphlets.

Lear was fascinated. 'Apropos of the Essays & Reviews', he noted in his diary the horror that Lord Stanley of Alderley had expressed to Fortescue:

'What is to become of us if you do away with miracles?' – said Lord S. of A. to C.F. – there is no faith – no nothing. 'And how rash of Jowett! He might have been Bp.!' – Poor fool Lord S. of A! How little you can understand the love of truth, which don't dwell in such meagre buzzims as your'n.

He disliked the extreme advocates on both sides, the High Churchmen and the Calvinists, and supported the liberal intellectual line taken by Jowett and his old friend Arthur Penrhyn Stanley, now a professor at Oxford and soon to be Dean of Westminster. When the Bishop of Salisbury prosecuted the vicar Rowland Williams (who had promoted the new German biblical criticism in the *Essays*) Lear wrote, 'Should Williams be condemned, I think you will not be surprised by my openly becoming a Unitarian some day.' In 1863, he was equally concerned about the attacks on the theologian John Colenso, who had been the first Anglican Bishop of Natal and had refused to accept that unbaptised Africans would go to hell: when the South African bishops tried to remove him from his post, he took the matter to the civil courts, and won the backing of the Privy Council. Colenso also wrote scrupulous, controversial studies of the Old Testament Pentateuch and the Book of Joshua, arguing that they could not be taken as literal truth, and commenting that massacres presented as 'works of God' were as terrible as the Indian Mutiny: the excesses and inconsistencies threw doubts on the historical truth of the whole Bible.

The Colenso affair enraged Lear: 'A broader creed, – a better form of worship – the cessation of nonsense and curses – and the recognition of a new state of matters brought about by centuries, science, destiny or what not, – will assuredly be demanded and come to pass whether Bishops and priests welcome the changes or resist them.' He was tired of the stupidity: 'I begin to be vastly weary of hearing people talk nonsense, – unanswered – not because they are unanswerable but because they talk in pulpits,' he wrote. Nonsense could only be answered by nonsense. Bishops should forbid people to come to church unless they answered two questions in the affirmative:

1st. Do you believe in Balaam's ass, Jonah's whale, Elisha's bears, and Lot's wife? 2nd. Do you believe that all mankind who do not believe in these creatures will be burned in everlasting fire, wholly without respect to their wisdom, charity or any other quality?

In the early 1860s he was appalled by the 'rage & horror' of religious factions that he met in polite Hastings. At the time he was reading Ernest Renan's *Vie de Jésus*, which argued that Christ's life should be subject to historical and textual criticism and was amused that Renan's title gave his fellow lodgers an impression of his piety, 'little conceiving the opposition of that volume to their views & their topics of faith'. He stuck to his views. Ten years later, he felt he had been knocking his head against a wall with regard to Holman Hunt, as he told Thomas Woolner. Thinking that Hunt possessed 'advanced or liberal principles' in religious matters:

I had spoken about the increase of rationalistic & antimiraculous thought, & hoped his future pictures would point or express such progress. Whereas I find I never made a greater mistake, & that on the contrary, he is becoming a literalist about all biblical lore, & has a horror of Darwin, Deutsch, & I suppose of Jowett

& A Stanley . . . meantime, if he should paint Balaam's Ass or Gideon's Fleece it will not surprise me.

He was alarmed, too, by the vogue for animal magnetism and spiritualism, and horrified when Fortescue and other intelligent people, including Dickens, Thackeray and Tennyson, flocked to the séances of the American medium Charles Forster, who claimed he was in touch with Virgil and Cervantes. In Lear's limericks judgement is social and human. It may be erring and arbitrary but it is certainly far from divine.

Lear protested almost too vehemently. The miracles he cited most – Balaam's ass, Jonah's whale, Elisha's bears and Lot's wife – touched his own fears, and his fascination with metamorphosis and change, speaking animals and vengeful justice. In particular Lear, who so feared drowning, recoiled at the horror of the whale carrying Jonah down into the depths: 'The waters compassed me about, even to the soul: the depth closed me round about, the weeds were wrapped about my head.'

But if his nonsense now feels full of undercurrents and psychic terrors, in the 1860s it just made children laugh, and carried adults back to the silliness of their youth. For a while, because of Lear, limericks were all the rage. Poets of Lear's generation and the next had a go: Rossetti, Lewis Carroll, later Kipling, and even, allegedly, Tennyson. Making up a limerick seemed so easy, old or young, drunk or sober, and it proved a perfect form for pornographic jollity in clubs and mess rooms across the empire.

A Book of Nonsense sold four thousand copies within six months but Routledge failed to pay and the Dalziels began to ask Lear to settle his account. In November 1862 he sold all the rights to Routledge for £200. He crowed with pleasure and relief all the way to the bank but George Routledge had the last laugh: the book sailed through twenty-four editions in Lear's lifetime. In different forms, it has never been out of print.

26: 'MR LEAR THE ARTIST'

When Frank Lushington's friend Granville Bradley left his card at Farringford, Tennyson invited him over 'to meet Lear, not the king but the artist'. This was what he wanted above all, not to be loved for his nonsense but to be taken seriously as 'Mr Lear the artist'.

The sketches he made on his travels – free, bold, alive – were not for sale; they were just the reference store, the library of his art. When he made them he was drawing only for himself, not to please others; his hand was sure and fast and the colour washes flowed over the lines like light itself, or the blue loom of storm. From these sketches Lear worked up his more finished studio watercolours and these specially commissioned versions of chosen scenes are often glowing, memorable works. His chief concern in the 1860s, however, was his oil painting. His oils – unlike his quick, spontaneous sketches – took an immense amount of time. He worked slowly, squaring up the original sketch so that it was easier to copy and drawing the design on his canvas in charcoal. Then he applied broad half-tone washes, especially where the picture would be shaded, and began to work. He could do the sky in one session but the main picture and especially the foreground required detailed work, tiny strokes, obsessive finishing.

Lear's great hope now was for the two canvases he worked at so painfully at Oatlands, *Cedars of Lebanon* and *Masada*, the latter of which was

exhibited at the British Institution in February 1861. He was planning
a gallery of his own at Stratford Place but was not sure exactly where
his work fitted in the current schools. He still moved in Pre-Raphaelite
circles, but was not comfortable with all its stars, deciding that Millais
was 'all outside & froth', vastly inferior to Hunt, 'like a crafty aged
French dancing-master, – & has neither depth nor softness in his character'. He disliked Effie Millais even more, 'her catching at Aristocratic
names, – her pity of bachelors – "it's just so melancholy!" (as if one half
of her 2 matrimonial ventures in life had turned out so happily!) – &
her drawling stoniness'. If Millais could charge 450 guineas for *Apple
Blossoms*, Lear thought, then *Cedars*, which he finished in May, should
be worth half as much again. He would put it on sale for £735 or more,
and not care if no one bought it. The painting has vanished today, but a
copy painted for the MP Charles Roundell gives some idea of what this
vast canvas was like.

Cedars of Lebanon (1862)

So *Cedars* was finished, but Lear worked on. By now he was tiring,
resenting being tied to his easel: 'No life is more *shocking* to me than the
sitting motionless like a petrified gorilla as to my body & limbs hour after

hour – my hand meanwhile peck peck pecking at billions of damnable little dots & lines, while my mind is fretting & fuming through every moment of the weary day's work.' Yet despite his comic rage, oil painting engrossed him: he liked the smell of the paint and linseed oil, the crumpled rags, the feel of the palette and brushes. (In Corfu that winter he was holding his palette at the window when his friend Colonel Bruce saluted as he marched by: returning the salute Lear got paint all over his hair and whiskers, 'which I must now wash in Turpentine or shave off'.) He was rethinking his views on the painters he admired, astonished that he could once have liked Poussin and Salvator Rosa, when he now liked Titian and Holbein more. But this had little impact on his own style, which remained recognisably the same. He felt he was on the right course – when *Cedars* was shown in Liverpool in late summer it was 'praised to the skies', he told Fortescue, 'the concluding paragraph being – "Mr. Lear has in this great picture not only achieved a professional success, but he has also conferred an obligation of the highest order on the whole Christian world" (!!!!!! – After that take care how you write to me.)'.

Lear found few autumn delights in London, except the sensation of 'a new spadmodic poet, by name Swinburne who seems to amaze small circles'. Then, to his surprise, at the end of his stay a Canadian relative by marriage arrived, Caroline Jones, the widow of his cousin Henry Chesmer, famous for her *'wonderful* eyes' and now married to a Quebec politician. Lear liked her, and took her down to see Ellen in Leatherhead: 'a sweetly kind creature is my cousin Caroline'. He was intrigued, too, by her lively, good-looking daughter Jessie, and her husband Major Foy, 'a chubby magnified cherub looking pudgy man –but a gentleman, & kindly & hospitable'. All in all, he enjoyed this surprise family meeting. And the next week he was off. He planned to spend the winter of 1861–2 in Corfu, without Frank, who became engaged this autumn to Kate Morgan, an old friend whom Lear had met in Eastbourne with the family and who had supported them at the time of Henry's death as 'a help & a pleasant sight to every body'. Lear made no comment. They would be married that December.

In Corfu, Lear thought of Emily Tennyson in an England full of 'snow, peasoups rain hail coalfires plumpudding and childblains', telling her that here, in glorious weather, 'oranges are a halfpenny a piece . . . Owls are Plentiful. Flights of grey gregarious gaggling grisogonous geese adorn the silver shining surface of the softly sounding sea.' He missed old friends like the Reids, Cortazzis and Edwards, not to mention Frank, and brooded over his struggles: 'Yet looking back – even as far as 6 years old – (at the clown & circus at Highgate,) & then to all since – how can it be otherwise? The wonder is, things are as well as they are through constant fighting.' But he liked the new governor, Sir Henry Storks, and found a lasting friend in his aide Evelyn Baring, Thomas Baring's young cousin. Even better, in December Julia Goldsmid took rooms in Corfu and stayed for three months: Lear saw her often, dined with her alone when he could, and grieved when she left. But he made no mention of marriage.

With all these distractions he was relatively calm when the post brought letters about Frank's wedding, which he hoped would let some light into 'the too close boskiness of Park House'. And another wedding was on the cards: Lady Waldegrave's husband Mr Harcourt died, leaving her free to marry Fortescue – if she would have him. After months of suspense, during which she seemed to lean towards Fortescue's boss at the Colonial Office, the Duke of Newcastle, she finally accepted his offer, making him feel 'the luckiest dog in the world'.

On Easter Sunday 1862 Lear sat on the cliffs at Palaiokastritsa, where he had sailed with Frank in *Midge*, in perfect quiet 'excepting only a dim hum of myriad ripples 500 feet below me, all round the giant rocks which rise perpendicularly from the sea: – which sea, perfectly calm and blue, stretches right out westward unbrokenly to the sky, cloudless that, save a streak of lilac cloud on the horizon'. He was fifty that May, and this island seemed the best place to be.

He came back to London in early June to a round of invitations and heavy eating and drinking ('o dear dear these dinners! – More amendments & resolves'). The diversions were constant, from gossip that

Ruskin was going mad to demands that he fill in his tax forms, from concerts with the Fairbairns to weekend trips to the country. One that he particularly enjoyed was his stay with Stephen Lushington at Ockham, where he met Mrs Gaskell and two of her daughters and spent a merry evening singing. He was not, however, so happy about his paintings. He had arranged for *Cedars of Lebanon* to be sent to the exhibition in South Kensington in May and was distressed to find that his pictures were hung too high, blaming this on the prejudice of the Royal Academicians against painters outside their group. Then he read a lukewarm review in *The Times* by Frank Lushington's friend and fellow Apostle, the powerful critic Tom Taylor, damning naturalistic painters influenced by 'Pre-Raffaelites', like John Brett, who merely mirrored the external scene, and adding: 'Mr Lear must be on his guard against descending to the same merely reflective function, though at the height at which his large landscape of "Corfu" (381) and the "Cedars of Lebanon" (382) are hung it is impossible to say if the remarks that we have applied to Mr Brett be applicable to him.' And that was all.

This summer and autumn, feeling bleak, Lear painted two oils linked to Tennyson's poem 'You ask me, why'. Commissioned by one of Fortescue's close friends, Henry Grenfell, MP for Stoke on Trent, the pair were complete contrasts, one being of Philae, already associated in his mind with the 'palms and temples of the South', and the other of Beachy Head, for the line 'Between the steep cliff and the coming wave' from 'Guinevere'. (Originally Lear had thought, appropriately, that he would illustrate 'my spirits falter in the mist'.) Sketching there in October, he groaned to Chichester Fortescue of the painful five-mile walk to get the 'vastly fine view he wanted'. The result, a study in black and white and silver, with the cliffs looming up like icebergs and only a streak of green on the mirror-like sea, had a chilly power, turning the Sussex coast into an Arctic drama.

As Lear sketched, he was not thinking of the poem's celebration of Britain's freedom of speech and good governance, but of the opening lines:

Beachy Head (1862)

You ask me, why, tho' ill at ease,
Within this region I subsist,
Whose spirits falter in the mist,
And languish for the purple seas.

His own spirits were faltering while he sketched these cliffs, the suicide's leap. He worried about the condemnation of *Cedars*, first by the Academicians who hung it so high and secondly in Taylor's 'cold-blooded criticism': 'What to do with the Cedars I do not know,' he wrote drily. 'Probably make a great coat of them.' Lear's hopes of a grand sale had faded: he couldn't even think how to pay for his frames, his colours and his rent. Perhaps he should slash his prices by half? He was almost broke, but within weeks the sale of his rights in the *Nonsense* to Routledge saved him, at least briefly. And once he had funds, he sailed off again to Corfu.

If he couldn't sell large pictures, why not try small ones to pay the bills? Three days after he arrived in Corfu he 'began to draw outlines of drawings "to be made –" – to the amount of 30!!!!!!!' Taking sixty sketches from his many travels, he made thirty small mounts and thirty larger. He stuck his paper onto these and for the next two days made thirty outlines a day, giving each one a number: within a fortnight he was calling these his 'Tyrants', writing to Winsor & Newton and ordering sixty frames from Foord's.

He worked punishingly hard, doing sketches for the smaller Tyrants through the storms and rain before Christmas and in the sunlit days afterwards: 'Paradise weather. Long as I have seen these mountains – yet their beauty today was so wonderful that I could fancy it new.' It was an odd kind of work, calling up all his memories, yet with no aspirations to high art. The Tyrants progressed painfully slowly. He went over the pencil outlines in grey watercolour, then rubbed out the pencil. Then to paint them, he took a single colour and moved from one to another, adding first a pale blue wash all along the line, then red, then yellow, then grey details, before gradually building up the picture with stronger colours, emphasising the distance and then highlighting the foreground. This was the way that he had watched the colourists work at Hullmandel's worshop, thirty years before.

Having finished his first thirty Tyrants, he began the second batch. The work became a 'terribly wearying incubus', but having begun, he had to finish. On 10 February he did, working out that the whole set had taken him sixty-three days: 'A singular spotch of energy'. Working in this way became a practice he returned to for years, whenever he needed money. Near the end of his life, Henry Strachey, the young brother-in-law of Lady Waldegrave's niece Constance, watched him in his studio:

He was then at work on a series of water-colours, and his method seemed to be to dip a brush into a large wide-necked bottle of water-colour, and when he had made one or two touches on the drawing, to carry it to the end of the room and put it on the floor, the performance being repeated until quite a row was arranged across the room.

Once he had finished his sixty watercolours, Lear sent out notes to all he knew, hoping to sell them for a very modest price, then framed and hung them round his gallery walls, knocking in the nails himself. 'There's a proof that an old cove of 50 has some energy still!'

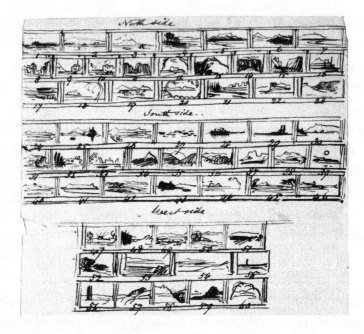

He had doubts about the success of his gallery, feeling that photography was now a rival to topographical prints, something that had dawned on him rather slowly. Six years ago he had bought a 'photographic machine' himself, but thought of photographs only as an aide-memoire. 'If I can come to use this mode of working,' he had explained to Ann, 'it will be of great service to me in copying plants, & in many things which distance, limited time, heat etc. would prevent.' Photography had developed rapidly in the last twenty years and many amateurs were now keen: Lewis Carroll bought his first camera in the same spring as Lear, becoming a master of the new medium, processing as well as taking his pictures. Lear's many friends now often pored over photographs, as well as prints, after dinner. But Lear was never happy with his experiments: two years after his first purchase he tried again, buying a new camera but selling it after a few months for £15 to Major Shakespear, who took many views of the island.

Despite opposition from his brother Lord Clermont, in which he sought Lear's help as an intermediary, Fortescue married Lady Waldegrave on

20 January 1863. He wrote to 'my dear Lear' at midnight before his wedding day: 'Today I am going to be married! I will not try to tell you what I feel tonight. How could I if I did try? I wonder that the world goes on as usual. I am almost overwhelmed.' The thought of this wedding made Lear feel more alone, but he had new friends like the de Veres, for whose daughter Mary he drew a set of coloured birds, and he became fond of Giorgio's family, paying for his sons' schooling, worrying about scarlet fever and giving the boys their medicine. He was thrilled, too, when the Shelleys arrived in their yacht and Percy Shelley copied his setting of 'O world! O life! O time!'

On the last day of February 1863 the Tyrants were finished. That day a letter came telling him that Frank and Kate Lushington had a daughter, Gertrude, and asking Lear to be her godfather. He looked back with some amazement at the misery of his time on the island with Frank, more than five years ago. By contrast the current year, with its string of cloudless days, had been calm, despite, or perhaps because of his hard work. He had not felt so serene for many years, he thought, putting this down to better climate, better health, getting over Ann's death and less anxiety about money, 'but I believe most of all to the better state of the "demon"— or rather to his greater absence'. Even his rooms were perfect: 'This home is a sort of Paradise this year: now & then the children below make a noise, but the most beautiful playing on the Piano of the Consul's wife is indeed a blessing. The only drawback is that she plays so little, & that the Instrument is below my bed room.' He had to give up his own piano as it was too expensive. This was a loss, but still, what could he do? He could not remember a happier winter.

His big pictures on display in Stratford Place had still found no takers. The Tyrants, however, did the trick: he sold them for ten or twelve guineas and when he did his accounts in March he reckoned he was owed precisely £289 8s. He wrote tactful letters to those who had not paid. Then, wondering how else he could make money, he decided to write another book, on the Ionian islands.

27: 'FROM ISLAND UNTO ISLAND'

At the end of March 1863 Lear packed a wooden crate with paintings, drawings and photographs. The crate went on the boat to England, but Lear did not. At the end of March he sold three more drawings, and worked out that he had 'enough tin to pay rent and shut up house for 8 weeks or thereabouts'. Then he set out round the Ionian islands.

He wanted to take this trip and make sketches for future paintings because the seven islands in British possession – Corfu, Paxos, Santa Maura, Cephalonia, Ithaca, Zante and Cerigo – were on the verge of being handed back to Greece. The islanders had asked for this for thirty years, in constant tension with the British establishment. 'They hold us in utter contempt', Frances McLellen had written on visiting Corfu in the 1830s, 'and we look on them as removed but one degree from donkeys.' Gladstone's visit to hear their grievances in 1858 had changed little. In 1862, inspired by Garibaldi's march to Rome and the founding of the Kingdom of Italy, the Greek military led a revolution and King Otto (the son of Ludwig of Bavaria) was deposed after thirty years' rule. But Greece still seemed destined to be ruled by foreigners. When a plebiscite was held to choose the next king nearly thirty names appeared on the ballot paper, including Garibaldi and 'an Orthodox king', but the vote was overwhelmingly for Prince Alfred, Victoria's second son, later Duke of Edinburgh.

This was not to be, however, as a protocol of 1832 – the year Otto was crowned – had decreed that no prince of Britain, France or Russia could take the throne. Then it was offered to Edward Stanley, later fifteenth Earl of Derby, but he too turned it down, so Palmerston manoeuvred the choice towards the sixteen-year-old Prince William of Denmark. Adding a jovial P.S. to a letter to Edgar Drummond about money, Lear wrote, 'You may not have heard (it is not generally known), that I refused the throne of Greece – King Lear the first – on account of the conduct of Goneril & Regan my daughters, wh. has disturbed me too much to allow of my attention to governing.' It was a joke, but a bitter one, as Lear the impoverished artist set out on his travels:

> O reason not the need! Our basest beggars
> Are in the poorest thing superfluous.
> Allow not nature more than nature needs,
> Man's life is cheap as beast's.

In Corfu a new row broke out when Storks, at Gladstone's order, removed two long-serving Ionian judges from the Supreme Council, a step that provoked Frank Lushington to publish a furious pamphlet in their support. Lear saw the island world he knew disintegrating around him. He packed for his trip, not forgetting the vital flea-powder, scribbling a quick limerick before heading for the quiet limestone island of Paxos:

> There was an old person of Páxo,
> Which complained when the fleas bit his back so;
> But they gave him a chair
> And impelled him to swear,
> Which relieved that old person of Páxo.

He sailed on the night of 4 April, looking back at Corfu under a bright full moon. Giorgio joined him in Paxos and for the next eight weeks they travelled the islands.

In each island Lear contacted the British Resident ministers, taking advantage of clean rooms, good meals and talk and books. He was welcomed everywhere and sketched every day, even Sundays, although the kindly Scottish Baron d'Everton on Santa Maura 'was awfully Sabbatical, & don't quite approve my sketching tomorrow evidently'.

He had strong opinions on what he found. Paxos was quiet and provincial. Santa Maura, despite the sea of olives spreading out like a morning view by Claude or Turner, was 'hideously dry', inland 'withered wrinkled, chasmy, rocky valley – gullies'. Initially Lear thought this island beautiful, but in the blazing heat he took against it, fearing fever around its lagoons and salt-pans. The next island, Ithaca, was grand and full of poetic resonance. Cerigo – the ancient Cythera – was gold with ripening corn; Zante was dazzling and elegant, but its people too violent; Cephalonia was beautiful but sombre, dominated by its Black Mountain. Everywhere he went he hunted for views to sketch, walking through shrublands of myrtle, arbutus and holm-oak, jotting reminders in his diary: 'Great naked slabs of rock. Twisted olives. Asphodels & lambs.' Once, when someone suggested going with him, Giorgio explained: 'My master is like one hunting dog – he looks there & here, & does not go straight, – he is always looking about as he goes, & cannot attend to anything: – so you would only be like one log of wood – & bother would be good for nothing.'

On Santa Maura he strode out to the rocky Cape Ducato, where Sappho leapt to her death, inspired by the dark grey cliffs, edged with foam, with vultures on a ridge and shards of pottery scattered round the ruined temples. At Metaxata, on Cephalonia, he searched for traces of a modern, not an ancient, poet:

Lord Byron's house was easily found – the small children knowing it. Every one I met said – 'Yes – we know it, ἀλλὰ θέλεις ἀγωράσει Μέρλαις;' [But would you like to buy some laces?] – to G.'s amusement. And at the house itself, (I was there in 1848 –) was nil save the white barrel earthen broken-handled jug – still there as then. —

Cape Lefkada (Cape Ducato), from *Views in the Seven Ionian Islands* (1863)

Poetry was mixed with politics, as it had been in Byron's life, and Lear was very conscious of the imminent end of British rule. He saw the civil power in action when Storks sailed in to hear a case, accompanied by Evelyn Baring, 'talkative & cheery', and he saw the remnants of military power in the soldiers who wined and dined him: 'good rough cheer, much beer & laughter'. As time went on he began to weary of the 'smoke, noise, cards, wine, bother' of the mess dinners that left him with terrible hangovers. Yet at fifty-one he felt fitter than he had for a long time. He walked all day, drinking at stone cisterns and eating picnics of bread, sausage, eggs, walnuts and almonds, stopping to sketch or write his journal by a path, on a rock or under a shady tree. For the past year he had been slowly reading though the *Iliad* in Greek and on Ithaca on 27 May 1863 he climbed high up to Korax, the crag of the raven, overlooking the spring of Arethusa, said to be where Odysseus met Eumaeus the swineherd when he returned to his island home:

Drew till 10, & we are now sitting at the fountain below the 'great rock;' a most exquisite cool spot – ('here are cool mosses deep,') popple popple ever, with green moss & maidenhair fern. All around are gray savage rocks, clad with Prickly

Oak – Ilex – Phyllorea, Πρινάρι [Kermes oak], & every sort of shrub & flower. The Squill leaves are grand, – the white & pink cistus lovely – salvia, mullein – what not. Blackbirds sing, pigeons flit, swallows shimmer, & as we came, a flock of goats was abundantly pretty. Κωραξ [Korax] is indeed a remarkable spot for beauty. The vast height & shut-in loneliness of the spot are very impressive, & as I drew from above opposite, the flight of wild pigeons to the little fountain, their wings shining in the morning sun, made the hollow gloom still grander.

Whether this island was Homer's Ithaca was disputed, but Lear was content to link the rock to the *Odyssey* and the cool mosses to Tennyson's 'Lotos Eaters'. His own drifting was a kind of lotus-eating, and sometimes he longed to live this way forever. In his diary he wrote,

It seems to me that I have to choose between 2 extremes of affection for nature – towards outward nature – i.e. — English, or Southern. – The former, oak, ash, beech, – downs & cliffs, – old associations, – friends near at hand, & many comforts not to be got elsewhere. The latter – olive – vine – flowers – the ancient life of Greece, warmth & light, better health – greater novelty – & less expense in life. On the other side are, in England, cold, damp & dullness, – constant hurry & hustle, – cessation from all varied Topographical interest, extreme expenses: – & at the South are ——— (cetera desunt).

Cetera desunt, 'the rest is missing', no disadvantages at all . . .

On 3 June he sailed back to Corfu through the islands 'now so well-known'. The familiar life opened up to receive him – letters, an invitation from the palace, a gathering at the de Veres', Evelyn Baring playing the piano. But the weather was ominous and a storm made the harbour a rolling sheet of foam. All the talk was of the end of their era: 'The acceptance of the Gk. Throne seems fixed – & one's impression is that the Islands will be ceded immediately: – & our occupation end by the end of the year.'

Two days later Lear took the boat to Italy. In Ancona, after struggling to undo the straps on all his luggage for a customs inspection in the blazing midday heat, he got sunstroke. He struggled north, but collapsed in Turin for ten days and arrived back in England giddy and low, worried that he had no news of Giorgio. People called to see him:

But nothing removes my sadness. It is dreadful: & this life is impossible – staying – hard-working all day – awaiting for comers – never going out – hearing the dim roar of the distant streets – only seeing those who come for a few minutes, no freedom, no air, – no light, – no friendliness. Better remain abroad wholly. Worst of all is the mortal folly of supposing Giorgio ill or dead: – it has often happened so before, but still weighs senselessly on me – without a shadow of foundation.

This penning out – & journals! The task seems too long.

It was a classic collapse. Yet within a few days he was dining out – 'very pleasant', 'utterly pleasant' and, at Thomas Baring's, 'very very pleasant' – and setting off to weekend house parties in country mansions. Eventually he retreated to Hastings to work. He had planned to write up his Ionian journal as he had for Albania, but this was too much and instead he decided to publish a large, elegant volume of twenty views with short introductions, like the second volume of his *Illustrated Excursions in Italy*. This, 'being *well done*, if at all, would keep up my prestige as a draftsman of Mediterranean scenery', he explained to Fortescue, 'and would, moreover, hold up or pave a way to my more general smaller sized Topography of Greece, to be one day printed with my Journals'.

To avoid the chore of lithography, Lear hoped to use photographs of black-and-white drawings, but although he tried drawing in pencil and charcoal and chalk, all the photographs were useless. He had to set about lithographs after all, complaining that he couldn't even go out to see the mountains, as he had when he slaved over Tyrants in Corfu. During these weeks he visited Ann's grave and went round Bowman's Lodge: 'As I stood in various parts of the large empty rooms, I could absolutely hear and see voices and persons, and could – (had I had a pen and ink and paper at the time,) have written out months and years of life nearly 50 years ago, exactly and positively.' Feeling distinctly odd at this annihilation of time he went home to finish another lithograph.

His twenty plates were dominated by Corfu, including the vista from Ascension; boats on the straits, their sails pale against the sea; the orange groves; the curving bay of Palaiokastritsa.

Palaiokastritsa, Corfu, from *Views in the Seven Ionian Islands* (1863)

For the other islands he chose views that summed up his most powerful memories: the precipices of Assos in Cephalonia; the 'gay white houses and tall and elegant campanili' of Zante; the 'cheerful calm' of Gaio in Paxos. But he could never quite banish the absurd. Of Zante's 'plain of currant vines', he noted:

The old nursery rhyme –

> 'If all the world were apple pie,
> And all the trees were bread and cheese' –

supposes a sort of Food-landscape hardly more remarkable than that presented by this vast green plain, which may be, in truth, called one unbroken continuance of future currant-dumplings and plum-puddings.

Even the flower-stems of the aloes were 'like asparagus-stalks on a gigantic scale'. The people amused him too. After the dark costumes of the northerly isles he warmed to the bright colours of Cerigo, where the women carried long sacks, slung from their shoulders, made of gorgeously coloured carpets. These sacks, open at one end, he explained, 'are universally used as cradles by the peasant-mothers of Cerigo during their outdoor labour; and in each of them is a baby Cerigot – if not quiet, at least as closely swathed and imprisoned as any chrysalis'.

By late October the book was finished, but then he had to write seeking subscriptions, another mighty labour: he never wanted to hold a pen again. Finally, *Views in the Seven Ionian Islands* appeared on 1 December, dedicated to Sir Henry Storks, the last High Commissioner. In a letter to Mrs Prescott, Lear drew himself as the 'old man with a Book', telling her he had left a copy for her at Waterloo station. All his friends liked it. 'What a beautiful book!' wrote Emily Tennyson on Christmas Eve. 'We are so glad – One can see the violet shadows on the Olive groves and the hot mist from the waters.'

In the summer of 1863, while Lear was working on his lithographs, William of Denmark accepted the Greek crown, becoming George I of Greece. Henry Storks dissolved the Ionian parliament and called a new one to vote formally on the cession of the islands. When George I visited London in September Lear wrote flippantly to Fortescue, asking him to 'write to Palmerston to ask the Queen to ask the King of Greece to give me a "place", specially created '& the title ὁ Αρχἀνοηδιφλναραποιὁς with permission to wear a fool's cape (or mitre) – 3 pounds of butter yearly and little pig, – and a small donkey to ride on. Please don't forget this as I have set my heart on it.'

Lear's portmanteau Greek word, *Archanoēdiphluaríapoios*, 'Arch-nonsense-chatter-maker', celebrated his role as the 'Arch' fool, the retainer with butter and pig and ass. But this was no comedy. On New Year's Day 1864, when it seemed that handing over the islands would take longer than expected, Lear suddenly felt he must go back. An acquaintance was leaving next day and in a whirl Lear set off. For a few weeks he took up his old island life, refusing to think of future winters:

'perhaps I may go about in an unfixed mode continually and evermore'. In particular he enjoyed his friendship with Evelyn Baring, sending illustrated letters – a letter snail, a letter cloud – and a phonetic letter enclosing photographs:

Deerbaringiphowndacuppelloffotografsthismawningwitchisendjoo thereiswun-ofeechsortsoyookankeepbothifyooliketodoosoanwenyoohaveabetterwunofyour-selfletmehavit.
    Yossin seerly
    DwdL

Having time for serious reading he turned to Renan, Colenso and *Phases of Faith* by Francis Newman (brother of the cardinal), describing his steps towards a radical Unitarianism. But he also read novels, history and travels: Abbé Michaud's novel of the Inquisition, *Le Maudit*, Froude's hostile study of Elizabeth I, Richard Burton's *Abeokuta and the Cameroon Mountains* and John Hanning Speke's account of his second journey to discover the source of the Nile.

Reading filled an uneasy time of waiting. Among the Corfiotes he found excitement, but also sorrow, confusion and unease, with servants, innkeepers and shopkeepers lamenting future loss of trade. They feared the loss of protection and as the garrisons took away cannon and blew up the forts, anti-British feeling rose. By the end of March his rooms were let to others. Sadly, Lear looked around:

The quiet of this house – the cheerful corner room – its green blinds – look out over the harbour – the large table – good fire etc – the long quiet study – an even light thru' all the day – the good order of things – bkfast – hearing George read, & so on . . . are among the scenes & times I fear not to return.

He packed amid explosions at the forts and spring thunderstorms. 'Goodbye,' he ended a letter to Fortescue, 'my last furniture is going. I shall sit upon an eggcup and eat my breakfast with a pen.' He wrote to the Prescotts' granddaughter, little Nora Decie, saying that he was going to join Captain Deverill's three geese and swim all the way to Piraeus.

On 4 April 1864, a year to the day since he sailed to the Ionian islands, Lear left Corfu: 'Once more I left the loveliest place in the world – with a pang.' The next morning he woke early and wrote a rough draft of a poem:

> She sits upon her Bulbul
> Through the long long hours of night –
> ~~Watching~~ And ~~Where~~ o'er the dark horizon gleams
> The Yashmack's fitful light.
> The ~~dark~~ lone Yaourt sails slowly down
> The deep & craggy dell –
> And from his lofty nest, loud screams
> The white plumed Asphodel.

Then he scrawled across the page, in large letters, 'Alas! indeed yes!—'

Lear went first to Athens, exploring the new excavations around the Acropolis and calling on the elderly philhellenes of Byron's generation, old General Church and the crusty George Finlay, author of the multi-volume *History of Greece*. But for Lear the city had lost its enchantment and instead of staying on, he sent for Giorgio and set off for Crete. He had read Robert Pashley's 1837 book *Travels in Crete*, and although the island was ruled by Turkey he felt he must cover it for his proposed 'topography of all Greece'.

The ship was full of pilgrims coming home from the Madonna of Tinos – site of a miraculous cure, a Greek Orthodox Lourdes – and their landing at Hania was chaotic. The land was hidden in cloud, the sea was rough, the women and children vomited, the hotel was filthy and the consul lived miles away. A young merchant, the Dutch consul Guarracino, came to his rescue by offering his comfortable house. Even better, Lear made friends with the English consul, Frank Drummond

Hay, and his beautiful Spanish wife. Toward the end of his Cretan visit, he sang Tennyson songs to the Hays, worked with Mrs Hay on translating Tennyson into Italian and made an alphabet and an illustrated set of numbers for their four-year-old daughter Madeleine. One afternoon he fell asleep on the sofa after a walk and woke 'to find little Madeleine lying by me with her arms round my neck kissing me and patting my eyes. Darling little child . . . what a blessing is this family!'

He tried to sketch every day but was bothered by perpetual wind and rain, retreating to read Pashley and novels of the 1840s found on hosts' bookshelves, such as *Vanity Fair* and then *Villette*, 'a very lovely book'. The hills were hard to draw and he thought Crete a 'sell', not a patch on Sicily. 'Its antiquities etc. *so* old as to be all but invisible; its buildings, monasteries, etc. nil; its Turkish towns fourth-rate. Rats O! and gnats.' It was some years before the excavation of Crete's Minoan civilisation and at Knossos Lear found only bushes and scattered brickwork. Yet as he moved eastwards along the coast to Heraklion and explored the inland hills, he made fine watercolour sketches of mountain views, monasteries and fountains, and drew comic doodles of the *moufflons*, the leaping mountain goats. The views Lear painted here were among his loveliest: swift, clear and serene, veiled with washes of colour.

He climbed through green valleys and drew under great oaks, gazing down across cornfields and groves of walnut and cherry. The climax was a view of Mount Ida, the nursery of Zeus, often veiled in cloud, but finally visible, 'a dream-like vast pile of pale pink and lilac, with endless gradations and widths of distance and the long curve of sand from Rethymnon hills to Armyro. So I drew till long after sunset, and then came to this place, where I washed in a cheese plate and sat down with what patience I could.' And the birds were here, making him a boy again:

the vast multitude of blackbirds, nightingales and many other sorts of birds . . . Far off, the cawing of the rooks, which brings back days – 'days that are no

Mount Ida from Phre, 7 p.m., 24 May 1864

more' – so long ago as 1823, when I first heard the voice of the rooks in Sussex . . . 'O life! O earth! O time! On whose last steps . . .' It is noon, and considering how unwell I was yesterday, happiness abounds.

His notes were full of people as well as places, and of food as well as views: dinners with the pasha, lunches with the Hays, evenings with Cretan families, meals in country monasteries, 'eggs, olives, caviar and *astonishing* wine!' At village feasts they ate crumbly brown bread, herbs and '*snails*' – the first time he and Giorgio had eaten them, finding them 'really very decent, boiled in oil'. As usual Lear had come armed with letters of introduction, aware that the island was full of different communities: Turks and Greeks, Albanians and Arabs, Jewish, Armenian and Maltese traders, and African soldiers from the Egyptian rule in the 1830s. Waves of occupation marked the island. In Heraklion, with its flat-topped houses and broken mosques, he noted, 'The Venetian cathedral, a ruined skeleton, speaks of former days.' In the hills, as he walked through groves of olives and gardens of oranges and lemons, he passed villages toppled by earthquakes or sacked in uprisings. His companion in the wild Sphakian mountains, the haunt of freedom fighters, was Captain Michael Korakis ('Crow'), a veteran of earlier rebellions. He was called 'the Garibaldi of Crete', Lear noted, but 'now in the Turkish government's pay – only they don't pay him.' Two years later, in 1866, Korakis would command twenty thousand partisans against the Turks. In this uprising, suppressed with terrible brutality, the Cretan rebels who were besieged at the monastery of Arkhadi blew it up rather than surrender. Lear's host, Abbot Gabriel Marinakis, 'a man of the world . . . very jolly and pleasant', gave the order himself, and died in the explosion.

Lear sensed the bloodshed ahead when one elderly man accosted him, 'When will our unhappy country be freed?' But despite the tensions, when he stood on the deck of the steamer at the end of May 1864, he already felt nostalgic: 'All Crete diminishes, fades, vanishes: but we see Ghonia, we see Platania, we see the pleasant Halepa, where we have spent so many happy days. We see the long range of Sphakian mountains, now nearly snowless. Last of all, lo! Ida fades.'

He had travelled from island to island. And sometimes it seemed that he would journey like this, 'for ever roaming with a hungry heart', to the very end of his life.

28: 'WHAT A CHARMING LIFE
AN ARTIST'S IS!'

There was an Old Man with an owl,
Who continued to bother and howl;
He sate on a rail, and imbibed bitter ale,
Which refreshed that Old Man and his owl.

Lear could not settle, but nowhere seemed right after Corfu. He needed
to winter abroad, but somewhere that British people gathered, so that he
could sell his pictures. In October 1864 he wrote whimsically to friends,
saying he would fly away south to someplace, he didn't know or much
care where, as long as it began with 'a Nem'. In the end he settled on
Nice, apologising that at least it was the next letter in the alphabet. The
next winter would be V for Venice, and then the promised M – for Malta.

In the summers he knew that it was vital to stay visible in Britain to
keep his reputation alive, and to catch up on the gossip and the exhibitions. Art, science and politics were discussed at the dinner tables as
Lear swung down the rope of familiar names – Baring, Bethell, Bruce,
Drummond, Fairbairn – and on down the alphabet to the Prescotts and
Tennysons, Fortescue and 'Lady W.', as Lear called her. He saw Frank
and Kate Lushington, whose first son, Harry, was born in August, and
he caught up, too, with his elderly sisters, Sarah and Ellen, who were
stricken by the sudden death of Sarah's son Fred in Arundel. On a 'hot

& lovely oldfashioned day' Lear took the train from Victoria to his funeral, passing Peppering on the new line, remembering Fred as a baby and himself as a boy. It was strange to see Fanny Coombe, as he did on every visit to London – now a grandmother.

Inevitably, Lear went to the Tennysons. Farringford, he thought, was 'one of the places I am really happy in', but Tennyson was unpredictable and Lear had his doubts about Farringford's bohemian chaos and reek of pipe tobacco and large wet dogs. Freshwater was changing, with the building of an enormous hotel, plans for three hundred houses, a new road and even talk of a railway, an idea that horrified Tennyson. Almost as bad, Lear thought, 'Pattledom has taken entire possession of the place – Camerons and Princeps building everywhere: Watts in a cottage (not Mrs W.) and Guests, Schreibers, Pollocks, and myriad more buzzing everywhere.' 'Mrs W.' was the sixteen-year-old actress Ellen Terry, who had married Watts, thirty years her senior, after he painted her portrait that spring, and soon regretted it, leaving him within a year: the Prinseps and Camerons had not welcomed his talented, outspoken child bride.

Lear was terrified of Julia Margaret Cameron, dashing between the houses in her Indian shawls with her fingers stained with photographic chemicals. Her daughter Julia had given her a camera the year before and she was already getting family, friends and servants to pose for her blurry scenes from history and poetry, creating her own negatives in wet collodion on glass plates. The following February Emily told Lear, 'Mrs Cameron is making endless Madonnas and May Queens and Foolish Virgins and Wise Virgins and I know not what besides. It is really wonderful how she puts her spirit into people.' Lear was not so sure. She was taking the first of her great portraits, which would include one of Holman Hunt in Eastern dress and many of Tennyson. (This summer Charles Dodgson also stayed in Freshwater, without his camera, asking her to take pictures for him of the prettiest children – in focus please.) Emily, Lear felt, was looking tired and Alfred, in expansive form, raved about England '"going down hill" – "best thing God can do is squash the planet flat"'. Lear sat with him reading scores of letters 'from fools – madmen – admirers – would-be employers'. The following morning, Tennyson was in one of his most irritating moods:

I believe no other woman in all this world could live with him for a month . . . It always wrings me to leave Farringford – yet I doubt – as once before – if I can go again. I suppose it is the Anomaly of high souls & philosophic writings combined with slovenliness, selfishness, & morbid folly that prevents my being happy there: – perhaps also – vexation at myself for not being more so.

In London Lear opened his gallery, sending a vignette of studio visitors to Holman Hunt. Four ladies rise to go after staying two hours looking at his pictures: 'What a treat my dear Mr Lear!', 'But how wrong to stay indoors, not good for your health', and 'how dreadful these interruptions must be!' Four more ladies enter:

The first 4 rush up to them:
All 8 ladies: – How charming! How fortunate! Dear Mary! Dear Jane! Dear Emily! Dear Sophia! &c.
5th Lady – How wrong of you dear Mr. Lear to be in doors this fine day!
6th Lady: – How you can ever work I cannot think! You really should not admit visitors at all hours!
7th Lady – But do let us only sit and look at these beautiful sketches!
8th Lady – O how charming! & we will not go to Lady O's.
The other 4 Ladies. – O then we also will all sit down again – it is so delightful.
Chorus of 8 ladies. What a charming life an artist's is!
Artist. – D—n!

More seriously, he felt, an artist's life was hard. His pictures could never be perfect, he told Hunt; they were deformed, born with 'one leg shorter than t'other', or a crooked nose: not strong examples of their species. He longed to study and produce work true to nature in the Pre-Raphaelite vein but the whole pattern of his life went against this: good topographical painting, he decided, was safer to aim at.

Lear took another three-year lease on Stratford Place to show his paintings while he was away, and worked on commissions of the Campagna, Greece and Corfu, and on colouring his Crete drawings. And seeing that his Tyrants had done well, he bought new colours and brushes and ordered mounts from Foord's for 'the absurd and utopian batch of 240 I propose doing next year'. To take his mind off this he plunged into Henry Walter Bates's account of the Amazon rainforests, which backed Darwin up in providing evidence of natural selection. Reading Bates, he fantasised about going to live in Ega, far up the great river, where jaguars roamed and huge butterflies flew. At Ega and in the Australian bush, he joked, there were 'abundance of caterpillars highly edible & refreshing – & thus life for its few remaining years, would be cheaply sustained'. But he did not sail away to eat caterpillars. He simply went to Nice.

In Nice he found rooms on the Promenade des Anglais, laid out his Tyrants in groups of eight and began penning out and colouring. He met the English residents – Helena Cortazzi was there, rousing no pangs – but after a month of working on the Tyrants he was desperate to be on the move. With Giorgio he walked along the coast, through Menton and Monaco and Alassio all the way to Genoa, sketching bays and cliffs and twisted rocks, jagged in the lines of his pen. It was icy, winds howled and rain poured, and modern progress, as well as the weather, was blasting the natural world. 'I tire sadly of this Corniche,' Lear wrote crossly, 'the lopsided views & blank gray sea – & this everlasting smash of Railway cuttings & blowings up & knocking down.' The sun came out briefly when they reached Genoa at Christmas and then back they tramped to Nice through more rain.

On his icy winter walk, and all through the spring, Lear made his sketches fast, with an almost abstract notation of line and distance, as if propelled into a new age. They had a clarity and strength that made them feel modern, strikingly unconventional.

He kept these sharp, bold drawings to himself: for his clients he re-

Oneglia, Riviera di Ponente, 11.15 am, 12 December 1864

turned to his familiar style, combining accuracy with drama and moody atmosphere. When he showed his Riviera watercolours in Nice, people crowded in with open purses – Lord and Lady Fitzwilliam handed him a cheque for £100 for six sketches.

His watercolours and his new Tyrants sold well in his London gallery too; the Prince of Wales came, and bought ten. But as usual in his London summers, he fretted about money. *Cedars of Lebanon* and other big pictures were still priced too high to attact buyers, and he resented the struggle. Within weeks he was impatient, dreaming of distant lands: 'I loathe London by the time I have been here a month. The walking – sketching – exploring – noveltyperceiving & beautyappreciating part of the Landscape painter's life is undoubtedly to be envied: – but then the contrast of the moneytrying to get smokydark London life – fuss – trouble & bustle is wholly odious, & every year more so.'

He endured the long English summer, but as soon as Lady Walde-grave, coming to the rescue again, commissioned a painting of Venice he accepted at once. Previously he had taken against Venice, lamenting its lack of trees, but when he arrived at the start of November 1865, he was entranced. 'How tremendously full of picturesqueness is every moment in Venetian canals.' He stayed in Danieli's hotel, rejoicing in the quiet after the noise of London: 'O! O! what a sunset & what a dream of wonderful beauty of Air & Architecture! – Earth & Heaven!! . . . *Silent* Venice!' He took gondolas along the canals and out to Murano, and made detailed drawings of the buildings, but often he set his pencils aside and settled for watercolour, pale washes of blue and grey, with amber tints and dark reflections. When the fog closed in, so that he could see no further than the boats at the quay, Venice vanished, but even then the atmosphere was beautiful.

Venice, 3.30 p.m., 18 November 1865

Lear owed his stay to Lady W. and he wrote to her exuberantly when he saw in *The Times* that Fortescue was now Chief Secretary for Ireland, appointed by Lord John Russell, Prime Minister after Palmerston's sudden death:

being of an undiplomatic & demonstrative nature in matters that give me pleasure, I threw the paper up into the air & jumped aloft myself – ending by taking a small fried whiting out of the plate before me & waving it round my foolish head triumphantly till the tail came off & the body and head flew bounce over to the other side of the table d'hôte room. Then only did I perceive that I was not alone, but that a party was at Bkft in a recess. Happily for me they were not English, & when I made an apology saying I had suddenly seen some good news of a friend of mine – these amiable Italians said – 'Bravissimo Signore! Ci rallegriamo anche noi! – se avessimo anche noi piccoli pesce li butteremo di quâ e la per la camera in simpatico con voi! – So we ended by all screaming with laughter.

It was a joyful dismemberment – the Italian family, equally delighted, wishing they too had little fish to throw across the room. But Lear did worry about Fortescue taking the position when Fenian attacks were on the rise. 'Read papers: Irish news looks really bad,' he noted in January 1866.

When he read the reports of Ireland Lear was in Malta. He had gone there largely to see Evelyn Baring and Sir Henry Storks, who had been governor there since 1864, and was furious to find that they had left two days earlier, to work on the commission on an uprising in Jamaica. 'No greater bore could have occurred,' he wrote in large scrawls with lines of exclamation marks. Resigned to the loss of 'Sir Storky', he took a room in a house across the bay from Valletta. He had toothache, his epilepsy was bad and the weather turned wild: 'Wonderfully shrilly-howly is the winds tonight, & how booming the sea!!!!!! . . . what a howling!!!!!!!'

Lear had always felt ambivalent about Malta. Stopping there briefly nearly twenty years before he had told Ann that he could never live there: 'there is hardly a bit of green in the whole island – a hot sandstone, wall, & bright white houses are all you can see from the highest places . . . the street scenery – so white, so bright, so clean, so balconied, is really beautiful, but there the charm ends.' Now, In January 1866 he complained that it was hard to capture the 'sparklingness' of the towns and the bareness of the landscape. But he made superb sketches, pure in line against a tawny wash. The highlight of his stay was his visit to Gozo, where the scenery, he told Lady W., 'may truly be called pomskizillious and gromphibberous, being as no words can describe its magnificence'. This was the legendary home of Calypso, who had detained Odysseus for years, and Lear played with her name in a single-sentence poem he sent to Henry Luard, the grandson of his early mentor Prideaux John Selby. 'Gozo my child', it began, 'is the isle of Calypso', the nymph who:

> . . . every morn in the sea did dip so
> Whereon Ulysses seeing her strip so
> And all her beautiful ringlets drip so
> From her beautiful head to her beautiful hipso
> Because her curls she never would clip so
> – Took to staying away from his ship so . . .

It seemed doubtful that any Calypso-like nymph would ever hold Lear in thrall. One evening, after writing letters and paying calls, he watched the full moon rise and scribbled a sketch in his diary with lines from Tennyson's 'The Palace of Art', slightly misquoted as usual:

> One seemed all dark and red – a tract of sand
> With someone pacing there alone
> Who pac'd for ever in a glimm'ring land
> Lit by a large low moon.

'It was most beautiful,' he wrote, 'the brilliance of the night, & its silence.'

29: 'THE "MARRIAGE" PHANTASY'

There was an Old Person of Harrow,
Who bought a mahogany barrow;
For he said to his wife, 'You're the love of my life!
And I'll wheel you all day in this barrow!'

Lear knew that there was an alternative to his wandering – to settle down, marry, have a family. His obsession with this idea, and his endless dithering, ruled his life in the mid-1860s, as his longing for Frank had dominated it ten years before. He felt out of step. Even in paintings he was faced with idealised visions of family life: Holman Hunt was now working laboriously, cursing the while, on *The Children's Holiday* for Thomas Fairbairn, literally moving the chair, table, damask table-cloth, dog, silver tea-urn and five plump children into the woods of their Sussex estate, and painting a surprised-looking Allison Fairbairn in a silver crinoline pouring the tea.

Frank Lushington and Chichester Fortescue had both gotten married, and at the end of this year Hunt married Fanny Waugh (Thomas Woolner had proposed to her the year before, and when she turned him down he married her sister Alice). 'Every marriage of people I care about rather seems to leave one on the bleak shore alone,' Lear confessed to Fortescue. As if in response, he had concocted his own dream of married life. The person he fixed on was Augusta Bethell, daughter of the Lord Chancellor, Richard Bethell, Lord Westbury.

Lear had known the family since the 1830s. He dined with them often in London and stayed at Hackwood, their estate near Basingstoke. But the friendship was not always congenial. As Lord Chancellor, Westbury was a ruthless reformer, favouring statute over the old common law. He led the Privy Council decision against the bishops' sacking of Rowland Williams, which pleased Lear – but he was sarcastic, boastful and self-centred, took a mistress openly and made his wife Ellinor ill and unhappy, as she lamented dolefully when he was out of earshot. Long ago, in 1858, Lear had suffered an intolerable evening showing them his Palestine sketches:

Tittering & laughing & bore – and Sir R talking Cicero & D Roberts – but no lifelike care for Palestine itself, tho' they asked to see views of it . . . At 11 I came away – I confess – very angry: but when I think of the life of poor Lady B. & the force she has to put on herself, – I do not wonder at her talking nonsense "Do you carry that large box always with you –" – &c

The Bethells set him on edge. A year later a real row had developed at dinner over Tennyson's 'Two Voices', in which one voice urges the other to suicide:

A still small voice spake unto me,
'Thou are so full of misery,
Were it not better not to be?'

This provoked 'a frightful discussion . . . wherein I lost my temper horridly', wrote Lear. And when the topic moved to religion, Sir Richard lost his temper too: 'he became vastly angry & blew me up – "Lear, if you grow so testy – no one will converse with you Lear! –" "You are quite a breed" on which he was perfectly right – only on the argument he was wholly wrong. Frightful indignation & irritation.'

They were worlds apart, and Westbury had no sympathy with Lear's humour:

He – Speaking of 'undique sequaces' – 'sequax,' – and saying 'let us remember the line and go and look for a translation,' quoth the landscape painter in a fit of absurdity, 'My Lord, I can remember it quite easily by thinking of wild ducks.'

'How of wild ducks, Lear?' said the Lord C. –

'Because they are *sea-quacks*,' said I.

'Lear,' said his Lordship, 'I abominate the forcible introduction of ridiculous images calculated to distract the mind from what it is contemplating.'

At the time Lear found this funny. But if his relationship with her father was so difficult, why did Lear fix on Gussie? He had known her since her childhood, and had watched the other children grow up; the boys Slingsby, Richard and Walter, and Emma, Gussie's older sister. Emma was now married to Mansfield Parkyns, famous for his book on travels in Nubia and Abyssinia in the 1840s, and a good amateur artist; eventually they had eight daughters. By contrast, Gussie was the invaluable daughter at home. She was round and sweet-faced, and easy to talk to, an echo of Emily Tennyson. Lear felt sorry for her, bullied as she was by her squabbling, 'disjointed' family. When she was in her late teens he thought of her as 'a dear good true little girl, – almost faultless'.

In fact Gussie was independent and clever, and by the early 1860s she had already published collections of folk tales, translations of works from Spain and Norway, and several stories 'for young people'. These were sentimental and moral, in good mid-Victorian vein, but the dialogue was lively and feeling intense, sometimes violent. In *Maud Latimer*, 1863, the heroine is a disobedient tomboy, given to storms and passions of tears, who accidentally blinds her sweet, golden-haired sister by pushing her near the fire so that her dress goes up in flames. Maud runs away to London and although she is saved by the kindness of strangers (and her sister, of course recovers), her wilfulness remains appealing – gripping reading for young girls.

So Gussie was no 'angel in the house', as Lear began to see her, after Coventry Patmore's popular poem. Yet as he listened to her play the piano, worried about her health and eyesight and walked with her

343

under the trees in Hackwood's park, he saw himself as a knight errant who could rescue her from her miserable home, as he had hoped to save Frank from Park House. On the other hand there was plenty against such a marriage. In 1862, Lear was fifty and Gussie twenty-four. He was not well off and knew his questionable status as a 'dirty landscape painter'. His epilepsy made him worry about living closely with someone, and he feared it might be passed on to children. And he dreaded giving up his work and travel. Most of all, he had never really got over Frank. When he and Frank walked home together after a jolly, 'anarchic' dinner in 1861 with the elderly Stephen Lushington Lear felt he was boring Frank and so 'cut away'. However, he wrote, 'it is best as it is. For a fanatical-frantic caring overmuch for those who care little for us, is a miserable folly. And after all ordinary natural pride revolts at selfish coldness.' He was on the rebound. It was the idea of marriage, not the woman, that he was in love with.

Augusta Bethell

In Lear's imagination and childhood memories marriage held as many threats as joys. In his limericks and poems, terror swirls around it. Judging by the grin on this wife's face, can 'mistake' be the right word?

There was an Old Man of Peru,
Who watched his wife making a stew;
But once by mistake, in a stove she did bake,
That unfortunate Man of Peru.

The diminutive, smiling husband is unfortunate indeed. But both husband and wife can suffer, and sometimes in Lear's verse the institution of marriage itself appears as a monster of nature, a walking, stalking, devouring, gnawing mistake.

There was an Old Person of Hyde,
Who walked by the shore with his bride,
Till a crab who came near fill'd their bosoms with fear,
And they said, 'Would we'd never left Hyde!'

In 1861, lonely after Ann's death, Lear had wondered, 'Would one have been as happy as one fancies if one had been married & had had children?' The past conditionals suggest a dream already abandoned, but marriage was still on his mind when he went down to Hackwood in June the following year and walked with 'dear little Gussie' in the woods. The family clearly knew something was up: every day they placed him next to Gussie at dinner and her father was determinedly agreeable, asking Lear to sing, walking with him and gossiping about the Cabinet and Corfu. The sun shone, the woods were green, the talk was good: there were tours round the old kitchen garden with the family, with Gussie's brother Wally pushing the now frail Lady Westbury in her bath chair. 'As pleasant a day as passed for *many* years,' Lear wrote on the last evening of his visit. But nothing was said.

The year passed. He returned to Corfu, sailed around the Ionian isles and spent his London summer working on his *Views*. But in the autumn of 1863 the dithering dance with Gussie was performed again, with the same tentative approach and recoil. Lady Westbury had died in March and Gussie was still grieving, hardly able to talk through her tears. Lear was as amenable as he could be, playing with Emma's six children, walking with Gussie's father and brothers in the woods, 'perhaps as lovely & grand a specimen of English lofty home scenery as can exist', singing after dinner and exchanging risqué stories with the men in the smoking room. But the issue went no further. 'A pleasant, but very sad visit. What will be the end of this odious matter?'

In early July 1864 he was at Hackwood once again, steeling himself to come to the point. Then, as always, he retreated: after a walk with Emma, who stressed the desolation of Gussie's life, he was on the point of fleeing. 'This visit will I fear be my last here. Poor Gussie! And how to decide? If her life is sad, – united to mine would it be less so? Or rather – would it not be more?' Next morning he was still in a whirl: 'The risk of trying the marriage – the marriage itself so gt. a risk of making 2 people more unhappy than before?' His reasoning now was that it was his duty to retreat to save Gussie from misery. This was a genuine fear as well as an excuse and a self-deception. He knew that she would be happy to be married, smiling like the woman wheeled in the barrow. This was a stock figure of old rhymes. But the earliest of such images from medieval manuscripts show the barrow full of souls being carted to Hell. Would he be wheeling a smiling Gussie into torment, or boxing into a life-in-death state from which there was no escape?

There was an Old Man on some rocks,
Who shut his wife up in a box;
When she said, 'Let me out,' he exclaimed, 'Without doubt,
You will pass all your life in that box.'

Lear seemed to welcome an excuse to stand back. In October, when Gussie's brother postponed a family dinner because Emma Parkyns was ill, he wrote to say he could not dine with them at all. 'Best so', he wrote in his diary, 'for, even at this late hour of life, the ridiculous flames of nature burn: best put out at once – hard as it is – over & over again, to welcome darkness.' Yet he could not quite put out the flames. He was back at Hackwood a year later, but it was a bad time to visit. That summer Gussie's father Lord Westbury had been embroiled in scandal after scandal. First he misled a House of Lords Committee about the dismissal of a fraudulent clerk, giving the vacant position to his own son Slingsby. Then there was a long court case in which he was held to have used undue influence on behalf of another son, Richard, an undischarged bankrupt. Westbury faced a vote of censure and in the week that Lear arrived, he was forced to give up the seals of office as Lord Chancellor. He was furious and humiliated, talking bombastically, hinting of further hidden scandals, boasting of his Italian mistress, Tizzy, and the estates he would gain in Italy. 'What a conversation!' thought Lear:

Was there ever such a man as this! . . . Alas! – I now see truly that all said of him is only too lenient – : the study of law – making black white – seems to have left

347

him no knowledge of right or wrong. If not for Gussie's sake – this is the last walk I will ever take with him.

The family's affairs were awful '& all seem in a trap – a snare – ruin'. In September he found things just as bad and clung to his self-deceiving belief that he must make a noble sacrifice. When Gussie played the piano: 'for a moment one's heart returned. But no. It would not do. Better suffer alone, than cause suffering in others.'

'And so ends Hackwood for ever', Lear wrote as he left. Not so. Six months later, in April 1866, he stopped at Corfu on his way back from Malta. Stunned afresh by the glory of the island, he walked up to Ascension and lay on a leafy platform under the olives, surrounded by wild flowers, looking down on the sea, 'one blue calm sheet of light'. It was, he said, 'A regular intoxication of beauty! . . . Can I give no idea of this Paradise island to others? Would Gussie like to live here?'

Two days later he sent her a long letter, 'but much beside the mark; also to Emily Tennyson – much more besider: but it is not possible to write as one would'. What Gussie herself felt remains a mystery.

On his first day back in London, he hung up his drawings, went to see Frank Lushington, who was out, and then headed straight to the Bethells at Lancaster Gate. Within a week he was there again, '& passed a pleasant evening. Pleasant did I say? This – the last dream – to burst in a bubble or flourish into reality – is indeed a strange matter.' At dinner he sat next to Gussie, but later, beneath his diagram of the seating plan he wrote some lines from *Maud*:

> Like a sudden spark
> Struck vainly in the night
> And *back returns the dark* –
> With no more hope of light.

Alas. The building seems to fade away & the dream to flit.

Next day, he wrote,

the 'marriage' phantasy 'will not let me be' – yet seems an intangible myth. To think of it no more, is to resolve on all the rest of life being passed thus – alone – & year by year getting more weary: – to envisage it, is to pursue a thread leading to doubt & perhaps more positive misery, & 'Meanwhile' – the 'ignoble toil' of these worrying drawings goes on – (as does the necessity of £200 a year rent).

He consulted Lady W. and Fortescue, who thought he should only marry if she brought him a solid £300 a year. Amid the late June thunderstorms he developed a tingling skin irritation and although Gussie sent a soothing letter, he was wretched. He visited Fortescue in the Gothic fantasy of Strawberry Hill, where he was trying to recreate the library of its builder, Horace Walpole. But among the crowd here Lear decided that he was not keen on English summer life, '& do greatly incline to shut up Stratford Place, & take my chances of wandering for some years'.

When Gussie visited his studio in September it was a pain rather than a pleasure to them both: 'For the gulf is not to be passed. Unhappiness only could follow if it were otherwise. Yet it seems hard too, & were I 10 years younger I would act differently.' From now on, he was 'not at home' to her sister Emma, dreading reopening of the subject. Just as the Yonghy-Bonghy-Bò would flee from his rejection by Lady Jingly Jones, so Lear bolted back to the travelling life:

> Down the slippery slopes of Myrtle,
>   Where the early pumpkins blow,
>   To the calm and silent sea
>   Fled the Yonghy-Bonghy-Bò.
> There, beyond the Bay of Gurtle,
> Lay a large and lively Turtle: –
>   'You're the Cove,' he said, 'for me;
>   On your back beyond the sea,
>   Turtle, you shall carry me!'

In December 1866 Lear was on his way to Egypt. He could not follow Bates up the Amazon, but he could follow Speke and Mansfield Parkyns up the Nile. This was what he could not give up, the liberty to travel, to paint, to drift in the 'sunlight dozy Lotos land'. In these years of indecision he wrote 'The Duck and the Kangaroo'. Problems were easier to solve in terms of animals and birds, even different in species, mismatched in size and uncertain in gender. The little duck longs to bound round the world escaping its dull life – 'a bore in this stagnant pond' – and easily deals with the Kangaroo's main objection, its unpleasantly cold, wet feet.

Said the Duck, 'As I sate on the rocks,
   I have thought over that completely,
And I bought four pairs of worsted socks
   Which fit my web-feet neatly.
And to keep out the cold I've bought a cloak,
And every day a cigar I'll smoke,
    All to follow my own dear true
    Love of a Kangaroo.

Said the Kangaroo, 'I'm ready!
   All in the moonlight pale;
But to balance me well, dear Duck, sit steady!
   And quite at the end of my tail!'
So away they went with a hop and a bound,
And they hopped the whole world three times round;
    And who so happy, – O who,
    As the Duck and the Kangaroo.

The person Lear was actually hopping round the world with was Giorgio Kokali. Giorgio was no duck (though he did wear a cloak and smoke cigars). If questioned, Lear simply said that Giorgio was 'a faithful serving man'. He was proud of him, fascinated by his Suliot past and intrigued by his large and often errant family. In some ways he treated Giorgio like a child, teaching him to read and write, putting up with his sulks, worrying if he was ill. He recorded his odd sayings and retailed them to friends: the way he asked in Santa Maura, '"if that Lady" – meaning Sappho – meant to drown herself, why did she take the trouble to go quite to the end of the promontory, when there were so many points nearer – unless indeed she came in a boat to the point?' Or in Crete, when a Turkish girl asked Giorgio why he didn't draw too: 'Don't you see, I am too short?' Giorgio took up Lear's interests, bug-hunting and collecting plants, and commenting on views and artists, and like Lear he was someone that children felt safe with: 'totally patient and good; all the children going to him in swarms by instinct'.

Yet Lear himself seemed often like a child. Giorgio cooked for him, cared for him, rushed to bring a cloak if it was cold, called him at four in the morning, scoured houses they were staying in for a good chamber-pot. When they were apart, Lear looked anxiously for his letters. Life with Giorgio did not assuage the marriage fantasy, but it was a comfort, and a partial consolation.

30: 'GRADUALLY EXTINGUIFIED'

There was an Old Man of Boulak,
Who sate on a Crocodile's back;
But they said, 'Tow'rds the night, he may probably bite,
Which might vex you, Old Man of Boulak!'

In the autumn of 1866, turning his back on Gussie, Lear felt impatient with Britain as a whole: people, politics, religion. 'Seriously, it does seem to me', he wrote to Henry Bruce, 'that those who have voices should use them now & then . . . tho' it is very likely that I am wrong & talking nonsense: those conditions not unfrequently occur to painters & poets & parrots, as well as priests.' The list of those who speak 'nonsense' was suggestive – painters, poets, parrots and priests. An old lithographer friend, Thomas McLean, who had printed Lear's *Views in Rome* and *Illustrated Excursions*, and his books of nonsense, now had a gallery in the Haymarket and offered to exhibit his new Tyrants. He rushed to finish them, slashed the prices of his big pictures and persuaded Edgar Drummond to buy his *Beirut*. Then, without even saying goodbye to his closest friends, he took the boat to Boulogne, making a note in his diary of the bottles left behind: 'Claret 8, Marsala 7, Sherry 4'. From Marseilles he explained to Fortescue that he had left abruptly because he was fed up with the smoke and noise and cold. England was fine for the wealthy, but 'an accursed place for those who have known liberty and have seen God's daylight daily in other countries'. Some day, he thought, he would quit the country altogether, 'even if I turn Mussulman & settle in Timbuctoo'.

He did not reach Timbuctoo. After a short stay in Marseilles, eyeing his companions at the table d'hôte – 'violent lively American damsel on the right' – Lear took the boat to Alexandria. On the way the boat stopped briefly in Malta, where he looked up friends and dined with John Peel, who had been Storks's Assistant Military Secretary. Peel told his younger brother about their boozy evening. Lear, he said, 'was as usual somewhat melancholy, and foretold the death of his remaining relatives, several in number and his own total blindness and impecuniosity like Micawber; however he brightened up, and concealed a good deal of liquor about his person, he is now up the Nile, and I owe him a letter'.

Giorgio – always ready to make such long-distance treks to join Lear – met him in Cairo. As his planned trip was alarmingly expensive, Lear borrowed from friends, a rash request, perilous to friendship, but the money came in. Once again the country entranced him: 'O sugar canes! O camels! O Egypt!' – but the whole trip was to fill him with visions of past glory lost, greatness extinguished. There were personal losses too: in Cairo, Lear heard of the death of Holman Hunt's wife Fanny, and wept for his friend, then shook off this sadness and joined the Nile boat on 31 December. Their journey up river was swift: Lear rose at dawn and stayed on deck, sketching the life on the river and the banks, where modern agriculture competed with temples and palms, 'a steam working engine, which grunts & whistles as it might do at King's Cross'. To his joy there were numberless birds, storks and pelicans, ducks and herons, ibis and pigeons – 'The myriads of pigeons! & when they fly, *their shadows on the ground!*' But all the time he felt the weight of the long-extinct civilisations, the great temples empty of all except swarms of wild bees, '& where one peeps into those dark death-silent halls of columns – a terror pervades the heart & head'.

Lear in Egypt, seated in the centre

He had promised his Montreal cousin Caroline Jones to meet up with her son Archie, who was touring the Mediterranean and planned to join the boat at Luxor. Lear wrote doubtfully before he set out: 'I hope to goodness he hasn't got a wooden leg, or stammer, or squints – I have never seen him, only out of affection for his mother I must stick to him.' When he arrived, Archie seemed amiable but his charm soon grew thin: he preferred shopping in the bazaars to exploring temples, which he said smelt awful; he whistled, drummed his fingers, scratched his name on temple walls. Then he fell ill and was moodily homesick. Having looked forward to the company, Lear thought, really, it was better to travel alone.

Archie was not the only transatlantic tourist. 'You can't imagine the extent of the American element in travel here!' Lear exclaimed to Lady W. Americans to English were twenty-five to one, and they went about in 'dozens and scores': one party refused to visit a temple on a Sunday because it was a 'heathen church', yet went without a murmur to see poor women, clad in nothing but necklaces and nose-rings, who were only made to dance by threats and large bribes. The English could unnerve him too, like the eccentric Lucie, Lady Duff Gordon, who had settled in Luxor five years before, who gossiped of the Prinseps family and G. F. Watts and took him round the English cemetery. He was impressed, but her habit of calling attention to the '"lovely rounded muscles and velvet skin" of naked men nearby – & absolutely naked cox and all', were, he decided, 'not what I like to admire in an Englishwoman'. There was a violence, as well as superiority, in the American and European gaze.

The river itself was peaceful, beyond corruption. The chief glory was the colour, changing from dawn to dusk.

Near Gau el Kebir, 6 p.m., 9 January 1867

At Luxor, when the sun set, the colours were 'perfectly astonishing . . . absolute Cadmium & Lemon light, with purple shades on the water's edge'. Lear felt this intensely at Philae (where Archie stunned him by saying he had seen it all in three hours): 'I have not made enough of the dark gray & black-sooted granite rox in the water – always too red & yellow in my drawing . . . & one feels acutely how little one has done to represent such beauty.' He never forgot the rocks and colours and birds of the Nile, the black storks poised on one leg, the lovely ibis, the watchful herons, and the pelicans, 'careless, foolish', and he celebrated them all in the opening to his later song, 'The Pelican Chorus':

> We live on the Nile. The Nile we love.
> By night we sleep on the cliffs above;

> By day we fish, and at eve we stand
> On long bare islands of yellow sand.
> And when the sun sinks slowly down
> And the great rock walls grow dark and brown,
> When the purple river rolls fast and dim
> And the Ivory Ibis starlike skim,
> Wing to wing we dance around, –
> Stamping our feet with a flumpy sound, –
> Opening our mouths as Pelicans ought,
> And this is the song we nightly snort: –
>   Ploffskin, Pluffskin, Pelican jee!
>   We think no Birds so happy as we!
>   Plumpskin, Ploshkin, Pelican jill!
>   We think so then, and we thought so still.

On the Nile, time and tenses turned upside down. In idle moments Lear read Herodotus; if the dinners were poor he read Darwin to console himself. Ancient history and natural history, extinction and evolution, ran side by side. Every day brought a welter of contrasts and surprises. Near Ibreem, at ten in the morning on 2 February 1867, one of the sailors close by was playing a violin 'to the utmost perfection':

no one could tell it was not a fiddle being tuned by a good performer – sliding into half scales & the resemblance is so absurd I am constantly grinning. How quiet is this river scene! One boat has been seen today, & that on the shore. 11. Reach Ibreem which on all sides is really fine, & I hope to get a good drawing of it: a sort of River Masada. But interest is divided between this & the Crocodile sandspit, where are some of these beasts – Castle – Crocodile – Crocodile – Castle – one don't know which way to look. Ibreem is past – & at 11.30 – lo! A vast Crocodile, at which G. fires & I fancy the second ball hit the brute, who walloped into the Nile. But then his head came up, tho he was a long time in getting to the sand again.

Their furthest point, Wadi Halfa, seemed to Lear the essence of Nubian scenery. The desert awed him with its utter loneliness and vast expanse of sand: a 'sad, stern, uncompromising landscape – dark ashy purple lines of hills, – piles of granite rocks – fringes of palm – & ever and anon aston-ishing ruins of oldest Temples: above all wonderful Abu Simbel, which took my breath away'. When he turned a corner at Abu Simbel and sud-denly saw the Rameses heads, he was so moved that he could not draw at all; his sketch of the heads is marked 'partly memory'. Overawed by the solitude and the weight of history he walked over the 'deep sinking gold apricot sand', and ventured inside the great temple, creeping on all fours down the slope between the columns into the darkness.

Abu Simbel, 9 February 1867

Lear and Giorgio were back in Cairo in early March, having dropped Archie at Luxor. He had planned to go on a second journey, to Gaza and Jerusalem and on to Tyre and Sidon, but by the time they reached Jerusalem, swamped by Easter pilgrims, he was so tired that he turned round, returned to Alexandria and waited for a boat to Europe.

It was too early for Lear to go back for his English summer, so he and Giorgio landed at Brindisi and spent a month meandering up the Italian coast to Ravenna and Rimini, and north-west to the Italian lakes. At Lake Garda, Lear was thrown back in time: flicking through an earlier visitors' book he saw that in 1833 J. D. Harding had praised the white wine, and a year later Dan Fowler and Robert Leake Gale (who had both emigrated to Amherst Island in Nova Scotia in 1843) had recommended the Hotel del Galline in Milan. 'I knew Dan's writing at once & poor Rob's,' wrote Lear. Remembering thirty years ago, when he had read Dan's letters from Italy with the Gale sisters, he added, 'Lucy and Elizabeth were happy then: now Lucy Francillon is a widow with 3 children, & poor Bessie an unhappy wife with 6!'

In England he avoided the Bethells and his own fantasy of marriage and children. Then, in October, a letter arrived from Gussie, 'wh puts me all nowhere again. & shortly after came Emma Parkyns: – go to Hinton it seems Somerset'. He was filled with odd thoughts: 'Gussie: – dreamland: – but it is a blessing – come of it what may'. Asked to stay in Hinton as long as he liked, he packed two trunks and wrote nervously,

It is absurd to think that at 54 years old I am within a point of doing what will fix the rest of my life – be it short or long – in one groove – good or bad. I do not say I am decided to take this leap in the dark, but I say that I am nearer to doing so than I ever was before.

Yet within a day of his arrival Emma took him aside and said that she did not think Gussie and he could live happily. It was a shock, given Emma's positive views of a year before, and '*broke up a dream* rudely & sadly'. Gussie's own feelings remain a mystery. That afternoon he walked with Lord Westbury: 'He says of G – she will never marry.' That was enough. On 7 November 1867, he left.

In the past few years of travelling and fretting about Gussie, Lear had often looked back to his early interest in natural history, which was revived by the recent flurry of debates about natural selection and evolution. In 1858, at the Royal Institution, T. H. Huxley had shocked his audience by comparing the skeletons and musculature of baboons, gorillas and humans, arguing that in structure man was no further from the gorilla than the gorilla from the baboon: the great difference was not physique, but the gift of speech. When Lear walked up to the zoo, he was fascinated by the orang utan, 'a very great brute'. (Queen Victoria had thought the same twenty years before, 'too wonderful . . . He is frightfully, and painfully, and disagreeably human.' In fact the one she saw was a female, called Jenny). Now *The Origin of Species* had led everyone to look at apes with some alarm. 'Is man an ape or an angel?' Disraeli asked at the Diocesan Society in Oxford in November 1864: 'My lord, I am on the side of the angels. I repudiate with indignation and abhorrence these new-fangled theories.'

Lear read Darwin happily on the Nile in 1867, but the ideas could be disturbing. Darwin and Alfred Russel Wallace, who developed similar theories at the same time, argued that all creatures passed certain variations on from one generation to the next: in the long struggle to preserve the species, the more advantageous variants would dominate, and the others would either be modified beyond recognition or die out completely. At this point, Lear was brooding on marriage and heredity, anxious not only about his epilepsy but about the threat of madness that he felt came with it. This fear had reached a peak on 30 April 1865 when his old friend, the banker Mr Prescott, cut his throat in the bathroom of his house at Roehampton, driven to despair by senile dementia. Lear was aghast and heartbroken for his family. He had become close to the Prescotts after meeting them in Rome in 1859 and discovering that Prescott had been his father's banker. (Their daughter Isabella had married Colonel Richard Decie of the Corfu garrison, and now they had a little boy and a baby, Ruth, to whom Lear gave an alphabet and sent sweet nonsense letters.) He felt the shock acutely because Sarah's husband Charles Street, now in his eighties, was suffering 'the same sad delusions as Mr Prescott'. It was the third recent case he had heard of. 'I have come to the conclusion', he told Emily Tennyson, trying to joke, 'that nobody ought to marry at all, & that no more people ought ever to be born, – & so we should be gradually extinguified, & the world would be left to triumphant chimpanzees, gorillas, cockroaches & crocodiles.'

*

In the mid-1860s, Lear began to write stories and poems that focused on animals, almost as parables of human dilemmas. In Nice in February 1865, he wote nonsense letters of this kind for Anna Duncan and her mother, Lady Duncan, whom he had known since his time in Rome. Playing on the nickname for the French, he told of being escorted home 'by two large and amiable Frogs', who took him by the arms and led him down the lane.

Nothing could exceed the genteel & intelligent expression of their counte-nances, except the urbanity of their deportment and the melancholy and oblivious sweetness of their voices. They informed me that they were the parents of nine and forty tadpoles of various ages and talents some of whom were expecting shortly to emigrate to Malvern and Mesopotamia.

Amused by his obliviously sweet-voiced Frogs, Lear spun out the story in another letter, in which they brought their offspring to see him: the tadpoles admired his new lamps but declined cold lamb and Marsala, saying that watercress or beetles would be pleasant, but they were not hungry. The jest became a comment on living abroad:

I did not quite know at first how to be civil to the tadpoles, as I found that owing to their long tails they could not sit on chairs as their parents did: I therefore put them into a wash hand basin, & they seemed happy enough.

Such kind attentions from foreign persons quite of a different race, & I may say nature from our own, are certainly most delightful: and none the less so for being unexpected. The Frogs were as good as to add that had I had any oil paintings they would have been glad to purchase one – but the damp of their abode would quite efface watercolour art.

He signed both letters, 'Believe me, Yours sincerely'.

Believe me. From now on, in Lear's poems and songs and stories, human traits would migrate more and more into the realm of animals, reptiles and birds. The frog story was about reproduction and nurture, but also about the sheer oddity of natural life, the mutations that meant tadpoles had tails while their frog parents had legs, the difficulties of living in a particular element, the clashes of instinct and culture. Darwin had shown Nature to be ruthless, pitilessly discarding the feeble and odd. He had written of the branching tree of nature, of 'strange and rare deviations of structure', and of variation, change and mutation across continents and ages. The phrases 'natural selection' and 'survival of the fittest' described a world that was mutable and exceedingly strange. Darwin's own books and letters contained innumerable Lear-like oddities, and some good portrayals of 'they', very human and home-bred. Writing to T. H. Huxley he described pigeon fanciers in a gin palace in the Borough, where 'it was hinted that Mr Bult had crossed his Pouters with Runts to gain size': 'and if you could have seen the solemn, the mysterious, and awful shakes of the head which all the fanciers gave at this scandalous proceeding, you would have recognised how little crossing has had to do with improving breeds, and how dangerous for endless generations the process was.' How Victorian the head-shakers seem in their concern for the purity of species: Mr Bult deserves a limerick.

Lear's own nonsense was open to the protean, changing Darwinian world. In the stories that he wrote at this time, he engaged playfully, but with a heartfelt subtext, with extinction and exploration. Beyond this, the lonely figures of his limericks and later poems raised a troubling question: if human as well as animal society was driven by a hunt for perfection in choosing a mate, what of the 'unfit'? Was there hope for the man with the very long nose? And were men and women any wiser than the beasts and the birds?

A month after the frog letters to the Duncans, Lear wrote a longer animal story – a black comedy, or comic tragedy, for Charlotte, Hugh and Reginald Wentworth-Fitzwilliam, the 'jolly, cheerful children' of Lord and Lady Fitzwilliam, generous purchasers of his pictures. (The family name jolted him, reminding him of Mrs Wentworth who had set him on his way with his first introductions to naturalists and to the zoo: 'Dear old Mrs Wentworth of Woolley would have rejoiced', he thought.) One day when he called on the family in Nice, no one was home, so he 'drew some birds & made some nonsenses for the children & came away'. Next he made them an alphabet, and then, taking a break from Tyrants, he spent a morning writing 'a most absurd lot of stories for the little Fs'.

The History of the Seven Families of the Lake Pipple-Popple gave him new freedoms. His narrative gifts stretched and capered; his dialogue flowed beyond the brusque limerick speech; he overturned the geography books and created his own lands and seas. 'In olden days', he began, 'that is to say, once upon a time, there lived in the Land of Gramblamble, Seven Families.' They lived by the Lake Pipple-popple, near to the City of Tosh – 'The names of all these places you have probably heard of and you have only not to look in your Geography books to find out all about them' – and each family, Parrots, Storks, Geese, Owls, Guinea-pigs, Cats and Fishes, had seven children. Mixing folk-tale and natural history writing, Lear logged habitat, habit and diet, ballasting all this with solemn nonsensical detail. A long parenthesis on the 'dangerous and delusive' Clangle-Wangle, for example, was a masterly imitation of 'scientific' description: 'Their speed is extreme, but their habits of life are domestic and pellucid. On summer evenings they may sometime be observed near the Lake Pipple-Popple, standing on their heads and humming their national melodies; they subsist entirely on vegetables, excepting when they eat veal, or mutton, or pork, or beef, or fish, or saltpetre.' He was nothing if not precise. The parrots from the blue-leaved Soffsky-Possky trees eat fruit, artichokes and striped beetles; the Storks eat buttered toast, the Owls make mice into

362

sago pudding, the Cats like sponge biscuits. The author draws punningly logical conclusions: 'The Geese, having webs for their feet, caught quantities of flies, which they ate for dinner.'

Like a good family of the empire, or rich parents funding the Grand Tour, the parents decided that their children should see the world, 'gave them each eight shillings and some good advice, some chocolate drops, and a small green morocco pocket book to set down their expenses in', and enjoined them not to quarrel. Injunctions, as fairy tales teach, are made to be disobeyed. Disasters follow with the speed of 'Ribands and Pigs'. The parrots immediately squabble over a single cherry, in a cascade of invented verbs:

On which all the Seven began to fight, and they scuffled,

and huffled,
and ruffled,
and shuffled,
and puffled,
and muffled,
and buffled,
and duffled,
and fluffled,
and guffled,
and bruffled, and

screamed, and shrieked and squealed, and squeaked, and clawed, and snapped, and bit, and bumped, and thumped, and dumped, and flumped each till they were all torn into little bits, and at last there was nothing left to record this painful incident, except the Cherry and seven small green feathers.

Each of the seven species has its fatal flaw, and while other threatened creatures, like the Clangle-Wangle and Plum-pudding flea, delight in the 'calamitous extinction', when the parents learn of their children's deaths, they buy pickling materials, make their wills and jump in. Like the countries that are not in the geography books, their remains are not displayed (with a picture) in the grand museum of Tosh.

In comic form, Lear told the story of the Fall, the defiance of the injunction not to eat the fruit, and the world of death to come. The joke was a playful answer to Tennyson's 'anomaly of high souls & philosophic writings' and his tirade about squashing the planet flat. But it was also a throwaway riposte to Darwin, a light-hearted 'On the Termination of Species'.

The Seven Families killed themselves through silliness. 'Very happily for me', Lear told Fortescue, somewhat unconvincingly, 'my queer natural elasticity of temperament does not at all lead me to the morbids – "suicide" or what not.' Yet there are plenty of suicides in his limericks, and in early August 1866, embarrassed about a book he thought he had left at a friend's house but then found in his pocket, he concocted a spoof news report of the 'sukycide' of the well-known author and landscape painter Edward Lear, who had thrown himself out of a fifth-storey window, 'to the extreme surprise & delight of some children playing on the pavement'.

Later that month he drew 'The Adventures of Mr Lear & the Polly & the Puseybite on their way to the Ritertite Mountains' for Emma Parkyns's children. In this short cartoon story, a mild satire on religious rows, with Lear the moderate squeezed between an evangelical parrot, mindlessly repeating prayers, and a High Church Puseyite, a weary Lear buys an umbrella for the rain. But when he sets out with his two companions, they meet disaster, indeed wholesale disassembly: 'Mr L & the P. & the P.B. incidentally fall over an unexpected Cataract & are all dashed to atoms.'

Two good-natured helpers, the Jebusites (biblical outsiders, driven from the promised land in Exodus), try hard, but cannot reconstruct the body parts 'perfectly as 3 individuals'. In this game of visual consequences – at once religious disarray and evolution gone wrong – the parrot has Mr Lear's head, the cat has the parrot's head and Lear's legs, and Lear's rotund torso is topped by a wobbly feline head.

In the end the friends tumble into a deep hole and vanish. Like the story of the parrots reduced to single feathers, this saga of fragmentation was another tale of extinction, the opposite of successful adaptation or magical metamorphosis.

In his youth Lear had drawn birds and beasts discovered on many expeditions, including Darwin's voyage on the *Beagle*. Recently, he had been reading about more journeys of exploration, including that of Bates in the Amazon and the two expeditions of John Hanning Speke and Richard Burton to search for the source of the Nile. When the first expedition in the late 1850s collapsed Speke went on alone to Lake Victoria, which he named after the queen, and was convinced that this must be the river's source. He returned to Africa in 1860 to confirm his theory. This was another dangerous, romantic journey: Speke fell in love with an African woman in Uganda, beat off Somalis armed with spears, and saved the life of a Buganda king's wife. This time, he found the outlet from the lake, the starting point of the great river that ran for 1200 miles through the desert.

Lear devoured the stories of mapping 'unexplored' areas, and the accounts of plant and animal collectors. Behind these, as he knew from his Knowsley days, ran a lust for possession, labelling, conquest and commerce. Bates, for example, had come back from the rain forest with thousands of specimens, most of them previously unknown insects and butterflies. In his book he wrote of the jungle and the river, the tribes and the animals, the insects and the birds, especially the toucan, flying heavily from the lower branches of the trees, a Lear-like curiosity, 'No one, on seeing a Toucan, can help asking what is the use of the enormous bill . . .' Was it once a web-footed bird, with a beak adapted to catch fish? It was hard to keep up with the new species. The Zoological Society was swamped by skins, specimens and pickled fish. In 1860 the founders of the London Acclimatisation Society argued that foreign species could be introduced and adapted to European conditions, improving local breeds. To prove that these strange creatures tasted good, the society's dinner at Almack's Assembly Rooms in 1862 included Bird's Nest Soup, Chinese sea-slugs (chopped into mush), 'Kangaroo steamer', spiced meat from the West Indies, Syrian pig, Canadian goose, the South American birds the guan and curassow, followed by 'Seaweed jelly'. The following year their sister society in Paris opened a Jardin d'Acclimatation, to display not only animals and plants but people from other lands.

Lear's disquiet about the raids of the botanists and zoologists, and the assumption of superiority over other races, found a voice in another story, 'absurd, but good fun', that he wrote before he left Hinton for the children of Gussie's brother Slingsby. In *The Four Little Children Who Went Round the World*, the children, Violet, Slingsby, Guy and Lionel, sail off in a boat painted blue with green spots. They sleep in a large tea-kettle and have a small cat to steer and an old Quangle Wangle to cook dinner and make the tea.

Their voyage is full of possible impossibilities, including churning sea-water to make butter, and their first landfall is an island with a single tree, 503 feet high. Having read so many travel books Lear had a sure grasp of their elaborate syntax, which he combined with the long sentences, persuasive detail and deceptive simplicity of his favourite childhood adventure, *Robinson Crusoe*. Here is Defoe:

All the Remedy that offer'd to my Thoughts at that Time, was, to get up into a thick bush Tree like a Firr, but thorny, which grew near me, and where I resolv'd to sit all Night, and consider the next Day what Death I should Dye, for as yet I saw no Prospect of Life; I walked about a Furlong from the Shore, to see if I could find any fresh Water to drink, which I did, to my great Joy; and having drank, and put a little Tobacco in my Mouth to prevent Hunger, I went to the Tree, and getting up into it, endeavour'd to place my self so, as that if I should sleep I might not fall . . .

And that is only half of the long sentence. Here is Lear, replacing the spiritual with the material – banishing death with 'the prospect of life':

When they had landed, they walked about, but found to their great surprise, that the island was quite full of veal-cutlets and chocolate-drops, and nothing else. So they all climbed up the single high tree to discover, if possible, if there were any people; but having remained on the top of the tree for a week, and not seeing anybody, they naturally concluded that there were no inhabitants, and accordingly when they came down, they loaded the boat with two thousand veal-cutlets and a million of chocolate-drops, and these afforded them sustenance for more than a month, during which time they pursued their voyage with the utmost delight and apathy.

The children find new species like the 'Co-operative Cauliflower', get stuck in narrow straits, join in feasts and give gifts of 'Black pins, Dried Figs, and Epsom Salts' to the natives. There are unfortunate incidents: the Cat and the Quangle Wangle bite off the tails of sixty-five red parrots, which Violet makes into an elaborate headdress with 'a lovely and glittering appearance, highly prepossessing and efficacious'.

Plumage interested Darwin. What were the shimmering crests and brilliant feathers for? Why were there specific forms for different species? Did a special fleck or dazzling spot make a difference? Lear, a wry observer of current London fashions, had often wondered what the point was of wearing elaborate plumes, much lampooned in *Punch*.

Lear now looked back to the eager, unthinking collecting of those at Knowsley with a colder eye. That summer he had tenderly visited old Colonel Hornby, who was slowly dying. The Hornbys were on his mind, and his story recalled the events in the journal that Elizabeth 'Pussy' Hornby had kept when she sailed in the Pacific on HMS *Asia* with her father Phipps in the 1840s, collecting specimens for Knowsley as they went. His tale also satirised the arrogance of empire, where the demands of outsiders prompt quick resentment, but his young imperialists survive their many crises and are finally rescued from a ferocious sea-monster by an elderly rhinoceros, who carries them home on his back. The four children return accompanied by the tokens of Knowsley, 'a crowd of Kangaroos and Gigantic Cranes' (all the smaller birds are cooked and eaten). But like all triumphant Victorian hunters and travellers, they need a trophy, something to stuff, something to show: 'As for the Rhinoceros, in token of their grateful adherence, they had him killed and stuffed directly, and then set him up outside the door of their father's house as a Diaphanous Doorscraper.'

The fate of the rhino is nonsensical but not comic: it casts a shadow backwards over the whole adventure. The great and generous rhino, reduced to a menial object on the doorstep (like the popular fashion for elephants' feet turned into holders for spirits and cigars), reproaches animal-hunter and colonist and collector all at once – all of whom, perhaps, should be 'gradually extinguified'. Like this surreal beast with its see-through skin, Lear's nonsense is both diaphanous and tough.

In his later limericks, Lear played, as he always had, with the borderlines between the animal and human world, sometimes with great tenderness and charm.

There was an Old Person of Bree,
Who frequented the depths of the sea;
She nurs'd the small fishes, and washed all the dishes,
And swam back again into Bree.

She is almost a shrimp-like mermaid but she has feet, in neat little shoes. An amphibian creature, she inhabits two elements at once. And in sliding between them she looks far from 'old'.

The shifting between realms marks many rhymes, and although people often fail in their efforts at instructing wild creatures and grow increasingly like their pupils, this closeness is healing and absorbing.

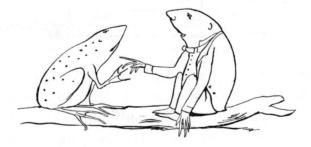

There was an Old Man in a Marsh,
Whose manners were futile and harsh;
He sate on a log, and sang songs to a frog,
That instructive Old Man in a Marsh.

Sometimes indeed, as the people don animal or insect shape, the effect is wholly enchanting.

> There was an old Person of Skye,
> Who waltz'd with a Bluebottle fly;
> They buzz'd a sweet tune, to the light of the moon,
> And entranced all the people of Skye.

But elsewhere, this inversion of size is more alarming.

> There was an Old Person in black,
> A Grasshopper jumped on his back;
> When it chirped in his ear, he was smitten with fear,
> That helpless Old Person in black.

Years later, thanking Fortescue for a New Year letter, Lear said what a pleasure it was; 'for the grasshopper has become a burden, and the quick-pace downhill transit to indifference and final apathy is more and more discernible as month follows month'. A man-sized insect chirruping in Lear's ear could be the voice of poetry, a perpetual pleasure – but it could also be a tinnitus-like distraction, a thing of nightmare, a warning that men too are mortal, and may face extinction, and that humans are far from the most important creatures in the world.

VI. CALLING

31: SAIL AWAY: CANNES, 1868–1869

When Lear left Gussie in Somerset in November 1867, she waved goodbye at the door, 'and so', he wrote, 'I went away – with a mind drearily tangled & numbed . . . What is left now but to go abroad as soon as possible – yet where to go?' He decided on Cannes and was there by the end of the month. It was freezing – 'O! O! O! how cold it is'. The only good thing was that he had found someone to grumble with; on 1 December, looking for good rooms, he wrote, 'Lo! All of a sudden I remember that the Simmonds are here!' This was the young John Addington Symonds and his wife Catherine, the daughter of Lear's Hastings friend Frederick North, whom he had known as a girl. He had noted her marriage, four years ago, and they had met on the boat at Nice and now they were here with their three-year-old daughter, Janet, and baby Charlotte, 'Lotta'.

Next day he called at the Pension Joseph, 'where the most amiable good Symonds & Catherine S. was at home. I fancy they liked my visit, tho' I was rather noisy methinx. Came home unwell & coughing much, so cayennepeppery is this air; yet better than ffogg.' Every day Lear saw the Symonds and walked and talked, sharing views on poetry and art and Italy, and swapping moans. Within a week of knowing them, Lear took a break after settling down to write up his Cretan journal, and composed an Eclogue, 'funny enough – & wrote it out'. It was a a catalogue of woes:

Edwardus. – What makes you look so black, so glum, so cross?
    Is it neuralgia, headache, or remorse?

Johannes. – What makes you look as cross, or even more so?
    Less like a man than is a broken Torso?

The mock eclogue appeals to Catherine as a judge of their 'foolish growlings' as the two men compete in damning the cold, the lodgings, the cooking, the piano-playing neighbours and German bands, the flies, the swells in their carriages who had not bought Lear's pictures. When Catherine forces a close, Johannes, she decides, has more excuse: her sentence is only that he nurse 'The baby for seven hours, and nothing worse'. Edwardus, however, told that his 'griefs are fudge, yourself a bore', is condemned

> To make large drawings nobody will buy –
> To paint oil pictures which will never dry –
> To write new books which nobody will read –
> To drink weak tea, on tough old pigs to feed –
> Till spring-time brings the birds and leaves and flowers,
> And time restores a world of happier hours.

The Symonds 'laughed hugely at the Ekklogg – & say they'll print it. Afterwards we talked of Ruskin, Byron, Shelley &c, &c.' Lear warmed to Johnny Symonds's learning and lack of vanity. But why, he wondered, did Catherine have 'a wildness in the eye – painful', and why was 'remorse' in her husband's list of ailments?

The truth was that their marriage was both solid and a sham. Symonds was twenty-seven, thirty years younger than Lear. His mother had died when he was four, the same age that Lear was when his mother rejected him. He too had been a sickly boy in a house full of aunts, governesses and sisters, but unlike Lear, he was more influenced by his father, an eminent physician and Greek scholar with a love of all things Italian. He was disturbed by the rough homosexuality he encountered at Harrow (where the headmaster had an affair with one of his friends), but at eighteen he fell in love with a Bristol chorister: 'For the first time in my life', he wrote in his memoir, 'I knew that I must take possession of the dream, and clasp it.' His father put an end to the infatuation, but at Oxford, where he won a prize for his essay on the Renaissance, gained a First and became a Fellow of Magdalen, he was caught up in yet another scandal. He left, and when he collapsed from stress the eminent doctor Sir Spencer Wells advised a cure through 'cohabitation with a hired mistress, or what was better, matrimony'. Symonds took this advice. He had already met and liked Catherine in Switzerland, and they were married in November 1864. He was nervous: his graphic, self-obsessed diary vividly conveys the pressure facing men of his day to control and smother their feelings, something Lear could understand. For a long time before his marriage, he wrote, 'I had treated the purely sexual appetite (that which drew me fatally to the male) as a beast to be suppressed and curbed, and latterly to be down trampled by the help of surgeons and their cautery of sexual organs,' and now, although he genuinely loved Catherine, he missed 'the coarse and hard vibrations of sex, those exquisite agonies of contact' he found with men.

Understandably, Catherine soon began to feel depressed and they left London for the Riviera, where Symonds's sister, Lady Strachey, had a house at Menton, and Catherine's half-sister, Lady Janet Kay-Shuttleworth, a villa in San Remo. But the sunshine did not help. In Cannes, where Symonds was diagnosed with consumption, he worked on his *Problem of Greek Ethics*, showing that 'what the Greeks called *paiderastia* or boy-love, was a phenomenon of one of the most brilliant periods of human culture'. And that winter he decided that although he wanted to be a husband and father he must follow his true self or go mad. The tension rubbed off on their daughter Janet: 'The little girl is unwell – and all is sad,' wrote Lear. Unlike most children, Janet shrieked and fled when she met Lear, and although she relaxed and grew fond of him he found her 'a queer, difficult child'.

For this troubled little girl Lear wrote his purest, most famous poem, with its lovely, halting, lilting lines. There was no fanfare, no rapturous

377

reception, no sense that this would be known the world over. It was just a tale of an odd couple who found happiness on the shore, hand in hand, under the moon. On 18 December 1867, he wrote, 'At 3.40 – walked to the Symonds with a picture poem for little Janet.'

The Owl and the Pussy-cat went to sea
 In a beautiful pea-green boat,
They took some honey, and plenty of money,
 Wrapped up in a five-pound note.
The Owl looked up to the stars above,
 And sang to a small guitar,
'O lovely Pussy! O Pussy my love,
 What a beautiful Pussy you are,
  You are,
  You are!
What a beautiful Pussy you are!'

Pussy said to the Owl, 'You elegant fowl!
 How charmingly sweet you sing!
O let us be married! too long we have tarried:
 But what shall we do for a ring?'
They sailed away, for a year and a day,
 To the land where the Bong-tree grows
And there in a wood a Piggy-wig stood
 With a ring at the end of his nose,
  His nose,
  His nose,
With a ring at the end of his nose.

'Dear pig, are you willing to sell for one shilling
    Your ring?' Said the Piggy, 'I will.'
So they took it away, and were married next day
    By the Turkey who lives on the hill.
They dined on mince, and slices of quince,
    Which they ate with a runcible spoon;
And hand in hand, on the edge of the sand,
    They danced by the light of the moon,
        The moon,
        The moon,
They danced by the light of the moon.

Slivers of darkness float within the nonsense and the pictures. In 'real' life, cats and birds are enemies and in the poem a tingle of threat remains. Their gender is indecipherable, yet the owl, the bird of wisdom, is the one who sings, while the pussy-cat, who sounds so feminine, steers the boat and proposes. When they reach the pig the cat seems to have grown, to be proud and predatory at once. Is this marriage actually a trap? No. Beneath the turkey's outspread wings the cat bows down. And then they are joined in the dance.

The Owl and the Pussy-cat take their year-long honeymoon before their wedding. Their poem has been read to children and sung at weddings ever since. But although we know it in the form above, that was not quite the poem given to Janet Symonds and the other children to whom Lear sent early drafts. All those copies had slight variations, in stanza form and wording: the runcible spoon was plain silver, the Bong Tree was a palm tree, the Turkey was absent (the Pig did the honours at the wedding), and the lovely, sighing repetition of 'the moon/ The moon/ The moon' was missing altogether. But the Turkey soon made an entrance in the drafts. On one copy Lear showed the foursome – owl, cat, pig and turkey – all dancing together, but he took out this picture when the poem was published. Without it the Owl and the Pussy-cat could dance on alone.

Lear's great poems and songs are not 'about' his life – they float free. But their gaiety and sadness feel even keener when set against the tensions he saw, and suffered.

That year, leaving the Owl and the Pussy-cat to sail away, he concentrated on his work. Cannes was full of Dukes and Lords and Ladies and Honorables and Bishops, but although they came to see his drawings, it was a while before he made any sales:

I suppose some will be sold eventually – nevertheless, considering the constant outgoing *ex*pense, this *sus*pense is not pleasant . . . The fuss the swells made today about asking me the prices of drawings! Poor old Lady Grey's regal ways – tho' she don't mean them ill. – But oh!! how sick I am of the upper 10,000! – I mean as acquaintances, for friends I have in their station, as in others.

Gradually he found purchasers, both here and in Britain, where to his joy in 1867 Lady Ashburton finally bought *Cedars* for two hundred guineas – less than a third of the price he had originally asked. Lady Lyttleton bought *Masada*, and Edgar Drummond, after some unsubtle bullying by Lear ('you may have it . . . & pay for it AT ANY TIME THAT BEST SUITS YOU'), bought his painting of *Beirut*.

Soon he had dinners to go to and people to walk with through the olives and vines. In spare moments he read the women's novels he loved, old favourites like Fanny Burney's *Evelina*, 'always a pleasure', and new works like *Romola*, George Eliot's drama of Savonarola's Florence, 'a powerful but painful book'. But he also read Walt Whitman's *Leaves of Grass*, first published in 1855: William Michael Rossetti was currently editing Whitman's poems, and Symonds would try for years to get Whitman to declare his homosexuality openly. On Christmas morning Lear noted that it was a cold, miserable day, 'but got some good out of queer Walt Whitman'.

At the end of the year, Symonds sprained his ankle on a walk with Lear, telling his sister Charlotte: 'Mr Lear, who is a whimsical Punster, had only just before invented this sorry riddle: "Why is this hillside like an old-fashioned waistcoat? Because it's a little jerkin". I had no notion I was to afford so painful an illustration of the conundrum's force.' The bad ankle was enough to send Johnny back to bed again, and back to his agony about how to live. His friend Henry Sidgwick told Lear that the problem was 'an affection of the brain . . . but this I have known before. Poor Catherine (North) is sadly harassed I fear – Poor thing.' Probably everyone in their circle knew of Symonds's 'affection of the brain', but this was an age where nothing was said in public. Lear may well have discussed his dilemma: he often sat with Johnny, who could not sleep and harped on dying or going mad. Symonds's last night in Cannes, he wrote, 'was the worst of my whole life. I lay awake motionless, my soul stagnant, feeling what is meant by spiritual blackness and darkness . . . Catherine, who kept hold of me, seemed far away. I was alone, so utterly desolate that I drank the very cup of terror of the grave.' Once he decided he could be a lover of men, the relief was huge, but in his poetry, coded as love of women, he mused 'on these last miseries of mankind':

> On souls that, fainting, feed a nameless thirst;
> On hearts that long, with self-loathed longing cursed;
> On loves that know themselves shameful and blind,
> Fierce cruel loves that crucify the mind.

Symonds would win fame as a vivid, popular poet and writer, author of the seven-volume *The Renaissance in Italy* (1875–86), friend of Robert Louis Stevenson, Walter Pater, Edmund Gosse and Leslie Stephen, and always a fervent advocate of 'Greek love'. Catherine accepted the situation and all her life, according to their third daughter Madge, Virginia Woolf's childhood friend, showed 'singular Sybilline fortitude'.

Lear knew that ferocious hiding of the self, and that desolate loneliness, but at this point his life was unusually tranquil. It had been a good year, he thought, pushing away the humiliation with Gussie. On New Year's Eve he summed it up: he had seen the second cataract of the Nile, wandered through Italy, sold several pictures and moved out of the 'gallery' of Stratford Place, letting McLean's show his pictures when he was away. This was 'certainly a goodly amount of items in one year – tho' how valuable each – who may say? Progress – or the contrary. Not, I think, the latter, but yet I doubt much of the former. Let me hope *some*: – and let me hope, leading to *more*, that some.'

He drew pictures for Janet and baby Lotta, and took a trip to Corsica, the basis for a book that would take up much time over the next two years. In the hot summer of 1868, he was working feverishly, 'So that rest there is none,' he sighed to Fortescue. 'When shall we fold our wings, and list to what the inner spirit says – there is no joy but calm? Never in this world I fear.' Perhaps, he joked, in the next existence they and Lady W. might sit placidly under a lotus tree eating ice creams and pelican pie, with their feet in a stream 'and with the birds and beasts of Paradise a sporting around us'. Yet it was hard to keep this dream alive. In one small poem, written that summer, even the birds and beasts – the fish from the syllabub sea, the little mice, the grasshoppers, butterfly, beetle and bee – seemed to flee him. The birds fly in a stream – where from, where to? – alighting for a moment and soaring away:

> Calico Pie
> The little birds fly
> Down to the calico tree,
> Their wings were blue,
> And they sang 'Tilly-loo!'
> Till away they flew, –
> And they never came back to me!
> They never came back!
> They never came back!
> They never came back to me!

All his life Lear had hidden essential aspects of his own nature: his epilepsy, of which he was ashamed; his troubled sexuality; his feeling of being an outsider. He had turned these anxieties outwards onto his perception of his body, convinced of his ugliness, exaggerating his bulk and spindly legs, bushy beard and bulbous nose. Like his limericks, the songs he now wrote were full of odd, self-conscious misfits. Even the tools on the brass stand at every Victorian fireside were mournfully body-conscious:

> 'Alas! Mrs Broom!' sighed the Tongs in his song,
> 'O is it because I'm so thin,
> And my legs are so long – Ding a dong! Ding a dong!
> That you don't care about me a pin?'

In 'The Broom, the Shovel, the Poker and the Tongs', the anxious coachman who drives the tools sees their pain and takes them home, where 'They put on the kettle, and little by little,/ They all became happy again.' It seemed to Lear, though, that domestic life rarely ended in tea and happiness: marriage was an off-rhyme, like kettle and little. He watched the Symonds suffer in Cannes, and he worried, too, about Frank and Kate Lushington in England. Over the years, without quite overcoming his longings, Lear had gradually established a calm, close friendship with Frank, and this grew steadily after Frank's marriage, when the possibility of ever living together finally receded. They corresponded often while Lear was abroad, and he had dinner with Frank and Kate in July 1868 before they set off for their Suffolk holiday. Their son Harry had died three years before ('a kind of awful doom seems to hang over that family,' wrote Emily Tennyson: 'A sort of martyr fate'). Their two girls, Gertrude and Millicent, were nice, Lear thought, '& F. & Kate seem happy – but their everlasting silence is horrible, & makes me foam and burst. They go on Friday morning & coolly say "we shan't see you again" – wh. I endorse coldly also.' He was horrified when their baby, Edmund Henry, died in mid-August, before his first birthday. 'Certainly, as far as I can see, possession of children is more of a sorrow in the long run, than the not having any.'

The following summer he stayed with the Lushingtons for a fortnight at Southwold on the Suffolk coast. Kate was pregnant again, and Frank was ill and tetchy; his sister Ellen was there too, 'little changed but broken in spirit', spreading 'dead mournful speechlessness'. Lear was supposed to stay nearby with Frank's brother Edmund and his wife Cecilia and daughter Zilly, but dreading the Park House gloom, he hastily booked a comfortable hotel. Every day he braced himself. There were diversions, including scandalised discussion of Harriet Beecher Stowe's article revealing Lady Byron's suspicions of incest between Byron and his half-sister Augusta, and walks across the cliffs and the commons, including a dramatic flight from a bull. Lear was drawn to the old town, the beach with its long pale shadows and creamy waves, the sea full of boats, and the marshes 'so remote & quaint & East Anglian that one feels as it were in the time of Edward the Confessor'. He tried to enjoy it, waking to see the dawn, 'beautiful semi-oriental colour on the broad sea & horizon at sunrise', but then the sea fog swept in and Lear went to bathe, 'or rather had a dip: but the shore is sharp & stony & very uncomfortable, & the act of dipping undesireable . . . Shall I live through 10 more days here? 13 left . . .'

It was worse on Sundays. Sadness rolled in like the sea mist, carrying ghosts of the Lushingtons gone: Louisa, Harry, Tom, little Eddy, Frank and Kate's children. 'It can't be good for the living to live with the dead,' Lear wrote. He warmed to Kate, who talked sensibly and openly, he thought, about the weight of the family melancholy, and told him one day, after Frank left the room, about his grief for the lost, 'how wonderfully they worry & torment him, as of old in Corfu. They are the scourge of the living, those dead people of P. House.' He was cheered only by the strange beauty of the coast and the joyful effect of his nonsense, hearing six-year-old Gertrude recite 'The Owl and the Pussy-cat' and 'Calico Pie', which she knew by heart. Next day: 'Rose 5.30 – gray: did little till 8 but a child's song.'

In this child's song, the two friends, Mr Daddy Long-legs and Mr Floppy Fly, play in the chilly wind among the pebbles, on a beach not unlike Southwold, at a child's game reversed, 'battlecock and shuttledore'. The fly shimmers in blue and gold, the daddy long-legs is famed for his silvery sound. But the fly cannot go to court 'because my legs/ Are so extremely short', while the daddy long-legs no longer sings even the smallest song, 'And this the dreadful reason is,/ My legs are grown too long!'

Gertrude Lushington, 1870

So Mr Daddy Long-legs
  And Mr Floppy Fly,
Sat down in silence by the sea,
  And gazed upon the sky.
They said, 'This is a dreadful thing!
  The world has all gone wrong,
Since one has legs too short by half
  The other much too long!

There was no dancing and no moon for Gertrude, but Lear did have an answer – first you find friends, and then you sail away.

Then Mr Daddy Long-legs
  And Mr Floppy Fly
Rushed downwards to the foamy sea
  With one sponge-taneous cry;
And there they found a little boat,
  Whose sails were pink and gray;
And off they sailed among the waves,
  Far, and far away.
They sailed across the silent main,
And reached the great Gromboolian plain;
And there they play for evermore
At battlecock and shuttledore.

'Much fun about my poem,' Lear wrote after a dinner party a month later. But despite the escape to a magic land, in the dying rhythm of this poem, with its silent sea and perpetual reversed game, there was something bleak even in an eternity of play.

32: 'THREE GROANS FOR CORSICA!'

There was a Young Lady of Corsica,
Who purchased a little brown saucy-cur
Which she fed upon ham, and hot raspberry jam,
That expensive Young Lady of Corsica.

In Cannes, in the spring sunshine of 1868, Lear penned out sketches and wrote up his journals of Crete and Egypt, hoping to publish all three. 'By degrees,' he told Lady W., 'I want to topographize & topographize all the journeyings of my life, so that I shall have been of some use after all to my fellow critters.' As soon as he sold some pictures and had some money, his restlessness returned. He moved to a different house, with a view west across the bay to the low, jagged Esterel hills. At times he thought of Cannes as a permanent winter home, at others he wondered if he should have gone to New Zealand instead (too far while the elderly Ellen was still living). He was bursting to move, getting into disputes, letting his tongue run away: 'I never can apply to remembering how hours of sedentary life make me boil over when I get away – a steam force which is let off by walking, but bursts out in rage & violence if it has no natural outlet.' It was not enough to walk by the sea, or in the pine woods counting caterpillars.

Thinking of his plan to 'topographise' his travelling life, Lear wanted to complete his unfinished journey to Nazareth and Galilee, but he was also tempted by Corsica, which was cheaper, and nearer: on clear days he could see the Corsican mountains floating on the horizon. He had become friends with the writer Prosper Mérimée, now in his mid-sixties and very frail, who spent the winters in Cannes, and when Lear read Mérimée's novella *Colomba*, about a Corsican vendetta, he was filled with curiosity. Mérimée gave him notes and introductions, and Symonds suggested they go together. On 7 April 1868 they took the steamer from Nice.

Corsica was a promising subject, easy for British tourists to reach yet still relatively unknown. In his first week in Ajaccio he went sketching with Catherine Symonds and planned his route with help from a new friend, Thomasina Campbell, 'a vast & manlike maiden' who had lived here for some years, collecting plants in the mountains and studying the fish around the coast. Now she was living at the Hôtel de France, finishing her *Notes on the Island of Corsica in 1868. Dedicated to those in search of Health and Enjoyment.* Lear became fond of her and drew a frontispiece of the forest of Valdoniello for her book. He was happy and optimistic. As for the people, he felt they were more dour than Italians, but intelligent and shrewd, like the Scots. 'The children are grave & thinking little animals,' he wrote, '& one can understand the Napoleon or any other Bonaparte cropping out of such ground.' Lear saw Napoleon's birthplace, read his letters and felt his life to be at one, in many places, with the island's history.

When he came to write his journal he was full of tips for artists who might follow, warning them about the climate – hot in the valleys, freezing on the peaks – and advising that as well as their drawing materials they should take 'an indian-rubber bath; above all, a small folding camp orient bed . . . in which I am sure of sleep anywhere'. A good servant was a bonus, and Lear paid tribute to his own:

George Kokali, a Suliot, speaking several languages, sober, honest, and active, saves me all trouble and gives none; now carrying a weight of cloaks and folios and daily bread for a twenty-mile walk or more, anon keeping off dogs and bystanders when I am drawing, or cooking and acting as house-servant when stationary; a man of few words, and constant work.

To cover the island quickly Lear hired a two-horse carriage and an objectionable-looking coachman called Peter. Miss Campbell saw them off, calling 'from the window cheerfully, "You should have taken my man Jean! All your luggage will fall off! Your horses will tumble! Everything will go wrong!"' Shrugging this off, Lear and Giorgio drove south into the mountains, range on range, their bare granite tops rising above dense woods, full, in Lear's view, of a lonely sadness.

They stayed in country inns, invariably run by widows, gazing 'into wide distances of Claude Lorraine landscape'. At every step, Lear wrote, 'there are studies for pictures, if only in the hedges, which are in some places literally blue with a beautiful climbing vetch'. Such details absorbed him, like the granite mottled with tints, 'green, white, yellow, orange and black lichen, tufts of a red kind of stonecrop, moss and ivy . . . enough work for months of artist-life'. He thought the forest of Bavella, where pines grew in ranks between great rock walls, 'one of the most wonderfully beautiful sights nature can produce'. The trees beat all he ever saw or dreamed of, he told Fanny Coombe:

The trees are many of them 150 feet high they say. The flowers would rather astonish you: sometimes you see a mile or so of pink – it is all rose cistus: the anemones, broom, crocus, lavender, vetch, cyclamen – all wild, along the sea side. The nightingales are by millions – ditto the blackbirds which inhabit the thick covering of myrtle, arbutus, that covers nearly all the island.

Sheltering from a thunderstorm Lear watched a shaft of sun touch the crags of Bavella, creating a golden haze above the vast gloom below where the dark pines stood out 'in deepest shadow against the pale granite cliffs dazzling in the sunlight'. 'No frenzy of the wildest dreams of a landscape painter', he wrote, 'could shape out ideal scenes of more magnificence and wonder.' Writing to Emily Tennyson he fantasised about building a house in one of these mighty pines. He drew a sketch of this up the side of his letter, lifting himself even higher than the Old Man of Philae in his palm tree.

The Forest of Bavella, 4 p.m., 29 April 1868. Notes: 'all/darkish/brown/green/
light/seen/through/blu'

There were disturbing scenes too. One day, walking up a mountain track, they saw Peter ahead, cursing and beating the horses, and
watched in horror as they backed towards the precipice, sending the
carriage careering into the ravine. 'A ghastly sight I can't get rid of. One
horse killed, the other horribly injured: the little beast of a driver not
so badly hurt as he ought to have been.' Miss Campbell's prophecy had
come true: all their luggage had tumbled far down among the rocks and
ferns. Back in Ajaccio Peter was replaced by the youthful Domenico 'of
Napoleonic and grave aspect', bringing with him a small spotty dog,
Flora, 'of amiable and watchful deportment'. Lear was happy, telling
Fanny, 'I eat trout no end, and drink no end of wine. Ajaccio is beautiful, dull & dirty, but there are some nice people here, & a house in a
garden would be Paradise: if I hadn't settled at Cannes I would come
here.' Then off they set again to the north, to the forest of Valdoniello,
enclosed by snowy mountains like wings. Their third, final tour was
to the eastern plain and the ports of Bastia and Calvi (where, to Lear's

delight, in the eighteenth century the people had driven off Genoa's German mercenaries by hurling bee-hives at their heads).

At the Hôtel de Londres, Lear dismissed Domenico and Flora fondly. Soon he was back in Cannes, gazing at the familiar Esterels, delicately perfect and lovely. He had made over three hundred sketches and in mid-June 1868 he headed for London to see about his book. Symonds gave him an introduction to the publisher George Smith, of Smith, Elder & Co.: he was interested but only if the costs were low, and suggested a single volume instead of two, with wood engravings instead of lithographs. Reluctantly, Lear agreed and set to work on revising his journal while travelling round his circle of friends. Tired though he was, he could still enjoy himself. At the Goldsmids in November he walked around the churchyard with a charming young woman: 'quoted Epitaphs – talked of Italy – religion, Philosophy – beetles – Via Reggio – toads – woodpeckers – & the immortality of the Soul – David, ladies trains, – Tennyson, mulberries, Calvinism, puns, landscapes, Tunny fish, Leghorn, Laurels & Lozenges'.

He felt alive, confident. He stayed on through the summer and autumn until all the woodcuts and drawings were ready. Then came a blow: 'Smithanelder, I saw at once, would have nothing to do with my book – his verdict was thus: "*Thus* expensively illustrated – your book *cannot* pay. *Less* expensively illustrated it won't be an 'illustrated book', & won't pay as a literary speculation."' Macmillan turned it down too, and gloomily he realised that he must publish it himself. The printer Robert Bush of Charing Cross agreed to do it, but with cheaper cuts. Lear had already spent £130 on the woodcuts, and now they would have to be done again.

The only option was to return to Cannes and find engravers in France. Back in the sunshine his mood lifted. He missed the Symonds, but met new people, like young Edmund Langton, '– fancy! Langton is nephew of DARWIN!!!!!!!!!' On Sunday evenings he asked Giorgio to stay and talk of his family and have a smoke and a drink, 'though he will not have more than a teaspoon of Marsala . . . I think this is right, that a man so far from home should feel that his employer has some interest in his life.'

As the weeks passed he started a new set of Corsican 'Tyrants', and transcribed his journal, striking a line through each page as he passed it. In the early months of 1869, when the mistral roared and the windows rattled, his epilepsy returned badly: one violent fit left him almost cataleptic for an hour. But as the sun warmed he took days off, wandering up into the hills with Giorgio and drawing as he loved to do: 'It was a *real* pleasure to me.' He went to Paris to see wood engravers although he knew that his drawings were too subtle and delicate for the hard line of woodcuts. Staying in his usual refuge, the Hôtel du Louvre, he looked caustically at the English people opposite him at dinner, who 'might have made a good Dickens chapter, but one can't record the nonsense . . . O this Corsica! 3 groans for Corsica!' Yet the engravings were underway, and if the style was heavier than usual, the scenes were still dramatically alive.

Ajaccio, from *Journal of a Landscape Painter in Corsica* (1870)

In late June Lear found rooms in Duchess Street in Marylebone and set out on his visits, including the fortnight with the Lushingtons at Southwold. Wherever he stayed, he worked, translating his French sources and writing 'Additional Notes' on Corsican geology, climate, people and history. In his Preface he explained that he had been led to the island by the wandering painter's need 'to find new places, and add fresh ideas of landscape to both mind and portfolio', quoting 'Ulysses' again, on 'the untravell'd world'.

Tennyson's poetry was still his guide, but he found it harder to get on with the poet himself. The previous year, when Tennyson had called on him in London, Lear thought that to hear him talk, 'one would fancy him a mere child and a foolish one too' – except on money matters – 'Verily o Poet! You are a wonder!' In Tennyson's view, however it was Lear who was childish with his riddles and puns and songs.

At the end of September 1869, Lear went to stay with Alfred and Emily in their newly built house, Aldworth, high on the Surrey downs. The year before he had been enraptured by the view stretching forty miles across the Weald to the Channel. Now driving up to 'Palazzo Tennyson' in a pony cart, he marvelled again. He walked cheerily with Tennyson through the woods, but next morning they had a row. Tennyson had chosen two colour sketches of Corsica, but then changed his mind, first wanting to exchange them for cheaper pencil drawings, then muttering that it would be better to spend the money on the house: after all, he said, it was Emily who wanted the pictures, not him. Lear fumed: 'I said he was given to worry & everyone knew it – & he said I was irritable & what not – & so we all exploded & went. Then I packed my things.' When he came downstairs Emily handed him a cheque for £10 for 'Morn broaden'd', patted and soothed him and sent him off for a walk. But although Lear apologised, Tennyson was still scalded by his '*Everyone* knows it'. Early next morning Lear left, with the great plain below covered in mist.

To cheer himself up, in a fit of extravagance he moved down the road to the new Langham's Hotel in Portland Place, fabulously modern, with bathrooms and hydraulic lifts. He corrected the proofs of his book, with Frank's help, and slowly the subscriptions came in. *Journal of a Landscape Painter in Corsica*, priced modestly at £1 and dedicated to Frank Lushington, would appear for the last Christmas of this fraught decade.

33: *DEGLI INGLESI*

There was an Old Man in a tree,
Whose whiskers were lovely to see;
But the birds of the air pluck'd them perfectly bare,
To make themselves nests in that tree.

On 10 December 1869, his Corsica book out at last, Lear was on the train, taking 'just 20 hours' from Folkestone. Arriving in Cannes he wrote in large letters, '*Of course*, George was there.' Everything was in order, '& such a dinner of mutton broth & roast lamb & cheese & olives! . . . I confess things seem like a dream, so very exact & good!' It was time for a new project. Two months earlier, when the American publisher James Fields asked to publish 'The Owl and the Pussy-cat', 'The Duck and the Kangaroo', and 'Mr Floppy Fly' in his children's magazine *Our Young Folks* (they appeared in February, March and April the following year), Lear had written firmly, 'You will I know kindly print my name in full "Edward Lear" – wh. will, when I get the Magazine, delight my feeble mind, & console me for remaining in this cold foggy place. After all, small as it may be, one does some good by contributing to the laughter of little children, if it is a harmless laughter.' Now he planned new laughter. On New Year's Day 1870 he told Fortescue: 'I shall look out and heap together all the nonsense I can for my new book which is to be entitled – Learical Lyrics and Puffles of Prose

&c., &c.' Over the year, the whimsical title vanished and the one book became two, *Nonsense Songs, Stories, Botany and Alphabets* and *More Nonsense*. And while these books grew, Lear found a new home, in Italy.

He had joked to Emily Tennyson about his nest in the pine tree but he was serious about building a house. This had been on his mind for some time. He had put money into government bonds for his old age but the interest was going on rent and London storage for his paintings – surely it could be better spent? First, he toyed with the idea of an English home. In 1868, when he heard that land near the Tennysons at Aldworth was £100 an acre, he wrote, 'My last mania is to buy some ten or so & build a house!' The following September, before their row, he saw one field there that would be 'absolutely delightful' to build on, but added, 'it by no means follows I could live "happily" – even if I built a house here'. Then he brooded over a house in Southwold, and, at Frank's suggestion, land near Bournemouth. But he knew it would not do. He looked around Nice and Cannes too, but in early 1870 the rumblings of the tension that would lead to the Franco-Prussian war made him wonder if France was a sensible place after all. At the end of February he crossed the border to San Remo in Italy, where his friends the Wyatts were considering settling. Here he met an English resident, Walter Congreve, who showed him land overlooking the sea. He heard of a house in Corfu; he thought of Ajaccio. But should he settle at all? Should he give up painting and travel? 'Good Gracious! What a bother about a place for a "comfortable life".'

In the clear March days when the air was like crystal and snow lay on the Esterels, Lear sent off two paintings to be entered for the Academy, *Valdoniello* and *Kasr es Saàd*, the first time he had done this for years. Then he went back to San Remo. Over a single weekend, everything happened in a flash. On 25 March, he looked at land above Walter Congreve's house, with a view out over the sea. Next morning he decided to buy, and later in the day met an architect, Anselmi. Within a couple of days he had sorted out terms and signed the contract. The land cost £400, and the house would be £1200, leaving him money to spare from his savings. First he was exhilarated: 'Very cold all day. Did little but write letters, & make plans of the House'. Then he panicked. Then he calmed again. A few weeks later, on May Day, he wrote to Thomas Woolner:

What do you think as I have been & gone & I grow so tired of noisy lodgings, & yet am so more & more unable to think of ever wintering in England – & so unable to bear the expense of two houses & two journeys annually, that I have bought a bit of ground at San Remo I am actually building a house there.

He drew a nonsense picture of his plans and joshed about living on figs in summer and worms in the winter, planting twenty-eight olive trees and an onion bed and having 'a stone terrace with a gray Parrot & 2 hedgehogs to walk up & down on it by day & by night'.

The Corso degli Inglesi circles up the hill in San Remo and then loops along the ridges that point down to the sea like the bent fingers of a hand. Here rich English families built villas surrounded by gardens, with turrets and balconies gazing down at the bays: by the end of the century, the curving road would be a ribbon of art nouveau 'Liberty' architecture. A narrow lane, the Via Hope, winds steeply down from the Corso to the shore. This was where Lear built his house, the Villa Emily – named, Lear insisted unconvincingly, for his New Zealand great-niece, Sarah's granddaughter, and not for Emily Tennyson. Below his garden lay a patch of land dotted with olives, and beyond it, across the road and the railway, the dazzle of the Mediterranean flared to the blue horizon. When Lear walked east, along the wide, new Corso Matteotti with its palazzi and smart shops, he reached the harbour and the fishing fleet. Behind, the old town, 'La Pigna', curled round the hill like its pinecone name, with narrow streets climbing like ladders to the church of the Madonna del Costa, a refuge from pirates and raiders. Could San Remo be the sanctuary he longed for?

In particular, the thought of the garden delighted him. The most notable things about the coast here, wrote the diplomat Ernest Satow,

Manypeeplia Upsidownia.

travelling on the Corniche train from Menton to San Remo, 'are lemon-groves on the seashore which look as if they were ready to be washed away at every moment'. Above them on the heights, all along this coast, where the Alpes-Maritimes meet the sea, the panes of glass-houses and nurseries glittered on the hillsides, raising flowers for the markets of the north. Inland, growers harvested roses, jasmine, mimosa, lavender and myrtle for the perfumeries of Grasse, and plant collectors roamed the mountains, home to hundreds of rare species. The Riviera was a paradise for botanists, and wealthy English plant lovers created grand gardens here like the Quaker merchant Thomas Hanbury, who had made a fortune buying silk in the Far East (and gave Wisley to the Royal Horticultural Society). At La Mortola, just over the Italian border, Hanbury grew citrus, medicinal and exotic plants: agave, aloes and salvias; monkey-puzzles from Chile; palms from Africa and India; bamboos from China; eucalyptus and yucca from Australia.

Lear knew Hanbury, who owned the empty plot below his own planned villa, and he had painted La Mortola in 1865: it was hardly possible, he thought, to imagine 'anything lovelier and more Italianly romantic'. All his botanical passions were revived. In the late spring of 1870 he was in Grasse collecting plants, and also inventing his own curious species. He sent drawings of his nonsense plants to his friend Mrs Ker, explaining that they only grew near Grasse, '& in the Humbly islands' where he had seen them long ago and had met a professor who gave him 'Generic & Specific names'. These plants would be his 'Nonsense Botany', an array of species like the *Cockatooca Superba* and the favourite, *Manypeeplia Upsidownia*, with its pendant persons, funny and fragile at once.

The Learical plants were comic but they also revealed Lear's deep knowledge of a plant's intricate organisation. In his drawings the stems branch in a host of ways, some with basal leaves, some with leaves sprouting from alternate sides, some with bracts climbing like the rising tiers of a cake. The flowers, too, flaunt different arrangements of petals and sepals: a single bell-shaped flower, like the *Baccopipia Gracilis*; tapering pyramids like the *Piggiwiggia Pyramidalis* or symmetrical five-petalled blooms like the clustering parrot-flowers of *Pollybirdia Singularis*. As in nature, each specimen is made up of multiple parts while remaining a clear example of a 'type', a distinctive, blooming individual, the union of the many and the one.

In the spring of 1870, impatient to have his own garden and waiting for the builders to start work, Lear rented rooms in San Remo for six months. To fill the time, he visited friends in Nice and Cannes and then headed to the hills to escape the steamy summer heat. One reason that he liked San Remo in comparison to the French towns, where villas mushroomed along the roads into the hills, was that the mountains behind rose like a wall and no roads led over them. As a carriage was out of the question, Lear and Giorgio set out to walk over the high ridges, with a mule called Roma to carry their packs, working their way across alpine meadows and through chestnut forests to the gorges of the river Roya, the border with France, and the town of Saorge. In the mountain inn Lear could not sleep for the song of nightingales outside his window, but this frontier town was a strange meeting place: at the table d'hôte, Lear found 'Messres Muller, Murphy, Chambers &c. &c,' and on his walk after supper he was pursued by the elderly Mrs Vigors, widow of Nicholas Vigors who had known him at the zoo when he was eighteen. 'Strange, to come to this out of the way place & find all this pumped up out of the depths of memory 40 years ago!' At last they looked up at the road winding up to the high Col du Tenda, 'like a long riband unrolled'. This was almost too much: on the climb Giorgio hurt his foot and Lear suffered bad palpitations – a doctor told him later that he had a weak heart, like his father. 'I have had advice about it,' he told Fortescue, '& they say I may live *any* time if I *don't run suddenly* or go *quickly upstairs*: but that if I do I am pretty sure to drop morto.' He wrote a note for Giorgio 'in case of my sudden death'.

Once over the pass, they travelled in more comfort, taking the omnibus on the Turin road to Cuneo, 'a large & very interesting place. Arcades, shops – silkworm cocoons for sale', and then winding south up a long valley to La Certosa di Pesio, an old Carthusian monastery that was now a smart 'hydropathic' hotel. It was a fashionable place, popular with writers (Stendhal had stayed there) and with minor royalty, American tourists and Piedmontese gentry, whom Lear found delightful, 'really charming people, so simple & kindly. Only I wish they weren't all counts. Who ever heard before of an omnibus stuffed quite full of counts – (8) & 2 Marquises?' With its dull pink walls, squares of lawn and cloisters open to the woods and the mountain above, the Certosa stood at the valley's head, where a brown stream rushed over the stones like a Cumbrian beck and insects hummed in the shade.

Later Lear came to love the whole area with its winding rivers and unexplored forests but to begin with he chafed against the narrow valley bounds. He found the place oppressive and climbed up to escape, drawing the Certosa's square buildings against the widening view behind, scribbling, 'oak, beech, all thick wood, chestnut, fern, moss'.

Within a week he adjusted to the regular, placid, pace of hotel life, creating his own routine in counterpoint. The new rhythm broke down when Lear decided that Giorgio, troubled by his injured foot and worried by news from home, should go back to Corfu to see his family. When he went to see him off in Turin on 17 July 1870, he learned that 'The horrid news has come that WAR has been declared between F & P.' Ahead lay Prussian victories, the siege of Metz and the defeat of the French at Sedan, then the long siege of Paris and the revolutionary months of the Commune: for the next year the horrors of war would thunder in the back of Lear's mind.

Lear's feet were still swollen after the walk: it was hard to get his shoes on, and he missed Giorgio badly. 'For all I write cheerfully,' he swore to Fortescue, 'I am as savage & black as 90000 bears . . .'

I live the queerest solitary life here in the company of 70 people. They are – many of them – very nice – but their hours don't suit me, & I HATE LIFE unless I **WORK** ALWAYS. I rise at 5. Coffee at 6. Write till 10. Bkft at Table d'hote. Walk till 11-30. Write till 6. Walk till 8. Dine alone. & bed at 10 or 9.30.

He had plenty of writing to do, including transcribing his Egyptian journals. He understood the quirky quality of his travel writing. A few years from now, writing to Amelia B. Edwards, who had illustrated her best-selling *A Thousand Miles up the Nile* with her own drawings and was a co-founder of the Egypt Exploration Fund, he tried to sound modest, but failed.

There is & must be a great drawback in *my* writing wh. your's on a similar subject would not have; – & this is that whatever *I* write would be *Edward Lear* – egotistical & unmitigated – fanciful – individual – correct or what not – but nevertheless always *Edward Lear*; – whereas what you write might be written by Mrs Tomkins, or Queen Boadicea, or Lady Jane Grey, or Rizpah of Gibeah, Joan of Ark or anybody else – because A. B. Edwards never appears at all.

The Egyptian journal would never be published. Instead, up in the mountains Lear was also gathering material for his new book of songs and nonsense, a work that could never be written by Mrs Tomkins or Joan of Arc. Before he left, he had already made fair copies of 'The Duck and the Kangaroo', 'Mr Daddy Long-legs and Mr Floppy Fly', and 'The Four Children Who Went Round the World'. At La Certosa he jotted in his diary: 'completed the Jumblies', 'Finished the poem of "Spikky Sparrow"'. His aim, as he had told James Fields, was to make children laugh and there were plenty of children at La Certosa, ready to be amused. 'Do the Carthusian friars look down on their old gardens & corridors?' Lear asked, '& if so, seeing there are 43 ladies, 19 nursery maids and some 50 children in said gardens & galleries— How do they bear the sight?'

Among the new guests in August were the 'English family' (actually American) the Terrys, with their four children, Margaret ('Daisy') and Alfred Terry, and their older half-sister and brother Mary and Francis Crawford. Lear had known the painter Luther 'Louis' Terry in London and Rome and found him as kindly and gentlemanly as ever: in 1861 he had married Louisa, the wealthy widow of the sculptor Thomas Crawford, and their apartment in the Palazzo Odescalchi was a cosmopolitan salon, one of the few places where the Italian elite and politicians mingled with artists. With their arrival, Lear's lonely summer became full: 'drew for little Daisy Terry', he wrote, 'Walked & sate with the Terrys.' In later life both Daisy and Mary recorded their impressions nostalgically. Daisy remembered how they were saved from the misery of sitting down with strangers at the table d'hôte by finding opposite them 'a rosy, gray-bearded, bald-headed, gold-spectacled little gentleman . . . something seemed to bubble and sparkle in his talk and his eyes twinkled benignly behind the shining glasses.' He helped Daisy with the rituals of hotel meals as she struggled with her large knife and fork, by slipping a drawing across the table. At seven, Daisy was 'a turbulent little creature', Mary wrote, 'always getting into trouble of some kind, and from that first day she learned to take her troubles to "Uncle Lear", who turned them into rhymes and pictures', like a bump on the forehead that became the third horn of the 'Uncareful Cow', rubbed away with camphor two hundred times a day. Lear gave Daisy a copy of 'The Duck and the Kangaroo', sang 'The Owl and the Pussy-cat' and walked with her in the forest, kicking chestnut burrs, which they called the 'yonghy bonghy bos'.

Every day Daisy and her small brother found a sketch and poem on their plates. These made up the alphabet of 'The Absolutely Abstemious Ass', drawn on scraps of paper and backs of letters, with afterthoughts like the crimson of the pensive owl's carpet bag.

The Goodnatured Grey Gull,
who carried the old Owl
and his Carpet-bag, across the river,
because he could not swim.

Mary was struck in particular by Lear's musical voice, and remembered that the 'strange meats and unmanageable cutlery of the *table d'hôte* inspired the marvellous botanical specimen "Manyforkia Spoonifolia" as well as most of the recipes for "Nonsense Cookery"'. (Gardening readers, like Maria Price La Touche, found the botany 'delicious', and called her zinc wheelbarrow 'Lady Jingly'.) Lear invented a special *Nonsense Gazette* for the Terry children, and, thinking perhaps of experts like La Mortola's Ludwig Winter, who was head gardener of the Botanical Garden at Poppelsdorf before moving to France, he attributed both plants and recipes to 'Professor Bosh'. The professor found the plants, the *Gazette* stated with precision, 'in the valley of Verrikwier, near the lake of Oddgrow, and on the summit of the hill Orfeltugg', and had also collected the recipes for Amblongus Pie, Crumblobblious Cutlets and Gosky Patties. The recipes echoed perfectly the practical, patronising tone of Mrs Beeton and her peers. The cook must simmer a mess of Amblongusses until they become 'a pale purple colour':

Then, having prepared the paste, insert the whole carefully, adding at the same time a small pigeon, 2 slices of beef, 4 cauliflowers, and any number of oysters.

Watch patiently till the crust begins to rise, and add a pinch of salt from time to time.

Serve up in a clean dish, and throw the whole out of the window as far as possible.

Food was always important to Lear, especially as he grew older: 'It is funny to see what attention I always pay to "dinner" details', he wrote at one point, 'but I have a notion that food is a great factor in our fooly life.' In his diary he noted meals at stately homes, at suppers with friends, in places on his travels. At one inn on the long walk to the Certosa, breakfast consisted of 'wonderful trout & potatoes – beefsteak – & wine & raspberries'. At home his daily diary ended with brief notes: 'dined on barley broth, & boiled mutton, cooked a la Giorgio Kokali – first rate'; 'came back by 6. when Giorgio gave me a very grand dinner of p. soup & grilled fowl'.

Sometimes botany and recipes combined. One later set of 'Flora Nonsensica' was full of transformed objects: a clothes-brush tree; a fork tree; a tree of chignons. Each had a quasi-scientific description, like the Biscuit Tree, 'never yet described or delineated':

As it never grows near rivers, nor near the sea, nor near mountains or vallies, or houses, its native place is wholly uncertain. When the flowers fall off, and the tree breaks out in biscuits, the effect is by no means disagreeable, especially to the hungry. If the Biscuits grow in pairs, they do not grow single, and if they ever fall off, they cannot be said to remain on.

In the summer Lear sent all the drawings to be lithographed in England, where Robert Bush would be his publisher again. On 30 August, as his eight weeks at La Certosa came to a close, he copied out the alphabet he had made for the Terry children, 'wrote out all the rest of the new Xmas book – & posted the *whole to Bush*'. This included all his new poems, the stories of 'The Seven Families' and 'The Four Little Children', the nonsense botany and cookery, and three alphabets. Sensibly, Bush persuaded him to leave the hundred new limericks for a separate book, *More Nonsense*, to be published the following autumn. Having sent all this off, Lear returned to the Corso degli Inglesi and waited anxiously for Giorgio: 'No steamer – no George – no nothing'; 'I wish George would come'; 'Where can G be?' Then Giorgio arrived, '& certainly, as one opens the window & looks out on the Lemon gardens to the city & mountain – S. Remo is a beautiful place'.

Putting the new book together was a simple matter compared to the agony of the Corsican journal, but in the storms of late autumn, Lear's anxiety grew. Doubts returned, fears that he should have spent the money on travel instead of on the house, should have gone to America or somewhere else far away. 'No sleep all night,' he recorded on 21 November:

Counted every hour, & rose at 6 worried & miserable – I review my whole life in such hours & full of evil as it undoubtedly is, I am obliged to conclude as I always do, that the great physical misery & 'particular skeleton' of all these long years, was not of my making – commenced when I was 5 or 6 years old, – & has influenced all the course of my existence. Blame there has been on my part no doubt – but the foundation of wretchedness was too solidly there, ever to have allowed of a greatly different chain of events & condition of living than has been my lot to bear.

It had taken time to reach this point of self-forgiveness. The 'particular skeleton' was his epilepsy, but the foundation of wretchedness also lay in his mother's rejection, his bullying at school, the unspecified abuse. This month his epilepsy was bad. His days were black. He thought of his family, the living and the lost: 'This was "Kate's" birthday: she would have been 56 had she lived'; 'This was poor Charles's birthday – he would have been 63 today.'

The dark mood passed as the weather improved and the builders worked on. Soon he and Giorgio were unpacking cases and putting thousands of drawings into cabinets 'just as if it were in Stratford Place'. James Field cheered him up by ordering five hundred copies of *Nonsense Songs, Stories, Botany and Alphabets* and he was pleased when his own copies arrived on 8 December: 'all my Autumn & Summer work at Certosa. – sent by Book Post from Bush. It is well got up & looks famous.' He found, to his great relief, that it was universally liked. In his anonymous review in the *Spectator* Richard Ford found some lapses and disliked the recipes, but he greatly admired the ballads, stories and botany:

The nonsense botany is genuine nonsense – extravagant enough to make the most prosaic man laugh; but yet nonsensical precisely because it recognizes the laws of sense, and directly traverses them . . . in spite of little failures here and there, the ideal of nonsense is attained by Mr Lear, who, in this respect, may be said to stand at the very summit of the human race.

34: NONSENSE SONGS AND MORE NONSENSE

We don't know whether Lear or Robert Bush chose the order for *Nonsense Songs, Stories, Botany and Alphabets*, but the first poem readers encountered was 'The Owl and the Pussy-cat', in which love and voyaging joined. As the poems followed in sequence that happy combination seemed more elusive. The Duck and the Kangaroo are friends, not lovers, and although their escape is joyful, the book's mood sobers with the 'The Daddy Long-legs and the Fly', playing forever on the shingly shore. But then the Jumblies sweeps melancholy away: they are so shouty and uncaring, so happy to launch their sieve full of holes, defying the storms and the warnings of 'they'.

> They went to sea in a Sieve, they did,
>   In a Sieve they went to sea:
>   In spite of all their friends could say,
>   On a winter's morn, on a stormy day,
>   In a Sieve they went to sea!
>   And when the Sieve turned round and round,
>   And every one cried, 'You'll all be drowned!'
>   They called aloud, 'Our Sieve ain't big,
>   But we don't care a button! We don't care a fig!
>   In a Sieve we'll go to sea!'

The Jumblies have no counterpart in nature, but they are marvellously persuasive. ('The Jumblies', Lear said to Emma Parkyns, who

407

loved the book, 'I believe with you, are real critters.') Lear makes them real by garlanding them with details, like their purchases in the Western Seas – an owl and a useful cart, some rice and a cranberry tart, and a hive of silvery bees:

> And they bought a Pig, and some green Jack-daws,
> And a lovely Monkey with lollipop paws,
> And forty bottles of Ring-Bo-Ree,
>   And no end of Stilton Cheese.

Drinking their Ring-Bo-Ree they never age: they return in 'twenty years or more', to the envy of all who hear their tales. As T. S. Eliot said, this is 'a poem of adventure and of nostalgia for the romance of foreign voyage and exploration', but only Lear could map these uncharted lands: the Gromboolian plain, the Torrible Zone, and the hills of the Chankly Bore.

When the poems shift from distant seas to domestic shores the desire for flight becomes more urgent still. The Nutcracker and the Sugartongs, fed up with their stupid existence, 'So idle and weary, so full of remorse', ride off on their stolen horses to a chorus of yelling and clattering and lady-like/ladle-like squeaks:

> The Cups and the Saucers danced madly about,
> The Plates and the Dishes looked out of the casement,
>   The Salt-cellar stood on his head with a shout,
> The Spoons with a clatter looked out of the lattice,
>   The Mustard-pot climbed up the Gooseberry Pies,
> The Soup-ladle peered through a heap of veal Patties,
>   And squeaked with a ladle-like scream of surprise.

These household things leap with clanging, hysterical life, imbued with the excitement that Lear felt when routines turned to chaos: the fire at Knowsley or the flood at Oatlands. But as the escapees flee, the tone changes and quietens:

> They galloped away to the beautiful shore;
> In silence they rode, and 'made no observation',
> Save this: 'We will never go back any more!'

With a final snap, like a vanishing act on the page, they ride out of hearing, 'Till far in the distance their forms disappearing,/ They faded away. – And they never came back!' We cannot follow them. Like the singer of 'Calico Pie', we are left behind – and they never come back.

If flight is the main imperative, sometimes, Lear suggests – if less convincingly – contentment can be bounded by a nest. His 'Mr and Mrs Spikky Sparrow' solve their headaches and lack of hats and slippers by dashing to Moses' wholesale shop, to buy a hat and bonnet 'and a gown with spots upon it'.

> Then when so completely drest,
> Back they flew, and reached their nest.
> Their children cried, 'O Ma and Pa!
> How truly beautiful you are!'
> Said they, 'We trust that cold or pain
> We shall never feel again!
> While, perched on tree, or house, or steeple,
> We now shall look like other people.
>   Witchy witchy witchy wee,
>   Twikky mikky bikky bee,
>   Zikky sikky tee!'

Might staying put in respectable comfort, 'like other people', yet sticking to your own nonsensical song, be happiness, of a sort? Perhaps,

but the two domestic poems that follow – the quarrelsome courtships of
'The Broom, the Shovel, the Poker and the Tongs' and 'The Table and
the Chair', undercut this idea. The impatience to move is clear when the
furniture with 'legs' try to walk:

> Said the Chair unto the Table,
> 'Now you *know* we are not able!
> How foolishly you talk,
> When you know we *cannot* walk!'
> Said the Table with a sigh,
> 'It can do no harm to try,
> I've as many legs as you,
> Why can't we walk on two?'

They do toddle off, with a cheerful bumpy sound, only to get lost 'in
going down an alley,/ To a castle in the valley'. Sometimes, Lear im-
plies, we need rescuing, bringing back. Travelling safely home is as vital
as escaping, and perhaps more difficult.

Nonsense Songs, which Lear never asked to be taken seriously, showed
him to be a lyrical poet whose metres were as varied as those of his hero
Tennyson, and whose moods could embrace yearning sadness as well
as wit. A lifetime of listening, reading, parodying, writing and singing
lay behind his musical use of intricate scansion and rhyme. The poems
moved like dances, their rhythms ranging from the slow, three-beat
ballad-waltz of the Owl and the Pussy-cat – 'They sailed away for a
year and a day' – to the simple four/three of 'Mr Daddy Long-legs' and
the hand-holding, foot-stamping chant of the Jumblies' choral dance:

> Far and few, far and few,
> Are the lands where the Jumblies live:
> Their heads are green, and their hands are blue,
> And they went to sea in a Sieve.

His subjects were as varied and alive as his verse. Into the slim volume in its dark blue binding, Lear crowded a host of creatures, animate, inanimate, real and imaginary. In poems and stories and alphabets he gathered flocks of birds, swarms of insects, shoals of Fizziggious Fish, an aquarium of reptiles and crustaceans and an army of animals. With them marched mundane things: cakes and ink-pots, dolls, hats and kites. Around them, in his botany, grew nonsense plants with formal names.

The land of Bosh was crowded, alive, overflowing. Yet it had room for more. As soon as *Nonsense Songs* was published in December 1871 he was writing new poems, 'The Courtship of the Yonghy-Bonghy-Bò' and 'Mr and Mrs Discobbolos', which he copied out on Christmas Eve. Here too, in bravura style, he explored the complexities of love and marriage and the perils of staying still and of taking flight. For Mr and Mrs Discobbolos – people-creatures, strange but human – married life is precarious. Their name echoes that of the Discobolos, the lost Greek bronze of the javelin thrower, and they aim high. They climb up, as so many Lear figures do:

> Mr and Mrs Discobbolos
>> Climbed to the top of a wall,
>> And they sate to watch the sunset sky
>> And to hear the Nupiter Piffkin cry
>> And the Biscuit Buffalo call.
> They took up a roll and some Camomile tea
> And both were as happy as happy could be –
>> Till Mrs Discobbolos said –
>> 'Oh! W! X! Y! Z!
>> It has just come into my head –
> Suppose we should happen to fall!!!!!
>> Darling Mr Discobbolos!'

It is never safe, with Lear, to say 'happy as happy could be'. Terror lies in the threat of falling, of breaking into pieces like the final, separate letters of the alphabet that form the refrain. One answer is simply to stay there, above the worry of life and household cares: from on high they see no trouble ahead, no 'Sorrow or any such thing'. But we feel the risk.

If Lear sighed for wall-top bliss, watching the sunset sky, he also remembered the loss of the dream. He kept in touch with Gussie, underlining the arrival of her letters in his diary, 'very sweet & good & dear little Gussie. – She is as good as good can be & we two ought to have been one, but can't be ever.' At a low point in the autumn of 1870 he plunged into self-pity:

I work without hope or heart, & am as depressed & wretched as at Corfu in 1855 – nay – more so, for then I had more hope, – now, alas, more experience instead – I see no loophole of light onward, 'tears, idle tears' are in my eyes – tho far from happy autumn fields. Ah! Gussie – But to look back is worse folly than any other – 'I must be *alone – until I die*'.

Yet rejection, as he knew from his own mixture of pain and relief when he left Hinton, could also feel like escape. The opening of 'The Courtship of the Yonghy-Bonghy-Bò' has a lyrical serenity but its folksong simplicity masks a poetic form of elaborate complexity, mirroring the depth of feeling. When Mr Bò, with his tiny body and big head and nursery-rhyme furniture – 'Two old chairs and half a candle – / One old jug without a handle' – comes across Lady Jingly Jones his loneliness and longing meet.

> 'Lady Jingly! Lady Jingly!
>   Sitting where the pumpkins blow,
>   Will you come and be my wife?'
>   Said the Yonghy-Bonghy-Bò.
> 'I am tired of living singly, –
> On this coast so wild and shingly, –
>   I'm a-weary of my life.'

He offers her practical things – prawns and fish, plentiful and cheap – but also a simple avowal worthy of Burns, 'As the sea, my love is deep!' (It's not clear which he feels is the most persuasive appeal.) It is no good, she weeps, he is too late – she is married already: 'his name is Handel/ Handel Jones, Esquire & Co.' If Mr Jones sounds more like a firm than a man, this is half the point. He belongs to the bourgeois life of 'they', and it is this that has blocked their romance.

The only option, as Lear himself felt, is to travel. And when Mr Bò flees on his large and lively turtle Lear quickens the pace *allegro vivace*, then slows it again on the tide:

> Through the silent-roaring ocean
>   Did the Turtle swiftly go;
>   Holding fast upon his shell
>   Rode the Yonghy-Bonghy-Bò.
> With a sad primaeval motion
> Towards the sunset isles of Boshen
>   Still the Turtle bore him well.
>   Holding fast upon his shell
>   'Lady Jingly Jones, farewell!'
>   Said the Yonghy-Bonghy-Bò,
>   Said the Yonghy-Bonghy-Bò.

The currents sweep him westwards to the isles of Boshen, where the refuge of 'Bosh', or nonsense, becomes the Hesperides, home of the blest. Lady Jingly Jones is left to sob alone.

From the Coast of Coromandel,
  Did that Lady never go;
    On that heap of stones she mourns
  For the Yonghy-Bonghy-Bò.

With that negative, 'never go', the poet condemns her. She is left on the shingly coast, trapped like Mariana or the Lady of Shalott, mourning a love denied consummation, a marriage that can never be.

Robert Bush was right to persuade Lear to leave his hundred new limericks for a second book, but when they were published at the end of 1872, in *More Nonsense, Pictures, Rhymes, Botany Etc.*, it was clear that the mystery of the songs coloured the limericks too.

There was a young lady in white,
  Who looked out at the depths of the night;
    But the birds of the air, filled her heart with despair,
  And oppressed that young lady in white.

Darkness crowds in on a ghostly figure stretching from a window to greet shadowy owls. The owls are not accusatory, but sympathetic, understanding. Despite her despair she looks into their eyes and her face reflects theirs – she looks as though she wants to join them, suspended, floating into the dark. In a note scribbled on his drawing, Lear said that he did not mind how the printer did the black, 'so long as you keep the figure quite white & the birds grey'.

Lear was an intelligent, self-aware depressive. Excitement ripples through his response to wide vistas, brilliant light, the great flight of birds. But he was easily knocked down and as he grew older the lows lasted longer than the highs. The triggers were darkness, cold, noisy crowds, loss of intimacy, memories of happiness lost. Abandonment, perhaps instilled by his childhood rejection, was the worst of his fears. Very early, he found a voice for this sense of loss in the Romantic poets, a mood he found again in Tennyson, another post-Romantic melancholic. Knowing his propensity for 'my distressing dark moods', Lear was also brave. He commanded himself: *'The morbids are not allowed!'* He tried to drag himself out of the pit. Work helped, walking helped, going out and seeing people helped, playing the piano helped – but sometimes not. He charted the course of his depressions baldly in his diary. All dissenting children were advised to keep a journal to record their self-improvement and lapses and often, as with Lear, these turned into a personal rather than religious record. Instead of struggles with the devil, Lear had his epilepsy, 'the Demon'; instead of meditations on death, he had death-like despair, 'the morbids'. He recorded moods, health, toothache, itchy skin, constipation; work and travel; people met, letters received, gossip heard; walks taken, books read, meals eaten.

What did he not record? Dreams, lusts, his feelings about words, his creative process – all these lie deep beneath the diary-words. But when his mind was 'off-duty', when he was writing nonsense to entertain or let off steam, fears and desires sometimes streamed up through the cracks into the light: 'Nonsense is the breath of my nostrils,' he wrote. In his limericks and songs, Lear wrote about his moods obliquely. More unusually, he drew them. He drew his longing to fly high, and those moments of ecstasy when one feels one can catch the moon.

There was an Old Person of Tring,
Who embellished his nose with a ring;
He gazed at the moon, every evening in June,
That ecstatic Old Person of Tring.

He drew, too, the fear of sinking, of drowning, of being like a jelly-fish, joining the fishes, a shapeless creature in the depth.

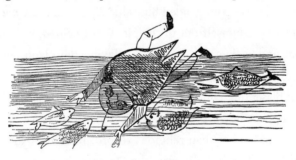

There was an Old Person of Ems,
Who casually fell in the Thames;
And when he was found, they said he was drowned,
That unlucky Old Person of Ems.

('Casually' is a key word for Lear, with its hidden root of falling, *cadere*, its sense of absent-mindedness and its hint of a nonsense opposite, 'causally'.) Many drawings evoke common words for mental and emotional collapse, words that actually make good therapeutic sense, describing what people feel is happening to them: 'under water', 'breakdown', 'going to pieces', being 'in bits'; and words for the fight to recover, 'pull myself together', 'make something of myself'. Lear drew the fragmented self and its attempted, often unsuccessful, reconstruction in Humpty Dumpty, in the Old Man of Nepaul, in the story of the Polly and the Puseybite. He also drew the depressive's urge to hide away, or to curl up. In *More Nonsense* many people hide their true selves, as their creator did, choosing not to face the world:

There was an Old Man of Hong Kong,
Who never did anything wrong;
He lay on his back, with his head in a sack,
That innocuous Old Man of Hong Kong.

In one drawing, in a letter to Evelyn Baring, written in a week of dreadful weather, Lear's own monogram became a person, coiled up in himself. 'Generally speaking', he wrote, 'I have been wrapped up like this all the week in a wholly abject and incapable state.'

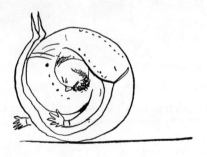

At the end of the 1860s, exhausted by the Corsican book, humiliated by affairs with Gussie, embarrassed by his confused, divided self, Lear felt more of an idiot than an inspired fool. He winced and pulled himself up, building his new house, writing his poems and reminding himself that he was known as an artist, a traveller and a writer, and that he was also loved for his nonsense. He enjoyed telling the story of a railway journey when he shared a carriage with two women who were reading the 1861 *Book of Nonsense* to children and he overheard a 'globular' gentleman explain that 'thousands of families were grateful to the author', who was really Edward, Lord Derby, as the author's name was an anagram of 'Edward Earl'. Outraged, Lear burst out that *he* was 'the painter & Author', only to be told that '"*There is no such person as Edward Lear*" "But" – says I "there is – & I am the man – & I wrote the book".' When they laughed, he showed the name in his hat, on his card and his handkerchief and left the amazed travellers 'to gnash their teeth in trouble & tumult':

When he drew the scene he took pains to show himself as 'real', and the doubter as the cartoon man. But even so he could only identify this fragile self, the 'no such person', by bits and pieces: hat, handkerchief, visiting card.

Lear's new limericks were full of familiar mishaps and violence – a mother beating daughters, an uncle fanning the head off his smiling niece – but in this book 'they' retreated somewhat from the assaults and frantic remonstrances of 1861. They bring the odd Persons hats to sit on, they sing ballads to soothe them, they are 'dazzled' by the Young Person of Ayr and 'entranced' when the Old Man of Skye does his waltz with the fly. When baffled, they ask meekly for explanations, only to be met by a matching incomprehension, or a stubborn silence:

There was an Old Person of Deal,
Who, in walking used only his heel;
When they said, 'Tell us why?' – he made no reply;
That mysterious Old Person of Deal.

Neither can fully understand each other, and perhaps they never will.

As 'they' fade, so the Persons grow bolder. The Old Person of Minety hurls apples and pears, and the Old Person of Stroud slaughters the crowd (as Lear often wished to do) when they push against her too thickly:

There was an Old Person of Stroud,
Who was horribly jammed in a crowd;
Some she slew with a kick, some she scrunched with a stick,
That impulsive Old Person of Stroud.

At last the Persons have power, of a kind. But the balance will always lie with 'they'. The fearsome old woman still hides under her hat. Yet while Lear's limericks can express defiance, onslaught, anger, despair, the urge to hide, even to die, they can also offer an exhilarating freedom, a rare joy. The nonsense man can fling open his window, spread his arms and let us in with 'Fil-jomble, fil-jumble'. He can play his fiddle, wreathed in smiles. He can let the birds nest in his beard. With one foot off the ground, his wide hat raised, he can become a male version of the Madonna della Misericordia who shelters the weak under her cloak.

There was an Old Man of Dee-side,
Whose hat was exceedingly wide;
But he said, 'Do not fail, if it happened to hail,
To come under my hat at Dee-side!'

Sometimes, too, hidden away, the men and women of the limericks can spin their dreams in peace. In the sunset, with her pen poised, this smartly dressed, smiling Young Person, like a female muse, can write her own version of the past.

There was a Young Person whose history
Was always considered a mystery;
She sate in a ditch, although no one knew which,
And composed a small treatise on history.

Between the publication of *Nonsense Songs* and the limericks of *More Nonsense*, Lear wrote two poems that hid the writer, not in a ditch, but in thickets of words and images. One was the mysterious 'The Scroobious Pip', whose illustrations, like a mixed-up medieval bestiary, suggest a shifting creature of stray man-beast parts – any metamorphosis seems possible.

The Pip, as in Lear's nesting fantasies, lives on the tallest tree, high above the world. Around him all the beasts and birds, fish and insects cry out in bemused frustration, trying to pin down this multiform creature:

'Tell us all about yourself we pray! –
For to know from yourself is our only wish –
Are you Beast or Insect, Bird or Fish?'

The Scroobious Pip looked softly round
And sang these words with a liquid sound –
'Plifatty flip – Pliffity flip –
My only name is the Scroobious Pip.'

The Pip hides himself, as Lear hid his inner being, his desires, his epilepsy, his loneliness. He looks on knowingly, replacing the demand

421

for identification only with his name, 'the Scroobious Pip', a name that recalls the seed at the heart of a fruit and also, perhaps, the power of drawing itself, the *'Scroo! Scroo!'* of the Albanian dervish. He is at home in any element. (In Lear's limericks many people are poised between earth and water, earth and air: indeed perhaps this suspension is the only way Lear finds to be 'at home'.) Surrounded by the call of birds and the splashing of fish, the Pip is an observer, a still centre. Lear does not dramatise the Pip himself, but the creatures he draws towards him, whirling as in a centrifuge, calling out in their quest to understand. The Pip, like the poet, is both part of, and apart from, the community of the world:

> And all the birds in the world came there,
> Flying in crowds all through the air.
> The Vulture and Eagle – the Cock and the Hen,
> The Ostrich, the Turkey, the Snipe and Wren,
> The Parrot chattered, the Blackbird sung,
> And the Owl looked wise but held his tongue,
> And when the Peacock began to scream
> The hullabaloo was quite extreme.
> And every bird he fluttered the tip
> Of his wing as he stared at the Scroobious Pip.

'The Scroobious Pip' was not published in Lear's lifetime. Nor was the second unfinished poem, 'Cold are the crabs'. This is a puzzle of 'utter nonsense', a poem about poetry itself, a palimpsest of remembered reading, a nonsense dance:

> Cold are the crabs that crawl on yonder hill,
> Colder the cucumbers that grow beneath
> And colder still the brazen chops that wreath
> The tedious gloom of philosophic pills!

Lear clearly delighted in the 'spot the poet' puzzle. The first line looks back to the second canto of Byron's *Childe Harold*, 'Cold as the crags upon his native coast', but one can also spy Pope, and Tennyson, and all through the poem, readers have found other voices – Wordsworth, Keats, Burns, Arnold, Shakespeare, Gray.

In this playful tribute with its solemn metre, even the cucumbers attain a dignity. Lear had fun with alliteration and carefully modulated assonance. His mismatched words generate energy, as they did in 'Ribands and pigs', as crabs, cucumbers and chops bump against archaic adjectives and the nonsense abstraction of tedious 'philosophic pills'. Then, suddenly, small living things disrupt the Romantic rhetoric.

> For when the tardy film of nectar fills
> The ample bowls of demons and of men,
> There lurks the feeble mouse, the homely hen,
> And there the Porcupine with all her quills.
> Yet much remains; – to weave a solemn strain
> That lingering sadly – slowly dies away,
> Daily departing with departing day.

That double 'departing' sounds like an ending, but in the final lines a warm-blooded, noisy, nonsense life rushes out again:

> Such such is life –
> Where early buffaloes in congress meet
> Than salt more salt, than sugar still more sweet,
> And pearly centipedes adjust their feet
> Where buffaloes bewail the loss of soap
> Where frantic walruses in clouds elope,
> And early Pipkins bid adieu to hope.

Such is life, salt and sweet. Even in the poem's half-made state the hidden poet, like the Scroobius Pip, is present in every line – like a child putting his hands across his eyes and pretending he isn't there. This was Lear's true way out of the morbids. In his drawings and limericks and songs he launched himself on stormy seas, sailing like the Jumblies to a realm beyond sense.

35: RESTLESS IN SAN REMO

In the year between *Nonsense Songs* and *More Nonsense*, Lear was busy with his house. His furniture, prints and books were shipped out from London duty free, thanks to Frank Lushington who was now 'the Judge', the London Police Magistrate, and wangled Lear a certificate of London residence. Another load arrived from Cannes by train and at the end of March 1871 Lear and Giorgio unpacked the crates and began arranging rooms. It was almost a year since he had bought the plot. The long, low house gleamed white against the slope. It had good rooms for friends to stay and, best of all, at last he had the perfect studio:

I never before had such a painting room – 32 feet by 20 – with a light I can work by at all hours, and a clear view south over the sea. Below it is a room of the same size, which I now use as a gallery, and am 'at home' once a week – Wednesday: though as Enoch Arden said in the troppicle Zone 'Still no sail, no sail'.

Lear told Holman Hunt about his new scheme for life: 'Neither too much *in*, nor altogether *out* of the world – my plan may ultimately succeed, if I can only work hard enough to send to every kind of exhibition in England, for that tack I am now (perforce) going to try.' He could settle down and be an artist again.

This proved harder than he hoped. Not only were sales slow, but he failed to get elected to the Old Water Colour Society, and his two large

Corsica pictures lingered unsold at Foord's, although he lowered the price to £50 each, without frames, instead of the £200 he thought they were worth. The summer before, to mark the move to the new house, he had offered to paint an oil for Lord Derby, his old patron's grandson, who had become the fifteenth earl on his father's death in 1869. The new earl, who had been one of the children that Lear wrote his first nonsense for in the nursery at Knowsley, sent a friendly letter declining a large painting – he had too many already – but asked for a smaller picture, or watercolours, for £100. After more correspondence he chose one of Corfu. Privately, the young earl noted that it was hard to refuse as Lear was always in want of money, 'and his request is quite as much an appeal for help as an offer to supply what he thinks may be wanted'. In Lear's view, however, this was a virtuous circle: the first painting in the house of his old age would have the same Knowsley patronage that had started his career. Luckily, when the Corfu picture arrived Derby noted, 'It pleases me much, and the cost (£100) does not seem expensive.' He became one of Lear's most loyal patrons in the coming years.

Villa Emily in the 1870s

Lear sent small oil paintings to be sold by Foord's, found other commissions to keep him going and, to his relief and delight, when he was really strapped for money, Sir Francis Goldsmid bought one of the two large Corsica paintings for £100. Lear's chief aim now was to return to his idea, first mooted almost twenty years ago, of illustrating Tennyson's poems. In the coming year he worked on five large oils, including paintings of Mount Athos and Mount Timohorit. Tennyson stayed in his mind, and among the many letters that made him feel surrounded by friends, the most precious were from Emily, 'singularly good & kind – that woman is 10,000 angels boiled down – an essence of goodness'.

What delighted him most was the utter quiet: only birdsong broke the silence, as he sat in his library, writing his letters. He paid calls on Lady Janet Kay-Shuttleworth next door and her daughter Janet Elizabeth ('Jenny' to friends, 'Puss' to her family), who was in her late twenties. Both were 'very kind and friendly'. Lear knew Janet Kay-Shuttleworth through his friendship with her stepfather, Frederick North: she was half-sister to Catherine Symonds and Marianne North ('Pop' to the family), and had known Charlotte Brontë and Elizabeth Gaskell, authors Lear greatly admired. When her marriage to the social reformer Sir James Kay-Shuttleworth collapsed in 1851, she had moved to San Remo with Jenny and her younger sons Lionel and Stewart and their Polish governess Miss Poplawska (whom Charlotte Brontë reckoned the most interesting person in the house, but the family thought dangerous). Lear liked her son Ughtred, who was now MP for Hastings, as his grandfather had been, and who visited with his new wife Blanche and took Lear's drawings back to England for him. He was also extremely fond of Marianne North, now travelling worldwide as a botanical painter, sending her a comic picture letter when he found he had refused to pay for a letter insufficiently stamped.

Yet despite Lady Kay-Shuttleworth's connections Lear disliked her aura of 'trouble' and illness, as well as her non-stop talking. He never felt at home in her Villa Ponente. By contrast, he became ever closer to

No. 3

Mr Lear stamps and dances for joy on securing Miss North's letter

Mr Lear stamps and dances for joy on securing Miss North's letter

Edward Lear. June 7. 1891

Walter Congreve and his sons. Congreve had taught at Rugby under Archibald Campbell Tait (who had since become Archbishop of Canterbury), and had been appointed Second Master at Marlborough when his first wife and their eldest son fell ill. Told to find a warmer climate, he took them to the Riviera, but they both died soon after they arrived. Walter stayed on, taking pupils, acting as a wine merchant, and building and renting villas. He remarried and had two more sons, but when Lear met the family the second Mrs Congreve was gravely ill. She died of cancer in October 1870, leaving Walter with two small boys, Hubert, who was twelve, and Arnold ('Arny'), aged eight. Walter was helped by their nanny, Ellen Walters, and only a couple of months after his wife's death, Lear noted waspishly that 'by the eye of proffisy I fancy I can see who may be a 3d Mrs C. – namely E – (but I may be wrong)'. Lady Kay-Shuttleworth worked this out too, coolly changing the subject when Congreve's name came up.

Hubert remembered running down the path to meet his father and finding him accompanied by 'a tall, heavily built gentleman, with a large curly beard and wearing well-made but unusually loose-fitting clothes, and what at the time struck me most of all, very large round spectacles'. He was disconcerted when Lear introduced himself with his long nonsense name, but Lear put his hand on his shoulder, saying, '"I am also

Derry Down Derry, who loves to make little folks merry, and I hope we shall be good friends." This was said with a wonderful charm of manner and voice, accompanied by such a genial, yet quizzical smile, as to put me at my ease at once.' He became an adopted uncle, giving the boys drawing lessons and reading his poems and stories: 'gt laughter thereat'. At lunchtime, he dropped in for a glass of Marsala, talking about travels, birds, botany and music, his conversation scattered with puns, and in the evenings he strolled over and stayed late, singing his Tennyson settings and comic songs, including their favourite, Thomas Hudson's 'The Cork Leg'. One morning in June he sketched the boys by the well in their garden, with Arny holding his much-loved cat.

Congreve's house was often full of visitors, including his brother Richard, a passionate republican and devotee of Auguste Comte: he was 'the (Unorthodox) Apostle of Positivism' as opposed to Congreve's other brother, 'the (Orthodox) Vicar of Tooting'. That winter a bevy of clerics were there, including Archbishop Tait. Lear went to church and groaned, and at Christmas he lent the archbishop *Nonsense Songs* 'as a pious and instructive work fitted for the season'.

The spring passed happily. He arranged for four pictures to be exhibited in the Academy show. Then he sat back to enjoy his Riviera garden, planting shrubs and flowers and seeds that friends sent from England and Sarah from New Zealand.

Lear's gardening was mostly pottering and planning – tying of creepers and picking up caterpillars, as he put it. He hired workmen to prune his thirty olive trees and a gardener to do the heavy work of digging, grubbing up huge aloes, making a pergola and planting tomatoes, peas, beans and vines. Making grander plans, he thought of buying another patch of land between his house and the Hôtel de Londres, but the owner decided not to sell. He enquired, too, about the empty plot below, which Thomas Hanbury had rented to the Kay-Shuttleworths, but Hanbury was in China and nothing could be done, and he wasn't worried, 'for even if Mr Hanbury builds, I look over the highest possible house'.

Giorgio, who had been with Lear now for sixteen years, did the indoor work and walked the half-mile to town to do the shopping. When he went to Corfu in the summer of 1871 Lear could not face rattling around on his own so he planned an Italian trip. For six weeks he toured old haunts, taking the train past the small Corniche towns he had walked through with Giorgio, with their towers and bridges, mulberries, olive groves and figs and golden sea, and then going south, crossing the Campagna to the capital: 'Rome 1837 – 1859 – & now 1871! But it is walking on graves.' He met old friends like Penry Williams, sweating in the heat as he toured his old neighbourhoods, then he set out for Frascati to see Margaret Knight, Duchess of Sermoneta – her invalid sister, Isabella, had died the previous year, another broken thread. From the cool Alban hills he crossed to Ancona and Rimini and the forests where Byron walked, before working his way north through Padua to Belluno and the Italian Tyrol, back to Milan and Turin and the beautiful, if fly-plagued, Certosa.

Frank Lushington came to stay in October, and after he left and the cold winds came, Lear took solace in nonsense, writing of the Scroobious Pip, the Discobbolos pair and the Yonghy-Bonghy-Bò. The latter, set to music, was a great success locally and he thought of asking Bush if he might bring out single ballads, 'or two or three at a time': 'It is queer (and you would say so if you saw me) that I am the man as is making some three or four thousand people laugh in England all at one time, – to say the least, for I hear 2,000 of the new Nonsense are sold.'

San Remo suited him, 'for we are all humdrum middle class coves and covesses, and no swells', and he was constantly dropping in on people, having guests for lunch and going out to dinner. 'Life is pretty easy as things go,' he wrote. 'My elth is tolerable', he told Fortescue and Lady W. on Christmas Day 1871, 'but I am 60 next May, & feel I am growing old. Going up & down stairs worries me, & I think of marrying some domestic henbird & then of building a nest in one of my many olive trees, whence I should only descend at remote intervals during the rest of my life.'

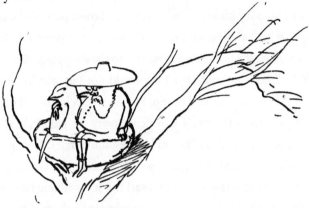

Instead of a wife, he acquired a cat. The first wandered off and when the second, Potiphar, 'Potta', disappeared in Corfu, where Giorgio took him the following summer, Miss Poplawska brought over his twin brother, with his cut-off tail. They called him Foss, short for 'Adelphos', Greek for 'brother'.

Lear's calm was shaken in the autumn of 1871 when his old friend Thomas Baring (Lord Northbrook since his father's death in 1866) reluctantly accepted the post of Viceroy of India and asked him if he would like to come out, at his expense, to live there for six months. India had long been a dream. Could he 'give up once more the chance of seeing Agra, Delhi and Darjiling? – I cannot decide at once'. He met Northbrook in Cannes the following March 1872, and enjoyed a jovial reunion with Evelyn Baring: 'Vastly good dinner, "too" much champagne perhaps.

Long sitting & smoking & stories. Later no end of stories & recollections of Corfu days.'

'This offer has greatly unsettled me,' he admitted to Fortescue a couple of months later. He felt there was something in him inherently antagonistic to travelling as part of a viceregal suite:

and indeed, though I am not in the strongest sense of the word Bohemian, I have just so much of that nature in me as it is perhaps impossible the artistic and poetic beast can be born without. Always accustomed as a boy to go my own ways uncontrolled, I cannot help fearing that I should run rusty and sulky by reason of retinues and routines.

Sometimes he thought he might just go with Giorgio, and ask Northbrook to fund him by commissioning drawings. At other times he thought he would not go at all: he had a new house, and to take flight so soon 'seems a kind of giddiness'.

In the end he decided to go and hurried back to London in the summer to collect orders for drawings. The trip also let him see his friends. The Lushingtons now had another daughter, Clare, another Lear godchild. Frank was tender towards his children, telling Emily Tennyson this autumn, 'Dear little Clare goes on pulling her way through the difficulties of teeth with a good deal of vigour . . . she is sharp enough for anything – she took to Lear as her godfather very kindly.' When he wrote this in November, their new son had been born on the first of the month: they thought of calling him 'Allsaints Lushington', Frank joked. In the end he was a solemn George Henry Fitzjames – soon known to all as a second Harry.

Lear left the Lushingtons and England tired but pleased. His many visits had paid off, winning £1000 of commissions. Despite a fall that left him feeling giddy and badly affected his right eye, making him worried about the pressures of the journey to India, in October he closed the house and sailed off, picking up Giorgio in Corfu. The sea was stormy, the ship was packed, the deck swam with vomit and Lear's temper was vile. In Egypt, whose scenery and people had always delighted him, he fell into uncharacteristic racist rants against 'brutal

Arabs', 'the devil nonsense of the loathsome aborigines' and 'Egyptian pests'. At Suez he drank in tales of the country's viciousness, lapping up the Prussian ambassador's story that the most popular entertainment at the opening of the canal had been 'a giant negro buggering seven boys in a row for two hours'. Such outbursts were very startling after so much self-concealment and reticence: Lear was heading for disaster. The boats at Suez were full and when a French boat for India arrived a week later and he booked a cabin, there was a muddle over Customs. A Customs officer demanded that his baggage be transferred from one barge to another to be checked; anxious about time, Lear began to argue; the officer then refused to look at his bags altogether and rode away. 'Nearly mad with worry, noise, delay & uncertainty', Lear impetuously ordered his luggage to be taken off the barge and sent to the station. By evening he and a shocked, vexed Giorgio were on the Alexandria train. Lear scrawled in large letters, '*The Indian bubble is burst.*'

Next day despair overwhelmed him. The breakdown of the trip was a calamity, he wrote, 'as at Jerusalem in 1867, & Larissa in 1849 – the abrupt change is afflicting, as savouring of insanity'. Was he going mad? And what was he to do about the £1000 commissions? He must plan the journey all over again.

In San Remo Lady Kay-Shuttleworth had died, and although Walter Congreve was still a good neighbour, Lear found him disconcertingly worldly. Scandal had surrounded him for the past two years. In the winter of 1871 Lear had heard rumours that Walter's servant Ellen, now in Nice, was pregnant and that he planned to marry her. He rushed to find details from the Congreves' visitor, Revd John Richard Green, author of *A Short History of the English People*, who implied that Ellen – 'a lascivious bitch' – would sleep with anyone, and was strongly against the marriage. (The following winter Walter told him that she had been fighting off brutal advances from the respectable Revd Green himself.) But it was clear that their relationship was serious, and Lear was concerned for the boys.

Fussing over the Congreves, dipping in and out of local gossip, in early 1873 Lear painted a set of Tyrants, read Horace Walpole's letters and Tom Moore's diaries, planned his garden and worked on his Tennyson paintings. He was bored: in April he was ill in bed, in May he had a swollen face. He felt crippled, emasculated, and the India plan seemed ridiculous and impossible. But in the heat of July he wrote wryly to Lady W. that he thought the sedentary life would kill him, after a lifetime of travel. He must pick himself up and go.

In these low days Lear turned to nonsense, writing two versions of 'The Pobble who has no Toes', and no nose either, judging from his bandaged face. Perhaps spurred by a news item reporting that the son of the Akhoond of Swat, near to the Hindu Kush, had quarrelled with his father, he also wrote an exuberant, foot-stamping, many-versed, poem, 'The Akond of Swat':

Who or why, or which, or what, is the Akond of SWAT? . . .

Do his people like him extremely well?
Or do they, whenever they can, rebel   or PLOT
                                                                    At the Akond of Swat?

If he catches them then, either old or young,
Does he have them chopped in pieces or hung or SHOT,
                                                                    The Akond of Swat?

India was on his mind. He began to get ready to go and spent the high summer sorting through three chests full of letters. He reckoned that he had over four hundred correspondents: it felt as if everyone since the invention of letters must have written to him, 'with a few exceptions perhaps, such as the prophet Ezekiel, Mary Queen of Scots & the Venerable Bede'. He was moved. 'It is quite impossible to record in detail what wonderful evidences of kindness to myself these multitudinous letters are!' he said. 'I destroy a great part, – but a great number remain – what I cannot bring myself to extinguish.'

Letters, however, could also bring pain. In September he learned that Gussie had finally married. Her husband, Adamson Parker, was old and an invalid – someone to take care of. Hit again by the vision of a lonely life, he wrote, 'I must leave this place.' Fancifully he told Fortescue that he had still always planned to propose to Gussie and his decision to go to India would have depended on her answer. 'So altogether I considered that to go to India for 18 months would really be my best course – as a change of scene may do me good, & besides, – living as I do from hand to mouth by my art, I dare not throw away the many commissions for paintings & drawings I already have for Indian subjects.'

Soon after he read Gussie's letter, Lear left for Genoa, full of nerves. In his diary, he wrote:

I have thought some time today that I would walk once more to San Remo from Genoa, & see Foss the forsaken, & Walter Congreve & Hubert & Arny once more, but I'm sure that would not be wise. // N.B. it would have been better not to have drunk those 2 bottles, but having drank them, let us forget that fact, & act sotto-sopra accordingly.

He spent the next three weeks in a hotel, and finally, on 24 October, he boarded the steamer *India*. There were last-minute anxieties about a day's delay in sailing, when he had all his luggage taken off the boat and nearly turned home. Next day, finally, he was off, meeting Giorgio in Naples, then sitting on deck in his warm cloak with 'good old George', heading across the great green sea to Bombay.

36: INDIA

When Lear reached Mumbai on 22 November 1873, he was excited to the point of shock: 'Extreme beauty of Bombay harbour! . . . Much surprised by the beauty of Bombay! . . . Violent and amazing delight at the varieties of life and dress here.' The short journey to the Esplanade Hotel, he said, drove him nearly mad from sheer wonder at the foliage, palms, flowers, beasts, colours and costumes and 'myriadism of impossible picturesqueness'. Even the woman who emptied the slops in the hotel was a wonder, her arms covered in bangles.

He would explore this new world for the next year and a half, criss-crossing the subcontinent by every kind of transport. He rode in trains and bullock carts, horse-drawn gharries, ehkkas – small pony-carts – and dhoolies, covered litters, and even a jampan, a sedan chair less bumpy than a dhooly, 'only when the men change the pole from one shoulder to t'other, it seems as if they were about to pitch you over into space'. He went from west to east, north to south, from the Himalayas to Sri Lanka, his long-dreamed-of Ceylon. He moved from torrid heat and monsoon rain to mountain ice and balmy shore. The travelling often tired him: he was cross and crusty, troubled by his bad eye, plagued by thoughts of going home. Equally often he was moved, amazed, astonished to be there, thrilled by passing scenes from a railway carriage which he noted hour by hour. 'What groves of Bananas! What groups of figures – (Crows on all cows bax) . . . Lovely river views! Every minute makes life more wonderful. Astounding effects of beauty on each side Railway, neck-twisting & eye-cracking.'

Using the old Anglicised names that Lear knew, the first great loop took him north-east up to Cawnpore and Lucknow, where he met Northbrook and Evelyn Baring, who had come out as Northbrook's secretary and who managed all Lear's arrangements. Giorgio had always wanted to see an elephant, and here, looking down from a hill at Lucknow, Lear drew a herd bathing in the river.

Lucknow, 1 p.m., 8 December 1873

Next he travelled down the Ganges to Benares and Calcutta. In the New Year of 1874 he went up to Darjeeling in the foothills of the Himalayas, then turned back south to Agra and Delhi, which he thought dirty and ruined by British barracks, but he still made 'Delhineations of the Dehlicate architecture as is all impressed on my mind as inDhelibly as the Dehliterious quality of the water of that city'. From here Lear trekked north again to Simla, the British summer capital in the hills, and then further north still, to Narkunda on the border with Tibet, an interminable four-day train journey that produced a string of limericks with dreadful rhymes:

> There lived a small puppy at Nārkunda,
> Who sought for the best tree to bārk under,
> Which he found, and said 'Now, I can call out Bow Wow
> Underneath the best Cedar in Nārkunda.'

In late April he worked his way nine hundred miles south again to Poona where the monsoons trapped him for two months. At last, when the rains stopped, he and Giorgio journeyed south, to Hyderabad and Madras, then across to the west, to Calicut in Kerala. The final stop, in late 1874, would be Ceylon.

Northbrook and Evelyn Baring could not have been kinder, but they were furiously busy. Northbrook was a liberal viceroy, determined to reduce tension by abolishing the new income tax and moderating the land tax on peasants, and working desperately to stave off famine in Bengal. And Lear had been right to think viceregal retinues were not for him. In the great camp at Lucknow he watched a parade in the ruined Residency, which had been destroyed in the Mutiny of 1857: 'Vast numbers of people. Immensely fine spectacle. Astonishing elephants.' But his luggage had vanished, causing 'a miserable hullabaloo', and he had to borrow clothes for the smart dinners. At Calcutta he found the strict protocol and packed social calendar of the governor's house hard to bear: 'No rest in Hustlefussabad.' At Hyderabad, although after a ball 'the 20 men who took up the carpets, & the 20 more who cleared the room were a sight to see', it was not for him. 'Boo! Bah! Ye Indian houses & humbugs!' Yet he fitted in well with the British society in Simla, where he spent nearly a month, in the Bombay hills and in Ootacamund, 'Ooty', the southern mountain retreat from Madras. The communities of the hill stations, with their villas, churches, croquet lawns and tea parties, reminded him of English spas, bizarrely set in Indian life: 'What strange scenes of ladies in Jampans! And liveried Coolies!

What groups of beautiful little English children, with Ayahs and Behr-ers!!!!! What women with nose-buttons, and rings, and spoons, and sky-blue breeches! Verily Simla is a queer place.'

Meeting the British residents, Lear came haloed in Northbrook's patronage and they found him a (mostly) cheery addition to their lives, singing his Tennyson songs, drawing alphabets and funny pictures for the children: he was delighted to find that 'The Owl and the Pussy-cat' was known in all the English schools in India. The hill stations were breathing spaces, in all senses. But on their travels Lear tried to avoid staying in private houses where he had to fit in and be polite to his hosts, or in hotels, which were generally squalid. He preferred the Dak houses, government-run bungalows on the main roads. When they arrived their luggage was simply put in any empty room: 'old George in 10 minutes used to get both of ours in neat order' and within half an hour the khamsamah, the cook, brought dinner and beer, or claret and sherry – Lear drank a lot on this trip.

In the bungalows he could get up as early as he liked and leave when he chose. As a British traveller he was in a bubble, floating above the people of the country, whom he never really came to know. Northbrook himself had identified this distance as a problem as soon as he arrived, noting how little his high-up civil servants knew the people, and ad-vising one new residency governor to get the views of district officers and those of Indians 'wherever we can get them to speak freely'. Lear went further than most, exploring the bazaars and temples of Poona and the villages around, drawing street scenes in Hyderabad, sketching men and women on mountain roads and beneath coastal palms and banyan trees. But he never really crossed the 'Borderline', as the young Kipling would put it ten years from now, 'away from Levees and Government House Lists past Trades Balls – far beyond everything and everybody you ever knew in your respectable life'.

This separation was intensified by his insistence on travelling with Giorgio rather than taking Indian servants: soon after he arrived he had been warned this was contrary to custom, and indeed, for the first time, there were mutterings about their relationship. But Giorgio knew him, understood his sudden fits and his need to sleep, could find his spectacles or false teeth, carry his sketches, hold down his sketch pad in a howling wind. They were an odd pair, this large, shambling, short-sighted, heavy-bearded man in his early sixties, and the craggy Suliot, now fifty-five and still proudly handsome, looking more like a couple than master and servant, quarrelling and making up, struggling on together, through varying landscapes, changing peoples, different languages. Lear found to his surprise that many people spoke English, the official language for the last forty years, with a 'curious fluent exactness'. This was useful, but he was sometimes disconcerted by the imposition of British education, so remote from their daily lives and own rich history. Towards the end of his stay he visited a school in Malabar: 'Heard upper class read Henry V, and they were examined in Ivanhoe. Is there, or is there not time thrown away in this sort of learning?' He tried to learn some Hindi, and some Tamil in the south – really just to ask the way – scattering his journals and letters with Indian terms and rolling the words and names round in his mind.

Nonsense was a refuge from boredom. After almost a fortnight of Poona downpours, he noted, 'Pouring rain – buckets – all day. Penned out all day . . . Wrote out the Cummerbund and sent it to the Bombay Times. The Monsoon has come upon us quoth the Lady of Shalott.'

> She sate upon her Dobie,
> To watch the Evening Star,
> And all the punkahs as they passed,
> Cried, 'My how fair you are!'
> Around her bower, with quivering leaves,
> The tall Kamsamahs grew,
> And Kitmutgars in wild festoons
> Hung down from Tchokis blue.

His lady swallowed by the angry Cummerbund has something of Carroll's 'Jabberwocky' of two years before, but Lear's ballad took its energy from the joyful translocation of words, giving them vibrant, sinister life. The Dobie, a washerman, becomes a seat, the punkah fans a chorus; the cook is a tree, the kitmutgars who wait at table are winding creepers, festooning the Tchoki chairs. The feast of words went on, with golden-finned Chuprassies (smarter servants), green Ayahs perching like parrots, a moaning Mussak (a water-bag), silvery Goreewallahs (grooms) and the angry Jampan howling, deep in his hateful lair. Lear was delighted when the *Bombay Times* printed it in their 'Whims of the Week'. Copying it out later he added a nonsense glossary, attributing the poem to a lady long resident in India, famed for her knowledge of its customs:

Cummerbund, a sort of Tiger or Leopard of immense size & ferocious nature
Dobie – a silk cushion
Punkah – a wandering minstrel
Khamsameh, a tree of the poplar kind
Kitmutgar – a sort of convolvulus.

Nonsense passed the time, but Lear was travelling as an artist, and everywhere he went, he carried his small sketch pad, making fast drawings, 'scraps' as he called them, and penning them out or leaving them until he came home to develop into larger watercolours. Giorgio kept the sketches in portfolios and boxes, until the rainy days in Poona, where they had tin cases made to preserve them better. As he travelled, Lear thought of earlier British artists in India, like Thomas Daniell and his nephew William, who had spent ten years here at the start of the century, publishing coloured aquatints in their six-part *Oriental Scenery*. For Lear, they had failed to capture India's brilliance. He remembered Daniell's view of the ghats in Benares, the steps where pilgrims gathered to bathe in the holy Ganges, as pallid, gray, sad, solemn. Yet when he saw them, he was dazzled by the rainbow colours of the crowds and found the river 'one of the most abundantly bruyant, and startlingly radiant places of infinite bustle and movement!!' Out in a boat, he put his pencil aside and took out his brush, making clear, pink-tinged, atmospheric sketches, outlining the buildings and the crowds later in sepia ink.

Benares, 2.30 p.m., 14 December 1873. Notes: 'A. Bathing rafts B. boats. C hazy blue. D sand. | E. Women above. F. Sheds on broken steps. G. green. H. cindery . . . light off sky. I. millions of pigeons J. gray L. gold. R. red'

India was almost beyond his grasp. He reached constantly for comparisons with places he had known: Cairo and Naples, Italian villas, Cumbrian mountains, Sussex parks, Nile cataracts, landscapes of Greece and Crete. All were inadequate for somewhere so magically, infuriatingly different. The watery area of Tollygunge in Calcutta, with boats moored along the banks, seen at dawn, was more like an English view, he thought, than a Nile scene, though his description gives the lie to this idea:

Remarked the beauty of white sheets, both in light and shadow – also black bodies and white waist cloths – also extreme featheriness of coconut palms – depths of brown gray shade – brilliancy of bananas and general misty grayness . . . General tone of the mosque and tank view, deep beautiful dark gray, relieved with vividly bright bits of light . . . Walk on slowly, drawing at times. Endlessly beautiful pictures of village life and Eastern vegetation.

Eastern vegetation was his great delight. In Calcutta he escaped the viceregal fuss to sketch in the Botanic Gardens, and all through India he

Tollygunge, Calcutta, painted between 24 December 1873 and 5 January 1874

made inspired studies of trees, bamboo and banyan, peepul and mango. By contrast, he found the architecture hard to draw and often bought photographs for reference. The styles of building were disconcertingly unfamiliar, like the temples of Benares, 'highly pagan and queer'. He coped better when the landscape framed the buildings, as it did the temples of Hurdwar, their pearly white and grey domes sharp against the green hills behind, or when the foreground detail was rich, as it was at Muttra, where palaces and mosques seemed to float above river banks full of bathers, fishermen, buffalo, crocodiles and turtles. (On one 'scrap' he drew an inset turtle, inscribed 'Turtles = Yonghy Bonghy Bò'.) The greatest challenge of all was the monument he had most wanted to see, the Taj Mahal. He thought it the most beautiful of all earthly buildings; 'Henceforth let the inhabitants of the world be divided into 2 classes, – them as has seen the Taj, – and them as hasn't.' Yet how to draw it? He made it a jewel in a garden, an Indian Villa d'Este, gleaming white at the end of an avenue of dark cypresses, 'with innumerable parrots flitting across, – like live Emeralds', above a dazzle of scarlet poinsettias and purple bougainvillea.

Trying to orient himself, Lear searched for comparisons in art, as well as in familiar scenery. Looking at plains and winding rivers, he

442

wrote of Poussinesque landscapes and Claude-like scenes, at once alike and utterly different. On the Malabar coast:

the infinite lines of low hills and high mountains are all quite a la Claude Lorraine distance, yet the texture of Cocoa-nuttery is something quite unlike. The rivers in this view are wonderfully beautiful while the sun is low; and all the colour, – changes of gray and misty lilac, and palest opal blue (not opal though, for that is clear whereas here all is misty and damp) makes a world of divinely exquisite beauty . . . such scenery may be compared to eating rich Plum Pudding continually.

In the Himalayas, he set aside the classical picturesque of Poussin and Claude for other models, painters of the sublime, such as Turner, his idol since childhood. In 1872 he had been reading Thornbury's life of Turner, 'A stupidly written book: – like Shakespeare, his works proclaim the man: & it don't really matter what Shakespeare or Turner were (though it would be pleasant to know), seeing they have left proofs of almightiness.' The other hero was the great American artist Frederic Church, whose paintings Lear had seen on show in London. He judged Church second only to Turner, he wrote later, '& one of his works "The Heart of the Andes" hangs always before me'.

He found touches of the sublime early in his trip, at the Marble Rocks of Nerbudda, where the river rushes through the limestone ravine, its glistening rocks reflected in the water. Greater visions were to come. He had commissions to paint Kanchenjunga, one of the highest mountains of the Himalayas, and when he arrived in Darjeeling in mid-January, in the depths of winter, he was overwhelmed: '*Wonderful wonderful* view of Kinchinjunga!!!!!' Next day he wrote nervously that it did not seem a very 'sympathetic' mountain: 'it is so far off, so very God-like & stupendous.' At sunrise it was a glory; in the afternoons 'a wonderful hash of Turneresque colour & mist & space'; by evening it was clear and rose-coloured again. Rising before dawn Lear drew half-frozen, kept going by Giorgio piling on cloaks and blankets. In his later paintings, he showed the mountain rising above a V-shaped gap in dense forest.

In the foreground he painted a Buddhist shrine, as if the road might lead to a sacred place beyond true comprehension.

Kinchenjunga from Darjeeling (1877)

Such magnificence was true Romantic sublimity, whose chief effect, in Burke's terms, was astonishment, when the mind was suspended, almost with terror.

Rather to his surprise, this mood returned when he saw the ruins of the seventh-century Hindu rock-temples, shrines and sculptures of Mahabalipuram on the Coromandel coast. These spoke to the heart of the poetical-topographer: 'The poetical character of this remarkably beautiful and interesting place is of a higher order than that of any I have yet seen in India, being so unique and ancient, and yet so unmixed by any sort of contamination of Modernism, still less of Anglo Saxonism.' The site opened his eyes to the drama of other southern glories, the great, sweeping rock of Trichinopoly, and the massive, melancholy, thousand-year-old temple of Tajore. He had found his own, unexpected sublime.

In November 1874, Lear and Giorgio sailed to Ceylon to get away from the Malabar heat. They were there for a month, but their stay was troubled and weary. They walked on the beaches and Lear sketched the bread-fruit trees and the boats, but it rained, and he was tired. At the start of December Giorgio became ill with dysentery. Lear nursed him, panicked when he saw a basin full of blood from a nosebleed, and watched him as he slept, 'good and patient always . . . I go to bed, but with no light heart. Pray God he may recover!' When he seemed better, Lear took him back to the mainland. But even the Malabar coast had lost its charm, so they took a boat from Cochin to Bombay, without stopping as Lear had planned at Mangalore or Goa. As consolation Lear read, often books he had read before. On New Year's Eve, he was drawing the Coorg mountains, complaining of a sore back and a cold, but enraptured by the country he was leaving:

Still getting out cargo at Cannamore; big barrels; still the clamour of savagery, the poppling of the sea, the grinding of the machinery, and the rising and falling of the cargo boats. A strange, foolish calmness of beautiful colour and sunshine over all. Thousands of seagulls sit on the waves, scores of bright red-brown falcons with white heads soar aloft . . . At 4.45 we go off and the land of Coorg fades into pale lilac distance. My back is so bad I am hardly able to go downstairs . . . Nevertheless, I must needs be thankful, and greatly so, that 1874 ends as it does, and that I have had such a year of active, constant pleasure, with so little suffering.

On New Year's Day, off Mangalore, he 'finished Jane Eyre'. On deck he sketched, writing on one sunset watercolour scrap, 'gold light off', 'green', 'orange', 'absolute Turner'. In Bombay, among the stack of post, a letter brought the terrible news that Giorgio's wife had died in Corfu. It was best, Lear thought, to go home straight away. On 12 January 1875, after fourteen months away, they sailed for Europe.

37: FAMILIES

There was an old man whose Giardino
Was always so cheerful and green O –
Every hour he could spare, – He sate in a chair
In the midst of his summer Giardino.

Arriving home at the Villa Emily in early 1875, Lear found that he had been burgled. The thieves had taken very little but had broken into trunks and made a horrible mess. But to his delight, 'The garden is beautiful with Oranges!!' For the first time he could give his own mandarin oranges to friends. When the sun warmed he filled pots and sowed seeds brought back from India, including a glorious purple morning glory from Bangalore. He put up arches and trellises, exchanged plants with neighbours – wallflowers for begonias – and bought new ones from nearby nurseries. In the spring he was up at five watering his seeds, and in June he could walk on the terrace in 'a wonder of loveliness' – geraniums and clematis, roses and passion flowers, lilies and carnations. His moods swooped up and down like changeable weather: cold, wretched, lonely; warm, content, busy. One day he walked over to Bordighera feeling that 'nothing could be lovelier than the sea and sky with Corsica clear as light, on the horizon'. As he penned out and coloured his Indian sketches and reread his diary the Durbah in Delhi and the ghats of Benares began to feel like a queer dream.

446

By now he was a fixture in San Remo. When Augusta Tozer, wife of Henry Tozer, whose *Researches in the Highlands of Turkey* Lear greatly admired and who became a good friend, passed through San Remo with her brother, the dashing diplomat Ernest Satow, 'Mr. Ed. Lear, artist' was one of the first people they met. Satow went out with this 'odd stout big man of 64' to help him choose a piano, walked with him, dined with him and pored over his sketches of Kanchenjunga and the red pagodas of Benares. Lear was out and about all the time, greeting friends who stayed in the hotels, calling on Sir Matthew and Lady Digby Wyatt, who had a villa up the hill, old friends whom he had known since his time in Rome and often visited in London. Digby Wyatt was an architect, secretary to the Great Exhibition in 1851, responsible for the construction of Paxton's Crystal Palace, and later the first Slade Professor of Fine Arts at Cambridge, and although he was now ill they had plenty to talk about, serious and frivolous. Lear often fell into nonsense with Mary Wyatt, his 'Dear Mrs Digby', and now, combining friendship with gardening, he sent her a long word-play letter.

Dear Lady Wyatt

If a*m int*errupting you please excuse me
as I *mint* to have asked you a question the other day
but forgot to *mint*-ion it. Can you tell me how to make
preserved or dry *mint*? I have got a
mint of
mint in my garden, but although I
a*m int*-erested in getting some of it dried for
pea soup, I a*m in t*errible ignorance of how to dry it,
and a*m in t*orture till I know how.

And so it ran on, the column widening to '*Mint*on pottery', the river '*Mint*cio' and Disraeli the new 'Prime *mint*-ster'.

From outside Lear appeared affable, interested, talented, funny, but in his diary, late at night or waking ill in the mornings, the loneliness poured out. 'Weary days', he wrote, 'wearisome work'. These were favourite terms of lament, recalling Tennyson's Mariana waiting for the lover who never comes: 'She said "I am aweary, aweary,/ I would that I were dead."' But Lear did not wish to be dead. He was too busy with his work and his garden, too alive to the sea and sky and olive-covered hills, too curious about the families close to him.

He thought too of his own family. To his great sadness Sarah had died in New Zealand while he was in India, but one joy of the spring of 1875 was a visit from her son Charles and his wife Sophy, who told him how active she had been to the last, working in her garden and playing the piano to her great-grandchildren. 'What a life!' Lear wrote. 'As her son says, she was indeed one of a million. This nephew & niece are a very loveable lot, & full of intellectual enjoyment.' Their visit made him think he must see Ellen, now frail and almost blind from cataracts, 'the only one remaining of all my thirteen sisters', sinking into darkness. He wanted to go back anyway, to show his Indian drawings. In early June 1875 he left for England.

In London Lear was touchingly, warmly, greeted. People poured into his rooms in Duchess Street and by the end of the month he had sold over £300 of drawings. Lady Ashburton asked for a large-scale painting of *Kinchenjunga*, offering £700, the most he had ever received for a picture, and he agreed to paint another seven-foot version for Henry Bruce, Lord Aberdare, and soon another for Northbrook. He was out to dinner, concerts, garden parties and lunches, meeting the Parkyns and Walter Bethell – 'they say Gussie is happy though' – and enjoying himself with Johnny and Catherine Symonds and Marianne North, whose dazzling paintings amazed him. On the odd occasions that he was alone, he ate at the zoo or at Simpson's in the Strand or walked nostalgically to the Blue Post, where he and Fortescue had always met. At the weekends he took the train to Leatherhead to see Ellen, putting up with her pious ways, or stayed with Bern Husey Hunt in Sussex, or at Strawberry Hill where Lady W., concerned with grander guests, whisked past him like a flash but Fortescue seemed completely unchanged. Yet Fortescue was

changed, at least in title: in April 1874 he had become Baron Carlingford. Lear had heard the news in Simla, writing at once:

> O! Chichester, my Carlingford!
> O! Parkinson, my Sam!
> O! SPQ, my Fortescue!
> How awful glad I am!
>
> For now you'll do no more hard work
> Because by sudden-pleasing jerk
> You're all at once a peer, –
> Whereby I cry, 'God bless the Queen!
> As was, & is, & still has been'.
> Yours ever, Edward Lear.

Delighted as he was to see Fortescue and to gossip about politics,
including Disraeli's move to make Victoria 'Empress of India' and
Dizzy's own transformation into the Earl of Beaconsfield, Lear felt
awkward among the Strawberry Hill glitterati. His closest friendship,
peaceful now, was with Frank Lushington. He saw the Lushingtons
the minute he arrived, ate with them in the evenings in London and
stayed with them at their new summer retreat in Kent. But four-year-
old Clare, always delicate, had died in May, and Lear was full of sympathy and tenderness towards little Harry and Mildred, now five, and
especially to Gertrude, who at twelve was old enough to join them at
supper. 'Gertrude is a duck,' he decided. Frank was proud of Lear's
achievements, telling Emily Tennyson, 'Lear is at 8 Duchess St, with
some exquisite drawings from India & elsewhere – I hope he is selling
them rather successfully & quickly – and in general spirits & looks he
seems to me better than 3 years ago.' At the end of his stay, Lear spent
his last three days with them, waving goodbye to Kate and the 'really
dear nice children' before he left for Folkestone. Back in Italy he still
felt attached to the family, as by a string, imagining them going back to
Norfolk Square, 'Frank & Kate, Gertrude, Milletts & 'arry'. Kate was

pregnant again, and in December Lear was godfather once more, to their new son, Franklin. When he collected his poems for a new book, he thought straight away of the Lushingtons: 'sat up very late writing out the two poems for Gertrude L'.

He kept in touch with friends through constant letters ('Letters are the only solace of my life at present', he had written once to Mary Wyatt, 'except sardines & omelettes'), and was delighted when they came to see him. In 1876 Johnny and Catherine Symonds walked admiringly round his garden, then Frank Lushington came, pacing on the terrace in the rain. Lear missed him badly when he left. Would they ever meet again, he asked, musing on the possibility of some afterlife where friends found each other: 'That all this trouble-whirl of sorrow and worry – all these entangled & dumb feelings are nil – I cannot believe.' To cheer himself up he took a picnic and went sketching: a ruined tower, the flickering shade of olive trees, green banks with yellow flowers '& red poppies & delicate shaking wild oats'. It was silent except for birdsong and he sat on a wall to write his journal, thinking of long-past Campagna days '& many many such later with the good Suliot'.

The house was alive with guests. Northbrook stopped on his way back from India – he had resigned as viceroy in January. Henry Bruce, Lord Aberdare, stayed nearby with three of his children and in July Charles Church came for a week; at some point Lear gave Church his journal of their trip to Greece in 1848, and a hundred sketches from that time. When the visitors had gone, Lear sketched and painted, wrote nonsense and drew his bizarre botany. In quieter evenings, perhaps in his 'Armchairia Comfortabilis', he read book after book – natural history books and memoirs, Carlyle's *Frederick the Great*, Sir John Kaye's *History of the Indian Mutiny*, and a pile of novels, from Disraeli's *Lothair* and Colonel Meadows Taylor's 'semi-historic' Indian sagas to the women writers he admired. *Middlemarch*, he thought, was 'a curiously clever book' with bits that 'do me good'; Gaskell's *Sylvia's Lovers* 'a wonderfully beautiful, but sad book'. In the autumn he noted, 'I am reading just now a good deal of Miss Edgeworth's books. Clever, undoubtedly – but not like Miss Austen or Mrs Gaskell's – or C Bronte's.'

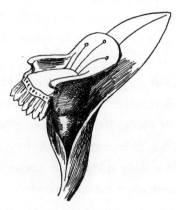

As Lear worked and read, life in the Villa Emily had been changing. Over the years he had become sucked into Giorgio's family problems. He worried about his children, after his wife and then his mother died, and sometimes wondered if he should bring them all to San Remo. He hesitated to suggest this, but he kept in touch by letter with Giorgio's eldest son, Nicola, and ten-year-old Dmitri, and was pleased when Giorgio returned from Corfu in the autumn of 1876 with his second son Lambi (Charalampos), who joined the household on wages of £5 a week. He fretted about Giorgio's health: when he was ill and a glass of vermouth helped, Lear dashed out to order three bottles. He felt responsible for them all – should he perhaps buy a small house in Corfu to leave to Giorgio? 'But must ask F.L. first.' (Frank was still his touchstone for all plans, as well as his legal and financial adviser.) They talked things over when Giorgio came in to smoke his cigar on Sunday evenings and they drank together – perhaps too much. 'Alack! alack!' Lear exclaimed that summer. 'The barrel of Marsala is near at an end.'

While he worried about the Kokali family Lear also became more involved with the Congreves. The boys had grown up in the years he had known them. The fourteen-year-old Arny – still very boyish – was thrilled to receive Lear's present of 'Wolff's Wild Animals' with its superb illustrations. Hubert, however, was now a young man – clever, energetic and handsome, 'well and strong, which it is a pleasure to see'. In May 1875, on Hubert's seventeenth birthday, Lear carried a bundle of small presents over to breakfast, 'a volume of Loudon's botany – H. & F.L.'s poems – a plant of saxifrage – & an opera glass'. He was offering small slices of his own life, his youthful botanical interests, his garden (which Hubert helped him with), the poems of the Lushington brothers, his love of music. He spent evenings at their house and the boys came over to his: 'Dinner good; & the boys – a nice good lot all – happy; – happier in looking at Parrots & Zoological drawings.'

A host of emotions, open and unacknowledged, clouded Lear's feelings for Hubert: in complex ways, he loved him. On his part, Hubert was fond of Lear and looked to him for advice. Much later he remembered Lear's drawing lessons, accompanied by running commentaries on art, nature, scenery and travels, as some of 'the most delightful experiences of my young days'. Sometimes they had lessons in the studio but often they went on sketching expeditions, with 'Lear plodding slowly along, old George following behind, laden with lunch, and drawing materials'. When they found a good subject, Lear would sit down, push up his spectacles and peer at the scene through his 'monocular glass', then draw mountain ranges, villages and foregrounds so fast and accurately that Hubert was left awe-struck.

More uncomfortably, Lear tried to act as a bridge between father and son. Walter was depressed, tired of being a property agent, anxious about his mistress Ellen Walters who was now working elsewhere. For a while he planned to go to Tasmania, although one day Hubert, flicking nervously through Lear's drawings, said that personally 'he had rather not go for 3 years as he could help his Father better as a man; also that he thought his father would never marry again – being 51!' In December, Walter told Lear that he would marry Ellen or no one, '"but shall not bring her here"!!' Over the New Year the tension grew, and impetuously, at the start of February 1877, Lear decided that Hubert should know the truth. Congreve agreed. It was a painful exchange. Hubert sobbed that he was sure Ellen was to blame: 'How can a fellow bear the sight of a woman who has caused the ruin of a whole family?' But when Lear begged forgiveness for causing him pain by telling him, he turned and kissed him, saying, 'It is not your fault.' In fact Hubert soon shook off the shock, Walter was grateful and Tasmania was forgotten.

That month, Giorgio, ill and agitated, demanded to return to his other children in Corfu. Lear agreed and decided to go with him, taking eighteen-year-old Hubert as a kind of treasurer to relieve him of worries about money and tickets. Lambi came too, and the odd quartet travelled down to Brindisi in icy weather, arriving in gales and snow. The gales strengthened, and seeing Lear become ill and anxious, Hubert persuaded him to let Giorgio and Lambi sail by themselves. Next day he and Lear went back across to Naples, where 'Lear at once began to revive'. Or appeared to. Privately, he was brooding on Giorgio's passionate farewell speech – that Lear had been good to him now for twenty-two years, that he felt he would never see him again – and his request that he might kiss him, *'per la prima e l'ultima volta'*. That first night in Naples Lear was not revived but distraught: 'Bed. Ill & tears – Mind & heart broken & distracted.'

Sharing Naples and Pompeii with Hubert worked a healing magic, and then on the train north they passed the valley of Frascati, with Lear's old haunt, Civitella, hidden in cloud and rain. Their week in Rome, in Hubert's rosy recollection, 'was one of the fullest and happiest we spent together. No one knew his Rome better than Lear, and in a week he had shown me more of the wonders and beauties of the old city and its surroundings than most people see in three months.' At their hotel, Lear sang Tennyson songs, bringing tears to an old lady's eyes when she realised that one setting she loved was Lear's own. But once Lear realised that lots of people were listening, he stood up abruptly, said good night and left: 'A sudden change of feeling and manner to casual acquaintances was one of his characteristics,' noted Hubert perceptively. On his last Roman evening he sang 'Lady Jingly Jones'. But there was no turtle to carry him away, and when he reached San Remo loneliness overwhelmed him. He had been playing at families, but they were not his own. He was left by his little heap of stones.

Another wrench came in July, when Lear was in England and Hubert wrote to say that he had decided to become a civil engineer. Soon he learned from the Congreve aunts that Hubert would study at King's College, London: his rooms were already arranged, '& not a word written to me about this!' Distraught at losing the person who made his San Remo days bright, Lear resolved 'and re-resolved' to overcome this:

Pain contracts & convulses me. But I am gradually getting to see that the past must be the past, & buried: yet I can by no means think of anything to put forward as the future. Meanwhile the present is a fearful blank – cutting off heartstrings the only serious order of the day . . . In vain I work for an hour – tears blind me. In vain I play on the Piano, – I get convulsed: – in vain I pace the large room – or try to sleep. True, all these symptoms happened also in 1855 – but then there was not the finality there is now – & then – there were unreal glimpses of light – ; now – back returns the dark, 'with no more hope of light'. God help me. I was never nearer to utter & total madness than now. Yet I don't mean to give way, & shall stave off worse things if I can.

Hubert had been a son, a companion, but also an embodiment of the handsome young men that he had loved ever since his time in Italy with Wilhelm Marstrand. But if he thought wretchedly of Frank in 1855, he also wrote 'back returns the dark' – the words he used when he gave up Gussie. Yet even in this self-dramatising misery, far from breaking down, Lear walked out, made calls, stayed to lunch, strolled through the park, slept in the afternoon and went to friends in Onslow Square in the evening: 'Contrary to my fears – a very pleasant dinner & song.'

Hubert wrote and Lear was comforted – slightly – but his spirit was sore. A fortnight later, staying with Bern Husey Hunt, walking, reading odd things that were lying around, thinking of time passing, he copied into his diary a verse from a poem, 'To a Beautiful Child', that had appeared in the *Eton College Magazine* in 1832:

May he that gave so beautiful a form
Protect and bless thee: May thy gentle heart
Be still as pure, as guileless, & as warm
As nobly worthy of thine outward part.
May'st thou be ever blest as now thou art.
Such are my prayers – nought else can I bestow;
May these suffice to blunt misfortune's dart,
And smooth thy passage through the world below –
And ne'er may I repent, that I have lov'd thee so.

Once Hubert began his studies, he wrote to Lear often and they spent time together in San Remo and in London: in 1880 Lear was almost dizzy with pride when he watched Hubert receiving prizes at King's. The day after the prizegiving was thundery and wet, dull until Hubert came in, 'all joyful at his College success, but as childlike & modest as ever'. They went out for supper to the zoo:

& ordering dinner, saw one side of the 'Society', & then dined very well – soup, salmon, cutlets, cold beef salad – omelette, cheese & a bottle of hock, for 12/-. Afterwards we saw all the other 'beasts' & walked back to 33 Norfolk Square by 8.30 – when, after tea, the Boy, H C left. Doubtless, a fine fellow & no mistake.

Hubert's recollections were even warmer, and in his memory there were no menus and no thunderstorms. 'You are just beginning the battle of life', Lear said, 'and we will spend the evening where I began it':

It was a beautiful evening in July and we dined in the open and sat under the trees till the gardens closed, he telling me all the story of his boyhood and early struggles, and of the meeting with Lord Derby in those gardens, and the outcome of that meeting – the now famous book, The Knowsley Menagerie. I never spent a more enjoyable evening with him, and Lear, when at his best, was the most inspiriting and delightful of companions. He was then absolutely natural and we were like youths together, despite the forty and more years that lay between us.

38: *LAUGHABLE LYRICS*

Lear liked showing off his house, and his longing for visitors — 'very few people come this way' — could be felt in the lovely 'Quangle Wangle's Hat', which he wrote soon after he moved in. Folk of the nonsense world, like the Fimble Fowl with a Corkscrew leg, as well as the birds, snails, bees and frogs, all make their way to the Crumpetty Tree:

> And the Golden Grouse came there,
>   And the Pobble who has no toes, –
> And the small Olympian bear, –
>   And the Dong with a luminous nose,
> And the Blue Baboon, who played the flute, –
> And the Orient Calf from the Land of Tute, –
> And the Attery Squash, and the Bisky Bat, –
> All came and built on the lovely Hat
>   Of the Quangle Wangle Quee.
>
> And the Quangle Wangle said
>   To himself on the Crumpetty Tree, –
> 'When all these creatures move
>   What a wonderful noise there'll be!'
> And at night by the light of the Mulberry moon
> They danced to the Flute of the Blue Baboon,
> On the broad green leaves of the Crumpetty Tree,

> And all were as happy as happy could be,
> With the Quangle Wangle Quee.

The names are alive – the Bisky, dusky Bat; the Attery Squash – will he squash the hat? They join in the treetop dance to the flute of the Blue Baboon. In 1876, a week after he wrote the poem out for his new book, Lear tried playing the flute, as he had done as a boy, '– but I can make little of it now a days'. Next day he played again, several times. His nonsense creatures, both less and more than 'characters', twirled in his head. They entered each other's poems, crept into alphabets, and became familiars, internal touchstones. When he took a shine to a visitor, Miss Poynter, he sighed, 'Too late – oh far too late, Mr Yonghy-Bonghy-Bò'; when he thought that the Tasmanian bush might actually suit Hubert Congreve, he added, 'but his aunt (Jobiska) thinks not'; when he brooded on the cost of furniture and new curtains he groaned,

> When all these people come to be paid
> What a horrible bore t'will be –
> Said the Quangle Wangle Quee.

At Christmas 1876, Fortescue spotted 'a pile of smart red and green books' in Bush's shop, 'and behold it was a new Nonsense Book' – *Laughable Lyrics: Fourth Book of Nonsense Poems, Songs, Botany, Music &c.* He bought several for Christmas presents and was glad, he told Lear, 'to meet again in full dress my old friend the Akond of Swat, whom I had learnt to know in the undress of MS'. 'I am very glad you like my new fooly- book,' Lear replied. All his poems of the last few years were there, Mr and Mrs Discobbolos, the Quangle-Wangle, the Pobble and the Pelicans, the Indian Akond and Cummerbund, as well as 'The New Vestments' and the latest ballad of all, 'The Dong with a Luminous Nose'. The Two Old Bachelors were on the cover, bashed by the Sage (who looks scarily like Lear in an angry mood). The Yonghy-Bonghy-Bò was on the title-page, riding his turtle. The cover said 'Fresh', the title-page 'Fourth': both were true.

In 'The Two Old Bachelors' Lear was in his lightest mode, turning linguistic muddle into narrative. When the hungry bachelors catch a muffin and a mouse, they think they could cook the latter, 'if we only had some Stuffin'!/ If we had but sage and onion we could do extremely well'. Lured by unhelpful directions, they embark on a mock-romantic quest, high among the rocks, where they find an ancient Sage 'areading of a most enormous book'. It is another of Lear's dramas of ascension and precipitous fall, of wisdom found at a price:

'You earnest Sage!' aloud they cried, 'your book you've read enough in! –
We wish to chop you into bits to make you into Stuffin'!' –

But that old Sage looked calmly up, and with his awful book
At those two Bachelors' bald heads a certain aim he took; –
And over crag and precipice they rolled promiscuous down, –
At once they rolled, and never stopped in lane or field or town, –
And when they reached their house, they found (beside their want of Stuffin')
The Mouse had fled; – and previously, had eaten up the Muffin.

They left their home in silence by the once convivial door.
And from that hour the Bachelors were never heard of more.

The poem ripples with tongue-rolling words, jokes and allusions: the 'once convivial door' echoes Mariana's 'unlifted was the clinking latch'; the teasing 'promiscuous' might at that date simply mean mixed, but already possessed a sexual edge. It gave Lear a thundering Miltonic line

458

(like the slaughter of the Piedmontese Protestants): 'As over crag and precipice they rolled promiscuous down', with the rocky 'cr' and 'pr' tumbling to land on the chord of the final round vowels.

The Bachelors are limerick men doubled, like the word they seek, sage/sage. Their silliness dooms them to fail and fall. In 'The New Vestments', another limerick-style figure gets a longer run on the page – and an extra foot in the line.

> There lived an old man in the Kingdom of Tess,
> Who invented a purely original dress;
> And when it was perfectly made and complete,
> He opened the door, and walked into the street.

How clever he is, the old man, what care he has taken – and how brave to walk into the street. Eccentric, original, obsessive, as Lear's old persons are, he steps into the world clothed in things that loomed large in Lear's life – food and animals – or their specimen 'skins'. He is both a mad preacher, as the word 'vestments' suggests, and a nursery-rhyme man, like Aikin Drum, whose hat was made of good cream cheese and his coat of good roast beef. But his garments are oddly sinister, corpses and meats and sweets combined.

> His Shirt was made up of no end of dead Mice,
> The warmth of whose skins was quite fluffy and nice; –
> His Drawers were of Rabbit-skins; – so were his Shoes; –
> His Stockings were skins, – but it is not known whose; –
> His Waistcoat and Trowsers were made of Pork Chops; –
> His Buttons were Jujubes and Chocolate Drops –

The straightforward sentences, very different to the baroque comedy of 'The Two Old Bachelors', sprinkled with conversational phrases – 'no end of', 'fluffy and nice', come to seem increasingly creepy. As Lear dresses his hero, garment by garment, line by line, he becomes a folklore figure, a predator, a sweet-toothed murderer. But then, in a trice, the poem shrinks him into a victim. 'They' turn upon him, not the bourgeois crowd, but the creatures Lear loved, 'Beasticles, Birdlings, and Boys'. Cows, monkeys, goats, dogs, children, pigs and cats rush from dark alleys, snatching and gobbling, stripping him down to his animal self:

> They swallowed the last of his Shirt with a squall, –
> Whereon he ran home with no clothes on at all.

> And he said to himself as he bolted the door,
> 'I will not wear a similar dress any more,
> Any more, any more, any more, never more!'

In 1875 Lear was reading the translation of Hans Christian Andersen's fictionalised autobiography *The Improvisatore*, pleased to discover that Andersen had lived in the same corner house that Fortescue had stayed in when they first met in Rome. His own version of Andersen's story 'The Emperor's New Clothes' is like a bad dream. It feels as if the affable Lear, clothed in his art, his Tennyson songs, his knowledge of natural history and faraway lands, was stripped of these clothes, leaving him bare, a figure of fun. It recalls his sense of being fat and hideous, his thick glasses and big nose, his baggy trousers, his buying of new clothes for Knowsley, his anxious packing of trunks for Hinton and packing again when his dream of Gussie was stripped away. These poems expose the old man of Tess and the two old bachelors as frauds as well as fools, ignorant of language, hopeless cooks, ridiculous tailors. Brutally, Lear pulls their self-esteem from under their feet, driving them to self-banishment. In both poems, the word 'never' sounds like a bell: 'And from that hour the Bachelors were never heard of more'; 'I will not wear a similar dress any more/Any more, any more, any more, never more!' They hide away, like the limerick person who lies with his head in a sack.

'The Two Old Bachelors' and 'The New Vestments' were boundingly dramatic. 'Lyric' was not the right word – but then nor was 'Laughable'. The violence was still there, in the bashing and stripping and crunching. It was there too in the whisking away of the Pobble's toes. Yet the Pobble's tale was genuinely lyrical in its mysterious, mournful tone, and so were 'The Courtship of the Yonghy-Bonghy-Bò' and 'The Pelican Chorus' – both of which he set to music.

'The Pelican Jee', as Lear called it, is different to Lear's other poems of longing and love. Not only are the lovers happy, but their relationship is seen from the outside, from the point of view of the parents – their love and loss lie at its heart. It is full, too, of a different love, for the glory of birds. At the feast for the Pelicans' daughter Dell, they flock to honour her:

> Herons and Gulls, and Cormorants black,
> Cranes, and Flamingoes with scarlet back,
> Plovers and Storks, and Geese in clouds,
> Swans and Dilberry Ducks in crowds.
> Thousands of Birds in wondrous flight!

The pelicans took Lear back to the Nile, to the gathering of birds on the sandbanks like a military court, 'serene geese & dux – & sentinel plovers – all without Heron guards'. As Lear watched, the herons reappeared and 'perhaps the funniest community came thro' the air, just then – 2 immense pelicans – & 20 cranes. These alighted near 2 other Pelicans who put up their heads (present arms) & then slept.' The poem's romantic suitor, the King of the Cranes, looks even further back, to Lord Derby's great cranes and to the Old Man of Dunblane:

There was an Old Man of Dunblane,
Who greatly resembled a Crane;
But they said, – 'Is it wrong, since your legs are so long,
To request you won't stay in Dunblane?'

In 'The Pelican Chorus', the Crane King dons human garb, far grander than that of Mr and Mrs Spikky Sparrow: 'Such a lovely tail! Its feathers float / Between the ends of his blue dress-coat'. Proudly, tenderly, without a ripple of wonder at the coupling between a tall elegant crane and a frumpy bird of another species, the Pelicans tell how the King won Dell's heart with gifts and tarts:

As soon as he saw our Daughter Dell,
In violent love that Crane King fell, –
On seeing her waddling form so fair,
With a wreath of shrimps in her short white hair.
And before the end of the next long day,
Our Dell had given her heart away;
For the King of the Cranes had won that heart,
With a Crocodile's egg and a large fish-tart.
She vowed to marry the King of the Cranes,
Leaving the Nile for stranger plains;
And away they flew in a gathering crowd
Of endless birds in a lengthening cloud.
    Ploffskin, Pluffskin, Pelican jee!
    We think no Birds so happy as we!

> Plumpskin, Ploshkin, Pelican jill!
> We think so then, and we thought so still!

The lovers disappear with the cloud of birds, streaming away to Lear's own 'stranger plains'. But if there is loss, the King and Queen Pelican feel no abandonment. They miss Dell, and mourn her, but are happy for her too, as they sit under the moon on their islands and rocks, where the present is past, and the past is here. Their 'never' is qualified by 'probably' – there is a chance, just a chance, that they will meet again.

> And far away in the twilight sky,
> We heard them singing a lessening cry, –
> Farther and farther till out of sight,
> And we stood alone in the silent night!
> Often since, in the nights of June,
> We sit on the sand and watch the moon; –
> She has gone to the great Gromboolian plain,
> And we probably never shall meet again!
> Oft, in the long still nights of June,
> We sit on the rocks and watch the moon; –
> – She dwells by the streams of the Chankly Bore,
> And we probably never shall see her more.
> Ploffskin, Pluffskin, Pelican jee!
> We think no Birds so happy as we!
> Plumpskin, Ploshkin, Pelican jill!
> We think so then, and we thought so still!

That 'probably' is lacking altogether in the poem that Lear finished two months later. On 24 August 1876 he worked on drawings of Hyderabad, 'After which I quite concluded "The Dong with the Luminous Nose" – & so also ends the new Christmas book.' Lear walked on his terrace in the evening cool, and, as he put it, 'mooned about'. 'The Dong' felt like a final word:

Wrote to F. Lushington enclosing the Dong, for Gertrude, also to R. J. Bush, with the Dong, his portrait, the music for Lady J Jones, & the Pelicans, & a list of Books to be sent, 55 in number. After wh – lunch on bread & cheese with Foss, & am now mostly mooning about . . . Later a walk on the Terrace, moonlight.

The year before, Lear had been astonished to learn that Edward Trelawny – the explorer of Albania, fighter for Greek independence, 'who with Byron burnt Shelley's remains' – was still alive: he had just missed him at the Wyatts' but would see him several times in the years ahead. The Dong, like Trelawny, is a Romantic relic roaming high Victorian terrain. The poem has the diction and rhythm of Tennyson, the doomed mood of 'The Lady of Shalott' or the darker Matthew Arnold. But it mixes these with earlier Romantic language, looking back to the lofty towers of Shelley and the bleak shore of Thomas Moore's 'The Beach' and to 'The Lake of the Dismal Swamp', where the 'meteor bright' is the firefly lamp of the lost girl, perhaps her ghost, paddling her white canoe. But if he heard these as he wrote, Lear's song is different. Its Gothic darkness is as wide as the world. Slowly it narrows in, pulling us with its wrenched syntax through the vast and gloomy dark to a pinpoint of flickering light:

When awful darkness and silence reign
   Over the great Gromboolian plain,
      Through the long, long wintry nights: –
When the angry breakers roar
As they beat on the rocky shore; –
      When storm-clouds brood on the towering heights
Of the Hills of the Chankly Bore: –

> Then, through the vast and gloomy dark,
> There moves what seems a fiery spark,
>   A lonely spark with silvery rays
>   Piercing the coal-black night, –
>   A Meteor strange and bright: –
> Hither and thither the vision strays,
>   A single lurid light.

> Slowly it wanders, – pauses – creeps, –
> Anon it sparkles, – flashes and leaps;
> And ever as onward it gleaming goes
> A light on the Bong-tree stems it throws.

The Dong, we learn, fell in love with a Jumbly Girl with her sky-blue hands and her sea-green-hair when the cheerful Jumblies landed and danced to his pipe all night. But then they sailed on:

> And the Dong was left on the cruel shore
> Gazing, – gazing for evermore, –
> Ever keeping his weary eyes on
> That pea-green sail on the far horizon.

The rhyme makes him funny. He knows he is a fool, a nonsense man, as he flatly admits: 'What little sense I once possessed/ Has quite gone out of my head!' He is driven beyond sense by refusal to abandon a dream. Ever since, he has looked for his Jumbly girl, even though he knows she has sailed. To guide him at night he weaves a huge nose from the bark of the Twangum tree, painted red, with a hollow space for a lamp, tied round his head with a bandage – like the Pobble's nose – 'To prevent the wind from blowing it out'.

> And now each night, and all night long,
> Over those plains still roams the Dong;
> And above the wail of the Chimp and Snipe
> You may hear the squeak of his plaintive pipe

While ever he seeks, but seeks in vain
To meet with his Jumbly Girl again;
Lonely and wild – all night he goes, –
The Dong with a Luminous Nose.
And all who watch at that midnight hour,
From Hall or Terrace, or lofty Tower,
Cry, as they trace the Meteor bright,
Moving along through the dreary night, –
 'This is the hour when forth he goes,
 The Dong with a luminous Nose!
 Yonder – over the plain he goes;
  He goes!
  He goes;
 The Dong with a luminous Nose!'

It would be simple to say that the noses that stretched and pointed and poked throughout Lear's work had finally fused into a single flaming organ. Yet the luminous nose is poetry itself, glimmering in the landscape of a sombre life. The great Gromboolian plain is not an empty, lonely land. It has halls and towers, full of people. But while 'they' live indoors by the fire, the Dong is an outsider, in all senses, lonely and wild. His folly is noble. He is a hero, driven by desire. He wanders hopefully, without hope, in a desperate refusal to despair.

VII. SWOOPING

39: SHOCKS

> There was an old person whose tears
> Fell fast for a series of years;
> He sat on a rug, and wept into a jug
> Which he very soon filled full of tears.

Lear was often unwell in his mid-sixties. He had shingles, asthma, giddiness, rheumatism, trouble with his bowels. His right eye, which he had damaged in the fall long ago, had never recovered and he worried that he would lose his sight. His epileptic fits were less frequent but more intense: 'Demon with violent indigestion but the fit tho' violent was short'; 'went out on the Terrace, where the cold gave me a chill, & went up to sleep then X5 super suddenly'. At one point his heart palpitations returned and he crawled into bed, 'perilously near a semi-paralysed state'. He felt mortal, and when Ellen told him that their brother Henry had died, aged eighty, he was badly upset – 'strangely as it may seem' – and decided to get to England as fast as he could.

England in 1877 both cheered and exhausted him. One day he walked past the house in Upper North Place, 'where Ann & I began our "Art Life" in 1828–9'. Another day, crossing Regent Street, he bumped into Hallam and Lionel Tennyson, now twenty-five and twenty-three: 'O days of Farringford! Giorni passate – perche no retorni!' Later he took them to drinks at the Criterion, and arranged to go down to Aldworth, where he found Tennyson in a genial, if growling, mood and Emily looking 'younger, & handsomer, & diviner than ever'.

That summer, after the shock of Hubert's decision to study at King's, Lear steadied himself. But he was badly shaken again when he heard that Giorgio was very ill in Corfu. He packed furiously and set off for Greece, steaming into Corfu harbour past the lilac coast and the islands where he and Frank used to sail. He found Giorgio sick and thin, and set about finding the family better rooms, leaving after a few days, happier in the thought that they could now live in comfort. But Giorgio was not well enough to come back until midsummer the following year, and then when Lear met him off the boat at Genoa he seemed a mere skeleton, hardly able to walk. He took him to convalesce in Mendrisio, across the Swiss border at the foot of Monte Generoso between lakes Lugano and Como, where they stayed in a hotel that was also a clinic, run by a Dr Pasta. Lear clambered up the mountain to sketch the ranges rippling to the Alps and the hazy views south across the plains, 'a vast scene, and one that might be made something of '.

Monte Rosa from Monte Generoso, 8 am, 6 July 1878

In October, back in San Remo, with Lambi to help, the old patterns resumed and Lear was sanguine. His garden was glorious, he told Fortescue, 'so that altogether I should be rather surprised if I am happier in Paradise than I am now'. Yet he ended on a different note, showing his anxiety by a plunge into nonsense:

A huge Hotel is to be built just below my garden. If it is on the left side it will shut out all my sea view: a calamity as afflicts me.

(The Akond of Swat would have left me all his pppropppprty, but he thought I was dead: so didn't. The mistake arose from someone officiously pointing out to him that King Lear died seven centuries ago, and that the poem referred to one of the Akhond's predecessors.)

King Lear had come to mind when he left Corfu – would he be dispossessed again? Would hotel shadows darken his garden and block out the sea, misty in the mornings and blue-black at night, with the silver track of the moon? Ever since he moved in Lear had talked to Lady Kay-Shuttleworth and Thomas Hanbury, first hoping to buy the land and then hoping to ensure that nothing high would be built on it. But now men were cutting down the olive trees and clearing the plot. The land had been sold to a German, Herr Wolfen, whom Lady Kay-Shuttleworth's daughter Jenny had introduced to Hanbury, and who planned to build a huge hotel. This made things worse: when German families fled across the border from France at the outbreak of the Franco-Prussian war Lear had seethed with an immigrant's resentment at a new wave of settlers. (Later, Henry Strachey remembered with amusement, Lear was pleased with his ploy of answering the door himself when he was supposed to be at home to show his pictures so that he could send away people he didn't like, 'and also keep out Germans. He seemed to have a great horror and fear that a German might be let in by accident.')

For the moment he planned to hide the eyesore with a wall, or to plant eucalyptus. Trying to forget the threat, Lear bustled back and forth, visiting Vice-Consul William Bevan and sitting with old-maidish kindness with the evangelical chaplain, Mr Fenton, whose sermons he had mocked but whose family he loved. There were new English arrivals in San Remo, including Hugh Montgomery and his wife, who became stalwart friends, and in Bordighera, where the writer George Macdonald and the unconventional botanist Clarence Bicknell both settled. Lear followed the gossip and flung himself into trivial pleasures like buying plants or chocolate, biscuits and bottles of Bass, and eating good meals with pears and quinces and champagne. He had money in the bank, his health was better and his depression lifted. There was no mention of tears or heartache, loneliness or the lost past. On New Year's Eve he wrote firmly, 'So ends 1878, which I ought to call a year of thanks, so much unexpected good has happened.'

There was an Old Person of Sheen,
Whose expression was calm and serene;
He sate in the water, and drank bottled porter,
That placid Old Person of Sheen.

It could not last. At the start of 1879 the blasting of rocks and rattling of carts on the land below were driving him mad: 'horribly out of humour with the Great Bee Stanbury and the Jenny Shuttlecock Hotel'. The worry came out in a quick rhyme:

O dear! How disgusting is life!
To improve it O what can we do?
Most disgusting is hustle & strife,
& of all things an ill fitting shoe –
   Shoe,
       O bother an ill fitting shoe!

The 'Devil's Hotel' rose, day by day, with scaffolding poles, gaping windows and hanging canvas. With the rashness that sometimes drove him, Lear immediately looked at new plots of land, working out what they would cost, examining his bank balance and listing people he could borrow from, making an offer for the Villa Berigo, higher up the hill, and then immediately withdrawing it. Ruefully, he pulled himself together and one April evening, with Bevan's eldest daughter, he composed a poetic self-portrait in response to a remark made by one of her friends.

'How pleasant to know Mr Lear!'
    Who has written such volumes of stuff!
Some think him ill-tempered and queer,
    But a few think him pleasant enough.

His mind is concrete and fastidious; –
    His nose is remarkably big; –
His visage is more or less hideous; –
    His beard it resembles a wig.

He has ears, and two eyes, and ten fingers, –
    (Leastways if you reckon two thumbs;)
Long ago he was one of the singers,
    But now he is one of the dumms.

He sits in a beautiful parlour,
    With hundreds of books on the wall;
He drinks a great deal of Marsala,
    But never gets tipsy at all.

He has many friends, laymen and clerical,
    Old Foss is the name of his cat;
His body is perfectly spherical; –
    He weareth a runcible hat.

When he walks in a waterproof white,
    The children run after him *so*!

473

Calling out, – 'He's come out in his night-
    gown, that crazy old Englishman, – O!'

He weeps by the side of the ocean,
    He weeps on the top of the hill;
He purchases pancakes and lotion,
    And chocolate shrimps from the mill.

He reads, but he cannot speak, Spanish,
    He cannot abide ginger-beer. –
Ere the days of his pilgrimage vanish, –
    How pleasant to know Mr Lear!

It was to be sung, he said, 'to the air "How cheerful along the gay mead"'. This was at once ironic and oddly appropriate, the tune being 'The Song of Eve' from Arne's mid-eighteenth-century opera *Abel*, celebrating the bursting life that never failed to thrill Lear, the flowers, the flocks, the trees and fruits, the 'myrtle that springs from the clod'. At the same time, Arne's song declared that this bounty was a fragile gift, which its creator could 'destroy with a nod'.

'How pleasant to know Mr Lear'. Drawing in Lear's letter to William Bevan,
14 January 1879

Lear sent his poem to several friends. It showed that he would never, really, be 'one of the dumms'. Everything was there: his work, his books, his friends, his Marsala, Foss and the rushing children, the nonsense 'runcible' and chocolate shrimps. And the tears. A fortnight after he wrote the poem he called round to the Bevans at teatime and finding a dozen children there, he sang 'The Owl and the Pussy-cat', 'but broke down in the Yonghy-Bonghy-Bò': 'I was sorry I could do no more to help the swarry.' He wept as the hotel's whitewashed walls glared into his studio.

On his way to Monte Generoso in July, Lear learned that Lady Waldegrave had died, suddenly, from a heart attack. Knowing that Fortescue would be distraught he wrote at once to ask him to stay. It would not happen this year: 'I am crushed to the earth,' Fortescue wrote, 'and have no energy to travel – and above all, I will not run away from my awful misery and suffering.'

Lear's suffering seemed small by comparison. In Mendrisio he tried to put the hotel, 'The Enemy,' out of his mind and on the whole he succeeded. Toward the end of his stay, Marianne North came to Como. She was on her way back to England from India, and they went on an excursion to Monte Civita near Monza to see a new hotel, talking endlessly and enjoying the views across the plain. 'There are few women to be compared with Marian North', Lear wrote, '& the day with her has been a wonderful light up.' He tried to keep this up when she visited him in San Remo a month later, plying her with little luxuries, showing her his Indian sketches and letting her know, as she left, how good he had been not to mention 'The Enemy' all day.

At this low point he took up Wilkie Collins's suggestion that he should finish the story of Mr and Mrs Discobbolos. In the new, second part, when the ever-expanding family have lived on their wall for twenty years, 'By all admired, and by some respected' – a nicely sly aside – Mrs Discobbolos wails for her children: 'Surely they should not pass their lives/ Without any chance of husbands or wives!' But her husband calls her a fiddledum head, a goose, an octopod: applied to their domestic life on the wall, Lear's 'runcible', usually affectionate, becomes a swear word, a term of abuse.

> Suddenly Mr Discobbolos
>   Slid from the top of the wall;
>   And beneath it he dug a dreadful trench, —
>   And filled it with Dynamite gunpowder gench, —
>   And aloud began to call, —
> 'Let the wild bee sing and the blue bird hum!
> For the end of our lives has certainly come!'
>   And Mrs Discobbolos said,
>   'O! W! X! Y! Z!
>   We shall presently all be dead
> On this ancient runcible wall, —
>   Terrible Mr Discobbolos!'
>
> Pensively, Mr Discobbolos
>   Sate with his back to the wall; —
>   He lighted a match, and fired the train, —
>   And the mortified mountains echoed again
>   To the sounds of an awful fall!
> And all the Discobbolos family flew
> In thousands of bits to the sky so blue,
>   And no one was left to have said,
>   'O! W! X! Y! Z!
>   Has it come into anyone's head
> That the end has happened to all
>   Of the whole of the Clan Discobbolos?'

'Pensively', Lear was blowing up the hotel, but the explosion, collapse and the awful fall contain all the crashes that had blighted his life, right back to his father's Stock Exchange collapse, which had scattered the Lear clan, after their twenty settled years in Bowman's Lodge.

In October Lear sent this terrible sequel to his American publisher James Fields. He told Fields about the hotel, and laughingly mentioned that someone had advised him to travel the world giving readings of nonsense to raise money to build another house: 'So look out for me and my cat some fine day – by a Boston steamer, on my way to San Francisco.' Then, at the end of his letter, he added a 'Statement' to the effect that the life of the celebrated Mr Lear, artist and writer of nonsense and travel, had been ruined, despite a written promise, by the construction of an immense hotel that condemned him to sunlessness in winter and destroyed his studio's light. He was preparing to move to New Zealand, and 'all the Sanremisi were not at all reticent in their remarks on the parties who are about to cause it'. If he was trying to blow himself up, he was succeeding. When Wilkie Collins leaked the statement to the press, the accused 'parties' were easily identifiable as Hanbury and the Kay-Shuttleworths: there were threats of libel actions and the Kay-Shuttleworth clan turned their backs. His friendship with Johnny and Catherine Symonds cooled drastically, and he lost touch with Marianne North, whom he loved. Corresponding with her friend Amelia Edwards he always asked, longingly, what had become of Marianne.

'Altogether I was never in a greater fix in all my life, & as it is so near the end of it, it is all the more disagreeable,' he groaned, a week after he sent his Statement to James Fields. But by the end of the month his friends were hatching a plan to solve his fix by building a new house. Northbrook offered a loan of £2000, and the young Earl of Derby commissioned yet more drawings. Other friends chipped in to swell the building fund and Lear planned to sell the Villa Emily, for a good price he thought, and send drawings to London to be sold. Chichester Fortescue was with Lear when he decided on the plot he would buy. For months Fortescue had been holed up in Lady Waldegrave's family home at Chewton, visiting her grave daily, weeping, kissing the clothes flung over the chair in her dressing room. His grief was compounded by recriminations that if he had only watched her, and seen how serious her illness was, he could have saved her. In December 1879 he forced himself to travel to Cannes for the wedding of Constance Braham, Lady Waldegrave's niece, to young Eddie Strachey, Johnny Symonds's nephew. Afterwards he made his way over to San Remo and stayed for two months at the Hôtel de Londres, next door to Lear, gradually regaining his cheerfulness. During his long visit they talked often of Tennyson. In his grief, Fortescue said, *In Memoriam* was constantly in his hands, 'soothing and strengthening both by its varied experience and expressions of sorrow and loss, and by the deep inward trust in God and a future life which is worked out'. Lear was warmly sympathetic, despite his own troubles.

Towards the end of Fortescue's stay, Lear sorted through boxes of sketches to sell; he took out 581 of them and decided to send four hundred to London: 'I seem by doing this to be cutting out parts of my own flesh, for I can never see them again.' At this point, Northbrook and Baring arrived. Appalled at the prospect of this loss, Northbrook offered to buy fifty drawings for £500. Although Lear would take no more money from him, he did agree to leave the drawings behind and sell more finished pictures instead. He could show them at 33 Norfolk Square, where Frank Lushington had asked him to stay for some months while Kate and the children were in the country for the summer.

London was a whirl: bewildering, noisy, confusing. He was bilious and tried to cure his bad stomach with neat whisky. He felt harassed and unsure. In June, Robert Bush went bankrupt, and it turned out that he had lost the plates for all the nonsense books he had published. 'Here's a shindy!' Lear wrote. It was even more vital to sell his paintings, and Lear sent letters to everyone he knew, posting four hundred cards: friends and patrons duly turned up, taking drawings away with them.

The Stripy Bird.

'I bought two, cost me £26,' said Lord Derby, rather tersely. There were lighter moments, like Hubert's prize-giving and the dinner at the zoo, and stays with good friends. He bought toys for the children, and drew alphabets and birds. They perched and swung and flew, glanced sideways and flaunted their feathers: green, brown, brilliant yellow and coy pink, and rather cross-looking in stripes.

Lear enjoyed his time with Frank and his evenings with Northbrook and with Fortescue. But once again he looked back to roads not taken. Watching Gussie he thought, 'What would not life have been with that woman!! But it was not to be.' Staying with her in Wimbledon, early one morning he looked out of his window and drew a small sketch, 'of a Chicken looking at the eggshell he had come from'. This prompted 'O Brother Chicken! Sister Chick!', with its wry acceptance of doubt:

> Can no one tell? Can no one solve, this mystery of Eggs?
> Or why we chirp and flap our wings, – or why we've all two legs?
> And since we cannot understand, –
>> May it not seem to me,
> That we were merely born by chance,
>> Egg-nostics for to be?

Lear did not look for answers. In his Paris hotel on his way home, he felt grateful, listing places where he had seen friends this summer:

So far I ought to be very thankful, – but – but – but – the past & the future often will outweigh the present – Leatherhead, Stratton, Aldworth, Compton, Dudbrook, Guy's Cliffe, Oxford, & Templehurst – for the past; – Sanremo the future.

Trust & go on hoping.

Bed at 11.

On the train he read Tennyson. Three days later he was home.

40: THE VILLA TENNYSON

The new villa was lower down the slope, just to the east. Its design copied that of the the Villa Emily almost exactly, to make it easier, Lear said, for Foss to find his way around, but the rooms were in reverse order, to fit the ground. In late February 1880 he could write: '*The walls of the Villa Oduardo was really begun yesterday*: certainly I am making a leap in a kind of darkness.' It had 'only the road & the Railway between it and the sea', he told Emily, so it was safe, 'unless the Fishes begin to build, or Noah's Ark comes to an Anchor below the site'. Fears sapped his confidence, old nightmares of Jonah and unfathomable depths.

Slowly the house rose, and in September he decided on a name – Villa Tennyson. The following spring, when he sent Lord Derby the last four drawings in repayment of his advance, he was packing paintings, books and furniture. When he moved, he said, 'thenceforward I hope to work harder & hardest at my 300 Topographical Poetical Illustrations of A Tennyson's poems – many of which are far advanced, – but all have had to be shunted along of the abominable Shuttleworth Hanbury Hotel'. He moved in in June 1881. 'We send our affectionate God bless you and the New House,' wrote Emily. The whole Tennyson family, with Alfred at the head, signed the letter wishing him well.

*

From time to time over the past thirty years Lear had returned to his 'Poetical Illustrations' of lines from Tennyson, first projected in 1852. In this strange, intensely personal – even eccentric – project, Lear looked back through his innumerable sketches to find scenes of real places that were suggested to him by lines of Tennyson's poetry, or that offered a visual equivalent to the mood and image. Then he drew these again to form a lengthy sequence. He had taken up the idea anew ten years ago, when he moved into the Villa Emily in 1871. At that point he had searched for his original list, writing it out again and beginning three oil paintings, of Philae for 'Moonlight on still waters', Kasr es Saàd for 'The crag that fronts the Even', and the Albanian mountains for 'Akrokeraunian Walls'. He had also made outline drawings on prepared wood: 'the small initiative preliminary pestilential pseudo perry derry pumpkinious beginnings for the Tennyson work'.

Lear's plan was to show the large paintings in his gallery and use the drawings to create a book, on the lines of Claude's *Liber Veritatis*, which he had pored over in Northbrook's library, and Turner's *Liber Studiorum* of 1807–9. He had a copy of the Turner with the seventy engravings in etching and mezzotint, as well as the new autotype edition, and the young lithographer Frank Underhill had made copies of five plates for him. He knew that Turner had returned to these early works towards the end of his life, painting some of the subjects afresh, including the shimmering *Norham Castle, Sunrise*. There was nothing wrong in reviving an earlier vision. It was a kind of return, an ending.

In the 1870s Lear had worked on five large oils related to particular Tennyson lines, telling his friends, and spoofing the quotations for fun. The effect was surreal – no. 5 could be a quotation from T. S. Eliot – but it was the kind of parody-puzzle Lear enjoyed, knowing that Tennyson fans could easily find the originals:

1. Tom Moorey
2. The Nasty crockery tott'ring falls
3. Like the wag that jumps at evening, – all along the sanded floor

4. To catch the whistling cripples on the beach
   With Topsy Turvy signs of screaming pay.
5. Spoonmeat with Bill Porter, in the hall
   With green pomegranates, & a shower of Bass.
This is frightful – but what can you expect from the Author of the Book of
   Nonsense?

The first two were 'Timohorit' and 'The vast Akrokeraunian walls'
from 'To E.L. on his travels in Greece'; the third, 'And the crag that
fronts the Even,/All along the shadowing shore', came from 'Eleanore',
and the final two from 'The Lotos Eaters': 'To watch the crisping ripples
on the beach,/and tender curving lines of creamy spray', and 'moonlight
on still waters between walls/Of gleaming granite, in a shadowy pass'.

Lear heard Tennyson's music tumbling in his head like the sea in a
shell pressed to the ear. Parody was irresistible. Evelyn Baring, insisting
on Lear's kindly, lovable self ('He was too warm-hearted to be satiri-
cal'), remembered him sobbing while he played 'Tears, idle tears', yet
sending round a sketch the next morning with a verse that was clearly
Tennyson, though clearly not:

Nluv, fluv bluv, ffluv biours,
Faith nunfaith kneer beekwl powers
Unfaith naught zwant a faith in all.

If read aloud, especially in the mournful, sonorous tones in which
Tennyson declaimed his work, this reproduces the original:

If Love, if Love be Love, if Love be ours
Faith and unfaith can ne'er be equal powers:
Unfaith in aught is want of faith in all.

Casting Lancelot's song from the *Idylls* into phonetic nonsense diction looks like mockery, but it let Lear spell – or unspell – his deepest beliefs, his need for love, his hope of faith. When he wrote to Fortescue in 1873 telling him about the five paintings, he padded out his letter with another parody. Here was Tennyson praising Lear's book on his travels in Albania and Greece:

> Illyrian woodlands, echoing falls
> Of water, sheets of summer glass,
> The long divine Peneian pass,
> The vast Akrokeraunian walls,
>
> Tomohrit, Athos, all things fair,
> With such a pencil, such a pen,
> You shadow forth to distant men,
> I read and felt that I was there . . .

And here were Lear's 'mysterious and beautiful verses', catching Tennyson's cadences and harmonies in a bathetic, concrete nonsense that was, paradoxically, more faithful to the actual Albanian trip: the dangerous dogs, stubborn mule and crashing plates.

> *Tom-Moory* Pathos; – all things bare, –
> With such a turkey! such a hen!
> And scrambling forms of distant men,
> O! – ain't you glad you were not there!
>
> Delirious Bulldogs; – echoing, calls
> My daughter, – green as summer grass: –
> The long supine Plebeian ass,
> The nasty crockery boring falls; –

The effect was both to make the original seem ridiculously overstated and to mock the tribute to himself. But in his drawings, Lear portrayed the 'Illyrian woodlands' with great seriousness, looking past the trees of Akhrida in Albania to the bays beyond.

Twenty-five years ago he had explained to Emily that he wanted to show that Tennyson's poetry,

(with regard to scenes) is as real and exquisite as it is relatively to higher and deeper matters: that his descriptions of certain spots are as positively true as if drawn from the places themselves, & that his words have the power of calling up images as distinct & correct as if they were written from those images, instead of giving rise to them.

'As if drawn from the places themselves', as if 'written from those images': it was Lear who had seen the places, not the poet. As he read and reread Tennyson's poems he found his own 'distinct & correct' images to illustrate them. In the process he compiled a pictorial autobiography, from the Sussex of his youth to his travels in Italy, Greece, Egypt, the Levant and India. By now he had drawn and painted watercolours and oils from his sketches many times. The Tennyson drawings were a way of seeing himself and his past through the 'subtle-thoughted, myriad-minded' power of recall that Tennyson himself had called on in his 'Ode to Memory':

> Thou who stealest fire,
> From the fountains of the past,
> To glorify the present; oh, haste,
> Visit my low desire!
> Strengthen me, enlighten me!
> I faint in this obscurity,
> Thou dewy dawn of memory.

In August 1876, as he opened packing cases and rifled through a clutter of belts and spades and garden scissors, he came upon the 'Tennyson' scenes of Civitella and Philae that his old friend Bill Nevill had bought years ago, now returned to him after Bill's death: 'Bottini's man came, & opened 2 cases. "Morn broadens", painted at Stretton (1853 I think) & "Palms & Temples" – at Eastbourne in 1855 – are now here: queer change – after their glory at Woodgreen & their happy obscurity – yet always beloved. At Langhams! They are very dirty though.'

In 1855 he had told Emily Tennyson proudly how these paintings hung each side of the drawing-room door in the Nevills' house in Stoke Newington. *'Morn Broadens'* was the first large Tennyson landscape sold, and although it went cheaply he was glad, he said, 'that it belongs to people who will always enjoy it'.

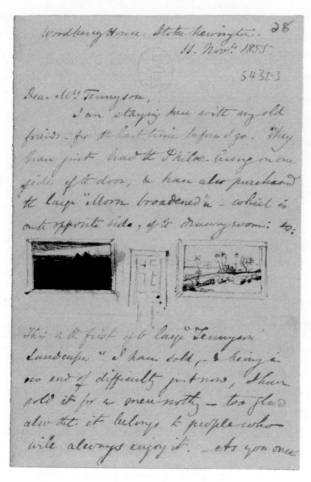

Letter from Lear to Emily Tennyson, 11 November 1855

Bill's sons had also sent Lear a packet of his letters: 'some are as far back as 1835 – from Knowsley!' That autumn, planning new Tyrants, he went through his sketches:

Worked all day long in looking over sketches – more than three cabinets full, so that today & yesterday I seem to have lived again every year of my life from 1824 – Sussex – Lancashire, the Rhine – Rome – Naples – Campagna, Abruzzi – Sicily, Calabria – Sicily again – Apulia – Corfu – Greece, Constantinople, Albania, Greece & Thessaly – Sinai, Egypt – Ionian Isles, Athos, Palestine, Malta, Cornice, Venice, the Lakes, Dalmatia, Crete, Corsica, India.

Long ago he had decided that 'in converting memories into tangible facts – recollections & past time as it were into pictures, – lies the chief use & charm of a painter's life'. The Tennyson work became a shifting lens focused on his own wanderings. When he drew sunlit plains and ruins glimpsed through a dark Roman arch – an eye of memory – he wrote beneath it the lines from 'Ulysses',

> For all experience is an Arch wherethro'
> Gleams the untravelled world, whose margin fades,
> For ever and for ever when I move.

And then, with a flourish, 'Campagna di Roma, Italy'.

Thinking about the paintings he had made throughout his travelling life brought not shocks exactly, but tremors from some fault-line deep beneath. He felt slightly behind the times: in London in 1876 he had gone to a show at the Watercolour Society; 'It interests me much – but principally in the various modes of execution – so much more liquid than my own. Glennie's distances are beautiful, but his foregrounds are wanting in much.' Arthur Glennie, one of Lear's many correspondents, had been known since the 1840s for his hazy, Italianate watercolours and Lear's work, too, seemed now to belong to that earlier era. In London Whistler was painting his *Nocturnes* in black and gold. Across the Channel, the exhibitions of the 'Impressionists', as the critic Louis Leroy called them sneeringly, were causing as much fuss as the Pre-Raphaelites had done a quarter of a century ago; Monet's painting of *Palm Trees at Bordighera* could not have been more different to Lear's.

Lear did not want to be 'new' or experimental. He wanted to achieve the Romantic, the sublime. When he was in London he always went to the National Gallery to see the Claudes and the Turners, but in 1876 he wrote, 'Depressed enough already – the glory & beauty of the Turners depressed me still more.' A year later, when he heard that the Aberdares were delighted with his *Kinchenjunga*, he was nonsensically self-deprecating: 'After all it is better to be the means of giving armless pleasure to a limited number of people, than to be the means of slaughtering indefinite thousands – though I grant the latter function requires the greater ability.' That summer, Europe was reeling at the violent suppression of the Bulgarian uprising against the Turks, in which over fifty villages were burned and ten to fifteen thousand Bulgarian citizens massacred. For Lear, art was life, but this bitter juxtaposition to mass death is disconcerting, and the truncated 'armless', with its sense of missing a limb vital to a painter, spoke of his own insecurity.

He was defensive: he felt his art to be trivial in comparison to the great and terrible events of the time, yet still important. He was embarrassed, too, at relying on the patronage of friends. In his letter to Aberdare he put the criticism into another's mouth, but he felt it: 'Said a foolish artist to me – "You can hardly be ranked as a Painter – because all you have done, or nearly all, – is merely the result of personal consideration, & you are comparatively if not wholly unknown to the public" – Says I to he, – that don't alter the qualities of my pictures.'

It did not matter if they were done to commission or bought in a gallery. If gallery pictures were 'cried up & well hung up' (which his had not been),

they are safe to be bought – be they by Whistler or anybody else. But the voice of fashion whether it issues hout of a Hart Cricket in a Paper, or hout of the mouth of a Duke or a Duchess – ain't by no means the voice of Truth. So you see o beloved growler – your ozbervations don't affect me a bit, who haven't got no ambition, nor any sort of Hiss Spree de Kor at all at all.

The cockney-Irish and the nonsense masked Lear's proud awareness that because he lacked *esprit de corps*, he saw and painted the world in his own way. In 1880 he was regaining his confidence. He finished *Kinchenjunga* for Northbrook and this summer saw it hung in his dining room, looking stunning. When he dined with Lady Ashburton in Knightsbridge, 'the most sunshiny-intellectual woman', he was amazed to see how good his *Cedars* and *Kinchenjunga* looked, and especially *Kasr es Saàd*, which he used to illustrate 'The crag that fronts the even' in his Tennyson series. It was let into a huge black frame, he told Fortescue, 'all the room being gilt leather'! It did his spirit good, he said mockingly, '& walked ever afterwards with a nelevated & superb deportment & a sweet smile on everybody I met'.

'The crag that fronts the Even'. Kasr es Saàd, Egypt (1856)

Lear always felt that there was a vein of poetry within his art, but doubted that it would come out. In the Tennyson drawings it did.

In the mountains in the summer of 1881 Lear drew outlines for fifty-four Tennyson designs, then penned them out and coloured them with wash. They illustrated lines from thirty-seven poems, all published before 1864: Lear took no lines from the later work, although Tennyson always sent him his new books and he read them as soon as they arrived. With wild ambition, he now planned three hundred illustrations, declaring whimsically:

When the 300 drawings are done, I shall sell them for £18,000: with which I shall buy a chocolate coloured carriage speckled with gold, and driven by a coachman in green vestments and silver spectacles, – wherein, sitting on a lofty cushion composed of muffins and volumes of the Apocrypha, I shall disport myself all about the London parks . . .

Perhaps he knew that his expansive plan was as much a fantasy as the cushion made of muffins. But he made many monochrome drawings in different sizes and tints over the next few years, and two sets of two hundred wash drawings, one small, a large postcard size, and one larger, ten inches by six. He still hoped that these could be reproduced for a book but to his deep disappointment, no reproduction process worked as he wanted: autotype was too uneven, lithography too feeble, photography too dark.

The whole sequence had an elegiac note, beginning with four sunset scenes for the final verse of 'Mariana', the hour of her greatest hopelessness, when 'the day/ Was sloping toward his western bower'. Several lines, like his favourite 'Palms and temples of the South' from 'The Palace of Art', had clusters of ten or more sketches, while 'The Daisy', inspired by the Tennysons' visit to the Riviera, a poem that Lear felt 'more than any other poem, presents a unbroken series of Landscape Portraits', had eighteen views. Even closer to his heart was the poem written for himself, 'To E.L., on his Travels in Greece'. For this he made nearly twenty different views, from the 'sheets of summer glass' of Lake Akhrida to Corfu and Kanchenjunga, and over and over again he drew Mount Athos, its peak above the woods, its monasteries perched on the cliffs.

The drawings became an obsession, and he now conceived of his progress, and of the drawings themselves, as a kind of metamorphosis. When he started, at Clive Vale Farm in 1852, he had told Hunt that the

'Athos – all things fair', The Monastery of St Dionysius, Mount Athos

drawings were 'in the Egg state'. Then he had drawn larger versions, 'caterpillars'. The detailed monochrome outlines he was working on now were 'chrysalisses' and eventually they would attain 'their final or Butterfly Condition'. The ideal watercolours, which never emerged, were 'perfect insects'. The lines and drawings hatched and swarmed around his mind. His eyesight was now poor and his diary was full of worry:

it is plain that owing to my very defective sight wh. cannot work without a distinct outline, – I have to make that outline so dark that it interferes with the light & clearness of the drawing, all through its future progress. It seems nearly impossible that I can *gradually* achieve colour & form together . . . Just now, it is on the cards whether or not I give up this 'cataract' – the 1st A 'finished' drawing! – a pretty 'kettle of fish!' – as the pious Baboo wrote.

With his sight in this state, he had to start with a fierce heavy outline that was hard to get rid of later. Yet many drawings, scratchy, thick or dark, are thrillingly evocative, almost abstract in their intensity. When he came to the line from *In Memoriam*, 'A looming bastion fringed with fire', one drawing of the Indian coast dispensed with outline altogether, becoming a Turner-like watercolour wash of fluid darkness against the sea with ghostly boats. His drawings translated Tennyson's sonorous, flowing lines into studies of light and dark, shadow and moon, river and cataract, snow and fire, distance and dusk.

'A looming bastion fringed with fire', the Coast of Travancore, India

The final Tennyson drawings were for 'Enoch Arden'. Lear's interest was not in Enoch's return after his shipwreck and long years on the desert island, when he comes home to find his wife remarried and resolves nobly not to interfere, but in the castaway, the exile, the tropical island itself. The line he chose was 'a mountain wooded to the peak'. His painting would show Enoch stranded on his homeward passage, like a lost migratory bird. In early 1877, when he was finishing his paintings of Kinchenjunga, Mount Timohorit and Kasr es Saàd, he told Fortescue: 'I try to look forward to hard work as the only mode of living in comfort, and a vast semi-composition of Enoch Arden – together with an equally large Himalayan subject, are the dreams of the future – not altogether dreams though – since the designs are already made.'

It was a vision of waiting, hoping, uncertainty. Fortescue was percipient. A few years later, when they were discussing life after death and how it seemed impossible for humanity to dispense with religion altogether, he told Lear, 'There is religion in your big Enoch Arden and your 150 Tennysonian subjects.'

The vast painting, which supposedly once hung in the Tennysons' dining room, is now lost. Did he ever finish it? On 15 December 1881, he wrote, 'At 8.30 the great case with the Canvas for Enoch Arden, is announced to be at hand. Every one of my steps in life have been denounced as silly & insane; perhaps this huge affair will be more truly & reasonably so than any previous.' A year later, when the young art student Henry Strachey admired Lear's gallery, with its beautiful watercolours and great canvas of Mount Athos, he noticed that

at the end of the gallery stood a huge canvas covered over with lines in squares, but with no drawing on it. This, he told me, was to be a picture of Enoch Arden on the desert island. My remark that this would be a great undertaking roused Mr Lear to declare warmly that an old man should never relax his efforts or fail to attempt great things because he was seventy.

In September 1883 Lear told Holman Hunt that he was working on a string of pictures, including 'a big Philae, & a bigger Athos & Bavella, & a biggissimo Enoch Arden', and the following spring Dmitri held him on a chair while he worked on the upper part of the picture, changing the place of the figures and going over the outlines in umber and turpentine. His drawings and preliminary watercolours show a figure seated on a rock or wandering down a forest path. Tall trees arch above him, a tropical landscape runs to the sea and jagged mountains rise beyond.

Enoch's island drew on landscapes Lear had painted over and over again: the bays of Greece, the mountains of Albania, the palms of Egypt, the banyan trees of India. In one sketch a skein of birds skims above the trees and a doodle among foliage reveals itself to be a parrot looking on. It was almost a reworking of Ann's portrait of him as a child in his *Robinson Crusoe* setting, a nonsense land like the Chankly Bore or the great Gromboolian plain. It was joyous as well as solitary.

'The foreground of my large Enoch Arden picture', he told Emily,

Lear's watercolour sketch for *Enoch Arden's Island*

is to be elaborately filled with all kinds of Ipomoeas, Passion-flowers etc. – The statistic-realistic idiot of this world will say, 'Why these flowers are of different countries! By no chance whatever do they ever grow in one place!' – On which the following discourse will occur.

E.L. 'Oh yes they do!'

Critic 'Where?'

E.L. 'Just 43 miles from the coast Enoch Arden's ship was bound to.'

Critic 'And where then was that coast?'

EL. 'Exactly 43 miles from Enoch Arden's Island.'

Critic explodes into several bits. Artist grins.

Enoch is alone, but he has hope. And the mountains and trees and flowers and birds surround him as he waits for a sail.

41: 'AS GREAT A FOOL AS EVER I WAS'

Lear trotted around San Remo, sociable, gossipy, inquisitive. This was very much a border town, with French spoken in the cafes and Italian in the markets, and a stream of English visitors. Some were invalids, like Ralph Touchett in Henry James's *Portrait of a Lady*, published that year, 'spending a dull, bright winter beneath a slow-moving white umbrella'; others, like James's Isabel Archer, were passing through, full of excitement, seeing San Remo as 'the threshold of Italy, the gate' to 'a land of promise'.

In the cold yet sunny winter of 1880–1, sitting comfortably in his library, Lear read in the *Telegraph* of blizzards and icy misery in England: 'With such wretchedness existing, why am I in such luxury?' He sent Frank a cheque for £5 for the poor of the London district where he was magistrate: 'of course one "can't afford" this, but if one is only to relieve others from one's superfluities, that can't be right. I have every comfort at present in all sorts of ways, & ought to help those who are wretched.' He replanted his mandarin orange trees from the Villa Emily, filled the garden with flowers and gave nosegays to departing visitors – he was heartbroken when his young gardener, Giuseppe, died of suspected tetanus. But he rejoiced in fine weather, wide views, birdsong and music, books and good dinners. He made new friends, like Revd E. Carus Selwyn, headmaster of Liverpool College, whom he met

494

in Monte Generoso and who became a regular correspondent, and the Watsons, for whom Lambi went to work: 'Watson is certainly a very likeable & delightful man; his brother in law is vastly less so.'

His letters were a lifeline, keeping him in touch with his many friends in England, and he still made careful notes of their arrival and his answers.

Letters received, late 1880, with 'A' for answered

He was overjoyed in May 1881 when Fortescue was made Lord Privy Seal – largely because of the name, which allowed many jokes and drawings. Fortescue's return to government was tough. Gladstone had appointed him to help him pass the Irish Land Bill, but he also had to cope with Gladstone's deal with the imprisoned Irish nationalist Charles Stewart Parnell, to allow Irish tenants to appeal for fair rent. Parnell was released from Kilmainham gaol after promising to co-operate and stop nationalist violence, but only four days after the 'Kilmainham treaty', two British officials were murdered in Phoenix Park in Dublin, causing great outrage in England. Lear sympathised with Fortescue's difficulties over Ireland, and his letters were now full of a new, avid interest in politics. He became tangled over the 'Eastern Question', concerning Russian aggression towards the Ottoman Empire. When Britain stood back, remembering the Crimea and protecting Indian shipping lanes by occupying Suez rather than engaging Russia, Lear was horrified. In response to Northbrook's comment that the Russian capture of Batumi on the Black Sea coast of Georgia might give them 'more responsibility', Lear noted, 'Certainly – & such would be the case if you gave them Anglesea or the I of Wight.' In his view, Gladstone, so fond of chopping down trees on his estate, was a reckless baboon:

> When 'grand old men' persist in folly
> In slaughtering men and chopping trees,
> What art can sooth the melancholy
> Of those whom futile 'statesmen' teaze?

Fortescue declined to join in: 'the old man' was his boss, after all. Lear wrote apologetically about his outpourings, while jokingly elevating his nonsense from a fool's cap to a mitre: 'Should you be injuiced by contemplating the remarkable development of my "Political knowledge and aspirations" to offer me some lucrative place under Government, be assured that I will take nothing but the Chancellor of Exchequership, or the Archbishoprick of Canterbury.'

He would never go back to Britain to see those friends. Young Lord Derby, who was always kind, invited him to come and stay and bring a 'room full of work with you. There is space still at Knowsley for a few more of your drawings, though I have a pretty good stock already.' Derby, however, was also realistic. When Lear asked if he could possibly send the rest of the money for the drawings, Derby wrote in his diary, 'I offered to do this, & he is heartily welcome', but, he thought,

in a world where nothing succeeds like success he has done himself much harm by his perpetual neediness. An artist who is always asking his friends to buy a picture and often to pay for it in advance, makes outsiders believe that he cannot know his business, which in Lear's case is certainly far from the truth. But *he has been out at elbows all his life*, and so will remain to the last.

A couple of years later Lear apologised for swamping Derby with notices about his London show, which had been moved from Christie's to Foord and Dickinson, acknowledging that the annual announcement about his gallery 'is as much an Advertisement-universal as Eno's Fruitsalt or Epp's Cocoa'. It was not meant, he insisted, to be a 'persistent request to my friends that they should buy more of my work, especially when their walls are pretty well covered'.

He was fearful of seeming to sponge on his rich patrons, yet he went on shamelessly trying to sell his work, enclosing lists of pictures and prices in letters to likely buyers and reminding friends, if they had admired a painting, that it was for sale. But he did become more choosy about his open Wednesdays in San Remo. Constance Strachey, who went over to see him from Cannes, noticed that sometimes he answered the door himself, to keep out dreaded Germans and others: 'If he did not like the appearance of a visitor, with a long face and woe in his voice he would explain that he never showed his pictures now, being much too ill. He would then shut the door and his cheerfulness would return.' He was fed up with crowds admiring his work and leaving without buying a thing. One guest he was keen to see, however, was Queen Victoria. In the spring of 1882 she spent a month in Menton, having fallen in love with the Riviera. Hanbury brought her baskets of flowers from La Mortola, and she drove along the Corniche road, enchanted by its grandeur and the sight of local shepherds with their white knee breeches and black hats. As she drew and sketched, perhaps she remembered Lear's lessons nearly forty years ago. (A friend warned Lear against holding forth about Germans while she was there: 'Says I, "I won't if I can help it."') In the end the visit proved too complicated to arrange, although Giorgio allegedly made piles of macaroons, which they knew Victoria loved, and crowds of people came hoping to see her. The following summer, in Monte Generoso, a small elderly lady peered at him through the restaurant door, then sent her husband to enquire if he was really 'Mr Lear', as if so, 'she would be glad to make your acquaintance again'. Lear was touched to find that it was the Princess Royal, 'the most absolute duck imaginable'.

Giorgio Kokali in 1881

Lear often felt he talked too much when he was out: he was drinking hard as well as working hard. Giorgio warned him about this, and investigated their regular supply of Marsala, which turned out to have been laced with spirits at the shop: put near the fire, it flamed up. Startled, Lear tried to cut down, guiltily buying the occasional bottle: 'Tried Barbera wine but did not like it at all – wh. would have been perhaps a good thing only there was Barolo to fall back on. Certainly the question of drink is a painful one to me.' The Barolo wine of Piedmont became his staple, supplemented with comforting bottles of Bass, and champagne, in quantities, if available.

If Lear was often tipsy – and his late night handwriting suggests that – he steered clear of becoming an alcoholic. Giorgio was the real victim of drink. Life in the Kokali family was turbulent and in 1879 Lambi was sent home for getting into debt, drinking and going to brothels. Now he and Nicola wanted to open a trattoria in Brindisi or Bari, the first stops for Corfiotes off the boat. Frustrated by their demands, Lear went south himself to see what the possibilities were. Despite his worries, he basked in his trip, staying with Arthur Glennie in Rome on the way; 'Strange place Rome! It seems a kind of dream to have been here.' In Brindisi the Corfu steamer lay below his hotel window, 'as does the *Sumatra* from India – All the water is like a silver mirror, & I wish I was going too! – It is impossible to be thankful enough for the blessings of the day, & for the whole past week. I hope I may be able to do some good for those 2 unhappy sons of my good servant.' He sketched a fishing boat sailing on the still harbour, found a place for the boys, and went home.

Money drained away. The Brindisi lease fell through and Lear learned from the British consul that trattorias opened and shut there in the wink of an eye. So the plan was dropped. Lambi came back to San Remo and went to work for the Watsons while Nicola, who was far from well, became a waiter at a nearby hotel. 'What a queer lot of Suliot incidents in my silly life, since reading of Suli in Byron before I was 10 years old!' Lear wrote in March 1882. Then Giorgio began drinking so heavily and behaving so wildly that Lear began to think he must dismiss him, even after their twenty-seven years together. In June, when the whole town closed in mourning for the death of Garibaldi, Giorgio was approaching collapse. He seemed a little 'ugly', thought Lear, and had 'queer and violent fits'. Then he disappeared. Nothing was heard until a telegram arrived from Giorgio, sent from Toulon early one morning, demanding that Lear send money to him in Marseilles, so that he could go to England. Desperate, Lear contacted the Greek consul in Toulon and sent Nicola to bring his father back. When he found him, Giorgio was in rags, thin and ill and nearly unconscious: he had been wandering in the hills, without food, and had almost lost his memory.

Nicola took Giorgio up to Monte Generoso to recover, and Lear settled back to work. 'I have still more to be thankful for,' he told Fortescue brightly, 'my health being MUCH better . . . I drink Barolo – fully as much "as is good for me" by way of precaution.' When he went up to Monte Generoso himself he tried to believe that Giorgio's alcoholic breakdowns were not serious, and set about enjoying himself: 'This place just now is not unlike the last Day, or universal judgement, – such heaps of unexpected persons keep turning up.' Fanny Kemble was there, and Mazzini's widow, and John Cross, George Eliot's widower . . . 'I constantly expect to see the Sultan, Mrs Gladstone, Sir Joshua Reynolds and the twelve apostles walk into the hotel.' He avoided the noisy mob of the table d'hôte by dining separately with friends and firmly turned the other guests, with their tentacular embraces and snapping conversation, into nonsense:

> The Octopods and reptiles
> They dine at six o'clock,
> And having dined, rush wildly out
> Like an electric shock.

Back in the Villa Tennyson, having smuggled precious alpine plants across the border in his pockets, Lear felt restored, writing casually, 'Georgio is *immensely* better & cheery. Garden now in extreme beauty. Ipomeas especially.' The Kokali quarrels continued but over the winter father and sons worked together. Foss, foolish and faithful, sat sedately under the canary's cage hoping for biscuits to fall through. At Christmas, when Henry Strachey came to stay, Lear gave him the second part of 'Mr and Mrs Discobbolos' for his father, Sir Edward, then collected a sheaf of carefully cut-out backs of old envelopes from his bureau. On these, for Henry's eight-year-old sister, he drew heraldic pictures of Foss: 'After he had done seven he said it was a great shame to caricature Foss and laid aside the pen.'

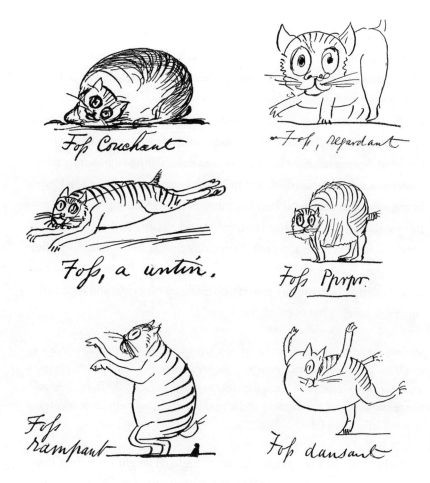

Fos Couchant

Fos, regardant

Fos, a untin.

Fos Pprpr.

Fos rampant

Fos dansant

Fos, Passant

In the new year of 1883 the Watsons sacked Lambi for stealing wine, pawning the cook's watch and having a woman in Pisa: after much prevarication, he slunk resentfully back to Corfu. Again, Lear shrugged off the drama: 'Watson may perhaps have been a little hasty, but Mrs Watson is beyond doubt very angelic & sensible.' His friendship with the Watsons survived: he drew birds for their daughter Beatrice, and laughed at her playing at being a Harpy with a waste-paper basket over her head. Spring brought friends, good evenings, long talks, sunny days.

Adamson Parker had died, and in March Gussie came out to San Remo bringing two nieces with her. Gussie was used to caring for people – her mother, her father, her husband – and if Lear had proposed she would doubtless have accepted. Every day he felt more undecided, but 'Alas! Alas! It cannot be,' he wrote. 'As a dream is a dream it is better to treat it as such.' On the day she left, he made up nosegays and took them up to the hotel. That evening, he wrote,

so ends the very last possible chance of a change of life. Many causes occasion this – my age, the least among them: – the knowledge of all my misery, physical and psychical – now & of late quite clear to me & unescapable from, – among the greatest. It was a hard effort at the last, & I could only not burst into tears before I left. When I did.

If Parker had died ten years ago, he thought, 'I might even then have hoped to have a good woman to nurse me at the last.' But he would never have asked her. The tears were less for Gussie than for his own hesitation and loss.

People he loved turned up one by one. A few weeks later, Frank Lushington came out to stay, bringing Gertrude with him, still to Lear 'an *absolutely delightful* girl; a perfect duck in all possible ways'. But during their visit Giorgio was far from well. After Frank left, Lear sat with him and coaxed him into the garden while the curtains were taken down and the carpets rolled up before the summer exodus. At the start of June Lear sent him to the mountains again with Nicola, and, glad of the calm, settled down to reading Crabb Robinson's memoirs and

Wilkie Collins's stories with immense pleasure (he had cried copiously over Collins's *The Frozen Deep* two years before). 'It is impossible to be thankful enough for the quiet and comfort of these last few days,' he wrote. Sitting on the terrace, he thought the garden 'wonderfully lovely, & daily more so'.

It was a shock then, when he and Dmitri went to Mendrisio in July, to see Giorgio coughing and pale. He came down to sit beside Lear while he played the piano and struggled along to Bella Vista to see the view, but it was clear that he was fading. Lear tried hard not to believe this, insisting that when Giorgio was shivering he should just put on warmer clothes, but his actions betrayed his distress: one day he went up to the high slopes and threw away all the alphabets he had used to teach 'poor Giorgio's 3 sons'. At three in the morning on 8 August 1883, Giorgio died, asking for Lear and saying, 'Nicola, Lambi, Dmitri.' Lear and Giorgio's sons closed his eyes and bound his hands. Astonished at how peaceful he looked, Lear went into the garden to write his diary in the dawn. 'O dear Giorgio you are gone', he wrote, 'but be as good a guide and angel to me as for so many years.'

He did not want to go home. He thought longingly of faraway places – South America, Japan or Java – but all he could manage was a long walk through Umbria and Tuscany, sketching as he went, with Dmitri carrying his portfolio, as his father had done. Giorgio was buried in Mendrisio, but Lear also bought a plot in the San Foce cemetery in San Remo, a few hundred yards from the Villa Emily, where he put up a large, pale, arched headstone in Giorgio's memory, using the Italian form of his surname 'Cocali'. The plot next to this, he bought for his own grave.

After Giorgio died, Lear went back to *In Memoriam*, quoting the opening stanza, as he had done many times before.

> I held it truth, with him who sings
> To one clear harp in divers tones,
> That men may rise on stepping-stones
> Of their dead selves to higher things.

503

Could one rise, he wondered, not on the dead selves of the self, but on the good selves of others? Could he make Giorgio a stepping stone? He shook off all memories of rows, tantrums and drunkenness and recalled only Giorgio's good side, writing emotionally to Emily Tennyson:

It is well for foolish people to say, – how can a mere servant be such a stepping stone? – but to one who for 30 years knew George's constant fidelity, activity, humility, goodness of disposition, – endless cheerfulness – honesty – patience, & untold other virtues. It is plain since his death, that as a 'stepping stone' he is ever of more value to my life now than in all the 30 years of his unbroken kindness & service.

I wish I could think that I had merited such a friend, & that I had never been hasty or cross; but if *anything* is known to those separated from us, then *all* may be known, & more allowance be made for faults than self-accusing memory may imagine.

Lear clung to this idea. It was impossible, he felt, to accept that life was all '"a dream & a waste": rather let me believe in the stepping-stone theory.' He made lists of stepping-stone people, including his sister Ann and his gardener Giuseppe, and hung their photos in his bedroom.

The Kokali troubles were not over. During the next two years Nicola became increasingly ill and Dmitri, whom Lear had taught Italian and English – they read *Robinson Crusoe* together – and who had looked after Lear so lovingly, was found stealing and sent back to Corfu. (Eventually he settled as a schoolteacher in a village on Paxos.) At the start of 1885 Nicola was the only one left in the Villa Tennyson, devoted to Lear but sick with consumption. He began spitting blood and in his illness revealed to a shocked Lear another side of Giorgio: a father whose returns to Corfu they had dreaded, who kept another woman, abused his wife and bullied his children. It was as if, in thirty years, Lear had never known him at all. Nicola died in March 1885, aged only thirty-four, and was buried in the plot in San Foce cemetery, his name added to his father's memorial.

*

Lear's sister Ellen had died soon after Giorgio, aged eighty-six. Her wealth went to the Boswell family but she had bought a house in Texas for Frederick, and left Lear a handy £500. More money came from the house. The Villa Emily had been let to a string of tenants but in late February 1884 he finally found a buyer: *the old Villa Emily is no longer mine,* he wrote, with heavy underlining. He had already reduced the price from £7000 to £3000, and in the end it went for 40,000 francs: £1,600. But still, it was a relief. At last, he thought, he could repay Northbrook's loan (although he did not manage this for another two years). But his old house still seemed part of his life: while it lay empty that spring, John and Catherine Symonds rented it to find a calm place for their daughter Madge to recover from typhoid fever.

As if collapsing after the farewell to the Villa Emily, Lear fell ill with pleurisy. It took him a long time to recover but with Dmitri pulling and pushing him into railway carriages like 'a sack of hay', in late May he managed to get up to Recoara near Vicenza, where he fell in love with Palladian architecture. He was shocked, though, by the bigotry of 'well-bred & educated' American Southerners staying at his hotel. One family, he wrote, 'electrified me by their opinion on "Slave Emancipation"':

The Civil War, in their view, had nothing to do with a hatred of slavery, though hatred of slavery was used as a factor in the matter. It was wholly in substance a political move against the Southern States. Not one of us, nor of thousands in America, would sit at table with a black man or woman! 'But', said I to one of the sons, 'you would sit in a room with your dog?' 'Dog? Yes, Sir! But you can't compare an inferior creature such as a negro is with a dog.'

Dodging such encounters when he could, Lear worked on his Tennyson project. He had wept – not difficult for Lear – when Tennyson was made a peer the previous December. (Though he did wonder, as a matter of interest, whether royalty and peers cut their own toe-nails: 'Thank the Lord that you are not a Centipede.') He was cheered in his work by the affectionate encouragement of Emily and Hallam. Lear had written sweetly in November 1883, when Hallam became engaged to Audrey Boyle, urging them to marry 'directly-suddenly' and to come along the Corniche for their wedding trip and stay next door in the Hotel Royal. He gave them one of his paintings as a wedding present.

He was cheered too by the response to his watercolours and drawings in Wardour Street: his friend Alfred Seymour told him he had never done anything better, picking out 'the poetical and mysterious' Calabrian Pentedattilo, and the 'lovely Corsican drawings'. But it was hard to concentrate. He mused on time passing: it seemed extraordinary to him that Frank Lushington and Chichester Fortescue were both now sixty-one. He brooded on faith, and a life hereafter. There had to be an afterlife, or at least the hope of one: 'We *know* nothing, but is that a reason we should not cling to a hope of reunion after death?' Playing his part among the British expats he went to church, stuck crossly between Fenton's evangelical sermons and the High Church effusions of the Revd Verschoyle. Where, he wondered, were the moderate followers of F. D. Maurice and Jowett and his old friend Arthur Penrhyn Stanley, whose death he sorely lamented? 'Is there no medium between damning Jews and Catholics to eternal burning and . . . walking among those dear candlestix?'

In 1884 he wrote a story-sequel to 'The Owl and the Pussy-cat', and when he was ill the following year he drafted another in verse. They had different settings but in both versions the Pussy-cat, now definitely female, dies suddenly, leaving her brood – like the Congreves and Kokalis, and, in his mind, Lear himself – as motherless children. In the story the Owl is shipwrecked and the children survive alone, 'though in a bereaved and bohemian condition'; in the poem, the widowed owl sings sadly to his old guitar:

> But with the feathers of his tail he wiped his weeping eyes,
> And in the hollow of a tree in Sila's inmost maze
> We made a happy home and here we pass our obvious days.

Lear too passed his days calmly. He had a new servant, Luigi Rusconi from Milan, who was quick and clever and played chess with him in the kitchen. He was busy with his work and his garden, played the piano and enjoyed his music: when the young lithographer Frank Underhill was coming out that autumn, Lear wrote, 'if you only play JIGGS I won't have you at all. Even Chopin worries & fidgets me – but Mozart, Handel, Mendelsohn, Hayden, Schubert & sichlike, I delight in.' Above all his friends' visits and letters kept him going. 'He really *lived* upon the letters of his distant friends more than any man I have ever known,' said Frank, 'all the more since he became unable to carry out his wish to go on & on over the untravelled world.'

He thought nostalgically of those travels. In April 1885, Foord and Dickinson showed his watercolour drawings of Egypt, on sale at a miserable £5, and when Amelia Edwards reviewed them kindly in the *Academy*, Lear asked her advice about his own journals. 'I don't say – mind – that my "Nile Diaries of a Landscape Painter" would be worth the 99th part of a grasshopper's eyelash,' he wrote tentatively, but they might be worth something if considered as part of his art. She offered to introduce him to her own publishers, Harpers, but he put the scheme aside: he had enough on his hands with his Tennyson drawings. He had already mounted all the smaller drawings on card and written the lines from the poems beneath them: these little sketches were now his 'Eggs' as the early work had been; next the 'Chrysalisses' needed mounting too. When the great heat came, he took these to the Villa Figini in Barzano, on the plains of Brianza between Milan and Como. He could see the Alps in the distance and in the pure, breezy air he felt he had never met 'any summer place so everlastingly green & lovely'. Yet he still planned his book, and that autumn wrote a dedication to Emily.

In the Villa Tennyson he worked on, played the piano and read Trollope. Having started with *Can You Forgive Her?* he went back to the earlier novels and began the whole Barchester series, 'wonderfully delightful books', sending to London for five books at a time and buying still more in San Remo. Trollope, so blessedly prolific, would keep Lear happy to the end of his life, a strange, homesick return to the vicarages and country houses of England. In November 1885, that country-house world came back to him when Fortescue came to stay. He had been out of office since Gladstone resigned in June over the Irish Home Rule Bill, and now that the days of long meetings and dining with the queen at Balmoral were over he had time on his hands. Frank Underhill, who was helping Lear with the Tennyson lithographs, had the guest room, so Fortescue stayed down the road in the Hotel Royal. When he arrived, he was still grieving for Lady W.: 'Slept badly last night, full of my love – I had her glove in my hand.' He was glad to see Lear, and to walk round his garden, 'a magical contrast to the bare bank covered in rubbish wh. I left in March 1880 – lovely convolvulus, daturas, begonias, scarlet passion flowers.'

The garden of the Villa Tennyson

After about a week Fortescue caught a chill from sitting outside watching the sunset and collapsed into bed. Lear went to see him daily in snowy December days, feeling pretty weak himself: 'very feeble lunch – chiefly bread & butter & Parmeggiano cheese; also a whole bottle of Marsala!!!!!!!! . . . Sate with Carlingford till nearly 6. He is much better – but dreadfully weak. Coming back, I fell over Foss in the dining room & hurt my nose a good deal. Luigi set me up again.' Soon Fortescue was up but Lear was down. On Christmas Day he staggered over to dine at the hotel, 'saying he would not have come for anyone else, "except Frank Lushington"'. He cheered up over dinner but next day he was in bed with bronchitis; now it was Fortescue's turn to sit by his sick friend. They talked and talked, of James Stuart Mill, irreligion and Calvinism, of the queen and John Brown, of the horrors of Bulgarian massacres, but 'all political talk is better avoided,' Lear decided, 'for official partisans can only see with the eyes of their party'.

As he slowly recovered, Lear thought of the lines from Gray's 'Elegy in a Country Churchyard':

> Some pious drops the closing eye requires;
> Even from the tomb the voice of Nature cries,
> Even in our ashes live their wonted fires.

After Fortescue left, he turned back to a poem of his own that he had tinkered with for years, 'Some Incidents in the Life of my Uncle Arly'. He had begun it long ago for Emma Baring, Northbrook's daughter, and had scribbled verses from time to time – on the flyleaf of Walpole's letters, which he read when he was ill in 1873, and in letters to friends.

All the drafts mentioned the cricket landing on his nose. Now, in February 1886, on a day of fierce east wind: 'I did not rise at all, but kept still, & with a good fire cough less, & feeling better generally, thank God – at 2–3 – broth, boiled mutton & tacoli – sort of peas – very good sort of food. Also jelly – but no wine. Kept always in bed & read – (also writing "my aged Uncle Arly").' A week later, he told Ruskin that he was writing the poem, adding, 'I esteem it a thing to be thankful for that I remain as great a fool as ever I was.'

The title contained his name, 'Uncle Arly'. But it also hinted at a willed obliqueness: it was unclear: 'Un-cleArly'. If 'How pleasant to

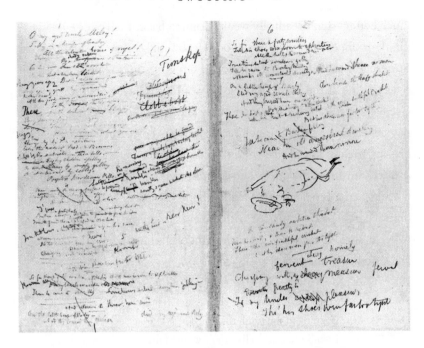

know Mr Lear' had been a teasing self-portrait, this was his whole life: his youthful love of natural history, his teaching and medical drawings, his forty-three years of wandering, from Bowman's Lodge to the Villa Emily. Always his cricket had chirruped in his ear, poetry's lasting power, the call that 'never – nevermore' would leave him. Lear's poem defied time, with its upside-down sunset and sunrise. It described age and childhood, mocking 'Twinkle, twinkle, little star' – as Lewis Carroll had done. It combined lyrical melody and down-to-earth chat. It was true to himself.

> O my agèd Uncle Arly! –
> Sitting on a heap of Barley
>   All the silent hours of night, –
> Close beside a leafy thicket: –
> On his nose there was a Cricket, –
> In his hat a Railway-Ticket; –
>   (But his shoes were far too tight.)

Long ago, in youth, he squander'd
All his goods away, and wander'd
   To the Timskoop Hills afar.
There, on golden sunsets blazing
Every morning found him gazing, –
Singing – 'Orb! you're quite amazing!
   How I wonder what you are!'

Like the ancient Medes and Persians,
Always by his own exertions
   He subsisted on those hills; –
Whiles, – by teaching children spelling, –
Or at times by merely yelling, –
Or at intervals by selling
   'Propter's Nicodemus Pills'.

Later, in his morning rambles
He perceived the moving brambles
   Something square and white disclose; –
'Twas a First-class Railway-Ticket;
But, on stooping down to pick it
Off the ground, – a pea-green Cricket
   Settled on my uncle's Nose.

Never – never more, – oh! never,
Did that Cricket leave him ever, –
   Dawn or evening, day or night; –
Clinging as a constant treasure, –
Chirping with a cheerious measure, –
Wholly to my uncle's pleasure, –
   (Though his shoes were far too tight.)

So for three-and-forty winters,
Till his shoes were worn to splinters,
   All those hills he wander'd o'er, –
Sometimes silent; – sometimes yelling; –
Till he came to Borly-Melling,

Near his old ancestral dwelling; –
    (But his shoes were far too tight.)

On a little heap of Barley
Died my agèd uncle Arly,
    And they buried him one night; –
Close beside the leafy thicket; –
There, – his hat and Railway-Ticket; –
There, – his ever-faithful Cricket; –
    (But his shoes were far too tight.)

He was pleased with his poem and sent it to several friends, often quoting Gray's 'Elegy' in his letters, 'even in our ashes live their wonted fires'. It was, he said, 'the last nonsense poem I shall ever write'.

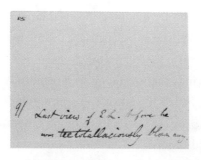

9/ Last view of EL. before he
was teetotallaciously blown away,

42: *PAX VOBISCUM*

A few months after finishing 'Uncle Arly', on the endpapers of his new
copy of Gordon Cummings's *At Home in Fiji* – his wanderlust now
confined to books – Lear wrote:

> Quacks vobiscum Uncle Arly
> Sitting on your heap of Barley
> Quacks vobiscum – every Duck
> Quacks vobiscum – two by two
> Quacks vobiscum – as they flew
> Through the morning sky so blue
> Quacks vobiscum – what a lark!

The birds were back, quacking in Latin the final blessing of the Mass,
'*Pax vobiscum*' – peace be with you. '*Pax vobiscum, serve fidem*' – keep
the faith.

Death did not frighten Lear, but he wanted to get things in order.
When he sold the Villa Emily he had made a will leaving £1500 to Sarah's
granddaughter Emily, and small sums to Hubert and Arny Congreve
and his godchildren Percy Coombe, Allan Nevill and Lizzie Senior; five
thousand drawings would go to Northbrook and his letters and diaries
to Fortescue. When Northbrook came to stay in April 1886, he gave
him several hundred drawings and watercolour sketches. (Northbrook

later had these beautifully mounted in seven large volumes, alongside the journals of the Abruzzi and Calabria, a tribute to his deep affection.) But that April Lear also asked him to witness a new will. This time, as well as more drawings that would go to Northbrook in their specially designed cabinets, he left the house to Sarah's granddaughter Emily in New Zealand, his painting materials to Frank Underhill and small legacies to Lambi and Dmitri. All his other papers and drawings would go to Frank Lushington. Emily's daughter Sophie remembered visiting Frank's house when she was a girl: 'He opened drawer after drawer of exquisite sketches, and now he would say, "Where will you go now, Egypt, Palestine, India, Italy, Greece"; and many other lovely places.' (Much later, in 1929, the bulk of these were sold.) Frank gave drawings to friends and patrons, including the Earl of Derby, and returned many letters to the writers or their families. But while Constance Strachey edited his correspondence with Chichester Fortescue, the letters to Frank himself disappeared and so did Lear's diaries of their time in Corfu. Perhaps Frank burned them, or Kate did after he died in 1901. Or are they still in some trunk, waiting to be discovered?

In February 1886 he was immensely pleased by a tribute from Ruskin in the February *Pall Mall Gazette*: 'I really do not know any author to whom I am half so grateful for my idle self, as Edward Lear. I shall put him first of my hundred authors.' His nonsense would live on, exerting a largely unrecognised influence on Modernist and later writers in Britain and America – on Eliot, Joyce, Auden and Stevie Smith, on Wallace Stevens, Elizabeth Bishop, Marianne Moore and John Ashbery, and many other poets, comedians, songwriters and illustrators. In a poll in 2012 a whole nation put 'The Owl and the Pussy-cat' at the top of their list: it was Britain's favourite poem. It took more time for Lear to be recognised as an artist: after Lady Ashburton's death, the great *Kinchenjunga* sold for £5 and as late as the 1950s his sketches and drawings could be picked up for peanuts. It is only in the last fifty years that his landscapes have been valued for their skill and their wistful, luminous beauty.

In the 1880s, when he thought of posterity, Lear thought of his paintings and, more and more, of his Tennyson drawings. He still worked on these, and on his paintings, but his health was a problem. In his garden in June 1886, 'the big magnolia flowers, also the nightingales and robins' were 'a satisfaction – but his boots were far too tight, i.e. my chest oppression and cough are a sad set off'. In the summer he went to Brianza, breathing better and cheerfully going back to his Marsala and Barolo, but the heat was tremendous, driving him into the mountains, to Mendrisio. In early September he took a trip to Lucerne, seeing the lakes and Alps that had inspired him when he first saw them fifty years ago, but here he fell seriously ill, and briefly his San Remo doctor, Dr Hassall, feared for his life. Within a month, he could shuffle across the room in his slippers, but when Frank saw him in November he was shocked. He told Hallam that 'my dear old Lear' was better, but 'sadly aged and feeble, very crippled at times with the rheumatism – totters about within the house – hardly ever goes out at all even on his terrace just outside the windows'. Luigi dressed and undressed him, putting him to bed at six. He was so disabled by rheumatism, he told Emily Tennyson, that often he was not up to writing at all. He managed a letter full of jokes to Fortescue, but ended, 'He only said, I'm very weary. The rheumatiz he said. He said, it's awful dull and dreary. I think I'll go to bed.'

Photographs filled the wall above Lear's fireplace, among them Emily Tennyson, Thomas and Evelyn Baring, Chichester Fortescue, Arthur Stanley, Charles Church, the doctor's wife Mrs Hassall, Gertrude Lushington and Gussie. 'There!' he wrote to Hallam, telling him of these. 'It ain't everybody as has such friends!' But while Lear treasured his old friends he withdrew more and more from San Remo society, confessing cheerfully to Wilkie Collins that 'of what is called the Colony here I know – I am happy to say – nothing. Neither perpetual church services (high & low – candlestix or cursing) are to my taste, nor are balls & Lawn Tennis among my weaknesses.' One day Constance and Eddie Strachey caught sight of him from the train going through San Remo. It was Sunday and he was walking dreamily away from the station, 'out of earshot of our calls. The sad, bent, loosely-clad figure with hands clasped behind him, we did not know was walking away from us then and for ever, for we never saw him again.'

He was far from well over the coming winter. Sometimes his hand-writing became wild. Once he fell out of bed in the dark, could not get up and lay there until day broke: 'Hardlines!' he wrote, but felt lucky that he was not badly hurt. He was pleased when friends called in, and by March 1887, when Northbrook and his daughter Emma Baring came to stay in San Remo, he could walk to the lower terrace and back and have lunch with them in style: their visit was 'a very great blessing, and I wish them back hourly'. Back they came a month later, walking in suddenly when he was already in bed, 'And sate knitting & talking till 10.30. A very great pleasure. We had great fits of laughter about the Welsh Epitaphs, making lots of others for fun.' These included one for Agnes Pears:

> Below the high Cathedral Stairs
> Lie the remains of Agnes Pears:
> Her name was Wiggs it was not Pears,
> But Pears was put to rhyme with stairs.

Foss kept him company, 'Foss always here'. Foss was supposed to be there in April when Lear had his photograph taken, sitting in a chair in his bedroom. He reported this exchange to Fortescue:

Manipulator (From the depths of the curtain and the black box): Mr Lear!
Mr Lear: How do you know my name?
Manipulator: I used to see you 35 years ago at Hullmandels, the lithographers. I was the boy. You ain't altered.

In the photograph Lear's arm is bent because he was holding Foss, who jumped down at the last minute. He wanted a photograph to give to his friends, including Gussie, to whom he had written when he was ill: she came out to see him, turning up without warning, 'more nice and charming than ever'. In an absurd repetition, he thought again whether he might, finally, ask her to marry him, and again did not. While she was there she read Wordsworth to him to pass the time, and on her return sent him a volume of the poems and a paper cutter, to cut the pages. In time she married again: when Lear died Frank sent the Wordsworth volume back to her and Gussie later gave it to her husband's young nephew, the artist Paul Nash, who proudly inscribed his name.

Lear in 1887

The days lengthened, the sun shone, and the passion flower and purple clematis were full of flowers. Lear passed his seventy-fifth birthday on 12 May 1887, and went back to Tennyson. The £500 that Ellen had left him had almost all gone on his experiments in reproducing the pictures, but he thought the proofs of the lithographs and autotype were always a failure: he had ordered the autotype company to send all his drawings back and now he was thinking of even more expensive processes, such as chromolithography and the new 'platinotype'. To cheer him, Hallam sent a young American publisher, Dana Estes, who was planning a Tennyson edition, to look at his drawings. Lear perked up but Estes, clearly taken aback, told Hallam tactfully that 'some portions are unfinished in detail, and would require very artistic treatment at the hands of an engraver or etcher'. He could see, he said, that publication was 'the dearest wish of the old gentleman's heart', and that Lear almost despaired this would happen. Lear was right. The only book, published two years after his death, was a private edition of one hundred copies using a selection of the drawings for 'The Daisy', 'The Palace of Art' and 'To E.L. on his Travels in Greece'. Tennyson signed all the copies, he said, for the sake of his old friend, Edward Lear.

Lear's last months were not sad. Luigi left 'in a vast tantrum', complaining of too much work, and Giuseppe Orsini arrived. Lear disliked him at first – he thought he smelled and looked like the hefty Irish 'Liberator' Daniel O'Connell – but Giuseppe turned out to be gentle, slow and devoted. Lear also had a young cook, Cesare, who raised pigeons, and he took great pleasure watching the ten birds '& their punctual ways – 2 hours exactly on their eggs – & 2 hours liberty'. (Giuseppe thought they had little watches under their wings that they wound up at night.) The birds' fluttering beauty among the full-blown roses pleased him: every day he looked from his window on 'the same goldengreen of the new terrace, the sparkle of pigeons' wings, the pulled blue of the sea breaking beyond. What continuance of heavenly weather!!' He lay, and read, and watched the birds.

In July he managed the jolting journey up to Andorno on the way to the Valle d'Aosta in the mountains north of Turin and even here, in the hot summer months with 'rumbly bumbly thunderstorms' and annoying clouds of flies, he worked on the Tennyson drawings. Often, though, his eyesight failed. He still wrote his letters. As Frank Lushington said, they kept up 'the affectionate regular correspondence we had maintained for many years, but by degrees his letters became shorter & showed failure of memory'. Gradually he gave up writing his diary. When he came home Foss was staggering around, stiff on one side. He died in early September, and was buried 'deep below the Figtree at the end of the Orange walk'. Foss was seventeen, a grand age for a cat, but Lear thought he was thirty, they had been together so long.

Lear grieved for Foss. He wrote letters, saw friends, and planned another two hundred Tennyson drawings in a larger size. 'Very absurd probably,' he admitted. Then he had a fall. It was not this, though, that caused the pains in his side, his doctor said, but too much champagne, 'a great and ridiculous bore, inasmuch as Frank Lushington has just sent me 30 Bottles as a present'. The champagne would have helped him celebrate: he was delighted this autumn when an article in the *Spectator* praised his nonsense books and picked out his drawings as 'enabling him to quadruple the laughable effect of his text by an inexhaustible profusion of the quaintest designs'. The review called him 'the parent of modern nonsense-writers'. 'Very nice indeed,' said Lear.

When the cold days came he sometimes walked on the terrace but often he just lay on the sofa, reading Trollope. He finished his household accounts, jotting down payments up to the end of November. Underneath these, a final entry read, 'Wrote to Frank Lushington, 6. January 1888'. Then he took to his bed. All the time he lay there, Giuseppe said, he talked of his friends. He became weaker, tender to all around him, Dr Hassall said, 'as by way of a leavetaking', and even when spoken to in English he generally answered in Italian. On 29 January 1888, just after midnight, he asked Giuseppe to take down a final message. Giuseppe sent this to Frank Lushington, writing a touch too eloquently, perhaps, to be really faithful, but claiming that 'with the greatest grief I act as interpreter of his last words – they are these precise and holy words'. '*Mio caro Giuseppe . . .*'

I feel that I am dying. You will render me a sacred service in telling my friends and relations that my last thought was for them, especially the Judge and Lord Northbrook and Lord Carlingford. I cannot find words sufficient to thank my good friends for the good they have always done me. I did not answer their letters because I could not write, as no sooner did I take a pen in my hand than I felt as if I were dying.

After that he slipped into unconsciousness. He died just after two in the morning. 'It was most peaceful,' Mrs Hassall told Constance Strachey, 'the great good heart simply ceasing to beat.'

Lear was buried among the cypresses and crumbling tombs in the cemetery of San Foce where light flashes off the sea beyond the wall and at noon insects hum and at dawn and dusk the birds sing. Italian law demanded a quick funeral, but it was sad, thought Mrs Hassall, that for a man who had so many friends, none could be there. Frank Lushington rushed out as soon as the telegram arrived and arranged for a headstone. Lear had wanted only his name and dates, but Frank thought 'none of his friends would have wanted him to rest without something more'. His inscription, describing Lear as 'landscape painter in many lands', ends with lines from Tennyson's 'To E. L., on his Travels in Greece'.

> *– all things fair,*
> *With such a pencil such a pen,*
> *You shadow'd forth to distant men*
> *I read and felt that I was there.*

His grave is next to the memorial to Giorgio and Nicola, their head-stones matching. Lear is not with the 'Colony', the rows of British expats who have a large space of their own. He is just round a corner, on a separate path. Slightly apart.

There was an Old Person of Hove,
Who frequented the depths of a grove
Where he studied his books, with the wrens and the rooks,
That tranquil Old Person of Hove.

Pax vobiscum, Mr Lear.

ACKNOWLEDGEMENTS

Like all admirers of Edward Lear, I am indebted for her work on his nonsense, art, life, and letters to the late Vivien Noakes, whose papers are now at Somerville College, Oxford. I have gained enormously, too, from current scholars, especially Hugh Haughton on nonsense, letters and language and Bob Peck on Lear's natural history; and it has been an extra pleasure to feel surrounded by enthusiastic colleagues like James Williams, Matt Bevis and Sara Lodge, who are all writing on Lear's poetry and intellectual culture. My sense of being part of a collaborative venture has been heightened by the support of Marco Graziosi, who is not only transcribing Lear's diaries, but also runs the 'Blog of Bosh', which contains bibliographies, guides to manuscripts, updates on recent sales and many articles.

I am grateful to the Lushington family, as heirs to the estate of Franklin Lushington, for permission to quote from unpublished Lear material, and to Dr Peter Gillies and Dr David Michell for permission to use documents in their possession. I would also like to thank the owners who have allowed me to reproduce paintings, as noted in the List of Illustrations, and the archivists, curators and dealers who have helped my search, particularly Ann Manuel at Somerville College, Oxford; Grace Timmins at the Tennyson Research Centre, Lincoln; Hope Mayo at the Houghton Library, Harvard; Colin Harrison and Katherine Wodehouse at the Ashmolean Museum, Oxford.

This has been an adventure, and I have many people to thank. Clem Fisher took me into the back rooms of the Liverpool World Museum and showed me the 'types' of Lear's birds and animals. Charles Lewsen has been warmly interested throughout; conversations with Sara Lodge have stirred me on; and I have enjoyed my correspondence with Susie

Winter, who is writing on Sarah Lear's life in New Zealand. The Rt Hon. the Earl of Derby kindly allowed me to see his collection and reproduce paintings and drawings; Stephen Lloyd guided me round Knowsley; and Christina Kokosalakis provided welcome assistance. Stephen Pollock gave expert advice on the nature of Lear's epilepsy; Charles Nugent shared his knowledge of Lear's watercolours and travels in the Lake District; Stephen Duckworth his experience of Athos; and David Taylor his research into the Lushington family. For ideas, talk and other good things my thanks go to Christine Carswell, Mary Evans, Will May, Wendy Rowland, Rona Sulkin, Peter Swaab and Marina Warner. And I am more than grateful to Nick Roe, who read the text with meticulous attention.

At Rogers, Coleridge and White, my agent Gill Coleridge has guided me through with great warmth, and Matt Turner is always invaluable. At Faber & Faber I am indebted to Julian Loose, my editor for many years, and since his departure I feel lucky to have been edited by Mitzi Angel, a fine publisher and ever-encouraging presence. I could not do without Kate Ward, who always manages the intricacies of production with skill, humour and grace. I'm grateful too to Pedro Nelson, Donna Payne and Kate Burton, and to Eleanor Rees and Peter McAdie for copy-editing and proofreading, Sarah Ereira for the index, and Stephen Page for his support. In New York I am grateful to Melanie Jackson, to Jonathan Galassi for his much-appreciated encouragement, and to all the team at Farrar, Straus and Giroux.

I owe special thanks to Julian Barnes, who gave me the push I needed to begin, and to the memory of the late Pat Kavanagh. Alison Samuel has always been a great person to talk to. And above all, thank you again to Hermione Lee, best of readers and best of friends, and to John Barnard. My children and grandchildren have been tolerant allies, reading nonsense aloud with gusto, and my deepest thanks go to Steve for untangling family histories, for travelling with me to Lear places at home and abroad, and, indeed, for everything.

LIST OF ILLUSTRATIONS

Unless noted below, all works are by Lear, and illustrations to the limericks, alphabets, stories, botany and nonsense songs are taken from early *Nonsense* books. Lear's drawings, watercolours and oils are scattered between many galleries and libraries. Several collections are now digitised in part or in full, notably those of the British Museum Department of Prints and Drawings; the Victoria & Albert Museum; the Ashmolean, Oxford; the Paul Mellon Collection, Yale Center for British Art; and the Houghton Library, Harvard University. The Houghton's great landscape archive is based on Northbrook's collection of approximately 3,530 drawings, bought in the 1930s by W. B. O. Field, still in Lear's two wooden storage cabinets, plus additional gifts from the former curator, Philip Hofer. The main categories are Drawings of Animals and Birds, *c.* 1831–36 (MS Typ 55.12); Landscape Drawings, 1834–84 (MS Typ 55.11, MS Typ 55.26, TypDr805.L513); and Miscellaneous Drawings, 1849–1866 (Typ 55.14), while other files contain drawings and proofs of the nonsense, and music.

9 'Brother Chicken', *Queery Leary Nonsense* (2nd edition, 1911)

13 Bowman's Lodge, Holloway

19 Portrait of Edward Lear, by Ann Lear (*c.*1821). Peter Lear, Gillies Collection, photo Stephen A'Court.

31 *Hexandria Monogynia* MS Typ 55.4, Houghton Library, Harvard University

33 'There was an old person so silly', Duncan manuscript (1864), *Bosh & Nonsense*, (1982)

35 *Peppering House* (1829). Private collection

46 *Feather and business card.* Courtesy of Charles Nugent. Photo Guy Peppiatt Fine Art

51 *Red and Yellow Macaw, Illustrations of the Family of Psittacidae, or Parrots* (1832)

55 'Parrots and People' (*c.* 1830–2). MS Typ 55.9 Houghton

59 *Culminated Toucan*, from John Gould, *A Monograph of the Ramphastidae* (1834)

60 *Eagle Owl*, from John Gould, *The Birds of Europe* (1837)

62 *Heads of Ara Ararauna (Linn.)* Courtesy of the Rt Hon. the Earl of Derby, 2017

66 Silhouette of Edward Lear, aged around twenty. National Portrait Gallery, London

69 *Spectacled Owl*, watercolour. Courtesy of the Rt Hon. the Earl of Derby, 2017

69 *Wattle-crowned Crane*, watercolour. Courtesy of the Rt Hon. the Earl of Derby, 2017

69 *Quebec Marmot*, watercolour. Courtesy of the Rt Hon. the Earl of Derby, 2017

70 *Malayan Giant Squirrel*, watercolour. Courtesy of the Rt Hon. the Earl of Derby, 2017

72 'Portraites of the inditchenous beestes of New Olland', Pierpont Morgan Museum and Library, New York, Gift of Mrs Paul Pennoyer, 1963

75 *Knowsley Hall, September 1835*. Courtesy of the Rt Hon. the Earl of Derby, 2017

81 *Head of a Chimpanzee* (17 October 1835). MS Typ 55.12, Houghton

82 *Ephialtes* (Scops-eared owl). Courtesy of the Rt Hon. the Earl of Derby, 2017

84 'When I dreamed I was young and innocent'. Pierpont Morgan Library, New York

87 *Miss Maniac*, MS Typ 55.6, Houghton

89 *Robin Grey*, H. W. Liebert, *Lear in the Original*, 1975

90 *St Kiven and the Gentle Kathleen*. Donald C. Gallup, 1973

95 'There was an Old Man of Tobago', H. W. Liebert, *Lear in the Original*, 1975

98 *Umbrellifera*, MS Typ 55.14, Houghton

103 *Scafell Pike from Styhead Pass* (1836). British Museum

109 *Rome from Monte Pincio* (1841) from *Views in Rome and its Environs* (1841)

116 *Temple of Venus and Rome*, (1840). Yale Center for British Art, Paul Mellon Fund

119 *Campagna of Rome from Villa Mattei*, from *Views in Rome and its Environs* (1841)

123 *Amalfi* (1838). Victoria & Albert Museum, London

126 Penry Williams, *Civitella Gazette*, 1839. British Museum

128 *Edward Lear* by Wilhelm Marstrand (1840). National Portrait Gallery

131 'Caius Marius in the marsh' (1841). Courtesy of Justin Schiller

135 *Romulus and Remus* (1841). Frederick R. Koch Collection, Beinecke

136 *Mr Lear recovers his hat* (1842). Frederick R. Koch Collection, Beinecke

137 '*L discovers Captn Hornby's office*'. H. W. Liebert, *Lear in the Original*, 1975

139 '*L . . . considers his horse far from tame*'. British Museum

142 *Lago di Fucino*, from *Illustrated Excursions in Italy* (1846)

145 *San Vittorino* (1845). MS Typ 55.26. Houghton

151 Cover of *A Book of Nonsense* (1861)

160 'There was an Old Man of New York', Frederick R. Koch Collection, Beinecke

166 *Syracuse quarries* (1847). MS Typ 55.26, Houghton

168 *Palizzi*, from *Journals of a Landscape Painter in Southern Calabria* (1852)

169 *Child in Calabrian costume*. Northbrook folios, Liverpool Central Library

172 Ann Lear by Mrs Arundale, 1847. Peter Lear Gillies Collection, photo Stephen A'Court

175 *Avlona* (detail), from *Journals of a Landscape Painter in Albania* (1851)

177 *Athens* (1848). MS Typ 55.26, Houghton Library, Harvard University

181 *Monastir*, from *Journals of a Landscape Painter in Albania* (1851)

185 *Khimara*, from *Journals of a Landscape Painter in Albania* (1851)

187 *Suli*, from *Journals of a Landscape Painter in Albania* (1851)

191 *Outside the Walls of Suez* (1849). Yale Center for British Art, Gift of Donald C. Gallup

192 *Near Wadi el-Sheikh* (1849). MS Typ 55.26, Houghton

194 Franklin Lushington, *c.* 1840. Private collection.

201 *Lear at the RA Schools*, Strachey, *Letters*

210 *The Mountains of Thermopylae*, 1852. Bristol Museum and Art Gallery

213 '*Illyrian woodlands*', *Akhrida, Albania*. MS Typ 55.7 Houghton

220 *'The vast Akrokeraunian Walls'*, *Khimara, Albania*. MS Typ 55.7 Houghton

222 *'Morn broadened.' Civitella di Subiaco (Italy)*. MS Typ 55.7, Houghton

228 *Philae* (1863). Yale Center for British Art, Paul Mellon Collection

234 *A shepherd at Kerkira* (1856). MS Typ 55.26, Houghton

236 *Corfu from Ascension* (1862). Yale Center for British Art, Gift of Donald C. Gallup

243 *The Monastery of Zografu*. Ashmolean Museum, University of Oxford

244 Lear, Lushington and friends. Lushington Family Album, MS Typ 1181, Houghton

247 Nuneham (1860) Berger Collection, Denver Art Museum, Colorado

248 *Lear and Fortescue at Ardee* (1857). Strachey, *Letters*

251 *Edward Lear* by Holman Hunt (1857). Lady Lever Art Gallery, Liverpool

259 *The theatre, Petra* (1858). Private collection

260 *Masada* (1858). Legion of Honour Museum, San Francisco

262 *'A was an Ass'*, Tatton alphabet (1849), facsimile 1926

263 *'W was a whale'*, Gertrude Lushington alphabet, MS Typ 55.14, Houghton

265 *'B was once a little bear'*. MS Typ 55.14, Houghton

265 *'M was once a little mouse'*. MS Typ 55.14, Houghton

268 *'Thistles & Moles'*, MS Typ 55.14 Houghton

283 'There was an Old Man of Lodore', Duncan manuscript (1864), *Bosh & Nonsense* (1982)

284 Oscar Gustave Rejlander, *The Tennysons at Farringford* (c. 1862). Museum of Reading

286 *Farringford* (1864). Tennyson Research Centre, Lincoln.

290 *The Temple of Apollo at Bassae* (c. 1854–5). The Fitzwilliam Museum, Cambridge

300 'There was a young lady of Lucca'. MS Typ 55. Houghton

311 *Lear the artist*. Strachey, *Letters*

312 *Cedars of Lebanon* (1862). Private collection: photo Charles Nahum Ltd

316 *Beachy Head* (1862). Private collection

318 Lear's Corfu gallery. Strachey, *Letters*

320 'There was an old man with a Book'. Ashmolean Museum, Oxford

323 *Cape Lefkada* (Cape Ducato), from *Views in the Seven Ionian Islands* (1863)

326 *Palaiokastritsa, Corfu*, from *Views in the Seven Ionian Islands* (1863)

331 *Mount Ida from Phre* (1864). British Museum

337 *Oneglia, Riviera di Ponente, 1864*. Ashmolean Museum, Oxford

338 *Venice* (1865). By kind permission of David Reid: photo Bonhams

344 Augusta Bethell. Private collection, Royal Academy Catalogue, 1985

354 Lear in Egypt. Courtesy of Henry Sotheran Ltd.

355 *Near Gau el Kebir* (1867). Yale Center for British Art, Gift of Donald C. Gallup

357 *Abu Simbel* (1867). Yale Center for British Art, Gift of Donald C. Gallup

360 Letter to Anna Duncan, 1865. Beinecke

383 *Calico Pie* (1868). MS Typ 55.14, Houghton

386 *Gertrude Lushington*, 1870. Lushington Family Album, MS Typ 1181, Houghton

391 *The Forest of Bavella, Corsica* (1868). MS Typ 55.26, Houghton

393 *Ajaccio*, from *Journal of a Landscape Painter in Corsica* (1870)

398 *Manypeeplia Upsidownia*. MS Typ 55.14, Houghton

403 *The Goodnatured Grey Gull*. MS Typ 55.14 Houghton

414 'There was a young lady in white'. MS 55.1, Houghton

418 'Lear shows his name'. Strachey, *Later Letters*

424 Lear and Foss. Strachey, *Later Letters*

425 Villa Emily (1870s). Strachey, *Later Letters*

427 *Mr Lear Stamps & Dances for Joy* (1871). Somerville College, Oxford

428 Lear watering the flowers. Strachey, *Later Letters*

430 Lear in a tree, Strachey, *Later Letters*

435 Lear and Giorgio on an elephant (1873). Strachey, *Later Letters*

436 *Lucknow* (1873). MS Typ 55.26, Houghton

441 *Benares* (1873). MS Typ 55.26, Houghton

442 *Tollygunge, Calcutta* (1873). Yale Center for British Art, Paul Mellon Collection

444 *Kinchenjunga from Darjeeling* (1875–7). National Museum of Wales, Cardiff

446 'There was an old man whose Giardino'. New York Public Library

469 'There was an old person whose tears'. New York Public Library

470 *Monte Rosa from Monte Generoso* (1878). MS Typ 55.26, Houghton

474 '*How pleasant to know Mr Lear*' (1879). British Library

478 'The Stripy Bird', *Queery Leary Nonsense* (1911)

480 '*For all remembrance is an arch'*. MS Typ 55.7, Houghton

482 Letter to Evelyn Baring. *Queery Leary Nonsense* (1911)

485 Letter to Emily Tennyson, 1855. Beinecke

488. *Kasr es Saàd (Egypt)* (1856). Legion of Honour Museum, San Francisco.

490 '*Athos – all things fair'. The Monastery of St Dionysius*, MS Typ 55.7, Houghton

491 '*A looming bastion fringed with fire', Coast of Travancore, India*. MS Typ 55.7, Houghton

493 Sketch for *Enoch Arden's Island*. Tennyson Research Centre, Lincoln

494 *A walk on a windy day*, 5, 1860. Beinecke

495 Letters received and answered. Diary, 1880. MS Eng 797.3, Houghton

496 Lear as Archbishop. Strachey, *Later Letters*

498 Giorgio Kokali. Strachey, *Later Letters*

501 *The Heraldic Blazon of Foss. Nonsense Songs and Stories* (1898)

508 The garden of Villa Tennyson (1881). Strachey, *Later Letters*

510 *Uncle Arly*, rough draft. Beinecke

517 Lear in 1887. Strachey, *Later Letters*

519 Foss's grave. Strachey, *Later Letters*

521 Gravestones of Giorgio and Nicola Cocali, and Edward Lear, San Remo. Strachey, *Later Letters*

ABBREVIATIONS

AT Alfred, Lord Tennyson
EL Edward Lear
ET Emily Tennyson
Ann Ann Lear
CF Chichester Fortescue
FC Fanny Coombe

FL Franklin Lushington
GC George Coombe
HC Hubert Congreve
HH Holman Hunt
Lady W Frances, Lady Waldegrave

Archives, Galleries and Collections

Baring	Baring Archive, Moorgate, London
Ashmolean	Ashmolean Museum, Oxford
Beinecke	Beinecke Library, Yale University
BL	British Library, London
BM	British Museum, London
Bodleian	Bodleian Library, Oxford
CUL	Cambridge University Library
Fitzwilliam	Fitzwilliam Museum, Cambridge
Glasgow	Glasgow University Special Collections
Houghton	Houghton Library, Harvard University
HRC	Harry Ransom Center, Austin, Texas
Huntington	Huntington Library, San Marino
John Rylands	John Rylands Library, University of Manchester
Liverpool	Liverpool Central Library Archives
LMA	London Metropolitan Archives (including Guildhall Library)
Morgan	Pierpont Morgan Library, New York
NLS	National Library of Scotland, Edinburgh
NMM	National Maritime Museum, Greenwich
NMS	National Museum of Scotland
NYPL	New York Public Library
Princeton	Special Collections, Princeton University Library
RA	Royal Academy, London
RSM	Royal Scottish Museum, Edinburgh
Taunton	Somerset Heritage Centre, Taunton
TRC	Tennyson Research Centre, Lincoln
V&A	Victoria & Albert Museum, London
VNA	Vivien Noakes Archive, Somerville College, Oxford

SELECT BIBLIOGRAPHY

For published works by Lear, manuscripts, articles and books on Lear and on nonsense generally, see Marco Graziosi's useful listings on nonsenselit.wordpress.com/bibliographies, and Peter Swaab, 'Edward Lear' in *Oxford Bibliographies* 2013, www.oxfordbibliographies.com; for the nonsense, see also the Select Bibliography in *Play*, 370–2; and for earlier criticism, Ann Colley, *Edward Lear and the Critics* (1993). For dispersal of Lear manuscripts and their collection, see Hope Mayo, 'The Edward Lear Collection at Harvard University', *Harvard Library Bulletin*, 22.2–3 (2011), 69–124.

In the list below, Lear's published and edited writings are presented chronologically, and other works alphabetically. Articles, essays and other books are cited in full in the relevant notes.

Edward Lear diary

D   Diary 1858–88, Houghton Library, Harvard University, MS Eng 797.3

Entries from 1858 to 1865 are transcribed by Marco Graziosi in 'The Edward Lear Diaries', https://leardiaries.wordpress.com/

Published works

Parrots	*Illustrations of the Family of Psittacidae, or Parrots* (1832)
Views	*Views in Rome and Its Environs* (1841)
BN (1846)	*A Book of Nonsense, by Derry down Derry* (1846, repr. 1855)
Excursions	*Illustrated Excursions in Italy*, 2 vols (1846)
Gleanings	*Gleanings from the Menagerie and Aviary at Knowsley Hall*, ed. J. E. Gray (1846)
Albania	*Journals of a Landscape Painter in Albania* (1851)
Calabria	*Journals of a Landscape Painter in Southern Calabria* (1852)
Tennyson Songs	*Poems and Songs by Alfred Tennyson, Set to Music by Edward Lear* (1853, expanded with five new songs, 1859)
BN (1861)	*A Book of Nonsense* (3rd edn, enlarged 1861)
Ionian Isles	*Views in the Seven Ionian Islands* (1863)

Corsica	*Journal of a Landscape Painter in Corsica* (1870)
NSSBA	*Nonsense Songs, Stories, Botany, and Alphabets* (1871)
MN	*More Nonsense, Pictures, Rhymes, Botany, &c.* (1872)
LaL	*Laughable Lyrics, A Fourth Book of Nonsense Poems, Songs, Botany, Music, &c.* (1877)

Posthumously published

	Poems of Alfred, Lord Tennyson, illustrated by Edward Lear (1889)
NSS	*Nonsense Songs and Stories* (1895)
QLN	*Queery Leary Nonsense*, ed. Lady Strachey (1911)
CNB	*The Complete Nonsense Book*, ed. Lady Strachey (1912)
Bird	*The Lear Coloured Bird Book for Children* (1912)
Jackson	*The Complete Nonsense of Edward Lear*, ed. Holbrook Jackson (1947)
T&Q	*Teapots and Quails, and Other New Nonsense*, ed. Angus Davidson and Philip Hofer (1953)
Original	*Lear in the Original*, ed. Herman W. Liebert (1975)
B&N	*Edward Lear: Bosh & Nonsense* (1982)
CN	*The Complete Verse and Other Nonsense*, ed. Vivien Noakes (2001, and as *The Complete Nonsense and Other Verse*, 2006)

Letters

L	*Letters of Edward Lear* [. . .] to Chichester Fortescue, etc., ed. Lady Strachey (1907)
LL	*Later Letters of Edward Lear* [. . .] to Chichester Fortescue, etc., ed. Lady Strachey (1911)
SL	*Edward Lear: Selected Letters*, ed. Vivien Noakes (1988)

Edited journals

Sicily	*Edward Lear in Sicily*, intr. Granville Proby (1938)
ELJ	*Edward Lear's Journals: A Selection*, ed. Herbert van Thal (1952)
IJ	*Edward Lear's Indian Journal*, ed. Ray Murphy (1953)
Lear's Corfu	*Lear's Corfu: An Anthology drawn from the Painter's Letters* (1965)
Crete	*Edward Lear: The Cretan Journal*, ed. Rowena Fowler (1984)
Levant	*Edward Lear in the Levant: Travels in Albania, Greece and Turkey in Europe, 1848–1849*, ed. Susan Hyman (1988)
CY	*Edward Lear: the Corfu Years: A Chronicle Presented through His Letters and Journals* (1988)
Swaab	'*Over the Land and Over the Sea': Edward Lear, Selected Nonsense and Travel Writings*, ed. Peter Swaab (2005)

Other works and sources

AT *Letters*   *The Letters of Alfred, Lord Tennyson*, ed. Cecil Y. Lang and Edgar F. Shannon, 3 vols (1982–90)

Bosh   'A Blog of Bosh', Marco Graziosi, https://nonsenselit.wordpress.com

Brown   Daniel Brown, *The Poetry of Victorian Scientists: Style, Science and Nonsense* (2013)

Byrom   Thomas Byrom, *Nonsense and Wonder: The Poems and Cartoons of Edward Lear* (1977)

Chitty   Susan Chitty, *That Singular Person Called Lear* (1988)

Colley   Ann C. Colley, *Wild Animal Skins in Victorian Britain* (2014)

Davidson   Angus Davidson, *Edward Lear: Landscape Painter and Nonsense Poet, 1812–1888* (1938)

Dehejia   Vidya Dehejia, *Impossible Picturesqueness: Edward Lear's Indian Watercolours, 1873–1875* (1988)

Deleuze   Gilles Deleuze, *The Logic of Sense*, trans. Mark Lester, ed. Constantin V. Boundas (2001)

Drummond   Maldwin Drummond, *After You Mr Lear: In the Wake of Edward Lear in Italy* (2007)

ET *Journal*   *Lady Tennyson's Journal*, ed. James O. Hoge (1981)

ET *Letters*   *The Letters of Emily Tennyson*, ed. James O. Hoge (1974)

Fisher   Clemency Fisher (ed.), *A Passion for Natural History: The Life and Legacy of the 13th Earl of Derby* (2002)

Fowler   Daniel Fowler, 'Autobiography' in *Daniel Fowler of Amherst Island, 1810–94* (catalogue, Kingston, Ontario, 1979)

Gaschke   Jenny Gaschke, *Edward Lear: Egyptian Sketches*, National Maritime Museum catalogue (2009)

Hark   Ina Rae Hark, *Edward Lear* (1982)

Harrison   Colin Harrison, *Edward Lear: Drawings and Watercolours* (1995)

HLB   *Harvard Library Bulletin*

Haughton   Hugh Haughton (ed.), *The Chatto Book of Nonsense Poetry* (1988)

Hofer   Philip Hofer, *Edward Lear as a Landscape Draughtsman* (1967)

Hunt   William Holman Hunt, *Pre-Raphaelitism and the Pre-Raphaelite Brotherhood*, 2 vols (1905)

Hyman   Susan Hyman, *Edward Lear's Birds* (1980)

Lecercle   Jean-Jacques Lecercle, *The Philosophy of Nonsense: The Intuitions of Victorian Nonsense Literature* (1994)

Lehmann   John Lehmann, *Edward Lear and His World* (1977)

Levi   Peter Levi, *Edward Lear: A Biography* (1995)

Lloyd   Stephen Lloyd (ed.), *Art, Animals and Politics: Knowsley and the Earls of Derby* (2016)

Lodge   Sara Lodge, *Inventing Mr Lear* (2018)

Montgomery   Michael Montgomery, *The Owl and the Pussy Cats* (2012)

Noakes   Vivien Noakes, *Edward Lear: The Life of a Wanderer* (1968, rev. 1979, 2004)

North   Marianne North, *Recollections of a Happy Life* (1892)

Nugent   Charles Nugent, *Edward Lear the Landscape Artist: Tours of Ireland and the English Lakes 1835 and 1836*, Wordsworth Trust exhibition catalogue (2009)

ODNB   *Oxford Dictionary of National Biography*

Original   Herman W. Liebert (ed.), *Lear in the Original: Drawings and Limericks by Edward Lear from his Book of Nonsense* (1975)

Painter   Vivien Noakes, *The Painter Edward Lear* (1991)

Peck   Robert McCracken Peck, *The Natural History of Edward Lear* (2016)

Pitman   Ruth Pitman, *Edward Lear's Tennyson* (1988)

Play   James Williams and Matthew Bevis (eds), *Edward Lear and the Play of Poetry* (2016)

RA   Vivien Noakes (ed.), *Edward Lear 1812–1888*, Royal Academy Exhibition catalogue (1985)

Regis   Amber K. Regis (ed.), *The Memoirs of John Addington Symonds: A Critical Edition* (2017)

RSV   *Rivista di Studi Vittoriani* 34–5 (2013), special issue, *Edward Lear in the Third Millennium, Explorations into His Art and Writing*, ed. Raffaella Antinucci and Anna Enrichetta Soccio

Sauer   Gordon C. Sauer, *John Gould: The Bird Man*, 5 vols, (1982–97)

Schiller   Justin Schiller, *Nonsensus: Cross-Referencing Edward Lear's Original 116 Limericks* (1988)

Sewell   Elizabeth Sewell, *The Field of Nonsense* (1952)

Shelves   William B. Osgood Field, *Edward Lear on My Shelves* (1933)

Tigges, *Exp.*   Wim Tigges (ed.), *Explorations in the Field of Nonsense* (1987)

Tigges, *Anat.* Wim Tigges, *An Anatomy of Literary Nonsense* (1988)

Waller   John O. Waller, *A Circle of Friends: The Tennysons and the Lushingtons of Park House* (1986)

Wilcox   Scott Wilcox, *Edward Lear and the Art of Travel* (2000)

Williams   James Williams, *Edward Lear* (2018)

Wonderland Jackie Wullschlager, *Inventing Wonderland: The Lives and Fantasies of Lewis Carroll, Edward Lear, J. M. Barrie, Kenneth Grahame and A. A. Milne* (1995)

NOTES

Unless otherwise indicated, all letters from EL to Ann are in the collection of Dr David Michell, and those to Fanny and George Coombe (FC, GC) are in the Warne Collection, V&A.

Prologue

'Lear could fly'. EL to Evelyn Baring, n.d. and 19 February 1864, *QLN* 9, 11.

'Auden' and 'Orwell'. W. H. Auden, *Collected Shorter Poems 1927–1957* (1966), 127; George Orwell, review of R. L. Megroz, *The Lear Omnibus*, in *Tribune*, 1945. For 'to encourage the bird' see Swaab.

'On his left, a sheet'. Elizabeth Bishop, 'The Sandpiper' (1956), from *The Complete Poems 1927–1979*.

1. One Foot Off the Ground

'O Brother Chicken!'. Written in June 1880, *CN* 432.

'*not wholly* responsible'. EL to CF, 27 June 1884, *LL* 311.

'Different lists are confused'. This list is from the Papers of Ellen Newsom, V&A. Lear sometimes said twenty-one (EL to CF, 18 July 1859), but at other times, e.g. to E. Carus Selwyn, he said nineteen. Family sources (never listing more than seventeen) include 'List of birth dates' of surviving children, and a Family Tree, *c.*1900. Some lists include an 'Olivier' who does not seem to have existed.

'The Lear family were nonconformists'. Haberdasher's Hall, 'Register of Births and Baptisms, 1785–1825' RG4/4343: online at BMDregisters.co.uk. On 1 November 1822, when Lear's sister Sarah married, John Coates, the registrar at Dr Williams' Library, registered Lear's birth as 13 May, in Holloway in the Parish of St Mary Islington: at the same time he registered the other twelve surviving children in the General Register of Births of Protestant Dissenters, RG4/4664. Birth certificate, V&A, RA 74. For 'bigots and fools': D 19 April 1859.

'He was born'. EL to HC, 12 May 1882, Noakes 268, n. 1, Houghton MS Eng 797.3.

'Memory's Arch'. D 4 August 1880.

'Lör'. *LL* 18, also EL to HC, 31 December 1882, and EL to E. Carus Selwyn, 'Late Letters of Edward Lear', *Cornhill* (1910), 396. Widely repeated by friends and early biographers.

'As for memory'. EL to E. Carus Selwyn, RA 74.

'gingerbread baker'. George Lear, 1666–1745: www.genealogy.com.

'sugar refining'. For Lear connections, partners and wills, see Bryan Mawer, 'Sugar Refiners and Bakers', mawer.clara.net.

'he married the nineteen-year-old Ann Clark Skerrett'. 24 August 1783, Wanstead Parish Church Register. Ann was descended from Eleanor Grainger, sixth child of Alice Brignall and John Grainger: Eleanor's granddaughter married Edward Skerrett. The money and land went to a different branch. 'Master of the Fruiterers'. Fruiterers Company Minute Book, 1799.

'Henry Chesmer'. Or 'Chesner'; son of Jeremiah Lear's sister Sarah, m. Thomas Chesner, Whitechapel, 1773. In 1811, Henry, a City import–export merchant was declared bankrupt after a failed deal involving Spanish wool; *London Gazette*, 28 February 1811. He moved to the West Indies and then Canada: the court case continued until 1829.

'when the stock exchange became a formal subscription body'. The proprietors raised 400 shares of £50 each. Jeremiah Lear was sworn in as broker, 12 March 1799, *Records of Corporation of London*, LMA, Brokers COL/BR; Share, 1801. *List of Proprietors of the New Stock Exchange*, LMA Guildhall CLC/B/004/B/01/MS14600.

'Heames Lane'. Replaced by the Seven Sisters Road, early 1830s.

'demolishing the house'. It was replaced by nine shops, backing onto the present Bowman's Mews. Bowman's Lodge Deeds, LMA B/MMN/6/27.

'old Bowman's Lodge'. D 17 October 1858.

'My room – ehi! ehi!'. D 10 September 1863.

'Elizabeth Duke'. Thomas Kitson Cromwell, *Walks through Islington*, 1835; in *A History of the County of Middlesex*: Victoria County History VI (1980). The water-proof patent was granted to J. R. Ackermann, 1801.

'I think a great deal'. EL to CF, 27 June 1884, *LL* 311.

'so very awful'. James Grant, *The Great Metropolis* (1837), II, 13. Jeremiah Lear's default: Stock Exchange, *Register of Defaulters*, LMA Guildhall CLC/B/004/G. Debt paid by William Smith Jr.

'King's Bench'. Told by Sarah Lear's daughter-in-law Sophie Street to her granddaughter Eleanor Bowen (née Gillies), 1907; Bowen transcript, Letter File 1, VNA.

'kept afloat'. Ann Lear had £800 p.a. (Bowen transcript); 'Josiah Lear' paid the rates late 1820–5: this may be a clerical error as no Josiah Lear appears in records of the Lear family. Henry and Frederick admitted as clerks, 29 July 1816, 1 April 1820: 'Lear F.', is noted in the *Times Register of Bankrupts* 1 July–30 September 1818 (26 2a) and October–31 December 1819 (402b) F. Henry in the army: D 8 October 1861, and Bowen transcript: bought out after swapping from infantry to cavalry and deserting.

'bacon and beans'. D 12 May 1881.

'Sarah teaching him to draw'. D 2 August 1865, 'forty-five years ago'.

'more or less stupefied'. D 15 August 1866. The entry ends, 'Thus, a sorrow so inborn & ingrained so to speak, was evidently part of what I had been born to suffer – & could not have been so far avoided willed I never so much so to do. And this is at times a great consolation to me in this life's struggle & strife.'

'a form of epilepsy'. Through its connections with the limbic system, epilepsy affecting the temporal lobe is also associated with the generation of primitive emotions. I am grateful to Steve Pollock for sharing his professional experience of treating epileptic patients, and to Charles Lewsen for discussions of Lear's condition.

'– & frightful dyspepsia'. D 11 January 1858.

'George W.'. D 2 September 1862.

'How I remember. D 21 August 1873.

'The strong will'. D 15 August 1866.

'It is wonderful'. D 14 February 1880.

'to be sure he was not smoking'. EL to Ann, 9 September 1848.

'a place earliest known'. D 9 February, 1867.

'She painted a portrait of him'. 'Portrait of Edwd. Painted by me when he was 9 years old.
A.L.' Peter Lear, Gillies Collection.

'agreeable in the face'. D 10 October 1866. Miniature by Frederick Harding.

'remembering my father'. D 7 June 1860.

'The earliest of all the morbidnesses.' D 23, 24 March 1877.

2. *With the Girls*

'spread around us'. *Edinburgh Review* 23 (April–September 1814), 205.

'Frederick Harding'. b. 25 June 1799, son of Ann Clark Skerrett's sister Sarah and her husband George Harding. After George died she married a Mr Knight: she appears in Lear's letters as 'Aunt Knight'. Frederick Harding later became a miniaturist, his portraits including one of Jeremiah Lear. He won prizes from the Society of Arts, 1814 and 1815, and exhibited at the RA and Society of British Artists 1825–57. Correspondence with Marco Graziosi.

'just fifty years'. D 19 June 1871. Ellen sent news of Harding's death: he worked out that Easter Monday 1822 was 8 April, and often marked this in his diary.

'in a crowd of horrid boys'. Annotation in Froude's *Thomas Carlyle* (1885), Noakes 11.

'when I heard that Ld Byron was dead'. D 18 September 1861.

'like Swift's Stullbruggs'. EL to CF, 2 September 1859, *L* 148. (misspelling of 'Struldbruggs')

'His elder sisters'. Bowen transcript, Somerville.

'I saw from the beach'. Thomas Moore, *Irish Melodies*, vol. 6.

'I lead as quiet a life'. EL to Lady W, 1 January 1863. Noakes 165.

'The Language Institution . . . founded in 1826'. *First Report of the Language Institution* (1826) 14; 'with a view of imparting to the Heathen the knowledge of Christianity'.

'a name-plate'. Davidson 5.

'Albert Durer'. EL to Ann, 28 November 1857.

'Hood's light verse'. As collected in *Whims and Oddities* (1826), 27, and in *Hood's Own, or Laughter from Year to Year,* and the *Comic Annual* series. See the brilliant study of Hood's work and influence, Sara Lodge, *Thomas Hood: Work, Play and Politics* (2007).

'In dreary silence'. *CN* 3–5, written 25 August 1825.

'Dear, and very dear relation'. 'To Miss Lear on her Birthday', *CN* 5–8.

'Major Wilby'. William Henry Wilby became a major in 1810, and lieutenant colonel in 1819.

'a proposal'. RA 76 says the proposal came from Sir Claudius Hunter (1775–1851), Lord Mayor 1811–12, whose first wife died in 1840: he married again in 1841. In 1856 Lear mentions meeting his daughter-in-law in Corfu, whose husband, Sir Paul, 'is the son of that Sir Claudius Hunter you were in love with so many years ago; so you see, that had you married Sir Claudius, this baronet would have been my nephew; but he is not, because you did not, or would not, marry his papa.' EL to Ann, 10 February 1856.

'Considering all I remember'. D 29 March 1868.

'at the age of 14'. EL to Charles Empson, 1 October 1831, *SL* 14.

'Dickens put George into the *Pickwick Papers*'. Quoted in Noakes 11.

'a little talk with Dickens'. Frederick Kitton, *Charles Dickens by Pen and Pencil* (1890).

'as full of beggars as Russell Square'. EL to Ann, 3 November 1837, 3 May 1838, *SL* 28, 42.

'Mrs D.' D 9 Jan 1865.

'How you used to swear!' EL to Ann, 17 January 1838.

'for bread and cheese'. 'By way of a Preface', *NSS* (1879, 9th edn 1894), xiv.

'passengers in the inn-yards'. Fowler 18.

'teaching well-off girls'. EL to FC, 15 April 1837. '2 mornings in the week, I have had a class of pupils in Grosvenor Square of 6 or 8 – & it has been quite delightful.'

'Every teacher'. Fowler 122–3.

'What is an album?'. By 'E.C.', 17 January 1824. See Samantha Matthews, '"O all pervading Album!"', in Christopher Bode (ed.), *Romantic Localities: Europe Writes Place* (2015).

'Albumean Persecution'. Lamb to Brian Waller Procter, 19 January 1828, *Works of Charles and Mary Lamb*, VII: *Letters*, ed. E. V. Lucas, 794–5.

'A Shabby Genteel Story'. W. M. Thackeray, *Fraser's Magazine* 22 (1840), 237, 402.

'several detailed studies suggest'. Houghton MS Typ 55.4, f.11, 16.

'Sarah . . . was the finest painter'. Album belonging to the Gillies family.

'gladly would I supply'. Sarah to Frederick, 12 September 1849, Michell.

'Drawn from nature'. Houghton MS Typ 55.4, f. 56, 58, 119; see also MS Typ 55.27.

'Eleanor's Geranium'. RA 78, Cat. 5b. Dated '18 June 1828'.

'This curious vegetable production'. Houghton MS Typ 55.4, loose image 9, verso.

'You are interested in Botany?' 1805, in Theresa M. Kelley, *Clandestine Marriage: Botany and Romantic Culture* (2012), 52; see also Ann B. Shteir, *Cultivating Women, Cultivating Science: Flora's Daughters and Botany in England, 1760–1860* (1996).

'*Hexandria Monogynia*'. Houghton MS Typ 55.4, loose image 9. 'Album of Drawings' *c.*1830, MS Typ 55.27, also contains over sixty images and seventeen pasted-in engravings.

'why should there not be a Bong Tree'. Richard Mabey, *The Cabaret of Plants* (2015), 1.

'There was an old person so silly'. *B&N*, 44; *CN* 112.

'A different, smaller notebook'. Notebook 1829, NLS Hugh Sharp Collection 594, MS 3321.

'other elegant, delicately careful paintings from the late 1820s'. See Houghton MS Typ 55.4. Lear paintings sold in 2012 included *A Greater Bird of Paradise* and *A Citron-crested Cockatoo and a Snake*: see Guy Peppiatt Fine Art Summer Catalogue 2012, cat. 40, 41.

'The Moral Zoologist'. *The Lady's Magazine*, 1800–5. University of Kent Special Collections.

3. 'O Sussex!'

'the curving loop of the Arun'. The river was diverted by the railway company in 1860, and the Burpham loop became a backwater, with the village wharf closing in 1887.

'involved in the town's finances'. Royal Bank of Scotland Archives. *Reports of Cases . . . in the House of Lords on Appeals and Writs of Error* (1839) IV, 101.

'William Jones'. (1745–1818), painter of the 1500 watercolours known as Jones' Icones. The cabinet was left to John Drewitt, and eventually donated in 1931 to the Hope Entomological Collection, Oxford University Museum of Natural History.

'How clearly just at the moment'. EL to FC, 27 November 1841.

'A drawing of Peppering House'. 1829; Private Collection, Nugent 3.

'the voice of the rooks'. D 13 May 1864.

'the bones, and several grinders'. Gideon Mantell, *The Fossils of the South Downs* (1822), 283–4.

'a rare coin'. *The Monthly Magazine*, 1826, 558; the reverse was inscribed 'E. Dux'.

'I was taken ill'. EL to Fanny Jane Dolly Coombe, 15 July 1832, *CN* 50.

'Ye who have hearts'. October 1826. Private collection.

'that insolent and rapacious oligarchy'. *A collection of Addresses, Squibs, Songs, &c. together with The political mountebank shewing the changeable opinions of Mr Cobbett, published during the contested election for the borough of Preston* (1826), 8. See also the editorial in *The Examiner*, 23 April 1826 on Parliament serving 'a proud and venal Oligarchy'.

'Methodist or Universalist/Unitarian hymns'. My thanks to Nicholas Roe.

'reading a Bible'. EL to CF, 25 July 1885, *LL* 336–7.

'Robert Curzon'. (1810–73), eventually the fourteenth Baron Zouche, a diplomat who brought back manuscripts from Orthodox monasteries, including Mount Athos.

'attacked the proposals for law reform'. 'Bentham, Brougham and Law Reform', *Westminster Review* XI (October 1829), 447–71.

'watercolours by Turner'. Cecilia Powell, 'Turner's Vignettes and the Making of Rogers' "Italy"', *Turner Studies*, vol. 3, no. 1 (1983).

'Nothing will persuade me'. James Hamilton, *Turner: a Life* (2007), 115.

'A very long day'. Hamilton, *Turner*, 274: manuscript diary at Farnley Hall. Fawkes/Wentworth marriages: Godfrey (Armytge) Wentworth (1773–1834) m. Amelia Fawkes 1794, 3s 5d; d. 1842; eldest son, Godfrey (d. 1865) m. Anne Fawkes 1822.

'a famous menagerie'. Caroline Grigson, *Menagerie: the History of Exotic Animals in Britain* (2016), 232.

'a grateful inscription'. 'To Mr and Mrs Wentworth,/and their family,/In acknowledgement of their kindness towards him/These drawings are respectfully and gratefully presented/by E. Lear/ 24th April 1830/35 Upper North Place/Gray's Inn Road'. RA 80.

'The Fudge Family in Paris'. Published 1818. See *Ronan Kelly, Bard of Erin: the Life of Thomas Moore* (2009).

'Peppering Roads'. 12 December 1829; *Sussex County Magazine*, January 1936; *CN* 16–17.

'their King Charles spaniel'. 'Ruby: Accidentally shot, November 23rd 1829', *CN* 22.

'turkeys attacking gulls'. 'Turkey Discipline', late autumn 1829, *CN* 14.

'3 parts crazy'. EL to Fanny Jane Dolly Coombe, 15 July 1832, *CN* 51.

'In a verse letter to Eliza'. 'I've just seen Mrs Hopkins', c.1830, *CN* 44.

'Troubadour'. This describes the singer's burial by an olive tree: 'The place was a thrice hallowed spot,/There he had drawn his golden lot/Of immortality; 'twas blest,/ A green and holy place of rest' (1825).

'little fat Person'. EL to FC, September 1830.

'cracked church bell'. The bell was replaced in 1922 with four bells bearing the names of Drewitt family members. 'Peppering Bell', *CN* 45–6 and n.

'O Sussex!' D 20 September 1862.

4. To the Zoo

'Siberian rubythroat'. McCracken Peck, 31. The paper for the drawing is watermarked 1829: see Guy Peppiatt Fine Art Winter Catalogue, 2012–13, cat. 42 43, 44.

'For all day I've been a-'. 'Letter to Harry Hinde', December 1830, *CN* 46–7.

'Zoological Society of London'. Members included aristocratic patrons and animal collectors. It soon merged with the Zoological Club of the Linnean Society led by Nicholas Vigors. For the early history, see Takashi Ito, *London Zoo and The Victorians, 1828–1859* (2014); Isobel Charman, *The Zoo: The Wild and Wonderful Tale of the Founding of London Zoo* (2016); Sofia Akerberg, *Knowledge and Pleasure at Regent's Park* (2001).

'guide for children'. *The Zoological Keepsake* (1830), in Diana Donald, *Picturing Animals in Britain* (2007), 181.

'*The Gardens and Menagerie*'. Vols I: *Quadrupeds* (1830), II: *Birds* (1831). Hyman 15–16.

'proof title page'. Zoological Society archives: see McCracken Peck, 42–4. The wrapper, for *Sketches of Animals in the Zoological Gardens Drawn from the Life by E. Lear*, to be published by 'R. Ackermann, 96 The Strand', can be dated between 1828 and 1832, when the form 'R. Ackermann' was dropped. Preliminary sketches: polar bear: album, NLS 594, Houghton MS Typ 55.27 f 21; 'peaceable kingdom', Houghton MS Typ 55.27 f. 47.

'cheap as dirt'. Audubon to Revd Bachmann, 1832, Sauer vol. 1, 88.

'a single species'. The only book on parrots was François Levaillant, *Histoire Nouvelle des Perroquets* (1768–1809), with 145 engravings based on paintings by Jacques Barraband, who had worked on designs for Gobelins tapestries and Sèvres porcelain: see McCracken Peck, 64.

'countless rough drawings'. See Hyman 20, 24, 25, 28–30.

'A huge Maccaw'. EL to Charles Empson, 1 October 1831, *SL* 14

'his own lithographic plates'. Michael Twyman, 'Lear and Lithography', in Nugent, 15.

'Hullmandel kept the blocks'. Michael Twyman, *Lasting Impressions – Lithography as Art* (1988), 62.

'a handful of natural history books'. These included William Swainson, *Zoological Illustrations* (1820–3) and Thomas Horsfield, *Zoological Researches in Java* (1824).

'Lear had to learn'. His 'first lithographic failure' was a drawing of a black-capped lory drawn from a model at Bruton Street. Houghton proof.

'He liked the freedom'. Lear later mastered tinted lithography and pen-and-ink sketches on transfer paper. Twyman, 'Lear and Lithography'; Nugent 11.

'Linnean Society'. Proposed as 'an Artist devoted to subjects of Natural History, and now employed in illustrating the Family of Parrots, and in other Zoological Works.'

'will then be framed'. W. Swainson to EL, 26 November 1831, on receipt of Part IX, Noakes 19: MS inserted in Ann's copy of *Parrots*, Houghton MS Typ 805L.32[A]. See EL to Arthur Aikin, Society of Arts, 1833: RSA B6/22 Lear.

'beautifully coloured'. Selby to William Jardine, 10 January 1831, CUL; Fisher, 165.

'pretty great difficulty'. EL to Charles Empson, 1 October 1831, *SL* 14–16.

'Their publication'. EL to Sir William Jardine, 23 January 1834, *SL* 19.

'giving little self-complacent stops'. Leigh Hunt, 'A Visit to the Zoological Gardens', *New Monthly Magazine*, 1836.

'curious, peering faces'. 'Visitors to the Parrot House', Houghton MS Typ 55.9 f. 60.

'when – lo!'. D 19 October 1848; *Albania* 295.

'4 black storks'. D 9 January 1867.

'your paternal beard'. EL to HH, 14 January 1860, HRC MS-2415.

'a man who without any prospects'. EL to GC, 19 April 1833.

'*Birds of Europe*'. Lear made sixty-eight plates. See Gould letters, Houghton MS Eng 797.

'exceedingly pleasant'. EL to Charles Empson, 1 October 1831, *SL* 15. 'Mrs Gould's Pet' was a short-tailed field vole: Houghton MS Typ 55.27 f. 12.

'esteemed & respected'. EL to John Gould, 28 August 1841, *SL* 53.

'they were always before me'. EL to GC, 19 April 1833. For sale of rights to Gould, EL to Jardine, 23 January 1834, *SL* 19. For dating of these visits see Sauer vol. I, Appendix C, 309–13.

'Exceedingly careful'. 'Scrawl', 5 April 1833, *CN* 48–9.

'Gould's book on toucans'. *A Monograph of the Ramphastidae, or Family of Toucans* (1833–5): Lear made ten of the thirty-four plates.

'While Lear felt disgruntled'. EL to FC, 17 March 1836, Nugent 214.

'Darwin's bird specimens'. Adrian Desmond and James Moore, *Darwin* (1991), 209, 222.

'always a hog'. D 27 November 1863.

'one I never liked'. D 7 February 1881.

'great expeditions'. Including drawings for the Society's *Transactions* (1835, 1841: vols I and V, ZSL) and fourteen watercolours (twelve birds and two mammals) for *The Zoology of Captain Beechey's Voyage* (1839).

'Selby's collaborator, Jardine'. Christine Jackson, *Prideaux John Selby: A Gentleman Naturalist* (1992), and *Sir William Jardine: A Life in Natural History* (2001). RA Cat. 80 notes a watercolour sketch for the Great Auk, signed by both Lear and Selby; Martin Bradley Collection, McGill University. Lear produced twenty plates for *Illustrations of Ornithology*, vols 2 and 4, and three for Jardine's *Illustrations of the Duck Tribe* (1840), as well as six plates in Thomas Campbell Eyton's *A Monograph of the Anatidae, or Duck Tribe* (1838).

'Parrots are my favourites'. EL to Jardine, 23 January 1834. Correspondence, 1833–6, William Jardine Papers, RSM: 3/64. Lear contributed plates to *Felinae* (1834), *Pigeons* (1835) and *Parrots* (1836. He dissuaded Jardine from copying the parrots in his own volume, as all rights now belonged to Gould.

'remembered their kindness'. For Selby, see EL to CF, 21 January 1862, *L* 222; for Jardine, EL to Sir Joseph Hooker, 3 June 1878, *SL* 252.

'only because I feel more pleasure'. EL to Fanny Jane Dolly Coombe, 15 July 1832 *SL* 18.

'*A Monograph of the Testudinata*'. 8 parts, 1833–6; the publisher failed before the final third of the plates were published, and unsold stock was bought by Henry Sotheran, published as *Tortoises, Terrapins and Turtles* (1872).

'drawn from nature'. Lear contributed seven drawings to Bell's *History of British Quadrupeds* (1837); Lear's copy, Houghton MS Typ 805L.37c, *Hyrax Capensis*, inscribed 'Drew Broad St. April 13th 1832'. In Houghton MS Typ 55.12 f. 4; several pages are labelled 'Zoo'. See McCracken Peck, 91–2, for correction of previous errors in dating. He also provided drawings of fossils and ammonites for William Buckland, *Geology and Mineralogy Considered with Reference to Natural Theology* (1836).

'I am up to my neck'. EL to GC, 19 April 1833.

'Bernard Senior'. (1811–94). In 1844, he took the name Husey Hunt to inherit the Husey estate at Compton Pauncefoot, Somerset; m. cousin Jane Blackmore 28 April 1840.

'*What* days, (& *what* nights)'. D 8 August 1881.

'some circumstances'. EL to GC, 19 April 1833.

'syphilitic disease'. D 20 February 1885.

'a very thin man'. EL to FC, 17 March 1836.

'decidedly caustic'. Fowler 102.

'A series of *conversazioni*'. [W. P. Frith], *A Victorian Canvas, The Memoirs of W. P. Frith*, ed. Neville Wallis (1957), 33.

'George Barnard'. M. Twyman, 'Charles Joseph Hullmandel: Lithographic Printer Extraordinary' in P. Gilmour, *Lasting Impressions – Lithography as Art* (1988), 46.

'Turner singing'. D 28 April 1871, and Henry Strachey, in Introduction, *NSS* x.

5. Knowsley

'the rain is coming down'. EL to GC, 24 June 1835.

'a lively rattling sportsman'. Amanda Askari, 'The 13th Earl of Derby's Equestrian Interests' in Fisher 30. Stanley was MP for Preston, then for Lancashire.

'spent a million'. Askari, 'The 13th Earl', 30.

'sent collectors'. Collectors included Thomas Bridges in South America, Joseph Burke in
South Africa and North America, John MacGillivray in Australia and Indonesia, Thomas
Whitfield in West Africa, and Derby's nephew, Vice-Admiral Phipps Hornby, helped by
his daughter Elizabeth in the Pacific and South America. See Colley, chs. 2 and 3 for Elizabeth Phipps-Hornby's diary; letter to Lord Derby, Liverpool 920 DER [13] 1/85/12.

'by shipping them.' Fisher 90.

'his museum'. A huge resource for nineteenth-century naturalists, still used today for identifying 'types'. See Clemency Fisher and Christine E. Jackson, 'The 13th Earl of Derby as a
Scientist', and Clemency Fisher, 'The Knowsley Aviary and Menagerie' in Fisher 45–51,
85–95. See also essays by Sir David Attenborough and Clemency Fisher in Stephen Lloyd
(ed.), *Art, Animals and Politics: Knowsley and the Earls of Derby* (2016).

'golden parakeet'. September 1831 (skin LM D. 735); Lord Derby's Parakeet, 1831 (skin LM
D. &93); Fisher 55, 126, 164. The skins are still in the Liverpool Museum.

'such as at the Gardens'. EL to FC, 19/20 June 1835.

'novelties'. EL to Jardine, 14 October 1835. NMS, GD 472 NRA 2475 Jardine.

'pencil studies'. See detailed sketches in album Houghton MS Typ 55.12.

'their cabinet skins'. I am immensely grateful to Clemency Fisher for showing me the
drawers full of parrots. The 'types' are in a special cabinet with a red tag attached, and an
orange tag outside, showing they must be the first to be saved in the event of fire.

'crowned crane'. September 1835, (skin LM.D.250); 'Orinoco goose'. July 1836, *Gleanings*
(skin, LM D. 198d); Fisher 98.

'woodchuck'. *Gleanings* Plate VII (skin LM.D.42a); 'Woolly Opossum', March 1834, (skin
LM D.194); 'black giant squirrel'. 1836, *Gleanings* Plate VI (alive in July 1836, but d. 27
December); 'Eastern quoll'. (skin LM D. 257), 1835; Fisher 111, 112, 130, 108.

'paying close attention'. See Colley, 110–12.

'I took the sketches very carefully'. EL to Derby, 2 June 1836, *SL* 22. The wildcat and turtle
both appear in *Gleanings*, Plates IV and XVII.

'to imitate the fur more nearly'. EL to Lord Derby, 17 December 1834, Knowsley.

'Portraites of the inditchenous beestes of New Ollond'. c.1838, MS Pierpont Morgan, *CN* 57.

'the Goulds set off to work there'. The Goulds' Australian works included *The Birds of Australia*, 7 vols (1840–8), *A Monograph of the Macropodidae, or Family of Kangaroos*, 2 vols
(1841–2) and *The Mammals of Australia*, 3 vols (1845–63).

'strict rules'. My thanks to Clemency Fisher for explaining this process.

'to establish a "type"'. Checking was often left to professionals like Gould, whose notorious speed and carelessness in recording which specimens he was using led to elaborate
tangles.

'Three birds were named after him'. The macaw, in Regent's Park Zoo, was identified as the 'Hyacinthine macaw': Charles Lucien Bonaparte named it after Lear in 1856, when he recognised Lear's accurate drawing as a new species; Bonaparte also named the cockatoo after him. The parakeet is now named *Platycercus tabuensis*.

'whiskered yarke'. The connection with nonsense names has been suggested by McCracken Peck and Fisher. The whiskered yarke, a monkey, is now called the white-faced saki; the eyebrowed rollulus is the Himalayan quail; the purplish guan is the crested guan; the aequitoon a Gambian antelope; the ging-e-jonga an eland, '*Oreas Derbianus*', and the jungli-bukra is the South Indian 'rib-faced deer'.

6. Tribes and Species

'Elizabeth Farren'. See Gill Perry, 'A Lady on the Stage and an Actress off It' in Lloyd 61–79. Derby, Charlotte and family shared the house with the 12th earl's younger children: Lucy (1799–1809), James (1800–1817) and Mary (1801–1858).

'linked through marriages'. The twelfth earl's sister Lucy m. Geoffrey Hornby 1772, given the Stanley living of Winwick: they had thirteen children. Stanley's sister Charlotte m. their oldest son Edmund Hornby, 1796, while Stanley m. his cousin Charlotte Margaret Hornby: their children were Edward (1799–1869), Charlotte (1801–53), Henry (1803–75), Emily (*b.* May 1804, *d.* November 1804), Louisa (1805–25), Eleanor Mary (1807–87), and Charles (1808–84).

'perfectly frozen'. EL to GC, 24 June 1835.

'Earl of Wilton'. *LL* Introduction, xix–xx, note of 1871 to CF.

'the uniform apathetic tone'. Davidson 17.

'Another!' EL to GC, 20 July 1835.

'the noise of children'. EL to CG, 20 July 1835.

'beyond all glorious'. EL to GC, 24 July 1835.

'the Stanleys of Alderley'. Revd Edward Stanley (1779–1849), Bishop of Norwich 1837; his sons were Arthur Penrhyn Stanley (1815–81), later Dean of Westminster, and Charles Edward Stanley, Royal Engineers, artist, d. Tasmania (1819–49). Edward Leycester Penrhyn (c.1790–1861) married Derby's daughter Charlotte in 1823.

'to give a stronger impulse'. *Proceedings of the British Association* 5. See Nugent 61–4.

'Dickens lampooned the BAAS'. *The Mudfog Papers*, *Bentley's Magazine* (1837–8) The presiding genius was Professor Woodensconce.

'We found there'. De Tocqueville, *Journey to Ireland July–August 1835*, ed. Emmet J. Larkin (1990), 14. Letter to his mother, 10 August 1835.

'chimpanzee in a dress'. 'Pan Troglodytes – chimpanzee with clothes on', *Anthropithecus Troglodytes* (African ape). Full length, Knowsley; close-up Houghton MS Typ. 55.12, f. 14, dated 17 October 1835.

'to Thomas Hood . . . and to George Cruikshank'. See Hood, 'A Strange Bird' (1831) and Cruikshank, 'Fellows of the Zoological Society' (1834) in Lodge, *Thomas Hood*, 120–5.

'Pythagorean Fancies'. In *Whims and Oddities*: Lodge, *Thomas Hood*, 120.

'scientific writing'. See Daniel Brown, *The Poetry of Victorian Scientists: Style, Science and Nonsense* (2015).

'Must go & draw a kangaroo'. EL to GC, 24 July 1835.

7. Make 'Em Laugh

'I think my stay here'. EL to GC, 24 June 1835.

'I feel like 5 nutmeg-graters'. EL to CF, 3 January 1858, *L* 76.

'Lady de T. and I'. EL to GC, 20 July 1835.

'The only way to be comfortable'. 12 August 1843, *Excursions* vol. 1, 57.

'The Bride's Farewell'. One of many songs by John Barnett (1802–90); see *The Musical World* (1844), 237–8: 'Fashionable ballads, like fashionable novels, are nowadays legion . . . the admirers of John Barnett will most likely purchase the ballads of John Barnett, be they good, bad, or indifferent.'

'Shall I tell what fetters'. John Lawson, *'The Maniac' with Other Poems* (1810). Other examples include Ann Taylor's 'The Maniac's Song' and Mary Robinson's 'The Maniac', written, after taking a 'considerable amount of laudanum', *Memoirs of the Late Mrs Robinson* (1801), vol. 2.

'Selina'. *The Lady's Magazine* (1804), 146; see also 'The Lament of Chatterton' (1846), *New Monthly Belle Assemblee*, 272.

'My mother did not speak'. *Original* 25, 146.

'a poem . . . by George Fenton'. 'A Dream', in *The Dublin University Magazine: A Literary and Political Journal* (February 1833), 145. I am indebted to 'Lear's Irish Sources' and 'Retrospection' in Bosh, 14 September 2008, 5 November 2014. George Livingstone Fenton became a chaplain in Bombay, returning in 1866, and was chaplain in San Remo 1869–85. A revised version of the poem appeared as 'Retrospection' in *The Mahabuleshwar Hills, and Other Poems. By an Indian Chaplain* (1876).

'folk tales'. 'Daniel O'Rourke' and 'Legend of Bottle Hill' in *Fairy Legends and Traditions of the South of Ireland* (1825, 1834).

'at the top of his voice'. Rowland E. Prothero, *The Life and Correspondence of Arthur Penrhyn Stanley, Late Dean of Westminster* (1884), vol. 1, 146–7. 'By the Lake', Thomas Moore, *Irish Melodies*, vol. 4 (1811).

'St Kiven and the Gentle Kathleen', published in five hundred copies, 1973. See Donald C. Gallup, 'Collecting Edward Lear', *Yale University Library Gazette* 61, no. 3/4 (1987), 125–42. Lear illustrated other songs from *Irish Melodies*, vol. 2 (1807), e.g. 'Go Where Glory Awaits Thee', 'Rich and Rare Were the Gems She Wore' and 'Eveleen's Bower'.

'trailing clouds of glory'. William Wordsworth, 'Ode: Intimations of Immortality' (1804). For a contrasting view of Lear and Romantic childhood, see Michael Heyman, 'Isles of Boshen: Edward Lear's Literary Nonsense in Context', PhD, Liverpool, 1999.

'Their innocent unconsciousness'. Lewis Carroll, *Letters*, 381.

'Never was there a man'. Mrs Hugh Fraser, *A Diplomat's Wife in Many Lands*, (1911), vol. 2, 25–7.

'I treasured it'. Robert Francillon, *Mid-Victorian Memories* (1914), 31.

'as Auden put it'. W. H. Auden, 'Edward Lear', *Collected Shorter Poems 1927–57*, (1966), 127.

'so much more amusing'. Davidson 15.

'Nonsense'. 'Rachel Revel', *Winter Evenings Pastimes* (1825), 50–2.

'Mr Abebika'. In full, this particular list, found on the reverse of the canvas of *The Temple of Rome* (1840), runs: 'Mr Abebika, Kratoponoko, Prizzikalo, Kattefello, Ablegorabalus, Ableborinto Phashyph, or Chakonoton the Cozovex, Dossi, Fossi, Sini, Tomentilla, Cornonilla, Polentilla, Battledore & Shuttlecock, Derry down Derry, Dumps, Otherwise – Edward Lear'. The long name varies, but Noakes 277 n. 18 says it is based on R. Stennett,

Aldiborontiphoskyphorniostikos: A Round Game for Merry Parties (1822). This surely derives from Henry Carey's *Chrononhotonthologos* (1734), with its ridiculous names: ('Aldiborontiphoscophornio!/Where left you Chrononhotonthologos?'), described in Noel Malcolm, *The Origins of English Nonsense* (1997).

'Long years ago'. Preface to *More Nonsense* (1871).

'Hey diddle diddle'. 'Humpty Dumpty' and 'Sing a Song of Sixpence' are in 'Mrs C. Beadon Edward Lear scrapbook', 1852–8, Houghton MS Typ 55.23.

'pasted into an album'. See *Original* 23–4 and Appendix 227. The large album (17 ½ by 11 ½ inches) has leaves for inserting swatches of material, and chintz for the back cover, inscribed 'R. Reynolds 10 King Street Manchester'.

'There was an Old Woman of Norwich'. The Hockliffe Project, http://hockliffe.dmu.ac.uk/ reproduces the book in full, and also the *Fifteen Young Ladies*. See Marco Graziosi, 'Limerick Books of the 1820s', www.nonsenselit.org, which also credits Jean Harrowven, *The Limerick Makers* (1976) and Iona and Peter Opie, *A Nursery Companion* (1980).

'our harsh Northern whistling'. Byron, *Beppo*, XLIV.

'to stuff the memory'. Catherine Sinclair, *Holiday House* (1839), Preface, iv.

8. Mountains

'My eyes are so sadly worse'. EL to John Gould, 31 October 1836, *SL* 23. For Gould's impatience and sense of Lear as a hired assistant, see letters between Gould and Jardine, late 1835 to 1836, Sauer vol. 1, 91–5, and EL to Jardine, 11 March 1836, Sauer vol. 1, 118.

'James Duffield Harding'. Harding (1797–1863), a pupil of Paul Sandby and Samuel Prout, was illustrator for *Landscape Annuals*, 1832 and 1833. See Wilcox 21–5.

'followed Harding's style'. See Nugent cat. 2, 6–9.

'Harding's pupils'. Fowler 15. Fowler and Gale emigrated to Amherst Island, Canada in 1843.

'almost brotherly'. Robert Edward Francillon, *Mid-Victorian Memories* (1914), 30–1. In 1838 Lucy Gale married James Francillon, later a judge in Gloucestershire, and Lear visited them often in Cheltenham.

'without *exception*'. EL to FC, [19 or 20 June 1835].

'red hot from Rome'. EL to FC, 19 June 1835.

'must have then been about twenty'. Frances K. Smith, *Daniel Fowler of Amherst Island, 1810–1894*, 18, 103. Fowler wrote, 'He was truly a remarkable man. He was painter, musician, traveller, author, linguist and humorist, not exactly the greatest in any of these departments, but an excellent second in all.'

'with Audubon'. Fisher 171. Lear enjoyed a lifetime friendship with Victor Audubon (1809–60).

'I never imagined any thing'. EL to Derby, 2 June 1836, *SL* 21.

'I never remember'. EL to FC, 24 August 1836.

'Edmund Hornby'. Edmund George Hornby (1799–1865), son of Edmund Hornby (1773–1857) and Derby's sister Charlotte. See Nugent 85.

'Mrs Hornby'. EL to FC, 24 August 1836. For this tour and Lear's sketches see Nugent.

'I have now been a month'. EL to GC, 6 September 1836.

'Mary Greville Howard'. See EL to Derby, 2 June 1836, *SL* 21. In 1874 she left Lear £100.

'where ghosts are as common as mice'. EL to FC, 24 August 1836.

'Conishead Priory'. EL to GC, 6 September 1836.

'I know every corner'. Nugent 115.

'he zig-zagged'. Judging from the numbering and dating of sketches, carefully examined by
 Nugent, Lear's route took him from Borrowdale up to Watendlath, Thirlmere and Dunmail Raise, and via Grisedale Tarn to Patterdale.

'Really it is impossible'. EL to John Gould, 31 October 1836, *SL* 24.

'*Wastwater*'. *Painter* 42–3. The lithograph is in the British Museum Department of Prints
 and Drawings: *View of Wastwater and the Screes from Wasdale Head* (1836–7).

'invited to stay on'. EL to FC, 3 January 1837.

'snow walls': EL to FC, 3 January 1837.

'unhinged & miserable'. EL to FC, 11 February 1837, on mourning paper.

'he had moved again'. EL to FC, 3 March 1837. In April Lear moved briefly to 21 Sherrard
 Street, Golden Square.

'executed in Rome'. EL to FC, 3 March 1837.

'in a chariot'. EL to FC, 19 May 1837.

'Phipps Hornby and his large family'. Captain (later Admiral) Sir Phipps Hornby (1785–
 1867), son of Revd Geoffrey Hornby of Winwick and Lucy Stanley. Superintendent of
 Plymouth Naval Hospital then of Woolwich Dockyard 1838, Commander of Pacific fleet,
 1847, admiral 1858. Eldest son John (b. 1820) cricketer, captain in the Royal Engineers,
 killed in Montreal, 8 April 1848, aged twenty-seven. His brother Geoffrey (1825–95) also
 became an admiral. The youngest brother, James (1826–1909) became headmaster of
 Eton. See the album, V&A E.752-788-1939, 'The Book of Bovisand/from Edward Lear/
 To Capn. & Mrs Hornby/& their family'. For this trip see EL to FC, 8 July 1837.

'I sail next Sunday'. EL to FC, 8 July 1837.

9. 'Rome Is Rome'

'drifted through Germany'. Houghton MS Typ 55.26 includes sketches of Luxembourg, 20
 July 1837; Moselle 26, 29 July; Eltz 8 August; Frankfurt 25 August.

'praises of the Beer'. EL to Ann, 3 November 1837, *SL* 24–30.

'Anna Jameson'. Julia Markus, *Dared and Done: The Marriage of Elizabeth Barrett and Robert
 Browning* (1995).

'the Academy'. After the Napoleonic wars the Royal Academy revived 'Rome Scholarships'
 and Severn galvanised British artists into founding a 'life Academy'. Thomas Lawrence,
 then President of the RA, hoped it 'might yet vie in usefulness and dignity with other
 foreign institutions', particularly the French. Lawrence to Severn, 23 December 1822, in
 Holger Hoock, *The King's Artists: The Royal Academy of Arts and the Politics of British
 Culture 1760–1840* (2003).

'Richard Wilson . . . William Pars . . . John Robert Cozens'. See Wilcox 25–7. Richard Wilson, in Italy 1750–7, provided sixty-eight drawings for the Earl of Dartmouth; Pars was
 sponsored by the Society of Dilettanti 1775–82; Cozens was in Italy 1776–79, 1782–3.

'The sculptors'. See Alison Yarrington, 'Anglo-Italian attitudes: Chantrey and Canova' in
 *The Lustrous Trade: Material Culture and the History of Sculpture in England and Italy,
 c.1700–c.1860* (2001). Thorwaldsen (1770–1844) lived in the Via Sistina: for his return, see
 Hans Christian Andersen, *The Story of My Life* (1852), 80–1.

'Gibby'. Lady Eastlake (ed.), *Life of John Gibson, RA. Sculptor* (1870), 107.

'I thank God'. *Biographical Dictionary of Sculptors* (1968), 171. For Theed, Gibson (1790–
 1866) and Wyatt (1795–1850) see *ODNB*, and *Biographical Dictionary of Sculptors in*

Britain, 1650–1851, website of the Henry Moore Foundation.

'extraordinary slovenliness'. William Dean Howells, *Italian Journeys* (1867), 151.

'five hundred foreign artists'. Jytte W. Keldborg, *Danish Artists in Olevano Romano, from the Golden Age to the 21st Century*, digital publication, 2011.

'"Ponte Molle" Society'. Founded in the 1820s.

'the country of my longing'. Andersen, *My Life*, 50–3.

'an unfortunate class of females'. *Metropolitan Magazine* (1834), 91.

'even & quiet man'. Penry Williams (c.1800–85). D 30 August 1863: 'always truthful & lovely'. Noakes 47, EL to Aberdare, 19 September 1884, Glamorgan DBR/ 153/20. Also D 29 January 1879.

'quiet, good-tempered'. EL to Ann, 29 March 1838. See Sarah Uwins, *A Memoir of Thomas Uwins*, 2 vols (1858).

'For improvement'. EL to Derby, 14 February 1838. *SL* 37–41.

'English Club'. *Murray's Handbook for Travellers in Central Italy*, 1850.

'whispering and eating biscuits'. *Murray's Handbook*, 42.

'English tradespeople'. C. T. McIntire, *England against the Papacy, 1858–61* (1983), 41.

'At last, dearest Louisa'. Arthur Clough, *Amours de Voyage*, 1849.

'All strangers'. EL to Ann, 29 March 1838.

'having disguised ourselves'. EL to Ann, 29 March 1838.

'One may be very gay'. EL to Ann, 27 January 1838.

'coming here'. EL to Ann, March 1838.

'Last Friday'. EL to FC and GC, 18, 26 March 1840.

'drawings and watercolours'. EL to Lord Derby, 5 June 1839, sending chalk drawings of Tivoli and Licenza, via Lady Susan Percy. For Lear's work for the Stanley and Hornby families see Edward Morris, 'Edward Lear in Italy 1837–1848' in Fisher 175–93.

'Joseph Lucien Bonaparte'. (1803–57), son of Napoleon's brother Giuseppe, King of Spain. Author of several zoological and ornithological works.

'staying with them at their villa'. EL to Gould, 17 October 1839, *SL* 49.

'thousands were shot'. EL to Derby, 14 February 1838, *SL* 37–41.

'Tivoli'. EL to Henry Catt, 11 April 1851, Houghton BMS Eng 707. For paintings see, for example, William Collins, *Villa d'Este, Tivoli* (1837), and Samuel Palmer, *The Villa d'Este from the Cypress Avenue* (1838).

'horribly fierce dogs'. EL to Ann, 27 January 1838.

'You have little notion'. EL to Ann, 29 October 1838.

10. Happy as a Hedgehog

'fleas'. EL to Ann, 12 May 1838.

'rollypoly babies'. EL to Ann, 28 May 1838.

'all noise, horror'. EL to Gould, 17 October 1839, *SL* 47.

'They yell and shout'. EL to Ann, 28 May 1838.

'Italy – especially Rome'. Samuel Palmer to Elizabeth Linnell, 22 December 1837, *The Letters of Samuel Palmer* (1974), vol. 1, 99. They shared lodgings with Lear and Uwins in the Hotel de la Ville de Rome, Naples (3 June 1838, *Letters*, vol. 1, 138).

'Much as I love England'. Samuel Palmer to Elizabeth Linnell, 14 July 1838. *Letters*, vol. I, 155.

'the sea at night'. Hannah Palmer to John, Mary and Elizabeth Linnell, 7 June 1838.

'filthy old mountain'. EL to Gould, 17 October 1839, *SL* 47.

'in high admiration'. Richard Colt Hoare, *A Classical Tour through Italy and Sicily* (1819), 149.

'crisper pencil'. Sketches: Corpo di Cava, 28 June, 19, 20 July 1838; Sorrento, 23 July; Houghton MS Typ 55.6. Two Corpo di Cava drawings dated 13 June 1838, are in the 'Italian Sketches', seven albums collected by Lord Northbrook, Hornby Library, Liverpool Central Library.

'*sempre contentissimi*'. Marco Graziosi, Bosh, 4 September 2016. Albergo Cappucini guest book, 18 July 1838, page shown in exhibition catalogue, *Alla ricerca del Sud: Tre secoli di viaggi ad Amalfinell'immaginario europeo*, ed. Dieter Richter (1989), 132.

'just as you see them now'. EL to Ann, 26 September 1838. He also advised Ann to read Bulwer-Lytton's *The Last Days of Pompeii* (1834).

'Rumours reached England'. Edwin Prince to Gould, 18 August 1838, Sauer vol. I, 271.

'Rome continues to fill'. EL to Ann, 29 October, 22 November 1838.

'sent money home'. EL to Gould, 17 October 1839, *SL* 48.

'a fooly Scotchwoman'. D 1885, *SL* 189. Sir William Knighton (1812–75).

'never very much alone'. EL to Ann, 26 September 1838.

'ancient stone walls'. EL to Ann, 11 May 1838.

'long been a favourite retreat'. The first devotees were Germans, Austrians and Scandinavians, following Thorwaldsen's friend Josef van Koch, who stayed here in 1804 and married a local girl.

'grandeur and mountain solitude' EL to Ann, 4 October 1838. Houghton MS Typ 55.6.130

'different nations'. Hannah Palmer to John and Mary Linnell, 30 June 1839, *Letters*, vol. 1, 350.

'The scenery here'. Hannah Palmer, 30 June 1839, *Letters*, vol. 1, 352.

'a quiet Sunday'. Hannah Palmer to John and Mary Linnell, 10 July 1839, *Letters*, vol. 1, 356.

'It takes a long while'. EL to Gould, 17 October 1839, *SL* 48.

'to put together a book'. The market had been established by Prout and Harding. David Roberts and John Frederick Lewis had published sketches of Spain in the mid-1830s, and would soon work in Egypt and the Middle East. See Wilcox 22, 160–1. Lear later particularly admired Lewis's 'oriental sketches': EL to Mrs Lewis, 22 June 1875, *SL* 247–8.

'annotated with jottings'. Piperno 5 February 1840, Houghton MS Typ 55.26.180; Roccagorga 6 February 1840, MS Typ 55.26.182.

'Olive'. Pitman 21.

'all the English artists'. EL to Gould, 17 October 1839, *SL* 48.

'Wilhelm Marstrand'. D 18 October 1873. For Marstrand see Hans Edvard Norregard-Nielsen, *The Golden Age of Danish Art* (exhibition catalogue, Copenhagen, 1995); Kaspar Monrad (ed.), *The Golden Age of Danish Painting* (1993).

'Lake Nemi'. D 7 April 1860.

'*Those Civitella days*'. D 16 January 1867.

'very considerable moustaches'. EL to Ann, 26 September 1838.

'All kinds of young men'. Regis, 347.

'Though I be not'. EL to Gould, 17 October 1839, *SL* 47.

'St Peter help me!' EL to FC, 1 December 1838.

'my old complaynt'. EL to FC, 8 December 1838.

'I wish to goodness'. EL to Gould, 27 February 1841, *SL* 51.

11. Third Person

'What I shall do'. EL to Gould, 27 February 1841, *SL* 51.

'apt to sprain your feet'. EL to Ann, 23 November 1857.

'four-page prospectus'. BL edition, with prospectus: extracts quoted in Swaab 118–20.

'publishing transaction'. EL to FC, 27 November 1841.

'I feel I ought to go'. EL to FC, 27 November 1841.

'foreignized'. EL to Derby, 5 June 1842, *SL* 54. Lear painted the Stanley crane, *Scops paradisae*, in September 1835: *Gleanings*, Plate XIV.

'I like the weather'. Byron, *Beppo*, XLVIII.

'John Drewitt'. d. 15 July 1842; bankruptcy commissioners at Norfolk Arms Hotel, Arundel to audit accounts and declare a dividend for creditors, *Hampshire Telegraph*, 3 October 1842.

'the family were leaving'. 1841 Census shows Fanny Coombe in Maltravers Street, Arundel; Fanny Jane Dolly with her grandmother.

'curiosities in the cabinet': EL to FC, 27 November 1841. Auction: 'A genuine library of books, valuable cabinet of insects, shells and other curiosities, the property of the late John Drewitt, arranged and collected by the celebrated naturalist, the late W Jones', *Hampshire Telegraph*, 15 August 1842.

'I hope you will dress very nicely'. EL to Ann, 27 August 1844.

'Gladstone'. Quoted in 'Edward Lear in Italy 1837–1848' in Fisher 179; 'an artist of great promise'. Murray's *Handbook for Travellers in Central Italy* (1843), 457, 459.

'the court jester'. See James Williams, 'Lear and the Fool' and, in his letters, Hugh Haughton, 'Playing with Letters, Lear's Episthilarity' in *Play* 16–50, 223–42, and 'Just Letters: Corresponding Poets', in *Letter Writing among Poets: From William Wordsworth to Elizabeth Bishop*, ed. Jonathan Ellis (2015), 57–80.

'Romulus and Remus'. 1841, MS Beinecke GEN MSS 601.

'*Caius Marius*'. October 1841, MS, Cotsen Children's Library, Princeton University: published in limited edition by Justin G. Schiller (1983).

'Mr Lear recovers his hat'. EL to Lady Susan Elizabeth Percy (1782–1847), 28 February 1842, Beinecke GEN MSS 601; and EL to Lady Susan Percy, 29 March 1844.

'fly with the birds'. See 'A Walk on a Windy Day', 1860, Beinecke GEN MSS 601.

'2 live tigers'. EL to GC, 24 July 1835.

'walking in Scotland'. VNA, Letter File, 1842, 'Hornby Notebook'.

'Woolwich Dockyard'. *Original* 176–84 (described as Greenwich).

'riding lessons'. Tour with Charles Knight, June 1842: 'Lear's Adventures on horseback', twenty-one drawings, BM 1970, 0411.26.

'a most elephantine nose'. EL to Charles Empson, 1 October 1831, *SL* 16.

'touring Sicily'. Twenty drawings, *Lear in Sicily* (1938). For a further collection of eight drawings in a friend's guestbook, see *Ye long nite* (1972), MSS Fitzwilliam, 1087/1–8.

'and surprised me'. Hunt, vol. 1, 332.

'capital watercresses'. 4 November 1848, *Albania* 321.

12. Excursions

'devouring his letters'. EL to Ann, 17 January 1838.

'if you are absolutely alone'. EL to CF, 1 May 1859, *L* 136.

'Peter Leopold Acland'. (1819–99), later Prebendary of Exeter Cathedral. Son of Sir Thomas Acland, a friend of the Hornbys, and a nephew of Sir Stamford Raffles.

'Just above Taormina'. EL to Derby, 5 June 1842, *SL* 59.

'that brilliant bird the Roller'. EL to Derby, 5 June 1842, *SL* 59.

'three provinces'. In Lear's map, these are Abruzzi Citeriore (eastern province, capital Chieti), Ulteriore Primo (northern province, with mountain range of Gran Sasso) and Ulteriore Secundo (the largest, western province, including Avezzano and Lake Fucino). See the short film on YouTube, 'Viaggio nell'Abruzzo romantic di Edward Lear', showing many of the palazzi he stayed in (Italia nostra Pescara, 2012).

'These people'. *Excursions* vol. 1, September 1843.

'Sir Richard Colt Hoare and Richard Keppel Craven'. Sir Richard Colt Hoare, *A Classical Tour through Italy and Sicily* (1819), and R. Keppel Craven, *Excursion in the Abruzzi and Northern Provinces of Naples* (1837).

'a wild chaos'. *Excursions* vol. 1. See Raffaella Antinucci, '". . . in those few bright (Abruzzi) days": Edward Lear's Landscaping Gaze and the Discovery of Abruzzo', *RSV* 159–88.

'crowded with peasants'. *Excursions* vol. 1, 26 July 1843.

'carrying a dead fox'. *Excursions* vol. 1, 13 August 1843.

'*Arabian Nights*'. The set, inscribed by Lear, was auctioned by Bloomsbury, 11 December 2014; see Marco Graziosi, Bosh, 17 December 2016.

'out before sunrise'. Extract copied from journal, 2 August 1844, University of Rochester, NY. Also letter to Gould, 12 August 1844. Houghton BMS Eng 707.

'Now you are not coming'. EL to Ann, 24 September 1844.

'You great fool!'. *Excursions* vol. 1, 126–7, 28 September 1844.

'Virgil'. EL to the poet Angelo Maria Ricci, 18 December 1844. Biblioteca Communale di Rieti, Fondo Ricci F=1=16/212. Lear said he must put this off because of his weak eyes and inability to reach some places. See also letter of 22 March 1845, and Bosh 5, 17 June 2013. Lear drew in the Alban and Volscian hills, March–April 1845.

'Lord Stanley'. For political career see Angus Hawkins, 'The 14th Earl of Derby' in Lloyd 200–20. As Colonial Secretary he oversaw the new colonies, Hong Kong, Natal and Sind.

'the *pifferi* also inspired'. Berlioz, *Harold en Italie* (1834). Berlioz and Mendelssohn travelled in Italy in 1831–2: Berlioz thought the *pifferi* music was that of the Sabines, *Aeneid* Book IX.

'Ruskin'. John Ruskin, *Modern Painters*, vol. 2 (1846), esp. Ch. 2, Sections 19 and 20.

'a treat'. EL to Ruskin, 16 February 1883, *SL* 262.

'snug and nice'. Queen Victoria to Leopold, 25 March 1845, *The Letters of Queen Victoria*, vol. 2 (1908), 35.

'& particularly a Terrace'. EL to CF, 29 December 1861, *L* 214. Albert met leading artists through his appointment in 1840 as President of the Fine Arts Committee.

'all whim and fancy'. Edwin Landseer to Lady Abercorn, in Vanessa Remington, 'Queen Victoria, Prince Albert and their relations with artists', www.royalcollection.org, 2012.

'teaches remarkably well'. Queen Victoria, A VIC/MAIN/QVJ (W), 15–18 July 1846 (Princess Beatrice's copies). See also Marina Warner, *Queen Victoria's Sketchbook* (1979), 117, 139.

'Helena's christening'. A VIC/MAIN/QVJ (W), 25 July 1846 (Princess Beatrice's copies).

'complaints'. EL to Ann, 6 February 1847.

'beautiful things'. *LL* xx–xxi.

'such nice letters'. EL to Ann, 6 February 1847.
'and should I never revisit'. *Excursions* vol. 2, 17 October 1844.

23. *Derry down Derry:* Nonsense, *1846*

'a good, clever, agreeable man'. Carlingford Diary 14 April 1845, BL Add MS 63664.
'I have enjoyed'. Carlingford Diary 11 May 1845, BL Add MS 63664.
'an advertisement'. *Excursions* vol. 2.
'*Book of Nonsense*'. Published 10 February 1846. The verses have 36 Old Men, 15 Old Persons (male) and one Old Sailor, 16 Young Ladies, 2 Old Ladies and one Young Girl.
'expanded edition of 1861'. Officially the third edition. As well as the second edition of 1854, there were other intervening reprints, mostly lost or destroyed. Howard M. Nixon, 'The Second Lithographic Edition of Lear's Book of Nonsense', *British Museum Quarterly* 28 (1964), 7–8.
'quite unlike the standard fare'. See Ann C. Colley, 'Edward Lear's Limericks and the Reversals of Nonsense', *Victorian Poetry* 26 (1988), 285–99.
'wrote and drew them fast'. For variations, see Schiller, *Nonsensus*.
'old person of Barnes'. EL to Mary Nicoll Wyatt, 24 December 1863, Beinecke GEN MSS 601.
'giving one manuscript'. The Phipps Hornby version, MS Koch, is published in *Original*, and MS Duncan, published in 1982 as *Bosh and Nonsense*, is in V&A, Warne.
'Derry down Derry'. John Brand, *Observations on Popular Antiquities* (1841).
'With hey dum dum'. www.wantagemummers.org.
'tradition of nonsense'. This line was followed by contemporaries like Sir Edward Strachey in his 'Nonsense as a Fine Art', *Quarterly Review*, 1888. For later studies see Ann Colley, *Edward Lear and the Critics* (1993) and James Williams, *RSV: 'Edward Lear's Luminous Prose'*, 139–158.
'local and historical references'. See Thomas Dilworth, 'Lear's Italian Limericks', *RSV* 51–78.
'Old Man of New York'. Drawing, Duncan MS, 1864, *B&N* 64.

24. *'Something Is About to Happen'*

'lithographs'. Transcribed from Lear's watercolours by J. W. Moore, printed in sets of 100 by Hullmandel and hand-coloured by professional watercolourists. Fisher 172.
'the annual experience'. [Richard Ford], 'Fanny Kemble and Lear in Italy', *Quarterly Review* 81 (June–September 1847), 464.
'The review seems written'. EL to Ann, 15 November 1847 (also 28 October 1847).
'crawling on'. EL to Ann, 25 December 1846, plus handwritten note of journey times.
'sounding slightly homesick'. EL to Ann, 31 December 1846, 24 January 1847.
'problems with her eyesight'. Ellen Newsom to Fanny, 25 March 1854, family letters. Photocopies of many family letters, especially to Sarah Street (née Lear), are in the Hocken Library, Otago, New Zealand, Misc-MS-0564.
'please God'. EL to Ann, 27 March 1847.
'like thistledown'. Mary Boswell to Frederick Lear, May 1850.
'To tell you the truth'. EL to Ann, 24 July 1847.
'perched himself at the top'. *Calabria* 5.
'an outsider'. EL to CF, 23 October 1881, *LL* 250.

'Many other causes'. EL to Ann, 6 February 1847.

'although no war'. EL to Ann, 27 August 1844.

'large and portly'. EL to Ann, 30 January 1847.

'climate & beauty'. EL to Ann, 27 March 1847.

'to half the grandees'. EL to Ann, 29 April 1847. (Also Proby MSS, Elton Hall, Peterborough.)

'entranced'. EL to Ann, 27 June 1847.

'one of his finest oil paintings'. *The City of Syracuse from the Ancient Quarries where the Athenians were Imprisoned BC 413*, exhibited at the Royal Academy in 1853, bought by Frederick Lygon, later sixth Earl Beauchamp, Madresfield Court, near Malvern.

'Sometimes I rolled back'. EL to Ann, 17 June 1847.

'full, full, full'. EL to Ann, 17 June, 11 July 1847.

'ending with'. *Calabria* 12.

'delight at Bruzzano'. *Calabria* 59.

'dense carpet-forests'. *Calabria* 56.

'cicadas'. *Calabria* 27.

'nest of crags'. *Calabria* 116.

'king of nine-pins'. *Calabria* 135.

'Supper and silkworms'. *Calabria* 58.

'like an armadillo'. *Calabria* 85.

'Calabria!' *Calabria* 2.

'pointed hats'. *Calabria* 106.

'Polsi'. *Calabria* 73.

'gooseberries were unreal'. *Calabria* 103.

'*Perche?*' *Calabria* 125.

'in the habit'. *Calabria* 154.

'revolution or no revolution'. *Calabria* 188.

'*Non ci sono più chiavi*'. *Calabria* 199.

'Gloom, gloom'. *Calabria* 205.

'Most people'. EL to Ann, 28 October 1847.

'exactly like looking at you'. EL to Ann, 15 November 1847. This was painted by her friend Mrs Arundale, who had studied at the RA Schools: Ann was staying with the Arundales in Brighton in early 1847.

'Calabrian moustaches'. EL to Ann, 5 December 1847.

'Lord Eastnor'. (1819–83), later third Earl Somers.

'Thomas Baring'. (1826–1904), later Earl of Northbrook. EL to CF, 12 February 1848, *L* 6.

'You see therefore'. EL to CF, 12 February 1848, *L* 8–9.

'I spent my last evening'. Charles Church (1823–1915). 'With Edward Lear in Greece', Introduction to Lear's journals, transcribed and edited by Church between 1907 and 1915, Westminster School Library. edwardlear.westminster.org.uk.

'What do you think of the Sicilians?'. EL to CF, 12 February 1848, *SL* 68.

'to make you understand'. EL to Ann, 9 April 1848.

'the whole tone'. EL to Ann, 9 April 1848.

15. 'Calmly, into the Dice-box'

'Daybreak and wailing'. 26 October 1848, *Albania* 280.

'Ulysses island'. EL to Ann, 19 April 1848.

'Venetian control'. *CY* Introduction, 9–14

'Land of Albania!'. Byron, *Childe Harold's Pilgrimage* (1812), Canto II, XXXVII.

'If I go to Albania'. EL to Ann, 14 May 1848.

'Poor old Rome'. EL to Ann, 3 June 1848.

'fields of pink hollyhocks'. 29 June, Church, 'With Edward Lear in Greece'.

'from 3 in the morning'. Church, 'With Edward Lear in Greece', introduction.

'on an Indiarubber bed'. EL to CF, 19 July 1848, *L* 10.

'books, jelly'. EL to Ann, 19 July 1848.

'good for knitting needles'. EL to Ann, 9 September 1848.

'sent money'. Cross and Fortescue each sent £40, Lord Ellesmere and Samuel Clowes £50.
    EL to Charles Church, 10 November 1848. VNA transcript.

'who entirely cover'. *Albania* 13.

'first pale and distinct'. *Albania* 13.

'abandon firearms'. *Albania* Introduction, 7–8.

'vast yet beautifully simple'. EL to CF, 26 August 1848, RA 107; William Martin Leake,
    Travels in the Morea (1830), *Travels in Northern Greece* (1835).

'sending sketches'. EL to Richard Ford, 27 November 1852, VNA.

'Make, I thought to myself'. 11 September, *Albania* 22.

'dragoman'. 14 September, *Albania* 35.

'Countless kestrils'. 13 September, *Albania* 27.

'*Yok, Yok!*'. 19 September, *Albania* 56.

'take to a fez'. *Albania* 67.

'drawing bolts'. 23 September, *Albania* 69.

'come what might of it'. *Albania* 91.

'luxury and inconvenience'. September 29, *Albania* 102.

'Tik-tok'. September 29, *Albania* 115.

'O khan of Tyrana'. 27 September, *Albania* 103.

'Four begin to form a sort of chorus'. 15 October, *Albania* 194.

'wildest of singular melodies'. 1 October, *Albania* 120.

'*vendette*'. 7 October, *Albania* 151.

'talk about pelicans'. 29 October, *Albania* 297.

'They were all pelicans!'. EL to Derby, 12 January 1849, *SL* 97.

'Shut out'. 22 October 1848, *Albania* 234.

'a dreary, blank scene'. 31 October 1848, *Albania* 304.

'In marble-paved pavilion'. Byron, *Childe Harold's Pilgrimage*, Canto II, LXII.

'the wild octave singing'. 8 May 1849, *Albania* 377.

'I gazed', 1848, *Albania* 364. After their defeat the surviving Suliots crossed to the Ionian
    islands, many returning at the start of the Greek War of Independence in 1820.

16. '*All that Amber*'

'The matter is a *secret*'. EL to Ann, 7 November 1848.

'high winds and hurricanes', and Greece and Malta. EL to Ann, 9, 17, 26 December 1848.

'Henry Lushington'. For the Malta appointment see Waller 151–60, 166–7, 174.

'I am quite crazy'. EL to CF, 12 February 1848, *L* 8.

'I shall never be surprised at anything'. EL to Ann, 11 January 1849.

'Riding a camel'. EL to Ann, 16 January 1849, *SL* 99.

'no romance of hardships'. EL to Ann, 11 January 1849.

'across gravelly plains to green oases'. *'Near Wadi El-Sheikh', 8 a.m., 30 January 1849*. Houghton Typ 55.7. 663.

'excessive & wonderful grandeur'. EL to Ann, 16 January 1849, *SL* 105.

'topographical artist'. FL, introduction to 'A Leaf from the Journals of a Landscape Painter', *Macmillan's Magazine* 90 (April 1897).

'I decided it would be more kind'. EL to Ann, 24 February 1849.

'wind up all my Thessaly'. EL to Ann, 2 January 1849.

'Here I am'. EL to Ann, 8 March 1849.

'his fellow traveller'. EL to Ann, 8 March 1849.

'Before visiting any country'. FL, introduction to 'A Leaf from the Journals'.

'Doctor Holland's narrative'. EL to Ann, 2 January 1849.

'One of the most delightful'. FL to ET, 13 April 1856, TRC 'Letters/ 5440.

'The two eldest Lushington brothers'. Edmund Law Lushington (1811–93), Henry Lushington (1812–55).

'I had rather address'. Donne to Richard Trench, May 1851, Catherine B. Johnson, *William Bodham Donne and His Friends* (1905), 165, quoted in W. C. Lubenow, *The Cambridge Apostles, 1820–1914: Liberalism, Imagination and Friendship* (1998), 64.

'one of the most touching'. *Tait's Edinburgh Magazine* 17 (August 1850). In addition, in 1847 Tennyson dedicated *The Princess* to Harry.

'to sketch as much as Lear'. The Benaki Museum in Athens holds two hundred of Lushington's drawings from this tour. *Levant* 122.

'I do not know'. EL to Ann, 4 April 1849.

'the ground has been literally covered'. EL to Ann, 4 April 1849.

'As for Lushington'. EL to Ann, 21 April 1849.

'one night in Greece'. FL, introduction to 'A Leaf from the Journals'.

'F.L., my Greek companion'. 24 April 1849, *Albania* 340.

'which F.L. had bequeathed'. 5 May 1849, *Albania* 360.

'Late at night'. 6 May 1849, *Albania* 371–2.

'Any one'. Greek journal, extract: Westminster School Library, Noakes 85.

'What scenery'. Greek journal extract, Westminster School Library.

17. The Brotherhood

'What to do'. EL to CF, 25 August 1848, *L* 13–14.

'Henry and his eldest son were described as painters'. US Census, 1860, Williamsburg, Brooklyn. Henry m. Jemima Pestell in Islington, 1828: children Henry, b. 1826, Jemima 1828, George 1831, George E. 1832, Anna 1835, Washington 1838, Susan 1841, Frederick 1845.

'Fred'. Sarah to Frederick, 12 September 1849, Family letters. US Census 1850. Frederick Lear m. Rosa Annie Smyth in Shoreditch, 1830.

'Adjouah'. Bowen transcript, Michell.

'if there was a Chapel.' Ann to Frederick, 1847, Family letters.

'What a funny dear old couple'. EL to Ann, 15 July 1856.

'He has arrived last'. Sarah to Frederick, 12 September 1849, Family letters.

'New Zealand'. Their emigration was paid for by a legacy from Charles Street's sister. For
  Sarah's impressions, see Ellen Newsom to Fanny, 25 March 1854, Family letters.
'The more I read travels'. EL to CF, 23 January 1853, *L* 28.
'I might see Sarah'. EL to Ann, 29 June, also 15 July 1856.
'viddies', EL to CF, 1 August 1849, *L* 16.
'in a constant state' EL to CF, 1 August 1849, *L* 15.
'Immense fun'. EL to CF, 1 August 1849, *L* 16.
'stuffed birds'. EL to Gould, August 1849, Houghton MS Eng 797.
'I tried with 51'. EL to CF, 20 January 1850, *L* 23–5.
'slavy labours'. D 8 December 1860.
'*heaps and loads*'. EL to Henry Catt, 11 April 1851, Houghton Ms Eng 797.
'Athenaeum'. EL to CF, 26 August 1851, *L* 22.
'Great Exhibition'. Ann to Fanny, May 1851, Family letters.
'oil of the road to the Acropolis'. Exhibited at British Institution 1852, as *The Acropolis of
  Athens, Sunrise, People Assembling on the Road to Piraeus*. Museum of Athens.
'He said last Sunday' and 'tew litters'. EL to CF 19 July 1851, *L* 19, 17.
'I hope to go on'. EL to CF, 19 July 1851, *L* 17.
'numbers grew to seven'. Other members by late 1849 were William Michael Rossetti, James
  Collinson, Frederic George Stephens and Thomas Woolner.
'Go to nature'. Ruskin, *Works*, vol. 3, 623–4, in Allen Staley, *The Pre-Raphaelite Landscape*
  (2001), 7.
'stated aims of the PRB'. William Michael Rossetti (ed.), *Dante Gabriel Rossetti: His Family-
  Letters, with a Memoir* (1895), vol. 1, 135. See also Hunt.
'Such men'. Charles Dickens, *Household Words*, 15 June 1850, 12–14.
'Ruskin, in two letters'. *The Times*, 15, 30 May 1851.
'overflowed with geniality'. Hunt, vol. 1, 328.
'It was curious'. Hunt, vol. 1, 329.
'In the intervals of working'. Hunt, vol. 1, 330–1.
'doesn't carry his own cuttlefish'. Hunt, vol. 1, 333.
'Brotherhood and their circle'. For the wider circle, and Lear's long association with PRB
  ideas, see Sara Lodge, '"My Dear Daddy": William Holman Hunt and Edward Lear',
  RSV 79–99. Also W. M. Rossetti, *Some Reminiscences of William Michael Rossetti* (1906),
  156–7. With Hunt, Rossetti, Ruskin and others Lear was briefly a member of the short-
  lived 'Hogarth Club': D 1 July 1859.
'pearly sheen'. As in *Fairlight Downs – Sunlight on the Sea* (summer 1852).
'traditional pigments'. See Carol Jacobi, *William Holman Hunt: Painter, Painting, Paint*
  (2006), 122.
'beyond doubt'. Hunt letter, 1852, John Rylands, Eng MS 1214/1: *RSV* 81.
'a wheel of sharp knives'. HH to EL, 24 January 1853, in Jacobi 97.
'where at least'. EL to CF, 23 January 1853, *L* 26–7.
'worked in his new Hunt-influenced style'. *View of Reggio* (Tate), *Venosa, Apulia* (Toledo
  Museum of Art, Ohio), *The Mountains of Thermopylae* (Bristol Museum and Art Gallery).
'off & on'. *Painter* 13.
'if the Thermopylae turns out right'. EL to HH, 19 December 1852, (Huntington) BL RP
  800/1.
'99 out of a hundred will blame'. EL to HH, 9 February 1853, *SL* 120.

'Altogether I foresee'. EL to HH, 9 February 1853, *SL* 120

'hop on one leg'. EL to HH, June 1853, *SL* 121.

'utterly impossible'. EL to HH, 11 July 1853, (Huntington) BL RP 800/1.

'bought some Southdown sheep'. North, vol. 1, 28.

'a drove of Apes'. EL to HH, 27 July 1853, (Huntington) BL RP 800/1. For his impatience with the sheep see EL to Lord Derby 15 June 1853, Liverpool 920 DER (13) 106/8.

'Giorgione & water'. EL to Hunt, 7 July 1854, (Huntington) BL RP 800/1. Lodge comments that 'veal' was PRB slang for a patron, *RSV* 85.

'did not always agree'. EL to Ann, 2 June 1856.

'As he that taketh away'. Hunt, vol. 1, 347.

'the skill and genius'. EL to Ann, 11 May 1856.

18. Meeting the Poet

'sing Tennyson's songs'. North, vol. 1, 29.

'two-volume *Poems*'. This included new works such as 'The Lady of Shalott', 'The Lotos Eaters' and 'The Palace of Art', and revised works, among them 'Mariana', 'Morte d'Arthur', 'Ulysses', 'Locksley Hall' and 'Break, break, break'.

'You will see and groan!' Robert Browning to Alfred Domett, 13 July 1842, F.G. Kenyon (ed.), *Robert Browning and Alfred Domett* (1906), 41.

'grander than Campbell'. Hallam Tennyson, *Alfred Lord Tennyson: A Memoir* (1897), vol. 2, 93.

'Locksley Hall'. Quotations from Christopher Ricks (ed.), *The Poems of Tennyson*, 3 vols (1987).

'I enjoy hardly any one thing'. EL to ET, 28 October 1855, *SL* 133.

'I am always fancying'. EL to CF, 21 December 1881, *LL* 257.

'*The Princess*'. The opening reflects the annual festival for the Maidstone Mechanics Institute at Park House: Waller 123–4. In the debate between brother and sister, well-informed readers saw 'Walter' as Frank and 'Lilia' as his spirited youngest sister Louisa.

'Mrs T also pleased me'. Thomas Carlyle to Jane Carlyle, 3 October 1850, AT *Letters*, vol. 1, 339.

'A thousand things'. EL to ET, 2 December 1851, *SL* 115. Emily had invited Lear to stay for the weekend, 4 December 1851: TRC/Letters 5398.

'more agreeable recollections'. ET to EL, 4 December [1851], ET *Letters* 56.

'It is a sad evil'. EL to ET, 18 November 1852, TRC/Letters 5402.

'I thought that if I tried'. EL to ET, 24 November 1885, Pitman 33.

'extracted and placed'. EL to ET, 5 October 1852, TRC/Letters 5399.

'There was a period'. Hallam Tennyson, *Memoir* (1897), vol. 1, 257. AT to Dawson, 21 November 1882, used by HT in relation to *The Princess*, 1847. Partially quoted by Pitman 30–1.

'on purpose to smoke on'. EL to ET, 12 October 1852, TRC/Letters 5400.

'A. said'. [November 1852], *Journal of Emily Tennyson*. Hallam was born 11 August 1852.

'all crookedwise'. EL to ET, [26 November 1852], TRC/Letters 5401.

Hunt's *Lady of Shalott* (1850), National Gallery of Victoria, Melbourne.

'I must now ask you'. Hunt, *Pre-Raphaelitism*, vol. 2, 124–5. Millais's designs included Mariana and the weeping Amy from 'Locksley Hall'; Rossetti contributed Sir Galahad.

'To E.L. on His Travels', *LL* v. See Anne Barton, 'Delirious Bulldogs and Nasty Crockery: Tennyson as Nonsense Poet', *VP* 47, 1 (2009), 313–30; Richard Maxwell, 'Palms and Temples: Edward Lear's Topographies' *VP* 48, 1 (2010), 73–94.

'one very fine picture'. AT to ET, 22 June 1864, AT *Letters*, vol. 1, 372.

'edged with broadening light'. EL to ET, 11 November 1855, TRC/Letters 5431.

'But stay here I *won't*'. EL to ET, 12 October [1853], TRC/Letters 5404.

'I have not shaved'. EL to Hunt, 12 October 1853, *SL* 123.

'settings of four Tennyson songs'. *Poems and Songs by Alfred Tennyson*, published by Cramer, Beale & Co. (1853).

'a set of songs'. EL to ET, November 1853. The first four were 'Tears, idle tears' and 'Sweet and low' from The Princess, and 'Edward Gray' and 'A Farewell'.

19. An Owl in the Desert

'so we have dinner parties'. EL to Ann, 7 February 1854. The island was flooded after the building of the Aswan dam, and the temples were removed to another island.

'Philae –'. RA cat. 147.

'all in broad stripes'. EL to Ann, 17 January 1854. His Nile sketches formed the basis for many paintings, and over 20 Tennyson illustrations.

'a very pleasant party'. EL to Ann, 7, 19 December 1853.

'Don't laugh!' EL to Ann, 23 December 1853.

'leghorn hat'. EL to Ann, 15 January 1854.

'like giant moths'. EL to Ann, 4 January 1854.

'Turtle doves'. EL to Ann, 15 January 1854.

'a great forest'. EL to Ann, 15 February 1854.

'like a ladies "goffrée" frill'. EL to Ann, 23 August 1854.

'she died in Frank's arms'. Waller 187.

'I have been wondering'. EL to CF, 20 April, 1862, *L* 234.

'We are united as a people . . . Let Hamlet stand aside'. Henry and Franklin Lushington, Preface to *La Nation Boutiquière & Other Poems Chiefly Political and Points of War* (1855), x, xxv. 'The Muster of the Guards' was published in a Macmillan Shilling Pamphlet, *Points of War* (1854), and included, with Henry's Inkerman poem, in *Two Battle Pieces*, Macmillan pamphlet (1855). See also Matthew Bevis, 'Fighting Talk' in *The Oxford Handbook of British and Irish War Poetry*, ed. Tim Kendall, 17.

'Lady Ashburton'. *Approach to Philae* (1854), Andrew Clayton-Payne website.

'& so completely uncertain'. EL to CF, n.d. 1855. *L* 294 dates this letter as 'September 1863', but I accept Noakes's redating, *SL* 131.

'By the bye'. CF to EL, 7 November 1855, SHC DD/SH/62/337 (2/13).

'Fortescue's influence'. CF to EL, n.d. 1855. Also ET to EL, 7 April 1855, ET *Letters* 75.

'album of drawings'. 'Edward Lear drawings of landscapes, animals and birds', inscribed to 'Cecilia Lushington from Mr. Lear, May 25th 1855'. Houghton MS Typ 55.13.

'invited Edmund, Tennyson and friends'. EL to Edmund Law Lushington, 6 June 1855, Glasgow MS Gen 557/2/161. Other guests included James Spedding, George Stovin Venables and B. L. Chapman.

'I of course would be happy'. AT to EL, 7, 8 June 1855, AT *Letters* vol. 2, 111.

'woundily like a spectator'. EL to AT, 9 June 1855, TRC 5415.

'As Frank's friend'. ET to EL, 27 July 1855, ET *Letters* 77–8.

'Mr Lear'. Cecilia to Edmund Lushington, 2 August 1855, Glasgow MS Gen/557/2/17/5.

'Frank will make it all easy for you'. ET to EL, 17 August 1855, ET *Letters* 79, and 30 August, TRC/Letters 5423.

'at heart grateful'. ET to EL, 7 September 1855, TRC/Letters 5424.

'more of himself, his secret feelings'. Carlingford Diary, 16 September 1855.

'wellest and freshest'. ET to EL, [late September 1855], ET *Letters* 83.

'Mr Lear's singing'. ET *Journal*, 17 October 1855.

'mostly pretty things'. Millais and Lady Charlotte Schreiber, quoted in Anne Ehrenpreis, 'Edward Lear Sings Tennyson's Songs', *Harvard Library Bulletin* 27 (1979), 72n.

'Alack! For Miss Cotton!' EL to ET, 29 October 1855.

'I am afraid'. ET to EL, 27 October 1855, ET *Letters* 87.

'You, Alfred & Frank'. EL to ET, 28 October 1855, *SL* 132–3.

'You are not alone'. ET to EL, 17 November [1855], ET *Letters* 89–90.

20. *Half a Life: Corfu and Athos*

'Was there ever such luck'. EL to Ann, 4 December 1855.

'begged Ann to write'. EL to Ann, 13, 18 December 1855.

'a necessity of existence'. FL and HSM [probably fellow Apostle, Henry Sumner Maine], *Memoir of Henry Fitzmaurice Hallam*, privately printed 1850, included in *Remains of Arthur Henry Hallam* (1853) TRC/BC/4611, lix.

'I suppose'. FL to ET, 13 April 1855, TRC/Letters/5440.

'no place in all the world is so lovely'. EL to Ann, 18 December 1855.

'Sir James Reid'. EL to Ann, 3 April 1856. Reid had been Chief Justice since the 1830s.

'Just now'. EL to Ann, 26 January 1856.

'School of Art in the university'. *CY*, Introduction, 13.

'a great addition'. CF to EL, 17 September 1856, *L* 37.

'the Court has taken a whim'. EL to Ann, 10 February 1856.

'We Corfiotes'. EL to Ann, 11 May 1856.

'music-hater'. FL to ET, 13 April 1856. TRC/Letters 5440

'all the fields'. EL to Ann, 3 April 1856.

'screwy & squashy'. EL to Ann, 27 April 1856.

'Carlyle's *Past & Present*'. FL to ET, 20 June 1856, TRC/Letters 5441.

'Last night the mountains'. EL to Ann, 29 June 1856.

'It seems but the other day'. EL to Ann, 15 July 1856.

'though I am beginning'. EL to Ann, 29 July 1856.

'not thought half as much of'. EL to William Michael Rossetti, 6 May 1854. Noakes 119.

'so full of poetry'. EL to HH, 11 May 1856, Noakes 119

'annual infants'. EL to CF, 23 January 1853, *L* 29.

'A world of thought'. D 1 October 1858.

'long desired Mount Athos'. EL to Ann, 29 July 1856.

'verifying Alfred's poem'. FL to ET, 14 September 1856, TRC/Letters 3909.

'a high peak'. EL to Ann, 8 October 1856.

'for any money'. EL to CF, 9 October 1856, *L* 41–2.

'many many thousand monks'. EL to ET, 9 October 1856, *SL* 138–9.

'The impetuosity of my nature'. EL to ET, 9 October 1856, *SL* 143.

'Major Shakespear'. EL to Ann, 30 November 1856.

'this queer Albanian trip'. EL to Ann, 9 January 1857.

'dancing and rushing'. EL to Ann, 22 March 1857.

'James "Jemmy" Edwards'. EL to Ann, 23 April 1857. Edwards was the godson of Thomas Lister Parker of Browsholme Hall, Yorkshire (now Lancashire): Lear had known Parker, a fellow of the Royal Society, since 1830, when he subscribed to the *Parrots*.

'Why are you coming?' EL to CF, 1 May 1857, *L* 50.

'poor, mean, dirty'. EL to Ann, 23 May 1857.

'the whitening of the ground'. EL to ET, 14 January 1861, *SL* 166.

'Why has Fanny Coombe'. EL to Ann, 19 June 1856: see also 29 June and 29 July.

'I have now letters'. EL to Ann, 15 December 1856.

'small dinners' EL to CF, 11 October 1861, *L* 198.

'of all things'. EL to ET, 6 March 1861, TRC/Letters 5481 (p/copy)

'painting of Nuneham'. *Nuneham* (1860), Denver.

'Captain James Dalzell'. EL to Ann, 28 December 1857, Michell.

'Frank's brother Tom'. Thomas Davies Lushington (1813–57). In 1850 m. half-cousin Mary, daughter of Charles May Lushington, a judge and Member of the Council at Madras.

'HURRAH!'. EL to Ann, [August 1857], Michell.

'three weeks in Ireland'. Carlingford Diary 29 August–2 October 1857. 'L is full of good feeling, an excellent friend, & values the obligation of friendship very high – but he is over sensitive & self-tormenting.' 6 September.

'a mixture of Socrates'. EL to Mrs Ford, 30 June 1865. Sotheby's catalogue, VNA Somerville, Letter file 1865.

'Thomas Fairbairn'. Fairbairn was a keen admirer of Hunt, commissioning *The Awakening Conscience* in 1853 and corresponding about changes to *The Scapegoat*.

'Wiliam Nevill'. Nevill bought *Philae* and *Civitella at Sunrise* (1855), now Worcester Art Museum, Mass., RA Cat. 147.

'The H's'. D 31 May 1860.

'All pleased'. ET *Journal*, 3 November 1857.

'These railway matters'. EL to Ann, 25 November 1857.

'The ludicrous sentiment'. EL to CF, 6 December 1857. *L* 65.

'Some Greek of St John'. EL to CF, 6 December 1857, *L* 67.

'rhinoceros-like insensibility'. EL to CF, 26 August 1851, *L* 22. For Bowen, Young and Corfu politics, see Sonia P. Anderson, 'Sir John Young, High Commissioner for the Ionian Islands, and His Private Letter Book, 1856–57' in *Every Traveller Needs a Compass*, ed. Neil Cooke and Vanessa Daubeny (2015), 9–10.

'Somehow I did nothing'. D 4 January 1858.

'one cannot help feeling'. EL to CF, 27 December 1857, *L* 72.

'millennial, corpse-like'. D 3 January, 3 February 1858. See also 7, 14, 27 February.

21. Bible Lands

'Tell them you introduce'. EL to HH, 7 February 1857, (Huntington) BL RP 800/1.

'but I suppose'. FL to ET, 18 January 1857, TRC/Letters 5445

'read as much as he could'. EL to Ann, 24 December 1857. For 'Pilgrim of Bordeaux' and a longer list of reading see EL to CF, 27 December 1857, *L* 69–70. Books mentioned include William Francis Lynch, *Narrative of the United States Expedition to the River Jordan and the Dead Sea* (1849); Edward Robinson, *Biblical Researches in Palestine and Adjacent Regions: A Journal of Travels in the Years 1838 and 1852* (1856); Félicien de Saulcy, *Narra-*

tive of a Tour around the Dead Sea, and in the Bible Lands (1853).

'David Roberts'. *The Holy Land, Syria, Idumea, Arabia, Egypt and Nubia*, 3 vols (1842–9).

'turquoises & emeralds'. EL to Ann, 28 December 1857.

'reassuring Ann'. EL to Ann, 2 February 1858.

'Brought up by women'. EL to CF, 9 March 1858, L 92.

'set off alone'. He had planned to go with Samuel Clowes (1821–98), son of Col. Clowes of Broughton Hall, Lancs, MP for Derbyshire 1868, High Sheriff 1888, an adventurous, military Derbyshire squire whom he had known at Knowsley.

'Weather frightful'. D 13 March 1858.

'some good Ministers'. Ellen to Fanny (Frederick's sister-in-law), 25 March 1854, Family letters.

'Stoke Newington'. EL to ET, 28 October 1855, TRC/Letters 5411.

'Anglo-Sunday'. D 22 September 1861.

'After dinner'. D 19 April 1859.

'Athanasian Creed'. Final section. *Book of Common Prayer.*

'or they would not say'. EL to CF, 21 October 1862, *L* 252.

'A man's life'. EL quoted in letter from Eleanor Newsom, 4 February 1873, Family letters.

'my own preference'. EL to HH, 15 October 1856, (Huntington) BL RP 800/1.

'*Phaedo*'. EL to CF, 3 January 1858, *L* 75.

'Renewal of Egyptian impressions'. D 19 March 1858.

'20 different languages'. EL to Ann, 29 March 1858.

'I saw all the places'. EL to Ann, 29 March 1858.

'of a kind I had not looked for'. EL to Ann, 29 March 1858. The preacher, Revd Barnes, son of the secretary to the Bishop of Exeter, was, said Lear, 'an old friend'.

'Martha, Martha'. Luke 10, 41–2.

'holy ground'. Thomas Seddon, *Memoir and Letters of the Late Thomas Seddon* (1858), quoted in Allen Saley, *The Pre-Raphaelite Landscape* (2001), 133.

'lo! the Dead Sea'. D 28 March 1858.

'Afterwards'. D 29 March 1858. His dinner companions were 'the usual party: Gibbs, Reginald Barnes [the preacher Lear had admired], Turner, Lord Dunglass – Sykes, McAnn.'

'Hubblebubble'. Quotations for the Palestine journey are from Lear's journal. Also printed as 'A Leaf from the Journal of a Landscape Painter', ed. Franklin Lushington for *Macmillan's Magazine* 75 (April 1897), 410–30.

'an ancient temple'. Identified today as the Temple of the Winged Lion. For precise location of Lear's sketches in Petra, see G. W. Bowerstock, *From Gibbon to Auden: Essays on the Classical Tradition* (2009), 101–8.

'you may imitate'. EL to Ann, 23 April 1858.

'a religion professing'. EL to Lady W, 27 May 1858, *SL* 156.

'natural grandeur'. RA cat. 112.

'his most ambitious painting'. *Cedars of Lebanon*. Watercolours include V&A P.4-1930; Ashmolean WA1942.169 (21 May 1858). See also Nicholas Tromans, 'The Orient in Perspective' in *The Lure of the East: British Orientalist Painting* (2008), 102–9.

22. *A Was an Ass*

'A was an Ass'. John Rylands Library, for Tatton children: published as *Facsimile of a Nonsense Alphabet* (1926). Known alphabets include: Massingberd 1851; Crake November

1857; Gage March 1858; Shakespeare March 1858; Reid March 1858; Blencow May 1859; Braham August 1860; Craven February 1862; Prescott December 1862; de Vere February 1865 (Fitzwilliam); Williams April 1866; Rawlinson June 1866; Drummond October 1866. Three were for unidentified children, published as *ABC* (1965), and 'A was an Ant' and 'A was an ape' (both in *NSSBA*), *CN* 492.

'Sir James Reid'. D 15 June 1858.

'Dear Sam'. *CN* 492.

'The pasting and the ironing'. ET to EL, 11 January 1856, TRC/Letters 5437. The TRC catalogue for the sale in 1980 noted: 'Mounted on canvas. Professionally removable'.

'3 Alphabets'. EL to CF, 10, 27 February 1858, *L* 88. For Colonel Edward and Arabella Gage ('very good people'), for Ida Néa Shakespear, and the Reids' two-year-old.

'Enthusiastic Elephant'. *CN* 259, for the Terry children, 25–31 August 1871.

'stories of Papa'. 'A was an Area Arch', *CN* 306–18, for the children of Revd Walter Clay, 1871. MS Princeton, Robert Taylor Collection, RTC01 (75).

'In one letter'. EL to Mrs Gurney Sutton, 7 May 1870, Beinecke GEN MSS 601.

'are you a tome'. EL to Mansfield Parkyns, [26 July 1865], Houghton BMS Eng 707.

'What would Neptune say'. EL to CF, 16 August 1863, *L* 288.

'What letter'. EL to CF, 13 September 1871, *LL* 141.

'mishearings and battles'. Adam Phillips, *The Beast in the Nursery* (1998), 47.

'immense lots of tangle'. *Excursions* vol. 2, 3 April 1845.

'horrible borrible'. EL to ET, 30 December 1861, TRC/Letters 5477.

'the perspective'. EL to CF, 1 February 1858, *L* 85.

'Ribands & pigs'. Undated, but the first seven verses are on paper watermarked 1849, the rest 1850. *CN* 493n. See Hugh Haughton, 'Edward Lear and the "Fiddleydiddlety" of Representation', *The Oxford Handbook of Victorian Poetry*, ed. Matthew Bevis (2013).

'pictogram letter'. Yale University Library, Tennyson papers, Box 3/161.

'if he dined alone'. D 29 July 1862.

23. *Home Again, Rome Again*

'Foord and Dickinson'. Sometimes spelled 'Dickenson'. For the company's connection with Turner and the Pre-Raphaelites, see 'The Frame Blog', archives, 19th century.

'sent details'. EL to CF, 25 November 1858, *L* 119.

'Knowsley'. He stayed at Knowsley Cottage with Wyndham Hornby, purchaser of one of his paintings of Corfu, son of Revd Geoffrey Hornby.

'the most beautiful things'. Thomas Woolner to ET, 22 October [1858], Noakes 139, citing Amy Woolner, *Thomas Woolner, R.A.* (1917), 154.

'*the* painter'. D 24 August 1858.

'Much conversation'. D 28 October 1858.

'many true & kind words'. D 18 September 1855.

'impatience blindness & misery'. D 12 October 1858.

'O! Mimber for the County Louth'. EL to CF, 4 November 1859, *L* 155–6, *CN* 152–3.

'A very ugly woman'. D 28 November 1858.

'& it does seem most wondrous'. D 2 December 1858.

'deep black bitter melancholy'. D 27 December 1858.

'Indeed, indeed'. D 24 December 1858.

'We are in the desert'. EL to Ann, 1 January 1859.

'4 male & 6 female Arabs'. EL to Ann, 19 February 1859.

'a great roaring watering place'. Elizabeth Barrett Browning to Isa Blagden, 15 February 1859, quoted in Alison Chapman and Jane Stabler, *Unfolding the South: Nineteenth-Century British Women Writers and Artists in Italy* (2003), 83.

'and one from Hosmer'. D 9 May 1859.

'The Cushman sings'. William Wetmore Story to Lowell, in Henry James, *William Wetmore Story and His Friends* (1903), vol. 1, 255. See D 28, 29 January 1859.

'Oh I so long'. Elizabeth Gaskell to William and Emelyn Story, July 1858, *The Letters of Mrs Gaskell*, ed. J. Chapple and A Pollard (1966), 515, 642.

'the lover of Italy'. James, *William Wetmore Story*, vol. 1, 246.

'everyone shook his hand and went away'. EL to Ann, 19 February 1859.

'very much like his mother'. D 6 February 1858.

'I shewed him'. D 29 March 1859.

'To tell truth'. EL to Charles Church, 15 March 1859. VNA, Somerville, Letter file 1859.

'All public news'. D 30 April 1859.

'three full "lots"'. D 9 May 1859.

'At present'. EL to CF, 12 June 1859, *L* 139.

'independentissimo'. EL to CF, 7 September 1859, *L* 152.

'puddle along the shingly beach'. EL to CF, 18 July 1859, *L* 146.

'I am tired'. 'The Courtship of the Yonghy-Bonghy-Bò', *CN* 325.

'There *is* no Peace'. 'First news from Villafranca', *The Poetical Works of Elizabeth Barrett Browning* (1932), 547.

'Tuscany'. EL to CF, 18 July 1859, *L* 147. In the negotiations Piedmont-Sardinia absorbed Lombardy: the duchies of Parma and Modena joined Piedmont against Austria.

'Bowels, stomach'. D 26, 27 December 1859.

'stagnation'. EL to CF, 6 January 1860, *L* 162.

'I deeply hate this place'. D 3 February 1860.

'Have I ever lied'. D 15 February 1860, and EL to Ann, 16 February, 11 March 1860.

'Better never to have been born'. D 21 February 1860. Translation from note to Marco Graziosi's transcription.

'actual as a wall'. D 4, 5 April 1860; EL to Ann, 11 April 1860.

'Charles Coleman'. Coleman's family had no sympathy for his Italian wife Fortunata and eight children. Lear wrote to his brother offering money to help pay his passage.

'foaming with spirit'. D 11 March 1860.

'What good does one get'. EL to ET, n.d. 1860, Noakes 146.

'No sir'. EL to Ann, 27 March 1860. Lear began to pack on 13 April.

'calmly enough'. D 25 May 1860.

24. No More

'the Lady of Astolât'. D 7 June 1859.

'looking out of the window'. 10 June 1859, ET *Journal* 136.

'computing moderately'. EL to CF, 12 June 1859, *L* 138.

'five more Tennyson songs'. These were 'Home they brought her warrior dead', 'As through the land at eve we went', 'Come not when I am dead', 'O let the solid ground not fail' and 'The time draws near', published by Cramer, Beale & Co., 1859. Lear had also planned to add 'Break, break, break' and 'O, that 'twere possible'. Houghton Typ 805 L.53. D 14 September 1858. (Robert Tear recorded these in 1984.)

'wonderfully beautiful'. 8 April 1859, ET *Journal* 134, and ET to EL, 16 April 1859. TRC/ Letters 5459.

'settings from *Idylls of the King*'. Others included 'Turn, fortune, turn' and 'Late, late, so late', also arranged with Rimbault's help. Lear's copy of the *Idylls*, signed by Tennyson 'July 12./59', was sold at Sotheby's New York, December 2015.

'Prinseps'. Sarah's husband, Henry Thoby Prinsep, was on the advisory Council of India. Their artist son Valentine was a friend of Millais, Burne-Jones and Rossetti.

'Virginia Woolf'. See Hermione Lee, *Virginia Woolf* (1996), 86–90.

'odious incense palaver' D 16 June 1860.

'most disagreeably querulous'. D 17 June 1860.

'polykettlejarring'. EL to ET, 16 February 1862, TRC/Letters 5491.

'We come no more'. D 16 June 1860.

'Pattledom'. D 11 February 1861.

'But all experience'. Pitman 125, and see Richard Cronin, 'Edward Lear and Tennyson's Nonsense' in *Tennyson among the Poets*, ed. Robert Douglas-Fairhurst and Seamus Perry (2009), 269.

'there is nothing'. EL to CF, 26 August 1851, *L* 20.

'his twenty-one years seemed'. D 15 October 1858.

'it is not easy to say why'. D 1 June 1870.

'Bother all painting'. EL to CF, 9 July 1860, *L* 141–4, *CN* 153–4.

'subscription'. See EL to HH, 9 December 1859.

'cedars of Lebanon'. D 9 July 1860.

'I am wretched.' D 26 July 1860. Colonel Charles Churchill, *Mount Lebanon. A Ten Years' Residence from 1842 to 1852*, 3 vols (1853).

'wonderfully fine'. D 15 July 1860; also 'Great & fine Cedars'. Lear was back again at Ockham on 30 September 1860.

'seized with incapacity to work'. D 28 November 1860.

'for truth and conscientious work'. *The Times*, 11 February 1861.

'Other reviews'. The *Morning Chronicle*, 11 February, thought it overpriced, sacrificing art for 'the absolute representation of a peculiar and arbitrarily chosen aspect of nature'. The *Illustrated London News*, 2 March, and the *Saturday Review*, 6 April, see Marco Graziosi, 'Reviews of Edward Lear's Masada', Bosh, 11 February 2011.

'diabolical Professor Tindall'. D 7 February 1861.

'Sir Francis Goldsmid' (1808–78). *Civitella* is now in the Clothworkers Hall, City of London. Goldsmid bought paintings of Mount Athos (1862), Piana Rocks and Bavella, Corsica (1869). Julia Goldsmid also bought several paintings and drawings.

'all my debts'. EL to ET, 6 March 1861, TRC/Letters 5482.

'poor dear'. D 25 September 1858.

'My kind love'. EL to Ann, 16 February 1860.

'She will bounce'. EL to Ann, 3 February 1859.

'Islington'. Ann moved in June to live here with 'Miss Randall and Miss Peel'. EL to Ann, June 1860, Michell.

'curious stories'. D 21 December 1860.

'Ann – dear Ann'. D 1 February 1861.

'what a blessing'. EL to ET, 6 March 1861, TRC/Letters 5482.

'her pain'. D 8 March 1861.

'sending Ellen to bed'. D 10 March 1861.

'a change'. EL to CF, 7 March 1861, *L* 183.

'all at sea'. EL to CF, 18 March 1861, *L* 184.

'Therefore wander'. D 5 April 1861.

'the Artillery ground'. D 9 May 1861.

'*Mandate mi un lettera*'. EL to Marstrand, 25 May 1861, Gillies.

'the *real* view of Turner'. D 12 June 1861.

'his heart bled for Browning'. D 29 June 1861.

'Mary had died'. D 17 June 1861.

'I suppose'. EL to CF, 26 August 1861, *L* 191. The most recent battle, on 10 August, was Wilson's Creek in Missouri, Frederick's home state, a Confederate victory. In 1863 Frederick's son Frank was taken prisoner: Henry's son died on sick leave in Boston, late 1864.

'Ever all she was to me'. D 17 January 1865.

25. '*Overconstrained to Folly*': Nonsense, *1861*

'always so quiet'. D 31 March 1861.

'Jemmy'. D 2 April 1861.

'Little Kathleen'. D 4 April 1861.

'so I took them on my knee'. D 27 May 1861. They turned out to be Mary and Robert Clive, children of his friend Robert Clive (not the same family as Archer Clive.) Lear was also friendly with George Clive (Under Secretary of State for the Home Department, 1859–62).

'no one in but the baby'. Visiting the Crakes, D 24 September 1861.

'Assuredly one'. D 1 September 1861.

'bosh requires a good deal of care'. EL to David Morier, 12 January 1871, *SL* 228.

'distracting Miss G.' EL to CF, 11 October 1861, *LL* 198. For Lear and Julia Goldsmid see Montgomery, 138–62, although I disagree that Lear thought of marriage.

'gt. Laughter'. D 30 September 1861. See 12 September: 'Looked over Nonsenses, & gave some nonsense prints to the little boy next door.'

'Dalziel brothers'. George Dalziel (1815–1902), from Newcastle, set up the firm in 1839, joined by his brothers Edward, John and Thomas, and his sister Margaret: from 1850 they worked closely with Routledge. [G. Dalziel and E. Dalziel], *The Brothers Dalziel: a record of fifty years' work . . . 1840–1890* (1901). D 1 February 1861, EL notes: 'I came to Dalzell's, & gave them 2 nonsenses to woodcut.'

'A wary Scotsman'. D 1 November 1861. For McLean relinquishing all rights, D 10 October 1861. The agreement in Routledge registers, 5 November 1861, notes that they will buy 'at 2/6 per copy, 13 as 12 less 15%', F. A. Mumby, *The House of Routledge* (1934).

'dropped three limericks'. These were 'The Old Sailor of Compton', 'The Old Man of Kildare' and 'The Old Man Of New York'.

'the large dresses'. EL to CF, 6 September 1863, *L* 290.

'now they can postulate'. EL to CF, 25 July 1877, *LL* 205–6.

'Incongruous'. See Cronin, 'Edward Lear and Tennyson's Nonsense', 263.

'so then I partly sleep'. EL to ET, 6 March 1861, TRC/Letters 5481.

'Perhaps it is better'. EL to CF, 18 October 1875, *LL* 187.

'easily bored'. EL to CF, 2 February 1862, *L* 225.

'I am come to a point', D 15 June 1862.

'dirty boots'. EL to ET, 15 December 1861, *SL* 173.

'Lewis Carroll'. Carroll had a go at limericks when he was thirteen; two are in *Useful and Instructive Poetry*. See Robert Douglas-Fairhurst, *The Story of Alice* (2015), 39–40.

'defied sense'. *Spectator*, 17 December 1870, archive.spectator.co.uk.

'*Water-Babies*'. EL to Charles Kingsley, 8 November 1871, *Notes and Queries* (June 1969): see Bosh, 1 June 2015.

'the rules "they" imposed'. For this social aspect see Ina Rae Hark, 'Edward Lear: Eccentricity and Victorian "Angst"', *Victorian Poetry* 16 (1978), 65–85.

'conformity is the first thing'. J. S. Mill, *On Liberty* (1859, 2nd edition), 110–11.

'little time for oddity'. Aldous Huxley described Lear's limericks as 'episodes from the eternal struggle between the genius or eccentric and his fellow beings': 'Edward Lear' in *On The Margin* (1923), 169.

'If an author pipe'. Christopher Ricks, 'Tennyson', *ODNB*.

'Darwin's researches'. *Journal* (1845), 361. Darwin's journal was originally the third part of the four-volume *Narrative of the Surveying Voyages of Her Majesty's Ships Adventure and Beagle* (1839); revised as *Journal of Researches into the Natural History and Geology of the Countries Visited during the Voyage of HMS Beagle round the World 1832–5.*

Essays and Reviews. Edited by J. W. Parker, dubbed 'the manifesto of Liberal Anglicanism'. Contributors included Benjamin Jowett, Frederick Temple, Baden Powell, Rowland Williams, H. B. Wilson, C. W. Goodwin and Mark Pattison.

'Apropos of the Essays & Reviews'. D 16 February 1861.

'Should Williams be condemned'. EL to CF, 2 February 1862, *L* 225.

'I begin to be vastly weary'. EL to Lady W, 15 March 1863, *L* 277, 276.

'Ernest Renan'. EL to CF, 9 August 1853, *L* 285.

'advanced or liberal principles'. EL to TW, 1 May 1870, *SL* 216.

'Jonah'. Book of Jonah 2, verse 5.

26. Mr Lear the Artist

'to meet Lear'. AT to Granville Bradley, Ann Thwaite, *Emily Tennyson* (2009) 305.

'took an immense amount of time'. See *Painter* 13–14.

'Millais'. D 23 April 1861.

'Charles Roundell'. MP for Grantham and Skipton. Picture, 1862, Charles Nahum Ltd. Roundell bought three more paintings of 1862: *Mont Blanc, Pont Pelissar, The Dead Sea* and *Cliffs of Cenc, Goʒo*. In 1872 he bought *Ravenna Forest.*

'No life is more *shocking*'. EL to CF, 29 August 1861, *L* 189; Taunton has 'damnable'.

'which I must now wash'. EL to CF, 21 January 1862, *L* 222.

'the concluding paragraph'. EL to CF, 5 September 1861, *L* 194.

'a new spadmodic poet'. EL to CF, 11 October 1861, *L* 198.

'Caroline Jones'. D 10 October 1861. After his first wife Sarah died Henry Chesmer m. Caroline in Montreal in 1818: in 1828, two years after his death, she married Senator Robert Jones, a Quebec politician. Lear met Jessie on 21 September, 'wonderfully like her father

& my aunt & father, but goodlooking & very lively & nice'.

'Major Foy', D 2 November 1861.

'a help and a pleasant sight'. Maria Lushington to ET, 29 September 1855, TRC/Letters 3925.

'snow, peasoups'. EL to ET, 15 December 1861 TRC 5490.

'looking back'. D 24 December 1861.

'the too close boskiness'. EL to ET, 16 February 1862, *SL* 174.

'the luckiest dog'. CF to EL, 19 September 1862, *L* 247.

'a dim hum'. EL to CF, 20 April 1862, *L* 234.

'o dear dear these dinners'. D 13 June 1862.

'met Mrs Gaskell'. D 28, 29 June 1862.

'Tom Taylor'. 'Pictures at the International Exhibition: V', *The Times*, 11 June 1862. Taylor's main criticism was aimed at John Brett. When Lear met Taylor he thought him 'superficial and bumptious & not altogether well bred', EL to HH, 5 July 1862, HRC MS-2415.

'vastly fine'. EL to CF, 3 October 1862, *L* 248–9.

'What to do'. EL to CF, 4 October 1862, *L* 249.

'began to draw outlines'. D 26 November 1862.

'Paradise weather'. D 28 December 1862.

'a singular spotch'. D 10 February 1863; 'spot' in letter to CF, 8 February 1863, *L* 271.

'He was then at work'. Henry Strachey, quoted by Sir Edward Strachey, Introduction, *NSS* ix.

'There's a proof'. EL to CF, 1 March 1863, *L* 274.

'photographic machine'. EL to Ann, 21 May 1856. See D 1 February 1858 for new camera.

'Lewis Carroll bought his first camera'. 18 March 1856: Lindsay Smith, *Lewis Carroll: Photography on the Move* (2015), 11.

'Major Shakespear'. John Davenport Shakespear. After fighting in the Crimea, Shakespear m. Louisa Sayer and was posted to Corfu in 1855. For Lear's sale of the camera, D 4 February 1858. Seventy of his photographs are in the Mon Repos Museum, Corfu. See also *Edward Lear: The Corfu Years*, ed. Philip Sherrard (1988).

'my dear Lear'. CF to EL, 19 January 1863, Taunton.

'the de Veres'. D 30 November 1862.

'coloured birds'. D 8 March 1863.

'the Shelleys'. D 7–23 March 1863.

'the "demon"'. D 31 January 1863.

'This home'. D 18 March 1863.

27. *'From Island unto Island'*

'enough tin', and limerick. EL to CF, 23 March 1863, *Lear's Corfu*, 34.

'utter contempt'. Frances McLellen, *Sketches of Corfu* (1835), quoted in *CY* Introduction, 16.

'You may not have heard'. EL to Edgar Drummond, 23 March 1863, *SL* 181–2.

'O reason not the need'. *King Lear*, II, iv, 267.

'a furious pamphlet'. Frank Lushington, *Ionian Judges*, June 1863.

'awfully Sabbatical'. D 11 April 1863.

'hideously dry'. D 18 April 1863.

'Great naked slabs of rock'. D 6 April 1863, Paxos.

'My master'. 29 April 1863, Ithaca.

'Lord Byron's house'. D 7 May 1863.

'smoke, noise'. D 7 May 1863.

'Korax'. D 27 April 1863. Translations are from Marco Graziosi's transcription, Bosh, 30 April 2013.

'It seems to me'. D 12 May 1863.

'the Gk. Throne'. D 3 June 1863.

'But nothing removes'. D 29 June 1863.

'being *well done*'. EL to CF, 9 August 1863, *L* 284.

'hoped to use photographs'. D 22 July 1863.

'I could absolutely hear'. EL to CF, 14 September 1863, *L* 292.

'*Views in the Seven Ionian Islands*'. For further reading he recommended *The Ionian Islands in the Year 1863*, by D. T. Ansted, whom he had helped in Corfu, and despite his dislike for George Bowen, he mentioned his contributions to Murray's *Handbook* (1845).

'old man with a Book'. EL to Mrs Prescott, 1863. Ashmolean Museum, Oxford.

'What a beautiful book!'. ET to EL, 24 December 1863, TRC/Letters 5503.

'to ask the Queen'. EL to CF, 6 September 1863, *L* 289.

'Arch-nonsense-chatter-maker'. I adopt the flexible translation used by James Williams, *Play* 19.

'perhaps I may go'. EL to CF, 15 January 1864, *L* 303.

'Deerbaring'. EL to Evelyn Baring, 1864, *SL* 195.

'The quiet of this house'. D February 1864.

'Goodbye'. EL to CF, 31 March 1864, *L* 308.

'little Nora Decie'. 3 April 1864. Ashmolean Library.

'Once more' and 'the Bulbul'. D 4 April 1864.

'George Finlay'. Lear had been reading Finlay's early volumes: D 7 February 1863.

'set off for Crete'. Lear's Crete journal, 4 April–4 May 1864, Houghton MS Typ 55.24. The third edition of Lear's *Cretan Journal* (*CJ*) transcribed by Rowena Fowler, contains an appendix on his drawings: for listings see Stephen Duckworth, 'Edward Lear and Crete' (2015), edwardlearandcrete.weebly.com, and *Edward Lear's Cretan Drawings* (2011) from the Gennadius Library, Athens, which holds 205 drawings.

'the women and children'. D 7 April 1864, *CJ* 26.

'Madeleine'. D 23 May 1864.

'*Villette*'. D 2 May 1864.

'Its antiquities etc.'. D 15 April, *CJ* 31.

'Knossos'. D 11 May 1864, CJ 66.

'a dream-like vast pile'. D 24 May 1864.

'the vast multitude of blackbirds'. D 15 May 1864.

'eggs, olives'. 21 April 1864, *CJ* 37.

'*snails*' D 8 May 1864.

'different communities'. Rowena Fowler, *CJ*, Introduction, 11.

'The Venetian cathedral'. D 10 May 1864, *CJ* 65.

'uprisings'. There were rebellions against Turkish rule in 1821–7, 1841 and 1858.

'Michael Korakis'. D 10 May 1864, *CJ* 112, n. 67.

'our unhappy country'. D 16 May 1864, translation from Greek, *CJ* 82.

'All Crete diminishes'. D 31 May 1864.

28. 'What a charming life an artist's is!'

'a Nem'. EL to Mrs Prescott, 12 October 1864, *SL* 198–9, Ashmolean.

'to his funeral'. D 18 July 1864.

'one of the places I am really happy in'. D 15 October 1864.

'Pattledom has taken entire possession'. EL to CF, 19 October 1864, *LL* 47.

'Mrs Cameron'. Julia Margaret Cameron (1815–79). ET to EL, 17 February 1865, TRC/ Letters 5508.

'the prettiest children'. Lewis Carroll to Julia Margaret Cameron, M. N. Cohen (ed.) *Letters of Lewis Carroll* (1979), vol. 1, 66.

'going down hill'. D 15 October 1864.

'Four ladies'. EL to HH, 6 October 1864, (Huntington) BL RP 800/1. This irresistible scene is also quoted, in full, in Noakes 174.

'his Crete drawings'. Lear penned out 196 Cretan sketches and coloured 48. D, throughout July 1864.

'absurd & utopian'. D 11 July 1864.

'Reading Bates'. Henry Walter Bates, *The Naturalist on the River Amazons* (1863). Bates found seven thousand species of ant and other insects, and 550 species of butterfly, around Ega above Para: EL to CF, 8 October 1864, *LL* 48; EL to ET, 10 May 1865, *SL* 204.

'the lopsided views'. D 12 December 1864.

'Lear made his sketches'. He made 145: EL to HH, 7 January 1865, *SL* 202.

'I loathe London'. EL to ET, 10 May 1865, *SL* 204–5.

'How tremendously full'. D 7 November 1865.

'O! O! what a sunset'. D 10 November 1865.

'undiplomatic & demonstrative nature'. EL to Lady W, 24 November 1865, *LL* 64.

'Fenian attacks'. Since the famine of 1847, resentment against the British had grown: the 1860s saw Fenian attacks on British forts in the United States and Canada, and uprisings in Ireland, quickly suppressed.. Fortescue introduced a new land bill to alleviate tension, but was out of office in July 1866, before he could see it through. He returned in 1868.

'Read papers'. D 31 January 1866.

'No greater bore'. D 9 December 1865.

'Wonderfully shrilly-howly'. D 20 December 1865.

'hardly a bit of green'. EL to Ann, 19 April 1848.

'sparklingness'. D 28 January 1866.

'visit to Gozo'. EL to Lady W, 30 March 1866, *LL* 60. See Joseph Attard Tabone, 'Edward Lear in Gozo, March 1866' in *Every Traveller Needs a Compass: Travel and Collecting in Egypt and the Near East*, ed. Neil Cooke Neil and Vanessa Daubney, 15–22.

'isle of Calypso'. EL to Henry Luard, 22 April 1866, HRC MS-2415; *CN* 210.

'It was most beautiful'. D 31 January 1866.

29. 'The "Marriage" Phantasy'

'Every marriage'. EL to CF, 22 August 1868, *LL* 105.

'Tittering'. D 16 November 1858.

'frightful discussion'. D 9 July 1859.

'sequax'. EL to CF, 21 October 1862, *L* 252–3.

'Mansfield Parkyns'. *Life in Abyssinia: Being Notes collected during three years' Residence and Travels* (1853, revised and expanded 1868).

'disjointed'. D 14 April 1861.

'a dear good true little girl'. D 19 September 1858.

'she had already published'. Her books include *Echoes of an Old Bell, and other Tales of Fairy Lore* (1865); *Maud Latimer: a Tale for Young People* (1863); translation of the French version of Fernan Caballero's *La Gaviota*, published as *The Sea-Gull* (1867); *Helen in Switzerland: A Tale for Young People* (1868); *Love and Life in Norway* (c.1870, translated with Augusta Plesmer); *A Village Maiden* (1871); *Millicent and her Cousins* (1881).

'angel in the house'. D 10 June 1859. Patmore's poem 'The Angel in the House', based on his courtship of and marriage to his wife Emily, was published in parts, 1854–62.

'cut away'. D 17 February 1861.

'Would one have been as happy?'. D 13 April 1862.

'dear little Gussie'. D 24–27 June, 1862.

'As pleasant a day'. D 27 July 1863.

'perhaps as lovely'. D 4 October 1863.

'A pleasant, but very sad visit'. D 6 October 1863.

'This visit will I fear'. D 8 July 1864.

'The risk of trying'. D 9 July 1864.

'woman wheeled in the barrow'. This figure appears in old nursery rhymes, as a woman to be 'bought', and also in *Sixteen Wonderful Women*: for these, and medieval images, see Bosh, 25 February, 17 July 2014.

'Best so'. D 9 October 1864.

'Was there ever such a man'. D 9 July 1865.

'for a moment'. D 23 September 1865.

'Would Gussie like to live here?'. D 18 April 1866.

'beside the mark'. D 20 April 1866.

'a pleasant evening'. D 29 May 1866.

'Like a sudden spark'. D 1 June 1866.

'the "marriage" phantasy'. D 2 June 1866.

'take my chances'. D 25 July 1966.

'For the gulf is not to be passed'. D 23 September 1866.

'not at home'. D 4 October 1866.

'Down the slippery slopes of Myrtle'. 'The Courtship of the Yonghy-Bonghy-Bò', *CN* 326.

'The Duck and the Kangaroo'. *CN* 207–9 and n. 304. Lear noted in his copy of *NSSBA* that this was written at Chewton Priory 'in 1865 or 1866' for the children of Sir Edward Strachey. The first surviving MS was for the family of George Clive, 19 October 1868

'a faithful serving man'. D 17 March 1863.

'if that Lady'. D 21 April 1863.

'Don't you see'. D 17 April 1864.

30. Gradually Extinguished

'Seriously, it does seem'. EL to Henry Bruce, 8 December 1866. Glamorgan DBR 153.

'Claret 8'. D 2 December 1867.

'even if I turn Mussulman'. EL to CF, 11 December 1866, *LL* 81.

'violent lively American damsel'. D 12 December 1866.

'as usual somewhat melancholy'. *Recollections of Lady Georgiana Peel* (1920), 239, quoted by Marco Grazioso, 'Edward Lear in Malta', Bosh, 11 January 2016.

'borrowed from friends'. EL to Lady W, 9 March 1867, *SL* 208. The plan was to travel up the Nile to Nubia, then to head for Jerusalem, Galilee and Nazareth and on to Tyre and Sidon and possibly Palmyra. Finding that the trip to Nubia would cost £400, Lear asked Lady Waldegrave, Monkton Milnes (Lord Houghton), Mrs Clive, Bernard Husey Hunt, Thomas Fairbairn, Johnny Cross, William Langton and Frank Lushington to lend him £100 each. Milnes had commissioned a painting of Nazareth, and Lear asked for half the money in advance; when he failed to reach Nazareth he returned the money and sent a drawing of Philae.

'O sugar canes!'. D 25 December 1866.

'Holman Hunt's wife'. Fanny died in Florence, two months after their son, Cyril Benoni, was born: her sister Edith looked after the baby, while Hunt stayed on in Italy alone.

'a steam working engine'. D 6 January 1867.

'& where one peeps'. D 16 January 1867.

'I hope to goodness'. EL to Mrs Digby, 30 December 1866, VNA Somerville, Letter File 1866, 751.

'the American element'. EL to Lady W, 9 March 1867, *LL* 83–4.

'lovely rounded muscles'. D 21 February 1867.

'perfectly astonishing'. D 18 January 1867.

'to represent such beauty'. D 28 January 1867.

'careless, foolish'. D 9 January 1867.

'to the utmost perfection'. D 2 February 1867.

'sad, stern, uncompromising'. EL to Lady W, 9 March 1867, *LL* 83.

'so tired that he turned round'. D 15 April 1867.

'I knew Dan's writing'. D 18 May 1867 [Ravenna 6 May].

'Gussie: – dreamland'. D 25 October 1867.

'It is absurd'. D 2 November 1867.

'*broke up a dream*'. D 3 November 1867.

'T. H. Huxley'. 'The Special Peculiarities of Man', 16 March 1858, in Desmond and Moore, *Darwin*, 465.

'a very great brute'. D 31 July 1864.

'too wonderful'. Quoted in Steve Jones, *The Darwin Archipelago* (2011).

'Disraeli'. Speech at Oxford Diocesan conference, 25 November 1864.

'driven to despair'. *Daily News*, 3 May 1865 (also *Morning Post*).

'close to the Prescotts'. Lear's letters to the Prescott and Decie families are in the Ashmolean.

'nobody ought to marry'. EL to ET, 10 May 1865, *SL* 204. Sarah Lear decided that Charles Street could travel with a 'guard and assistant'. The third case was H. G. Mildmay.

'Nothing could exceed'. This and the following letter to Lady Duncan were written on 3 and 7 January 1865. Beinecke MSS GEN 601. They were published in *Bosh & Nonsense* in 1983, with a manuscript of limericks that Lear drew for Anna's eleven-year-old sister Ada. (Ada is often described as the recipient of the frog letters.)

'pigeon fanciers'. Charles Darwin to T. H. Huxley, 27 November 1859, *Life and Letters of Charles Darwin*, ed. Francis Darwin, 1887.

'Dear old Mrs Wentworth'. D 11 February 1865.

'drew some birds'. D 1 February 1865.

'made them an alphabet'. D 10 February 1865.

'absurd lot of stories'. D 13 February 1865.

'Very happily for me'. EL to CF, 9 August 1867, *LL* 86.

'satire on religious rows'. Sara Lodge, 'Edward Lear and Dissent', *Play* 85–6.

'John Hanning Speke and Richard Burton'. John Hanning Speke, *The Discovery of the Source of the Nile* (1863). For the feud, see Tim Jeal, *Explorers of the Nile* (2011).

'toucan'. Henry Walter Bates, *In The Heart of the Amazon Forest* (selection, 2007).

'London Acclimatisation Society'. Richard Girling, *The Man Who Ate the Zoo: a Life of Frank Buckland* (2016), 174–5.

'Here is Defoe'. *Robinson Crusoe*, 47.

'elaborate plumes'. For discussion of 'borrowed plumes' see Matt Bevis, 'Lear's Lines of Flight', *Journal of the British Academy* I (2013), 45–8.

'Elizabeth "Pussy" Hornby'. See Colley 87–91.

'elephants' feet'. Colley 91.

'the grasshopper has become a burden'. EL to CF, 7 January 1884, *LL* 295.

31. Sail Away: Cannes 1868–1869

'and so I went away'. D 7 November 1867.

'O! O! O!' D 8 December 1867.

'All of a sudden'. D 1 December 1867.

'the most amiable good Symonds'. D 2 December 1867.

'Ekklogg'. D 9 December 1867.

'For the first time in my life'. Regis (ed.), *Memoirs*, 156.

'cohabitation'. Regis (ed.), *Memoirs*, 257.

'the purely sexual appetite'. Regis (ed.), *Memoirs*, 259–60.

'Janet Kay-Shuttleworth'. (1817–72). Her mother Janet (née Marjoribanks) m. Frederick North after the death of her first husband, Robert Shuttleworth of Gawthorpe Hall: Sir James Kay added his wife's surname in 1842. They had five children, and in 1851 she moved to the Villa Ponente, San Remo, while Sir James remained in Manchester.

'What the Greeks called *paiderastia*'. J. A. Symonds, *A Problem in Greek Ethics: Studies in Sexual Inversion* (2002 edn), 11.

'The little girl is unwell'. D 14 December 1867.

'walked to the Symonds'. D 18 December 1867.

'The Owl and the Pussy-cat', *CN* 238–9. Vivien Noakes notes that the whereabouts of this MS, owned by Symond's granddaughter Dame Janet Vaughan and sold in 1937, are unknown. The drawings from original MS are in *QLN*, see *CN* n. 510–11. Lear sent copies to Lady W, 9 January 1868 (Morgan), to George Clive's family, 19 October 1869 (Houghton MS Typ 55.14), and an unillustrated one to Mrs Fields, 14 October 1869 (Morgan). Copies were also made for the children of Lord Edgcumbe, 24 January 1868, Lear's neighbour Giacinta Galleti, June 1886, and for the Nevills (nd).

'early drafts'. See Daniel Karlin, '"The Owl and the Pussy-cat", and Other Poems of Love and Marriage', *Play* 202–22, especially the variations, 205.

'I suppose some will be sold'. D 20 December 1867.

'you may have it'. EL to Edgar Drummond, 22 September 1866, *SL* 207.

'women's novels'. D 19 December 1867, 15 January 1868.

'Walt Whitman'. D 25 December 1867. William Michael Rossetti selected and edited *Poems by Walt Whitman* (1868); Symonds's *Walt Whitman: A Study* was published in 1893.

'Mr Lear, who is a whimsical Punster'. Symonds to his sister Charlotte, 1 January 1868, Horatio F. Brown, *John Addington Symonds* (1908), 252.

'an affection of the brain'. D 5 January 1868.

'the worst of my whole life'. Regis (ed.), *Memoir*, 342.

'Fierce cruel loves.' J. A. Symonds, 'Stella Maris', *Vagabunduli Libellus* (1884).

'singular Sybilline Fortitude'. *ODNB*, quoting Margaret Symonds, *Out of the Past* (1924), 163; see also K. Furse, *Hearts and Pomegranates* (1940).

'certainly a goodly amount'. D 31 December 1868.

'drew pictures for Janet and baby Lotta'. D 24 January 1868.

'rest there is none'. EL to CF, 16 August 1869, *LL* 106.

'a kind of awful doom'. ET to EL, 17 February 1865, ET *Letters* 188; also D 3 February 1865. Lear was godfather to all the Lushington children: Henry 1862–5; Louisa Gertrude, b. 1863; Edmund Henry, 1867–8; Mildred, b. 1870; Clare Emily, 1871–5; George, b. 1872, Franklin b. 1876.

'their everlasting silence'. D 11 July 1868. See also D 11 October 1868.

'Certainly, as far as I can see'. EL to CF, 22 August 1868, SHC.

'little changed'. D 28 August 1869.

'so remote & quaint'. D 8 September 1869.

'beautiful semi-oriental colour'. D 29 August 1869.

'It can't be good'. D 9 September 1869.

'how wonderfully they worry'. D 7 September 1869.

'Rose 5.30'. D 8 September 1869.

'Much fun about my poem'. D 10 October 1869.

32. *'Three Groans for Corsica!'*

'By degrees'. EL to Lady W, 9 January 1868, *LL* 91.

'I never can apply'. D 14 March 1868.

'*Colomba*'. *Corsica*, Preface.

'a vast & manlike maiden'. EL to ET, 6 May 1868, *SL* 213. Her book was *Southward Ho! Notes on the Island of Corsica in 1868* (1868).

'The children are grave'. EL to ET, 6 May 1868, *SL* 212.

'George Kokali'. *Corsica*, Preface.

'one of the most wonderfully beautiful sights.' EL to Lady W, 6 May 1868, *LL* 103.

'The trees'. EL to FC, 5 May 1868, Beinecke GEN MSS 601.

'in deepest shadow'. *Corsica* 93.

'he fantasised'. EL to ET, 6 May 1868, *SL* 213.

'A ghastly sight'. EL to Lady W, 6 May 1868.

'I eat trout'. EL to FC, 5 May 1868, Beinecke GEN MSS 601.

'Smith, Elder & Co.'. D 27 July 1868.

'quoted Epitaphs'. D 2 November 1868.

'Smithanelder'. D 7 December 1868.

'Langton is nephew of DARWIN'. D 10 January 1869. Darwin's aunt Emily Darwin married Charles Langton: his first wife was her cousin Charlotte Wedgwood.

'though he will not have more'. D 10 January 1869.

'a *real* pleasure'. D 16 May 1869.

'a good Dickens chapter'. D 21 June 1869.

'to find new places'. *Corsica* 1.

'one would fancy him a mere child'. D 13 November 1868.

'& so we all exploded'. D 27 September 1869.

'subscriptions came in'. Familiar names included the Clive family, Clowes, Edwards, Fairbairn, Goldsmid, Vernon and Godfrey Lushington, Nevill, Prescott, Potter and Percy Shelley.

33. Degli Inglesi

'*Of course*, George was there'. D 14 December 1869.

'my name in full'. EL to James Fields, 18 November 1869, *SL* 215.

'Learical Lyrics'. EL to CF, 1 January 1870, *LL* 112.

'My last mania'. D 28 September 1868. He wrote to enquire about the land on 6 October.

'it by no means follows'. D September 1869.

'Good Gracious!'. D 28 February 1870.

'Very cold all day'. D 30 March 1870.

'a stone terrace'. EL to Thomas Woolner, 1 May 1870, *Thomas Woolner*, 284, *SL* 216.

'lemon-groves'. *A Diplomat in Japan, Part II: The Diaries of Ernest Satow, 1870–88*, ed. Ian Ruxton (2009), 141.

'Thomas Hanbury'. See Charles Quest-Ritson, *The English Garden Abr*oad (1992) and Michael Nelson, *Queen Victoria and the Discovery of the Riviera* (2007).

'La Mortola'. D 17 August 1876. The painting, dated 30 December 1865, was sold at Christies, 16 November 2006. Lear also called on Hanbury in London in 1869.

'to his friend Mrs Ker'. EL to Mrs Ker, Beinecke GEN MSS MISC 10549741.

'Roya'. D 26, 27 June 1870.

'I have had advice'. EL to CF 31 July 1870, *LL* 123.

'my sudden death'. D 9 July 1870.

'Piedmontese gentry'. EL to CF, 31 July 1870, *LL* 123.

'the Certosa'. Since the 1930s the Certosa has been run by the Padri Missionari della Consolata di Torino as a religious foundation and retreat.

'Unless I WORK'. EL to CF, 31 July 1870, *LL* 122.

'There is & must be'. EL to Amelia Edwards, 26 October 1885, A. B. Edwards papers, Somerville.

'fair copies'. See for example, D 6–8 June 1870.

'completed the Jumblies'. D 7, 8 July 1870.

'the Carthusian friars'. EL to 15th Earl Derby, 26 July 1870.

'Luther Terry'. D 2 August 1870.

'drew for little Daisy Terry'. D 18 August 1870.

'rosy, gray-bearded'. Mrs Winthrop Chanler, *Roman Spring* (1934), 29–30, Noakes 211.

'a turbulent little creature'. Mrs Hugh Fraser, *A Diplomat's Wife in Many Lands* (1910), vol. 2, 333.

'strange meats'. ibid.

'Lady Jingly'. Maria Price La Touche to Mrs Severn, June 1886, *The Letters of a Noble Woman*, ed. Margaret Ferrier Young (1908), 121.

'Amblongus Pie'. *CN* 249–50. The printed version has 'Bottlephorkia spoonifolia'.

'It is funny'. D 19 February 1884.

'dined on barley broth'. D 5 March 1866; 18 December 1869.

'Biscuit Tree'. *T&Q* 57. 'Flora Nonsensica', 1871, Houghton MS Typ. 55.14.

'wrote out all the rest'. D 30 August 1870.

'& certainly' D 2 November 1870.

'Counted every hour'. D 21 November 1870.

'Charles's birthday'. D 24, 30 November 1870.

'just as if it were in Stratford Place'. EL to Lady Wyatt, 4, 11 December 1870, Morgan MA 6421

'all my Autumn & Summer Work'. D 8 December 1870.

'genuine nonsense'. *Spectator*, 17 December 1870. Archive.spectator.co.uk.

34. Nonsense Songs *and* More Nonsense

'real critters'. EL to Emma Parkyns, 18 December 1871, *SL* 233.

'poem of adventure'. T. S. Eliot, 'The Music of Poetry' (1942), *On Poetry and Poets* (1957), 30.

'whose metres were as varied'. For stanza form, scansion and rhyme-schemes see Haughton, 'Edward Lear and "The Fiddlediddlety of Representation"', *Oxford Handbook of Victorian Poetry* (2013) 351–69.

'dear little Gussie'. D 33 July 1870.

'I work without hope'. D 23 November 1870.

'In a note'. Houghton MS Typ 55.1.

'the breath of my nostrils'. EL to Nora Bruce, Florida State University, Special Collections, 24 December 1870.

'Generally speaking'. EL to EB, Introduction, *QLN* 12.

'Edward Earl'. EL to Lady W, 17 October 1866, *LL* 78–9.

'the Albanian dervish'. A connection made by James Williams; see Matthew Bevis, 'Edward Lear's Lines of Flight', *Journal of the British Academy* 1, 31–69 (2012).

'Cold as the crags'. See note, *CN* 526; also Pope, 'Cold is the breast that warmed the world before', and Tennyson's 'Tithonus': 'Cold thy rosy shadows bathe me, cold/Are all thy lights, and cold my wrinkled feet/Upon thy glimmering thresholds'. For Pope, see Byrom, 230; for 'Tithonus', Anne Stillman, 'T. S. Eliot plays Edward Lear', *Play* 272. The poem was published as a sonnet sixty-five years after Lear died in *T&Q*, 62. In *CN* it has twenty lines. In Houghton MS Typ. 55.14, the last four lines are written sideways up the page.

35. Restless in San Remo

'such a painting room'. EL to Lady W, 24 April 1871, *LL* 133.

'neither too much *in*'. EL to HH, 7 July 1870 (Huntington) BL RP 800/1.

'he chose one'. For this exchange, and the fifteenth earl's importance as a patron in Lear's late years, see Colin Harrison, 'Edward Lear's Landscapes at Knowsley' in Lloyd 179–84.

'Lear was always in want of money'. Derby diary, Liverpool, 920 DER (15) Diaries 10; 14 July 1870.

'It pleases me much'. Liverpool, 920 DER (15) Diaries 10; 18 October 1870.

'Goldsmid bought one'. D 14 January 1871.

'singularly good'. D 10 February 1872.

'very kind & friendly'. D 19 December 1870.

'Polish governess'. Rosa Poplawska. Charlotte Brontë to Ellen Nussey, 19 March 1850, Margaret Smith, ed., *Letters of Charlotte Bronte, 1848–51* (1995), 367.

'her son Ughtred'. EL to Lady W, 22 January 1871, *LL* 129. The drawings were a gift for Princess Louise, and two for Alfred Drummond. See Ughtred Kay-Shuttleworth to Sir James, 24 December 1870, 16, 21 January 1871, and Blanche Kay-Shuttleworth to Sir James, 28 November 1871: JRL, GB 133 JKS/1/1/857, 858, 859, 873.

'a 3d Mrs. C.' D 14 December 1870.

'a tall, heavily built gentleman'. Hubert Congreve, Preface, *LL* 17–18.

'gt laughter'. D 8 December 1870.

'sketched the boys'. D 27 June to 4 and 5 July 1871: the drawing was for their aunt, Miss Congreve, to whom Lear wrote on 7 July. See Bosh, 30 November 2015.

'a pious and instructive work'. EL to Nora Bruce, 24 December 1870, Florida State University.

'four pictures'. The RA exhibits were: *Cattaro in Dalmatia*; *On the Nile near Assioot*; *On the Nile, Nagadeh*; and *On the Nile, near Ballas*.

'for even if Mr Hanbury builds'. D 2 August 1870.

'Rome 1837'. D 23 July 1871.

'solace in nonsense'. 'Mr and Mrs Discobbolos', copy 24 December 1871; 'Yonghy-Bonghy-Bò', written out 11 December 1871, 'The Scroobious Pip', begun November/December, continued January 1872; CN 521–6.

'It is queer'. EF to CF, 31 December 1872, LL 123.

'coves and covesses'. EL to CF, 28 February 1872, LL 145. On Christmas Day 1871 he told CF and Lady W: 'San Remo is fullish: Knatchbulls, Philip Miles', Calls, a'Courts, Monteiths, Ldy K Buchanan & Co – Ldy. Isabella Hope & Co – Pitts, Levern Gowers, Galtons & what not'. SL 235.

'Life is pretty easy'. D 29 October 1871.

'My elth is tolerable'. EL to CF, 25 December 1871, *LL* 142.

'give up once more the chance'. D 9 March 1872.

'Vastly good dinner'. D 24 March 1872.

'travelling as part of a viceregal suite'. EL to CF, 26 May 1872, *LL* 148–9.

'a giant negro'. D 20 October 1872, in Greek, translated in Levi 259.

'*The Indian bubble*'. D 21 October 1872.

'as at Jerusalem'. D 22 October 1872.

'Ellen'. D 13 and 23 December 1871 (Giorgio heard the rumours from a local man) and 13 February 1872. See Montgomery 239–41, where Green is wrongly identified as the local Anglican vicar, corrected by Marco Graziosi, Bosh, 19 February 2016.

'the sedentary life'. EL to Lady W, 6 July 1873, *LL* 153–4.

'with a few exceptions'. EL to CF, 12 September 1873, *LL* 156.

'impossible to record'. D 19 August 1873.

'I must leave this place'. D 20 September 1873.

'altogether I considered'. EL to CF, 15 October 1873, SHC DD/SH/62/337 (2/341): Noakes 225.

'I have thought'. D 27 September 1843.

'good old George'. D 26 October 1873.

36. India

'beauty of Bombay harbour'. All quotations in this paragraph, D 22 November 1873.

'when the men change the pole'. *IJ* 11 April 1874, edited version of Lear's Indian Journals 1875–8, Houghton MS Eng 797.4. I have used the names that Lear used: modern versions include Mumbai (Bombay), Kanpur (Cawnpore), Varanasi (Benares), Kolkata (Calcutta), Pune (Poona), Chennai (Madras), Mathura (Muttra), Kozhikode (Calicut).

'What groves'. D 21 December 1873.

'Delhineations'. EL to CF, 24 April 1874, *LL* 171.

'Vast numbers'. D 2 December 1873.

'a miserable hullabaloo'. D 5 December 1873.

'At Hyderabad'. D 27 July 1874.

'What strange scenes'. *IJ* 123, 19 April 1874.

'old George'. EL to CF, 12 June 1874 (from Poona), *SL* 242.

'to speak freely'. *ODNB*, quoting Northbrook to Lord Hobart, 19 May 1872, Baring Archive, Northbrook MSS, MS Eur. C. 144/13.

'away from Levees'. Rudyard Kipling, 'His Chance in Life', *Plain Tales from the Hills* (1886). For the lack of understanding that Northbrook noted, see also Kipling's 'Tod's Amendment' about a new Land Bill.

'fluent exactness' *IJ* 103, 18 March 1874.

'Henry V'. *IJ* 203, 23 September 1874.

'The feast of words'. For the correct meanings, *CN* 533. For the swapping of English and Indian terms – a kind of 'linguistic kedgeree' – see the review of *Hobson-Jobson, A Glossary of Anglo-Indian Words or Phrases* quoted by Marco Graziosi, Bosh, 12 June 2004.

'later he added'. Houghton MS Typ 55.16.

'making fast drawings'. Over 2000 are at Houghton, including some from the return voyage, MS Typ 55.11 and 55.26. The Houghton collection also includes forty-nine drawings in Northbrook's bound volume, *Vol II. Central India 1875*. MS Typ 55.5.

'Remarked the beauty'. *IJ* 52, 31 December 1873, also quoted in Dehejia, 23.

'fuss'. D 30 January 1873, 2 January 1874.

'highly pagan and queer'. *IJ* 45, 12 December 1873.

'Taj Mahal'. *IJ* 79, 16 February 1874.

'A stupidly written book'. D 2 February 1872.

'on show in London'. e.g. D 23 July 1863. Pictures exhibited included *The Heart of the Andes* (1859), *The Icebergs* (1861), *Cotopaxi* (1862) and *Chimborazo* (1864).

'& one of his works'. He admired Church's 'unfailing force' and his ability to paint 'Arctic scenes, South American magnificences & endless other distinctly various phases of nature': EL to James Fields, 18 January 1880, RA cat. 20.

'Marble Rocks'. Lear made seven 'scraps', five larger sketches and four full-scale watercolours. Houghton MS Typ 55.26, 1494–1504; Scraps 2440–2449.

'Kinchinjunga'. Quotations are from *IJ* 63–5, 17–22 January 1874. Lear bought photographs in Darjeeling as an aide-memoire.

'his later paintings'. Lear painted three large oils, for Northbrook, Lord Aberdare and Lady Ashburton. The latter two show the Buddhist shrine.

'The poetical character'. *IJ* 180, 1 November 1874.

'good and patient always'. D 7 December 1874.

'Still getting out cargo'. D 30 1 December 1874, *IJ* 231–2.

'absolute Turner'. Houghton MS Typ 55.26. 3478 (Scrap 1157, 'En route to Bombay').

37. Families

'Oranges'. D 30 January 1875.

'odd stout big man'. *A Diplomat in Japan*, 143, 148: 21 December 1875–3 January 1876. Lear met and liked Tozer, by now curator of the Taylor Institution in Oxford in 1872, and painted many pictures for him, now in the Ashmolean.

'*mint*'. EL to Lady Wyatt, 16 April 1875, *CN* 407.

'As her son says'. D 1 April 1875.

'the only one remaining'. EL to CF, 24 May 1875, Taunton (Passage not in *LL*.)

'they say Gussie is happy'. D 1, 15 July 1875.

'Strawberry Hill'. D 10 July 1875.

'O Chichester!' *CN* 404.

'Gertrude is a duck'. D 25 September 1875; succeeding quotations 27, 28 September.

'Lear is at 8 Duchess St'. FL to ET, *c*.July 1875, TRC/Letters 3912.

'Frank & Kate'. D 30 September 1875.

'sat up very late'. D 30 June 1876.

'Letters are the only solace'. EL to Lady Wyatt, 11 December 1870, *SL* 226.

'That all this trouble-whirl'. D 21 May 1876.

'had resigned'. Northbrook resigned partly to extract his son from an affair, but also at the Foreign Office's insistence on the Tariff Act, abolishing duties on Indian cotton imports to please Lancashire manufacturers, and at their aggressive stance towards Afghanistan.

'pile of novels'. *Lothair*, D 9 June; *Middlemarch*, D 10 June; *Sylvia's Lovers*, D 19 August; Edgeworth, D 8 October 1875.

'vermouth'. D 21 November 1875.

'must ask F.L.'. D 9 June 1875.

'Alack! Alack!' D 29 August 1875.

'Wolff's Wild Animals'. Joseph Wolf (1820–99), a German artist specialising in natural history illustration, worked for the British Museum in 1848, illustrating works for the Zoological Society, and for David Livingstone, Alfred Wallace and Henry Walter Bates – much admired by Gould and the Pre-Raphaelites; Clemency Fisher, *ODNB*.

'well and strong'. D 4 October 1875.

'Loudon's botany'. D 19 May 1875. Jane Loudon, wife of the landscape designer and writer John Claudius Loudon, published a series of botanical books in the 1840s.

'Dinner good'. D 7 May 1875.

'delightful experiences'. All quotations from Hubert Congreve, Preface, *LL* 22–37.

'Tasmania'. D 15 April 1876.

'but shall not bring her here'. D 30 December 1876.

'How can a fellow bear'. D 28 February 1876.

'demanded to return'. D 26 February 1877.

'Ill & tears'. D 3, 4 March 1877. Lear recorded G's speech in Italian.

'& not a word'. D 25 July 1877.

'Meanwhile the present'. D 2 August 1877.

'May he that gave so beautiful a form'. D 19 August 1877. Lear's copy makes slight errors in punctuation, but is otherwise faithful to the *Eton College Magazine*, June–November 1832 (Google Books). The poem is signed 'H.' This is the only place I have yet found it.

'ordering dinner'. D 1 July 1880.

'You are just beginning'. Hubert Congreve, Introduction, *LL* 35–6. Twenty-four letters from Lear to Hubert are in the Robert H. Taylor Collection of English and American Literature, Princeton, Box 11 Folder 9. Several have drawings, including one showing Lear carried on a litter by three young friends, Hubert, Arny and their cousin. Hubert did become an engineer, working for the Manchester Ship Canal Company from 1887 and eventually becoming Chief Engineer. In 1911, worried by the Company's finances and by recent strikes, he climbed a high bridge, shot himself and dropped into the canal.

38. Laughable Lyrics

'The Quangle Wangle's Hat'. Written for Arthur Buchanan, 26–27 May 1872, copied for Gertrude Lushington 8 June (Edinburgh).

'but I can make little of it'. D 21, 22 April 1876. He wrote out 'Vestments' and 'Quangle-Wangle's Hat' for Bush on 9 April.

'Too late'. D 8 December 1875.

'aunt (Jobiska)'. D 30 April 1876.

'Quangle Wangle Quee'. D 9 November 1875.

'smart red and green books'. CF to EL, 22 December 1876, *LL* 198.

'fooly-book'. EL to CF, 25 December 1876, SHC DD/SH/62/337 (2/367).

'The New Vestments'. See Carol Rumens, *Guardian*, 30 December 2013.

'sandbanks'. D 9 January 1867, also quoted *CN* 535.

'The Dong'. D 24 August 1876.

'Wrote to F. Lushington'. D 27 August 1876.

'who with Byron'. EL to CF, 26 September 1875, *LL* 186–7. Trelawny died in 1881, aged 88.

39. Shocks

'Demon'. D 9 September 1875; 9, 19 March 1876.

'crawled into bed'. D 18 June 1876.

'strangely as it may seem'. D 21 April 1877.

'where Ann & I began'. D 25 July 1877.

'Tennyson'. D 2 July; 19, 21 June, 7–9 July.

'a vast scene'. D 1 August, 24 July 1878.

'happier in Paradise'. EL to CF, 28 October 1878, *LL* 211. In 1875 Hanbury wrote that he would only let the land on a building lease for ninety-nine years and would build three low villas.

'keep out Germans'. Henry Strachey, quoted in Introduction, *NSS* xi.

'horribly out of humour'. D 3 January 1879.

'O dear'. D 3 January 1879.

'Devil's Hotel'. D 9 October 1880; triumvirate, EL to CF, 16 April 1879, Taunton.

'How cheerful'. EL to Bevan, 14 January 1879; copied, D 9 April 1879.

'The Song of Eve'. See Alexandra Ault, BL 'Untold Lives' blog, 12 May 2016, and for the music, Marco Graziosi, Bosh, 29 May 2016, and Hymnary.org.

'sent his poem'. EL to Bevan, 14 January 1879, BL Add MS 61891 ff. 104–9.

'I was sorry'. D 26 April 1879.

'I am crushed'. CF to EL, 25 July 1879, *LL* 223.

'There are few women'. D 18 September 1879.

'The Enemy'. North, *Recollections*, vol. 2, 83–5.

'So look out for me'. EL to James Fields, 14 October 1879; next day he sent the poem and statement to Wilkie Collins, who sent it to the *World* (D 2 November 1879).

'all the Sanremisi'. EL to James Fields, 15 October 1879, *SL* 255: *Athenaeum*, 1 November 1879, printed an abridged version.

'Altogether I was never in a greater fix'. D 22 October 1879.

'young Earl of Derby'. See Derby diaries: Liverpool, 920 DER (15) Diaries 10, 11 12; 14 July 1870, 18 October 1871, 4 July 1872.

'soothing and strengthening'. CF to EL, 6 October 1879, *LL* 226.

'I seem by doing this'. D 24 February 1880.

'Northbrook and Baring'. D 11–14 March 1880.

'33 Norfolk Square'. EL to ET, 16 February 1880, TRC/Letters 5538.

'Here's a shindy!' EL to CF, 7 June 1880, *LL* 231. Bush had published *Corsica*, 1870; *Nonsense Songs etc.*, 1871, *More Nonsense*, 1872, and *Laughable Lyrics*, 1877. No new editions appeared until Routledge bought the rights to these after Lear's death.

'Watching Gussie'. D 12, 26 June 1880.

'a Chicken'. D 13 June 1880.

'So far'. D 25 August 1880.

40. The Villa Tennyson

'*The walls*'. D 26 February 1880.

'only the road'. EL to ET, 16 February 1880, TRC/Letters 5538.

'decided on a name'. EL to CF, 4 September 1880, Taunton.

'When he moved'. EL to 15th Earl of Derby, 13 April 1881, *SL* 256.

'God bless you'. ET to EL, 7 June 1881, TRC/Letters 5543.

'the small initiative'. D 23 June 1871; Pitman 28–9.

'Claude's *Liber Veritas*'. D 26 August 1867, at Stratton. Turner purchase, facsimile: D 27 July 1863.

'the new autotype edition'. Published in 1871 by the Autotype Fine Art Company: 2nd edn 1880 with notes by Revd Stopford Brooke.

'early works'. As part of the Turner bequest, twenty-four of these were included in an exhibition of 102 watercolours at the Marlborough Gallery in 1857, and were on display at South Kensington museum (now the V&A) soon afterwards. Two volumes of photographs, published 1861 and 1862, returned to National Gallery, 1878. Matthew Imms, 'Liber Studiorum: Drawings and Related Works', in David Blayney Brown (ed.), *J. M. W. Turner: Sketchbooks, Drawings and Watercolours* (2012), www.tate.org.

'Tom Moorey'. EL to Mrs Richard Ward, 22 July 1873, *SL* 239 and note.

'Nluv, fluv'. Evelyn Baring, Introduction to *QLN*, 8.

'Delirious bulldogs'. EL to CF, 28 February 1872, *LL* 161. See Anne Barton, 'Delirious Bulldogs and Nasty Crockery: Tennyson as a Nonsense Poet', *Victorian Poetry*, 47.1 (Spring 2009), 313–30.

'Akhrida'. (Ohrid, Macedonia). Drawing at head of chapter. Houghton MS Typ 55.7. 105.

'with regard to scenes'. EL to ET, 5 October 1852, *SL* 116–17.

'Bottini's man'. D 24 August 1876.

'he was glad'. EL to ET, 11 November 1855, Beinecke GEN MSS 601.

'Bill's sons had also sent'. D 18 November 1876.

'Worked all day'. D 17 October 1876.

'in converting memories'. EL to LW, 5 January 1862, 1862 *L* 216.

'lines from "Ulysses"'. Houghton MS Typ 55.7. 88, Pitman 125. See also Cronin, 'Edward Lear and Tennyson's Nonsense', 269.

'It interests me much'. D 19 June 1875. Arthur Glennie (1803–90) was known for hazy Italianate landscapes.

'*Palm Trees at Bordighera*'. (1884), Metropolitan Museum of Art, New York.

'the glory & beauty of the Turners'. D 1 August 1877.

'giving armless pleasure'. EL to Henry Bruce, Lord Aberdare, 23 August 1877, *SL* 251.

'dined with Lady Ashburton'. D 21 June 1880.

'gilt leather'. EL to CF, 7 June 1880, *LL* 231.

'When the 300 drawings are done'. EL to CF, 14 April 1881, *LL* 238–9.

'no reproduction process'. See Pitman, Appendix, 214–15.

'Mariana'. Four pictures: pine trees at Cannes; Albegna on the Genoese Riviera; the woods of India; temples almost standing in the water, Houghton MS Typ 55.7. 1–4.

'drew Mount Athos'. Sketches, Houghton Library, MS Typ 55.7.

'the Egg state'. EL to HH, 27 October 1880, Noakes 248. The small versions were at the Tennyson Research Centre until 1980 when they were separated and sold. A set of photographs was used by Judith Pitman for her book in 1988.

'Chrysalisses'. D 20 November 1885; also see EL to Underhill, 19 August 1885, *SL* 270–2. A manuscript list of the drawings and lines is in Yale University Library, Tennyson Papers, *Purchase from Colonel E. S. M. Prinsep / Box 8 / 359*

'it is plain'. D 16 October 1880.

'A looming bastion'. Houghton MS Typ 55.7.181, the Coast of Travancore, India.

'Enoch Arden'. Houghton MS Typ 55.7 (200).

'I try to look forward'. EL to CF, 14 April 1877, *LL* 203.

'There is religion'. CF to EL, 29 September 1882, *LL* 270.

'At 8.30'. D 15 December 1881.

'Lear's gallery'. Henry Strachey, quoted in Introduction, *NSS* ix.

'a big Philae'. EL to HH, 24 September 1883, (Huntington) BL RP 800/1.

'the following spring'. D 8 May 1884.

'parrot'. For this detail, see Bevis, 'Lines of Flight', 63–6. The watercolours are at TRC, the drawings at Harvard, MS Typ 55.7.

'The foreground'. EL to ET, 1 June 1884, TRC/Letters 5556.

41. *'As Great a Fool as Ever I Was'*

'Henry James'. *The Portrait of a Lady*, 1881, ch. 21.

'such wretchedness'. Cheque to FL. D 22, 23, 24 January 1881.

'Giuseppe'. D 20, 21 February 1881.

'Watson'. D 28 April 1881. Selwyn published his 'Later Letters of Edward Lear' in the *Cornhill*

Magazine, 1910, a reminiscence with copious extracts; this promoted a re-evaluation of Lear, in the *Spectator*, 26 March 1910.

'When "grand old men"'. EL to CF, 9 February 1884, *CN* 452.

'Should you be injuiced'. EL to CF, 30 April 1885, *LL* 335.

'room full of work', Derby to EL, January 1882, *Shelves*, 96–7.

'in a world'. Derby diary, 14 January 1880, Liverpool 920 DER (15).

'Advertisement-universal' EL to 15th Earl of Derby, 26 June 1884, *SL* 265; for Derby's response to earlier letter, Derby diary, 18 March 1884, Liverpool 920 DER (15).

'trying to sell his work'. E.g. EL to Angela Burdett-Coutts, 7 February 1883, *SL* 260–1.

'If he did not like'. *LL*, Introduction, xxxiii.

'Victoria'. RA VIC/MAIN/QVJ (W) 5 April 1882 (Princess Beatrice's copies).

'A friend warned Lear'. EL to CF, 30 March 1882, 10 April 1882, *LL* 258, 262.

'Princess Royal'. D 2 August 1882.

'the question of drink'. D 23 November 1880.

'Lambi was sent home'. D 28 September, 8–10 October 1879.

'Strange place Rome!' D 13 May 1881.

'as does the *Sumatra*'. D 15-16 May 1881.

'queer & violent fits'. D 14 June 1882.

'he disappeared'. D 30 June 1882.

'more to be thankful for'. EL to CF, 2 July 1882, *LL* 265.

'This place just now'. EL to CF, 31 August 1882, *LL* 266–7.

'The Octopods and reptiles'. D 13 September 1882, *CN* 444.

'Georgio is *immensely* better'. D 30 September 1882.

'After he had done seven'. Henry Strachey, quoted in Introduction, *NSS* xii.

'Watson may perhaps'. D 20 January 1883.

'Alas, Alas!' D 20, 21 March 1883.

'nosegays'. D 21 March 1883.

'a good woman'. EL to CF, 8 April 1883, Taunton.

'absolutely delightful'. D 27 May 1883.

'It is impossible'. D 14 June 1883.

'wonderfully lovely'. D 30 June 1883.

'poor Giorgio's 3 sons'. D 24 July 1883.

'O dear Giorgio' Written later, at the bottom of D 8 August 1883.

'stepping-stones'. Earlier mention, D 5 December 1858.

'It is well'. EL to ET, 18 August 1883.

'a dream and a waste'. D 3 March 1886.

'*the old Villa Emily*'. D 23 February 1884.

'John and Catherine Symonds'. D 13 May 1884. During their stay Symonds finished his study of medieval Latin poetry, *Wine, Women and Song*, dedicated to Robert Louis Stevenson.

'a sack of hay'. EL to CF, 4 June 1884, *LL* 309.

'Slave Emancipation'. EL to CF, 8 September 1884, *LL* 315.

'Tennyson was made a peer'. EL to ET, 13 December 1883, TRC/Letters 5550. He was created Baron Tennyson of Aldworth and Freshwater in late 1883 and took his seat in the Lords in March 1884.

'Centipede', EL to CF, 23 December 1883, *LL* 293. Lear had finished the first set of two hundred drawings by late 1883.

'directly-suddenly'. EL to Hallam, 21 November 1883, VNA transcript.

'poetical and mysterious'. EL to CF, 28 September 1884, *LL* 318.

'We *know* nothing'. EL to CF, 25 December 1882, *LL* 282.

'Is there no medium'. EL to CF, 3 May 1885, Taunton, VNA transcript, Somerville.

'But with the feathers of his tail'. *CN* 545, draft April 1885.

'chess'. D 29 December 1885, 6 January 1886, etc.

'if you only play JIGGS'. EL to Frank Underhill, 28 October 1885, *SL* n. 287.

'He really *lived*'. FL to HT, 7 March 1888, TRC/Letters 5580.

Amelia Edwards. Her review appeared in *The Academy Magazine*: EL to Amelia Edwards, 18, 26 October 1885, Amelia B. Edwards Papers 102, 103, Somerville.

'any summer place'. EL to Underhill, 189 August 1885, *SL* 271.

'dedication to Emily'. 21 November 1885, Pitman 33.

'Barchester series'. D 14 November 1885.

'Slept badly'. Carlingford Diary, 25–26 November 1885: VNA notes.

'fell over Foss'. D 12 December 1885.

'saying'. Carlingford Diary, 25 December 1885, VNA notes.

'political talk'. D 5 January 1886.

'Elegy'. D 31 January 1886.

'Uncle Arly'. See *CN* 549–50. Drafts: 1873, on the endpapers of *The Letters of Horace Walpole*, vols 8 and 9 (Beinecke); amended 1884, finished February–March and copied 5 March 1886. MSS sent to Wilkie Collins, 7 March 1886, MS Typ 55.22.

'Kept always in bed.' D 22 February 1886.

'I esteem it'. EL to Ruskin, 1 March 1886, *SL* 276.

'Un-*cleArly*'. This point is made with his usual insight by Byrom, 219.

'poetry's lasting power'. For a comparison with Keats, 'On the Grasshopper and the Cricket' (1817), see Bevis, 'Lines of Flight', 66.

'the last nonsense poem'. Sent to Fortescue, FL, Mrs Kettlewell & Lady Wyatt, 11 March 1886.

42. Pax Vobiscum

'*Pax vobiscum*'. He bought C. F. Gordon Cumming's *At Home in Fiji* in June 1886: copy owned by Sir David Attenborough.

'small sums'. List of legacies, 15 October 1877, on final page of 1877 diary.

'He opened drawer after drawer'. Bowen transcript, Letter File 1, VNA, Somerville.

'in 1929'. Sold at auction by the Lushington family, and mostly acquired by the dealers Cradock and Barnard. The Northbrook drawings of India, also sold in 1929, were eventually given to Houghton. See Donald C. Gallup, 'Collecting Edward Lear', *Yale University Library Gazette* 61 (April 1987), 125–42, and Hope Mayo, 'The Edward Lear Collection at Harvard University', *Harvard Library Bulletin* (2011), 69–124.

'Earl of Derby'. Frank Lushington's list is in his letter to the 15th Earl of Derby, 9 April 1889, Liverpool DER (15) 43/24/75. For Lear's landscapes at Knowsley sent by FL, see Edward Morris, 'Landscapes by Edward Lear', in Fisher 185–209.

'my hundred authors'. Letter from John Ruskin to the *Pall Mall Gazette*, 15 February 1886.

'influence'. See the excellent essays in the final section of *Play*: Anne Stillman on T. S. Eliot, Adam Piette on Joyce, Seamus Perry on Auden, Will May on Stevie Smith, Stephen Ross on John Ashbery. (Marianne Moore and Elizabeth Bishop were also admirers.) Also see

Marco Graziosi's article, 'Mr Lear, Humpty Dumpty and Finnegan', Bosh, 8 January
2011, and posts on Lennon, McCartney, 4 January, 25 May 2016, and Syd Barrett, 27 December 2015. Among many illustrators, Maurice Sendak gave 'A Book of Nonsense' to
one of his creatures to hold in *Where the Wild Things Are.*

'the big magnolia flowers'. D June 1886.

'Brianza'. D 2 July 1886.

'sadly aged'. FL to HT, 14 November 1886, TRC/Letters 5569; see also FL to Lady Reid, 6
November 1886.

'He only said'. EL to CF, 10 December 1886, *LL* 353.

'There!' EL to HT, 30 May 1887, TRC/Letters 5573.

'the Colony'. EL to Wilkie Collins, 7 March 1886, Pierpont Morgan.

'The sad, bent, loosely-clad figure'. *L* xv–xvi.

'Hardlines!' D 13 January 1887.

'a very great blessing'. EL to CF, 1 April 1887, *LL* 354.

'Agnes Pears'. D 20 April 1887.

'Foss always here'. D 1 February 1887.

'had his photograph taken'. D 28 April 1887.

'more nice and charming'. D 2 April 1887.

'sent him a volume'. D 20 June 1887.

'Paul Nash'. Gussie m. Thomas Nash, who was writing a life of her father. Note on title
page states that she gave this to Lear, 4 April 1887, and to Paul Nash *c.*1908. Princeton.

'platinotype'. The new, platinum photographic print process, patented in 1873.

'very artistic treatment'. Estes to HT 8 May 1887, TRC/Letters 5578; D 7 May 1887, and EL
to HT 27 April 1887, TRC/Letters 5572.

'private edition'. Published by Boussod, Valadon & Co. in London. It contained sixteen full-
page illustrations. Pitman, 31 n.

'in a vast tantrum'. D 23 December 1886.

'pigeons'. EL to the Hon. Mrs Augusta Parker, 18 June 1887. *SL* 281, also D 22 May 1887.

'the same goldengreen'. D 3 July 1887.

'rumbly bumbly'. D 28 July 1887.

'the affectionate regular correspondence'. *SL* xviii.

'deep below the Figtree'. EL to Aberdare, 29 November 1887, *SL* 282. '*Qui sotto e sepolto il
mio buon/Gatto Foss. Era 30 anni in casa/mia, e mori il 26 Novembre 1887, di eta 31 anni*'.

'Very absurd'. EL to CF, 21 October 1887, SHC DD/SH/62/337 (2/641).

'a great and ridiculous bore'. EL to CF, 10 November 1887, *LL* 358.

'an inexhaustible profusion'. *Spectator*, 8 September 1887, 11.

'Very nice indeed'. EL to CF, 10 November 1887, *LL* 358.

'by way of a leavetaking'. FL to HT, 4 February 1888. TRC/Letters 5577.

'*Mio caro Giuseppe*'. FL to CF, 6 February 1888, *LL* 362, translated by Constance Strachey.

'It was most peaceful'. Mrs Hassall to Constance Stracey, 21 January 1911.

'none of his friends'. FL to HT, 8 March 1888, TRC/Letters 5580. Frank's affectionate obit-
uary appeared in the *Saturday Review*, 4 February 1888.

INDEX

Page numbers in *italics* refer to illustrations.

Aberdare, Henry Bruce, first Lord, 247, 249, 333, 352, 448, 450

Ackermann, Rudolph, 29, 48, 52, 53

Acland, Peter Leopold, 139

Adelaide, Queen, 53

Albania: Akhridha, 180, 484; birds, 55–6, 180, 184, 196; Byron in, 176, 186–7; EL's journal, 188, 201, 204, 219, 325, 483; EL's sketches, 181–2, 198, 268, 422; EL's travels, 6, 138, 176, 180–6, 197–8, 240–1, 245; Elbasan, 181–2; Khimara, 175, 184–6, *185*; lament for the dead, 175, 185; Skodra, 183–4; Suli, 188, 198

Ali Pasha, 186–7, 188

Amalfi, *123*, 124

Andersen, Hans Christian, 113, 460

animals and birds: Balkan birds, 180; birds in Egypt, 56, 225–6, 255, 353, 355, 461; birds named after EL, 71; camels, *189*, 190, 257; chimpanzee, *81*; Corfu birds, 314; cranes, 68, 69, 226, *461*, *462*; eagle owl, *60*; EL's love of birds, 45, 55–6; EL's youthful drawings, 2, 5; elephants, *435*, *436*, 437; frog story, *360*, 360–1; geese, 57, 226, 314, 363, 461; horses, 137, 138, *139*, 140, 143, 177, 391; human relationship with, 80–3, 361, 369–72; kangaroos, 74; owls, *60*, *69*, 82, 140, 176, 314, 414–15; parrots and macaws, 5, 45, 50, *51*, *55*, 62, *363*; pelicans, 56, *175*, 184, 226, 355–6; pigs swimming, 237; plumage, 368; 'Portraites of the inditchenous beestes of New Ollond', *72*; Quebec marmot, *69*; ravens, 3; rhinoceros, *369*; squirrel, *70*; tortoises, 63, 245, 249; toucans, 5, *59*, 366; turkeys and gulls, 41; wattle-crowned crane, *69*

Apostles, 194–5, 215, 235, 315

Ashburton, Harriet, Lady, 228, 380, 448, 488, 514

Audubon, John James, 49–50, 53, 101; *Birds of America*, 49

Baalbec, 261

Babbage, Charles, 80

Baring, Emma, 509, 516

Baring, Evelyn, *see* Cromer

Baring, Thomas, *see* Northbrook

Bassae, Temple of Apollo, 196, 289, *290*

Bates, Henry Walter, 336, 349, 366

Batsworth Park, 24, 35, 38, 40

Bavella, Corsica, 390, *391*

Beechey's voyage, 61

Beirut, 192, 261, 272

Bell, Thomas, 53; *History of Quadrupeds*, 63; *A Monograph of the Testudinata*, 63

Bennet, Edward, 48, 49, 53

Bethell, Augusta 'Gussie': appearance, 343, *344*; character, 343; EL considers marriage with, 341, 343–4, 346–9, 352, 358, 517; EL's departure, 358, 375, 382, 417, 454, 460; EL's visit, 479; family background, 342–3, 502; husband's death, 502; letters from, 358, 412, 434; letters to, 516; marriages, 434, 448, 517; photograph, 515; visits EL, 502, 516–17; writings, 343; *Maud Latimer*, 343

Bethell, Emma, *see* Parkyns

Bethell, Sir Richard, *see* Westbury

Bethell, Slingsby, 343, 347, 367

Bevan, William, 471, *474*

Bevan family, 473, 475

Bewick, Thomas, 48; *History of British Birds*, 61

Bicknell, Clarence, 472

Bishop, Elizabeth, 6, 514

Bonaparte family, 117

Bonatti family, 184

Book of Nonsense: authorship disputed, 418; copy sent to Hunt, 209; cover, *151*; editions, 151, 310; limericks, 300–3; origins, 93, 146; publication, 151–2, 262, 299; readership, 304–5; rights, 310, 316; sales, 299, 304, 310, 429; There was an Old Man of Whitehaven, 3–4

Boswell, Mary (EL's sister): childhood, 10, 11, 13, 22–3; death, 294; home, 202; marriage, 24; money from EL, 203

Boswell, Richard Shuter (EL's brother-in-law), 24, 202

Bowen, George, 173, 174, 175, 234, 236, 250

Bowman's Lodge: birth of EL, 12; demolition, 12; EL revisits, 12–13, 325; EL's childhood, 13–14, 21, 510; Lear family move from, 15, 26, 84, 476; Lear family return to, 18; site, 12, *13*

Bradyll family, 101

Brett, John, 315

British Association for the Advancement of Science (BAAS), 79–80

British Institution, 39, 210, 291, 312

Brontë, Charlotte, 250, 276, 426, 451

Brown, Ford Madox, 208, 271

Browning, Elizabeth Barrett, 110, 165, 275, 279, 281, 294

Browning, Robert: birth, 10; EL meets, 275, 281; Florence life, 110, 165; Rome life, 275; view of Tennyson's revisions, 214; wife's death, 294

Bruce, Colonel, 277, 313

Bruce, Henry, *see* Aberdare

Burton, Sir Richard, 225, 366; *Abeokuta and the Cameroon Mountains*, 328; *Mecca*, 250

Bush, Robert: bankruptcy, 478; EL's ballad project, 429; printing Corsican journal, 392; printing Nonsense books, 405, 406, 407, 414, 457, 478

Byron, Lord: Albania visit, 176, 186–7; death, 22, 175; EL's childhood reading, 18, 25, 499; influence on EL, 21, 22, 37, 96, 133, 255, 282, 322–3, 429; love of Italian, 128; marriage, 290; parodies of, 25, 289, 422; scandal, 384; Shelley's death, 464

Cameron, Julia Margaret (*née* Pattle), 285–6, 334

Campbell, Thomasina, 389, 390, 391; *Notes on the Island of Corsica*, 389

Cannes: EL enjoying, 27, 288, 392; EL's arrivals, 375, 395; EL's departure, 424; EL's plans, 388, 391, 396; EL's sales, 380, 388; social life, 380–1, 400, 430, 477; Symonds family in, 375, 377, 381, 384

Canning, Sir Stratford (*later* Lord Canning), 176, 250

Canning, Lady, 176, 177

Carlingford, Lord, *see* Fortescue

Carlyle, Thomas, 216, 230, 281; *Frederick the Great*, 450; *Past and Present*, 239

Carroll, Lewis, *see* Dodgson

Cartwright, George, 38, 117

Certosa di Pesio, 401, 402, 404–5, 406, 429

Cesare (cook), 518

Ceylon, 435, 437, 444–5

Chambers, Robert, 400; *Vestiges of the Natural History of Creation*, 307

Chesmer, Henry (EL's cousin), 12, 313

Church, Charles: Corfu visit, 239; family background, 173, 194; EL's visit, 249; memories of EL, 214; Nile travel plans, 222; photograph of, 515; trapped in Salonica, 179; travel to Athens, 173; travelling with EL, 176–7, 198, 450; visiting EL, 450

Church, Frederic, 443

Church, Sir Richard, 173, 329

Civitella: EL's paintings, 289, 291, 484; EL's prints, 132; EL's commissions, 289; EL's visits, 125, 127, 128, 144, 215, 221; sketching parties, 125–6, *126*, 144

Claude Lorrain: idealised scenes, 112, 322; influence on EL, 119, 167–8, 207, 390, 443, 487; Italian scenes, 119, 125; Ruskin on, 147; *Liber Veritatis*, 119, 481

Clive family, 298

Clough, Arthur, 114, 238; *Amours de Voyage*, 114–15, 289

Clowes, Samuel, 274, 287

Coleman, Charles, 113, 281

Colenso, John, 308–9, 328

Collins, Wilkie, 230, 475, 477, 503, 515; *The Frozen Deep*, 503

Collins, William, 18, 26

Congreve, Arnold (Arny), 427, 434, 513

Congreve, Hubert: childhood, 427, 434; EL's will, 513; memories of EL, 427, 452, 453, 455; relationship with EL, 452–3, 454–5, 479; studies, 454, 455, 470, 479; Tasmania plan, 452, 453, 457; travelling with EL, 453–4

Congreve, Walter, 396, 427–8, 432, 452–3

Coombe, Fanny (*née* Drewitt): children, 42, 62–3, 133; EL's visits, 249, 270, 334; husband's death, 249; letters from, 246; letters to, 36, 42, 64, 68, 78, 106, 117, 129, 132, 133–4, 390, 391; marriage, 42; poems for, 85–6; relationship with EL, 36, 40, 41, 42, 117, 130

Coombe, George: children, 42, 62–3, 133; death, 249; illness, 133; letters to, 58, 63, 66, 75, 84; marriage, 42

Coombe, Percy, 42, 133, 513

Corfu: birds, 314; Bowen's invitation to EL, 173, 174; British community, 175–6; British departure, 328; EL's departures, 262, 275, 328–9; EL's diaries, 514; EL's first visit, 175–6; EL's friends, 239–40, 262; EL's opinions of, 245, 250, 348; EL's pictures, 209, 235–6, *236*, 239, 245, 248, 251, 315, 316–17, 320, *326*, 336, 425, 489; EL's unhappiness over Frank Lushington, 235, 412; EL's visits, 234–40, 243–5, 246, 250, 262, 313–14, 316–17, 320–1, 324, 327–8; Frank Lushington's position as judge, 230, 235, 262, 272; Giorgio in, 274, 278, 282; Giorgio's family, 239, 280, 401, 445, 451, 453, 504; Giorgio's illness, 470; Giorgio's visits, 401, 429, 430, 431, 453; Ionian Academy, 173, 237; palace, 234, 236, 237, 245, 250, 252, 304, 324; Palaiokastritsa bay, 258, 314, *326*; political scene, 175, 234–5, 262, 320; sailing, 238; scenery, 176, 235, 238, 239, 348

Corpo di Cava, 122

Corsica: Ajaccio, 396; Bavella, 390, *391*; EL's colour sketches for Tennyson, 394; EL's drawings, 265, 506; EL's pictures, 425, 426; EL's travels, 382, 389–92; *Journal of a Landscape Painter in Corsica*, 382, 393, *393*, 394, 395, 405, 417; 'Tyrants', 393; Valdoniello, 389, 391

Cortazzi, Helena, 239–40, 272, 299, 336

Cortazzi family, 239, 240, 244, 314

Crawford, Mary (*later* Fraser), 92, 402

Crawford, Thomas, 402

Crete, 329–32, 351, 388

Crimean war, 227–8, 234, 241, 277, 305, 306

Cromer, Evelyn Baring, first Earl of: career, 314, 339, 436, 437; character, 323; friendship with EL, 314, 328, 430–1, 515; letters to, 328, 417; memories of EL, 482; piano playing, 324

Cross, John, 189–93, 198, 500

Cruikshank, George, 81–2, 87

Cruikshank, Robert, 94

Cushman, Charlotte, 276, 281

Dalziel brothers (engravers), 299, 310

Damascus, 261, 289

Daniell, Thomas, 440

Darwin, Charles: *Beagle* voyage, 307, 365; controversy, 307; EL reading, 356, 359; EL's responses to, 361, 364; home, 99; identification of his Galapagos bird specimens, 61; interest in plumage, 368; natural selection, 307, 336, 361; rooms in Gt Marlborough St, 105; *On the Origin of Species*, 307–8, 309

de Tabley, John Leicester, Lord, 39

de Tabley, Lady, 78, 85

de Vere family, 319, 324

Decie family, 328, 359

Derby, Edward Smith Stanley, 12th Earl of, 66, 67, 745

Derby, Edward Smith Stanley, 13th Earl of (*earlier* Lord Stanley): commission for EL to draw in Rome, 105–6; death, 205; EL's drawings for, 65, 67, 68, 70–1, 77, 117; EL's watercolours for, 67–71, 117; family background, 66–7, 74–5; *Gleanings from the Menagerie and Aviary at Knowsley Hall*, 161, 455; health, 131; *Illustrated Excursions* dedication, 146–7; inheritance of Derby title, 65, 66; letters to, 113–14, 117–18, 132–3, 140, 184; life at Knowsley, 76–7; natural history collections, 50, 67–9; *Parrots* subscription, 49; president of Zoological Society, 65; relationship with EL, 68, 92, 101, 105–6, 132–3, 203–4, 455; zoo at Knowsley, 65, 67–71, 80–1, 161, 461

Derby, Edward Smith Stanley, 14th Earl of (*earlier* Lord Stanley), 67, 145–6, 149, 211, 247

Derby, Edward Stanley, 15th Earl of: EL's death, 514; Greek throne question, 321; patronage of EL, 425, 477, 479, 480; view of EL's neediness, 497

Dickens, Charles, 10, 27–8, 79, 310; *Household Words*, 207; *Pickwick Papers*, 28

Disraeli, Benjamin, 146, 211, 247, 359, 447, 449; *Lothair*, 450

Dodgson, Charles (Lewis Carroll), 17, 91, 284, 334, 439

Domenico (coachman), 391–2

Drewitt, Eliza, 36, 37, 40–1, 63, 85–6

Drewitt, Fanny, *see* Coombe

Drewitt, John, 35–6, 133

Drewitt, Robert, 36, 37, 40, 63, 129, 133

Drewitt family, 35–7, 40–2, 59, 99, 133

Drummond, Edgar, 321, 333, 352, 380

Duff Gordon, Lucie, Lady, 355

Duncan, Lady, 153, 360, 362

Eastnor, Lord, *see* Somers

Edward, Prince of Wales (*later* Edward VII), 276–7, 337

Edwards, Amelia B., 402, 477, 507

Edwards, James ('Jemmy'), 245, 314

Egg, Augustus, 65, 208, 271

Egremont, George Wyndham, third Earl of, 38–9, 49

Egypt: Abu Simbel, 18, *357*; Alexandria, 190, 255; birds, 56, 225–6, 255, 353, 355, 461; Cairo, 190, 255, 353, 357; EL in, 349, *354*, 431–2; EL's journal, 388, 402, 507; EL's pictures, 198, 230, 262, 507; *Kasr es Saàd*, *488*; Luxor, 226, 354, 355, 357; Nile, 5, 224–5, 350, 353, *355*, 355–6, 359, 382, 461; Philae, 224–5, *228*, 355; Sinai, 191–2; Sphinx. 190; Suez, *191*, 432, 496; Wadi Halfa, 356–7

Eliot, George, 254, 500; *Romola*, 380

Eliot, T. S., 408, 481, 514

Estes, Dana, 517–18

Excursions, see Illustrated Excursions

Fairbairn, Thomas, 249, 315, 333, 341

Fawkes, Walter Ramsden, 39, 61

Fenton, George, 90, 471, 506

Fields, James, 395, 402, 476, 477

Finlay, George, 329

Fitzwilliam, Lord and Lady, 39, 337, 362

Florence, 28, 110–11, 162, 165, 275, 294

Foord and Dickinson: EL's show, 497, 507; framers, 270, 317, 336; picture dealers, 270, 425, 426

Ford, Richard, 161–2, 406

Fortescue, Chichester Parkinson, Baron Carlingford: appearance, 193, *248*; career, 150, 165, 167, 230, 247, 273, 314, 338–9, 495–6, 508; character, 150, 193; correspondence with EL, 514; descriptions of EL, 150–1, 232, 237, 248, 304; EL's bequest, 513; friendships, 172, 315; house at Ardee, 248, 267, 272–3; illness, 508–9; letters from, 205, 229, 274, 319, 457, 475; letters to, 139, 173, 177, 179, 190, 201, 203, 204, 205, 210, 215, 240, 242, 245, 246, 255, 269, 278, 287, 289, 293, 301, 313, 315, 325, 327, 328, 341, 352–3, 364, 371–2, 382, 395–6, 400, 401, 430, 431, 434, 457, 470–1, 475, 483, 488, 491, 496, 500, 515, 516; marriage, 314, 318–19, 333, 338, 341, 475; monogram, 269; nephew, 225, 247; relationship with EL, 224, 230, 232, 248, 272, 278, 333, 349, 448–9, 477–8, 479, 491–2, 506, 515; relationship with Lady Waldegrave, 229–30, 232, 301, 314, 318–19, 333; religious controversy, 308; séance-going, 310; title, 247, 448–9; travelling with EL, 150, 460; visiting San Remo, 477–8, 508–9; wife's death, 475, 477–8, 508

Foss (cat): arrival, 430; cut-off tail, 2, 118; death, 518–19; grave, *519*; heraldic pictures of, 500, *501*; left behind while EL travels, 434; life with EL, *424*, 464, *474*, *496*, 500, 509, 516; move to Villa Tennyson, 480; name, 430

Fowler, Daniel: Continental sketching tour, 99; emigration, 358; family background, 99; marriage, 99, 358; memories of EL, 76, 100; travelling with EL, 106, 109; view of art teaching, 29; view of Hullmandel, 64

Fowler, Elizabeth (*née* Gale), 99, 358

Francillon, Lucy (*née* Gale), 99, 297, 358

Francillon, Robert, 92, 99

Franco-Prussian war, 396, 401, 471

Fraser, Mary, 92

Gale, Robert Leake, 22, 92, 99–100, 109, 358

Gale family, 99, 100, 358

Garibaldi, 164, 174, 277, 281–2, 320, 499

Gaskell, Elizabeth, 276, 315, 426, 450–1; *Life of Charlotte Brontë*, 250, 276; *Sylvia's Lovers*, 450

George I, King of Greece (*formerly* William of Denmark), 321, 327

Gibson, John, 112, 113, 274

Giorgio, *see* Kokali

Giuseppe (gardener), 494, 504

Gladstone, William, 134, 291, 320, 321, 495–6, 508

Gleanings from the Menagerie and Aviary at Knowsley Hall, 161, 455

Glennie, Arthur, 486, 499

Goldsmid, Sir Francis, 291, 299, 392, 426

Goldsmid, Julia, 299, 314

Gould, Elizabeth, 58

Gould, John: Australian trip, 71; buys *Parrots* stock and rights, 58; career, 57–8, 61; Continental trips with EL, 58, 59, 64, 105; death, 61; EL's work with, 58, 59, 61, 68, 98; letters to, 104, 105, 127, 130; taxidermist, 50, 57, 67; *Birds of Europe*, 58, 59; *A Century of Birds from the Himalaya Mountains*, 57–8

Gray, John Edward, 161

Gray, Thomas, 18, 423; 'Elegy in a Country Churchyard', 509, 512

Greece: Athens, 176, *177*, 197, 201, 329; Bassae, 196; EL's travels, 176–7, 179, 193, 195–8, 450; flowers, 196; Marathon, 177; Morea, 195–6; Mount Athos, 179, 240–3, *243*; Mount Olympus, 198; Mount Parnassus, 197; scenery, 198; Thermopylae, 177; throne, 320–1, 324, 327

Green, Revd John Richard, 432

Greening, Henry, 63–4

Grenfell, Henry, 315

Hallam, Arthur, 195, 215, 235

Hallam, Henry, 195, 235

Hanbury, Thomas, 399, 429, 471, 477, 480, 497–8

Harding, Frederick, 21, 22

Harding, James Duffield, 98–9, 358; *Elementary Art*, 99

Harris, John, *The Adventures of Fifteen Young Ladies* and *A History of Sixteen Wonderful Old Women*, 94, 95

Harvey, William, 48, 50

Hassall, Dr, 515, 519

Hassall, Mrs, 515, 520

Hay, Frank Drummond, 329–30

Headfort, Lady (Lady McN), 250

Himalayas, 435, 436, 443–4

Hoare, Richard Colt, 122, 141

Hood, Thomas, 25, 81–2, 154; 'The Demon Ship', 87; 'Pythagorean Fancies', 81; *Whims and Oddities*, 87

Hornby, Edmund, 101

Hornby, Elizabeth 'Pussy', 369

Hornby, Phipps, 106, 136–7, 153, 293, 369

Hornby, Robert, 76, 105, 146, 203–4, 249

Hornby family: Cortazzi connections, 239; Knowsley visits, 75–7; puffin shooting, 79; relationship with EL, 77, 101, 104, 133, 369; voyage to Egypt, 225

Hosmer, Harriet 'Hatty', 276

Howard, Fulke and Mary Greville, 102

Howard, Lady, 202, 203

Hullmandel, Charles: assistants, 52, 317, 516; EL's party, 99; EL's work, 52; friendship with EL, 99, 105; Harding's illustrations, 98; hire of stone blocks, 52; illness, 105; influence, 64, 65; printing Gould's works, 58; printing *Illustrated Excursions in Italy*, 146; printing *Views in Rome and Its Environs*, 132; stones for lithographs, 131; studio, 52, 64, 65, 99, 105; *The Art of Drawing on Stone*, 52

Hunt, Leigh, 54

Hunt, William Holman: beard, 56; career, 206; descriptions of EL, 96, 138, 208, 209; friendship with EL, 208–9, 211, 225, 226, 249, 270–2, 294; influence on EL, 208–11, 271; letters to, 222, 223, 240, 335, 424, 489–90, 492; Lushington family friendship, 290; marriage, 341, 353; monogram, 269; portrait by Cameron, 334; portrait of EL, *251*; PRB, 206; relationship with Annie Miller, 271–2; religious views, 254, 272, 309–10; travels, 209, 226, 294; use of colours, 207–8; working with EL, 165, 206–8, 210, 271; works: *The Awakening Conscience*, 211–12, 271; *The Children's Holiday*, 341; *The Lady of Shalott*, 219, 271; *The Light of the World*, 211–12, 225; *Rienzi*, 206; *The Scapegoat*, 211; *Strayed Sheep*, 207

Husey Hunt, Bernard (Bern, *formerly* Senior): Alpine holiday with EL, 226; EL's executor, 252; EL's visits, 249, 253, 448, 454; loan to EL, 274; social life with EL, 63, 100

Huxley, T. H., 358, 361, 307

Illustrated Excursions in Italy: copy for Emily Tennyson, 216; dedications, 146–7, 149; plans for publication, 141, 146–7; preface, 149; publication, 146–7, 352; review, 161–2; second volume, 149, 151, 325; subscribers, 146; *Lago di Fucino*, *142*

Illustrations of the Family of Psittacidae, or Parrots, 49–54, *51*, 57–8, 61, 65, 114, 132

India: Benares, 436, 440, *441*, 442, 446; Bombay, 435, 445; Calcutta, 436, 437, 441, *442*; Delhi, 436, 446; EL's arrival, 435; EL's journey attempt, 430–2; EL's journey to, 434; EL's travels, 435–43, 444–5; Hyderabad, 437, 438, 463; Lucknow, 247, *436*, 437; Mahabalipuram, 444; Malabar coast, 443, 445; Mutiny, 247, 305, 309, 437; Nerbudda, 443; Ootacamund ('Ooty'), 437; Poona, 437, 438, 439, 440; railway travel, 131, 435–7; Simla, 436, 437–8; Taj Mahal, 442; transport, *435*; Viceroy, 430, 450

Ionian Academy, 173, 237

Ionian islands: British protectorate, 175, 234, 320, 321, 323, 324, 327; Cephalonia, 175, 320, 322, 326; Cerigo (Cythera), 320, 322, 327; cession to Greece, 320, 324, 327; Corfu, *see* Corfu; EL's book (*Views in the Seven Ionian Islands*), 319, *323*, 325–7, *326*, 346; EL's travels, 175, 320, 321–4, 346; Ithaca, 175, 320, 322, 323–4; Napoleonic wars, 173, 175; Paxos, 320, 321–2, 326, 504; Samos, 322, 326; Santa Maura, 189, 320, 322, 351; Supreme Council, 321; Supreme Court, 230; Zante, 320, 322, 326

Italy: Abruzzi, 137, 140–4, 145, 149, 164; Amalfi coast, 124, 144; Barzano, 507; Basilicata, 171–2; Bologna, 28, 110; Calabria, 165, 167–71, *169*; La Certosa di Pesio, 401, 402, 404–5, 406, 429; Como, 109–10; EL's railway trip, 429; EL's walking holidays from San Remo, 400–1; Florence, 28, 110–11, 162, 165, 275, 294; Lake Garda, 357–8; Milan, 109, 110; Monte Generoso, *470*, 475, 495, 498, 500; Naples, 121, 148, 167, 189, 239, 453; political scene, 164–5, 171, 173–4, 277, 279; Recoara, 505; Risorgimento, 189, 277; Rome, *see* Rome; San Remo, *see* San Remo; Tuscany, 279, 503; Umbria, 503; Venice, 245, 337–9

Jardine, Sir William, 49, 54, 62, 68; *Illustrations of Ornithology*, 62; *Naturalist's Library*, 62

Jerusalem, 192, 251, 256, 260–1, 357, 432

Jones, Archie (EL's cousin), 354, 355, 357

Jones, Caroline (EL's cousin), 313, 354

Journal of a Landscape Painter in Corsica, 389, *393*, 393–4, 395, 405, 417

Journal of a Landscape Painter in Greece & Albania, 188, 204, 219, 483

Journals of a Landscape Painter in Southern Calabria and the Kingdom of Naples, 167–70, *168*, 208, 514

Jowett, Benjamin, 308, 309, 506

Kay-Shuttleworth, Janet, Lady, 377, 426–7, 432, 471

Kay-Shuttleworth, Janet (Jenny), 426, 471, 472

Kay-Shuttleworth family, 426, 429, 477, 480

Kemble, Fanny, 161, 500

Ker, Mrs, 399

Kingsley, Charles, 305

Knight, Charles, 114, 137, 140, 143

Knight, Isabella, 114, 280–1, 429

Knight, Margaret, Duchess of Sermoneta, 114. 429

Knight family, 114, 274

Knighton family, 110, 111, 115, 125

Knowsley Hall: EL's nonsense rhymes, 84–5, 93, 146, 153, 154, 425; EL's visits, 65, 66, 68, 75–9, 92–3, 104–6, 131–3, 136, 145–6, 249, 270, 304, 460; EL's watercolour of view from, 66; EL's work, 67–8, 425, 497; fire, 78–9, 85, 408; *Gleanings from the Menagerie and Aviary at Knowsley Hall*, 161, 455; house, 66, 74–5, *75*; natural history collections, 50, 67–9, 366, 369; nursery and schoolroom, 91, 425; patronage, 76, 425; social life at, 76–9, 92–3; zoo, 67–71, 74, 76, 80–1, 161, 461

Kokali, Dmitri, 451, 492, 503, 504, 505, 514

Kokali, Giorgio (George): appearance, *498*; Cannes arrival, 395; death, 503, 504; drinking, 499–500; family, 64, 239, 280, 319, 401, 445, 451, 453, 499, 504; EL's concerns for, 325, 499–500; grave, 503, *521*; health, 242, 400, 401, 445, 451, 453, 470, 502; relationship with EL, 322, 328, 351, 392, 438–9, 451, 453, 498, 499–50, 504; returning to Corfu, 278, 282, 401, 430, 453; Rome arrival, 274; San Remo arrival, 405; travelling with EL, 241, 252, 257–9, 282, 321, 329, 331, 336, 353, 357, 390, 393, 431, 432, 434, *435*, 436–40, 443–5; wife's death, 445; working for EL, 239, 275–7, 280–1, 389, 395, 404, 406, 424, 429, 438, 452, 498

Kokali, Charalambos ('Lambi'): bad behaviour, 499, 502; father's death, 503; father's illness, 453; legacy from EL, 514; trattoria plan, 499; working for EL, 451, 470; working for Watsons, 495, 499, 502

Kokali, Nicola, 451, 499, 500, 502–3, 504, 521

Korakis, Captain Michael, 332

Kourkoumeli family, 236

Landseer, Edwin, 65, 148, 211

Langton, Edmund, 392

Laughable Lyrics: Fourth Book of Nonsense Poems, Songs, Botany, Music &c., 457

Lear, Ann (EL's mother): children, 9–10; death, 134; family background, 11, 26; home (Bowman's Lodge), 12; marriage, 10, 11; money from EL, 64, 125; move to Gravesend, 27; rejection of EL, 15–16, 19–20, 22, 376, 406; relationship with EL, 64

Lear, Ann (EL's sister): Academy visit, 212; Bath visit, 106; care of EL, 15–16, 18–19, 24–8, 130, 293, 294; character, 16, 22, 28, 130; childhood, 10, 11, 34, 292; clothes, 134; death, 12, 293–4, 297, 298, 319, 345; drawing plants, 32; education of EL, 18, 22–3, 24; EL visits, 274, 292–3; grave, 325; Great Exhibition visit, 204–5; health, 162, 291–3; letters from, 163, 274; letters to, 24–5, 28, 38, 58, 91, 111, 113, 116–17, 119, 120–1, 124, 129, 139, 149, 162–5, 174, 176, 178, 188, 189, 190, 193, 196, 203, 224, 225, 235, 237–8, 244, 246, 248, 249–50, 252, 260, 292, 318, 339; life in Belgium and France, 109; life in Islington, 292; life with EL, 27–8, 33, 64; Margate visits, 18, 274; marriage question, 27; money, 27; mother's death, 134; move to Gray's Inn Road (Upper North Place), 27, 33, 45, 469; old age, 291–3; photograph of, 504; portrait, *172*; portrait of EL, 18–19, *19*, 492; possibility of joining EL in Italy, 117, 134, 144, 164; possibility of living with EL, 162–3, 202; reading, 25, 34; religion, 22, 163, 254; scrapbooks, 33; sisters' marriages, 24; staying with friends, 163; study of art, 25, 212; thirty-fifth birthday, 26–7; verse diary from EL, 40

Lear, Catherine (EL's sister), 10, 27

Lear, Charles (EL's brother), 10, 21, 202, 406

Lear, Cordelia (EL's sister), 10, 29

Lear, Edward: family background, 9–14; birth, 10, 12; childhood, 12–20, 215; reading, 16, 18, 21, 25; education by sisters, 16, 18, 22–3, 24–5, 34; school, 22, 24, 36; living with sister Ann off Gray's Inn Road (Upper North Place), 27, 33, 45, 469; art teaching, 29, 148; scrapbooks, 33; Sussex visits, 33–8, 40–2; drawing and painting at London Zoo, 45–9, 54–5; *Parrots*, 49–54; move to 61 Albany Street, 53–4; work for Gould, 58–61; growing reputation, 63; father's death, 64; move to 28 Southampton Row, 64; at Sass's School of Art, 64–5; Derby's patronage, 65, 76; Knowsley visits, 67–73, 74–9, 92–3, 104–6, 131–3, 145–6; takes up landscape painting, 98–9; party at Southampton Row, 99–100; Dublin visit, 100–1; trip to Lake District, 101–4; move to 36 Great Marlborough Street, 105; Rome commission, 105–6; journey to Rome, 109–11; rooms in Via del Babuino, 111, 124–5; life in Rome, 111–18, 127; enjoying the Campagna, 118–19; travels through Italy, 120–4; move to rooms in Via St Felice, 125, 162; sketching in Civitella and Olevano, 125–6, 144; relationship with Marstrand, 127–9; return to London, 131; publication of *Views in Rome and Its Environs*, 132; move to Rome, 132–4, travel writing, 139; trip to Sicily, 139–40; riding in the Abruzzi, 140–4; life in Rome, 144; mother's death, 144; second trip to the Abruzzi, 144–5; tour of Volscian mountains, 145; third trip to the Abruzzi, 145; return to England, 145–6; publication of *Illustrated Excursions in Italy*, 146–7; drawing lessons for Queen Victoria, 147–9; second volume of *Excursions*, 149; friendship with Fortescue, 150–1; publication of *A Book of Nonsense*, 151–4; publication of *Gleanings from the Menagerie and Aviary at Knowsley Hall*, 161; return to Rome, 162; walking in Sicily with Proby, 165–7; walking in Calabria with Proby, 167–71; walking in Basilicata with Proby, 171–2; return to Rome, 172; life in Rome, 172–4; leaves Rome, 174; in Malta, 175; sailing through Ionian islands, 175; arrival in Corfu, 175–6; in Athens, 176; riding through Greece, 176–7; in Constantinople, 177–8; steamer journey to Salonica, 178–9; solo journey through Albania and north-western Greece, 179–87; second journey through north-western Greece, 188; planned journey to the Holy Land, 189, 251–2; in Malta, 189–90; travels in Egypt, 190–2; travelling in Greece with Frank Lushington, 193–4, 195–7; love for Frank Lushington, 197; second journey through Albania, 197; return to England, 198; career plans, 201; Sass's School of Art, 203–4; Royal Academy Schools, 203, 204, 206; rooms at 17 Stratford Place, 204, 207, 209; publication of *Journals of a Landscape Painter in Greece and Albania*, 204; staying in Devon and Cornwall, 205; encounters with PRB, 206–8, 211–12; work with Holman Hunt, 206–10, 271; publication of *Journals of a Landscape Painter in Southern Calabria and the Kingdom of Naples*, 167–8, 208; move to 65 Oxford Street, 209; in Sussex, 213; first meeting with Tennyson, 216; friendship with Emily Tennyson, 216, 217; travelling to Egypt, 223; in Egypt, 224–6; walking in Alps, 226; in London, 226–9; Henry Lushington's death, 231–2; journey to Corfu with Frank, 233, 234; in Corfu, 234–40,

244–5; despair over relationship with Frank, 235; journey to Mount Athos, 240–3; trips to Albania, 245; in Venice, 245; return to England, 245–8, 249; plans for seasonal residence, 245–6; in Ireland, 248; return to Corfu, 250; journey to Palestine, 255–7; travelling to Petra, 257–8; attacked at Petra, 258–60; return to Jerusalem, 260; journey to Lebanon, 261; life in Corfu, 262–3; social life in England, 270–1; working with Hunt, 271; return to Rome, 272, 274; suite in palazzo on Via Condotti, 274; life in Rome, 274–7; departure for London, 277–8; journals of Athos, Palestine and Lebanon, 278; return to Rome, 279–81; leaving Rome, 281–2; return to England, 283; staying with Tennysons, 283–6; working on paintings, 289–91, 311–13; visitors to studio at Stratford Place, 291, 303, 335; death of sister Ann, 292–4; in Florence, 294; new *Book of Nonsense*, 298–303; response to Darwin debate, 307–8, 358–9; 'gallery' at Stratford Place, 312, 317–18, *318*, 319, 335, 336, 349, 382; in Corfu, 314; in London, 314–15; paintings exhibited and reviewed, 315; working on 'Tyrants', 316–17, 319; trip round Ionian islands, 320, 321–4; return to England through Italy, 324–5; collapse, 325; *Views in the Seven Ionian Islands*, 325–7; return to Corfu, 327–8; leaving Corfu, 328–9; in Athens, 329; trip to Crete, 329–32; deciding where to live, 333; gallery visitors, 335; lease on Stratford Place, 336; winter in Nice, 336–7; summer in London, 337; Venice trip, 337–9; in Malta, 339–40; considering marriage, 341; considering marriage to Gussie Bethell, 343–9, 358; travelling up the Nile, 349–50, 353–7; relationship with Giorgio, 351; journey up Italian coast, 357–8; *The History of the Seven Families of the Lake Pipple-Popple*, 362–4; *The Four Little Children Who Went Round the World*, 367–9; life in Cannes, 375–6, 380–2, 388, 392; journal of Crete, 375, 388; 'The Owl and the Pussy-cat', 378–80; trip to Corsica, 382, 389–92; Corsican journal, 382, 389, 392–4; journal of Egypt, 388, 402, 507; rooms in Duchess Street, 393, 448, 449; staying in Langham Hotel, 394; publication of *Journal of a Landscape Painter in Corsica*, 394; return to Cannes, 395; *Nonsense Songs, Stories, Botany and Alphabets*, 396, *398*, 405–6, 407–11; *More Nonsense*, 396, 405, 414, 417, 421; plans to build a house in San Remo, 396–400; walking in Italy, 400–1; staying at Certosa, 401–5; moving in to new house (Villa Emily), 424, 426; life in

Lear, Edward (*cont.*)
San Remo, 426–30, 432–3, 447–8; failed trip to India, 430–2; journey to India, 434; travels in India, 435–44, 445; in Himalayas, 443; in Ceylon, 444–5; return to San Remo, 446; in London, 448–9; return to San Remo, 449; life in San Remo, 450–3; travelling in Italy with Hubert Congreve, 453–4; relationship with Hubert, 454–5; *Laughable Lyrics*, 457–66; summer in England, 469; Giorgio's illness in Corfu, 470; view from Villa Emily spoiled by new hotel building, 471–3, 475, 476–7; Statement to James Fields, 476–7; plans to build new house, 477; trying to raise money for new house, 478–9; new house (Villa Tennyson), 480; feeling behind the times, 486–7; Tennyson illustrations, 488–93, 505; life in San Remo, 494–5, 500–3; Giorgio's death, 503–4; sale of Villa Emily, 505; 'Uncle Arly', 509–12; old age, 513–18; last months, 518–19; death of Foss, 518–19; death, 520; funeral, 520; grave, 503, 520–1, *521*; wills, 252, 513, 514, 517

ALPHABETS: EL's childhood reading, 16; EL's gifts of, 74, 262–5; A was an Ass, *262*; The Absolutely Abstemious Ass, 403; B was once a little bear, *265*; The Enthusiastic Elephant, *264*; The Goodnatured Grey Gull, *403*; H was Papa's new Hat, 264; The Kicking Kangaroo, *74*; M was once a little mouse, *265*; W was a Whale, *263*

APPEARANCE: adolescence, 36–7, 41; as Archbishop, *496*; beard, 223, 226, 272, 300, 383, 403, 427, 439; childhood, 18–19, *19*; clothes, 45, 77, 180–1, 190, 427, 437, 460; clumsiness, 137; domed head, 57; gangly, 54–5; hair thinnng, 272, 403; hat, 225; in a tree, *430*; legs, 36, *126*, 137, 383; moustaches, *128*, 172, 222–3, 272; nose, 5, 19, *126*, 137, 272, 300, 383, 460; photographs, *244*, *248*, *354*, 516, *517*; portraits, *19*, *66*, *128*, 248, *251*, *424*; shambling, 439; spectacles, 55, 57, 272, 403, 427, 439, 460; tall and ungainly, 100; weight, 226, 272, 294, 300, 383, 427; worry about appearance, 272, 383, 460

BOOKS: *Gleanings from the Menagerie and Aviary at Knowsley Hall*, 161, 455; *Illustrated Excursions in Italy*, 141, *142*, 145, 146–7, 149, 151, 161–2, 216, 325, 352; *Illustrations of the Family of Psittacidae, or Parrots*, 49–54, *51*, 57–8, 61, 65, 114, 132; *Journal of a Landscape Painter in Corsica*, 389, *393*, 393–4, 395, 405, 417; *Journal of a Landscape Painter in Greece & Albania*, 188, 204, 219, 483; *Journals of a Landscape Painter in Southern Calabria and the Kingdom of Naples*, 167–70, *168*, 208, 514; *Views in Rome and its Environs*, *119*, 132, 147, 151, 352; *Views in the Seven Ionian Islands*, *323*, 325–7, *326*, 346; *see also* NONSENSE

BOTANICAL INTERESTS: 'Armchairia Comfortabilis', 450, *451*; collecting plants, 399; early life, 32–3; flowers and trees, 33; gardening, 399, 428–9, *428*, *446*, 447, 470–1, 494; *Manypeeplia Upsidownia*, 32, *398*, 399; nonsense botany, 2, 32, *398*, 399–400, 404–5, 406, 450; seeds from India, 446; seeds from New Zealand, 448

HEALTH: asthma, 16, 226, 280, 469; box of medicines, 252; bronchitis, 16, 18, 509; centipede bite, 177; collapse, 58, 324–5; cough, 515; depression, 209, 226–7, 271, 412, 415, 417, 472, 487; drinking, 498–9, 500, 508, epilepsy (the demon), 16–18, 21, 98, 207, 272, 274, 319, 339, 344, 359, 383, 393, 406, 415, 421, 469; eye injured in fall, 431, 469; eyesight, 2, 16, 18, 98, 162, 439, 469, 490, 518; falls, 431, 509, 519; fever, 177–8, 242; giddiness, 469; heart, 400, 469; lungs and throat, 223; palpitations, 400, 469; pleurisy, 505; possible childhood abuse, 21, 22; quinine pills, 179; rheumatism, 469, 515; rumours of illness in Amalfi, 124; 'severe cold', 192; shingles, 469; shoulder injury, 177; skin irritation, 349; sore back, 445; sunstroke, 324; swollen face, 433; syphilitic diseases, 64; toothache, 339

HOUSES: building house at San Remo (Villa Emily), 396–7; building house at San Remo (Villa Tennyson), 480; buying land at San Remo, 396–7; moving into Villa Emily, 424, 456, 481; moving into Villa Tennyson, 480; plans to build a house, 396; plans to move from Villa Emily, 473, 477; sale of Villa Emily, 477, 505, 513; setting up home in San Remo, 424

INTERESTS: cats, 430, *see also* Foss; chess, 507; food, 326, 331, 395, 404, 455, 459, 508, 509; gardening, 399, 428–9, *428*, *446*, 447, 470–1, 494; godchildren, 22, 42, 319, 431, 450, 513; languages, 128, 141, 209, 225, 239, 250, 255, 280, 323, 330, 504, 520; letters, 149, 208, 246, 426, 433–4, 450, *495*, 507, 518; politics, 37, 163–4, 174, 496, 509; reading, 16, 18, 21, 25, 193–4, 238–9, 250, 251, 254–5, 292, 309, 313, 323, 328, 330, 336, 356, 366, 380, 433, 443, 450–1, 460, 502–3, 507–8, 519; religious views, 10, 23, 37, 163, 242, 252–5, 256, 304–10, 506, 509; shooting, 252; social life, 246–7, 270

LIMERICKS: birds in limericks, 56–7; characters of nonsense people, 154–60, 307, 418–21; defying social rules, 305; origins, 94–6; There lived a small puppy at Nārkunda, 437; There was an Old Derry down Derry, 151; There was an Old Lady of Prague, 153; There was an Old Lady whose folly, 97; There was an Old Man at a casement, 304; There was an Old Man in a boat, 303; There was an Old Man in a Marsh, 370; There was an Old Man in a tree, 395; There was an Old Man of th' Abruzzi, 155; There was an Old Man of Apulia, 15; There was an Old Man of Bohemia, 152; There was an Old Man of Boulak, 352; There was an Old Man of the Cape, 83; There was an Old Man of Dee-side, 420; There was an Old Man of Dunblane, 461; There was an Old Man of Hong Kong, 417; There was an Old Man of the Isles, 297, 303; There was an Old Man of Lodore, 283; There was an Old Man of Marseilles, 2; There was an Old Man of Melrose, 301, 302; There was an Old Man of Nepaul, 160, 417; There was an Old Man of New York, 160, 300; There was an Old Man of the North, 157; There was an Old Man of Peru, 345; There was an Old Man of Spithead, 1; There was an Old Man of Tobago, 94–5, 95; There was an Old Man of Vesuvius, 120; There was an Old Man of the West, 150; There was an Old Man of Whitehaven, 3, 3–4, 301; There was an Old Man on a Hill, 300; There was an Old Man on some rocks, 347; There was an Old Man who said 'How, –, 197, 300; There was an old man whose Giardino, 446; There was an Old Man with a beard, 56; There was an Old Man with a Book, 320, 327; There was an Old Man with a nose, 270; There was an Old Man with an owl, 333; There was an Old Person in black, 371; There was an Old Person of Bray, 83; There was an Old Person of Bree, 370; There was an Old Person of Cromer, 300, 300–1; There was an Old Person of Deal, 419; There was an Old Person of Ems, 416; There was an Old Person of Ewell, 302, 303; There was an Old Person of Gretna, 161; There was an Old Person of Harrow, 341; There was an Old Person of Hove, 521; There was an Old Person of Hyde, 345; There was an Old Person of Nice, 57; There was an old person of Páxo, 321; There was an Old Person of Philae, 224, 300; There was an Old Person of Rhodes, 159; There was an Old Person of Sheen, 472; There was an old Person of Skye, 371; There was an Old Person of Stroud, 419; There was an Old Person of Tartary, 158; There was an Old Person of Tring, 416; There was an old person so silly, 33; There was an old person whose tears, 469; There was an Old Woman of Norwich, 95; There was a Young Girl of Majorca, 5; There was a young lady in white, 414, 414–15; There was a Young Lady of Corsica, 388; There was a young Lady of Lucca, 300; There was a Young Lady of Norway, 157; There was a Young Lady of Wales, 159; There was a Young Lady whose bonnet, 45, 302; There was a Young Person of Smyrna, 302; There was a Young Person whose history, 420, 421

MONEY: bequest from Mrs Courtney Warner, 203; bequest from sister Ellen, 505, 517; borrowing from friends, 274, 353; building house at San Remo, 396–7; buying land at San Remo, 396–7; commissions, 105–6, 125, 149, 228, 248, 260, 271, 289, 336, 337, 426, 431, 432, 434, 443, 477, 487; cost of woodcuts, 299, 392; debts, 203, 291; Derby patronage, 65, 76, 127, 135, 147, 425; earnings from teaching, 125; efforts to sell work, 497; first sales of drawings, 28–9; gifts from friends, 178, 189; government bonds, 396; hire of stone blocks for lithographs, 52, 53; Knowsley group's Rome commission, 105–6; living abroad, 245; loan from Husey Hunt, 274; loan from Northbrook, 477, 478, 505; marriage question, 349; open Wednesdays in San Remo, 497; owed money, 319; patrons, 2–3, 65, 76, 127, 135, 203, 246, 285, 289, 425, 478, 487, 497, 514; paying Arab assailants in Petra, 259–60; payments for paintings, 68; plan to sell four hundred sketches, 478; plan to show pictures at Norfolk Square, 478; prices, 316; refuses loans, 278; rent, 237, 316, 320, 349, 396; reproduction costs, 517; Rome studio, 172; sale of Villa Emily, 505; sales in Nice, 337; sales of books, 132, 162, 304–5; sales of Corfu views, 237; sales of drawings, 125, 320, 448, 478–9, 507; sales of Nonsense books, 299, 304–5, 310, 429; sales of paintings, 209, 211, 237, 248, 276, 289, 291, 337, 380, 394, 425, 426, 448, 479; sales of rights, 58, 310, 316; sales of 'Tyrants', 319, 337; sales slow, 414; sending money for the London poor, 494; sending money to mother, 64; sending money to sister Mary, 203; sending money to sisters for Christmas, 172; sent money by friends for travelling, 178; sketches in India, 478; storage of paintings, 396; subscribers and subscriptions,

MONEY (*cont.*)
49, 53, 105, 114, 132, 146, 208, 289, 327, 394; tax forms, 315; teenage poverty, 26, 27; travel costs, 125, 257; travelling expenses paid, 189; wages, 451; worries, 161, 203, 405

MUSICAL INTERESTS: accordion, 23, 79, 85, 102, 262; Appendix of music to *Excursions*, 146; compositions, 23, 25, 146, 212, 213, 214, 223, 232, 284, 319, 428, 453; flute, 19, 23, 63, 79, 85, 102, 126, 221, 457; guitar, 23, 85, 102, 106, 173, 214, 221, 291; piano, 20, 23, 85, 102, 213, 214, 229, 262, 271, 286, 319, 415, 447, 454, *482*, 507; reputation on Corfu, 238; singing, 23, 79, 85, 173, 213, 229, 286, 299, 330, 403, 453, 475; singing criticized, 232

NATURAL HISTORY ARTIST: bird paintings, 33–4, 45, 59, 98; early works, 30–1, *31*; feather and business card, *46*; *Illustrations of the Family of Psittacidae, or Parrots*, 49–54, *51*, 57–8, 61, 65, 114, 132; Knowsley collection, 67–73, *69*, *70*, *72*; reptiles and animals, 61; works for Gould, 58–61

NONSENSE WRITER AND POET: cartoon misadventures, 135–8, *137*; comic Roman histories, *135*; first nonsense rhymes, 91–7, 153; influence of nonsense writing, 514; nonsense botany, 2, 32, *358*, 399–400, 404–5, 406, 450, *451*; nonsense cookery, 2, 32, 404–5, 406; publishers, 299, 305, 310, 395, 405, 406, 407, 414, 457, 478; words and letters, 265–9, 328; written fast, 152; 'The Adventures of Mr Lear & the Polly & the Puseybite', 364–5, *365*, 417; 'The Akond of Swat', 433, 457, 471; *Book of Nonsense*, 4, 93, *151*, 209, 262, 299–303, 304, 310, 316, 418; 'The Broom, the Shovel, the Poker and the Tongs', 383–4, 410; 'Calico Pie', 382, *383*, 385, 409; 'Cold are the crabs', 422–3; 'The Courtship of the Yonghy-Bonghy-Bò', 278, 349, 411, 412–14, *412*, 429, 442, 457, 461, 475; 'The Cummerbund', 439–40, 457; 'The Dong with a Luminous Nose', 1, 457, 463–6; 'The Duck and the Kangaroo', 350, 395, 402, 403, 407; *The Four Little Children Who Went Round the World*, 367–9, *367*, *368*, *369*, 402, 405; 'Gozo my child is the isle of Calypso', 340; *The History of the Seven Families of the Lake Pipple-Popple*, 362–4, *363*, 405; 'The Jumblies', 5, 402, 407, 407–8, 410; *Laughable Lyrics*, 457; *More Nonsense*, 396, 405, 414, 417, 421; 'Mr and Mrs Discobbolos', 266, 411, 429, 457; 'Mr and Mrs Discobbolos' second part, 475–6, 500; 'Mr and Mrs Spikky Sparrow' ,

402, *409*, 462; 'Mr Daddy Long-legs and Mr Floppy Fly', 385–7, *385*, 395, 402, 407, 410; 'Mr Lear recovers his hat', 135–6, *136*; 'The New Vestments', 457, 459–60; *Nonsense Gazette*, 404; *Nonsense Songs, Stories, Botany and Alphabets*, 396, *398*, 405–6, 407–11, 421, 428; 'The Nutcracker and the Sugartongs', 408–9; 'The Owl and the Pussy-cat', *375*, 378–80, *378*, *379*, 385, 395, 403, 407, 410, 438, 475, 506, 514; 'The Owl and the Pussy-cat' sequels, 506; 'The Pelican Chorus', 355–6, 457, 461–3, *462*; 'The Pobble who has no Toes', *433*, 457, 461, 465; 'Quacks vobiscum Uncle Arly', 513; 'Quangle Wangle's Hat', 73, *456*, 456–7; 'Ribands and pigs', 233–4, *234*; 'The Scroobious Pip', ix, 421–2, *421*, 423, 429; 'She sits upon her Bulbul', 329; 'Some Incidents in the Life of my Uncle Arly', 509–12, *510*; 'The Table and the Chair', 410; *The Tragical Life and Death of Caius Marius*, *131*, 135; 'The Two Old Bachelors', 457–60, *458*, 460

PAINTER AND ARTIST: brushes and colours, 270, 289, 336; chalks, 99, 103, 122, 325; commissions, 105–6, 125, 149, 228, 248, 260, 271, 289, 336, 337, 426, 431, 432, 434, 443, 477, 487; Corfu gallery, *318*; drawings of people, 237; engravers, 299; exhibitions, 207, 211, 212, 245, 249, 280, 289, 291, 311–12, 315, 352, 396, 428, 497, 506, 507; first sales of drawings, 28–9; frames, 270, 316, 317, 336, 488; landscape painting, 98–9, 104, 127; lithographs, 52–3, 58, 63, 131–2, 138, 141, 161, 299, 325, 517; oils, 122, 165, 209, 212, 225, 242, 271, 289, 311, 313, 315, 426, 481; 'Mr Lear the artist', *311*; orders for lithographs and watercolours, 105; pencil sketches, 122; photography, 318, 325; picture dealers, 270; purchasers, 246–7, 362, 380; reputation, 62, 63, 79, 134, 333, 514; sales of paintings, 209, 211, 237, 248, 276, 289, 291, 337, 380, 394, 425, 426, 448, 479; sales of drawings, 125, 320, 448, 478–9, 507; sepia ink, 122, 440; sketches, 70–1, 101, 103–4, 192, 198, 218, 311, 336, 339, 440, 478, 481, 486, 507, 514; use of colours, 209–10, 261; watercolour sketches, 61, 191, 225, 330, 513–14; watercolours, 62, 67, 68, *69*, 122, 198, 225, 271, 289, 311, 317, 337, 440, 490; woodcuts, 392, 393; working methods, 32, 50, 122, 127, 311, 312–13, 317

PAINTINGS AND DRAWINGS: drawings for nursery rhymes, 268; illustrations of songs, 88–91, *89*, *90*, *91*; pictogram letters, 268–9; self-portraits, *57*, 86, *424*; Tennyson illustrations, *see* TENNYSON ILLUSTRATIONS;

travel sketches, 137–8, 336–7; 'Tyrants', 316–17, *318*, 319, 325, 336, 337, 352, 362, 393, 433, 486; works: *Abu Simbel, 151; Ajaccio, 393; Amalfi,* 123; *The Approach to Philae, 228; Athens, 177; Avlona, 175; Beachy Head,* 315, *316;* Beirut, 289, 352, 380; *Benares,* 440, *441; Campagna of Rome from Villa Mattei, 119; Cape Lefkada* (Cape Ducato), 322, *323; Cedars of Lebanon,* 280, 289–91, 311, *312,* 313, 315, 316, 337, 380, 488; *The City of Syracuse from the Ancient Quarries,* 165, 208, 209, 210–11, 213, 249; *Civitella,* 189, 291; *Claude Lorrain's House on the Tiber,* 207; *Coast of Travancore, India, 491; Corfu from the Village of Ascension, Evening, 236,* 248, 251, 315, 326; *The Forest of Bavella, 391; Kasr es Saàd,* 396, 481, *488,* 491; *Khimara, 185; Kinchenjunga,* 443–4, *444,* 448, 487, 488, 491, 514; *Knowsley Hall from the west, 75; Lago di Fucino, 142; Lucknow, 436; Masada,* 260, 271, 291, 311–12, 380; *Miss Maniac, 87; The Monastery of St Dionysius, Mount Athos, 490; The Monastery of Zografu, Athos,* 243; *Monastir, 181; Monte Rosa from Monte Generoso, 470;* Mount Athos, 242, *243,* 245, 248, 262, 298, 426, 489, *490,* 492; *Mount Ida from Phre,* 330, *331; Mount Parnassus,* 209, 237; *The Mountains of Thermopylae,* 209–10, *210; Mr Lear stamps and dances for joy, 427; Near Gau el Kebir, 355; Near Wadi el-Sheikh, 192, Nuneham,* 246–7, *247; Oneglia, Riviera di Ponente, 337; Outside the Walls of Suez, 191; Palaiokastritsa, Corfu, 326; Palizzi,* 168; *Petra, the theatre,* 259; Philae paintings, 225, *228,* 237, 289, 315, 481, 484, 492; *Rome from Monte Pincio, 109; San Vittorino, 145; Scafell Pike,* 103; *A shepherd at Kerkira, 234;* 'The Stripy Bird', *478; Suli, 187; Syracuse quarries, 166,* 207; *The Temple of Apollo at Bassae,* 196, 289, *290; Temple of Venus and Rome, 116; Tollygunge, Calcutta, 441, 442; Umbrellifera,* 102; *Valdoniello,* 396; *Venice, 338; A walk on a windy day, 494; Wastwater* (watercolour), 104; *Wastwater & the Screes, from Wastdale* (print), 104; 'When I dreamed I was young and innocent', *84*

PERSONALITY: agreeable and genial, 100, 150; changes in mood, 20, 274, 397; companionable, 150; depression, 209, 226–7, 271, 412, 415, 417, 472, 487; diary, 415; 519; feelings of panic, 84; fitting into any group, 40, 100; Hunt's description, 138; loneliness, 18, 84, 92, 139, 289, 421, 447, 454; love for Frank, 197; love of England, 133; making people laugh, 22, 84, 92–3, 138, 429; marriage question, 129–30, 239–40, 314, 341–51, 359, 517; memory, 287–8, 486; monogram, 269, *417;* 'the morbids', 20, 288, 364, 415, 423; nostalgia, 36, 133, 215, 332, 408, 507; real feeling, 151; relationship with children, 91–2, 297–8; self-description, 58, 133–5, 251, 473–4; self-portraits, *57,* 86, *137, 418, 424, 427, 430,* 473–4, *474;* self-presentation, 136–7, 447; sexuality, 21, 64, 129, 383; stepping-stone people, 504; *"There is no such person as Edward Lear", 418;* uses of humour, 84–5, 134, 229; weeping, 22, 235, 353, 474, 475, 482, 505; wills, 252, 513, 514, 517; worrying, 164, 203, 289, 405, 450, 472, 490

POEMS AND SONGS: album rhymes, 30; comic saga, 25–6; parodies, 25–6, 37, 84–8, 90, 289, 482–4; picture-poems, 267–8; poems for Drewitt family, 41–2; sister Ann's birthday poem, 26–7; verse diary, 40; verse letters, 38, 41, 91–2, 289; work titles and first lines: Eclogue, 375–6; 'Farewell Mother! Tears are streaming', 84–5; 'How pleasant to know Mr Lear!', 473–5, *474,* 509–10; 'I slept – and back to my early days', 90; 'Nluv, fluv bluv, ffluv biours', 482–3; 'O Brother Chicken! Sister Chick!', *9,* 479; O! Chichester, my Carlingford!, 449; O! dear! How disgusting is life!, 472; O! Mimber for the County Louth, 273; 'Peppering Roads', 40–1; 'Ribands and Pigs', 267–8, *268;* 'The Sunny Side of Durham', 26; '*Tom-Moory* Pathos; – all things bare', 483–4; 'Ye who have hearts – aloud rejoice', 37

TENNYSON ILLUSTRATIONS: project, 5, 216–19, 287, 484, 488–9, 507, 508, 517–18; titles: 'Athos – all things fair', 483, *490;* 'The crag that fronts the Even', 481, 482, *488; Enoch Arden's Island,* 491–3, *493;* 'For all remembrance is an arch', *480,* 486; 'Illyrian woodlands', *213,* 220, 483, 484; 'A looming bastion fringed with fire', 490–1, *491;* 'Moonlight on still waters', 481, 482; 'Morn broaden'd on the borders of the dark, 221, *222,* 394, *485;* 'Palms and temples of the South', 223, 225, *485,* 489; 'To watch the crisping ripples on the beach', 482; 'Tomohrit', 482; 'The vast Akrokeraunian walls', 220, 481, 482

TRAVELS: advice to travellers, 178–9; Albania, 180–6, 197–8, 240–1, 245; Amsterdam, 59; Basilicata, 171–2; Brussels, 109; Calabria, 167–71; childhood reading, 18, 21; Constantinople, 177–8; Dublin, 79–80, 100–1; Egypt, 190–2, 224–6, 349–50, 353–7, 431–2; Florence, 110–11,

TRAVELS (*cont.*)
162, 294; Germany, 109; Greece, 176–7, 188, 193–4, 195–7; India, 435–45; Ireland, 89, 248; Italy, *see* Italy; Jerusalem, 256, 260–1, 357; Lake District, 101–5; Lebanon, 261; Luxembourg, 109; Malta, 175, 187, 189–90, 339–40, 353; Naples, 121–2, 171, 453; Palestine, 255–8, 260–1; Paris, 105, 274; Petra, 257–60; railway travel, 131, 162, 249–50, 279, 298; 'roaming with a hungry heart', 332; Rome, *see* Rome; Salonica, 178, 179; Sicily, 137–8, 139–40, 165–7; Vienna, 249

Lear, Eleanor (Ellen, EL's sister), *see* Newsom

Lear, Florence (EL's sister), 10, 27, 105, 117

Lear, Frederick (Fred, EL's brother), 10, 15, 31, 202, 252, 294

Lear, George (from Arundel), 27–8, 63

Lear, Harriett (EL's sister), 10, 17–18, 117, 202, 203, 292

Lear, Henry (EL's brother), 10, 13, 15, 201–2, 294, 469

Lear, Jeremiah (EL's father): absence, 19–20; career, 11–12, 14–15, 22, 25; collection of pictures and prints, 24; death, 64; EL's memories of, 20; family background, 11; financial difficulties, 14–15, 476; health, 400; marriage, 10, 11; retirement to Gravesend, 27

Lear, Jeremiah (of Batsworth Park), 24, 27, 35

Lear, Kate (EL's sister), 105, 406

Lear, Mary (EL's sister), *see* Boswell

Lear, Sarah (EL's sister), *see* Street

Lebanon, 261, 278, 289

Linnean Society, 49, 53, 63, 79

Liverpool exhibitions, 245, 280, 313

London: Buckingham Palace, 148; Crystal Palace, 230, 447; EL's attitude to, 28, 337, 478; EL's lodgings with sister Ann, 27; EL's teenage life, 27–9; exhibitions, 98, 112, 245, 486; fashions, 368; Great Exhibition, 204–5, 447; Lear family background, 11; menageries and zoos, 47; political scene, 174; the poor, 27, 494; Royal Society, 291; Season, 67, 246; social connections, 39; social life, 270, 291, 304, 314, 448; Zoo, 45, 47–8, 54, 65, 80, 101

Luard, Henry, 340

Lushington, Cecilia (*née* Tennyson), 195, 204, 215–16, 230, 231, 384

Lushington, Cissy, 204

Lushington, Eddy, 230, 243, 385

Lushington, Edmund, 194–5, 204, 215–16, 230, 231, 384

Lushington, Ellen, 204, 226, 233, 384

Lushington, Emily, 189, 194, 204, 231

Lushington, Franklin (Frank): Albania travels, 240, 245; appearance, 193, *194*, *244*; brother Henry's death, 231, 233, 313; career, 230, 233, 234–5, 262, 272, 321, 424, 494; champagne for EL, 519; character, 193, 204, 230, 232, 243, 250, 251; children, 319, 333, 384, 385, 431, 449; Cornwall with EL, 205; education, 194; EL's grave, 520; EL's home plans, 396; EL's love for, 197, 222, 224, 235, 285, 341, 344, 509; EL's visits, 384, 393, 431, 478–9; EL's wills, 252, 514, 517; family background, 194–5; *Journal* dedication, 394; journey to Corfu with EL, 234; letters to, 241, 463, 514, 518, 519–20; Malta visits, 190; marriage, 313, 314, 341, 384; memories of EL, 196, 238, 241, 248, 449, 515; poems, 227–8, 452; relationship with EL, 222, 232, 235, 236–9, 243–4, 250, 251, 272, 344, 384, 449, 451; relationship with Henry Hallam, 195, 235; review of *In Memoriam*, 195; sister Louisa's death, 226; Temple chambers, 272, 288; Tennyson visits, 216, 232, 285–6; travelling with EL, 193–7, 238, 245, 262, 470; view of EL's work, 191–2; visiting EL, 429, 450, 502; warlike enthusiasm, 227–8; yacht, 238, 245, 314

Lushington, Gertrude, 319, 384–7, *386*, 449–50, 463, 502, 515

Lushington, Henry (Harry), 189–90, 194–5, 227, 231, 313, 385

Lushington, Kate (*née* Morgan): children, 319, 333, 384, 385, 431, 449–50, 478; Frank's death, 514; marriage, 313, 384

Lushington, Louisa, 190, 226, 385

Lushington, Maria, 189–90, 194

Lushington, Stephen, 290, 315, 344

Lushington, Tom, 248, 385

Lushington family, 194–5, 204, 215–16, 230–2, 272, 385

Lyell, Charles, *Principles of Geology*, 80

Lyttleton, Lady, 380

Macdonald, George, 471

Malta: EL's visits, 174, 175, 187, 189–90, 198, 339–40, 353; Lushington family in, 189–90, 197, 226, 231; scenery, 175

Manchester exhibitions, 245, 249, 280

Marseilles, 352–3

Marshall, John, 94

Marstrand, Wilhelm ('Willi'), 127–9, 294, 454

Martineau, Robert Braithwaite, 207, 208, 271

McLean, Thomas; gallery, 352; picture dealer, 270, 352, 382; publication of *A Book of Nonsense*, 151, 352; publication of *Illustrated*

Excursions in Italy, 146, 352; publication of *Views in Rome*, 132, 352; publishing, 299, 305

Mérimée, Prosper, 389

Mill, John Stuart, 306, 509

Millais, John Everett: friendship with EL, 208, 212; lordly character, 208; marriage, 230, 312; monogram, 269; opinion of EL's singing, 232; PRB, 206, 312; RA Schools, 206; Sass's school, 65; *Apple Blossoms*, 312; *Christ in the House of His Parents*, 207; *Isabella*, 206

Monte Generoso, *470*, 475, 495, 498, 500

Montgomery, Hugh, 471

Moore, Thomas, 25, 433, 481; ballad of St Kevin, 90, *91*; 'The Beach', 464; 'The Boat', 23; 'The Fudge Family in Paris', 40; *Irish Melodies*, 23; 'The Lake of the Dismal Swamp', 464; 'Oft in the Stilly Night', 211

More Nonsense, 396, 405, 417, 421

Mount Athos: EL's journal, 278; EL's pictures, 242, *243*, 245, 248, 262, 298, 426, 489, *490*, 492; EL's planned visits, 179, 193, 220, 240; EL's visit, 241–3, 253

Mount Tomohrit, 426, 482

Moxon, Edward, 219, 249, 271

Murchison, Sir Roderick, 192

Naples: EL's dislike of, 121–2; EL's journal, 167; EL's visits, 121–2, 167, 171, 174, 434, 453; English in, 115, 173, 189; Kingdom of, 164, 173

Nash, Paul, 517

Nevill, Allan, 22, 105, 249, 513

Nevill, Ralph, 22, 105

Nevill, William (Bill), 22, 104–5, 249, 484

Nevill family, 117, 252, 293, 484–5

New Zealand, 202–3, 245, 292, 294, 448, 477

Newsom, Eleanor (Ellen, EL's sister): brother Henry's death, 469; childhood, 10, 22–3; death, 505; education, 22–3; home, 202, 203; husband's death, 292; marriage, 24; nephew's death, 333; New Zealand, 203, 245; old age, 333, 388, 448; religion, 22, 202, 252; will, 505

Newsom, William (EL's brother-in-law), 24, 202, 203, 292

Nice, 336–7, 360, 362, 396, 400

Nonsense Songs, Stories, Botany and Alphabets, 396, 406, 407–14, 421, 428

North, Catherine, *see* Symonds

North, Frederick, Earl of Guilford, 237

North, Frederick (Hastings MP), 211, 213

North, Marianne, 213, 426, *427*, 448, 475, 477

Northbrook, Thomas Baring, first Earl of: appearance, 174; character, 2, 172; commis-sions, 431, 448, 488; daughter Emma, 509, 516; 'Eastern Question', 496; EL's bequests, 513, 514; EL's gift of drawings and water-colour sketches, 513–14; EL's Indian travels, 430–1, 436–8; EL's last words, 520; EL's visits, 325; first meeting with EL in Rome, 172; generosity, 478; letters to, 2; library, 481; loan to EL, 477, 478, 505; photograph, 515; Viceroy of India, 430–1, 437–8; visiting EL, 450, 478–9, 516

Northumberland, Duke of, 49, 114

Odysseus, 323, 340

Orsini, Giuseppe, 518, 519–20

Palmer, Anny, 121–2, 126, *126*

Palmer, Samuel, 121–4, 126, *126*

Palmerston, Lord, 144–5, 247, 321, 327, 338

Parker, Adamson, 434, 502

Parkyns, Emma (*née* Bethell), 343, 346–7, 349, 358, 364, 407–8

Parkyns, Mansfield, 343, 349

Parrots, see Illustrations of the Family of Psittacidae

Peel, John, 353

Penrhyn, Edward Leycester, 79

Peppering House, *35*, 36, 40–2, 59, 130, 288

Percy, Lady Susannah ('Susan'), 114, 135–6

Petra, 258–60, *259*

Philae: EL at, 224–5, 355; limerick, *224*, 226, 300, 390; paintings, 225, *228*, 237, 289, 315, 481, 484, 492

Pius IX, Pope, 164–5, 173, 174, 274

Poplawska, Miss (governess), 426, 430

Poussin, Gaspard Dughet ('Gaspar'), 122, 168

Poussin, Nicolas, 112, 147, 168, 313, 443

Poynter, Miss, 457

Pre-Raphaelite Brotherhood (PRB): aims, 206–7; attacks on, 207, 306, 487; influence on EL, 209, 211–12, 222, 312, 335; monogram, 269; Tenny-son illustrations, 219

Prescott family, 327, 328, 333, 359

Prinsep, Henry Thoby, 285, 334, 355

Prinsep, Sara (*née* Pattle), 285, 334, 355

Proby, John, 137, 165–72, 173, 270

Prout, Samuel, 98, 112

Reid, Sir James, 236, *244*, 262, 287, 297, 314

Reid, Lady *244*, 247, 297, 314

Rimbault, Edward Francis, 284

Roberts, David, 251, 278, 342

Rogers, Samuel, *Italy*, 38, 112, 217

Rome: Academy, 111; Campagna, 118–19, *119*, 165; EL's apartment on Via Condotti, 274–5; EL's departures, 277–8, 282; EL's life in, 275–7, 280–1; EL's move to, 132, 274, 360, 447; EL's return to, 279–80; EL's visits, 111–19, 124–9, 429, 453, 460, 499; English community, 114–15, 277, 280; political scene, 277, 281–2; *Temple of Venus and Rome, 116*; visit by Prince of Wales, 276–7

Rosa, Salvator, 112, 122, 168, 170, 313

Rossetti, Dante Gabriel, 206, 249, 271, 290, 310; *Girlhood of the Virgin Mary*, 206; *Helen of Troy*, 271

Rossetti, William, 208, 210, 271, 380

Routledge, Warne & Routledge, 299, 305, 310, 316

Royal Academy: exhibitions, 207, 211, 212, 396, 428; Schools, 65, *201*, 203–4, 206

Rusconi, Luigi, 507, 509, 515, 518

Ruskin, John, 207, 209, 315, 376, 509, 514; *Modern Painters*, 147, 206

Russell, Lord John, 147, 338

Russell, Odo, 281

San Remo: cemetery, 503, 520; EL's house plans, 396–7, 477, 480; EL's life in, 430, 447, 454, 494, 497–8, 515–16; EL's rented rooms, 400; English residents, 90, 377, 397, 426–7, 471–2, 515; English visitors, 494; flowers and trees, 399; hotel spoiling EL's view, 471, 472–3, 475, 476–7; landscape, 400; Villa Emily, *see* Villa Emily; Villa Tennyson, 480, 494, 500, 504, 507–8, *508*

Sandbach, Sam, 262

Sappho, 175, 322, 351

Sass's School of Art, 64–5, 110, 203–4

Satow, Ernest, 397, 447

Schreiber, Charlotte, 232

Seddon, Thomas, 208, 225, 256

Selby, Prideaux John, 49, 53, 61–2, 340; *British Ornithology*, 61–2; *Illustrations of Ornithology*, 62

Selwyn, Revd E. Carus, 494–5

Senefelder, Alois, 52; *A Complete Course of Lithography*, 52

Senior, Bernard, *see* Husey Hunt

Senior, Lizzie, 513

Seymour, Alfred, 506

Shakespear family, *244*, 318

Sharpe, Richard Scrafton, *Anecdotes and Adventures of Fifteen Gentlemen*, 94, 95, 154

Shelley, Percy Bysshe, 25, 37, 282, 294, 464

Shelley, Percy (son of poet), 25, 319

Sicily, 137–8, 139–40, 165–7, 173, 282

Simeon, Cornwall, 150–1

Simeon, Sir John, 232

Sinclair, Catherine, *Holiday House*, 96

Smith, Elder & Co., 299, 392

Smith Stanley, *see* Derby

Somers, Lord, 172, 203, 285

Somers, Virginia, Lady, 203, 285

Speke, John Hanning, 328, 349, 366

Stanley, Arthur Penrhyn, 79, 89–90, 101, 308, 506, 515

Stanley, Edward, Reverend, 79, 89, 101

Stanley, Lord, *see* Derby

Stanley of Alderley, Lord, 308

Stebbins, Emma, 281

Storks, Sir Henry, 314, 321, 323, 327, 339, 353

Story, William Wetmore, 275–6, 279

Story family, 275, 276, 279

Stowe, Harriet Beecher, 281, 384

Strachey, Constance (*née* Braham), 317, 497, 514, 515, 520

Strachey, Eddie, 477, 515

Strachey, Sir Edward, 500

Strachey, Henry, 317, 471, 492, 500

Strachey, Mary Isabella, Lady (*née* Symonds), 377

Street, Charles (EL's brother-in-law), 24, 35, 40, 49, 202, 359

Street, Charles Henry (EL's nephew). 40, 91–2

Street, Emily (EL's great-niece), 292, 397, 514

Street, Fred (EL's nephew), 40, 91–2

Street, Sarah (EL's sister): artist, 16, 18, 31, 33; botanist and gardener, 31, 202, 428; childhood, 10, 11; children, 40, 91–2, 202, 333; death, 448; education, 22–3; EL's letters, 117; EL's visits, 35, 40, 58; emigration to New Zealand, 202–3; grandchildren, 202, 397, 513, 514; Great Exhibition visit, 204–5; husband's illness, 202–3, 359; marriage, 24; neighbours, 49; return from New Zealand, 292; sister Mary's death, 294; son Fred's death, 333; teaching EL to draw, 16, 18

Sussex: Arundel, 24, 35, 37, 40, 49, 133; Batsworth Park, 24, 35, 38, 40; countryside, 36, 38, 99; Parham, 38, 99; Peppering House, 35–7, 40–2, 133; social connections for EL, 37–8

Symonds, Catherine (*née* North): childhood, 213, 375; children, 375, 377, 381, 382, 505; friendship with EL, 375–6, 448, 450, 477; half-sister, 426; life in Cannes, 375; marriage, 375, 376, 377, 381; relationship with husband, 377, 381, 384; renting EL's house, 505; sketching with EL, 389

Symonds, John Addington: career, 377, 381; character, 377; childhood, 376–7; children, 375,

377, 381, 382, 505; education, 376–7; friendship
with EL, 375–6, 392, 448, 450, 477; health,
377, 381; life in Cannes, 375; marriage, 375,
376, 377, 381; relationship with wife, 377, 381,
384; renting EL's house, 505; sexuality, 129,
377, 380–1; travels in Corsica with Prosper
Mérimée, 389; *Problem of Greek Ethics*, 377;
The Renaissance in Italy, 381

Tait, Archibald Campbell, 427, 428

Taylor, Tom, 315, 316

Tennyson, Alfred: Aldworth, 394, 396; appearance, 216, *284*, 285; brother Horatio, 293;
character, 216, 285, 334–5, 394; childhood, 215;
children, 216, 219; EL's illustrations, 5, 216–19,
287, 480–1, 484, 488–91, 507, 508, 517–18; EL's
parodies, 482–4; EL's settings, 212, 214, 223,
232, 284, 428, 453; EL's visits, 217, 232–3, 278,
283–6, 293, 334, 394; Farringford, 231, 283,
284, 285, *286*, 334; finances, 289; friendship
with Lushington family, 215–16; illustrators,
219, 271; Italian trip, 216; limericks, 310; love
for Arthur Hallam, 195, 215, 235; marriage,
215–16; meetings with EL, 218–19, 295;
monogram, 269; Moxon's illustrated edition,
219, 249, 271; peerage, 505; Poet Laureate, 215,
219; portrait by Cameron, 334; relationship
with EL, 216, 219–21, 283, 285–7, 334, 394, 518;
responses to landscape, 218; revising work,
214; voice, 482; works: 'Charge of the Light
Brigade', 227; 'The Daisy', 489, 518; 'A Dream
of Fair Women', 221; 'Eleanore', 482; 'Enoch
Arden', 492; 'Guinevere', 283, 315; *Idylls of
the King*, 283, 284, 483; *In Memoriam*, 195, 215,
240, 478, 490, 503; 'The Lady of Shalott',
214, 219, 283, 414, 439, 464; 'Locksley Hall',
213, 214, 289; 'The Lotos Eaters', 214, 324,
482; 'Mariana', 214, 448, 458, 489; *Maud*, 231,
306, 348; 'Ode to Memory', 484; 'The Palace
of Art', 340, 489, 518; *Poems* (1843), 213–14;
The Princess, 240; 'Tears, idle tears', 212, 215,
223, 412; 'To E.L. on His Travels in Greece',
219–21, 482, 489, 518, 520; 'Two Voices', 342;
'Ulysses', 213, 287, 394, 486; 'You ask me,
why', 223, 315–16

Tennyson, Emily (*née* Sellwood): appearance and
character, 216, 283–4, *284*, 334; children, 216,
219; EL's dedications to, 223, 507; EL's visits,
232–3, 293, 394; letters from, 231–2, 233, 327,
480; letters to, 222, 223, 230, 231, 243, 267, 281,
303, 304, 314, 359, 390, 396, 449, *485*, 515; marriage, 215–16; memories of EL, 215, 249, 286;
photograph, 515; relationship with EL, 217–18,

224, 226, 230, 233, 283–4, 394, 505; view of
Lushington family, 204, 232

Tennyson, Hallam: childhood, 219, 234, 263,
284; EL's alphabet for, 263; EL's old age,
517–18; engagement and marriage, 506; father's
responses to landscape, 218; letters to, 506, 515;
relationship with EL, 469, 505

Tennyson, Lionel, 263, 268, *284*, 469

Terry, Ellen, 334

Terry family, 74, 402–5

Thackeray, William Makepeace, 208, 269, 279,
285, 310; 'The Rose and the Ring', 279; 'A
Shabby Genteel Story', 30

Theed, William, 111, 112, 113, 120

Thorwaldsen, Bertel, 112

Thrupp, Frederick, 113, 125, 132

Tozer, Augusta, 447

Tozer, Henry, *Researches in the Highlands of
Turkey*, 447

Trelawny, Edward, 464

Trollope, Anthony, 229, 238, 507–8, 519; *Can You
Forgive Her?*, 507

Turner, J. M. W.: engravings for *Italy*, 38, 112;
friendships, 39, 65; influence on EL, 101, 119,
443, 487; patronage, 38–9; Ruskin on, 147;
Scott illustrations, 217; social life, 65; working
style, 218; works: *Liber Studiorum*, 481; *Norham
Castle, Sunrise*, 481; *Rain, Steam and Speed*,
131; *The Reichenbach Falls*, 226

Underhill, Frank, 481, 507, 508, 514

Uwins, James, 113, 120–4, 125, 139, 239, 274

Uwins, Thomas, 113, 122

Venables, George Stovin, 231, 235, 272

Victoria, Queen: accession, 106; children, 147,
148, 276, 320, 498; drawing lessons from EL,
147–9; Empress of India, 449; Italian trip,
497–8; Sussex visit, 37; view of orang utan,
359; *Views in Rome* subscription, 132

Views in Rome and its Environs, *119*, 132, 147,
151, 352

Views in the Seven Ionian Islands, *323*, 325–7, *326*,
346

Vigors, Nicholas, 49, 50, 53, 62, 400

Villa Emily: building, 396–7; burglary, 446; design,
480; garden, 397, 399, *425*, 428, 446, 470, 494;
hotel spoiling EL's view, 471, 472–3, 475,
476–7; library, 426; life at, 426, 451, 481; name,
397; sale of, 477, 505, 513; site, 397, *425*, 503;
studio, 424

Villa Tennyson, 480, 494, 500, 504, 507–8, *508*

Waldegrave, Frances, Lady (Lady W.): advice to EL, 349; death, 475, 477, 508; EL's work for, 246–7, 260, 271, 294, 337–8; family background, 229; letters to, 338–9, 340, 354, 388, 430, 433; marriages, 229, 314, 318–19; photograph of, 301; relationship with Fortescue, 229, 232, 314, 318–19, 333, 338, 382; society hostess, 229–30, 448

Wallace, Alfred Russel, 359

Watson family, 495, 499, 502

Watts, G. F., 285, 334, 355

Waugh, Fanny, 271, 341, 353

Wentworth, Mrs (of Woolley), 39–40, 48–9, 61, 362

Wentworth-Fitzwilliam family, 362

Westbury, Ellinor, Lady, 342, 346

Westbury, Richard Bethell, Lord, 209, 341–3, 346–8, 358

Whistler, James McNeill, 486, 487

Whitman, Walt, 380–1

Williams, Penry: career, 113; friendship with EL, 274, 281, 429; influence on EL, 113, 125, 207; sketching trips, 125, 126; studio in Rome, 113, 274; 'View of the Serpentara', 126

Williams, Rowland, 308, 342

Woolner, Thomas: friendship with EL, 208, 212, 309, 397; marriage, 341; PRB, 208; social life, 249, 271; view of EL's Palestine pictures, 271

Wyatt, Sir Matthew and Lady Digby, 396, 447, 450, 464

Wyatt, Richard James, 112, 113, 125, 144

Young, Sir John, 237

Young, Lady, 237, 245

Zielske, Madame, 29, 49

Zoological Society of London, 45, 47–9, 57, 61, 65, 81, 366; *The Gardens and Menagerie of the Zoological Society Delineated*, 48